THE MACMILLAN READER

Judith Nadell
Glassboro State College

John Langan
Atlantic Community College

Macmillan Publishing Company
New York

Macmillan Publishing Company
866 Third Avenue, New York, New York 10022

Library of Congress Cataloging-in-Publication Data

The Macmillan reader.

   Includes index.
   1. College readers.   2. English language — Rhetoric.
I. Nadell, Judith.   II. Langan, John,
PE1417.M34   1987   808'.0427   86-8494
ISBN 0-02-386010-3

Printing: 1 2 3 4 5 6 7   Year: 7 8 9 0 1 2 3

ACKNOWLEDGMENTS

"Allene Talmey." Betty Rollin, from *Am I Getting Paid for This?* Copyright © 1982
by Betty Rollin and Ida Rollin. By permission of Little, Brown and Company.

"The American Way of Death." Jessica Mitford, from *The American Way of Death.*
Copyright © 1963, 1978 by Jessica Mitford. Reprinted by permission of Simon &
Schuster, Inc.

"At a Nuclear Age." Ellen Goodman, from *At Large.* Copyright © 1981 by The
Washington Post Company. Reprinted by permission of Summit Books, a division
of Simon & Schuster, Inc.

"Beauty: When the Other Dancer Is the Self." Copyright © 1983 by Alice Walker.
Reprinted from her volume *In Search of Our Mothers' Gardens* by permission of
Harcourt Brace Jovanovich, Inc.

"The Beekeeper." Sue Hubbell, from *The New York Times,* August 2, 1984. Copyright © 1984 by The New York Times Company. Reprinted by permission.

"The Boy Scout Handbook." From *The Boy Scout Handbook and Other Observations*
by Paul Fussell. Copyright © 1982 by Paul Fussell. Reprinted by permission of
Oxford University Press, Inc.

ISBN 0-02-386010-3

Acknowledgments   iii

"The Brown Wasps." Loren Eiseley, from *The Night Country.* Copyright © 1971 Loren Eiseley. Reprinted with the permission of Charles Scribner's Sons.

"The Bubble Gum Store." Calvin Trillin, from *The New Yorker,* January 21, 1975. Reprinted by permission; copyright © 1975 The New Yorker Magazine, Inc.

"Channelled Whelk." From *Gift from the Sea,* by Anne Morrow Lindbergh. Copyright © 1955 by Anne Morrow Lindbergh. Reprinted by permission of Pantheon Books, a division of Random House, Inc.

"Children at Risk." Vance Packard, from *Our Endangered Children.* Copyright © 1977 by Vance Packard. By permission of Little, Brown, and Company.

"Children's Hospital." From *Children's Hospital,* by Peggy Anderson. Copyright © 1985 by Peggy Anderson. Reprinted by permission of Harper & Row, Publishers, Inc.

"College Pressures." William Zinsser, from *Blair and Ketchum's Country Journal,* April, 1979. Copyright © 1979 by William K. Zinsser. Reprinted by permission of the author.

"Communication in the Year 2000." From *Media: The Second God,* by Tony Schwartz. Copyright © 1981 by Tony Schwartz. Reprinted by permission of Random House, Inc.

"The Damned Human Race." Excerpt from "The Lowest Animal" by Mark Twain. From *Letters From the Earth,* edited by Bernard DeVoto. Copyright © 1962 by the Mark Twain Company. Reprinted by permission of Harper & Row, Publishers, Inc.

"Darkness at Noon." Harold Krents, from *The New York Times,* May 26, 1976, Op-Ed. Copyright © 1976/84 by The New York Times Company. Reprinted by permission.

"Entropy." K. C. Cole, from *The New York Times,* March 18, 1982. Copyright © 1982 by The New York Times Company. Reprinted by permission.

"The Faltering Family." George Gallup, Jr., from *Forecast 2000,* by George Gallup, Jr. with William Proctor. Copyright © 1984 by George Gallup, Jr. Reprinted by permission of William Morrow & Company, Inc.

"Handled with Care." Bob Greene, from *American Beat.* Copyright © 1983 by John Deadline Enterprises, Inc. Reprinted by permission of The Sterling Lord Agency, Inc.

"The Health Care System." From *The Medusa and the Snail,* by Lewis Thomas. Copyright © 1975 by Lewis Thomas. Originally published in *The New England Journal of Medicine.* Reprinted by permission of Viking Penguin, Inc.

"High Noon." Art Spikol, from *Philadelphia* Magazine, April 1976. Reprinted by permission of *Philadelphia* Magazine.

"Horace's Compromise." From *Horace's Compromise* by Theodore R. Sizer. Copyright © 1984 by Theodore R. Sizer. Reprinted by permission of Houghton Mifflin Company.

Acknowledgments   v

For Our Parents

PREFACE

"Does the world really need another reader?" That may have been your reaction when you first saw this book. Such a response wouldn't surprise us at all. Our bookshelves sag under the weight of all the readers we've used over the years, as perhaps yours do. The texts as a whole were serviceable, but we came to feel we wanted more than was being offered. For one thing, most readers contained an all too predictable blend of selections, with many of the same pieces cropping up from one book to the next. Equally troubling was the fact that the books provided students with little direction on ways to think, read, and write about the selections. We wanted a different kind of reader—one that would offer fresh examples of professional prose and would take a more active role in helping students become stronger reader, thinkers, and writers.

Our first concern, then, has been to enliven the mix of selections that commonly appear in readers by finding contemporary pieces not yet tapped by other anthologists. Although *The Macmillan Reader* does include many popular and classic essays, a number of the fifty-five selections were discovered only after a lengthy search for stimulating new material. Among these are "Handled with Care" by Bob Greene, "Allene Talmey" by Betty Rollin, "Wanting an Orange" by Larry Woiwode, "The Bubble Gum Store" by Calvin Trillin, "Channelled Whelk" by Anne Morrow Lindbergh, "Children's Hospital" by Peggy Anderson, "Horace's Compromise" by Theodore Sizer, "The Beekeeper" by Sue Hubbell, "In Depth, but Shallowly" by Dave Barry, and "High Noon" by Art Spikol.

Although our priority has been to find engaging new pieces, we've been careful to choose selections that range widely in subject matter and approach, from the humorous to the informative, from personal meditation to polemic. In addition, all the essays have been class-tested. We've made sure that each selection captures students' interest and illustrates clearly a specific method of development.

Just as our first concern has been the quality of the selections, so our second concern has been the quality of instruction accompanying the selections. Our aim has been to prepare a reader that projects the voice of a real teacher working with students in a knowledgeable and helpful way. And so we have designed *The Macmillan Reader* with several important instructional features: comprehensive chapters on the reading and writing processes, detailed introductions for each group of rhetorical selections, and a wide variety of questions, activities, and assignments. The following pages explain how these features will help students read more critically, think more logically, and write more skillfully.

Our first chapter, "The Reading Process," discusses the importance of reading and offers students a brief program for becoming better, more perceptive readers. The chapter describes a three-part process for reading with close attention, careful thought, and a high level of interpretive skill. Each step explains how to proceed and often includes questions that students can ask as they work at strengthening their grasp of the material. The three-step process not only will sharpen students' understanding of the selections in the book but also will promote the rigorous thinking needed to write effective essays.

A special activity at the end of the reading chapter gives students a chance to use the process just studied. First, they read an essay by Pulitzer Prize-winning journalist Ellen Goodman; then detailed commentary shows them how to apply the reading techniques to the selection. Last, they respond to a number of sample questions, all of them similar to the kind that follow each selection in the book. The chapter thus gives more than lip service to sharpening students' reading skills; it presents a class-tested plan for developing higher-level reading abilities and offers students an opportunity to apply what they have learned.

The second chapter, "The Writing Process," introduces students to essay writing. The chapter emphasizes that writing is a process, a gradual transformation of random ideas and free-form thoughts into polished prose. We have divided the process into six stages: prewriting; stating the thesis; developing the thesis with solid evidence; organizing the evidence; writing and connecting the parts of the essay; and revising. But right from the start, we let students know that the composing process is ultimately a personal matter and that each writer will adopt his or her own version of the sequence described in the chapter. We explain each stage in detail, illustrating central concepts with examples of student work. And a series of activities allows students to practice the skills involved in each stage.

To demonstrate the connection between the reading and writing processes, the writing chapter ends with an annotated student paper written in response to Ellen Goodman's "At a Nuclear Age," the essay presented in the reading chapter. The student paper embodies many of the principles discussed in the writing chapter and so prepares students for the essays they will compose. A commentary follows the student paper, explaining the strengths of the essay and pointing out spots that could use additional work.

The next nine chapters of *The Macmillan Reader* contain forty-nine selections grouped according to nine rhetorical patterns: description; narration; exemplification; process analysis; comparison-contrast; cause-effect; definition; division-classification; and argumentation-persuasion. We have sequenced the chapters to reflect a progression from the more experiential to the more analytic modes. But because each chapter is self-contained, the patterns may be covered in any order. If a thematic approach is preferred, the alternative table of contents near the end of the book will help organize an effective course.

The Macmillan Reader treats the rhetorical modes as discrete patterns because such an approach helps students grasp the distinctive characteristics of each mode. We also stress, though, that writers rarely set out to compose an essay in a particular pattern. Rather, they choose a mode or combination of modes because it helps them meet a broader rhetorical purpose. Each of the nine rhetorical chapters has the following format:

- **A comprehensive explanation of the particular method of development** begins the chapter. We have divided the explanation into three sections. First, we describe the general characteristics of the pattern; we then explain when to use the pattern; and finally, we offer practical suggestions for writing an essay or part of an essay in that mode. Throughout the explanation, we remind students that a writer's purpose and audience determine which pattern, or mixture of patterns, to use in an essay.
- A **student essay** using the pattern under discussion is then presented. Written in response to one of the professional selections in the chapter, each essay illustrates clearly the unique features of that method of development. In selecting student papers, we looked for strong, interesting essays that would encourage other students to write with equal thought, vigor, and attention to revision.
- **Commentary** on each student essay helps students evaluate the paper, identify its strengths, and locate areas that could be sharpened. A special feature of the commentary is a "before" and "after" version of the part of the student essay; these two versions help students appreciate the crucial role that revision plays in the writing process.
- Two kinds of **additional writing assignments** are included at the end of each rhetorical chapter: "General Assignments" and "Assignments with a Specific Audience and Purpose." The first group encourages students to discover their own approach when using a specific method of development; the second develops their sensitivity to concrete writing situations
- The **professional selections** in the rhetorical chapters are accompanied by the following:
    1. A *biographical note and preview*. The biographical information gives students a perspective on the author, and the preview creates interest in the piece.
    2. *Questions for Close Reading*. The first question asks students to identify the thesis of the selection. The next three questions prompt students to return to the selection to

focus further on the content of the piece. The fifth question provides work in vocabulary development

3. *Questions about the Writer's Craft.* The first question in this series helps students discover for themselves some of the features of the rhetorical pattern used in the selection. The other three questions treat such stylistic matters as tone, purpose, audience, figures of speech, and organization.

4. *Questions for Further Thought.* These questions ask students to reflect on a variety of issues related to the selection. The questions will inspire lively classroom discussion and help students refine their thoughts before beginning to write.

5. *Writing Assignments.* Four writing assignments, all using the selection as a springboard, follow each professional selection. The first two assignments ask students to write an essay organized around the same pattern of organization as the selection. The last two assignments, which may be written using any pattern of development, are particularly helpful for instructors preferring a thematic approach in the course. At times, one of these last two assignments will call for some basic research, such as interviewing people or consulting periodicals. In addition to making the assignments as stimulating as possible, we've also been careful to supply students with guidelines for tackling the assignments.

The Macmillan Reader includes a number of other features. A "For Further Reading" section near the end of the book contains five additional selections representing a variety of topics and rhetorical patterns. For easy reference, a glossary lists all the terms and concepts presented in the text. And a comprehensive *Instructor's Manual* contains the following: detailed answers to the "Questions for Close Reading" and "Questions about the Writer's Craft"; suggested activities; pointers about using the book; and a syllabus showing how *The Macmillan Reader* can be used in conjunction with *The Macmillan College Handbook.*

To summarize, *The Macmillan Reader* has been designed to support students through all phases of their work in a freshman writing class. As students read the selections, a series of questions encourages them to do close, analytical work. And as students shape their own essays, the book keeps them in touch with the principles of sound thinking and logical writing. In short, we think you'll find that *The Macmillan Reader* is indeed different from other readers; it provides students with clear guidelines for reading critically, thinking logically, and writing skillfully.

ACKNOWLEDGMENTS

We are pleased that prepublication reviews of the manuscript were so strong that the book has been christened with the name of one of the country's oldest and most prestigious college publishers.

We would like to thank Eben W. Ludlow, Executive Editor at Macmillan, for his enthusiastic commitment and insightful advice as we worked on the book. Our appreciation also goes to Wendy Polhemus at Macmillan for her skillful attention to the countless details involved in the production process. The following writing teachers reviewed the manuscript and provided valuable suggestions that guided our work:

Chris Anson, University of Minnesota
Barry Maid, University of Arkansas at Little Rock
Elizabeth Metzger, University of South Florida
Steve Odden, University of Wisconsin at Stevens Point
Marie Secor, The Pennsylvania State University
Carl Singleton, Fort Hays State University
Judith A. Stanford, Merrimack College

We are especially indebted to Janet M. Goldstein, Cynthia M. Leary, Linda McMeniman, and Maryann Porch. Creative teachers of composition, each of them contributed in meaningful ways to the book's final shape. And we owe thanks to Dorothy Carroll for her efficiency and patient good humor when typing and retyping the manuscript. Finally, we are thankful to our students. Their reaction to various drafts of the manuscript helped focus our efforts to fine-tune the material. To the ten students whose writing is included in the book, we owe special thanks. Their thoughtful and carefully revised essays demonstrate vividly the potential of student writing and the power of the composing process.

Judith Nadell
John Langan

CONTENTS

PROCESS ANALYSIS   231

Introduction:
What Is Process Analysis?   When to Use
Process Analysis   Suggestions for Using
Process Analysis in an Essay
Student Essay and Commentary   240

THE
READING
PROCESS

More than two hundred years ago, the celebrated essayist Joseph Addison wrote, "Of all the diversions of life, there is none so proper to fill up its empty spaces as the reading of useful and entertaining authors." Addison might have also added that reading is challenging and eye-opening. Reading *is* magical. We can perhaps best see this magic in the faces of young children who suddenly realize that all those mysterious, odd-shaped symbols on the page are the passport to vivid scenes and exciting adventures. The pride and pleasure children feel when they first learn to read stem from the power reading gives them. Without consciously realizing it, they know at some level that reading gives them access to worlds that would otherwise remain closed.

But children often lose this sense of wonder as they grow older. They begin to associate reading with tests and homework— both to be avoided at all costs. And there is another reason why many people dislike reading. Quite simply, as pleasurable as reading can be, it requires work. It is almost impossible to remain passive while reading. Even a slick, easy-to-digest bestseller de-

1

mands that the reader decode, visualize, react to, and interpret what is on the page. The more challenging the reading material, the more actively involved the reader must be.

The selections in this book demand active reading on your part. The essays, representing a broad mix of styles and subjects, range from the classic to the contemporary. Despite this variety, there is a common thread that binds the selections together. Each has something important to say; each is intended to stimulate thinking.

The selections serve other purposes as well. They will help you develop a strong repertoire of reading skills — abilities that will benefit you throughout life. The three sets of questions following each selection demonstrate that reading occurs at several different levels, moving from a literal to an increasingly analytic and interpretive level. Giving serious thought to the questions will help you achieve a high level of reading proficiency.

As you become more adept at reading the selections, you will also find that your writing abilities will be sharpened. For one thing, the selections provide a rich source of background material for the essays you will write. Second, as you develop an understanding of the techniques experienced writers use, you will learn to apply these strategies in your own essays, for — as novelist Saul Bellow has observed — "A writer is a reader moved to emulation."

Here are some suggestions intended to enlarge your understanding of the selections in this book. The suggestions will also develop your reading skills in general, helping you approach a wide variety of written material with ease and assurance.

STEP 1: READ THE SELECTION

Ideally, you should get settled in a quiet place that encourages concentration. If you can focus your attention while sprawled on a bed or curled up in a chair, that's fine. But if you find that being very comfortable is more conducive to daydreaming and dozing off than it is to studying, be sure to avoid getting too relaxed.

Once you are settled, it's time to read the selection. To ensure a good first reading, try the following hints:

• Get an overview of the piece and its author. Start by reading the preview and biographical note that precede the selection. The preview introduces you to the general subject of the essay and often raises questions to consider as you read the selection. The biographical note, by providing information about the author's background, helps you evaluate the writer's credibility as well as his or her slant on the subject. If you know, for example, that Theodore Sizer was the innovative Dean of the School of Education at Harvard University you have an idea of his perspective and reliability as a source of information for "Horace's Dilemma," an essay which explores problems in public education.

You should then study briefly the title of the selection. A good title often expresses the main idea of the piece, giving you insight into the selection even before reading it. The title "Making Medical Mistakes," for instance, signals that the essay will focus on the issue of doctors' fallibility. A title may also hint at the tone of a selection. "How to Live to Be 200" points to an essay that is light in spirit, whereas "College Pressures" suggests a piece with a more serious mood.

- Read the selection straight through purely for pleasure. Allow yourself to be drawn into the world the author has created. Just as you first see a painting from the doorway of a room and form an overall impression without perceiving the details of the image, so you should form a preliminary, subjective feeling about the selection. Because you bring your own experiences and viewpoints to the piece, your reading will be unique. As Emerson said, "Take the book, my friend, and read your eyes out; you will never find there what I find."

- After finishing the selection, focus your first impressions by asking yourself — very simply — if you like the selection or not. Try to think of a few words that describe the piece and your reaction to it.

STEP 2: DEEPEN YOUR SENSE OF THE SELECTION

At this point, you are ready to move further into the selection. This second reading will help you identify the specific features of the selection that triggered your initial reaction. Here are some suggestions on how to proceed:

- Mark off the selection's main idea or thesis, often found near the beginning or end of the piece. If the thesis is not stated explicitly, write down your own version of the selection's main idea.
- Locate the main supporting evidence used to develop the thesis. You may even want to number in the margin each area of support.
- Go back to any unclear passages you encountered during the first reading. The feeling you now have for the whole piece will probably help you make sense of these spots that were previously confusing. On the other hand, this second reading may reveal that the writer's thinking in places is not as clear as it could be.
- Ask yourself if your initial impression of the selection has changed in any way. Take a minute to write "Yes" or "No" beside any points with which you strongly agree or disagree. Your reaction to these points often explains your feelings about the aptness of the selection's ideas.

STEP 3: EVALUATE THE SELECTION

Now that you have a good grasp of the essay, you may want to read it again, especially if the essay is complex or lengthy. This time, your goal is to make some judgments about the effectiveness of the piece. You might find it helpful at this point to get together with other students to discuss the selection. Comparing viewpoints often opens up a piece, enabling you to gain a clearer perspective on the selection and its author.

Keep in mind that evaluating the selection should be done only after you feel you have a solid hold on the piece. A negative, even a positive, reaction is valid only if it is not based on a misreading of the selection. At first, you may feel uncomfortable evaluating the work of a professional writer. But remember: written material set in type only *seems* perfect; all writing can be fine-tuned. If you can identify what does and does not work in others' writing, you are taking an important first step toward developing your own power as a writer.

To evaluate the essay, ask yourself the following questions:

1. *Is there adequate and logical support for the selection's thesis?* Does the author provide valid and logical support for the thesis? Are the supporting facts, arguments, and examples pertinent and convincing?
2. *Is the selection unified?* Does everything in the selection belong? Are there any digressions or off-target detours?
3. *Does the selection move smoothly from beginning to middle to end?* What techniques does the writer use to create an easy flow between ideas? Are any parts of the selection abrupt and jarring?
4. *Are various stylistic techniques used effectively in the selection?* What pattern or combination of patterns does the writer use to develop the piece? Is the method of development effective? Do the writer's sentence structure and paragraph development contribute to the impact of the selection? Are the author's tone and point of view appropriate? Does the writer use figures of speech to good effect? (The glossary at the back of the book explains these and other terms.)
5. *Does the selection make the reader think?* Does the piece offer a new way of thinking about an issue? Are the ideas in the selection worthy of consideration?

It takes some work to follow the three steps described in this chapter. But the selections in *The Macmillan Reader* are worth the effort. Bear in mind that the selections reprinted here did not spring full-blown from the pens of their authors. The selections are the result of hours of work — hours of writing, rethinking, and revising. As a reader, you should show the same willingness to work with the selections, to read them carefully and thoughtfully. Henry David Thoreau, an avid reader and prolific writer, emphasized the importance of this kind of attentive reading when he advised that "books must be read as deliberately and reservedly as they were written."

To understand the implications of such thoughtful reading, try applying the three-step process just described to the professional essay that follows. That means you should start by reading the preview and biographical note that precede the selection. Then, after looking at the title of the piece, you should read the selection straight through once, pausing to collect your first impressions. Next, reread the selection, paying special attention to the essay's thesis and supporting evidence. Finally, so that you can evaluate the selection, ask yourself the five questions listed on the previous page. Brief answers are provided so you can assess your responses.

Ellen Goodman

The recipient in 1980 of a Pulitzer Prize for distinguished commentary, Ellen Goodman was educated at Radcliffe College. Goodman worked for Newsweek *and the* Detroit Free Press *before joining the staff of the* Boston Globe *in the mid-1970s. A resident of the Boston area, Goodman writes a popular column which is syndicated in newspapers throughout the country. Goodman's pieces appear in a number of national publications, including* The Village Voice *and* McCalls. *Collections of her columns have been published in* Close to Home *(1979),* Turning Points *(1979), and* At Large *(1981).*

At a Nuclear Age

Our age is different from other times. We have medical technology, space exploration, and global communication. But these developments are not what set our age apart from all others. The one factor that most distinguishes this era is that we alone have the capacity to destroy the entire world. How does this knowledge affect us? In the following selection, Ellen Goodman writes about the shadow that haunts us, especially those with the most to lose — the young.

The girl is worrying about The Bomb. 1

It is, a friend assures me, a passing thing. It is, he says, just a 2 symbol of childhood feelings of impotence in a wider and scary world.

But I think it is a symbol of her fear of the bomb. 3

I saw her staring into space when the idea goose-bumped 4 across her body. She shivered and said simply, "I was worrying about the bomb."

I wanted to say the right thing to her. It is a parental flaw, 5 wanting to say the right thing. We always want to say the right thing and end up telling them to brush their hair. So, about the

7

bomb, I said: "It is worth worrying about." That was dumb . . . unsatisfactory.

She asked for a second opinion. It's what resourceful children 6 do when the first answer is dumb or the source is as historically unreliable as a parent. She looked across the table and questioned a friend of ours: "Do you think I will die from old age, disease, or the bomb?"

My friend was taken aback, but he is congenitally reassuring. 7 At least, he has been reassuring me since I was eighteen and worried about making a fool of myself in *Damn Yankees*. He said then that I would be great. My friend is often more reassuring than accurate.

So, of course, he told the girl that there wouldn't be a nuclear 8 war because it would be disastrous for everyone. People were too sane to drop the bomb.

The girl, however, has had a good deal of experience with the 9 use of ultimate weapons on school playgrounds. She is not convinced that the reasonable human mind is a deterrent to violence.

So it was my turn again. This time the best I could do was wryly 10 point out one of the values of living in Boston, one which goes unadvertised by realtors. In the event of a nuclear war, anyone this close to MIT will never know what hit her.

Double dumb. 11

What I wanted to be, of course, was both honest and reassur- 12 ing, both accurate and comforting. But it is sometimes impossible to be both. Ground Zero is not a great comfort, especially if you are eleven years old.

This isn't the first time I have flunked my own self-adminis- 13 tered, self-corrected, take-home parenting test. Maybe I'm a tough grader, maybe we all are, or maybe the world has raised the standards over our heads.

It's not just about the bomb. It's hard to be simultaneously 14 realistic and comforting about almost anything that makes life stable, or the future certain.

When we were young, most of us were fed three square meals 15 of certainties. I don't know if our parents believed them all or if they just thought that security, like milk, was good for children. But it was a pretty constant and even nourishing diet.

We didn't hear much about bad times, bad marriages, bad 16 wars. The survivors of the Depression didn't talk much about it; the survivors of World War II were proud; divorce was a secret scandal.

Most of us grew up expecting a stable world. I don't think we   17
were betrayed; at worst, most of our parents believed they could
build us that world. They thought we needed to be assured instead
of prepared. Instead, we were surprised.

The way we live is unexpectedly, surprisingly, insecure. We   18
live in a state of flux.

And lurking in the background is the epitome of human fool-   19
ishness and insecurity: The Bomb.

All these things cannot help but affect the way we live with our   20
own children. I suspect that they, too, want a stable, secure world.
They want consistency; they want answers to questions and solutions for problems.

But we can't give them what we don't have. Instead we offer   21
ambiguity, contingency plans, history, alternatives. And we call
this "preparation for the real world."

I don't know whether they are learning insecurity and fear, or   22
learning how to cope. Or perhaps learning how to cope with insecurity and fear. But I suppose we do what parents always do: our
best. We try to share what we know of the world and what we
assume they will need to know.

With any luck we will have been too pessimistic.   23

The five questions that follow will help crystallize your reaction to Goodman's essay.

1. Is there adequate and logical support for the selection's thesis?

The best explicit statement of Goodman's thesis may be, "The way we
live is unexpectedly, surprisingly insecure. We live in a state of flux.
And lurking in the background is the epitome of human foolishness
and insecurity: The Bomb." Yet these two sentences are not the most
complete statement of Goodman's main idea because they do not mention the major concern of her piece — trying to give children a sense of
security in a world governed by the possibility of annihilation. Stating
the thesis in your own words may be best: "It is difficult for parents to
provide a sense of security in today's world when children must live
with the specter of nuclear war."

Goodman dramatizes her thesis with a single strong example —
her daughter's fears and questions. She also gives examples of parents'
answers to their children's questions, showing how inadequate such

responses are. Finally, Goodman compares a pre-Bomb childhood with a modern one and points out how much easier it was to provide certainties when such an overwhelming threat did not exist.

2. Is the selection unified?

At first, paragraphs 15–17 seem like a digression. Yet these paragraphs are important because they contrast the simplicity of the world Goodman experienced growing up with the world her daughter must face. The chatty aside in paragraph 7, though, is jarring. Goodman includes the paragraph to show that her "congenitally reassuring" friend tends not to be convincing—not to Goodman at eighteen, not to her daughter at eleven. But the paragraph, with its focus on Goodman and its reference to *Damn Yankees*, distracts from the unity of the piece.

3. Does the selection move smoothly from beginning to middle to end?

Goodman's essay progresses from the dinner-table conversation with her daughter (paragraphs 1–12) to her thoughts about why our children face such an uncertain world. In keeping with conventional newspaper format and her informal style, Goodman writes short, crisp paragraphs—paragraphs that are much briefer than those appropriate for most student writing. And she is careful about providing transitional words to ease the reader from one idea to another: "*But* I think . . . ," "The girl, *however* . . . ," "*So* it was my turn *again*. . . ." She also uses transitional sentences that echo previous ideas while also introducing new points: "It's not just about the bomb . . . ," "All these things cannot help but affect. . . ."

4. Are various stylistic techniques used effectively in the selection?

Goodman develops her essay by using several patterns of organization. For example, *narration* and *examples* are used in the first twelve paragraphs, while *comparison-contrast* provides the focus for paragraphs 15–17. She uses short, dramatic sentences to begin the essay ("The girl is worrying about The Bomb") and to punctuate her ideas ("Double dumb"; "We live in a state of flux"). The essay concludes with a similarly spare but striking sentence: "With any luck we will have been too pessimistic." Goodman achieves an informal tone through the use of the first person ("I think . . . ," "I saw . . . ") and colloquial language ("never know what hit her"; "that was dumb"; "I have flunked"). In paragraph 15, Goodman uses figurative language ("three square meals of certainty" and "security, like milk, was considered good for children") to dramatize how much simpler life was a generation ago. Finally, Goodman leavens her weighty subject with dashes of humor, as when she states, "It is a parental flaw, wanting to say the right thing."

5. Does the selection make the reader think?

Goodman's essay treats a broad issue that is crucial to all of us — the nuclear peril. Her specific area of interest is the dilemma parents face dealing with their children's fears. Although Goodman offers no solutions, her personal account sharpens our awareness of the problem.

If, for each essay you read, you give serious thought to the evaluative questions above, you will be prepared to respond to the *Questions for Close Reading*, *Questions about the Writer's Craft*, and *Questions for Further Thought* that follow each selection. Given below are several sample questions based on the Goodman essay; they are similar to the sort you will encounter in this book. To encourage you to dig even deeper into the selection, answers are not provided for these questions. Still, you should give each question a mental run-through to see how well you would do on an actual assignment.

Questions for Close Reading

1. What is the reason Goodman's daughter rejects the family friend's contention that people are too sane ever to drop the bomb?
2. Why does living in Boston create special anxiety for a child concerned about nuclear war?

Questions about the Writer's Craft

1. How would you characterize the tone of Goodman's essay? Is it formal and objective? Informal and subjective? What techniques does Goodman use to achieve this tone?
2. Why does Goodman begin and end her essay with a brief, one-sentence paragraph? What is the effect of such short paragraphs?

Questions for Further Thought

1. What specifically can parents do to minimize the anxiety their children feel living in a nuclear age?
2. Do you think that made-for-television movies, which dramatize the impact of nuclear war, have any value? Or are they sensationalized, popular entertainment, having no real significance?

The benefits of active reading are many. Books in general and the selections in *The Macmillan Reader* in particular will bring you face to face with issues that concern all of us as thinking and feeling beings. If you study closely the selections and the questions that follow them, you will be on your way to discovering ideas for your own papers. The next chapter, "The Writing Process," offers practical suggestions for turning these ideas into well-organized, thoughtful essays.

THE
WRITING
PROCESS

Not many people retire at thirty-eight. But Michel Montaigne, a sixteenth-century French attorney, did exactly that. Montaigne retired at such a young age because he wanted time to read, think, and write about all the subjects that interested him. After spending years getting his ideas down on paper, Montaigne finally published his short prose pieces. He called them essays — meaning trials or attempts.

All writing is, in fact, an attempt to transform ideas into words, thus giving order and meaning to life. By using the term *essay*, Montaigne acknowledged that a written piece is never really complete or finished. Of course, writers have to stop at some point, especially if they have deadlines to meet. But, as all experienced writers know, even after they dot the final *i*, cross the final *t*, and say "That's it," there is always something that could have been expressed just a little better.

Because writing is an evolutionary process, it can be time-consuming. Changes of direction, even false starts, are not uncommon. Although no suggested approach can eliminate the work needed to prepare effective essays, a number of strategies can make the process less confusing and more satisfying. The six-stage sequence detailed in this chapter provides a series of steps you can take when writing essays. The sequence can help you discover the pleasure and sense of accomplishment that come from expressing your ideas with clarity and force.

The suggested sequence is, above all, flexible. Most people develop personalized approaches to writing. Some mull over a topic, then move quickly into a promising first draft; others work best if they outline their essays in detail before beginning to write. Between these extremes are a number of variations. Whatever approach you use, familiarity with a proven writing sequence should be helpful. Remember, though, that the sequence described here can be streamlined, juggled, or otherwise modified to fit individual needs and styles. The six stages in the sequence are as follows:

1. Prewriting
2. Stating the thesis
3. Supporting the thesis with solid evidence
4. Organizing the evidence
5. Writing and connecting the parts of the essay
6. Revising the essay

STAGE 1: PREWRITING

Prewriting, the first stage of the writing process, is probably the most crucial factor in creating effective papers. Yet many people often disregard this stage, starting to write without first thinking through what they plan to say. This full-steam-ahead approach rarely leads to an effective essay. Such an approach is a little like building a house without a blueprint and *then* discovering all kinds of structural defects in the building. Prewriting provides a blueprint for your writing. It focuses your thinking early in the writing process, steering you away from many potential writing pitfalls.

Prewriting also helps reduce the anxiety you may feel when you stare at a blank page, wondering how to start and what to say. Since prewriting consists of a series of small steps, it makes the writing process less intimidating and more manageable.

Finally, because prewriting is tentative and exploratory, it can spark your powers of invention. By giving yourself time to explore a subject in an unhurried, imaginative way, you increase the possibility of discovering what interests you most about a topic. When prewriting, you do the following:

- Understand the boundaries of the assignment
- Discover the limited subject of the essay
- Generate raw material about the limited subject
- Organize the raw material

Each of these steps will be discussed in turn. But first, here is a practical tip: Many writers find it helpful to use pencil and scratch paper during the prewriting stage. Less intimidating than typewriter or pen and perfectly white paper, the pencil and scratch paper reinforce the notion that prewriting is intended to be open and inventive.

Understand the Boundaries of the Assignment

You should not start writing a paper until you know what is expected of you. First of all, clarify the *kind of paper* the instructor has in mind. Assume the instructor asks you to discuss the key ideas in a selection you have read. What, you might wonder, does the instructor want you to do? Should you include a brief summary of the selection? Should you compare the author's ideas with your view of the subject? Should you try to determine if the author's view is supported by valid evidence? In other words, what specifically are the instructor's expectations for such an assignment?

If you are not sure about an assignment, ask your instructor — not the student behind you, who is probably as confused as you — to make the requirements clear. Most instructors are more than willing to provide an explanation. They would rather take a few minutes of class time to explain an assignment than spend hours reading dozens of student essays that miss the mark.

Second, try to find out *how long* the paper should be. Many instructors will indicate the approximate length of the papers they assign. If you have such guidelines, be sure to follow them. If no length requirements have been provided, you should discuss with the instructor what you plan to cover and indicate how long you think your paper will be. The instructor will either give you the go-ahead or will help you refine the direction and scope of your work.

Once you feel confident about the requirements of the assignment, you are ready to begin planning your approach to the paper. At this point, you should focus on the *purpose* of the essay. Two papers about political campaigns would have very different purposes if one were written for a business class and the other for an English course. Your purpose in the first case might be to analyze the costs involved in conducting a campaign; your purpose in the second might be to offer personal observations about one candidate's attempt to get elected. Taking the time to think about your purpose will shape the paper even further by helping you identify the appropriate *tone* for the essay. You might decide, for instance, that the essay for the business class should be straightforward and serious, filled with facts and statistics. But because the purpose of your English paper is different, you might choose to write a light, humorous account of one eccentric politician.

In addition to establishing the essay's purpose and tone, you also need to consider for whom the essay is being written. Identifying the *audience* will help you set additional boundaries for the paper. If you keep in mind what your audience needs to know, you can determine which information to include and which to leave out. A paper on food additives, for instance, would take one form if submitted to your chemistry professor and a very different shape if written as a column for the college newspaper. The chemistry paper probably would be highly technical, complete with scientific data and chemical equations. The column, however, would probably be informal in tone and might include specific examples of common food additives and provide suggestions for avoiding them. In short, it helps to imagine the audience as you plan your paper. What do they already know? What do you want them to know? What do they expect from you? How can they be convinced that you know what you are talking about? Keeping these questions in mind is an important part of the writing process — no matter who makes up your audience.

Discover the Limited Subject of Your Essay

Now that you have a firm grasp of the assignment's boundaries and the best way to approach your work, you are ready to focus on a specific, limited aspect of the general assignment. Too broad a subject can result in a diffuse, rambling essay, so you want to be sure to restrict the general subject of the essay before starting to write.

The following examples show the difference between general subjects that are too broad for an essay and limited subjects that are appropriate and workable.

General Subject	Less General	Limited
Education	Computers in education	How computers improve on human teachers
Transportation	Bus travel	The unspoken rules of riding in a bus
Work	Planning for a career	Preparing for the jobs of the future

How do you move from a general to a narrow or focused subject? Imagine that you were given an assignment to prepare a straightforward, informative essay to be read by your instructor and other members of your English class. The assignment is as follows:

> In the essay "At a Nuclear Age," Ellen Goodman contends that the world today is a difficult, even dangerous, place for children. Write an essay that provides evidence for or against Goodman's point.

Some students might feel unsure about how to proceed with such a general, open-ended assignment. But there are two techniques that can be used to limit a general subject such as this one. Keeping your purpose and audience in mind, you may question or brainstorm the general subject. These two techniques — both explained in detail below — have a paradoxical effect. They encourage you to roam freely over a subject, but they also help focus and restrict the discussion by revealing which aspects of the subject interest you most.

1. Questioning the general subject. One way to arrive at a limited subject is to ask a series of questions beginning with words such as *who, how, why,* and *what.* For example, look at the way the questioning technique serves as a powerful tool for limiting the general assignment based on Goodman's essay.

> *General Assignment:* We live in a world that is difficult, even dangerous, for children.

Question	Limited Subject
Who is to blame for the difficult conditions under which children grow up?	An essay describing the effect on children of a weakening family structure
How can parents provide their children with some sense of security in a world filled with uncertainties?	An essay giving examples of the ways parents can give children a surer sense of control over their lives
Why do some people claim that our world offers children more security than other periods in history?	An essay comparing the harsh world of children in the past with the relatively easy world of childhood today
What things, other than nuclear war, contribute to the dangers children face?	An essay describing the range of problems that make it difficult to raise children today

2. Brainstorming the general subject. Another way to focus on a limited subject is to list, using brief words and phrases, all the points the general subject brings to mind. The idea is to capture all the free-floating ideas you have about the general subject; one of them may make an excellent limited subject. When brainstorming, do not try to organize or censor your ideas. List anything that occurs to you, as soon as it comes to mind. Even the most fleeting or random thought about the general subject can point the way to an appropriate limited subject. Here is an example of brainstorming based on the Goodman assignment:

> *General Subject:* We live in a world that is difficult, even dangerous, for children.

- Effect of widespread divorce rate on children
- Child abuse growing

- Families move frequently, making it difficult for children to feel secure
- Widespread drug abuse affects kids
- Children confused by lack of discipline
- Adults' declining respect for education harms kids
- Problems raising children today
- Two-career families mean absent parents
- TV presents distorted values to kids

As a result of these prewriting activities, the following limited subject emerged: "The special problems that parents face raising children today."

Generate Raw Material about the Limited Subject

Sometimes, the limited subject seems promising but ends up yielding little of value. After focusing on a limited subject, you next need to find out if you have enough to say about the subject to write an interesting essay. To see if you do, you can use any or all of the following techniques.

1. Freewrite on your limited subject. Freewriting means writing down in rough sentences or phrases everything that comes to mind about your limited subject. To capture this continuous stream of thought, write nonstop for ten minutes or more; pay no attention to organization, spelling, or grammar. Simply get the ideas down on paper. If your mind goes blank, repeat words until another thought emerges. When looking at a mass of freewriting, you may spot ideas that warrant development.

The brief freewriting sample that follows hints at some ideas that will be expanded later in a student essay.

Limited Subject: The special problems that parents face raising children today

Parents today have tough problems to face. Lots of dangers. Drugs and alcohol for one thing. Also crimes of violence against kids. Parents also have to keep up with cost of living, everything costs more, kids want and expect more. Television? Another thing is *Playboy, Pent-*

house. Sexy ads on TV, movies deal with sex. Kids grow up too fast, too fast, too fast. Drugs. Little kids can't handle knowing too much at an early age. Both parents at work much of the day. Another problem is getting kids to do homework, lots of other things to do. Malls, arcades, stereos in kids' rooms. When I was young, we did homework after dinner, no excuses accepted by my parents. . . .

2. Brainstorm your limited subject. Earlier, brainstorming helped you arrive at a specific, limited subject. Now brainstorming can help generate raw material about the limited subject. Once again, let your mind wander freely and list every idea, fact, and example that occurs to you about your limited subject. Use single words and phrases so you do not get bogged down writing full sentences. Be spontaneous; don't worry whether ideas fit together or whether the points you list make sense. When you are finished, you'll probably find that you generated a great deal of material about the limited subject.

Here is an example of brainstorming on the limited subject that emerged from the Goodman assignment:

Limited Subject: The special problems that parents face raising children today

- Prices of everything have increased
- Explicit sex on TV, in movies, in magazines
- Crimes of violence against children
- Violence in movies and on television
- More distractions, places for kids to go like shopping malls
- TV and stereos in kids' rooms
- Dangers such as drugs
- Schools not as good as they once were
- Pressures on kids to drink
- Trying to raise kids when both parents work

3. Map out the limited subject. Instead of freewriting or brainstorming, it may be helpful to use an informal system of mapping or diagramming to generate raw material. Tree diagrams (with ideas growing out from each other), balloons, or arrows can be used to make a visual outline of your random thoughts about a topic. These visual techniques can prompt imaginative exploration of a subject, especially if you are the kind of person who instinctively begins to doodle while thinking about a subject.

4. Use group discussion. Brainstorming can sometimes be conducted as a group activity. Thrashing out ideas with other people stretches the imagination, prompting you to go in directions you may not have considered otherwise. Because group brainstorming occurs in an atmosphere of creative competition, the process often yields a wealth of prewriting material.

5. Go to the library. Depending on your topic, you may find it helpful to look in the card catalog subject file for the titles of books concerned with your limited subject. At this stage in the writing process, it is not necessary to read the books you find. Just skim them and, perhaps, take a few brief notes on ideas and points that could be useful to you. You may also look in the *Readers' Guide to Periodical Literature* or another more specialized index to find the titles of magazine articles related to your limited topic. A third approach might be to check the library's vertical file for pamphlets on your limited subject.

When researching the Goodman assignment, for instance, you might look under the following headings in the *Readers' Guide:*

Drug abuse
Mass media
Family
Parent-child relationship:
    Child abuse
    Children — Management and training
    Children of divorced parents
    Children of working mothers
School and the home

Organize the Raw Material

Once a good deal of raw material has been generated, you are ready to impose form and order on your unorganized ideas. A good way to do this involves preparing a *scratch outline*. When making a scratch outline, you first eliminate points not closely related to your limited subject and add any points needed to develop this focused topic. Then you group related ideas until the essay's general plan of organization begins to emerge.

Making a scratch outline gives you a preliminary idea of what should be discarded or added, what should come first, what should come last, and what sections need more development. You are not creating a formal outline but a flexible one that can be reshaped easily along the way. Here is an example of a scratch outline that begins to organize the material for the Goodman assignment.

Limited Subject: The special problems that parents face raising children today

1 More distractions from schoolwork
- Stereos, televisions in room at home
- Places to go — malls, video arcades, fast food restaurants
2 More sexually-explicit materials around
- Magazines and books
- Television
- Movies
3 More life-threatening dangers
- Violent crimes against children
- Drugs
- Drinking

By the time your prewriting is finished, you will have accumulated a good deal of raw material that can be shaped into an organized essay. The work done during prewriting is crucial since it provides a solid foundation for the next stages in the writing process. But don't think that once prewriting is completed, invention and imaginative exploration are no longer needed. As you will see, a willingness to remain open to new ideas is crucial in all phases of the writing process.

Activities: Prewrite

1. Five general subjects are listed at the top of the next page. Use the techniques indicated in parentheses to limit each general topic to a more focused subject.

Medicine (questioning)
Sports (freewriting)
Women (brainstorming)
Leisure (mapping)
Law (group discussion)

2. Each set below contains five scrambled items for a scratch outline. Number the items in each set from 1 (broadest subject) to 5 (most limited subject).

Set A	Set B
Abortion	Business majors
Controversial social issues	Students divided by major
Cutting off state abortion funds	College students
Federal funding for abortions	Kinds of students on campus
Social issues	Why many students major in business

STAGE 2: STAGING THE THESIS

The process of prewriting — discovering a limited subject and generating ideas about it — prepares you for the next stage in writing an essay: stating the paper's thesis or controlling idea. The thesis, representing your slant on a subject, should focus on an interesting and significant issue, one that engages your energies and merits your time and consideration. Because the thesis is the hub of an essay — the central point around which all other material revolves — it helps the reader get a solid grasp of the essay. The thesis is equally valuable to you as a writer, for it helps determine what does and does not belong in the essay. In short, for reader and writer alike, the thesis signals the essay's scope and direction.

Writing a sound thesis usually does not happen all at once. Willingness to work at shaping a thesis is a crucial part of your job as a writer. Typically, the thesis evolves over time. You may have a clear idea of your thesis near the beginning of the prewriting stage. Or you may have to sift through your prewriting material to identify the thesis. In either case, the first thesis formulated may change as the writing process continues. You may find, after writing a while, that the thesis is faulty and that you cannot write a strong essay around it. Or the act of writing may reveal feelings, thoughts, examples and facts which force you to reexamine your thesis. This process of clarification and revision is normal and necessary.

A thesis statement, generally expressed in one or two sentences, often has two parts. It presents the *limited subject* of your paper as well as your *attitude* about the limited subject. Here are some examples of the way you might move from general subject to limited subject to thesis statement. Note that in each thesis, the limited subject has been underlined once and the attitude toward the limited subject has been underlined twice.

General Subject	Limited Subject	Thesis
Education	How computers improve on human teachers	Computer programs in mathematics can individualize instruction more effectively than the average teacher can.
Transportation	The unspoken rules of riding on a bus	Violating the unspoken rules of bus travel is risky.
Work	Preparing for the jobs of the future	Computer jobs of the future will demand good communication skills.
Our anti-child world	Special problems that parents face raising children today	Being a parent today is much more difficult than it was a generation ago.

As you can see, the thesis statement is an important step toward making the essay sharply focused. For this reason, you want to be careful that you do not run into the three common problems described on the next page.

Making an announcement. Some people merely announce the limited subject of their paper and forget to indicate their attitude toward the subject. Such statements are announcements of intent, not thesis statements.

Compare the following three announcements with the thesis statements beside them.

Announcements	Thesis Statements
My essay will discuss whether a student pub should exist on campus.	This college should not allow a student pub on campus.
Handgun legislation is the subject of this paper.	Banning handguns is the first step toward controlling crime in America.
I want to discuss cable television	Cable television has not delivered on its promise to provide an alternative to network programming.

Making a factual statement. An essay should focus on an issue worthy of consideration. If a fact is used as a thesis, you have no place to go. A fact is a fact. It does not invite much discussion. Since there is not much to develop, there is really no essay to write.

Studying the following two groups will help you see the difference between factual and thesis statements.

Factual Statements	Thesis Statements
Many people today are worried about toxic dumpsites.	Businesses that pollute the environment should be required to finance clean-up programs.
Many movies today are violent.	Movie violence provides a healthy outlet for aggression.
America's population is growing older.	The aging of the American population will eventually create an economic crisis.

Making a broad statement. You also want to avoid stating your thesis in vague, general, or sweeping terms. For one thing, broad statements make it easy for readers to misinterpret the point of your essay and the scope of your discussion. Moreover, if you start with a broad thesis, you are saddled with the impossible task of trying to develop a book-length idea with an essay that runs only several pages.

The following examples contrast statements that are too broad with thesis statements that are focused effectively.

Broad Statements	Thesis Statements
A high school education is often meaningless nowadays.	High school diplomas have been devalued by grade inflation.
The newspaper industry is catering to the taste of the American public.	The success of *USA Today* proves that people want their newspapers easy to read and entertaining.
The computer revolution is not all that we have been led to believe it is.	Home computers are still an impractical purchase for most people.

Although every good essay has a thesis as its center, there is considerable freedom regarding the presentation of this central idea. Often, the thesis is stated explicitly near the beginning of an essay. But sometimes, the thesis is not stated at all; it may be implied. Other times, the thesis may be delayed until the middle or end of an essay. Moreover, the thesis may be reiterated—with subtle variations—at several spots in an essay. The important point to remember is that every essay must have a controlling idea. That central concept is the essay's reason for being.

Activities: State the Thesis

1. Four possible thesis statements are listed for each of the limited subjects on the next page. Indicate whether each thesis is an announcement (A), a factual statement (FS), too broad a statement (TB), or an acceptable thesis (OK).

Limited Subject: The ethics of treating severely handicapped infants

Some babies born with severe handicaps have been allowed to die.
There are many serious issues involved in the treatment of handicapped newborns.
The government should pass legislation requiring medical treatment for handicapped newborns.
This essay will analyze the controversy surrounding the treatment of severely handicapped babies who would die without medical care.

Limited Subject: Privacy and computerized records

Computers raise some significant and crucial questions for all of us.
Computerized records keep track of consumer spending habits, credit records, travel patterns, and other personal information.
Computerized records have turned our private lives into public property.
In this paper, the relationship between computerized records and the right to privacy will be discussed.

2. Each of the following sets lists the key points in an essay. Based on the information provided, prepare a possible thesis for each essay.

Set A

- One evidence of this growing conservatism is the increased popularity of fraternities and sororities.
- Beauty contests, ROTC training, and corporate recruiting — once rejected by students on many campuses — are again popular.
- Most important, many students no longer choose careers that enable them to contribute to society but select, instead, fields with money-making potential.

Set B

- We do not know, first of all, how engineering new forms of life might affect the earth's delicate ecological balance.
- Another danger of genetic research is its potential for unleashing new forms of disease on the population.
- Even beneficial attempts to eliminate genetic defects could contribute to the dangerous idea that only perfect individuals are entitled to live.

3. Supplied here are four sets of general and limited subjects. Generate an appropriate thesis statement for each set of subjects.

General Subject	Limited Subject
Music	Fads in music
Psychology	The power struggles in a classroom
Politics	The separation of church and state
Health	Doctors' attitude toward patients

STAGE 3: DEVELOPING THE THESIS WITH SOLID EVIDENCE

After creating a thesis statement, you are ready to develop the evidence needed to support the essay's central idea. This supporting material lends substance to your viewpoint and gives your writing the specificity that makes an essay enjoyable to read. In traditional college essays of 500–1,500 words (the approximate length of many essays assigned in English and other classes), you usually need at least three major points of evidence to develop the thesis. These major points — each focusing on related but separate aspects of the thesis — eventually will become the supporting paragraphs in the body of the essay.

Where do you find the evidence to support the thesis? Where do you find the essay's major supporting points and secondary details, examples, and facts? A great deal of supporting evidence is generated during the prewriting stage when you brainstorm, freewrite, use the mapping technique, and discuss your ideas with others. The library, with its abundance of material, is another rich source for supporting evidence. Moreover, the patterns of development described in later chapters of *The Macmillan Reader* often point the way to specific kinds of support and evidence.

Regardless of its source, strong supporting evidence has the following characteristics.

It is unified.   All the supporting evidence in an essay must be appropriate and on target, clearly supporting the thesis of the paper. No matter how riveting certain details might be, supporting material that does not relate directly to the central point of the essay should be eliminated. Such off-target details distract the reader from the paper's controlling idea.

The importance of unified evidence is demonstrated by the following paragraphs, both on the subject of the benefits of cable television. As you will see, the first paragraph lacks unity because it contains points unrelated to the paragraph's main idea. Specifically, the comments about the foul language on cable television and the "clean" shows on network television are off target. Although these observations bring up interesting points, their inclusion in this paragraph shifts the focus of the writer's thought. If the writer wants to present a balanced view of the pros and cons of cable versus network television, these points *should* be discussed, but they should be covered in another paragraph. By way of contrast, the second paragraph is unified and tightly woven because all its supporting evidence is appropriate and relevant.

Nonunified Support

Cable television is a substantial improvement over network television. For one thing, the movies shown on cable are better than those on network TV. Cable movies are usually only months old, they have not been edited by censors, and they are not interrupted by commercials. In addition, the specials on cable television are superior to the ones the networks grind out. Cable viewers may enjoy such pop stars as Bruce Springsteen, Tina Turner, or Eddie Murphy in concert. One problem with the comedians, though, is that the foul language many of them use makes it hard to watch these shows with children. The networks, on the other hand, generally present "clean" shows that parents and children can watch together. But the networks continue to broadcast tired Bob Hope variety shows and boring awards ceremonies. Finally, programs on cable TV are scheduled at various times over the month. People who work night shifts or attend evening classes can see movies in the afternoon, and viewers who miss the first twenty minutes of a program can always catch them later. It's not surprising that cable viewership is growing while network ratings have taken a plunge.

Unified Support

Cable television is a substantial improvement over network television. For one thing, the movies shown on cable are better than those on network TV. Cable movies are usually only months old, they have not been edited by censors, and they are not interrupted by commercials. In addition, the specials on cable television are superior to the ones the networks grind out. Cable viewers may enjoy such pop stars as Bruce Springsteen, Tina Turner, or Eddie Murphy in concert. The networks, on the other hand, continue to broadcast tired Bob Hope variety shows and boring awards ceremonies. Finally, programs on cable TV are scheduled at various times over the month. People who work night shifts or attend evening classes can see movies in the afternoon, and viewers who miss the first twenty minutes of a show can always catch them later. It's not surprising that cable viewership is growing while network ratings have taken a plunge.

It is adequate. Readers will not automatically accept the idea expressed in your thesis; they have to be convinced that your point is valid. The credibility of your position depends, in part, on whether you provide enough evidence to support your viewpoint. To illustrate the importance of adequate support in the creation of a strong paper, look at the following paragraphs, both on the subject of limited-service gas stations. You will see how additional supporting evidence makes the second paragraph stronger and more convincing than the first.

Inadequate Support

Gas stations still provide gas, but they no longer provide service. At many stations, attendants have stopped pumping gas. Motorists pull up to a combination convenience store and gas island where the attendant is enclosed in a glass booth with a tray for taking money. The driver must get out of the car, pump the gas, and walk over to the booth to pay. That's a real inconvenience, especially when compared with the way service stations used to be run. Friendly service seems to have faded into the past.

Adequate Support

Gas stations still provide gas, but they no longer provide service. At many stations, attendants have stopped pumping gas. Motorists pull up to a combination convenience store and gas island where the attendant is enclosed in a glass booth with a tray for taking money. The driver must get out of the car, pump the gas, and walk over to the booth to pay. Even at stations that still employ "pump jockeys," the workers seldom ask, "Check your oil?" They rarely wash windshields, although they may grudgingly point out the location of the bucket and squeegee. Finally, many gas stations have eliminated on-duty mechanics. The skillful mechanic who could replace a belt or fix a tire in a few minutes has been replaced by a teenager in a jumpsuit who doesn't know a carburetor from a charge card. Is the demise of service the result of a decrease in owner-operated businesses and the rise in chain operations? Is it part of a general lack of courtesy in our society? Whatever the reason, it's clear that most gas stations today are mere fuel stops that provide minimal service.

It is specific.   For writing to be vivid and energetic, supporting evidence must be specific. When evidence is stated in broad, general terms, writing tends to be boring and lifeless. Specific writing, though, is likely to be energetic because it focuses on concrete details. In the following paragraphs about flexible working hours, note how interesting the second paragraph is — particularly when compared to the vague generalities of the first paragraph.

Nonspecific Support

Employees should be allowed more freedom in setting their own work schedules. One benefit of such a change would concern traffic problems. Hours would be different, so traffic patterns, especially around urban areas, would be altered too. This would eliminate the difficulties that confront motorists in these areas now. In addition, employers would benefit from the change. They would soon see that they could make more money, and this might reduce any objections they would have to flexible hours. Employees' work would be improved, and this effect would reach all the way to the national economy. A final benefit would involve working parents. Two-career families might solve many of the tough problems they now face, for the new hours would significantly affect the family. Children, therefore, would be less of a problem. Emotionally, parents would feel better. Making work hours more flexible is a step we should take now.

Specific Support

Employees should be allowed more freedom in setting their own work hours. One benefit of such a change would be a reduction in traffic problems. If employees could report to work any time between 6 A.M. and 11 A.M., for example, rush hour would vanish, traffic jams would be eliminated, and accidents would be reduced. In addition, employers would benefit from the new system. Expensive office buildings could be used for twelve or fifteen hours a day rather than eight. Productivity would rise, too, because studies show that contented employees tend to work harder and take fewer days off. Most important, flexible hours would solve some dilemmas that many working parents face. Child care, for instance, could be handled more easily if parents were freed from the 9-to-5 schedule. Money spent on day care might be saved, and the guilt that arises from leaving a child with outsiders would be reduced. Flexible hours seem to be a sensible alternative to the current rigid system.

An essay without solid evidence is unlikely to convince readers of the validity of the writer's views. Such writing also tends to be flat and dull, more apt to put readers to sleep than to engage their interest. Taking the time to accumulate supporting material that is specific, adequate, and appropriate is an important step toward writing effective essays.

Activities: Develop the Thesis with Solid Evidence

1. For each of the two thesis statements below, develop three points of relevant support.

   Thesis: The trend toward disposable, throw-away products has gone too far.

   Thesis: All first-year college students should be required to participate in an orientation program conducted the week before the start of the academic year.

2. Each of the following sets includes a thesis statement and four points of support. In each set, identify the one point that is off target.

   ### Set A
   Thesis: Colleges should put less emphasis on sports.

   Encourages grade fixing
   Creates a strong following among former graduates
   Distracts from real goals of education
   Causes extensive and expensive injuries

   ### Set B
   Thesis: America is becoming a homogenized country.

   Regional accents vanishing
   Chain stores blanket country
   Americans proud of their ethnic identities
   Metropolitan areas almost indistinguishable from one another

STAGE 4: ORGANIZING THE EVIDENCE

The next step in writing a paper involves organizing the essay's supporting evidence. Evidence that is presented in a random way is bound to confuse the reader, making it difficult to demonstrate the soundness of the essay's thesis. Although some writers can move almost immediately into a clear, logical draft (they usually say they have done the organizing in their heads), such individuals are rare. Most people need to spend some time organizing their thoughts; otherwise, they tend to lose their way in a tangle of ideas. Organizing and planning demand hard thought, but they provide the surest route to a clear, well-reasoned essay.

Using Rhetorical Patterns of Development

Organizing means finding the most effective sequence for your points. But how do you decide which piece of supporting evidence should be first, next, and last? The process of ordering points is not arbitrary; experience shows that certain sequences lead to strong essays. The rhetorical modes or patterns of development described in *The Macmillan Reader* suggest useful strategies for organizing or sequencing material. Some selections in this book use a single organizational pattern as they unfold. More often, though, the selections (and the essays you will write) use a mix of patterns, with one predominant mode providing the organizational focus for the piece. For example, an essay that argues a debatable issue might start with a *narrative* to dramatize the controversy, then move to a *definition* of terms, then *compare* and *contrast* various viewpoints. Still, the essay as a whole would be categorized as argumentation-persuasion because its purpose is to advance a particular position on a controversial issue.

You may be asked at times to organize an essay around a single pattern of development. Such assignments ensure that you understand the unique demands of that pattern. Helpful as such assignments are, you should keep in mind that writing usually begins not with a specific mode but with a specific purpose. The pattern or combination of patterns used to organize the piece evolves as you work to fulfill that larger purpose.

The following list summarizes the purpose of each of the nine patterns discussed in this book.

Pattern	Purpose
Description	To detail what a person, place, or object is like
Narration	To relate an event
Exemplification	To provide specifics or instances
Process analysis	To explain how something is done
Comparison-contrast	To point out similarities and differences
Cause-effect	To analyze reasons and consequences
Division-classification	To divide something into parts or to place related things into separate categories
Definition	To explain the meaning of a term or concept
Argumentation-persuasion	To convince readers about a controversial point of view

Using Three Basic Organizational Techniques

No matter which pattern of development is selected, you need to know three general methods for organizing supporting evidence. The three methods are explained below.

Chronological method. Some essays are best organized chronologically; that is, the supporting material follows a clear time sequence. Usually, the sequence starts with what happened first and ends with what happened last. Sometimes, however, chronological sequences can be juggled to create flashback or flashforward effects, powerful techniques that will be discussed later in the chapter on narration. Process essays and narrative essays are most apt to use the chronological method of organization.

Spatial method. Arranging supporting evidence in spatial order means discussing details as they occur in space. This strategy is most often used in descriptive essays. Let's imagine you are planning to write an essay describing the time you spent as a child playing near a fondly remembered tree in the neighborhood park. To organize the essay spatially, you might start by describing the games you and your friends played at the foot of the tree. Next, you might recall the sense of fun and power you experienced sitting on a large branch in the middle of the tree. Finally, you might end by describing the view of the world from the top of the tree.

Although there is flexibility regarding spatial arrangement (the essay could, for example, start at the top of the tree), you should choose an organizational plan that the reader can follow easily. And once a specific spatial sequence is chosen, you should usually stay with that sequence to the end of the paper.

Emphatic method. In emphatic order, the most compelling, most striking evidence is saved for last. This arrangement works well because it is based on the psychological principle that people remember best what they experience last. To use emphatic order effectively, you should organize the points so that momentum builds, leading inevitably to the most significant point in the essay. Emphatic order is an effective strategy for organizing material in cause-effect, comparison-contrast, division-classification, and argumentation-persuasion essays.

It might be helpful at this point to see how the supporting evidence in an essay could be arranged using these three methods. Assume, for example, that you want to develop the following thesis for the Goodman assignment discussed earlier in this chapter: "Being a parent today is much more difficult than it was a generation ago." The ordering principles selected will depend on your purpose for writing the essay. If you want to emphasize the difficulties parents face at various stages in their children's lives, you will probably select a chronological sequence. If you want to focus on the challenges parents face when children are at home, at school, and in the world at large, you most likely will choose a spatial sequence. If you want to show the range of problems parents face (from less to more serious), you will probably use an emphatic sequence. As you can see, the essay's purpose helps determine which of the three organizational methods is most effective.

Preparing an Outline

For many people, outlining can be an effective way to determine the sequence of ideas in a paper. Because an outline is a skeletal version of a paper, it clarifies the relationship among the points in an essay, highlighting any weaknesses in logic *before* the paper is actually written. Moreover, a strong outline can function as a road map that can be referred to once writing begins.

As with previous stages in the writing process, outlining is flexible and adaptable. An outline may be highly structured or informal, brief or detailed; it may evolve in a straightforward fashion, or it may shift as the flow of ideas develops. Moreover, while preparing an outline, you may uncover areas where supporting material is weak. If that happens, more brainstorming, freewriting, library research, or group thinking may be appropriate.

Since outlining can be an invaluable step in crafting a paper, you'll probably want to spend some time discovering the kind of outline that works best for you. Keep in mind that the complexity and amount of detail in an outline will vary according to the length of the paper and the instructor's requirements. Often a scratch outline — an example of which appears on page 22 — will serve you well. Other times, a more formal outline may be required to sequence your thoughts. The suggestions that follow will help if you decide to prepare a fairly structured outline. As always, feel free to modify these guidelines to fit your needs.

- Keeping in mind the essay's purpose, tone, and audience, write the thesis statement at the top of your outlining page. As long as you focus on your purpose, tone, audience, and thesis, you will stay on track.
- Cross out supporting material that seems off target or that does not develop the essay's thesis.
- Analyze the remaining supporting evidence and distinguish between major points, secondary points, and specific details.
- Label with Roman numerals (I, II, III, and so on) the major points that develop the thesis.
- Label secondary points with capital letters (A, B, C, and so on). Be sure to group the secondary points under the appropriate major points.
- Label specific details (facts, statistics, examples) with num-

bers (1, 2, 3, and so on). Be sure to group the details under the appropriate secondary points.
- Add any supporting evidence needed to develop the thesis. This additional evidence includes major points, secondary points, and specific points. .
- Evaluate all the elements in the outline, including the thesis and the various levels of support. Make whatever changes are needed until you are satisfied that you have organized your material in a logical fashion.

Here is an example of a formal outline for an essay written in response to the Goodman assignment discussed earlier:

Purpose and tone: To write an informative essay that is serious and straightforward
Audience: Instructor and class members
Thesis: Being a parent today is much more difficult than it was a generation ago.

I. More distractions from schoolwork
   A. At home
      1. Stereo
      2. Television
   B. Outside home
      1. Malls
      2. Video arcades
      3. Fast-food restaurants
II. Sexually explicit materials
   A. In print
      1. Sex magazines
      2. Pornographic books
   B. In movies
      1. Seduction scenes
      2. Sex as casual sport
   C. On television
      1. Soap operas
      2. R-rated movies on cable
III. Increase in life-threatening dangers
   A. Violent crimes against children
   B. Drugs
   C. Alcohol

A brief suggestion: You might find it helpful to show your outline to several people (your instructor, friends, roommates, class members) before beginning to prepare the essay. Their reactions often reveal whether the organization proposed is appropriate for your purpose and audience; their comments can highlight areas that need additional work.

If you are asked to submit an outline along with your essay, you may feel tempted to prepare the outline *after* the paper has been finished. Reversing the process in such a way defeats the purpose of outlining. If you adapt the outlining suggestions to suit your needs, outlining will not deteriorate into a mechanical exercise or meaningless busywork. Instead, outlining can guide your writing, providing a sound structure for the work that follows.

Activities: Organizing the Evidence

Following each thesis statement below is a scrambled list of supporting points for an essay. Prepare an outline for each potential essay, being sure to distinguish between major and secondary points.

1. Thesis: Our schools, now in crisis, could be improved in several ways.

Certification requirements for teachers
Schedules
Teachers
Longer school year
Merit pay for outstanding teachers
Curriculum
Better textbooks for classroom use
Longer school days
More challenging content in courses

2. Thesis: Supermarket fruits and vegetables are far from being natural products.

Dyes used to brighten colors
Techniques for growing produce
Pesticide sprays in the fields
Preservative treatments in the warehouse or market
Wax coatings to create shininess
Use of chemical fertilizers
Cosmetic treatments in the warehouse or market
Injections to retard spoilage
Chemical dips to extend shelf life

STAGE 5: WRITING AND CONNECTING THE PARTS OF THE ESSAY

Now — after prewriting, writing a thesis, generating supporting evidence, and organizing the evidence — you are ready to write the first draft of the essay. Because the groundwork has been completed, you will find that writing the draft will probably proceed fairly smoothly. But even at this stage, don't be surprised if your thoughts continue to change and evolve. Writing is a process of clarification, a continuous refining of ideas. Don't be discouraged if the first draft proceeds slowly in spots, if a point no longer seems to fit, or if you must return to a prewriting activity to generate additional evidence. This stopping and starting is normal. However, keep in mind that if you do need to generate new evidence during the draft stage, you should evaluate the new material carefully. Does it support the thesis of the essay? Is it suitable, given the essay's purpose and audience? If you answer "yes" to these questions, go ahead and use the added evidence with confidence. Just be sure to make any necessary rearrangements in the outline you may be using to guide the preparation of the first draft.

Some students get stuck while preparing the draft because they try to edit their writing as they go along. Remember: a draft is a work-in-progress. It is not intended to be perfect. You will have time later on to polish your writing. For now, just let your ideas flow. You should be concerned only with getting down on paper a basic version of your essay. That means you shouldn't stop to look up spelling, check grammar, or fine-tune sentence structure. To help free you from the tyranny of perfection while writing the draft, try using pencil and yellow lined paper rather than pen or typewriter and white paper.

At times, students have trouble with the beginning of the draft because they think they have to write the introductory paragraph before anything else. There is no rule that says you have to write the introduction first. Instead, you may find it helpful to follow the sequence below.

- Write the essay's supporting paragraphs
- Connect the supporting paragraphs
- Write the introduction

- Write the conclusion
- Create a title for the essay

Working in this sequence encourages you to focus on the supporting paragraphs of the essay. These key paragraphs, in turn, influence how you tie your points together and what you say in your introduction and conclusion.

Write the Essay's Supporting Paragraphs

The major supporting points in your outline, previously marked with Roman numerals, often become the *topic sentences* for each of the supporting paragraphs in the essay. The topic sentence in each paragraph functions as a kind of mini-thesis for the paragraph. One or two sentences in length, the topic sentence is often — but not always — the first sentence in a paragraph. Regardless of its length or placement, the topic sentence states the main idea of the paragraph, with the rest of the paragraph developing this central point. Like a thesis statement, the topic sentence signals the subject of the paragraph and often indicates your attitude toward the subject. In the topic sentences below, the subject of the paragraph is underlined once and the attitude toward the subject is underlined twice.

Students often select their majors for the wrong reasons.
The ocean dumping of radioactive waste is a ticking time bomb.
Several contemporary rock groups show unexpected sensitivity to social issues.
Political candidates are being sold like products.

After writing the topic sentences, you begin developing these key ideas into full paragraphs. The material listed in your outline provides a blueprint to follow, telling you what details to include and in what order the specifics should be arranged.

Sometimes you may develop (or recast) the topic sentence after writing the body of the paragraph. Occasionally, if you feel confident that your paragraph has a clear direction, you may eliminate a topic sentence and simply imply the focus of the paragraph. Topic sentences are, in short, flexible elements that can be altered in many ways — as long as each paragraph is unified and serves to develop the essay's thesis.

Connect the Parts of the Essay

Once you have written the body paragraphs, you need to ensure that movement between paragraphs is smooth and logical, making it easy for the reader to follow the development of your thinking. The primary way to create an essay that flows easily and clearly is to use connecting devices. Such devices signal the relationships among your ideas and make the evidence in your essay stick together or cohere. If you did not provide links between paragraphs when you wrote the body of the essay, this is the time to add connecting devices. A light touch should be your goal when providing linkages. Too many connectives call attention to themselves, making the progression of ideas plodding and mechanical. Here are some linking devices to consider.

1. Transitions.   Transitions are words and phrases that give simple, clear signals to readers, telling them how the ideas in a paper are connected. Among such signals are the following:

Time	Space	Addition	Examples
First	Above	Moreover	For instance
Next	Below	Also	For example
After	Next to	Furthermore	To illustrate
Finally	Behind	In addition	As an example

Contrast	Comparison	Summary
But	Similarly	Therefore
However	Also	Thus
Rather	Likewise	In short
On the other hand	Too	In conclusion

On the next page is one earlier paragraph from this chapter. Note how the italicized transitions link ideas together.

In addition to establishing your essay's purpose, you *also* need to consider for whom you are writing the essay. Identifying the audience will help you set additional boundaries for the paper. If you keep in mind what your audience needs to know about the subject, you can determine which information to include and which to leave out. A paper on food additives, *for instance*, would take one form if submitted to your chemistry professor and a very different shape if written as a column for your college newspaper. The chemistry paper probably would be highly technical, complete with scientific data and chemical equations. The column, *however*, would probably be informal in tone and might include specific examples of common food additives and provide suggestions for avoiding them.

2. Linking sentences. Linking sentences tie paragraphs together by mentioning what has gone before and what is yet to come. Such sentences remind readers of the material they have just read and introduce them to new ideas. Look closely again at the paragraph reprinted above. Note how the first sentence in the paragraph links back to the preceding paragraph's discussion of purpose, while also signaling that the new paragraph will focus on the importance of audience-awareness.

3. Repeated words, synonyms, and pronouns. Repeating key words, using synonyms, and using pronouns all help create a tightly woven network of ideas within an essay. The repetition of important words produces an echo effect which firmly plants key ideas in the reader's mind. You need to be careful, though, to use repetition carefully so that the essay does not *sound* repetitious. Synonyms — words that are similar in meaning to key words or phrases — also link parts of the essay and make it possible to avoid using a particular expression too many times. Finally, pronouns are another way to weave ideas together. They are automatic connecting devices, gently forcing readers to think back to the original word (or antecedent) the pronoun replaces. Be sure to keep your pronouns clear and precise; there should be no ambiguity about the pronoun's antecedent.

Reprinted here is another paragraph from this chapter. Repeated words have been underlined once, synonyms underlined twice, and pronouns italicized to illustrate how these techniques were used to link the ideas in a paragraph.

The process of prewriting—discovering a limited subject and generating ideas about *it*—prepares you for the next stage in writing an essay: stating the paper's <u>thesis</u> or <u>controlling idea</u>. The <u>thesis</u>, representing your slant on a subject, should focus on an interesting and significant issue, *one* that engages your energies and merits your time and consideration. Because the <u>thesis</u> is the <u>hub</u> of an essay—the <u>central</u> <u>point</u> around which all other material revolves—*it* helps the reader to get a solid grasp of the essay. The <u>thesis</u> is equally valuable to you as a writer, for *it* helps determine what does and does not belong in the essay. In short, for reader and writer alike, the <u>thesis</u> signals the essay's scope and direction.

Write the Introduction to the Essay

After you provide clear connecting devices in the supporting paragraphs, your next step involves preparing the essay's introduction. The introduction is crucial because it serves three important purposes. First, it introduces the subject of your paper. Second, it arouses the audience's interest, making them want to read more about your subject. Third, it presents the thesis—your special angle on the topic.

The length of the introduction will vary according to the scope and purpose of your paper. Most essays you write, though, will be served best by a one- or two-paragraph introduction. Incorporating all the key information into one or two paragraphs is a challenge, but there are several proven methods you can use to prepare effective introductions. These methods, illustrated briefly below, can be used singly or in combination. Note that the thesis statement in each introduction has been underlined.

A Broad Statement Narrowing to a Limited Subject

For generations, morality has been molded primarily by parents, religion, and schools. Children traditionally acquired their ideas about what is right and wrong, which goals are important in life, and how other people should be treated from these three sources. But now there is another powerful force influencing youngsters. <u>Television is implanting in children negative values about sex, work, and family life.</u>

A Brief Anecdote

At a local high school recently, students in a psychology course were given a hint of what it is like to be the parents of a newborn. Each "parent" had to carry a raw egg around at all times to symbolize the responsibilities of parenthood. The egg could not be left alone; it limited the "parents'" activities; it placed a full-time emotional burden on "Mom" and "Dad." This class exercise illustrates a common problem facing the majority of new mothers and fathers. Most people receive little preparation for the job of being parents.

An Idea or Situation That Is the Opposite of the One to Be Developed

We hear a great deal about the disastrous effect of divorce on children. We are deluged with advice on ways to make divorce as painless as possible for youngsters; we listen to heartbreaking stories about the confused, grieving children of divorced parents. Little attention has been paid, however, to a radically different kind of divorce. If children are deeply unhappy with their homelife, they should be allowed to "divorce" their parents.

A Series of Short, Stimulating Questions

What happens if your child is caught vandalizing school property? What happens if your child goes for a joyride in a stolen car and accidentally hits a pedestrian? Are you, as a parent, liable for your children's mistakes? Will you end up being sued for hundreds of thousands of dollars in damages? Parents have begun to think seriously about such questions because the laws concerning the limits of parental responsibility are changing rapidly. With unfortunate frequency, courts are beginning to hold parents liable for their children's mistakes.

A Thought-Provoking Quotation

Educator Neil Postman believes that television has blurred the line between childhood and adulthood. According to Postman, "All the secrets that a print culture kept from children . . . are revealed all at once by media that do not, and cannot, exclude any audience." This media barrage of information once intended only for adults has changed childhood for the worse.

A Dramatic Fact or Statistic

Seventy percent of the respondents in a poll conducted by columnist Ann Landers stated that, if they could live their lives over, they would choose not to have children. This startling statistic makes one wonder what these people believed parenthood would be like. <u>Most</u> <u>parents</u>, <u>it</u> <u>seems</u>, <u>have</u> <u>unrealistic</u> <u>expectations</u> <u>about</u> <u>their</u> <u>children</u>. Parents want their children automatically to accept their values, follow their paths, and succeed where they failed.

Introductory paragraphs sometimes end with a *plan of development*. The plan of development may be part of the thesis (as in the first introduction above) or it may immediately follow the thesis (as in the last introduction above). A plan of development gives the reader a quick preview of the essay's major points and signals the order in which the points will be discussed. Because the plan of development highlights the organizational structure of the essay, it helps focus attention on the logical progression of ideas in the essay. A plan of development may not be needed in a brief essay, for your audience will often be able to keep track of your ideas without this extra help. In a longer essay, though, a plan of development can be a unifying device because it points to the main ideas the reader will soon encounter.

Write the Conclusion to the Essay

You have probably read pieces that sputtered to a tired close. Perhaps there was no conclusion at all, making the piece end abruptly, in a jarring, disorienting way. Or there may have been a conclusion, but it was weak and lifeless, evidence that the writer ran out of steam and wanted to finish the piece as quickly as possible. But a strong conclusion is an important part of an effective essay. Generally one or two paragraphs in length, the conclusion should give the reader a feeling of completeness and finality. Because people remember most clearly the points they read last, the conclusion is a good spot to remind readers of your thesis. You can also use the conclusion to express a final thought about your subject.

Illustrated briefly here are several methods for writing sound conclusions. These techniques may be used singly or in combination.

A Summary
Parent-child divorce should not be seen as frivolous and impractical. Studies show that such divorces can save marriages, create a calmer atmosphere at home, and help troubled children develop a

new outlook on life. Perhaps such an extreme measure is exactly what is needed to keep families together during these confusing times.

A Prediction

The growing tendency on the part of the judicial system to hold parents responsible for the reactions of their wayward children can have a disturbing impact on all of us. Parents will feel bitter toward their own children and cynical about a system that allows such an injustice. Children, continuing to escape the consequences of their actions, will become even more lawless and destructive. Society cannot afford two such possibilities.

A Quotation

The comic W. C. Fields is reputed to have said, "Anyone who hates children and dogs can't be all bad." Most people do not share Fields' cynical views. If anything, they hold an idealized vision of childhood as a time of purity. But television, by exposing children to worlds they would be better off not knowing about, has stripped children of the innocence that should be their birthright.

A Recommendation or Call for Action

It is a mistake to leave parenting to instinct. Instead, we should make parenting skills a required course in schools. In addition, a nationwide hotline should be established to help parents deal with crises. Such training and continuing support would help adults deal more effectively with many of the problems they face as parents.

Create a Title for the Essay

Some professional writers say that they began a certain piece with only a title in mind. But for most people, a title is a finishing touch. Although creating a title for your paper is usually one of the last steps in writing an essay, it should not be done haphazardly. It may take time to write an effective title — one that hints at the thesis of the essay and snares the reader's interest.

Good titles may make use of the following techniques: repetition of sounds ("Why I Want a Wife"); twists on familiar sayings ("To Win or Not to Win: That Is the Question"); and humor ("How to Say Nothing in 500 Words"). More often, though, titles are straightforward phrases derived from the essay's subject or thesis: "Shooting an Elephant" and "TV Addiction," for example.

Pulling It All Together

Now that you understand how to write the various parts of an essay, you might find it helpful to see a diagram that illustrates how the different paragraphs can fit together. Keep in mind that not every essay you write will take this shape. As your purpose, audience, and tone change, so will the structure of your essay. An introduction or conclusion, for instance, may be developed in more than one paragraph; the thesis statement may be implied or delayed until the middle or end of the essay; not all paragraphs will have topic sentences; and several supporting paragraphs may be needed to develop an important point. Despite these variations, the diagram below shows one helpful format for structuring a traditional college essay. Feel free to adapt the format to suit your needs.

As you can see, a well-written essay grows in an organic way, each part of the essay emerging from and influencing the others. By paying attention to supporting paragraphs, connecting devices,

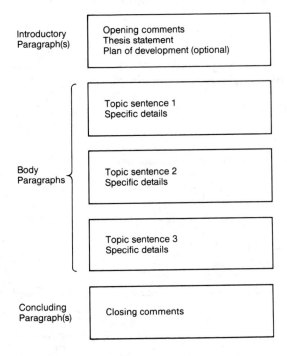

openings, closings, and titles, you will craft an essay with its own clear logic and inner integrity.

Activity: Write and Connect the Parts of the Essay

Following is an outline for a potential essay. The thesis statement, major points, secondary points, and supporting details are given. Write an essay, using this outline as a guide, but feel free to make changes as needed.

Assume that your essay will appear as an informative article in a local high school newspaper. Your audience consists of high school students about to start their first jobs; you want to tell these students what the world of work is like. The tone of the essay should be personable and friendly; you want to sound helpful, not frightening. The essay should include the following: a title; an introduction that includes the thesis and, if needed, a plan of development; supporting paragraphs, some of which are focused by topic sentences; expanded specific details; transitions and linking sentences; a conclusion.

If you would rather prepare an essay on a different subject, that's fine. Be sure, however, that your essay includes a title, an introduction, and so on. Also, before writing the essay, clarify to yourself the essay's purpose, audience, and tone.

Thesis: Most employers are neither angels nor ogres; they are simply human beings with varying degrees of management skill.

I. Bosses who exercise strict control
   A. Bosses who enjoy exercising authority
      1. Give orders at every opportunity
      2. Want to make all decisions themselves
   B. Worriers
      1. Watch employees closely to prevent mistakes
      2. Redo employees' work until it is perfect
II. Bosses who have relinquished control
   A. Absentee bosses
      1. Never available at critical moments
      2. Employees forced to make all decisions
   B. Burned-out bosses
      1. Uninterested in how job is done
      2. Unreliable — never on time, many supposed sick days

III. Bosses with good management skills
  A. Skilled supervisors
    1. Good at giving feedback
    2. Willing to delegate authority
  B. Mentors
    1. Help employees get promotions
    2. Provide emotional support

STAGE 6: REVISING THE ESSAY

In the final stage of the writing process, you revise and then proofread what you have prepared. Revision, which often marks the difference between satisfactory and superior work, means that you examine your essay carefully, reworking areas that could be improved. Alexander Pope's comment that "True ease in writing comes from art, not chance" is as true today as it was more than two hundred years ago. A piece that seems effortlessly clear is often the result of sustained work, not good luck or even inborn talent.

By now, you have probably abandoned any preconceptions you might have had about good writers sitting down and creating a finished product in one easy step. Perhaps it is comforting to know that people who make their living as writers — reporters, novelists, columnists, textbook authors — seldom submit a piece of writing that has not undergone revision. They recognize that raw, unrevised work does not do justice to their ability as writers.

As you have seen, writing involves ongoing change. Even during this final stage, ideas continue to reshape themselves. Revision (literally, "reseeing") means casting a clear eye on your work, bolstering weak spots, eliminating deadwood, bridging gaps in logic, and generating more material if needed. More specifically, revision may involve rewording your thesis statement and topic sentences. It may also involve reshaping whole paragraphs, adding or deleting material, strengthening links. Other times, you may need to edit sentences, substituting new words and phrases for old ones.

Here are several suggestions to ease you through the revising process. First, try to set your essay aside for a while. When you return to your work, you will have a fresh, more objective perspective. Also, when revising, be sure to leave time to read your essay aloud. Hearing how your work sounds often identifies spots where your sentences are awkward and your thinking unclear. And having someone else read aloud what you have written can be especially helpful. Finally, consider using the group process to get reaction to your essay. Ask people several focused questions about your paper, perhaps using the checklist on the opposite page. The feedback you receive can be invaluable when revising.

To give you a clearer sense of what revision entails, you might find it interesting to see how the paragraphs you just read were originally written. After some time had elapsed, the paragraphs were revised, based partly on helpful feedback from friends and colleagues. As you compare the two versions, note that some ideas were dropped, others expanded, new points introduced, and some paragraphs and sentences reshuffled and polished.

Unrevised Version

In the final stage of the writing process, you revise and proofread what you have prepared. Revising means examining your essay carefully and reworking areas that could be improved. Revision is an ongoing process; you have probably made a number of changes in the essay already. You will now find it helpful to set the essay aside for a while. "Forgetting" what you have written allows you to return to the essay with a fresh perspective.

Revision may mean rewording your thesis statement and topic sentences. It may also mean reworking whole paragraphs, adding or deleting supporting material, strengthening connecting links, tightening an introduction or conclusion. Other times, you may edit specific sentences, substituting new words and phrases for old ones.

Because revision demands careful thought, it takes time. But revision is often the difference between mediocre and superior work. Perhaps it's comforting to know that people who make their living writing—reporters, novelists, magazine writers, technical writers—seldom submit a piece of writing that has not undergone revision. They know that raw, unrevised work does not do justice to their real ability as writers.

Proofreading is a more mechanical task than revising, but it, too, is essential. Once you feel satisfied that the essay is sound, you should reread the final draft closely, correcting any grammar, spelling, and punctuation problems that remain. You should keep a dictionary and an English handbook nearby while you proofread. Although proofing may seem to involve relatively minor matters, an accumulation of small errors can make an otherwise good essay weak and ineffective. You do not want readers to be distracted from the main point of your essay by misspelled words or misplaced commas. When proofing, many people tend to see what they think is on the page rather than what really is there. Reading the essay backwards, starting with the last word first, can help locate errors that might otherwise go undetected.

The brief checklist that follows will help when revising and proofreading your essay.

Checklist for Revision and Proofreading

- What is the central idea of the essay? Is it stated explicitly? Where? If not stated explicitly, where is the essay's thesis implied?
- What pattern or combination of patterns is used to develop the essay? Why was that method of development chosen? Is it effective?
- What organizing principle has been used to sequence the supporting paragraphs? Is the principle effective?
- In what way does each supporting paragraph develop the essay's thesis?
- Is the evidence in each supporting paragraph unified, specific, and adequate? Which points of evidence are especially effective?
- What connecting devices are used within and between paragraphs? Are the devices effective?
- What techniques are used to open and close the essay? Are the techniques effective?
- Have all grammar, punctuation, and spelling problems been eliminated?

The six-stage writing process is not meant to be a fixed, unchanging formula for preparing essays. As you gain more experience writing papers, you will learn how to adapt the stages to fit your personal needs as well as the demands of specific assignments.

You will also learn how to move through the stages more quickly, taking shortcuts when appropriate. But until you feel real confidence as a writer, the six-stage process can provide a welcome series of steps to follow.

Just as the six-stage process may be adapted, the format for the traditional college essay may also be modified. Still, the basic pattern described in this chapter offers a strategy for organizing a variety of writing assignments — from term papers to lab reports. Once you feel comfortable with the structure, you have a starting place, a foundation on which to plan your variations. The rich variations possible are evident in the student essays and professional selections in the book. Finally, you should keep in mind that even when using a specific format, you always have room to give your spirit and imagination free play. The language you use, the details you select, the perspective you offer are highly personal and uniquely yours. They are what make your essay different from everyone else's.

Student Essay and Commentary

The student essay that follows was written by Harriet Davids, a thirty-eight-year-old college student who is the mother of two young teenagers. Harriet set out to write an informative paper with a straightforward, serious tone. While preparing her essay, Harriet kept in mind that her audience included the course instructor as well as other students in the class — most of whom are considerably younger than she. To jog your memory, this is the assignment that provided the springboard for Harriet's essay:

> In the essay "At a Nuclear Age," Ellen Goodman contends that the world today is a difficult, even dangerous, place for children. Write an essay that provides evidence for or against Goodman's point.

The essay has been annotated so you can see how it illustrates the essay format described in this chapter. As you read the essay, try to determine how well it reflects the principles of effective writing. The commentary following the paper will help you look at Harriet's essay more closely.

Challenges for Today's Parents

INTRODUCTION   Reruns of situation comedies from the fifties and early sixties dramatize the kinds of problems that parents used to have with their children. The Cleavers scold Beaver for not washing his hands before dinner; the Andersons ground Bud for not doing his homework; the Nelsons dock little Ricky's allowance because he keeps forgetting to clean his room. But times have changed dramatically. Being a parent today is much more difficult than it was a generation ago. Parents nowadays must protect their children from a growing number of distractions, from sexually explicit material, and from life-threatening situations.

Thesis

Plan of development

FIRST SUPPORTING PARAGRAPH   Today's parents must try, first of all, to control all the new distractions that tempt children away from schoolwork. At home, a child may have a room furnished with a stereo and television. Not many young people can resist the urge to listen to an album or watch MTV--especially if it is time to do schoolwork. Outside the home, the distractions are even more alluring. Children no longer "hang out" on a neighborhood corner within earshot of Mom or Dad's reminder to come in and do homework. Instead, they congregate in vast shopping malls, buzzing video arcades, and gleaming fast-food restaurants. Parents and school assignments have obvious difficulty competing with such enticing alternatives.

Topic sentence

SECOND SUPPORTING PARAGRAPH   Besides dealing with these distractions, parents also have to shield their children from a flood of sexually explicit materials. Today, children can find sex magazines and pornographic paperbacks in the same corner store that once offered only comics and candy. Children will not see the fuzzily photographed nudes that a previous generation did but will encounter the hard-core raunchiness of <u>Hustler</u> or <u>Penthouse</u>. Moreover, the movies young people attend often focus on highly sexual situations. It is difficult to teach children traditional values when films show teachers seducing students and young people treating sex as a casual sport. An even more diffi-

Topic sentence

cult matter for parents is the heavily sexual content of programs on television. With just a flick of the dial, children can see soap opera stars cavorting in bed or watch cable programs where nudity is common.

THIRD SUPPORTING PARAGRAPH

Topic sentence

Most disturbing to parents today, however, is the increase in life-threatening dangers that face young people. When children are small, parents fear that their youngsters may be victims of violence. Every news program seems to carry a report about a mass murderer who preys on young girls, a deviant who has buried six boys in his cellar, or an organized child pornography ring that molests preschoolers. When children are older, parents begin to worry about their kids' use of drugs. Peer pressure to experiment with drugs is often stronger than parents' warnings. This pressure to experiment can be fatal if the drugs have been mixed with dangerous chemicals. Finally, even if young people escape the hazards associated with drugs, they must still resist the pressure to drink. Although alcohol has always held an attraction for teenagers, reports indicate that they are drinking more than ever before. As many parents know, the consequences of this attraction can be deadly--especially when drinking is combined with driving.

CONCLUSION

Within one generation, the world as a place to raise children has changed dramatically. One wonders how yesterday's parents would have dealt with today's problems. Could the Andersons have kept Bud away from MTV? Could the Nelsons have shielded little Ricky from sexually explicit material? Could the Cleavers have protected Beaver from drugs and alcohol? Parents must be aware of all these distractions and dangers, yet be willing to give their children the freedom they need to become responsible adults. It is not an easy task.

"Challenges for Today's Parents" is an essay with many positive points. Although the paper — like most writing — could be shaped and polished further, it is clear that Harriet understands the basic principles of essay writing.

The essay's *introduction* arouses the reader's interest by recalling television shows that are almost a part of our cultural heritage. Harriet begins with these examples from the past because they present such a sharp contrast to the idea expressed in the *thesis*: "Being a parent today is much more difficult than it was a generation ago." This reversing of direction is a common and effective technique for starting an essay. Note, too, the way Harriet's thesis states the paper's subject (being a parent) as well as her attitude toward the subject (the job is more demanding than it was years ago).

Harriet follows her thesis statement with a *plan of development* that anticipates the three major points to be covered in the essay's supporting paragraphs. But the plan of development is somewhat mechanical, with the major points being trotted past the reader in one long, awkward sentence. To deal with this problem, Harriet could have rewritten the sentence or simply eliminated the plan of development, ending the introduction after the thesis.

Organizing her essay around a series of interesting and specific examples, Harriet uses *emphatic order* to sequence the paper's three main points. By beginning the third supporting paragraph with these words (*"Most disturbing* to parents today . . . "), Harriet signals that she feels particular concern about the physical dangers children face. Moreover, Harriet uses basic organizational strategies to order the supporting examples within each paragraph. The details in the first supporting paragraph are organized *spatially*, starting with distractions at home and moving to those outside the home. In the second supporting paragraph, Harriet sequences her examples *emphatically*. She starts with sexually explicit publications and ends with the "even more difficult matter" of sexuality on television. The final supporting paragraph is organized *chronologically*; it begins by discussing dangers to small children and concludes by talking about teenagers.

The essay displays Harriet's familiarity with other kinds of organizational techniques. Each supporting paragraph opens with a *topic sentence*, while *connecting devices* are used throughout the paper to link ideas. For example, these are some of the connecting devices that tie together the essay's ideas: *transitions* ("Instead, they congregate in vast shopping malls . . . "; "Moreover, the movies young people attend often focus on highly sexual situations"); *repetition* ("sexual situations" and "sexual content"); *synonyms* ("distractions . . . enticing alternatives" and "life threatening . . . fatal"); *pronouns* ("young people . . . they"); and *linking sentences* ("Besides dealing with these distractions, parents also have to shield their children from a flood of sexually explicit material"). In the last case, note how the connecting device eases the progression from one paragraph to the next.

In spots, though, the structure of Harriet's essay is a bit predictable. It might have been better had she rewritten one of the paragraphs, perhaps embedding the topic sentence in the middle of the paragraph or saving it for the end. Harriet's use of connecting devices is also somewhat routine ("Today's parents must try, *first of all* . . . "). Still, an essay with a clear focus and obvious links is preferable to one with a confusing or inaccessible structure. Harriet can continue to work on making the design of her essays more subtle as she gains writing experience.

Given the essay's *purpose* and *audience*, Harriet provides evidence that is unified, specific, and adequate. But assume that Harriet had been asked by her daughters' school newspaper to write a humorous column about the difficulties that parents face raising children. Because of the shift in tone, purpose, and audience, Harriet would have proceeded differently. She might have drawn on her experience as a mother of two young teenagers and spent several paragraphs detailing the ploys she uses to pull her daughters away from stereos and MTV. This material, with its personalized perspective and light tone, would be appropriate, considering Harriet's readers and objective.

The *conclusion* of "Challenges for Today's Parents" brings the essay to a satisfying close by reminding readers of the paper's controlling idea and three main points. The final paragraph also extends the scope of the essay by introducing a new but related issue: that parents have to strike a balance between their need to provide limitations and their children's need for freedom.

Harriet's conclusion, like the rest of her essay, went through a number of changes before reaching its final form. Take a moment to compare the final version shown above with the first draft version reprinted here.

Unrevised Version
Most people love their children and work hard at being good parents. But the job gets harder in a world that is, in many ways, hostile to young people. Even Holden Caulfield, with his rage against

a phony society, didn't face the confusing pressures of our world. Today's parents must somehow find ways to give children a reasonable amount of freedom, yet still exercise greater caution than before.

You probably observed that the original concluding paragraph seemed like a tired afterthought. It had trouble bringing the essay to a satisfying finish. When Harriet read her paper aloud during a group feedback session, she realized she had to rework the conclusion, so it would pull the essay together more smoothly. Note how she proceeded.

After eliminating the shopworn opening sentence ("Most people love their children . . . "), Harriet added three interesting questions ("Could the Andersons . . . Could the Nelsons . . . Could the Cleavers . . . ?"). Because these three rhythmical questions echo the essay's main points and recall the material first encountered in the introduction, they help round out and unify Harriet's paper.

When revising the final paragraph, Harriet also took into account a comment made by another student during the feedback session. The student felt that Harriet's reference to Holden Caulfield was distracting. As the student pointed out, Harriet's paper focuses on children of all ages, not just on teens. The allusion to *The Catcher in the Rye* misrepresented the focus of the essay. Harriet's decision to omit the reference in the revised conclusion helped the paper come together as a unified whole.

These are just several changes Harriet made when reworking her essay. Harriet's revisions reflect her understanding that writing is a process. It take time. Harriet also knows that the effort can yield highly satisfying results, for writer and reader alike.

DESCRIPTION

WHAT IS DESCRIPTION?

Animals live — or die — by their senses. Being able to scent danger, detect the slightest rustle, spot the lion camouflaged among the tawny grass is crucial to survival. Although human senses are weak compared to those of most other animals, and although we compensate for this weakness by favoring our brains over our sensory organs, we are still animal enough to respond in a strong way to sensory stimulation. The sweet perfume of a candy shop takes us back to childhood; the stale medicine smell of the campus infirmary reminds us of long vigils at a hospital while a grandmother lay dying; the clang and thud of a city sets our nerves on edge; a splendid meal, pleasing to both eye and palate, usually revives even the most beleaguered among us.

Without any sensory stimulation, we sink into a less-than-human state. Neglected babies, left alone with no human touch, no colors, no lullaby sounds, become withdrawn and unresponsive. And prisoners dread solitary confinement, knowing that the sensory deprivation can be unbearable, even to the point of madness.

Because sensory impressions are so important, descriptive writing has a power and a basic appeal that is unlike any other kind of writing. Description can be defined as the expression — in vivid word pictures — of what the five human senses experience. A richly rendered description freezes a subject in time, evoking sights, smells, sounds, textures, and tastes in such a way that the reader becomes one with the writer's world and vision.

WHEN TO USE DESCRIPTION

Description can be a supportive technique that develops part of an essay, or description can be the dominant technique used within an entire essay. Your purpose in writing will determine the amount of description you use. The following examples show how description can help make a point in an essay organized chiefly around another pattern of development.

- You could describe a violent family confrontation that ended in murder at the beginning of an *argumentation-persuasion* essay urging handgun control legislation.
- You might describe a pack of stray, starving dogs in a *causal analysis* that explains the consequences of pet overpopulation.
- In a *process analysis* explaining how to make ice cream that outclasses the packaged brands sold in grocery stores, you might describe the simple, functional beauty of an old-fashioned, hand-cranked ice cream maker.
- In a *narrative* essay that recounts a busy day in the life of a street musician, you could use description to detail the energy of the musician and the crowd milling around him.

Just as your purpose determines how much or how little description to use, you have a great deal of freedom deciding *what* to describe. Description is especially suited to objects (your car or desk, for example), but you can also describe a person, place, time, and phenomenon or concept. Effective descriptions might be written about a friend who runs marathons (person), the kitchen of a fast-food restaurant (place), a period when you were unemployed (time), the "flight or fight" syndrome (phenomenon or concept).

Depending on your approach to the subject, description can be divided into two types: *objective* and *subjective*. In an *objective description*, you describe the subject but do not reveal your attitude or feelings about it. Instead, you are concerned with transmitting a straightforward and literal portrait of the subject, without fusing your own point of view onto the description. For example, a reporter may write an unemotional account of a township meeting that ended in a fistfight between town council members and residents. Or a marine biologist may write a factual report describing the way sea mammals are killed by the plastic refuse (sandwich wrappings, straws, fishing lines) that humans throw into the ocean. Reporters as well as technical and scientific writers specialize in objective description; their jobs depend on their ability to detail experiences without emotional bias.

By way of contrast, in a *subjective description*, you want to convey a highly personal vision of the subject; you want to evoke a strong emotional response in the reader. Subjective descriptions are often reflective pieces or character studies. For example, you might describe the abundance of plant life in an inner-city community garden, using the piece to reflect on the human need to connect with the soil. Or you might write a character study of your grandfather, describing the contradictions between his imposing appearance and his gentle nature.

Subjective descriptions vary in tone, according to your attitude toward your subject. You could write a serious, respectful piece about a high-powered woman who runs a center for disturbed children. But the essay could also be an amusing description of your roommate's fastidious need for order. In all cases, though, a subjective description is concerned with a personal view of the subject.

Descriptive language changes, depending on whether your purpose is primarily objective or subjective. If the description is objective, the language is straightforward, precise, and factual. Such *denotative* language is concerned with neutral dictionary meanings. For example, if you wanted to describe as dispassionately as possible the violent behavior of fans at a football game, you might write about the "large crowd" and its "mass movement onto the field." But if you were disturbed by the fans' behavior and decided to write a highly subjective piece making your outrage clear, you might write about the "swelling mob" and their "rowdy stampede onto the field." In the latter case, the language used would be *connotative*, emotionally charged with your feelings about what happened.

Subjective and objective descriptions often overlap. Sometimes a single sentence will contain objective *and* subjective elements ("Although his hands were large and misshapen by arthritis, they were gentle to the touch, inspiring confidence and trust"). Other times, part of an essay may provide a factual description (the physical appearance of a summer cabin your family rented), while another part of the essay may be highly subjective (how you felt in the cabin, sitting in front of a fire on a rainy day).

SUGGESTIONS FOR USING DESCRIPTION IN AN ESSAY

The following suggestions will be helpful whether you use description as a dominant or supportive pattern of development.

1. Focus a descriptive essay around a dominant impression. Like other kinds of writing, a descriptive essay must have a main idea or point. The point usually centers on the *dominant impression* you have about your subject. Suppose you decide to write a paper about your unforgettable ninth-grade history teacher, Mrs. Hazzard. You want to write an essay that conveys Mrs. Hazzard's unconventional, flamboyant nature. The essay could, of course, focus on a different dominant impression—how insensitive she could be to students, for example. What is important is that you establish for yourself the dominant impression of the essay. Because many descriptive essays do not have thesis statements, the essay's dominant impression may be implied. Still, there never should be any question about what the dominant impression is.

2. Be selective in your choice of details. The power of description—especially description with a subjective slant—hinges on the details chosen to support the dominant impression. You should include only those details that contribute to this impression and leave out all others, no matter how vivid or interesting they might be. If you are describing how flamboyant Mrs. Hazzard could be, the details in the following paragraph would be appropriate.

A large-boned woman, Mrs. Hazzard wore her bright red hair piled on top of her head where it perched precariously. By the end of class, wayward strands of hair tumbled down and fell into eyes fringed by spiky false eyelashes. Mrs. Hazzard's nails, filed into crisp points, were painted either bloody burgundy or neon pink. Plastic bangle bracelets, also either burgundy or pink, clattered up and down her ample arms as she scrawled on the board the historical dates that had, she claimed, "changed the world."

The details you chose — the heavy eye makeup, the stilettolike nails, the gaudy bracelets — contribute to the impression of a flamboyant, unusual person. Even if you remembered times that Mrs. Hazzard seemed perfectly conventional and understated, you would most likely omit those details because they would detract from the unity your essay achieves by being rooted in a single, dominant impression.

You must also be selective in the number of details you include in the essay. Having a dominant impression helps you eliminate many inappropriate details, but there will still be choices to make. For example, you would not want to describe in exhaustive detail everything in a messy room:

The brown desk, made of a grained plastic laminate, is directly under a small window covered by a torn yellow-and-gold plaid curtain. In the left corner of the desk are four crumbled balls of blue-lined yellow paper, three red markers, two fine-point blue pens, an ink eraser, and four letters, two bearing special wildlife stamps. A green down-filled vest and a red cable knit sweater are thrown over the back of the bright blue metal bridge chair pushed under the desk. Under the chair is an oval braided rug, its once brilliant blues and greens spotted by old coffee stains.

Your readers will be reluctant to wade through these undifferentiated specifics. Even more important, such obsessive detailing dilutes the focus of the essay. You end up with a seemingly endless list of specifics, rather than a carefully crafted picture in words. In this regard, sculptors and writers are similar — what they take away is as important as what they leave in.

Perhaps you are wondering how to generate the details that support your dominant impression. As you can imagine, you have to develop heightened powers of observation and recall. To sharpen these key faculties, it can be helpful to make up a chart with separate columns for each of the five senses. If you can observe your subject directly, enter in the appropriate columns what you see, hear, taste, and so on. If you are attempting to remember something from the past, try to recollect details under each of these sense headings. Ask yourself questions ("How did it smell? What did I hear?") and list each memory recaptured. You will be surprised how this simple technique can tune you in to your experiences, helping uncover the specific details needed to develop your dominant impression.

3. Organize the descriptive details.   It is important to select the organizational pattern (or combination of patterns) that best supports your dominant impression. The paragraphs that make up a descriptive essay are most frequently organized *spatially* (from top to bottom, from interior to exterior, from near to far) or *chronologically* (as the subject is experienced in time). But the paragraphs can also be organized *emphatically* (ending with the most striking elements of your subject). Or you may decide to sequence the paragraphs according to *sensory impressions* (first smell, then taste, then touch, and so on). Although descriptive paragraphs do not always have topic sentences, each paragraph should have its own clear focus.

You might, for instance, use a spatial pattern to organize a description of a large city, detailing your view of the city from the air, from a taxi, and from your vantage point as you walked around the city. A description of your first day at a new job might move chronologically from how you felt when you woke up that morning to the events that occurred during the course of the day. In a paper describing a bout with the flu, you might arrange details emphatically, starting with a description of your low-level aches and pains, concluding with an account of the raging fever that made you feel as though you were burning up. An essay about a neighborhood garbage dump, euphemistically called an "ecology landfill" by its owners, could be organized by sense impression: the sights of the dump, its smells, its sounds.

4. Use vivid and varied language.   The connotative language used in subjective descriptions must be rich and evocative. Vague, dull generalizations cannot convey the highly personal impression you wish to share with your readers. The words selected must have the power to etch in their minds the same picture that you have in yours. For this reason, you must use language that involves the readers' senses. Consider, for instance, the differences in the following pairs of descriptions:

The food was unappetizing.	The stew congealed into an oval pool of milky-brown fat.
The toothpaste was refreshing.	The toothpaste, tasting minty sweet, felt good against slippery teeth, free finally from braces.
Filled to the roof with passengers and baggage, the car moved slowly down the road.	Burdened with its load of clamoring children and well-worn suitcases, the car labored down the interstate on bald tires and worn shocks, emitting puffs of blue exhaust and an occasional backfire.

The general, abstract sentences on the left are not effective. Unlike the concrete, sensory-packed images on the right, these vague sentences fail to create a strong impression or engage the reader. While all good writing is a blend of abstract and concrete language, descriptive writing demands an abundance of specific sensory language.

Description often uses an especially vivid and creative form of language called *figures of speech*. Figures of speech involve nonliteral, imaginative comparisons between two usually dissimilar things. *Similes* use the words *like* or *as* when making the comparisons; *metaphors* imply that two things are alike; and *personification* involves attributing human characteristics to inanimate things.

The examples that follow show how effective figurative language can be in descriptive writing.

Moving as jerkily as a marionette on strings, the old man picked himself up off the sidewalk and staggered down the street. (simile)

Stalking their prey, the hall monitors remained hidden in the corridors, motionless and ready to spring on any unsuspecting student who dared to sneak into class late. (metaphor)

The scoop of vanilla ice cream, plain and unadorned, cried out for hot fudge sauce and a sprinkling of sliced pecans. (personification)

When writing descriptive passages, you also want to be sure to vary your sentence structure; you do not want to use the same subject-verb pattern in all your sentences. In the second example above, for instance, the revised sentence could have been written as follows: "The hall monitors stalked their prey. They remained hidden in the corridors. They remained motionless and ready to spring on any unsuspecting student who dared to sneak into class late." But note how much richer and more interesting the sentence is when the descriptive elements are embedded in the sentence, eliminating what would otherwise be a clipped and predictable subject-verb pattern.

Henry James, American novelist and master of description, gave this advice to beginning writers: "Try to be one of the people on whom nothing is lost." If you work to become the kind of writer "on whom nothing is lost," you will find you have a rich mine of sensory impressions to explore and transmute into written form. To develop your descriptive powers, you must be alert to your inner and outer worlds. And you must develop sensitivity to the nuances of language, finding just the right words to convey the essence of your experiences. It is no wonder, then, that descriptive writing can be a source of such pleasure for writer and reader alike.

STUDENT ESSAY AND COMMENTARY

The following student essay was written by Marie Martinez in response to this assignment:

The essay "Once More to the Lake" is an evocative piece about a spot that had special meaning in E. B. White's life.

Write an essay about a place that holds rich significance for you, centering the description on a dominant impression.

While reading Marie's paper, try to determine how well it applies the principles concerning the use of description. The commentary following the paper will help you look at Marie's essay more closely.

Salt Marsh

In one of his journals, Thoreau told of the difficulty he had escap- 1
ing the obligations and cares of society: "It sometimes happens that I cannot easily shake off the village. The thought of some work will run in my head and I am not where my body is--I am out of my senses. In my walks I . . . return to my senses." All of us feel out of our senses at times. Overwhelmed by problems or everyday annoyances, we lose touch with sensory pleasures as we spend our days in noisy cities and stuffy classrooms. Just as Thoreau walked in the woods to return to his senses, I have a special place where I return to mine: the salt marsh behind my grandparents' house.

My grandparents live on the East Coast, a mile or so inland from 2
the sea. Between the ocean and the mainland is a wide fringe of salt marsh. A salt marsh is not a swamp, but an expanse of dark spongy soil threaded with salt-water creeks and clothed in a kind of grass called salt meadow hay. All the water in the marsh rises and falls daily with the ocean tides, an endless cycle that changes the look of the marsh--partly flooded or mostly dry--as the day progresses.

Heading out to the marsh from my grandparents' house, I follow 3
a short path through the woods. As I walk along, a sharp smell of salt mixed with the rich aroma of peaty soil fills my nostrils. I am always amazed by the way the path changes with the seasons. Sometimes I walk in the brilliant green of spring, sometimes in the tawny gold of autumn, sometimes in the grayish-tan of winter. No matter the season, the grass flanking the trail is often flattened into swirls, like the paintings by Van Gogh where thick brushstrokes of paint curve and recurve in circular patterns. No people come here. The peacefulness heals me like a soothing drug.

After a few minutes, the trail suddenly opens up to a view that 4
calms me no matter how upset or discouraged I might be: a line of tall waving reeds bordering and nearly hiding the salt marsh creek. To get to the creek, I part the reeds.

The creek is a narrow body of water, no more than fifteen feet   5
wide, and it ebbs and flows as the ocean currents sweep toward the
land or rush back toward the sea. The creek winds in a sinuous pattern so that I cannot see its beginning or end, the places where it
trickles into the marsh or spills into the open ocean. Little brown birds
dip in and out of the reeds on the far shore of the creek, making a
special "tweep-tweep" sound peculiar to the marsh. When I stand at
low tide on the shore of the creek, I am on a miniature cliff, for the
bank of the creek falls abruptly and steeply into the water. Below me,
green grasses wave and shimmer under the water while tiny minnows flash their silvery sides as they dart through the underwater
tangles.

The creek water is often much warmer than the ocean, so I can   6
swim there in three seasons. Sitting on the edge of the creek, I scoop
some water in my hand, rubbing my face and neck, then ease into the
water. Where the creek is shallow, my feet sink into a foot of muck that
feels like mashed potatoes mixed with motor oil. But once I become
accustomed to it, I enjoy squishing the slimy mud through my toes.
Sometimes I feel brushing past my legs the blue crabs that live in the
creek. Other times, I hear the splash of a turtle or otter as it slips from
the shore into the water. Otherwise, it is silent. The salty water is
buoyant and lifts my spirits as I stroke through it to reach the middle
of the creek. There in the center, I float weightlessly, surrounded by
tall reeds that reduce the world to water and sky. I am at peace.

The salt marsh is not the kind of dramatic landscape found on   7
picture postcards. There are no soaring mountains, sandy beaches, or
lush valleys. The marsh is a flat world that some consider dull and
uninviting. I am glad most people do not respond to the marsh's
subtle beauty because that means I can be alone there. Just as the
rising tide sweeps over the marsh, floating debris out to ocean, the
marsh washes away my concerns and restores me to my senses.

Marie responded to the assignment by writing a moving tribute to a place having special meaning for her — the salt marsh near
her grandparents' home. Like most *descriptive pieces*, Marie's essay is
organized around a *dominant impression*: the peaceful solitude and
gentle natural beauty of the marsh. The essay's introduction provides a context for the dominant impression by comparing the
pleasure Marie experiences in the marsh to the happiness Thoreau
felt in his walks around Walden Pond.

Before developing the essay's dominant impression, Marie
uses the second paragraph to present a *definition* of a salt marsh.
This *objective description* clarifies that a salt marsh — with its spongy

soil, haylike grass and ebbing tides — is not to be confused with a swamp. Because she offers such a factual definition, readers are now in a position to understand what Marie is talking about; they have the background needed to enjoy the personalized view that follows.

At times, Marie develops her dominant impression explicitly, as when she writes "No people come here" (paragraph 3) and "I am at peace" (6). But Marie generally uses the more subtle techniques characteristic of *subjective description* to convey her dominant impression. First of all, she fills the essay with strong *connotative language*, rich with *sensory images.* In the third paragraph, she describes what she smells (the "sharp smell of salt mixed with the rich aroma of peaty soil") and what she sees ("brilliant green," "tawny gold," and "grayish-tan"). The fifth paragraph tells us that she hears the chirping sounds of small birds. And the sixth paragraph includes vigorous descriptions of how the marsh feels to Marie's touch. She splashes water on her face and neck; she relishes digging her toes into the mud at the bottom of the creek; she delights in the delicate brushing of crabs against her legs.

You might have noted that *figurative language* and *varied sentence patterns* also play an important role in conveying the descriptive power of Marie's essay. Marie develops a *simile* in the third paragraph when she compares the flattened swirls of swamp grass to the brush strokes in a painting by Van Gogh. Later in the paper, she uses another simile when she writes that the thick mud in the creek feels "like mashed potatoes mixed with oil." Marie adds further impact to her description by varying the length of her sentences. Long, fairly elaborate sentences are interspersed with short, dramatic statements. In the third paragraph, for example, the long sentence describing the circular swirls of swamp grass is followed by the brief statement "No people come here." And the sixth paragraph uses two short sentences ("Otherwise, it is silent" and "I am at peace") to punctuate the longer sentences in the paragraph.

We can follow Marie's journey through the marsh with ease because she *organizes her descriptive details* effectively. She uses a combination of *spatial, chronological*, and *emphatic* patterns to sequence her experience. Perhaps you realized that the four paragraphs making up the body of the essay focus on the different spots that Marie reaches: first, the path behind her grandparents' house (3); then the area bordering the creek (4); next, her view of the creek

(5); and last, the creek itself with its extraordinary restorative powers (6). Clear *signals* (marked by italics here) indicate the passage of time as well as Marie's location, thus clarifying the sequence of her journey: "*As* I walk along, a sharp smell . . . fills my nostrils" (3); "*After* a few minutes, the trail suddenly opens up . . ." (4); "*Below* me, green grasses wave . . ." (5); and "*There* in the center, I float weightlessly . . ." (6).

Although the four paragraphs in the body of the essay focus on the distinctive qualities of each location, Marie runs into a minor problem generating appropriate material for the third paragraph. Take a moment to reread the last sentence in that paragraph. Comparing the peace of the marsh to the effect of a "soothing drug" is jarring. The effectiveness of Marie's essay hinges on her ability to create a picture of a pure, natural world. This reference to drugs is inappropriate. Now, reread the paragraph aloud, stopping after "No people come here." Note how much more effective the paragraph is, how much more in keeping it is with the essay's dominant impression.

The concluding paragraph brings the essay to a graceful close. The powerful *simile* found in the last sentence contains an implied reference to Thoreau and her statement about the joy to be found in special places having restorative powers. Such an allusion echoes, with good effect, the paper's opening comments.

When Marie met with some classmates during a group feedback session, the students agreed that Marie's first draft was strong and moving. But they also said that they had difficulty following her route through the marsh; they found her third paragraph especially confusing. The original draft of the third paragraph is reprinted below.

Unrevised Version

As I head out to the marsh from the house, I follow a short trail through the woods. A smell of salt mixed with the aroma of soil fills my nostrils. The end of the trail suddenly opens up to a view that calms me no matter how upset or discouraged I might be: a line of tall waving reeds bordering the salt marsh creek. Civilization seems far away as I walk the path of flattened grass and finally reach my goal, the salt marsh creek hidden behind the tall waving reeds. The path changes with the seasons; sometimes I walk in the brilliant green of spring, sometimes in the tawny gold of autumn, sometimes in the quiet grayish-tan of winter. In some areas, the grass is flattened into swirls that make the marsh resemble one of those paintings by Van Gogh. No people come here. The peacefulness heals me like a soothing drug. The path stops at the line of tall waving reeds, standing upright at the border of the creek. I part the reeds to get to the creek.

When Marie looked more carefully at the paragraph, she realized it was indeed baffling. For one thing, in the paragraph's third and fourth sentences, she wrote that she came to the end of the path and reached the reeds bordering the creek. But in the following sentences she said she was on the path again. Then, at the end of the paragraph, she indicated she was once more back at the creek and the reeds, as if she had just arrived there. Marie resolved this confusion when editing her paper. She reorganized the information in the single paragraph into two separate paragraphs — one describing the walk along the path, the other describing her arrival at the creek. This restructuring, especially when combined with the addition of clearer transitions, eliminated the confusion.

While editing her essay, Marie also decided to intensify the sensory images in her original version of the paragraph. The "smell of salt mixed with the aroma of soil" was changed to the "sharp smell of salt mixed with the rich aroma of peaty soil." And when she added the phrase, "thick brushstrokes of paint curving and recurving in circular patterns," she made the comparison between the grass swirls and a Van Gogh painting more vivid.

These represent some of the changes Marie made while revising her paper. Her skillful editing provided the polish needed to make an already strong essay even more powerful and evocative.

All the selections ahead use description to make their subjects come alive and to provide supporting evidence for a controlling idea or impression. Larry Woiwode's "Wanting an Orange" is an exuberant and sensuous account of one of life's small pleasures, while Russell Baker's "In My Day" is a wistful memoir of the author's aging mother. "The Bubble Gum Store," by Calvin Trillin, celebrates the mom-and-pop grocery and the warm traditional values it represents. In "Once More to the Lake," E. B. White recalls his youth when visiting a childhood vacation spot with his son. Finally, Peggy Anderson's "Children's Hospital" describes an environment especially designed to heal and nurture.

Larry Woiwode

Larry Woiwode (1941–   ) was born and raised in Carrington, North Dakota. He is a freelance writer whose short stories, poems, and essays have appeared in The New Yorker, Atlantic Monthly, The New York Times, *and the* Paris Review. *His first two novels,* What I'm Going to Do, I Think *(1969) and* Beyond the Bedroom Wall: A Family Album *(1975), won prestigious literary awards; his most recent novel is* Poppa John *(1981). The following essay originally appeared in the* Paris Review.

Wanting an Orange

When we look back on our childhoods, it is often the small things we remember most vividly — swinging on a backyard gate, the taste of dreaded lima beans, a grandfather's way of being funny. In this essay, Larry Woiwode celebrates such a seemingly minor experience — the eating of an orange. Using a multitude of sensory details, he shows how youthful enthusiasm can transform the commonplace into sacred ritual.

Oh, those oranges arriving in the midst of the North Dakota 1
winters of the forties — the mere color of them, carried through the
door in a net bag or a crate from out of the white winter landscape.
Their appearance was enough to set my brother and me to thinking
that it might be about time to develop an illness, which was the
surest way of receiving a steady supply of them.

"Mom, we think we're getting a cold." 2

"*We?* You mean, you two want an orange?" 3

This was difficult for us to answer or dispute; the matter 4
seemed moved beyond our mere wanting.

"If you want an orange," she would say, "why don't you ask 5
for one?"

"We want an orange." 6

"'We' again. '*We want an orange.*'" 7

72

"May we have an orange, please."   8
"That's the way you know I like you to ask for one. Now, why   9
don't each of you ask for one in that same way, but separately?"
"Mom . . . " And so on. There was no depth of degradation   10
that we wouldn't descend to in order to get one. If the oranges
hadn't wended their way northward by Thanksgiving, they were
sure to arrive before the Christmas season, stacked first in crates at
the depot, filling that musty place, where pews sat back to back,
with a springtime acidity, as if the building had been rinsed with a
renewing elixir that set it right for yet another year. Then the crates
would appear at the local grocery store, often with the top slats
pried back on a few of them, so that we were aware of a resinous
smell of fresh wood in addition to the already orangy atmosphere
that foretold the season more explicitly than any calendar.

And in the broken-open crates (as if burst by the power of the   11
oranges themselves), one or two of the lovely spheres would lie free
of the tissue they came wrapped in — always purple tissue, as if that
were the only color that could contain the populations of them in
their nestled positions. The crates bore paper labels at one end — of
an orange against a blue background, or of a blue goose against an
orange background — signifying the colorful otherworld (unlike
our wintry one) that these phenomena had arisen from. Each orange, stripped of its protective wrapping, as vivid in your vision as a
pebbled sun, encouraged you to picture a whole pyramid of them
in a bowl on your dining room table, glowing in the light, as if
giving off the warmth that came through the windows from the real
winter sun. And all of them came stamped with a blue-purple name
as foreign as the otherworld that you might imagine as their place
of origin, so that on Christmas day you would find yourself digging
past everything else in your Christmas stocking, as if tunneling
down to the country of China, in order to reach the rounded bulge
at the tip of the toe which meant that you had received a personal
reminder of another state of existence, wholly separate from your
own.

The packed heft and texture, finally, of an orange in your   12
hand — that is it! — and the eruption of smell and the watery fireworks as a knife, in the hand of someone skilled, like our mother,
goes slicing through the skin so perfect for slicing. This gaseous
spray can form a mist like smoke, which can then be lit with a match
to create actual fireworks if there is a chance to hide alone with a

match (matches being forbidden) and the peel from one. Sputtery ignitions can also be produced by squeezing a peel near a candle (at least one candle is generally always going at Christmastime), and the leftover peels are set on the stove top to scent the house.

And the ingenious way in which oranges come packed into their globes! The green nib at the top, like a detonator, can be bitten off, as if disarming the orange, in order to clear a place for you to sink a tooth under the peel. This is the best way to start. If you bite at the peel too much, your front teeth will feel scraped, like dry bone, and your lips will begin to burn from the bitter oil. Better to sink a tooth into this greenish or creamy depression, and then pick at that point with the nail of your thumb, removing a little piece of the peel at a time. Later, you might want to practice to see how large a piece you can remove intact. The peel can also be undone in one continuous ribbon, a feat which maybe your father is able to perform, so that after the orange is freed, looking yellowish, the peel, rewound, will stand in its original shape, although empty. 13

The yellowish whole of the orange can now be divided into sections, usually about a dozen, by beginning with a division down the middle; after this, each section, enclosed in its papery skin, will be able to be lifted and torn loose more easily. There is a stem up the center of the sections like a mushroom stalk, but tougher; this can be eaten. A special variety of orange, without any pits, has an extra growth, or nubbin, like half of a tiny orange, tucked into its bottom. This nubbin is nearly as bitter as the peel, but it can be eaten, too; don't worry. Some of the sections will have miniature sections embedded in them and clinging as if for life, giving the impression that babies are being hatched, and should you happen to find some of these you've found the sweetest morsels of any. 14

If you prefer to have your orange sliced in half, as some people do, the edges of the peel will abrade the corners of your mouth, making them feel raw, as you eat down into the white of the rind (which is the only way to do it) until you can see daylight through the orangy bubbles composing its outside. Your eyes might burn; there is no proper way to eat an orange. If there are pits, they can get in the way, and the slower you eat an orange, the more you'll find your fingers sticking together. And no matter how carefully you eat one, or bite into a quarter, juice can always fly or slip from a corner of your mouth; this happens to everyone. Close your eyes to be on 15 the safe side, and for the eruption in your mouth of the slivers of watery meat, which should be broken and rolled fine over your tongue for the essence of orange. And if indeed you have sensed yourself coming down with a cold, there is a chance that you will feel it driven from your head — your nose and sinuses suddenly opening — in the midst of the scent of a peel and eating an orange.

And oranges can also be eaten whole — rolled into a spongy   16 mass and punctured with a pencil (if you don't find this offensive) or a knife, and then sucked upon. Then, once the juice is gone, you can disembowel the orange as you wish and eat away its pulpy remains, and eat once more into the whitish interior of the peel, which scours the coating from your teeth and makes your numbing lips and the tip of your tongue start to tingle and swell up from behind, until, in the light from the windows (shining through an empty glass bowl), you see orange again from the inside. Oh, oranges, solid *o*'s, light from afar in the midst of the freeze, and not unlike that unspherical fruit which first went from Eve to Adam and from there (to abbreviate matters) to my brother and me.

"Mom, we think we're getting a cold."   17

"You mean, you want an orange?"   18

This is difficult to answer or dispute or even to acknowledge,   19 finally, with the fullness that the subject deserves, and that each orange bears, within its own makeup, into this hard-edged yet insubstantial, incomplete, cold, wintry world.

Questions for Close Reading

1. What is the thesis (or dominant impression) of the selection? Locate the sentence(s) in which Woiwode states his main idea. If he does not state the thesis explicitly, express it in your own words.
2. Why were Woiwode and his brother, growing up as children in North Dakota, so fond of oranges? What was it about the oranges that made them so appealing?
3. How could the oranges be enjoyed even before they were eaten? What uses, for example, did the author and his brother find for the peel?
4. According to Woiwode, there is no one way to eat an orange. Why is this? How many ways does he describe?
5. Refer to your dictionary as needed to define the following words used in the selection: *degradation* (paragraph 10), *wended* (10), *elixir* (10), *ingenious* (13), *detonator* (13), *morsels* (14), and *disembowel* (16).

Questions about the Writer's Craft

1. Descriptive writing often appeals to our senses, especially to the sense of sight. Which of the senses does "Wanting an Orange" focus on? Why?
2. What method or combination of methods (chronological, sensory, spatial, or emphatic) does Woiwode use to organize his description?
3. Figurative language is another tool the author uses to make his description memorable. One example is the comparison of the green nib at the top of an orange to a detonator in paragraph 13. Find other examples of metaphors and similes in the essay. What qualities of an orange does Woiwode evoke with these images?
4. Why does Woiwode begin this description of an orange by recounting a typical conversation of his youth, one between himself, his brother, and his mother? How does this opening serve as an enticing introduction? In what way does the conversation help support the thesis?

Questions for Further Thought

1. After reading Woiwode's description of oranges, do you feel differently about them? Are there other foods or ordinary things you now realize you take for granted?
2. Do you still remember and treasure any childhood experiences, even those as mundane as eating a favorite food? What memories of special events or objects from childhood do you have that would correspond to Woiwode's of eating oranges?
3. Anything can be special if we pay attention, if we suddenly see it in a close-up or new way. Are there any objects or events in your life that, like the orange, would benefit from such careful examination and appreciation? Could any of these objects and events take on symbolic significance, like the orange?
4. Eating an orange is a simple pleasure. Have we lost sight of such basic appreciations? Do we rely too much on manufactured products, such as electronic gadgets and gourmet delicacies, for our enjoyments?

Writing Assignments Using Description as a Method of Development

1. Write an essay celebrating another food, household item, or ordinary object that people take for granted but that is actually very special and precious, even magical. For example, a pencil, candy bar, paper clip, or favorite pair of shoes or jeans could be the subject of your ode. Use vivid sensory description to convey the significance and vitality of your topic.

2. Describe a recurring event of your childhood that was much anticipated by you and other members of your family. The essay could focus on a cherished family ritual like the celebration of Christmas, a birthday, or Thanksgiving. Or you might write about a family vacation, an annual trip to see a particular sports team play, or even the yearly spring cleaning. Evoke the specialness of this ritual by describing how you anticipated it and the details of the day when it came. If food played an important part in the event, be sure to include the appropriate sensory details.

Writing Assignments Using Other Methods of Development

3. Woiwode describes in great detail how to eat an orange. Pick some other food you enjoy and write an essay describing the process of enjoying it to the fullest. For example, you might write about how to eat an ice cream cone, spaghetti, pizza, tacos, lobster or crab, bacon and eggs, or a Chinese dish.

4. Most people don't pay enough attention to the ordinary things of life. Write an essay arguing this point of view, giving reasons why we should be more observant, even reverent, about the details of what is around us. Support your essay by giving examples of the benefits and advantages of being an aware and appreciative person.

Russell Baker

In his regular column "The Observer" for The New York Times, *Russell Baker applies his unique brand of humor to social commentary. Born in Virginia in 1925, Baker received his B.A. from Johns Hopkins University and spent several years working as a reporter for the* Baltimore Sun *before joining the* Times *in the mid-'50s. In 1979, Baker won a Pulitzer Prize, journalism's highest honor. Baker's columns have been collected in several books, including* So This Is Depravity *(1980). The following selection is from his 1982 autobiography,* Growing Up, *which became a bestseller and received critical acclaim.*

In My Day

We often expect the most from — and are most intolerant of — the people we counted on when we were young. In the following selection, Russell Baker describes his aging mother and the tangled feelings she arouses in him as she takes refuge in her memories. Her mental deterioration leads Baker to ponder the weaving of past and present that flows through all families.

At the age of eighty my mother had her last bad fall, and after 1 that her mind wandered free through time. Some days she went to weddings and funerals that had taken place half a century earlier. On others she presided over family dinners cooked on Sunday afternoons for children who were now gray with age. Through all this she lay in bed but moved across time, traveling among the dead decades with a speed and ease beyond the gift of physical science.

"Where's Russell?" she asked one day when I came to visit at 2 the nursing home.

"I'm Russell," I said. 3

She gazed at this improbably overgrown figure out of an in- 4 conceivable future and promptly dismissed it.

"Russell's only this big," she said, holding her hand, palm 5
down, two feet from the floor. That day she was a young country
wife with chickens in the backyard and a view of hazy blue Virginia
mountains behind the apple orchard, and I was a stranger old
enough to be her father.

Early one morning she phoned me in New York. "Are you 6
coming to my funeral today?" she asked.

It was an awkward question with which to be awakened. 7
"What are you talking about, for God's sake?" was the best reply I
could manage.

"I'm being buried today," she declared briskly, as though 8
announcing an important social event.

"I'll phone you back," I said and hung up, and when I did 9
phone back she was all right, although she wasn't all right, of
course, and we all knew she wasn't.

She had always been a small woman — short, light-boned, del- 10
icately structured — but now, under the white hospital sheet, she
was becoming tiny. I thought of a doll with huge, fierce eyes. There
had always been a fierceness in her. It showed in that angry, challenging thrust of the chin when she issued an opinion, and a great
one she had always been for issuing opinions.

"I tell people exactly what's on my mind," she has been fond 11
of boasting. "I tell them what I think, whether they like it or not."
Often they had not liked it. She could be sarcastic to people in
whom she detected evidence of the ignoramus or the fool.

"It's not always good policy to tell people exactly what's on 12
your mind," I used to caution her.

"If they don't like it, that's too bad," was her customary reply, 13
"because that's the way I am."

And so she was. A formidable woman. Determined to speak 14
her mind, determined to have her way, determined to bend those
who opposed her. In that time when I had known her best, my
mother had hurled herself at life with chin thrust forward, eyes
blazing, and an energy that made her seem always on the run.

She ran after squawking chickens, an axe in her hand, deter- 15
mined on a beheading that would put dinner in the pot. She ran
when she made the beds, ran when she set the table. One Thanksgiving she burned herself badly when, running up from the cellar
oven with the ceremonial turkey, she tripped on the stairs and
tumbled back down, ending at the bottom in the debris of giblets,

hot gravy, and battered turkey. Life was combat, and victory was not to the lazy, the timid, the slugabed, the drugstore cowboy, the libertine, the mushmouth afraid to tell people exactly what was on his mind whether people liked it or not. She ran.

But now the running was over. For a time I could not accept   16
the inevitable. As I sat by her bed, my impulse was to argue her back to reality. On my first visit to the hospital in Baltimore, she asked who I was.

"Russell," I said.   17
"Russell's way out west," she advised me.   18
"No, I'm right here."   19
"Guess where I came from today?" was her response.   20
"Where?"   21
"All the way from New Jersey."   22
"When?"   23
"Tonight."   24
"No. You've been in the hospital for three days," I insisted.   25
"I suggest the thing to do is calm down a little bit," she   26
replied. "Go over to the house and shut the door."

Now she was years deep into the past, living in the neighbor-   27
hood where she had settled forty years earlier, and she had just been talking with Mrs. Hoffman, a neighbor across the street.

"It's like Mrs. Hoffman said today: The children always   28
wander back to where they come from," she remarked.
"Mrs. Hoffman has been dead for fifteen years."   29
"Russ got married today," she replied.   30
"I got married in 1950" I said, which was the fact.   31
"The house is unlocked," she said.   32

So it went until a doctor came by to give one of those oral   33
quizzes that medical men apply in such cases. She failed catastroph-ically, giving wrong answers or none at all to "What day is this?" "Do you know where you are?" "How old are you?" and so on. Then, a surprise.

"When is your birthday?" he asked.   34
"November 5, 1897," she said. Correct. Absolutely correct.   35
"How do you remember that?" the doctor asked.   36
"Because I was born on Guy Fawkes Day," she said.   37
"Guy Fawkes?" asked the doctor, "Who is Guy Fawkes?"   38
She replied with a rhyme I had heard her recite time and again   39
over the years when the subject of her birth date arose:

"Please to remember the Fifth of November,
Gunpowder treason and plot.
I see no reason why gunpowder treason
Should ever be forgot."

Then she glared at this young doctor so ill informed about Guy
Fawkes' failed scheme to blow King James off his throne with
barrels of gunpowder in 1605. She had been a schoolteacher, after
all, and knew how to glare at a dolt. "You may know a lot about
medicine, but you obviously don't know any history," she said.
Having told him exactly what was on her mind, she left us again.

The doctors diagnosed a hopeless senility. Not unusual, they
said. "Hardening of the arteries" was the explanation for laymen. I
thought it was more complicated than that. For ten years or more
the ferocity with which she had once attacked life had been turning
to a rage against the weakness, the boredom, and the absence of
love that too much age had brought her. Now, after the last bad fall,
she seemed to have broken chains that imprisoned her in a life she
had come to hate and to return to a time inhabited by people who
loved her, a time in which she was needed. Gradually I understood.
It was the first time in years I had seen her happy.

She had written a letter three years earlier which explained
more than "hardening of the arteries." I had gone down from New
York to Baltimore, where she lived, for one of my infrequent visits
and, afterwards, had written her with some banal advice to look for
the silver lining, to count her blessings instead of burdening others
with her miseries. I suppose what it really amounted to was a threat
that if she was not more cheerful during my visits I would not come
to see her very often. Sons are capable of such letters. This one was
written out of a childish faith in the eternal strength of parents, a
naive belief that age and wear could be overcome by an effort of
will, that all she needed was a good pep talk to recharge a flagging
spirit. It was such a foolish, innocent idea, but one thinks of parents
differently from other people. Other people can become frail and
break, but not parents.

She wrote back in an unusually cheery vein intended to demonstrate, I suppose, that she was mending her ways. She was never a
woman to apologize, but for one moment with the pen in her hand
she came very close. Referring to my visit, she wrote: "If I seemed
unhappy to you at times—" Here she drew back, reconsidered,
and said something quite different:

"If I seemed unhappy to you at times, I am, but there's really   43
nothing anyone can do about it, because I'm just so very tired and
lonely that I'll just go to sleep and forget it." She was then seventy-
eight.

Now, three years later, after the last bad fall, she had managed   44
to forget the fatigue and loneliness and, in these free-wheeling
excursions back through time, to recapture happiness. I soon
stopped trying to wrest her back to what I considered the real world
and tried to travel along with her on those fantastic swoops into the
past. One day when I arrived at her bedside she was radiant.

"Feeling good today," I said.   45

"Why shouldn't I feel good?" she asked. "Papa's going to take   46
me up to Baltimore on the boat today."

At that moment she was a young girl standing on a wharf at   47
Merry Point, Virginia, waiting for the Chesapeake Bay steamer
with her father, who had been dead sixty-one years. William How-
ard Taft was in the White House, Europe still drowsed in the dusk
of the great century of peace, America was a young country, and the
future stretched before it in beams of crystal sunlight. "The greatest country on God's green earth," her father might have said, if I
had been able to step into my mother's time machine and join him
on the wharf with the satchels packed for Baltimore.

I could imagine her there quite clearly. She was wearing a blue   48
dress with big puffy sleeves and long black stockings. There was a
ribbon in her hair and a big bow tied on the side of her head. There
had been a childhood photograph in her bedroom which showed
all this, although the colors of course had been added years later by
a restorer who tinted the picture.

About her father, my grandfather, I could only guess, and   49
indeed, about the girl on the wharf with the bow in her hair, I was
merely sentimentalizing. Of my mother's childhood and her people, of their time and place, I knew very little. A world had lived and
died, and though it was part of my blood and bone I knew little
more about it than I knew of the world of the pharaohs. It was
useless now to ask for help from my mother. The orbits of her mind
rarely touched present interrogators for more than a moment.

Sitting at her bedside, forever out of touch with her, I won-   50
dered about my own children, and their children, and children in
general, and about the disconnections between children and par-

ents that prevent them from knowing each other. Children rarely want to know who their parents were before they were parents, and when age finally stirs their curiosity there is no parent left to tell them. If a parent does lift the curtain a bit, it is often only to stun the young with some exemplary tale of how much harder life was in the old days.

I had been guilty of this when my children were small in the   51
early 1960s and living the affluent life. It galled me that their childhoods should be, as I thought, so easy when my own had been, as I thought, so hard. I had developed the habit, when they complained about the steak being overcooked or the television being cut off, of lecturing them on the harshness of life in my day.

"In my day all we got for dinner was macaroni and cheese, and   52
we were glad to get it."

"In my day we didn't have any television."   53

"In my day . . . "   54

"In my day . . . "   55

At dinner one evening a son had offended me with a inade-   56
quate report card, and as I leaned back and cleared my throat to lecture, he gazed at me with an expression of unutterable resignation and said, "Tell me how it was in your days, Dad."

I was angry with him for that, but angrier with myself for   57
having become one of those ancient bores whose highly selective memories of the past become transparently dishonest even to small children. I tried to break the habit, but must have failed. A few years later my son was referring to me when I was out of earshot as "the old-timer." Between us there was a dispute about time. He looked upon the time that had been my future in a disturbing way. My future was his past, and being young, he was indifferent to the past.

As I hovered over my mother's bed listening for muffled sig-   58
nals from her childhood, I realized that this same dispute had existed between her and me. When she was young, with life ahead of her, I had been her future and resented it. Instinctively, I wanted to break free, cease being a creature defined by her time, consign her future to the past, and create my own. Well, I had finally done that, and then with my own children I had seen my exciting future become their boring past.

These hopeless end-of-the-line visits with my mother made me   59
wish I had not thrown off my own past so carelessly. We all come

from the past, and children ought to know what it was that went into their making, to know that life is a braided cord of humanity stretching up from time long gone, and that it cannot be defined by the span of a single journey from diaper to shroud.

Questions for Close Reading

1. What is the thesis (or dominant impression) of the selection? Locate the sentence(s) in which Baker states his main idea. If he does not state the thesis explicitly, express it in your own words.
2. What was Mrs. Baker's philosophy of life? How did it change in her old age?
3. Why does Baker feel "forever out of touch" with his mother? Does he feel equally out of touch with his children?
4. Why does Baker stop trying to get his eighty-year-old mother to return to the real world? Is he being kind or unkind?
5. Refer to your dictionary as needed to define the following words used in the selection: *inconceivable* (paragraph 4), *libertine* (15), *banal* (41), *wrest* (44), *exemplary* (50), *galled* (51), and *consign* (58).

Questions about the Writer's Craft

1. How does the series of scenes in "In My Day" develop the dominant impression of the essay?
2. Baker describes his mother by using details about her actions and her appearance as well as by quoting things she said. Both are typical techniques for revealing character in a descriptive piece. Which technique is more effective in conveying Mrs. Baker's personality?
3. Baker repeats the word *ran* as he describes his mother's energy in paragraph 15. He also speaks several times of her *falls*. What is the purpose of repeating these words? What do they suggest about the pattern of his mother's life?
4. In paragraph 28, Mrs. Baker says, "The children always wander back to where they come from." How is this comment by Baker's mother ironic? Find some other examples of irony in the essay.

Questions for Further Thought

1. Baker writes, "Other people can become frail and break, but not parents" (41). What does he mean? What illusions do we have about our parents?

2. On the whole, would you say Russell Baker has been a good son? A good father? What do you think he would do differently if he had another chance? Will reading this essay affect your behavior toward your parents or children?
3. Baker feels that there is no way for parents and children truly to know each other. Do you agree or not—and why?
4. Is it inevitable that children will reject their parents' values and their parents' lives? What forms might this rejection take?

Writing Assignments Using Description as a Method of Development

1. Write a description of a parent or relative at a certain age, for example, "My Brother at Fourteen" or "My Mother at Fifty-Five." Your description should create a dominant impression by conveying the person's characteristic approach to life. Be sure to select lively details that support this dominant impression.
2. Describe one or more active, vital older people who have not retreated into the past to find happiness. Your examples could be people you know, people you have heard about, or people in the public eye. Choose vivid details that show how such people's actions and attitudes keep them "young." Draw some conclusions about what older people can do to stay involved with life.

Writing Assignments Using Other Methods of Development

3. Russell Baker's essay concerns a crisis within his family. Write an essay about a crisis situation within a family—your own or someone else's. The crisis might be a divorce, serious or chronic illness, loss of a job, financial difficulties, or some other serious problem. Your essay might explore the causes and/or effects of the crisis; it might outline the steps the family has taken to deal with the crisis; it might be a narrative that points to some conclusion about how people deal with crises.
4. In the past, most elderly parents lived in an extended family— children, grandchildren, and other relatives were all part of the household. Now, many old people are isolated from families. In addition, our culture does not revere older people as many cultures do; we seem to care little about their experience, wisdom, and traditions. In what way might these factors affect the mental and physical health of older people? Write an essay showing how society's attitudes toward older people have affected their lives.

Calvin Trillin

Calvin Trillin is a celebrated essayist who writes primarily about two diverse topics—politics and food. Born in 1935 in Kansas City, Missouri, Trillin was educated at Yale University. Since 1963, he has been a staff writer for The New Yorker; *he also contributes regularly to* The Nation. *Some of Trillin's social commentaries are collected in the book* With All Disrespect *(1985), and his books on food include* American Fried *(1974),* Alice, Let's Eat *(1974), and* Third Helpings *(1983). The following essay first appeared in* The New Yorker.

The Bubble Gum Store

In this age of multi-level shopping malls and huge supermarkets, what was once an American institution has become nearly extinct—the "mom-and-pop" grocery store. But in some neighborhoods, a few of these old stores still survive. Calvin Trillin pays tribute to one such place. The store, complete with homemade cookies and gumball machines, is run by a young couple interested not so much in high profits as in a spirit of neighborly warmth.

A year or so ago, I became aware that a corner grocery store in   1
our neighborhood was being operated with peculiar warmth. I
don't mean that the other storekeepers are unfriendly. The
laundry, for instance, is run by a pleasant couple with whom we
exchange inquiries about the family in an en-route-to-the-subway
sort of way. One of the checkers at the supermarket is a kindly
woman who has always been a favorite of my daughters, both of
whom are still young enough to consider a bank of gumball machines the store's other attraction, although the relentless line at a
supermarket checkout counter is designed to put a quick end to
conversation after the money has been collected. (By the time I
have reached the register, I have often been made slightly irritable
anyway by counting thirteen or fourteen items in the shopping cart

of the woman ahead of me in the eight-items-or-under express line — thirteen or fourteen even if she counts, as I'm certain she would if I ever worked up the courage to challenge her, a selection of tonic water and Dr. Pepper and Tab as one item of soft drinks.) We have friends and neighbors who run retail businesses in the neighborhood, so we may find ourselves in an antique shop around the corner or a saloon on the square just saying hello or delivering something for a school fair rather than transacting retail business. Our neighborhood is on the edge of what has remained a strongly Italian section of Greenwich Village, and many of the Italian food shops retain the warmth of businesses run by families who have reason to be proud of what they sell — places like Frank's Pork Store, where a few bottles of liquor and some paper cups are left on a counter around Christmas week, so that the customers aren't put in the position of offering each other holiday greetings empty-handed. I might as well admit that because a spectacular delicacy called "hot cooked salami" is produced by Frank's every morning I would probably patronize the place if it were run by the kind of people who kept their thumbs on the scale and snarled at my daughters. It stands to reason that a baker of fresh bread or a maker of homemade chocolates could be forgiven a sullenness intolerable in a purveyor of canned goods.

We live in a neighborhood, at any rate, where civility and informality and friendliness in shops are sufficiently widespread to be taken for granted; we have our grouches, but they are few enough to permit us to husband most of our pure Manhattanite venom for use against Con Edison or the Telephone Company or one of those faceless voices that speak for the uptown department stores. Still, the atmosphere in the corner grocery store seemed unique. The people who ran it, a couple named Ken and Eve, were young, but the store was old-fashioned — a tiny, crowded room with a worn linoleum floor and a marble counter that had been placed toward the rear, so that the customers tended to collect in the center of the store rather than to pause briefly at a register on their way out. Ken and Eve seemed to call all of the customers by name, and the conversation often drew in anyone who just happened to be standing in front of the counter waiting to pay for a quart of milk or studying the canned goods along the wall trying to find the appropriate soup. The customers chatted among themselves, some of them apparently having been introduced by Ken,

2

who (sometimes as a disembodied voice from behind the meat-slic-
ing machine) had a habit of saying, "Hey, you two might as well
know each other — you're neighbors." Somehow, space had been
found in the center of the store for a rocking chair — a wooden one,
with worn spots on the arms and a worn pad on the seat — and it
was often occupied. At first glance, the place seemed to have the
predictable inventory — when I try to envision the inside of a New
York corner store, my mind fills with walls of cat food — but on the
counter were two or three plates of homemade cookies. And what a
gumball machine! Inside of it, a cheerful little man with a necktie
and a grocer's apron stood waiting with his scoop in hand. For only
a penny, he would nod, turn to the cupboard on his left, open it,
withdraw a gumball, and, turning in the other direction, drop it
down a chute that led to the outside world. My daughters were
captivated. From the start, they referred to Ken and Eve's as the
Bubble Gum Store, and that is what we have called it ever since.

   I know that part of my interest in the Bubble Gum Store was   3
based on regret that my daughters had missed growing up near an
old-fashioned grocery on our own corner that had closed just before we moved into the neighborhood — a store that a friend of
ours who spent part of her childhood on the block can still recall in
detail. It was a regret tinged with irritation for a while when the
tenants who replaced the grocer seemed to be a succession of the
kind of shops that these days have names held together by a con-
traction of the uncontractable "and" — Rings 'n' Things, 'n'
names like that. I was also interested to find Ken and Eve — a
bright, open, obviously educated couple — running an old-fashioned store. It even occurred to me that, considering the way a large
percentage of New York families arrived in the city, Ken might have
had a grandfather who in order to get a toehold in the New World
slaved away for years in such a store (as Greek and Portuguese
immigrants are doing in our neighborhood now), giving his son
the opportunity to amass enough capital to send Ken comfortably
to college — so that he could run a corner grocery store. In the
cultural flip-flops of the sixties, of course, New York abounded in
such minor generational ironies — middle-aged couples who
shuddered at having to return from Long Island to the lower East
Side every other Sunday to visit a father who had never left his
tenement, only to find that their own son, having had the blessings
of the Great Neck school system and superior orthodontics be-

stowed on him, made directly for a lower-East Side tenement that differed from his grandfather's only in its lack of cleanliness. The likelihood that Ken and Eve were in the Bubble Gum Store more or less by choice, of course, distinguished them from any earlier generation of storekeepers — or, for that matter, from most of the other merchants in our neighborhood. I suppose there are aspects of the grocery business that are satisfying to the Portuguese couple running a place a few blocks from the Bubble Gum Store, but I suspect that their store represents to them mainly a way to pay the rent and educate their children. Ken and Eve really seemed to be having a good time.

As it turned out, Ken and Eve had thought they might enjoy 4 running a corner store in our neighborhood partly because they had so enjoyed the neighborhood. In recent years, neighborhoodism has been growing in New York, particularly in neighborhoods dominated by brownstones rather than high-rises — the Village, Chelsea, a half-dozen partly renovated areas in Brooklyn. The new version of neighborhoodism, often led by middle-class house renovators, is geographical rather than ethnic; it is organized around residence on a block rather than membership in, say, an Italian Catholic Church. I have always thought that when one of the new tree-planting, block-party-holding, neighbor-meeting block associations is scratched deeply, what scratches back has some attributes of the old, exclusionary, property-crazed homeowners associations. On the other hand, I like the block parties. Geographical neighborhoodism does reflect some of the reasons that New Yorkers who have some choice about where to live may choose the agonies of renovating a brownstone in Chelsea or Cobble Hill rather than move into an apartment in a West Side high-rise — a manageable number of people on the block, next-door neighbors, buildings constructed on a scale that human beings can grasp, the casual neighborliness that comes with sitting on a stoop for a chat on a spring evening rather than exchanging quick hellos between floors in an elevator. What some people are seeking in the low-rise neighborhoods of New York is not adventure or the bright lights but some qualified urban version of what people in other parts of America would consider a normal life.

Ken has not been a consistent block-association activist; al- 5 though he is not overtly political, Eve always says that at heart he is too much of an anarchist to sit through the meetings. But even before he began running the Bubble Gum Store he took great pleasure in the block it is on — a lively Village mixture of renovated brownstones and unrenovated brownstones and small apartment buildings occupied by Irish and Italian families who have lived in them for three or four generations. He lived and worked on the block as a building superintendent. My guess about his background had not been far off, although he is the first person in his family to run a store. His grandfather was an immigrant, his father has prospered in a manufacturing business, his brother is an architect. Ken dropped out of college and tried a number of jobs, none of which he liked, until he more or less settled down to being a super. Eve lived on the same block. She was working in an insurance-company office after having spent several years teaching retarded adults. She was introduced to Ken by the president of the block association.

Ken did not feel philosophically or psychologically prepared 6 to hold the kind of job that might traditionally be associated with his background; he often says he has "a little trouble with authority." The man who had run the corner grocery store on the block for years, an Armenian immigrant, was about ready to retire. ("He was not an uninteresting man, and he ran a profitable store," Ken says, "but he didn't have a good time.") Both Ken and Eve liked the idea of doing something they could do together. Ken liked the idea of not having a boss. Ken's father was willing to put up some money for the purchase. And the corner store had the final appeal of being right on the corner of their own block. Ken now says, "Down to the corner was about as far as I wanted to go."

For an American who finds himself running a small grocery 7 store these days, the normal channels for ambition are expansion or escape. "A whole bunch of things pressure you to become bigger," Ken says. "The nature of business in America is to grow. The customers want more variety. You can buy things cheaper from suppliers in large quantities." Ken and Eve had a different sort of ambition. They did want to make a profit, of course, and Ken says that they have greatly improved on the volume of the previous owner. But they are horrified at anything they believe might detract from the intimacy of the store, and they have no interest in the chain-grocery business. When they talk about how the store is doing, they discuss not just sales volume but whether the atmosphere is quite right or how well the store is filling its role as a place where neighbors can have a relaxed and impromptu chat. In that sense, as Ken and Eve are quick to acknowledge, the store is "artificial" — something they can see themselves doing, something they do because it interests them rather than because the alternative is penury. Ken tends to analyze reasons for, say, having gumball machines the way block-association organizers analyze reasons for having block parties.

There are, as it happens, four gum machines now in the Bubble   8 Gum Store. Ken says he bought the first one while he was looking for ways to "warm the place up a little." He says a gumball machine can be seen as an investment, the way, say, printing up advertising circulars would be an investment — although he sees the return in this case as being in "depth rather than breadth" of patronage. Ken and Eve also consider the gumball machines a way to attract the children of the old Irish and Italian families in the neighborhood — families they are particularly interested in attracting, since they believe the patronage now has an overrepresentation of younger people who live in the Village because they enjoy the informality and an underrepresentation of older people who live in the Village because they were born there. Adults use the machines, too; it is not unusual for a customer to slap a nickel on the counter and say, out of the corner of his mouth, "Gimme five singles" or "Break this five for me." But the kids, by hitting a home run on the baseball gum machine or a hole in one on the golf gum machine, are eligible for stickers that, according to a complicated formula, can be traded in for candy bars or super-hero decals. There is no sign announcing such a system, of course; Ken says it is "not for strangers." Ken and Eve can name three or four other reasons for having gumball machines in a corner store. Among them is that Ken happens to be a sucker for gumball machines.

Three years of ownership by Ken and Eve have brought some   9 physical changes to the Bubble Gum Store — although not enough of them to alter my impression that it is dominated by cat food. On the side of the building Ken now has a long flower box about six feet off the ground — high enough, he says, to foil dogs and to force anyone who wants to steal a flower to do so with a conscious effort rather than a casual swipe. The store-front windows on either side of the entrance still have brands of beer spelled out in neon, but one of them also has an attractive gold-leaf window sign that includes the names of Ken and Eve on intertwined hearts. (Ken has just become a notary public — partly, he claims, because the notary symbol will look terrific on the other window.) The Bubble Gum Store has conventional freezers and coolers jammed into it, but one of them is covered with pictures that Ken took of customers with a Polaroid he got once as a gift, and one of them is festooned with decals of the sort that can be won by a quick pair of hands at the golf gumball machine. A few waiters' trays and old-fashioned advertisements and old cracker boxes are around, but not enough to give the impression that the place sells knick-knacks rather than milk and eggs. The air space in the Bubble Gum Store seems just about fully occupied. There is a clown who can be made to cycle across the store on a tightrope, and a couple of hanging ceramic pieces done by Ken's mother, and a rope that is often climbed by a wooden bear, and a mop that I took to be part of some sort of artistic assemblage until Eve informed me that it was a mop display.

Ken and Eve do a pretty good take-out-sandwich business at   10
noon with people who work in the neighborhood, and, partly because Ken enjoys preparing salads, they can pull out of the delicatessen case a lot of food not found in the ordinary corner store — marinated mushrooms, for instance, and garlic carrots, and stringbeans vinaigrette. They also keep some steak and hamburger in the deli case, on the theory that someone ought to be able to assemble a full meal in the store if necessary. I have occasionally assembled a full meal there myself, but it consists entirely of homemade cookies — Rosie's Cinnamon Butter Crunchies, Meg's Scottish Short Bread, Karen's Nut Brownies, Jean's Banana Nut Bread, and, for dessert, Keen Specials, which are to chocolate-chip cookies what Frank's hot cooked salami is to salami. The idea of selling homemade cookies began, Ken told me, when they told a friend who had become seriously interested in baking that they would sell what she baked on consignment. Then Ken saw that carrying cookies on consignment was one way of keeping traffic in the store; it guarantees the presence of the cookiemakers checking on their cookies, if no one else. The cookie system is the most obvious way that the distinctions between buyers and sellers become blurred at the Bubble Gum Store; the Rosie who makes Rosie's Cinnamon Butter Crunchies is a customer and a supplier and a friend and, as it happens, the block-association president who introduced Ken and Eve.

A bookcase full of books next to the door also came about   11
more or less accidentally, Eve told me—starting when a new
cooler freed some space there and it was decided that whatever
went into the space ought to be something that could be stolen
without inflicting serious financial damage. That led to the idea of
using the space for something free, and that led to the idea of an
informal book-trading pool—unidentified as that, of course, because it, too, is not for strangers. Ken says that some people only
bring books and some people only take books and a few do both.
Some people, he thinks, use the book supply to rationalize spending a few more cents per item in the Bubble Gum Store than they
might spend at the supermarket, but so many people seem uncomfortable about taking hardcover books that Ken periodically goes
around the corner to a store that seems to specialize in secondhand
books and whipping-and-bondage magazines, and trades his hard-
covers in for paperbacks.

Ken and Eve were pleased with how the bookshelves worked   12
out, and they liked the response to their bean-guessing contest.
(The winner got two tickets to a Bette Midler show; second prize
was, naturally, the beans.) They think they're getting better and
better at the more routine aspects of running the store—knowing
how much ice cream to order and maintaining the right kind of
variety. They still poke around other grocery stores looking for
items they might want to stock. The challenge of improving the
store is, of course, part of the enjoyment. Sooner or later, of course,
Ken and Eve are likely to decide that they are doing what they set
out to do about as well as it can be done. Then, I suspect, my
daughters and I will again be without an old-fashioned corner
store.

Questions for Close Reading

1. What is the thesis (or dominant impression) of the selection? Locate
   the sentence(s) in which Trillin states his main idea. If he does not state
   the thesis explicitly, express it in your own words.
2. What does the Bubble Gum Store have in common with the ordinary
   small grocery or convenience store? In what ways is it different?
3. What does Trillin mean by "neighborhoodism"? How has this phenomenon of "neighborhoodism" changed since Trillin's youth?

4. What does Trillin imply, in the last paragraph, about the reason Ken and Eve might eventually sell the neighborhood store? What does this tell you about their motives for being in the grocery business?
5. Refer to your dictionary as needed to define the following words used in the selection: *purveyor* (paragraph 1), *amass* (3), *ethnic* (4), *exclusionary* (4), *overtly* (5), *impromptu* (7), *patronage* (8), *assemblage* (9), and *periodically* (11).

Questions about the Writer's Craft

1. Ken and Eve's store obviously is very special to Trillin. Why, then, does he begin his essay with a long description of other stores, especially stores and storekeepers he doesn't like?
2. Trillin writes long sentences that develop into lengthy paragraphs. What effect do these long sentences have on you? What effect do they have on the tone of the essay?
3. Where in the essay does Trillin make the transition from discussing his curiosity about the Bubble Gum Store and its owners to describing them in detail? What words help him make this transition?
4. Within the description of "The Bubble Gum Store," Trillin includes some short narratives. What does his recounting of the history of the store and of Ken's background add to the essay? How does it support the thesis?

Questions for Further Thought

1. Have you ever visited a store such as the one run by Ken and Eve? Are there any similar ones in your home neighborhood or near your college? Would you be attracted to such a store, or do you prefer modern, quick-service convenience stores?
2. Are you surprised at the warmth between Ken and Eve and their customers? What kind of relationship do you typically have with store clerks and owners — cool and impersonal, or friendly and warm? Are you satisfied with the level of interaction, or do you, like Trillin, long for and appreciate more neighborly store owners?
3. Ken and Eve take pride in their work as store owners. In general, do you feel that people today take pride in doing a job well and in investing in improvements for their own sake? If not, how could people be encouraged to raise their standards for themselves?
4. One reason for the Bubble Gum Store's appeal is its small size. We are often led to believe big is better, but is it really? Are there other areas of life in which "small is beautiful"?

Writing Assignments Using Description as a Method of Development

1. Write a description of a person you know who obviously enjoys his or her work, as Ken and Eve do. Support your thesis with a detailed description of the place where the person works. Your description should reveal the person's attitudes and values.
2. You may have a place in your life that makes you feel wanted, comfortable, important, like the store Trillin describes. This special place could be a church, restaurant, a retail store, a friend's home, a "hangout." Write a description of this place, evoking through the use of detail the decor, atmosphere, and people that make the place unique and meaningful for you.

Writing Assignments Using Other Methods of Development

3. Write a brief report to the owner of a business you patronize suggesting ways to make that store, restaurant, or office more hospitable and inviting to customers. Give examples showing how each of your recommendations would attract more customers.
4. Take a position arguing against Trillin's admiration of the quaint, old-time Bubble Gum Store and its young, educated shopkeepers. Write an essay contending that Ken and Eve should use their talents for something more substantial than a corner store. Or, argue that devoting one's life to preserving an old-style grocery store is a waste of energy. Be an advocate for the new, the speedy, and the progressive, supporting your paper with well-reasoned arguments and examples. The essay may have a serious or humorous tone.

E. B. White

Elwyn Brooks White (1899–1985) is considered one of America's finest essayists. For many years, White was a member of The New Yorker *magazine staff and wrote the magazine's popular column, "The Talk of the Town." He also wrote children's books, including the classic* Charlotte's Web *(1952) and was the coauthor with William Strunk, Jr., of the renowned guide for writers,* The Elements of Style *(1959). But most memorable are the essays White produced during his life—gems of clarity, wit, and heartfelt expression. White's contribution to literature earned him many awards, including the Presidential Medal of Freedom and the National Medal for Literature. The classic essay reprinted here is taken from* The Essays of E. B. White *(1977).*

Once More to the Lake

In this celebrated essay, E. B. White describes his return to a vacation spot he had known intimately in his childhood, a cabin on a lake in Maine. This time White is accompanied by his son. In many ways the lake, the cabin, and the surrounding fields and woods are the same, but in other respects they are different. With great skill, White describes his past and present experiences at the lake, exploring the nature of life cycles and of change itself.

One summer, along about 1904, my father rented a camp on a   1
lake in Maine and took us all there for the month of August. We all got ringworm from some kittens and had to rub Pond's Extract on our arms and legs night and morning, and my father rolled over in a canoe with all his clothes on; but outside of that the vacation was a success and from then on none of us ever thought there was any place in the world like that lake in Maine. We returned summer after summer—always on August 1 for one month. I have since become a salt-water man, but sometimes in summer there are days when the restlessness of the tides and the fearful cold of the sea

water and the incessant wind that blows across the afternoon and into the evening make me wish for the placidity of a lake in the woods. A few weeks ago this feeling got so strong I bought myself a couple of bass hooks and a spinner and returned to the lake where we used to go, for a week's fishing and to revisit old haunts.

I took along my son, who had never had any fresh water up his   2 nose and who had seen lily pads only from train windows. On the journey over to the lake I began to wonder what it would be like. I wondered how time would have marred this unique, this holy spot — the coves and streams, the hills that the sun set behind, the camps and the paths behind the camps. I was sure that the tarred road would have found it out, and I wondered in what other ways it would be desolate. It is strange how much you can remember about places like that once you allow your mind to return into the grooves that lead back. You remember one thing, and that suddenly reminds you of another thing. I guess I remembered clearest of all the early mornings, when the lake was cool and motionless, remembered how the bedroom smelled of the lumber it was made of and of the wet woods whose scent entered through the screen. The partitions in the camp were thin and did not extend clear to the top of the rooms, and as I was always the first up I would dress softly so as not to wake the others, and sneak out into the sweet outdoors and start out in the canoe, keeping close along the shore in the long shadows of the pines. I remembered being very careful never to rub my paddle against the gunwale for fear of disturbing the stillness of the cathedral.

The lake had never been what you would call a wild lake. There   3 were cottages sprinkled around the shores, and it was in farming country although the shores of the lake were quite heavily wooded. Some of the cottages were owned by nearby farmers, and you would live at the shore and eat your meals at the farmhouse. That's what our family did. But although it wasn't wild, it was a fairly large and undisturbed lake and there were places in it that, to a child at least, seemed infinitely remote and primeval.

I was right about the tar: it led to within half a mile of the   4 shore. But when I got back there, with my boy, and we settled into a camp near a farmhouse and into the kind of summertime I had known, I could tell that it was going to be pretty much the same as it had been before — I knew it, lying in bed the first morning, smelling the bedroom and hearing the boy sneak quietly out and go off along the shore in a boat. I began to sustain the illusion that he was I, and therefore, by simple transposition, that I was my father. This sensation persisted, kept cropping up all the time we were there. It was not an entirely new feeling, but in this setting it grew much stronger. I seemed to be living a dual existence. I would be in the middle of some simple act, I would be picking up a bait box or laying down a table fork, or I would be saying something, and suddenly it would be not I but my father who was saying the words or making the gesture. It gave me a creepy sensation.

We went fishing the first morning. I felt the same damp moss   5 covering the worms in the bait can, and saw the dragonfly alight on the tip of my rod as it hovered a few inches from the surface of the water. It was the arrival of this fly that convinced me beyond any doubt that everything was as it always had been, that the years were a mirage and that there had been no years. The small waves were the same, chucking the rowboat under the chin as we fished at anchor, and the boat was the same boat, the same color green and the ribs broken in the same places, and under the floorboards the same fresh-water leavings and débris — the dead helgramite, the wisps of moss, the rusty discarded fishhook, the dried blood from yester-day's catch. We stared silently at the tips of our rods, at the dragon-flies that came and went. I lowered the tip of mine into the water, tentatively, pensively dislodging the fly, which darted two feet away, poised, darted two feet back, and came to rest again a little farther up the rod. There had been no years between the ducking of this dragonfly and the other one — the one that was part of mem-ory. I looked at the boy, who was silently watching his fly, and it was my hands that held his rod, my eyes watching. I felt dizzy and didn't know which rod I was at the end of.

We caught two bass, hauling them in briskly as though they   6 were mackerel, pulling them over the side of the boat in a business-like manner without any landing net, and stunning them with a blow on the back of the head. When we got back for a swim before lunch, the lake was exactly where we had left it, the same number of inches from the dock, and there was only the merest suggestion of a breeze. This seemed an utterly enchanted sea, this lake you could leave to its own devices for a few hours and come back to, and find that it had not stirred, this constant and trustworthy body of water. In the shallows, the dark, water-soaked sticks and twigs, smooth and old, were undulating in clusters on the bottom against the clean ribbed sand, and the track of the mussel was plain. A school of minnows swam by, each minnow with its small individual shadow, doubling the attendance, so clear and sharp in the sunlight. Some of the other campers were in swimming, along the shore, one of them with a cake of soap, and the water felt thin and clear and unsubstantial. Over the years there had been this person with the cake of soap, this cultist, and here he was. There had been no years.

Up to the farmhouse to dinner through the teeming, dusty 7 field, the road under our sneakers was only a two-track road. The middle track was missing, the one with the marks of the hooves and the splotches of dried, flaky manure. There had always been three tracks to choose from in choosing which track to walk in; now the choice was narrowed down to two. For a moment I missed terribly the middle alternative. But the way led past the tennis court, and something about the way it lay there in the sun reassured me; the tape had loosened along the backline, the alleys were green with plantains and other weeds, and the net (installed in June and removed in September) sagged in the dry noon, and the whole place steamed with midday heat and hunger and emptiness. There was a choice of pie for dessert, and one was blueberry and one was apple, and the waitresses were the same country girls, there having been no passage of time, only the illusion of it as in a dropped curtain — the waitresses were still fifteen; their hair had been washed, that was the only difference — they had been to the movies and seen the pretty girls with the clean hair.

Summertime, oh, summertime, pattern of life indelible, the 8 fade-proof lake, the woods unshatterable, the pasture with the sweetfern and the juniper forever and ever, summer without end; this was the background, and the life along the shore was the design, the cottagers with their innocent and tranquil design, their tiny docks with the flagpole and the American flag floating against the white clouds in the blue sky, the little paths over the roots of the trees leading from camp to camp and the paths leading back to the outhouses and the can of lime for sprinkling, and at the souvenir counters at the store the miniature birch-bark canoes and the postcards that showed things looking a little better than they looked. This was the American family at play, escaping the city heat, wondering whether the newcomers in the camp at the head of the cove were "common" or "nice," wondering whether it was true that the people who drove up for Sunday dinner at the farmhouse were turned away because there wasn't enough chicken.

It seemed to me, as I kept remembering all this, that those 9 times and those summers had been infinitely precious and worth saving. There had been jollity and peace and goodness. The arriving (at the beginning of August) had been so big a business in itself, at the railway station the farm wagon drawn up, the first smell of the pine-laden air, the first glimpse of the smiling farmer, and the great importance of the trunks and your father's enormous authority in such matters, and the feel of the wagon under you for the long ten-mile haul, and at the top of the last long hill catching the first view of the lake after eleven months of not seeing this cherished body of water. The shouts and cries of the other campers when they saw you, and the trunks to be unpacked, to give up their rich burden. (Arriving was less exciting nowadays, when you sneaked up in your car and parked it under a tree near the camp and took out the bags and in five minutes it was all over, no fuss, no loud wonderful fuss about trunks.)

Peace and goodness and jollity. The only thing that was wrong 10 now, really, was the sound of the place, an unfamiliar nervous sound of the outboard motors. This was the note that jarred, the one thing that would sometimes break the illusion and set the years moving. In those other summertimes all motors were inboard; and when they were at a little distance, the noise they made was a sedative, an ingredient of summer sleep. They were one-cylinder and two-cylinder engines, and some were make-and-break and some were jump-spark, but they all made a sleepy sound across the lake. The one-lungers throbbed and fluttered, and the twin-cylinder ones purred and purred, and that was a quiet sound, too. But now the campers all had outboards. In the daytime, in the hot mornings, these motors made a petulant, irritable sound; at night, in the still evening when the afterglow lit the water, they whined about one's ears like mosquitoes. My boy loved our rented outboard, and his great desire was to achieve single-handed mastery over it, and authority, and he soon learned the trick of choking it a little (but not too much), and the adjustment of the needle valve. Watching him I would remember the things you could do with the old one-cylinder engine with the heavy flywheel, how you could have it eating out of your hand if you got really close to it spiritually. Motorboats in those days didn't have clutches, and you would make a landing by shutting off the motor at the proper time and coasting in with a dead rudder. But there was a way of reversing them, if you learned the trick, by cutting the switch and putting it on again exactly on the final dying revolution of the flywheel, so that it would kick back against compression and begin reversing. Approaching a dock in a strong following breeze, it was difficult to slow up sufficiently by the ordinary coasting method, and if a boy felt he had complete mastery over his motor, he was tempted to keep it running beyond its time and then reverse it a few feet from the dock. It took a cool nerve, because if you threw the switch a twentieth of a second too soon you would catch the flywheel when it still had speed enough to go up past center, and the boat would leap ahead, charging bullfashion at the dock.

    We had a good week at the camp. The bass were biting well and 11
the sun shone endlessly, day after day. We would be tired at night and lie down in the accumulated heat of the little bedrooms after the long hot day and the breeze would stir almost imperceptibly outside and the smell of the swamp drift in through the rusty screens. Sleep would come easily and in the morning the red squirrel would be on the roof, tapping out his gay routine. I kept remembering everything, lying in bed in the mornings — the small steamboat that had a long rounded stern like the lip of a Ubangi, and how quietly she ran on the moonlight sails, when the older boys played their mandolins and the girls sang and we ate doughnuts dipped in sugar, and how sweet the music was on the water in the shining night, and what it had felt like to think about girls then. After breakfast we would go up to the store and the things were in the same place — the minnows in a bottle, the plugs and spinners disarranged and pawed over by the youngsters from the boys' camp, the Fig Newtons and the Beeman's gum. Outside, the road was tarred and cars stood in front of the store. Inside, all was just as it had always been, except there was more Coca-Cola and not so much Moxie and root beer and birch beer and sarsaparilla. We would walk out with the bottle of pop apiece and sometimes the pop would backfire up our noses and hurt. We explored the streams, quietly, where the turtles slid off the sunny logs and dug their way into the soft bottom; and we lay on the town wharf and

fed worms to the tame bass. Everywhere we went I had trouble making out which was I, the one walking at my side, the one walking in my pants.

One afternoon while we were there at the lake a thunderstorm   12
came up. It was like the revival of an old melodrama that I had seen long ago with childish awe. The second-act climax of the drama of the electrical disturbance over a lake in America had not changed in any important respect. This was the big scene, still the big scene. The whole thing was so familiar, the first feeling of oppression and heat and a general air around camp of not wanting to go very far away. In midafternoon (it was all the same) a curious darkening of the sky, and a lull in everything that had made life tick; and then the way the boats suddenly swung the other way at their moorings with the coming of a breeze out of the new quarter, and the premonitory rumble. Then the kettle drum, then the snare, then the bass drum and cymbals, then crackling light against the dark, and the gods grinning and licking their chops in the hills. Afterward the calm, the rain steadily rustling in the calm lake, the return of light and hope and spirits, and the campers running out in joy and relief to go swimming in the rain, their bright cries perpetuating the death-less joke about how they were getting simply drenched, and the children screaming with delight at the new sensation of bathing in the rain, and the joke about getting drenched linking the genera-tions in a strong indestructible chain. And the comedian who waded in carrying an umbrella.

When the others went swimming, my son said he was going in,   13
too. He pulled his dripping trunks from the line where they had hung all through the shower and wrung them out. Languidly, and with no thought of going in, I watched him, his hard little body, skinny and bare, saw him wince slightly as he pulled up around his vitals the small, soggy, icy garment. As he buckled the swollen belt, suddenly my groin felt the chill of death.

Questions for Close Reading

1. What is the thesis (or dominant impression) of the selection? Locate the sentence(s) in which White states his main idea. If he does not state the thesis explicitly, express it in your own words.
2. Why does White return to the lake in Maine he had visited as a child?

Why do you think he has waited to revisit it until he has a young son to bring along?

3. Several times in the essay, White notes that he felt as if he were his own father — and that his son became his childhood self. What event first prompts this sensation? What actions and thoughts cause it to recur?

4. How is the latest visit to the lake similar to White's childhood summers? What differences does White notice? What effects do the differences have on him?

5. Refer to your dictionary as needed to define the following words used in the selection: *incessant* (paragraph 1), *placidity* (1), *primeval* (3), *transposition* (4), *undulating* (6), *indelible* (8), *petulant* (10), and *languidly* (13).

Questions about the Writer's Craft

1. Through vivid language, descriptive writing evokes the experiences of the five senses. In "Once More to the Lake," White overlays two sets of sensory details: those of the present-day lake and those of the lake as it was in his boyhood. Which set of details is more objective? Which seems sharper and more powerful? Why?

2. White chooses many words and phrases with religious connotations as he describes the lake. Give some examples. Why does he use such language?

3. In paragraph 12, White describes a thunderstorm. Explain the metaphors he uses in this passage.

4. White's thought concerning "the chill of death" in the final paragraph may seem surprising. What brings on this feeling? Why does he feel it "in his groin"? Where has this idea been hinted at previously in the essay?

Questions for Further Thought

1. In paragraph 9, White says about his boyhood visits to the lake that "those times and those summers had been infinitely precious and worth saving." From your own perspective, what makes an experience worth savoring and storing in the memory in all its detail?

2. When White refers to his son, he never uses the boy's first name (he calls him "the boy" or "my boy"); only in the last scene does he call him "my son." Why does White use this impersonal form of reference? Could this essay have been written if the author's child had been a girl?

3. In your opinion, was the visit to the lake a good experience for White — or a bad one? In general, is it or is it not a good idea to try to relive the past?

4. This essay touches on a universal human feeling—the sensation that time is slipping by, that our lives are spinning out their allotted spans every moment of the day. When do people first become aware of their own mortality? What events or phases of life heighten this feeling?

Writing Assignments Using Description as a Method of Development

1. Write a descriptive essay about a special place in your life. It need not be a natural setting like White's lake; it could be a place in a city or house, for example, that has meant a great deal to you or has had an effect on your life. Use sensory details and figurative language, as White does, to give energy to your description. Explain the effects the place has on you, but avoid long narrative passages concerning events that may have occurred there.
2. In a way, White was fortunate that his lake had remained virtually unchanged—no loggers had cut the trees, no one had built condominiums on the shore, no pollution had contaminated the water. But many other beautiful settings have been destroyed or are threatened with destruction. Write a descriptive essay about a place or site that is "infinitely precious and worth saving." Your dominant theme should be the qualities or aspects of your subject which make it worthy of being preserved intact for future generations.

Writing Assignments Using Other Methods of Development

3. In the midst of our daily routines, we are sometimes suddenly reminded of the nearness of death: limp animals lie on the road, a politician is assassinated, a celebrity dies an untimely death, a classmate is killed in a car crash. Write an essay about a time when you were forced to think about mortality. Explain what happened and describe your thoughts and feelings afterwards.
4. Have your older relatives made an attempt to transfer the special experiences of their younger years to you in some way? Or have you done the same with your own children? You may have visited a special place, as White did, or listened to stories, or looked at photographs or objects. Write an essay recounting such a moment (or moments) and explain the motivations of the older generation—and the effects on the younger one.

Peggy Anderson

*Peggy Anderson was born and raised in Chicago and edu-
cated at Augustana College in Rock Island, Illinois. She
served in the Peace Corps in Togo, West Africa, and later
worked as a writer for the Peace Corps in Washington. Now a
freelance writer, Anderson has published articles in* Family
Circle, The New York Times, *and* Ms. *She is also the author
of three books:* The Daughters *(1974), a profile of the
Daughters of the American Revolution;* Nurse *(1977),
which was made into a television movie and series; and* Children's Hospital *(1985), from which this selection is taken.*

Children's Hospital

*Most hospitals are the dreariest of places, but the children's
hospital described by Peggy Anderson is attractive and
friendly. With its impressive atrium, brightly trimmed rooms,
and ample play and gathering areas, the hospital imparts a
sense of community and hope to young patients and their
visitors.*

Children's Hospital stands beside a busy boulevard in a major   1
American city. Its nearest neighbors are a massive civic center, a
high-rise hotel, and the medical school and hospital of a distinguished university. For decades Children's was housed in a turn-of-
the-century edifice of red brick which had grown dingier and more
cramped with every passing year. The new facility is a classy, modern, energy-efficient structure of gleaming brown, striped horizon-
tally by brown-tinted windows, with three times the square footage
of the old building and space for twice the number of intensive care
beds. Its defining characteristic is a one-million-cubic-foot atrium
which rises from the lobby through all nine floors and lets in the sky
through a stepped glass roof. The new Children's was designed to
please children and to allay their fears. To a visitor, the dominant
impressions are of openness, color, and natural light.

It is light that first strikes a person coming into the hospital in   2
the daytime. One has passed through an entrance, one is definitely
inside, yet the light makes the lobby feel out-of-doors. As if drawn
by pulleys, the visitor's eye climbs the nine stories to the source.
Only when the light has been accounted for does one look around
at ground level and begin to appreciate the lobby itself.

It's enormous. It compares favorably in size with the multi-   3
purpose lobbies of the newest hotels. Like many hotel lobbies, the
lobby at Children's features live trees and a working fountain.
Wooden planters, a quarry tile floor, and molded plastic benches in
orange and yellow contribute further to the visitor's sense of being
in a park.

But in common with few if any hotels, the Children's lobby is   4
occupied on one side by a McDonald's restaurant. Seating is arranged in the manner of a sidewalk café. Across the floor from
McDonald's is a carpeted play pit where a child who feels well
enough may roughhouse with siblings in reasonable safety, or a
patient in a wheelchair may picnic quietly with parents. At some
remove from the pit and right next to the main entrance stands a
distorting mirror that could have come straight from a fun house.

The rear of the ground floor is occupied by the hospital cafete-   5
ria. Beneath the cafeteria and lobby is a two-level parking garage.
The floor below that is the province of computers, equipment, and
building engineers. Short wings off the lobby house the Emergency
Room, a small chapel, the day surgery unit, and a branch bank as
well as the Admissions Office. Floors One through Three are for
offices and outpatient clinics.

Four is given over to the operating room complex and four   6
intensive care units. Five and Six are likewise for inpatients. On
each of these floors the choicest space has been designated for the
children. Head nurses' offices do not have windows at Children's,
nor do many doctors' offices. But half of one wall in every patient
room is a large window overlooking either the city or the center
court. Each wall opposite contains a window through which patients may see into the hall. Every playroom at Children's has huge
windows. Some playrooms actually jut out into the court like enclosed balconies with windows on three sides.

Halls play an important role on the first six floors at Chil-   7
dren's. The major hallways all overlook the court through tempered glass partitions. From a distance that honors privacy, these

halls afford a look into patient rooms, playrooms, clinic waiting rooms, and offices around the court from lobby to skylight. This view diminishes the mystery one usually associates with hospitals. To a parent or child immersed in private misery, the view also offers perspective. Other children are sick enough to be in here too, it says. Some may be worse off. Some are getting well. The view provides a glimpse of institutional business-as-usual which can serve as a reminder that while one's personal world may have stopped, the larger world goes on as dependably as the tides. At night someone standing in a main hallway at Children's can look up through the skylight and see stars.

The tops of the tempered glass partitions do not meet the hall ceilings. For this reason and because planners sought to isolate sick children as little as possible from life around them, sounds of the hospital reach the hallways from many parts of the building. Somewhere a baby cries. Somewhere a toddler laughs. Somewhere a mother reprimands a clinic patient springing for the elevator. "*Anthony! You get back here!*"   8

Somewhere a child demands a milkshake *and* french fries. The fall of water from the lobby fountain reaches the sixth floor. So does the aggregate of voices from the lobby—a hum of many people with many different missions, much like the buzz one hears in a shopping mall on a weekday afternoon. Together the sounds impart an air of informality and normalcy.   9

Varnished benches of light wood run along the low walls supporting the glass partitions. Though most units have small waiting rooms off the halls, the benches get heavier use. Patients come out to sit on them for a change of scene. Parents give themselves moments alone on the benches. Aunts and uncles and grandparents spread out on them while waiting their turn to visit a child. Doctors or social workers or the chaplain join families on the benches to talk. Secretaries relax on the benches with sandwiches or yogurt. Parents wait out surgery there.   10

As hours pass, or days, the groups in the halls become small cultures. Each has its own habits, its own personality, its own pitch. Cigarette stubs and ashes build up in disposable silvery ashtrays. People stretch out and nap. Group weather brightens or darkens with news. When the news is grave, the sorrow touches anyone who passes. But the halls are long. The benches are long. No one culture can dominate. Traffic continues to go by. Nurses and doctors talk   11 to each other in ordinary voices. Usually in the hallways at Children's, and often in the units themselves, there is notable absence of hush.

Color abounds on the first six floors. In some rooms painters   12
made big orange circles on ceilings. They stenciled big yellow C's and D's on clean and dirty linen bins. Floor experts laid red and blue paths of linoleum tiles in the halls and added red and blue baseboards to match. For clinic waiting areas Purchasing ordered child-sized tables and chairs in orange and green. The color is meant to lift heavy spirits, as is the lilt of popular music which permeates the hospital day and night so unobtrusively as to escape conscious notice.

For all the resemblance they bear in mood to the floors below,   13
the top three floors of Children's might as well be in another city. Floors seven through nine are for research. They are not for patients but for scientists, not for parents but for technicians. On these floors decorators bothered little with color. The rooms are white. The halls are white. The linoleum is gray with white flecks. Hospital sounds seem remote. One imagines bacteria shushing each other in saucers. On three floors of odoriferous laboratories, small and large medical questions are being addressed with such aids as microscopes, scalpels, chemical solutions, government grants, dogs, cats, mice, rabbits, petri dishes, and equations that only scientists comprehend. For all this activity, the atmosphere of these floors feels quiet and white, as after heavy snow.

Questions for Close Reading

1. What is the thesis (or dominant impression) of the selection? Locate the sentence(s) in which Anderson states her main idea. If she does not state the thesis explicitly, express it in your own words.
2. How have the builders of Children's Hospital brought light into the structure? What other aspects of outdoors have they included inside?
3. Anderson says that halls play an important role in the hospital. What is that role? How are the halls different from those of most hospitals?
4. How has color been used throughout the nine floors of Children's Hospital? What is the purpose of the various colors or their absence?
5. Refer to your dictionary as needed to define the following words used in the selection: *edifice* (paragraph 1), *atrium* (1), *siblings* (4), *province* (5), *aggregate* (9), *abounds* (12), *unobtrusively* (12), and *odoriferous* (13).

Questions about the Writer's Craft

1. Anderson says that the dominant impression of the hospital is one of "openness, color, and natural light." What details in the description support that overall impression? Are there any that do not?
2. How does the author use transitions to keep the reader oriented in space throughout the description? Where does the author use repeated words to provide coherence between paragraphs?
3. Anderson's description is primarily visual, but she also refers to the other senses. Where does she point out smells and sounds? How do these details contribute to the overall impression of the hospital being a pleasant, comfortable place?
4. Why does Anderson describe the upper floors of the hospital in only one paragraph? Does this paragraph make an effective conclusion?

Questions for Further Thought

1. The new Children's Hospital "was designed to please children and to allay their fears." Which of the features do you think children will find most appealing? Can you think of other improvements that would add to the hospital's friendly feeling?
2. Why do you think the designers did not decorate the research floors the same way as the patient care floors? What is the effect of the whiteness of the walls?
3. According to psychologists, colors affect our moods; green is calming, red is stimulating, and so on. How responsive are you to colors in your environment? When have you been particularly aware of color or the lighting in your surroundings?
4. In such institutional buildings as schools, hospitals, and government facilities, do you feel enough attention is paid to the visual appeal of the rooms and halls and to the comfort of the users? What positive or negative experiences have you had with such institutional architecture?

Writing Assignments Using Description as a Method of Development

1. Write a description of another children's place, such as a playground, day care center, school, or swimming pool. Include vigorous sensory details that show why the place is appealing to children, or why it is not.
2. Prepare a descriptive essay about a building or room you find uncomfortable, unattractive, and inhospitable. The specifics in your essay should convey your belief that the building or room needs significant changes to make it more appealing to the people who must work in it or use it.

Writing Assignments Using Other Methods of Development

3. Write a narrative essay about the time you spent at a clinic, court, hospital, or other institutional setting. Explain what happened during the visit, being sure to convey whether the experience was a stressful or comfortable one.

4. You have probably visited someone who has been hospitalized, or perhaps you have been a patient yourself. Prepare an essay explaining how to cheer up a patient. Or write an essay showing how to be a cooperative — or difficult — patient. The essay may be serious or light in tone.

Additional Writing Topics
DESCRIPTION

General Assignments

Write an essay using description to develop any of the following topics. Remember that an effective description focuses on a dominant impression and arranges details in a way that best supports that impression. Your details—vivid and appealing to the senses—should be carefully chosen so that the essay is not overburdened with material of secondary importance. When writing, keep in mind that varied sentence structure and imaginative figures of speech are ways to make a descriptive piece compelling.

1. A favorite item of clothing
2. The world as a certain kind of animal sees it
3. An athletic shoe or high-heeled shoes
4. An individualist's appearance
5. A coffee shop, bus shelter, newsstand, or some other small place
6. A parade or victory celebration
7. A banana, squash, or other fruit or vegetable
8. A particular drawer
9. A house plant
10. A "media event"
11. A dorm room
12. An elderly person
13. An attractive man or woman
14. A prosthetic device or wheelchair
15. A TV, film, or music celebrity
16. A student lounge
17. A once-in-a-lifetime event
18. The inside of something, such as a cave, boat, shed, or machine
19. A friend, roommate, or other person you know well
20. An essential gadget or a useless gadget

Assignments with a Specific Audience and Purpose

1. You have been asked to speak to next year's freshman class at your college on the topic of the registration process. The more the students know what to expect, the less confused or frustrated they will be. De-

scribe what registration day is like, using specific details and lively language to make the experience vivid and realistic. Choose an adjective that represents your dominant impression of the experience and keep that in mind as you write.

2. As a subscriber to a dating service, you have been asked to submit a description of the kind of person you'd like to meet. Describe your ideal date. Focus on specific information about physical appearance, personal habits, character traits, and interests.

3. Your college has decided to tear down a campus structure and replace it with a new version (it could be a dorm, a dining hall, a special landmark, or any other structure). Write a letter of protest to the administration, describing the place so vividly and appealingly that its value and need for preservation are unquestionable.

4. You have recently joined the staff of the campus newspaper, and you have been asked to write an entertaining column of social news and gossip. As your first column, you are supposed to write a description of a recent campus event — a mixer, party, concert, or other social activity. Write the description, focusing on the places in which the event was held, the appearance of the people who attended, and so on. Your column could be straightforward or tongue-in-cheek.

5. Some students at your college have complained that the college catalog is inaccurate. Its course descriptions are too scanty, misleading, or both. You are on the team charged with revising the catalog. Write an *accurate* description of a course (or courses) with which you are familiar. Tell exactly what the course is about, who teaches it, and how it is run.

6. As a resident of a particular town, you are angered by the appearance of (and activities taking place in) a certain spot — a video game arcade, an adult bookstore, a bar, a bus or train station, or any other place. Write a letter to the town council, describing in detail the undesirable nature of this place.

NARRATION

WHAT IS NARRATION?

Human beings are instinctively storytellers. In prehistoric times, our ancestors huddled around a campfire to hear tales of hunting and magic. In ancient times, warriors gathered in halls to listen to bards praise in song the exploits of epic heroes. Things are no different today. Boisterous children invariably settle down to listen when their parents read to them; millions of people tune in day after day to the ongoing drama of their favorite soap operas; vacationers sit motionless on the beach, caught up in the latest best-sellers; and all of us enjoy saying, "Just listen to what happened to me today." Our hunger for storytelling is a basic part of us.

Narration means telling a single story or several related stories, often to make a point. As you will see, the story can be a means to an end, a way to support a main idea or thesis. For instance, to demonstrate that television has become the constant companion of many children, you might narrate the story of a typical child's day in front of the television — starting with frantic cartoons in the morning and ending with dizzy situation comedies at night. Or to support the point that the college registration process should be reformed, you could tell the tale of a chaotic morning spent trying to enroll in classes.

Narration is powerful. Every public speaker, from politician to classroom teacher, knows that stories can capture the attention of bored listeners in a way that nothing else can. Narration speaks to us strongly because it is about us; we want to know what happened to others, not simply because we are curious, but because their experiences shed light on the nature of our own existence. Narration lends power to opinions, triggers the flow of memory, and evokes places and times in ways that are compelling and affecting.

WHEN TO USE NARRATION

Since narratives tell a story, you may think that narratives can be found only in novels or short stories. But the narrative technique is often used as a supplemental pattern of development to help make a point in various kinds of essays. A *persuasive* essay urging more rigorous security at airports might begin with a brief narrative about an armed terrorist who had no difficulty boarding a plane. An essay attempting to *define* the nature of skillful teaching might include a narrative about the stimulating way a respected high school teacher conducted class. In an essay discussing the *effects* of an overburdened judicial system, you might use a narrative about one criminal's successful attempt to plea bargain a murder charge.

Most of this chapter, however, is concerned with using a single extended narrative as the predominant method of development in an essay that makes a point. In such a case, you narrate a story, either your own or someone else's, sharing with the reader your personal perspective on what happened. The narrative might be about the unexpected pleasure you felt when you spent an afternoon with your three-year-old nephew; you might focus on the feelings of vulnerability and powerlessness your roommate experienced after being mugged. It doesn't matter whose story is recounted as long as the narrative conveys the essence of what was experienced.

SUGGESTIONS FOR USING NARRATION IN AN ESSAY

The following suggestions will be helpful whether you use narration as a dominant or supportive pattern of development.

1. Determine the point of the narrative. In *The Adventures of Huckleberry Finn*, Mark Twain warned: "Persons attempting to find a motive in this narrative will be prosecuted; persons attempting to find a moral in it will be banished; persons attempting to find a plot in it will be shot." Twain was, of course, being ironic, for his novel's richness lies in its "motives" and "morals." Similarly, the narratives you write should have a meaning and purpose. Your readers want to be pulled into the narrative action, but they also want to feel that the tale has direction and focus. You should, then, make clear to yourself the point you want to make or the feeling you want to convey.

Suppose you decided to write about a frightening time you got locked in a mall late at night. Your narrative would focus on the way the mall looked after hours, what you did during that time, how you felt. But you would also use the narrative to make a point. Perhaps you would want to make the point that fear can be instructive. On the other hand, your point might be that malls have a disturbing, surreal underside. You could state this thesis or narrative point explicitly ("After hours, the mall shed its cheerful daytime demeanor for a more sinister quality"). Or you could refrain from stating the thesis directly, relying on your details and language ("The mannequins stared at me with glazed eyes and frozen smiles"; "The steel grates pulled over each store glinted in the cold light, making each shop look like a prison cell") to convey the point of the narrative.

2. Select details that advance the narrative point. You know from experience that nothing is more boring than listening to a storyteller who gets sidetracked and drags out a story with nonessential details. If a friend started to tell about the time his car broke down in the middle of an expressway — but interrupted his story to complain at length about the slipshod work done by his auto repair shop — you might clench your teeth in annoyance, wishing your friend would hurry up and get back to the interesting part of the story.

Brainstorming ("What happened? When? Where? Who was involved? Why did it happen?") is invaluable in helping you amass narrative details. After generating the details, you have to cull out the nonessential, devoting your energies to the key specifics needed to advance your narrative point. When telling a story, an effective narrative pace is maintained by focusing on the point and eliminating details that do not support that point. A good narrative depends not only on what is included, but also on what has been left out.

But how do you determine which specifics to omit, which to treat briefly, and which to emphasize? Knowing your audience and having a clear sense of your narrative point are crucial. Assume you were writing a narrative about a disastrous get-acquainted dance sponsored by your college the first week of the academic year. In addition to telling what happened at the dance, you would want the narrative to make a point; perhaps you want to emphasize that, despite the college's good intentions, such "official" events actually make it difficult to meet people. With that purpose in mind, you might write about how stiff and unnatural students seemed, all dressed up in their best clothes; you might narrate snatches of strained conversation you overheard; you might describe the way males gathered on one side of the room, females on the other — reverting to behaviors supposedly abandoned in fifth grade. All these details would support your narrative point.

Because you are steering your readers toward a particular point, you do not want to get waylaid by detours that lead away from that point. You would, then, leave out details about the topnotch band and the appetizing refreshments at the dance. The music and food may have been surprisingly good, but these details do not advance the point you want to make and so should be omitted.

In addition to considering your point or purpose, you also need to keep your audience in mind when selecting narrative details. If the audience consists of your instructor and other students — all of them familiar with the new student center where the dance was held — specific details about the center would probably not have to be provided. But imagine that the essay is going to appear in the quarterly magazine published by the college's community relations office. Many readers of the magazine are former graduates who have not been on campus for a number of years. They will most likely need some additional details about the student center: its location on campus, how many people it holds, how it is furnished.

As you are writing, then, you should keep asking yourself a number of questions: "Is this detail or character or snippet of conversation essential to my purpose? Does my audience need this particular detail to know what I'm talking about?" Borderline details which have some importance but do not deserve lengthy treatment should be summarized ("Two hours went by . . . "). Passing over such specifics quickly allows you to move the story along to its finish. Just as movies use the "quick cut" as storytelling shorthand (the camera lingers on the bags of money being loaded into the armored truck that will soon be held up by a gang of thieves but pans rapidly over the interior of the truck), you need to strike a balance between summarized and fully developed narrative detail.

Sometimes, especially if the narrative recreates an event from the past, you will not be able to remember what happened detail for detail. In such a case, you should take advantage of what is called *dramatic license*. Using as a guide your powers of recall as well as the perspective you now have of that particular time, feel free to reshape actual events to suit your narrative point.

3. Select and organize the narrative sequence.   All of us know the traditional beginning of fairy tales: "Once upon a time. . . ." Every narrative must begin somewhere, present a span of time, and end at a certain point. Frequently, you will want to use a straightforward time order, following the event chronologically from beginning to end: first this happened, next this happened, finally this happened.

But sometimes a strict chronological recounting may not serve your narrative purpose — especially if the high point of the narrative gets lost somewhere in the middle of the time sequence. To avoid that possibility, you may want to disrupt the chronology, plunge the reader into the middle of the story, and then return in a *flashback* to the beginning of the tale. You are probably familiar with the way flashback is used on television and in film. You see the main character being clapped into jail; then you are returned to "why it all happened" before learning how the rest of the story unfolds. A narrative can also use a *flashforward* to tell a story. You get a glimpse of the future (the student graduating with honors during a commencement ceremony) before the story continues in the present (the student agonizing over whether or not to drop out of school). These techniques add substance and texture to the narrative; they shift the story onto several time planes rather than following a straight, linear path from beginning to end. Here are examples of how flashback and flashforward can be used in narrative writing:

> Standing behind the wooden counter, Greg wielded his knife expertly as he shucked clams--one every ten seconds--with practiced ease. The scene contrasted sharply with his first day on the job, when his hands broke out in blisters and when splitting each shell was like prying open a safe. (Flashback)

> Rushing off to move my car from the no-parking zone, I waved a quick goodbye to Karen as she climbed the steps to the bus. I didn't know then that by the time I picked her up at the bus station later that day, she had made a decision that would affect both our lives. (Flashforward)

Whether or not you choose to include flashbacks or flashforwards, remember to limit the time span covered by the narrative. Otherwise, you will have trouble generating the details needed to give the story depth and meaning.

Regardless of the time sequence you select, you also want to guard against organizing the narrative so that it trails off into minor, anticlimactic details. Effective narratives drive toward a strong finish.

Finally, readers should be able to follow with ease your organization of the narrative action. Although narrative paragraphs often do not have topic sentences, each paragraph should be organized clearly. Describing each distinct time phase in separate paragraphs — with or without topic sentences — helps the reader grasp the flow of events. You should also be sure to use frequent time signposts when recounting a story. Words such as *now, then, next, after,* and *later* ensure that your reader will not get lost as the story progresses.

4. Make the narrative vigorous and immediate.   A compelling narrative provides abundant specific details, making readers feel as if they are experiencing the story being told. Readers must be able to see, hear, touch, smell, and taste the event being narrated. *Vivid sensory description* is, therefore, an essential part of an effective narrative. Not only do these specific sensory details make writing a pleasure to read — we all enjoy learning the particulars about people, places, and things — but they also give the narrative the stamp of reality. The specifics convince the reader that the event being described actually did, or could, occur. Compare the following excerpts from a narrative essay; the first version is lifeless and dull, while the revised version grabs readers with its sense of foreboding:

> That eventful day started out like every other summer day. My sister Tricia and I made several elaborate mudpies which we decorated with care. A little later on, as we were spraying each other with the garden hose, we heard my father walk up the path.

> That sad summer day started out uneventfully enough. My sister Tricia and I spent a few hours mixing and decorating mudpies. Our hands caked with dry mud, we sprinkled each lopsided pie with alternating rows of dandelion and clover petals. Later when the sun got hotter, we tossed our white T-shirts over the red picket fence-- forgetting my grandmother's frequent warnings to be more ladylike. Feeling as tough as boys, our sweaty backs bared to the sun, we doused each other with icy sprays from the garden hose. Caught up in the primitive pleasure of it all, we barely heard my father as he walked up the garden path, the gravel crunching under his heavy work boots.

The power of many narratives is rooted in a special kind of tension that "hooks" the audience and makes them want to follow the story to its end. This narrative tension is often a by-product of some form of *conflict* within the story. The conflict may be between the narrator and other people in the story or between a pivotal character and societal institutions. Many dramatic narratives revolve around an internal conflict experienced by the narrator or key person in the story.

Another way to create an aura of narrative immediacy is to use *dialogue* while telling a story. Our sense of other people comes, in part, from what they say and from the way they sound. Conversational exchanges allow the reader to experience characters directly, gaining better understanding of the people in the narrative. Compare the following fragments of a narrative, one with dialogue and one without:

When I finally found my way back to the campsite, the trail guide commented on my disheveled appearance.

When I finally found my way back to the campsite, the trail guide took one look at me and drawled, "What on earth happened to you, Daniel Boone? You look like you've been dragged through a haystack backwards."

A final way to make narratives lively and vigorous is to use *varied sentence structure*. Sentences that plod along predictably (subject-verb, subject-verb) put readers to sleep. Experiment with your sentences by juggling length and sentence type; mix long and short sentences, simple and complex. Comparing the following original and revised versions will give you an idea how effective varied sentence rhythm can be in narrative writing.

Original
The store manager went to the walk-in refrigerator every day. The heavy metal door clanged shut behind her. Visions of her freezing to death among the hanging carcasses crept into my mind. Finally, the shiny door swung open and she waddled out.

Revised
Each time the store manager went to the walk-in refrigerator, the heavy metal door clanged shut behind her. Visions of her freezing to death among the hanging carcasses crept into my mind until the shiny door finally swung open and out she waddled.

Original
The yellow-and-blue-striped fish struggled on the line. Its scales shimmered in the sunlight and its tail waved frantically. The fish gave my brother a real fight.

Revised
The yellow-and-blue-striped fish struggled on the line, scales shimmering in the sunlight, tail waving frantically, giving my brother a real fight.

5. Narrate the story using a consistent point of view. All stories have a *narrator*: the person who tells the story. If you, as narrator, tell a story as you experienced it, the story is written in the *first person point of view* ("I saw the dog pull loose . . . "). But if you, as narrator, observed the event and want to tell how someone else experienced it, you would use the *third person point of view* ("Anne saw the dog pull loose . . . "). Each point of view has advantages and limitations. First person can recreate with power the event as you, the narrator, actually experienced it. This point of view is limited, though, in its ability to describe the inner reactions of other people involved in the event. By way of contrast, third person makes it easier for you as narrator to provide insight into all the participants; however, this increased objectivity may undercut some of the subjective immediacy typical of the "I was there" point of view.

Effective narratives may be exciting or charming or moving; writing them can be great fun and devilishly difficult at the same time. It is no mean feat to recreate an event, drawing on your powers of recall as well as your skill with language to make the narrative action come alive.

Although some narratives relate experiences unfamiliar to your audience, most narrative essays tread familiar ground, telling tales of joy, love, loss, frustration, fear — all common emotions experienced during a life. Do not think, however, that writing about the familiar makes your story predictable. On the contrary, all of us feel an energizing shock of recognition whenever the human condition is written about with grace and power. Narratives can take the ordinary or uneventful and transmute it into something significant, even extraordinary. As Willa Cather, an American novelist, wrote: "There are only two or three human stories and they go on repeating themselves as fiercely as if they had never happened before." The challenge lies in applying your own vision to the tale, thereby making it unique.

STUDENT ESSAY AND COMMENTARY

The student essay that follows was written by Paul Monahan in response to this assignment:

> In "Shooting an Elephant," George Orwell tells about an incident which forced him to act in a manner that ran

counter to his better instincts. Write a narrative about a
time when you faced a disturbing conflict and ended up
doing something you later regretted.

While reading Paul's paper, try to determine how well it applies the principles concerning the use of narration. The commentary following the paper will help you look at Paul's essay more
closely.

If Only

Having worked at a 7-Eleven store for two years, I thought I had   1
become successful at what our manager calls "customer relations." I
firmly believed that a friendly smile and an automatic "sir,"
"ma'am," and "thank you" would see me through any situation that
might arise, from soothing impatient or unpleasant people to apolo-
gizing for giving out the wrong change. But the other night an old
woman shattered my belief that a glib response could smooth over
the rough spots of dealing with other human beings.

The moment she entered, the woman presented a sharp contrast   2
to our shiny store with its bright lighting and neatly arranged
shelves. Walking as if each step were painful, she slowly pushed open
the glass door and hobbled down the nearest aisle. She coughed
dryly, wheezing with each breath. On a forty-degree night, she was
wearing only a faded print dress, a thin, light-beige sweater too small
to button, and black vinyl slippers with the backs cut out to expose
calloused heels. There were no stockings or socks on her splotchy,
blue-veined legs.

After strolling around the store for several minutes, the old   3
woman stopped in front of the rows of canned vegetables. She picked
up some Del Monte corn niblets and stared with a strange intensity at
the label. At that point, I decided to be a good, courteous employee
and asked her if she needed help. As I stood close to her, my smile
became harder to maintain; her red-rimmed eyes were partially
closed by yellowish crusts; her hands were covered with layer upon
layer of grime, and the stale smell of sweat rose in a thick vaporous
cloud from her clothes.

"I need some food," she muttered in reply to my bright, "Can I   4
help you?"

"Are you looking for corn, ma'am?"   5

"I need some food," she repeated. "Any kind."   6

"Well, the corn is ninety-five cents," I said in my most helpful   7
voice. "Or, if you like, we have a special on bologna today."

"I can't pay," she said.   8
For a second, I was tempted to say, "Take the corn." But the   9
employee rules flooded into my mind: Remain polite, but do not let
customers get the best of you. Let them know that you are in control.
For a moment, I even entertained the idea that this was some sort of
test, and that this woman was someone from the head office, testing
my loyalty. I responded dutifully, "I'm sorry, ma'am, but I can't give
away anything free."

The old woman's face collapsed a bit more, if that were possible,   10
and her hands trembled as she put the can back on the shelf. She
shuffled past me toward the door, her torn and dirty clothing barely
covering her bent back.

Moments after she left, I rushed out the door with the can of corn,   11
but I never spotted her. For the rest of my shift, the image of the
woman haunted me. I had been young, healthy, and smug. She had
been old, sick, and desperate. Wishing with all my heart that I had
acted like a human being rather than a robot, I was saddened to
realize how fragile a hold we have on our better instincts.

Paul chose to write "If Only" from the first person (I was
there) *point of view*, a logical choice because he appears as a main
character in his own story. It is not always necessary to state the
narrative point of an essay; it can be implied. But Paul decided to
express the controlling idea of his narrative in two spots — in the
introduction ("But the other night an old woman shattered my
belief that a glib response could smooth over the rough spots of
dealing with other human beings") and in the conclusion where he
expands his idea about rote responses taking precedence over im-
pulses of kindness and compassion. All the *narrative details* in the
essay contribute to the point of the piece; Paul does not include any
extraneous information that would detract from the major idea he
wants to convey.

The narrative is *originated chronologically*, from the moment
the woman enters the store to Paul's reaction after she leaves. Paul
limits the time span of the narrative. The entire incident probably
occurs in under ten minutes, yet the introduction serves as a kind of
flashback by providing some necessary background about Paul's
past experiences. To help the reader follow the course of the narrative, Paul uses time signals: "*The moment* she entered, the woman
presented a sharp contrast . . . " (paragraph 2); "*At that point*, I
decided to be a good, courteous employee . . . " (3); "*For the rest*

of my shift, the image of the woman haunted me . . . " (11). And
he breaks his narrative into separate paragraphs, each paragraph
dealing with a distinct block of time: the woman's actions when she
first enters the store, the encounter that takes place after several
minutes, the woman's reaction, Paul's delayed reaction.

A number of techniques are used to add energy and interest to
the narrative. Paul concentrates on the *conflicts* that occurred —
between him and the woman and between his fear of breaking the
rules and his human instinct to help someone in trouble. The first
conflict is dramatized through *dialogue*, the words Paul and the
woman spoke. (Note that a new line is used to indicate a shift from
one speaker to another.) Paul also uses *descriptive detail* to give the
narrative sharp immediacy. For instance, the sentence "her red-
rimmed eyes were partially closed by yellowish crusts . . . " (3)
recreates vividly the woman's appearance while also suggesting
Paul's response to the woman. Moreover, Paul achieves a vigorous
narrative pace by *varying the length and structure of his sentences.* In
the second paragraph, a short sentence ("There were no stockings
or socks on her splotchy, blue-veined legs") alternates with a longer
one ("On a forty-degree night, she was wearing only a faded print
dress, a thin, light-beige sweater too small to button, and black
vinyl slippers with the backs cut out to expose calloused heels").
Some sentences in the essay open with a subject and verb ("She
coughed dryly . . . "), while others start with dependent clauses
or phrases ("As I stood close to her, my smile became harder to
maintain"; "Walking as if each step were painful, she slowly
pushed open the glass door . . . "), or with a prepositional phrase
("For a second, I was tempted . . . ").

Comparing the final version of the essay's third paragraph,
shown above, with the preliminary version reprinted below reveals
some of the decisions Paul made while revising the essay.

Unrevised Version
After sneezing and hacking her way around the store, the old
woman stopped in front of the vegetable shelves. She picked up a can
of corn and stared at the label. She stayed like this for several minutes. Then I walked over to her and asked if I could be of help.

After putting the original draft aside for a while, Paul reread
his paper and added the following sentence to the third paragraph:
"I decided to be a good, courteous employee." These few words

introduce an appropriate note of irony and serve to echo the controlling idea of the piece. When revising the paragraph, Paul also decided to enlarge the descriptive detail, thus, giving readers a more compelling picture of the woman.

You probably noted that the sentences in the first draft were choppy and clipped, whereas the revised paragraph has an easy, graceful rhythm. The stilted quality in the original was eliminated when Paul expanded some sentences and combined others. Much of the time, revision involves paring down excess material. In this case, though, Paul made the right decision to elaborate his sentences.

As he reworked the third paragraph, Paul omitted the words "sneezing and hacking," realizing they were too comic or light for his subject. Still, there is something jarring about the first sentence in the revised paragraph. Paul's use of the word "strolling" does not work because the word implies a leisurely grace inconsistent with the impression he wants to convey. Changing "strolling" to "shuffling" would bring the image more into line with the essay's overall feeling.

Despite this slight problem, Paul's revisions are solid and right on the mark. The changes he made strengthened his essay, turning it into a more evocative, more polished piece of narrative writing.

The following selections are examples of skillfully written narratives, each with vivid characters and scenes, dramatic conflicts and vigorous language. George Orwell's "Shooting an Elephant" has become a classic with its unforgettable confrontations among a man, his conscience, a crowd, and a rampaging animal. Bob Greene's "Handled with Care" tells about people's surprising reactions when a naked woman wanders through the streets of Chicago. In "Little Deaths," T. H. Watkins joins a professional trapper on his rounds and learns something important about the complexity of life. Langston Hughes in the essay "Salvation" recounts his wrenching loss of innocence. Finally, Theodore Sizer's "Horace's Compromise" follows a typical day in the life of a high school teacher.

George Orwell

*Born Eric Blair in the British colony of India, George Orwell
(1903–1950) is probably best known as the author of Nineteen Eighty-Four (1949), a frightening portrayal of a totalitarian society watched over by the ubiquitous Big Brother.
Orwell was also the author of numerous books and essays,
many based on his diverse life experiences. He served with the
Indian imperial police in Burma, worked at various jobs in
London and Paris, and fought in the Spanish Civil War. His
experiences in Burma are the basis for the following essay,
which is taken from his collection* Shooting an Elephant and
Other Essays *(1950).*

Shooting an Elephant

*At one time or another, most of us have done something just so
people would not laugh at or think badly of us. In this essay,
George Orwell describes how he felt pressured into taking an
action against his better judgment — killing an elephant that
had strayed into the center of a town in India. In addition to
its powerful insights into human behavior, Orwell's essay also
presents a vivid and horrifying picture of the death of an
animal.*

In Moulmein, in Lower Burma, I was hated by large numbers   1
of people — the only time in my life that I have been important
enough for this to happen to me. I was sub-divisional police officer
of the town, and in an aimless, petty kind of way anti-European
feeling was very bitter. No one had the guts to raise a riot, but if a
European woman went through the bazaars alone somebody
would probably spit betel juice over her dress. As a police officer I
was an obvious target and was baited whenever it seemed safe to do
so. When a nimble Burman tripped me up on the football field and
the referee (another Burman) looked the other way, the crowd
yelled with hideous laughter. This happened more than once. In

the end the sneering yellow faces of young men that met me everywhere, the insults hooted after me when I was at a safe distance, got
badly on my nerves. The young Buddhist priests were the worst of
all. There were several thousand of them in the town and none of
them seemed to have anything to do except stand on street corners
and jeer at Europeans.

All this was perplexing and upsetting. For at that time I had   2
already made up my mind that imperialism was an evil thing and
the sooner I chucked up my job and got out of it the better.
Theoretically — and secretly, of course — I was all for the Burmese
and all against their oppressors, the British. As for the job I was
doing, I hated it more bitterly than I can perhaps make clear. In a
job like that you see the dirty work of Empire at close quarters. The
wretched prisoners huddling in the stinking cages of the lock-ups,
the grey, cowed faces of the long-term convicts, the scarred buttocks of the men who had been flogged with bamboos — all these
oppressed me with an intolerable sense of guilt. But I could get
nothing into perspective. I was young and ill-educated and I had
had to think out my problems in the utter silence that is imposed on
every Englishman in the East. I did not even know that the British
Empire is dying, still less did I know that it is a great deal better than
the younger empires that are going to supplant it. All I knew was
that I was stuck between my hatred of the empire I served and my
rage against the evil-spirited little beasts who tried to make my job
impossible. With one part of my mind I thought of the British Raj
as an unbreakable tyranny, as something clamped down, in *saecula
saeculorum*,[1] upon the will of prostrate peoples; with another part I
thought that the greatest joy in the world would be to drive a
bayonet into a Buddhist priest's guts. Feelings like these are the
normal by-products of imperialism; ask any Anglo-Indian official,
if you can catch him off duty.

One day something happened which in a roundabout way was   3
enlightening. It was a tiny incident in itself, but it gave me a better
glimpse than I had had before of the real nature of imperialism —
the real movies for which despotic governments act. Early one
morning the sub-inspector at a police station the other end of the
town rang me up on the 'phone and said that an elephant was
ravaging the bazaar. Would I please come and do something about

[1]For ever and ever.

it? I did not know what I could do, but I wanted to see what was happening and I got on to a pony and started out. I took my rifle, an old .44 Winchester and much too small to kill an elephant, but I thought the noise might be useful *in terrorem*.[2] Various Burmans stopped me on the way and told me about the elephant's doings. It was not, of course, a wild elephant, but a tame one which had gone "must." It had been chained up, as tame elephants always are when their attack of "must" is due, but on the previous night it had broken its chain and escaped. Its mahout, the only person who could manage it when it was in that state, had set out in pursuit, but had taken the wrong direction and was now twelve hours' journey away, and in the morning the elephant had suddenly reappeared in the town. The Burmese population had no weapons and were quite helpless against it. It had already destroyed somebody's bamboo hut, killed a cow and raided some fruit-stalls and devoured the stock; also it had met the municipal rubbish van and, when the driver jumped out and took to his heels, had turned the van over and inflicted violences upon it.

The Burmese sub-inspector and some Indian constables were   4
waiting for me in the quarter where the elephant had been seen. It was a very poor quarter, a labyrinth of squalid bamboo huts, thatched with palm-leaf, winding all over a steep hillside. I remember that it was a cloudy, stuffy morning at the beginning of the rains. We began questioning the people as to where the elephant had gone and, as usual, failed to get any definite information. That is invariably the case in the East; a story always sounds clear enough at a distance, but the nearer you get to the scene of events the vaguer it becomes. Some of the people said that the elephant had gone in one direction, some said that he had gone in another, some professed not even to have heard of any elephant. I had almost made up my mind that the whole story was a pack of lies, when we heard yells a little distance away. There was a loud, scandalized cry of "Go away, child! Go away this instant!" and an old woman with a switch in her hand came round the corner of a hut, violently shooing away a crowd of naked children. Some more women followed, clicking their tongues and exclaiming; evidently there was something that the children ought not to have seen. I rounded the hut and saw a man's dead body sprawling in the mud. He was an

[2]As a warning.

Indian, a black Dravidian coolie, almost naked, and he could not have been dead many minutes. The people said that the elephant had come suddenly upon him round the corner of the hut, caught him with its trunk, put its foot on his back and ground him into the earth. This was the rainy season and the ground was soft, and his face had scored a trench a foot deep and a couple of yards long. He was lying on his belly with arms crucified and head sharply twisted to one side. His face was coated with mud, the eyes wide open, the teeth bared and grinning with an expression of unendurable agony. (Never tell me, by the way, that the dead look peaceful. Most of the corpses I have seen looked devilish.) The friction of the great beast's foot had stripped the skin from his back as neatly as one skins a rabbit. As soon as I saw the dead man I sent an orderly to a friend's house nearby to borrow an elephant rifle. I had already sent back the pony, not wanting it to go mad with fright and throw me if it smelt the elephant.

The orderly came back in a few minutes with a rifle and five 5 cartridges, and meanwhile some Burmans had arrived and told us that the elephant was in the paddy fields below, only a few hundred yards away. As I started forward practically the whole population of the quarter flocked out of the houses and followed me. They had seen the rifle and were all shouting excitedly that I was going to shoot the elephant. They had not shown much interest in the elephant when he was merely ravaging their homes, but it was different now that he was going to be shot. It was a bit of fun to them, as it would be to an English crowd; besides they wanted the meat. It made me vaguely uneasy. I had no intention of shooting the elephant — I had merely sent for the rifle to defend myself if necessary — and it is always unnerving to have a crowd following you. I marched down the hill, looking and feeling a fool, with the rifle over my shoulder and an ever-growing army of people jostling at my heels. At the bottom, when you got away from the huts, there was a metalled road and beyond that a miry waste of paddy fields a thousand yards across, not yet ploughed but soggy from the first rains and dotted with coarse grass. The elephant was standing eight yards from the road, his left side towards us. He took not the slightest notice of the crowd's approach. He was tearing up bunches of grass, beating them against his knees to clean them and stuffing them into his mouth.

I had halted on the road. As soon as I saw the elephant I knew 6 with perfect certainty that I ought not to shoot him. It is a serious matter to shoot a working elephant — it is comparable to destroying a huge and costly piece of machinery — and obviously one ought not to do it if it can possibly be avoided. And at that distance, peacefully eating, the elephant looked no more dangerous than a cow. I thought then and I think now that his attack of "must" was already passing off; in which case he would merely wander harmlessly about until the mahout came back and caught him. Moreover, I did not in the least want to shoot him. I decided that I would watch him for a little while to make sure that he did not turn savage again, and then go home.

But at that moment I glanced round at the crowd that had followed me. It was an immense crowd, two thousand at the least and growing every minute. It blocked the road for a long distance on either side. I looked at the sea of yellow faces above the garish clothes — faces all happy and excited over this bit of fun, all certain that the elephant was going to be shot. They were watching me as they would watch a conjurer about to perform a trick. They did not like me, but with the magical rifle in my hands I was momentarily worth watching. And suddenly I realized that I should have to shoot the elephant after all. The people expected it of me and I had got to do it; I could feel their two thousand wills pressing me forward, irresistibly. And it was at this moment, as I stood there with the rifle in my hands, that I first grasped the hollowness, the futility of the white man's dominion in the East. Here was I, the white man with his gun, standing in front of the unarmed native crowd — seemingly the leading actor of the piece; but in reality I was only an absurd puppet pushed to and fro by the will of those yellow faces behind. I perceived in this moment that when the white man turns tyrant it is his own freedom that he destroys. He becomes a sort of hollow, posing dummy, the conventionalized figure of a sahib. For it is the condition of his rule that he shall spend his life in trying to impress the "natives," and so in every crisis he has got to do what the "natives" expect of him. He wears a mask, and his face grows to fit it. I had got to shoot the elephant. I had committed myself to doing it when I sent for the rifle. A sahib has got to act like a sahib; he has got to appear resolute, to know his own mind and do definite things. To come all that way, rifle in hand, with two thousand people marching at my heels, and then to trail feebly away, having done nothing — no, that was impossible.

7

The crowd would laugh at me. And my whole life, every white man's life in the East, was one long struggle not to be laughed at.

But I did not want to shoot the elephant. I watched him   8 beating his bunch of grass against his knees, with that preoccupied grandmotherly air that elephants have. It seemed to me that it would be murder to shoot him. At that age I was not squeamish about killing animals, but I had never shot an elephant and never wanted to. (Somehow it always seems worse to kill a *large* animal.) Besides, there was the beast's owner to be considered. Alive, the elephant was worth at least a hundred pounds; dead, he would only be worth the value of his tusks, five pounds, possibly. But I had got to act quickly. I turned to some experienced-looking Burmans who had been there when we arrived, and asked them how the elephant had been behaving. They all said the same thing: he took no notice of you if you left him alone, but he might charge if you went too close to him.

It was perfectly clear to me what I ought to do. I ought to walk   9 up to within, say, twenty-five yards of the elephant and test his behavior. If he charged, I could shoot; if he took no notice of me, it would be safe to leave him until the mahout came back. But also I knew that I was going to do no such thing. I was a poor shot with a rifle and the ground was soft mud into which one would sink at every step. If the elephant charged and I missed him, I should have about as much chance as a toad under a steam-roller. But even then I was not thinking particularly of my own skin, only of the watchful yellow faces behind. For at that moment, with the crowd watching me, I was not afraid in the ordinary sense, as I would have been if I had been alone. A white man mustn't be frightened in front of "natives"; and so, in general, he isn't frightened. The sole thought in my mind was that if anything went wrong those two thousand Burmans would see me pursued, caught, trampled on and reduced to a grinning corpse like that Indian up the hill. And if that happened it was quite probable that some of them would laugh. That would never do. There was only one alternative. I shoved the cartridges into the magazine and lay down on the road to get a better aim.

The crowd grew very still, and a deep, low, happy sigh, as of   10 people who see the theatre curtain go up at last, breathed from innumerable throats. They were going to have their bit of fun after all. The rifle was a beautiful German thing with cross-hair sights. I did not then know that in shooting an elephant one would shoot to cut an imaginary bar running from ear-hole to ear-hole. I ought, therefore, as the elephant was sideway on, to have aimed straight at his ear-hole; actually I aimed several inches in front of this, thinking the brain would be further forward.

When I pulled the trigger I did not hear the bang or feel the kick—one never does when a shot goes home—but I heard the devilish roar of glee that went up from the crowd. In that instant, in too short a time, one would have thought, even for the bullet to get there, a mysterious, terrible change had come over the elephant. He neither stirred nor fell, but every line of his body had altered. He looked suddenly stricken, shrunken, immensely old, as though the frightful impact of the bullet had paralyzed him without knocking him down. At last, after what seemed a long time—it might have been five seconds, I dare say—he sagged flabbily to his knees. His mouth slobbered. An enormous senility seemed to have settled upon him. One could have imagined him thousands of years old. I fired again into the same spot. At the second shot he did not collapse but climbed with desperate slowness to his feet and stood weakly upright, with legs sagging and head drooping. I fired a third time. That was the shot that did for him. You could see the agony of it jolt his whole body and knock the last remnant of strength from his legs. But in falling he seemed for a moment to rise, for as his hind legs collapsed beneath him he seemed to tower upward like a huge rock toppling, his trunk reaching skywards like a tree. He trumpeted, for the first and only time. And then down he came, his belly towards me, with a crash that seemed to shake the ground even where I lay. 11

I got up. The Burmans were already racing past me across the mud. It was obvious that the elephant would never rise again, but he was not dead. He was breathing very rhythmically with long rattling gasps, his great mound of a side painfully rising and falling. His mouth was wide open—I could see far down into caverns of pale pink throat. I waited a long time for him to die, but his breathing did not weaken. Finally I fired my two remaining shots into the spot where I thought his heart must be. The thick blood welled out of him like red velvet, but still he did not die. His body did not even jerk when the shots hit him, the tortured breathing continued without a pause. He was dying, very slowly and in great agony, but in some world remote from me where not even a bullet 12 could damage him further. I felt that I had got to put an end to that dreadful noise. It seemed dreadful to see the great beast lying there, powerless to move and yet powerless to die, and not even to be able to finish him. I sent back for my small rifle and poured shot after shot into his heart and down his throat. They seemed to make no impression. The tortured gasps continued as steadily as the ticking of a clock.

In the end I could not stand it any longer and went away. I heard later that it took him half an hour to die. Burmans were bringing dahs and baskets even before I left, and I was told they had stripped the body almost to the bones by the afternoon. 13

Afterwards, of course, there were endless discussions about the shooting of the elephant. The owner was furious, but he was only an Indian and could do nothing. Besides, legally I had done the right thing, for a mad elephant has to be killed, like a mad dog, if its owner fails to control it. Among the Europeans opinion was divided. The older men said I was right, the younger men said it was a damn shame to shoot an elephant for killing a coolie, because an elephant was worth more than any damn Coringhee coolie. And afterwards I was very glad that the coolie had been killed; it put me legally in the right and it gave me a sufficient pretext for shooting the elephant. I often wondered whether any of the others grasped that I had done it solely to avoid looking a fool. 14

Questions for Close Reading

1. What is the thesis (or narrative point) of the selection? Locate the sentence(s) in which Orwell states his main idea. If he does not state the thesis explicitly, express it in your own words.
2. How did Orwell feel about the Burmans? What words does Orwell use to describe them?
3. What reasons does Orwell give for shooting the elephant?
4. In paragraph 3, Orwell says that the elephant incident gave him a better understanding of "the real motives for which despotic governments act." What do you think he means? Before you answer, reread paragraph 7 carefully.
5. Refer to your dictionary as needed to define the following words used in the selection: *imperialism* (paragraph 2), *prostrate* (2), *despotic* (3), *mahout* (3), *miry* (5), *conjurer* (7), *futility* (7), and *sahib* (7).

Questions about the Writer's Craft

1. Most effective narratives encompass a restricted time span. How much time elapses from the moment Orwell gets his gun to the time the elephant dies? What time signals does Orwell provide to help the reader follow the sequence of events in this limited time span?
2. Orwell does not actually begin his narrative until the third paragraph. What purposes do the first two paragraphs serve?
3. In paragraph 6, Orwell says that shooting a working elephant "is comparable to destroying a huge and costly piece of machinery." This kind of comparison is called an *analogy* — describing something unfamiliar, often abstract, in terms of something more familiar and concrete. Where else in "Shooting an Elephant" does Orwell use analogies to make a point? Find at least three additional examples in the essay.
4. Much of the power of Orwell's narrative comes from his ability to convey sensory impressions — what he saw, heard, smelled. Orwell's description becomes most vivid when he writes about the death of the elephant in paragraphs 11 and 12. Find some evocative words and phrases that give the description its power.

Questions for Further Thought

1. In the first paragraph of "Shooting an Elephant," Orwell tells us he was "hated by large numbers of people — the only time in my life that I have been important enough for this to happen to me." What is Orwell implying about people's attitudes toward authority? Do you think Orwell has a valid point? To decide, think about the people who have power over you and how you feel about their authority.
2. The Burmese population was eager to see Orwell shoot the elephant. Why do you believe this incident held such significance for them?
3. In paragraph 7, Orwell comments that "when the white man turns tyrant it it his own freedom that he destroys." This is a *paradox*: a statement that seems to contradict itself. Explain the meaning of this paradox.
4. At the end of his essay, Orwell says he is glad the elephant had killed someone because it put him "legally in the right" for shooting the animal. Think of actions today considered legally right that you, or others, feel are morally wrong.

Writing Assignments Using Narration as a Method of Development

1. In "Shooting an Elephant," Orwell tells us that his "whole life . . . was one long struggle not to be laughed at." Write a narrative

essay about an incident in your life when you did something you didn't want to do (or wouldn't normally do) simply to avoid being laughed at. Like Orwell, use vivid details to make the incident come alive.

2. Write a narrative essay about an experience that gave you, like Orwell, a deeper insight into your own nature. You may have discovered, for instance, that you can be naive, compassionate, petty, cowardly, brave, rebellious, hypocritical, or surprisingly good at something.

Writing Assignments Using Other Methods of Development

3. Was Orwell justified in shooting the elephant? Write an essay arguing that Orwell was justified *or* that he was not. To develop your thesis, cite several specific reasons, each supported by details drawn from the essay. Here are some points you might consider: the legality of Orwell's act; the temperament of the elephant; the influence of the crowd; Orwell's state of mind; the aftermath of the elephant's death; the actual death of the elephant.

4. Orwell's essay concerns, in part, the all-too-human tendency to cover up indecision and confusion just to maintain a facade of authority. Write an essay about the way people in authority often *pretend.*to know what they are doing rather than seem insecure to those subordinate to them. You might consider discussing examples of such behavior that you have seen in parents, teachers, police officers, politicians, or other authority figures. You may use actual incidents you have witnessed or hypothetical examples of common responses.

Bob Greene

Bob Greene is a journalist whose column for the Chicago Tribune *is syndicated in more than two hundred newspapers across the country. Greene also serves as a contributing editor of* Esquire *magazine, which carries his "American Beat" column each month. His bestselling 1984 book,* Good Morning, Merry Sunshine, *recounts his experiences as a father. His observations of American life have been published in two books,* American Beat *(1983), from which the following essay is taken, and* Cheeseburgers *(1985).*

Handled with Care

Life in cities is tough, cruel, harsh, dangerous — or so we are told all the time by the media. We come to expect wrenching stories of vulnerable people ignored or even injured by hardened passersby on city streets. But in the following essay, Bob Greene describes what actually happened one day in Chicago when a woman took off her clothes on a busy downtown street.

The day the lady took her clothes off on Michigan Avenue, 1 people were leaving downtown as usual. The workday had come to an end; men and women were heading for bus and train stations, in a hurry to get home.

She walked south on Michigan; she was wearing a white robe, 2 as if she had been to the beach. She was blond and in her thirties.

As she passed the Radisson Hotel, Roosevelt Williams, a door- 3 man, was opening the door of a cab for one of the hotel's guests. The woman did not really pause while she walked; she merely shrugged the robe off, and it fell to the sidewalk.

She was wearing what appeared to be the bottom of a blue 4 bikini bathing suit, although one woman who was directly next to her said it was just underwear. She wore nothing else.

Williams at first did not believe what he was seeing. If you 5 hang around long enough, you will see everything: robberies, muggings, street fights, murders. But a naked woman on North Michigan Avenue? Williams had not seen that before and neither, apparently, had the other people on the street.

It was strange; her white robe lay on the sidewalk, and by all 6 accounts she was smiling. But no one spoke to her. A report in the newspaper the next day quoted someone: "The cars were stopping, the people on the buses were staring, people were shouting, and people were taking pictures." But that is not what other people who were there that afternoon said.

The atmosphere was not carnival-like, they said. Rather, they 7 said, it was as if something very sad was taking place. It took only a moment for people to realize that this was not some stunt designed to promote a product or a movie. Without anyone telling them, they understood that the woman was troubled, and that what she was doing had nothing to do with sexual titillation; it was more of a cry for help.

The cry for help came in a way that such cries often come. The 8 woman was violating one of the basic premises of the social fabric. She was doing something that is not done. She was not shooting anyone, or breaking a window, or shouting in anger. Rather, in a way that everyone understood, she was signaling that things were not right.

The line is so thin between matters being manageable and 9 being out of hand. One day a person may be barely all right; the next the same person may have crossed over. Here is something from the author John Barth:

> She paused amid the kitchen to drink a glass of water; at that instant, losing a grip of 50 years, the next-room-ceiling plaster crashed. Or he merely sat in an empty study, in March-day glare, listening to the universe rustle in his head, when suddenly a five-foot shelf let go. For ages the fault creeps secret through the rock; in a second, ledge and railings, tourists and turbines all thunder over Niagara. Which snowflake triggers the avalanche? A house explodes; a star. In your spouse, so apparently resigned, murder twitches like a fetus. At some trifling new assessment, all the colonies rebel.

The woman continued to walk past Tribune Tower. People 10 who saw her said that the look on her face was almost peaceful. She did not seem to think she was doing anything unusual; she was described as appearing "blissful." Whatever the reaction on the street was, she seemed calm, as if she believed herself to be in control.

She walked over the Michigan Avenue bridge. Again, people 11 who were there report that no one harassed her; no one jeered at her or attempted to touch her. At some point on the bridge, she removed her bikini bottom. Now she was completely undressed, and still she walked.

"It was as if people knew not to bother her," said one woman 12 who was there. "To tell it, it sounds like something very lewd and sensational was going on. But it wasn't like that at all. It was as if people knew that something very . . . fragile . . . was taking place. I was impressed with the maturity with which people were handling it. No one spoke to her, but you could tell that they wished someone would help her."

Back in front of the Radisson, a police officer had picked up 13 the woman's robe. He was on his portable radio, advising his colleagues that the woman was walking over the bridge.

When the police caught up with the woman, she was just 14 standing there, naked in downtown Chicago, still smiling. The first thing the police did was hand her some covering and ask her to put it on; the show was over.

People who were there said that there was no reaction from the 15 people who were watching. They said that the juvenile behavior you might expect in such a situation just didn't happen. After all, when a man walks out on a ledge in a suicide attempt, there are always people down below who call for him to jump. But this day, by all accounts, nothing like that took place. No one called for her to stay undressed; no one cursed the police officers for stopping her.

"It was as if everyone was relieved," said a woman who saw it. 16 "They were embarrassed by it; it made them feel bad. They were glad that someone had stopped her. And she was still smiling. She seemed to be off somewhere."

The police charged her with no crime; they took her to Read 17 Mental Health Center, where she was reported to have signed herself in voluntarily. Within minutes things were back to as they always are on Michigan Avenue; there was no reminder of the naked lady who had reminded people how fragile is the everyday world in which we live.

Questions for Close Reading

1. What is the thesis (or narrative point) of the selection? Locate the sentence(s) in which Greene states his main idea. If he does not state the thesis explicitly, express it in your own words.
2. What does the newspaper say about this event? Why does its report differ from Greene's?
3. How do the other passersby react to the woman's disrobing on the street? How do the police treat the woman?
4. Why does Greene interpret the woman's disrobing as a call for help?
5. Refer to your dictionary as needed to define the following words used in the selection: *titillation* (paragraph 7), *trifling* (9), and *blissful* (10).

Questions about the Writer's Craft

1. What is the source of the narrative tension that keeps you reading this essay? What conflict underlies this narrative?
2. Why does Greene use the title, "Handled with Care"? What is being "handled with care" in this case?
3. What does the quotation from John Barth add to the essay? Why does Greene interrupt his narrative with this quotation, rather than include it in a concluding interpretive paragraph?
4. How does Greene know what happened that day? Would you believe his account over that of the newspaper? Why? What in this essay makes it different from a straightforward newspaper report?

Questions for Further Thought

1. Why do you think none of the bystanders interfered with the woman's actions? Do you agree with the person who said the onlookers handled it "with maturity"? What could or should people have done before the police came?
2. Should people "get involved" when strangers are in trouble? Are we our brothers' or sisters' keepers?
3. What is so "very sad" about this woman's action? If this woman is so sad, why do you think she had a "blissful" appearance?
4. The author writes, "The line is so thin between matters being manageable and being out of hand." Do you agree? Do you know of anyone who has abruptly given in to feeling that life is unmanageable?

Writing Assignments Using Narration as a Method of Development

1. "Handled with Care" is an example of a "slice of life" narrative. It consists of a single incident, vividly told, that illustrates the author's

main point. Think of a similar incident that suggests a larger meaning. The incident may be one you have experienced or heard about. Brainstorm to gather the details, and then write a narrative essay in the third person. In addition to relating the incident, be sure to clarify—through implicit or explicit means — the significance of the experience.

2. Greene's essay uses a quotation to focus the events of the narrative effectively. Find a quotation or a familiar saying which appeals to you or seems wise and true. Write a narrative essay in which an incident or event illustrates the quotation. Some examples of quotations on which essays might be based include the following:

- What a tangled web we weave/When first we practice to deceive. (Walter Scott)
- When the going gets tough, the tough get going.
- Trees that bend with the wind live longer. (fortune cookie)
- Experience is a tough teacher. She tests first and teaches afterwards. (Salada tea bag "tag line")

Writing Assignments Using Other Methods of Development

3. Write an essay explaining the reasons for the bystanders' reaction to the naked woman. You may choose to analyze one cause in depth, or you may examine several causes; for example, city dwellers' habitual treatment of others, people's attitudes toward aberrant behavior, and so on.

4. Write an essay arguing that we should or should not get involved when we see people in trouble, whether or not they ask for help. Explain in what cases we should offer assistance, if any, and what we should do if we do not offer help. You might consider any of the following: a person in tears, a street person asleep on a sidewalk, an immigrant wearing light native clothes and sandals on a wintry day, a person talking to himself or herself or screaming or cursing at the air.

T. H. Watkins

T. H. Watkins is a historian and environmentalist who has written nine books and numerous articles for such magazines as American Heritage, Cry California, The American West, *and* The Sierra Club Bulletin. *One of his books,* California: An Illustrated History *(1973), was nominated for a Pulitzer Prize. He currently lives on a houseboat moored in San Francisco Bay. This selection first appeared in* The Sierra Club Bulletin.

Little Deaths

We Americans coddle our pets; yet every year, thousands of cats and dogs are abandoned by their owners. We take our children to zoos to see the beauty of wild animals, but we wear furs from the pelts of nearly extinct species. In this selection, T. H. Watkins describes an expedition he took with his cousin, a professional trapper whose job is to "clear the varmints" from the land. As Watkins accompanies his cousin, he experiences some conflicting emotions.

It has been more than ten years since the day my cousin let me 1
walk his traplines with him. We never see each other now. Our worlds, never very close, have grown even farther apart. He left California several years ago to become a trapping supervisor somewhere in Nevada, while I have joined the ranks of those who would cheerfully eliminate his way of life. He would, rightly enough, consider me one of his natural enemies, and it is not likely that we would have much to say if we did meet. Still, I am grateful to him for giving me a glimpse into the reality of a world normally hidden from us, a dark little world where death is the only commonplace.

At the time, my cousin was a lowly field trapper at the beck and 2
call of any rancher or farmer who made an official complaint to the trapping service about varmint troubles — coyotes or wildcats getting after newborn lambs, foxes sneaking into chicken coops, that

141

sort of thing. His current assignment was to trap out the varmint population of some ranchland high in the Diablo Hills southeast of Oakland, a country of rolling grassland, scrub oak, and chaparral dominated by the 3,000-foot upthrust of Mount Diablo. His base was a house trailer planted on the edge of one of the ranches he was servicing near Livermore, although he got into Oakland quite a lot for weekend visits to a lady of his acquaintance. I lived in Oakland at the time, and he usually made a point of stopping by to see my children, of whom he was particularly fond.

I was then a practicing student of western history and thoroughly intrigued by the glittering adventure that pervaded my reading — especially in the stories of the mountain men, those grizzled, anarchic beings with a lust for far places and far things, stubborn individualists who had lived freer than any Indian and had followed their quest for beaver pelts into nearly all the mysterious blanks of the American West, from Taos, New Mexico, to Puget Sound, from the Marys River of the northern Rockies to the Colorado River of the Southwest; hopelessly romantic creatures with a predilection for Indian women, a talent for profanity, and a thirst for liquor profound enough to melt rivets. And here was my cousin, the literary — if not lineal — descendant of the mountain man. True, he was neither grizzled nor given much to profanity, nor had he, so far as I knew, ever offered his blanket to an Indian woman. Still, he was a *trapper*, by God, and when on one of his visits he invited me to accompany him on his rounds, I was entranced with the notion.

Late one spring afternoon I bundled wife and children into the car and drove down to Livermore and out to the ranch where he was staying. After a dinner cooked in the trailer's tiny kitchen, my wife and the children bedded down in the trailer's two little bunks. "When we get back tomorrow afternoon," my cousin told the children. "I'll take you out and show you some spring lambs. You'd like that, right?" he added, giving them a pinch and tickle that set them to giggling in delight. He and I bundled up in sleeping bags on the ground outside.

It was pitch black when he woke me that next morning at five o'clock. After shocking ourselves out of sleep by bathing our faces in water from the outside faucet, we got into his pickup and drove off for breakfast at an all-night diner on the road. Dawn was insinuating itself over the dark hills by the time we finished breakfast,

and had laid a neon streak across the sky when we finally turned off
the highway and began climbing a rutted dirt road that led to the
first trapline (we would be walking two traplines, my cousin explained, one on the western side of the hills, one on the eastern;
these were two of the six he had scattered over the whole range, each
of them containing between 15 and 20 traps and each checked out
and reset or moved to a new location every ten days or so). As we
bumped and rattled up the road, daylight slowly illuminated the
hills. For two or three months in the spring, before the summer sun
turns them warm and brown, these hills look as if they had been
transplanted whole from Ireland or Wales. They are a celebration
of green, all shades of green, from the black-green of manzanita
leaves to the bright, pool-table green of the grasses. Isolated
bunches of cows and sheep stood almost motionless, like ornaments added for the effect of contrast, and morning mist crept
around the base of trees and shrouded dark hollows with the ghost
of its presence. Through all this, the exposed earth of the road cut
like a red scar, and the sounds of the pickup's engine and the
country-western music yammering out of its radio intruded themselves on the earth's silence gracelessly.

   We talked of my cousin's father, whom he worshipped and   6
emulated. My cousin was, in fact, almost literally following in his
father's footsteps, for "the old man" had been a state trapper himself and was now a trapping supervisor. Before that, back in the
deep of the Depression, he had been a lion hunter for the state,
when a mountain lion's ears were good as money, and before that
he had "cowboyed some," as he put it; at one time, according to
family tradition, his grandfather's ranch had encompassed much of
what became the town of San Bernardino in Southern California.
At one point in his life, he had led jaguar-hunting trips to the
jungles of northwestern Mexico, and he was still a noteworthy
hunter, though now he confined himself principally to an occasional deer, antelope, or bear. My cousin had grown up in a house
where skins of various types served as rugs and couchthrows, where
stuffed heads glared unblinkingly from the walls, where sleek
hounds were always in-and-out, where hunting magazines dominated the tables, hunting talk dominated the conversations, and
everywhere was the peculiarly masculine smell of newly oiled guns,
all kinds of guns — pistols (including an old Colt once used by my
cousin's great-grandfather, legend had it, to kill a man), rifles,

shotguns. It was a family that had been killing things for a long time, sometimes for meat, sometimes for a living, sometimes for what was called the sport of it, and one of my cousin's consuming ambitions was to bag a bighorn sheep, something his father had never managed to do.

I had never killed anything in my life except fish, and since fish   7
neither scream, grunt, squeal, nor moan when done in, it had never seemed like killing at all. In any case, I was by no means prepared for the first sight of what my cousin did to earn his bread. I don't know what I had expected with my romantic notions of the trapper's life, but surely it was something other than what I learned when we crawled up the road through increasingly heavy underbrush and stopped to check out the first of my cousin's traps.

We got out of the truck and beat our way through the brush to   8
a spot perhaps 30 feet from the road. I did not see the animal until we were nearly on top of it. It was a raccoon, the first raccoon I had ever seen in person, and at that moment I wished that I never had seen one. It was dead, had been dead for several days, my cousin informed me. "Hunger, thirst, and shock is what kills them, mostly," he said in response to my question. "That, and exhaustion, I reckon." The animal seemed ridiculously tiny in death. It lay on its side, its small mouth, crawling with ants, open in a bared-tooth grin, and its right rear leg in the clutch of the steel trap. It was easy to see how the animal had exhausted itself; it had been at its leg. A strip of flesh perhaps three inches in width had been gnawed away, leaving the white bone and a length of tendon exposed. Tiny flies sang about the ragged wound and over the pool of dried blood beneath the leg. There was a stink in the air, and it suddenly seemed very, very warm to me there in the morning shadows of the brush.

"Once in a while," my cousin said, prying open the curved   9
jaws of the trap, "one of them will chew his way loose, and if he doesn't lose too much blood he can live. I caught a three-legged coyote once. Too stupid to learn, I guess."

"Do you ever find one of them still alive?" I asked.   10
"Sometimes."   11
"What do you do with them?"   12
He looked up at me. "Do with them? I shoot them," he said,   13
patting the holstered pistol at his waist. He lifted the freed raccoon by the hind legs and swung it off into the brush. "Buzzard meat," he said. He then grabbed the steel stake to which the trap was

attached by a chain and worked it out of the ground. "I've had this line going for over a month, now. The area's just about trapped out." He carried the trap back to the road, threw it in the back of the pickup, and we drove up the increasingly rough road to the next trap. It was empty, as was the one after it. I was beginning to hope they would all be empty, but the fourth one contained a small skunk, a black-and-white pussycat of a creature that had managed to get three of its feet in the trap at once and lay huddled in death like a child's stuffed toy. It, too, was disengaged and tossed into the brush. A little further up the ridge, and we found a fox, to my cousin's visible relief. "Great," he said. "That has to be the mate to the one I got a couple of weeks ago. Pregnant, too. There won't be any little foxes running around this year." Into the brush the animal went.

By the time we reached the top of the long ridge on which my cousin had set his traps, the morning had slipped toward noon and our count had risen to seven animals: three raccoons, three skunks, and the pregnant fox. There was only one trap left now, but it was occupied by the prize of the morning, a bobcat. "I'll be damned," my cousin said, "I've been after that bugger all month. Just about give up hope." The bobcat had not died well, but in anger. The marks of its rage and anguish were laid out in a torn circle of earth described by the length of the chain that had linked the animal to its death. Even the brush had been ripped and clawed at, leaves and twigs stripped from branches, leaving sweeping scars. Yellow tufts of the animal's fur lay scattered on the ground, as if the bobcat had torn at its own body for betraying it, and its death-mask was a silent howl of outrage. My cousin took it out of the trap and heaved it down the side of the hill. Buzzard meat.

We had to go back down the hills and around the range in order to come up the eastern slopes and check out the second trapline, and on the way we stopped at a small roadhouse in Clayton for a hamburger and a beer. I found I could eat, which surprised me a little, and I certainly had a thirst for the beer. We sat side-by-side at the bar, not saying much. Something Wallace Stegner had once written kept flashing through my mind. "Like most of my contemporaries," he had said, "I grew up careless. I grew up killing things." I wondered if my cousin would know what Stegner had been talking about, and decided it would be best not to bring it up. I could have cancelled out right there, I suppose, asking him to take me back to his camp, explaining that I had seen enough, too much, of the trapper's life. I could always plead exhaustion. After all, the day's hiking had been more real exercise than I had had in months, and I was, in fact, tired. A stubborn kernel of pride would not let me do it. I would see the day through to the end.

So the ritual continued. We climbed back up into the hills on   16
the east side of the range in the oven-heat of a strong spring sun. The day's count rose even more as the pickup bounced its way up the ragged weedgrown road: two more skunks, another fox, two more raccoons. The work went more slowly than the morning's run, for this was a new line, and each trap had to be reset. My cousin performed this task with an efficient swiftness and the kind of quiet pride any craftsman takes in his skill, snapping and locking the jaws of the traps, covering them with a thin scattering of earth and twigs, sprinkling the ground about with dog urine from a plastic squeeze bottle to cover up the man-smell. By the time we were ready to approach the last three traps of the line, it was well after three o'clock. We were very high by then, well up on the slopes of Mount Diablo itself, and we had to abandon the pickup to hike the rest of the way on foot. We broke out of the brush and walked along a spur of the hills. About 1,500 feet below us and some miles to the east, we could see the towns of Pittsburg and Martinez sending an urban haze into the air. Ahead of me, my cousin suddenly stopped.

"Wait a minute. Listen," he said.   17

A distant thrashing and rattling sound came from the slope   18
below us. That's where the trap is," he said. "Might be a bobcat, but I didn't expect to get him so soon. Come on."

The slope was very steep, and we slid much of the way down to   19
the trap on our bottoms, slapped at and tangled by brush. The animal was not a bobcat. It was a dog, a large, dirty-white mongrel whose foreleg was gripped in the trap. The dog snarled at us as we approached it. Saliva had gathered at its lips and there was a wildness in its eyes.

"*Dammit*," my cousin said. He had owned dogs all his life. "A   20
wild dog. Probably abandoned by somebody. They do it all the time. Dogs turn wild and start running in packs. Some people ought to be shot."

I didn't know what he wanted to do. He hadn't pulled out his   21
gun. "Can we turn him loose? Maybe he isn't wild. Maybe he just wandered up here on his own."

My cousin looked at me. "Maybe. There's a noose-pole in the 22
back of the truck—a kind of a long stick with a loop of rope at the
end. Why don't you get it?"

I scrambled back up the slope and made my way back to the 23
pickup, where I found the noose-pole. As thick as a broomhandle
and about five feet in length, it looked like a primitive fishing-pole.
When I got back down to the trap, the dog was still snarling vi-
ciously. My cousin took the pole from me, opened the loop at the
end, and extended it toward the dog. "If I can hook him," he said,
"I'll hold his head down while you open the trap. You've seen how I
do it."

It was useless. The dog fought at the loop frantically in a 24
madness of pain and fear. After perhaps 15 minutes, my cousin laid
the pole down. "He just isn't going to take it."

"What'll we do?" I asked, though I'm sure I knew. 25

He shrugged. "Can't just leave him here to die." He un- 26
snapped his holster and pulled out the gun. He duck-walked to
within a couple of feet of the animal, which watched him suspiciously. "I'll try to do it with one shot," he said. The gun's dis-
charge slammed into the silence of the mountain. The dog howled
once, a long, penetrating song of despair that ran in echoes down
the hill. My cousin nudged the animal with his boot. It was dead.
He opened the trap, freed the leg, and heaved the body down the
slope. The crashing of its fall seemed to go on for a long time. My
cousin reset the trap. "Come on," he said. "It's getting late."

The last trap of the day held a dead raccoon. 27

My cousin was pleased with the day's work. "If it keeps up like 28
this," he said as we rattled down the highway toward his trailer, "I
could be out of here in a month."

"What's the hurry?" 29

He indicated a small housing development by the side of the 30
road. "Too much civilization around here for me. Too many people. I need to get back up into the mountains."

There was plenty of light left when we got back, and true to his 31
promise, my cousin took the children out into the fields to see a
newborn lamb. While its mother bleated in protest, he ran one
down and brought it to my children so they could pet it. I watched
his face as he held the little creature. There was no hint in it of all the
death we had harvested that day, no hint of the half-eaten legs we
had seen, no hint of the fearful thrashing agony the animals had

endured before dying. No hint, even, of the death-howl of the dirty white dog that may or may not have been wild. There was neither irony nor cynicism in him. He held the lamb with open, honest delight at the wonder my children found in touching this small, warm, live thing.

My cousin is not an evil man. We are none of us evil men.   32

Questions for Close Reading

1. What is the thesis (or narrative point) of the selection? Locate the sentence(s) in which Watkins states his main idea. If he does not state the thesis explicitly, express it in your own words.
2. Watkins explains that even ten years ago, he and his cousin were not close or much alike. Why, then, was Watkins so eager to accompany his cousin on a trapping expedition? What fascination did trapping hold for Watkins?
3. Although Watkins does not approve of what his cousin does for a living, he is fair to him. Find places in the essay where Watkins points out (a) his cousin's good qualities, (b) his cousin's reasons for trapping.
4. What is the difference between the incident of the trapped dog and the other trapping incidents described in the essay? Why do you think Watkins describes the episode with the dog at such length?
5. Refer to your dictionary as needed to define the following words used in the selection: *chaparral* (paragraph 2), *anarchic* (3), *predilection* (3), *lineal* (3), *emulated* (6), and *encompassed* (6).

Questions about the Writer's Craft

1. Narratives rely on vivid description for much of their impact. As a narrator, Watkins is a master of sensory detail, particularly when he wants us to see the death agonies of the trapped animals. Locate two paragraphs in which his descriptions of death are especially vivid. Which words and phrases in these paragraphs make you understand the pain and horror of the animals' deaths?
2. What are some of the time signals that Watkins uses to indicate the sequence of events in his essay?
3. Watkins skillfully employs *simile*, a technique that uses the words *like* or *as* to highlight the similarities between two seemingly unlike objects. One example of simile can be found in paragraph 13, where Watkins describes the dead skunk as looking "like a child's stuffed toy." Find two more examples of similes in "Little Deaths."
4. How does Watkins use dialogue to reveal his cousin's attitudes toward animals? How do these comments help us understand Watkins' thesis?

Questions for Further Thought

1. In what ways are the animals' deaths "little" deaths? In what ways are they significant deaths? What else might have "died" during Watkins' experience?
2. The last paragraph of the selection reads, "My cousin is not an evil man. We are none of us evil men." Do you think Watkins is correct about his cousin? About humanity in general?
3. How might Watkins' cousin, so gentle with young children and a newborn lamb, justify to himself what he does for a living? Is there necessarily a conflict between the two sides of his character?
4. The essay raises the question of justifiable killing. Was the trapper justified in killing the animals because they were "varmints"? Should human needs and desires take precedence over an animal's right to live?

Writing Assignments Using Narrative as a Method of Development

1. As Watkins has done, write a narrative about a moment of harsh discovery in your life. Describe how someone or something you had idealized turned out to be sharply different from what you had expected. Be sure you describe briefly, perhaps in the introduction, your original expectations.
2. Undoubtedly, Watkins feels that his cousin treats life too casually. Write a narrative about a time when you treated life too lightly. The life could be an animal's, another person's, even your own. Use specific details to tell what happened.

Writing Assignments Using Other Methods of Development

3. Write an essay on either the pros or cons of hunting. To prepare for this assignment, look up "Hunting" or "Wildlife Management" in the *Readers' Guide to Periodical Literature*. In addition, you might talk to people you know about their attitudes toward hunting. Then take a position. Direct your essay to a confirmed nonhunter and prove that hunting is beneficial. Or direct the essay to an enthusiastic hunter and support the nonhunting position.
4. The philosopher Hannah Arendt refers in her writings to "the banality of evil." Evil may sometimes be part of the most ordinary, most normal people or activities. Write an essay about one commonly accepted activity that you believe is evil—or at least immoral. Offer detailed support about how or why this activity is wrong. You may consider any of the following: killing animals for fur or food; our treatment of old people or children; our neglect or abuse of our environment.

Langston Hughes

One of the foremost members of the 1920s literary movement known as the Harlem Renaissance, Langston Hughes (1902–1967) committed himself to portraying the richness of black life in America. A poet and a writer of short stories, Hughes was greatly influenced by the rhythms of blues and jazz. In his later years, he published two autobiographical works, The Big Sea *(1940) and* I Wonder as I Wander *(1956), and he wrote a history of the National Association for the Advancement of Colored People (NAACP). The following selection is from* The Big Sea.

Salvation

Disillusionment is part of growing up. As children, we start out expecting the best from people and life. But as we grow older, experiences tend to chip away at our cherished beliefs and trusting expectations. In "Salvation," Langston Hughes uses humor and poignancy to recount a time in his own childhood when he faced such a moment of disillusionment.

I was saved from sin when I was going on thirteen. But not 1 really saved. It happened like this. There was a big revival at my Auntie Reed's church. Every night for weeks there had been much preaching, singing, praying, and shouting, and some very hardened sinners had been brought to Christ, and the membership of the church had grown by leaps and bounds. Then just before the revival ended, they held a special meeting for children, "to bring the young lambs to the fold." My aunt spoke of it for days ahead. That night I was escorted to the front row and placed on the mourners' bench with all the other young sinners, who had not yet been brought to Jesus.

My aunt told me that when you were saved you saw a light, and 2 something happened to you inside! And Jesus came into your life! And God was with you from then on! She said you could see and hear and feel Jesus in your soul. I believed her. I had heard a great many old people say the same thing and it seemed to me they ought to know. So I sat there calmly in the hot, crowded church, waiting for Jesus to come to me.

The preacher preached a wonderful rhythmical sermon, all 3 moans and shouts and lonely cries and dire pictures of hell, and then he sang a song about the ninety and nine safe in the fold, but one little lamb was left out in the cold. Then he said: "Won't you come? Won't you come to Jesus? Young lambs, won't you come?" And he held out his arms to all us young sinners there on the mourners' bench. And the little girls cried. And some of them jumped up and went to Jesus right away. But most of us just sat there.

A great many old people came and knelt around us and prayed, 4 old women with jet-black faces and braided hair, old men with work-gnarled hands. And the church sang a song about the lower lights are burning, some poor sinners to be saved. And the whole building rocked with prayer and song.

Still I kept waiting to *see* Jesus. 5

Finally all the young people had gone to the altar and were 6 saved, but one boy and me. He was a rounder's son named Westley. Westley and I were surrounded by sisters and deacons praying. It was very hot in the church, and getting late now. Finally Westley said to me in a whisper: "God damn! I'm tired o' sitting here. Let's get up and be saved." So he got up and was saved.

Then I was left all alone on the mourners' bench. My aunt 7 came and knelt at my knees and cried, while prayers and songs swirled all around me in the little church. The whole congregation prayed for me alone, in a mighty wail of moans and voices. And I kept waiting serenely for Jesus, waiting, waiting—but he didn't come. I wanted to see him, but nothing happened to me. Nothing! I wanted something to happen to me, but nothing happened.

I heard the songs and the minister saying: "Why don't you 8 come? My dear child, why don't you come to Jesus? Jesus is waiting for you. He wants you. Why don't you come? Sister Reed, what is this child's name?"

"Langston," my aunt sobbed. 9

"Langston, why don't you come? Why don't you come and be 10 saved? Oh, Lamb of God! Why don't you come?"

Now it was really getting late. I began to be ashamed of myself, 11 holding everything up so long. I began to wonder what God thought about Westley, who certainly hadn't seen Jesus either, but who was now sitting proudly on the platform, swinging his knickerbockered legs and grinning down at me, surrounded by deacons and old women on their knees praying. God had not struck Westley dead for taking his name in vain or for lying in the temple. So I decided that maybe to save further trouble, I'd better lie, too, and say that Jesus had come, and get and be saved.

So I got up. 12

Suddenly the whole room broke into a sea of shouting, as they 13 saw me rise. Waves of rejoicing swept the place. Women leaped in the air. My aunt threw her arms around me. The minister took me by the hand and led me to the platform.

When things quieted down, in a hushed silence, punctuated 14 by a few ecstatic "Amens," all the new young lambs were blessed in the name of God. Then joyous singing filled the room.

That night, for the last time in my life but one — for I was a big 15 boy twelve years old — I cried. I cried, in bed alone, and couldn't stop. I buried my head under the quilts, but my aunt heard me. She woke up and told my uncle I was crying because the Holy Ghost had come into my life, and because I had seen Jesus. But I was really crying because I couldn't bear to tell her that I had lied, that I had deceived everybody in the church, and I hadn't seen Jesus, and that now I didn't believe there was a Jesus any more, since he didn't come to help me.

Questions for Close Reading

1. What is the thesis (or narrative point) of "Salvation"? If the thesis is not explicitly stated, express it in your own words.
2. During the revival meeting, what pressures are put on the young Langston to get up and be saved?
3. How does Westley's attitude differ from Langston's?
4. Does the narrator's Auntie Reed really understand him? Why can't he tell her the truth about his experience in the church?
5. Refer to your dictionary as needed to define the following words in the selection: *revival* (paragraph 1), *knickerbockered* (11), *punctuated* (14), and *ecstatic* (14).

Questions about the Writer's Craft

1. The power of a narrative can often be traced to a conflict within the event being recounted. What conflict does the narrator of "Salvation" experience? How does this conflict create tension in the reader?
2. What key role does Westley serve in the resolution of the narrator's dilemma? How does the inclusion of Westley in the story help us to understand Langston better?
3. The thirteenth paragraph develops a metaphor of the church as an ocean. What images create this metaphor? What does the metaphor tell us about Hughes' feelings and those of the church people at this point?
4. The singing of hymns is a major part of this religious service. Why does the narrator reveal the subjects and even the lyrics of some of the hymns?

Questions for Further Thought

1. What did Hughes expect to happen when he was "saved"? Was he led to have unrealistic expectations about this religious moment? Do you think children often understand religious ideas differently than adults?
2. Given the circumstances, do you think young Langston Hughes did the right thing?
3. Young people often feel excessively pressured by family and community to adopt certain values, beliefs, or traditions. What are some examples of this pressure from your own experience? Should young people accept that the older generation knows more about what to believe and do?
4. Is disillusionment with adults and with society's institutions a necessary part of growing up? Why or why not?

Writing Assignments Using Narration as a Method of Development

1. Sometimes we feel deception is our best route to protecting those we care about. Write a narrative about an occasion when you felt you had to go along with what was expected of you because otherwise you would hurt the feelings of people important to you. Describe the pressures on you and show whether your deception was effective or not.
2. Write a narrative essay about a chain of events that caused you to become disillusioned about a person or institution you had held in high esteem. Begin as Hughes does by presenting your initial beliefs. Relate the sequence of events that brought about a change in your evaluation of the person or organization. In the conclusion, explain the short- and long-term effects of the incident.

Writing Assignments Using Other Methods of Development

3. Hughes writes, "My aunt told me that when you were saved, you saw a light, and something happened to you inside! And Jesus came into your life!" What causes people to change their beliefs? Can such changes come from waiting calmly, as Hughes tried to do in church, or must they come from a more active process? Write an essay explaining why or how a change or conversion in beliefs might take place. You may use process analysis, causal analysis, or some other organizational pattern to develop your thesis. Be sure to include specific examples of what you are describing.

4. Write a persuasive essay arguing either that lying is sometimes right or that lying is always wrong. Support your thesis by showing the consequences of your position for society and the individual. Apply your thesis to particular situations and show how lying was or was not the right course of action.

Theodore Sizer

*One of America's leading educators, Theodore Sizer chaired
A Study of High Schools, a national inquiry into the education of adolescents. Sizer's 1984 book, Horace's Compromise, is the first in a series to emerge from that study; the
selection below is from the book's prologue. Sizer is a former
headmaster at the Phillips Exeter Academy and has also
served as dean of Harvard's Graduate School of Education.
He is currently the head of the Education Department at
Brown University.*

Horace's Compromise

*Students often view their teachers one dimensionally: people
who spend their whole lives talking in front of blackboards, or
hunched over desks with red pens in hand. Teachers are supposedly rewarded by their contact with youth, their long vacations, and their lifelong involvement with their favorite academic subject. In the following selection, Theodore Sizer
follows a high school teacher through a typical day. The portrait that emerges is complex and contradictory, anything but
one dimensional.*

Here is an English teacher, Horace Smith. He's fifty-three, a   1
twenty-eight-year veteran of high school classrooms, what one calls
an old pro. He's proud, respected, and committed to his practice.
He'd do nothing else. Teaching is too much fun, too rewarding, to
yield to another line of work.

Horace has been at Franklin High in a suburb of a big city for   2
nineteen years. He served for eight years as English department
chairman, but turned the job over to a colleague, because he felt
that even the minimal administrative chores of that post interfered
with the teaching he loved best.

He arises at 5:45 A.M., careful not to awaken either his wife or   3
grown daughter. He likes to be at school by 7:00, and the drive

155

there from his home takes forty minutes. He wishes he owned a home near the school, but he can't afford it. Only a few of his colleagues live in the school's town, and they are the wives of executives whose salaries can handle the mortgages. His wife's job at the liquor store that she, he, and her brother own doesn't start until 10:00 A.M., and their daughter, a new associate in a law firm in the city, likes to sleep until the last possible minute and skip breakfast. He washes and dresses on tiptoe.

Horace prepares the coffee, makes some toast, and leaves the house at 6:20. He's not the first at school. The custodians and other, usually older, teachers are already there, "puttering around," one of the teachers says.   4

The teachers' room is large, really two rooms. The inner portion, windowless, is arranged in a honeycomb of carrels, one for each older teacher. Younger or newer teachers share carrels. Each has a built-in desk and a chair. Most have file cabinets. The walls on three sides, five feet high, are festooned with posters, photographs, lists, little sayings, notes from colleagues on issues long past. Horace: Call home. Horace: The following students in the chorus are excused from your Period 7 class — Adelson, Cartwright, Donato . . .   5

Horace goes to his carrel, puts down his briefcase, picks up his mug, and walks to the coffee pot at the corner of the outer portion of the teachers' room, a space well lit by wide windows and fitted with a clutter of tables, vinyl-covered sofas, and chairs. The space is a familiar, comfortable jumble, fragrant with the smell of cigarettes smoked hours before. Horace lights up a fresh one, almost involuntarily, as a way perhaps to counteract yesterday's dead vapors. After pouring himself some coffee, he chats with some colleagues, mostly other English teachers.   6

The warning bell rings at 7:20. Horace smothers his cigarette, takes his still partly filled cup back to his carrel and adds it to the shuffle on his desk, collects some books and papers, and, with his briefcase, carries them down the hall to his classroom. Students are already clattering in, friendly, noisy, most of them ignoring him completely — not thoughtlessly, but without thinking. Horace often thinks of the importance of this semantic difference. Many adults are thoughtless about us teachers. Most students, however, just don't know we're here at all, people to think about. Innocents, he concludes.   7

7:30, and its bell. There are seventeen students here; there   8 should be twenty-two. Bill Adams is ill; Horace has been told that by the office. Joyce Lezcowitz is at her grandmother's funeral; Horace hasn't been officially told that, but he knows it to be true. He marks Joyce "Ex Ab" — excused absence — on his attendance list. Looking up from the list, he sees two more students arrive, hustling to seats. You're late. Sorry . . . Sorry . . . The bus . . . Horace ignores the apologies and excuses and checks the two off on his list. One name is yet unaccounted for. Where is Jimmy Tibbetts? Silence. Tibbetts gets an "Abs" after his name.

Horace gets the class's attention by making some announce- 9 ments about next week's test and about the method by which copies of the next play being read will be shared. This inordinately concerns some students and holds no interest for others. Mr. Smith, how can I finish the play when both Rosalie and I have to work after school? Mr. Smith, Sandy and I are on different buses. Can we switch partners? All these sorts of queries are from girls. There is whispering among some students. You got it? Horace asks, abruptly. Silence, signaling affirmation. Horace knows it is an illusion. Some character will come up two days later and guiltlessly assert that he has no play book, doesn't know how to get one, and has never heard of the plans to share the limited copies. Horace makes a mental note to inform Adams, Lezcowitz, and Tibbetts of the text-sharing plan.

This is a class of juniors, mostly seventeen. The department 10 syllabus calls for Shakespeare during this marking period, and *Romeo and Juliet* is the choice this year. The students have been assigned to read Act IV for this week, and Horace and his colleagues all get them to read the play out loud. The previous class had been memorable: Juliet's suicide had provoked much mirth. *Romeo, I come!* The kids thought it funny, clumsily melodramatic. Several, sniggering, saw a sexual meaning. Horace knew this to be inevitable; he had taught the play many times before.

We'll start at Scene Four. A rustle of books. Two kids looking 11 helplessly around. They had forgotten their books, even though in-class reading had been a daily exercise for three weeks. Mr. Smith, I forgot my book. You've got to remember, Alice . . . *remember!* All this with a smile as well as honest exasperation. Share with George. Alice gets up and moves her desk next to that of George. They solemnly peer into George's book while two girls across the classroom giggle.

Gloria, you're Lady Capulet. Mary, the Nurse. George, you're 12 old man Capulet. Gloria starts, reading without punctuation: *Hold take these keys and fetch more species Nurse.* Horace: Gloria. Those commas. They mean something. Use them. Now, again. *Hold. Take these keys. And fetch more spices. Nurse.* Horace swallows. Better . . . Go on, Mary. *They call for dates and quinces in the pastry.* What's a quince? a voice asks. Someone answers, It's a fruit, Fruit! Horace ignores this digression but is reminded how he doesn't like this group of kids. Individually, they're nice, but the chemistry of them together doesn't work. Classes are too much a game for them. Go on . . . George?

Come. Stir! Stir! Stir! The second cock hath crow'd. Horace   13
knows that reference to "cock" will give an opening to some jokester, and he squelches it before it can begin, by being sure he is looking at the class and not at his book as the words are read.

The curfew bell hath rung. 'Tis three o'clock. Look to the bak'd   14
meats, good Angelica . . . George reads accurately, but with little accentuation.

Mary: *Go, you cot-quean, go . . .* Horace interrupts, and ex-   15
plains "cot-quean," a touch of contempt by the Nurse for the meddling Capulet. Horace does not go into the word's etymology, although he knows it. He feels that such a digression would be lost on this group, if not on his third-period class. He'll tell them. And so he returns: George, you're still Capulet. Reply to that cheeky Nurse.

The reading goes on for about forty minutes, to 8:15. The   16
play's repartee among the musicians and Peter was a struggle, and Horace cut off the reading-out-loud before the end of the fifth scene. He assigns Act V for the next period and explains what will be on the *Romeo and Juliet* test. Mr. Smith, Ms. Viola isn't giving a test to her class. The statement is, of course, an accusing question. Well, we are. Ms. Viola's class will get something else, don't you worry. The bell rings.

The students rush out as the next class tries to push in. The   17
newcomers are freshmen and give way to the eleventh-graders. They get into their seats expectantly, without quite the swagger of the older kids. Even though this is March, some of these students are still overwhelmed by the size of the high school.

There should be thirty students in this class, but twenty-seven   18
are present. He marks three absences on his sheet. The students watch him; there is no chatter, but a good deal of squirming. These

kids have the Wriggles, Horace has often said. The bell rings: 8:24.

Horace tells the students to open their textbooks to page 104   19 and read the paragraph at its top. Two students have no textbook. Horace tells them to share with their neighbors. *Always* bring your textbook to class. We never know when we'll need them. The severity in his voice causes quiet. The students read.

Horace asks: Betty, which of the words in the first sentence is   20 an adverb? Silence. Betty stares at her book. More silence. Betty, what is an adverb? Silence. Bill, help Betty. It's sort of a verb that tells you about things. Horace pauses: Not quite, Bill, but close. Phil, you try. Phil: An adverb modifies a verb . . . Horace: O.K., Phil, but what does "modify" mean? Silence. A voice: "Darkly." Who said that? Horace asks. The sentence was "Heathcliff was a darkly brooding character." I did, Taffy says. O.K., Horace follows, you're correct, Taffy, but tell us why "darkly" is an adverb, what it does. Taffy: It modifies "character." No, Taffy, try again. Heathcliff? No. Brooding? Yes, now why? Is "brooding" a verb? Silence.

Horace goes to the board, writes the sentence with chalk. He   21 underlines darkly. Betty writes a note to her neighbor.

The class proceeds with this slow trudge through a paragraph   22 from the textbook, searching for adverbs. Horace presses ahead patiently, almost dumbly at times. He is so familiar with the mistakes that ninth-graders make that he can sense them coming even before their utterance. Adverbs are always tougher to teach than adjectives. What frustrates him most are the partly correct answers; Horace worries that if he signals that a reply is somewhat accurate, all the students will think it is entirely accurate. At the same time, if he takes some minutes to sort out the truth from the falsity, the entire train of thought will be lost. He can never pursue any one student's errors to completion without losing all the others. Teaching grammar to classes like this is slow business, Horace feels. The bell rings. The students rush out, now more boisterous.

This is an Assembly Day, Horace remembers with pleasure. He   23 leaves his papers on his desk, turns off the lights, shuts the door, and returns to the teachers' room. He can avoid assemblies; only the deans have to go. It's some student concert, in any event.

The teachers' room is full. Horace takes pleasure in it and   24 wonders how his colleagues in schools in the city make do without such a sanctuary. Having a personal carrel is a luxury, he knows. He'd lose his here, he also knows, if enrollments went up again. The teachers' room was one happy consequence of the "baby bust."

The card game is going, set up on a square coffee table sur-   25
rounded by a sofa and chairs. The kibitzers outnumber the players; all have coffee, some are smoking. The chatter is incessant, joshingly insulting. The staff members like one another.

Horace takes his mug, empties the cold leavings into the drain   26
of the water fountain, and refills it. He puts a quarter in the large Maxwell House can supplied for that purpose, an honor system. He never pays for his early cup; Horace feels that if you come early, you get one on the house. He moves toward a clutch of fellow English and social studies teachers, and they gossip, mostly about a bit of trouble at the previous night's basketball game. No one was injured — that rarely happens at this high school — but indecorous words had been shouted back and forth, and Coke cans rolled on the gym floor. Someone could have been hurt. No teacher is much exercised about the incident. The talk is about things of more immediate importance to people: personal lives, essences even more transitory, Horace knows, than the odors of their collective cigarettes.

Horace looks about for Ms. Viola to find out whether it's true   27
that she's not going to give a test on *Romeo and Juliet*. She isn't in sight, and Horace remembers why: she is a nonsmoker and is offended by smoke. He leaves his group and goes to Viola's carrel, where he finds her. She is put off by his query. Of course she is giving a test. Horace's lame explanation that a student told him differently doesn't help.

9:53. The third-period class of juniors. *Romeo and Juliet* again.   28
Announcements over the public address system fill the first portion of the period, but Horace and a bunch of kids who call themselves "theater jocks" ignore them and talk about how to read Shakespeare well. They have to speak loudly to overpower the p.a. The rest of the class chatter among themselves. The readings from the play are lively, and Horace is able to exhibit his etymological talents with a disquisition on "cot-quean." The students are well engaged by the scene involving the musicians and Peter until the class is interrupted by a proctor from the principal's office, collecting ab-

sence slips for the first-class periods. Nonetheless, the lesson ends with a widespread sense of good feeling. Horace never gets around to giving out the assignment, talking about the upcoming test, or arranging for play books to be shared.

10:47, the Advanced Placement class. They are reading   29 *Ulysses*, a novel with which Horace himself had trouble. Its circumlocutions are more precious than clever, he thinks, but he can't let on. Joyce is likely to be on the AP Exam, which will put him on a pedestal.

There are eighteen seniors in this class, but only five arrive.   30 Horace remembers: This is United Nations Week at the local college, and a group of the high school's seniors is taking part, representing places like Mauritius and Libya. Many of the students in the UN Club are also those in Advanced Placement classes. Horace welcomes this remnant of five and suggests they use the hour to read. Although he is annoyed at losing several teaching days with this class, he is still quietly grateful for the respite this morning.

11:36. Lunch. Horace buys a salad on the cafeteria line — as a   31 teacher he can jump ahead of students — and he takes it to the faculty dining room. He nods to the assistant principal on duty as he passes by. He takes a place at an empty table and is almost immediately joined by three physical education teachers, all of them coaches of varsity teams, who are noisily wrangling about the previous night's basketball game controversy. Horace listens, entertained. The coaches are having a good time, arguing with heat because they know the issue is really inconsequential and thus their disagreement will not mean much. Lunch is relaxing for Horace.

12:17. A free period. Horace checks with a colleague in the   32 book storeroom about copies of a text soon to be used by the ninth-graders. Can he get more copies? His specific allotment is settled after some minutes' discussion. Horace returns to the teachers' room, to his carrel. He finds a note to call a Mrs. Altschuler, who turns out to be the stepmother of a former student. She asks, on behalf of her stepson, whether Horace will write a character reference for the young man to use in his search for a job. Horace agrees. Horace also finds a note to call the office. Was Tibbetts in your Period One class? No, Horace tells the assistant principal; that's why I marked him absent on the attendance sheet. The assistant principal overlooks this sarcasm. Well, he says, Tibbetts wasn't marked absent at any other class. Horace replies, That's someone else's problem. He was not in my class. The assistant principal: You're sure? Horace: Of course I'm sure.

The minutes of the free period remaining are spent in organiz-   33
ing a set of papers that is to be returned to Horace's third junior English class. Horace sometimes alternates weeks when he collects homework so as not totally to bury himself. He feels guilty about this. The sixth-period class had its turn this week. Horace had skimmed these exercises — a series of questions on Shakespeare's life — and hastily graded them, but using only a plus, check, or minus. He hadn't had time enough to do more.

1:11. More *Romeo and Juliet*. This section is less rambunctious   34
than the first-period group and less interesting than that of the third period. The students are actually rather dull, perhaps because the class meets at the end of the day. Everyone is ready to leave; there is little energy for Montagues and Capulets. However, as with other sections, the kids are responsive when spoken to individually. It is their blandness when they are in a group that Horace finds trying. At least they aren't hell raisers, the way some last-period-of-the-day sections can be. The final bell rings at 2:00.

Horace has learned to stay in his classroom at the day's end so   35
that students who want to consult with him can always find him there. Several appear today. One wants Horace to speak on his behalf to a prospective employer. Another needs to get an assignment. A couple of other students come by actually just to come by. They have no special errand, but seem to like to check in and chat. These youngsters puzzle Horace. They always seem to need reassurance.

Three students from the Theater Club arrive with questions   36
about scenery for the upcoming play. (Horace is the faculty adviser to the stage crew.) Their shared construction work on sets behind the scenes gives Horace great pleasure. He knows these kids and likes their company.

By the time Horace finishes in his classroom, it is 2:30. He   37
drops his papers and books at his carrel, selecting some — papers given him by his Advanced Placement students two days previously that he has yet to find time to read — to put in his briefcase. He does not check in on the card game, now winding down, in the outer section of the teachers' room but, rather, goes briefly to the auditorium to watch the Theater Club actors starting their re-

hearsals. The play is Wilder's *Our Town*. Horace is both grateful and wistful that the production requires virtually no set to be constructed. The challenge for his stage crew, Horace knows, will be in the lighting.

Horace drives directly to his liquor store, arriving shortly after 4:00. He gives his brother-in-law some help in the stockroom and helps at the counter during the usual 4:30-to-6:30 surge of customers. His wife had earlier left for home and has supper ready for them both and their daughter at 7:45.   38

After dinner, Horace works for an hour on the papers he has brought home and on the Joyce classes he knows are ahead of him once the UN Mock Assembly is over. He has two telephone calls from students, one who has been ill and wants an assignment and another who wants to talk about the lighting for *Our Town*. The latter, an eager but shy boy, calls Horace often.   39

Horace turns in at 10:45, can't sleep, and watches the 11:00 news while his wife sleeps. He finally drifts off just before midnight.   40

Horace has high standards. Almost above all, he believes in the importance of writing, having his students learn to use language well. He believes in "coaching" — in having his students write and be criticized, often. Horace has his five classes of fewer than thirty students each, a total of 120. (He is lucky; his colleagues in inner cities like New York, San Diego, Detroit, and St. Louis have a school board – union negotiated "load" base of 175 students.) Horace believes that each student should write something for criticism at least twice a week — but he is realistic. As a rule, his students write once a week.   41

Most of Horace's students are juniors and seniors, young people who should be beyond sentence and paragraph exercises and who should be working on short essays, written arguments with moderately complex sequencing and, if not grace exactly, at least clarity. A page or two would be a minimum — but Horace is realistic. He assigns but one or two paragraphs.   42

Being a veteran teacher, Horace takes only fifteen to twenty minutes to check over each student's daily homework, to read the week's theme, and to write an analysis of it. (The "good" papers take a shorter time, usually, and the work of inept or demoralized   43 students takes much longer.) Horace wonders how his inner-city colleagues, who usually have a far greater percentage of demoralized students, manage. Horace is realistic: even in his accommodating suburban school, fifteen minutes is too much to spend. He compromises, averaging five minutes for each student's work by cutting all but the most essential corners (the *reading* of the paragraphs in the themes takes but a few seconds; it is the thoughtful criticizing, in red ballpoint pen in the margins and elsewhere, that takes the minutes).

So, to check homework and to read and criticize one para-   44 graph per week per student with the maximum feasible corner-cutting takes six hundred minutes, or ten hours, assuming no coffee breaks or flagging attention (which is some assumption, considering how enervating is most students' forced and misspelled prose).

Horace's fifty-some-minute classes consume about twenty-   45 three hours per week. Administrative chores chew up another hour and a half. Horace cares about his teaching and feels that he should take a half-hour to prepare for each class meeting, particularly for his classes with older students, who are swiftly moving over quite abstract and unfamiliar material, and his class of ninth-graders, which requires teaching that is highly individualized. However, he is realistic. He will compromise by spending no more than ten minutes' preparation time, on average, per class. (In effect, he concentrates his "prep" time on the Advanced Placement class, and teaches the others from old notes.) Three of his sections are ostensibly of the same course, but because the students are different in each case, he knows that he cannot satisfactorily clone each lesson plan twice and teach to his satisfaction. (Horace is uneasy with this compromise but feels he can live with it.) Horace's class preparation time per week: four hours.

Horace loves the theater, and when the principal begged him   46 to help out with the afternoon drama program, he agreed. He is paid $800 extra per year to help the student stage crews prepare sets. This takes him in all about four hours per week, save for the ten days before the shows, when he and his crew happily work for hours on end.

Of course, Horace would like time to work on the curriculum   47 with this colleagues. He would like to visit their classes and to work with them on the English department program. He would like to meet his students' parents, to read in his field, and, most important for him, to counsel students as they need such counseling one on one. Being a popular teacher, he is asked to write over fifty recommendations for college admissions offices each year, a Christmas vacation task that usually takes three full days. (He knows he is good at it now. When he was less experienced, the reference writing used to take him a full week. He can now quickly crank out the expected felicitous verbiage.) Yet Horace feels uneasy writing the crucial references for students with whom he has rarely exchanged ten consecutive sentences of private conversation. However, he is realistic: one does what one can and hopes that one is not sending the colleges too many lies.

And so before Horace assigns his one or two paragraphs per week, he is committed for over thirty-two hours of teaching, administration, class preparation, and extracurricular drama work. Collecting one short piece of writing per week from students and spending a bare five minutes per week on each student's weekly work adds ten hours, yielding a forty-two-hour work week. Lunch periods, supervisory duties frequently, if irregularly, assigned, coffee breaks, travel to and from school, and time for the courtesies, civilities, and biological necessities of life are all in addition.   48

For this, Horace, a twenty-eight-year veteran, is paid $27,300, a good salary for a teacher in his district.   49

Questions for Close Reading

1. What is the thesis (or narrative point) of the selection? Locate the sentence(s) in which Sizer states his main idea. If he does not state the thesis explicitly, express it in your own words.
2. Sizer lets us know in several places that Horace is an "old pro." How can we tell?
3. How much of Horace Smith's teaching day is consumed by activities other than teaching? What are these activities? How many of them directly help students learn?
4. What are the rewards of Horace Smith's job? What specific things bring him satisfaction?
5. Refer to your dictionary as needed to define the following words from the selection: *semantic* (paragraph 7), *inordinately* (9), *melodramatic* (10), *kibitzers* (25), *indecorous* (26), *etymological* (28), *circumlocutions* (29), *felicitous* (47), and *verbiage* (47).

Questions about the Writer's Craft

1. Narratives usually include direct reports of words exchanged between people. Where does Sizer relate conversations between Horace and other people? Why do you think Sizer ignores the rules about using quotation marks for dialogue and instead runs the conversations together in a paragraph?
2. What is Sizer's purpose in relating all the little details of an ordinary teacher's day — from whether he pays for his coffee to who is absent from his classes?
3. "Horace's Compromise" is actually the introductory chapter of a book Sizer, the former Dean of Harvard University Graduate School of Education, wrote to argue that American high schools are in need of reform. Why do you think he chose to begin this kind of book by telling Horace's story?
4. After Horace "drifts off" around midnight, Sizer concludes with a few pages of discussion about Horace. What does this commentary add to your understanding of Horace's life? Of Sizer's purpose in writing the essay?

Questions for Further Thought

1. Why does Sizer use "Horace's Compromise" as his title? Since the word "compromise" has negative overtones, is he criticizing Horace in any way?
2. Does the description of Horace's day make it seem as if his day is hard or easy? Would it be hard or easy to be a new teacher? Did this essay alter your previous opinion about how hard high school teachers work?
3. In Horace's classes, students forget books, call out comments, and giggle. Should Horace be a stricter disciplinarian? Are discipline standards in today's high schools generally too relaxed?
4. Do you think the high school Horace teaches at is typical? Overall, is high school education in the U.S. something the teachers and the taxpayers can be proud of?

Writing Assignments Using Narration as a Method of Development

1. Write a narrative about a "day in the life" of a high school student, a college student, or a particular kind of employee. Even if you base the essay on your own experience, write the narrative in the third person. Begin with awakening, end with going to sleep, and conclude with a summary evaluating the day and determining whether the day was successful in terms of the person's own goals. (If a day would be too

much to describe, limit yourself to a morning, afternoon, or evening.) Provide vigorous narrative specifics about key events, remembering not to get sidetracked by minor occurrences.

2. Despite the difficulties of Horace's job, Sizer makes clear that Horace has touched the lives of many students. Write an essay recounting a single time or a series of times that someone taught you something significant. The person might be a classroom teacher, but he or she could also be a parent or grandparent, a brother or sister, a religious or youth leader, or a friend. Use lively narrative details, dialogue, and description to make the event(s) immediate and dramatic.

Writing Assignments Using Other Methods of Development

3. Employees or students are often caught in a web of pressures from different sources. For example, Horace Smith encounters various daily requests and demands from parents, other teachers, students, and administrators. Write an essay identifying and classifying the pressures experienced by students or a particular type of employee (cafeteria workers or bank tellers, for example). You might include pressures from supervisors, peers, or other outside parties, as well as pressures from within.

4. As Horace Smith's department head, write a memo to either Horace or the school principal evaluating Horace's work. In preparation for this evaluation, you have observed Horace during the day Sizer describes. Include a summary of his performance and indicate what Horace is doing well and what areas he needs to improve.

Additional Writing Topics
NARRATIVE

General Assignments

Prepare an essay on any of the following topics, using narration as the paper's dominant method of development. Be sure to select details that advance the narrative purpose of the essay; you may even want to experiment with flashback or flashforward. In any case, keep the sequence of events clear by using transitional cues. Within the limited time span covered, use vigorous details and varied sentence structure to enliven the narrative. Tell the story from a consistent point of view.

1. An emergency that brought out the best or worst in me
2. The hazards of taking children out to eat
3. An incident that made me believe in fate
4. My best or worst day at school or work
5. A major decision
6. An encounter with a machine
7. An important learning experience
8. A narrow escape
9. My first date, day on the job, or first anything
10. A memorable childhood experience
11. A fairy tale the way I would like to see it told
12. A painful moment
13. An incredible but true story
14. A significant family event
15. An experience in which a certain emotion (pride, anger, regret, or some other) was predominant

Assignments with a Specific Audience and Purpose

1. A friend comes to you with a question of ethics. Your friend has seen someone cheat, or shoplift, or perform some dishonest action. Should your friend speak up to the teacher, the store owner, the employer? Convince your friend that he or she should act by narrating an incident in which someone did (or did not) speak up in such a situation. Tell what happened as a result.
2. As fundraiser for a particular organization (SPCA, Red Cross, Big Brothers/Sisters, and so on), you are sending a newsletter to contribu-

tors. Support your cause by telling the story of one time when your organization made all the difference — the blood donation that saved a life, the animal that was saved from the gas chamber, and so on.

3. You have had a disturbing encounter with one of the people who seems to have "fallen through the cracks" of society — a street person, an unwanted child, or anyone else who is alone and abandoned. Write a letter to the local newspaper describing this encounter. Your purpose is to arouse people's indignation and compassion and to get help for such unfortunates.

4. Write an article for your old high school newspaper. The article will be read primarily be seniors who are planning to go away to college next year. In the article, narrate a story that points to some truth about the "breaking away" stage of life — that first experience of moving away from home.

5. Your best friend has had a terrible experience with a teacher, employer, doctor, repairperson (or any other kind of professional) and is completely disillusioned. Balance the cynical picture your friend has by narrating a story that shows the "flip side" of this profession — a good experience you had when such a person went all out to help you.

6. Your younger brother or sister can't wait to be your age. Tell your sibling that your age isn't as wonderful as he or she thinks by narrating a story that shows the disadvantage of being your age. Make the story one that a young person could understand.

EXEMPLIFICATION

WHAT IS EXEMPLIFICATION?

If someone asked you, "Have you been to any good restaurants lately?" you probably wouldn't answer "Yes" and then immediately change the subject. You would go on, most likely, to explain your answer with examples. You might give the names of restaurants you had enjoyed and talk briefly about the specific things you liked: the attractive prices, the tasty main courses, the pleasant service, the tempting desserts. Such examples and details are needed if you want to convince others that your opinion—in this or any matter—is valid. Similarly, when you talk about larger and more important issues, people will not pay much attention to your opinion if all you do is string together vague generalizations: "We have to do something about acid rain. We have a real problem. The impact of acid rain on the environment has been considerable. Acid rain has serious effects on all of us." Without specific supporting examples, such an argument is a toothless tiger, blustery but ineffective. People must have examples (the forests in the Adirondacks are dying; yesterday's rainfall was fifty times more acidic than nor-

171

mal; Pine Lake, in the northern part of the state, was once a great fishing spot but now has no fish population) to be convinced that your point is well-founded.

Examples are equally important when writing an essay. These "for instances" are at the heart of effective writing, giving your work substance and solidity. Don't think that you are padding the essay when you use examples, or that general statements and abstract phrasing somehow elevate your paper, making it sound more impressive. The best writing is concrete and down-to-earth. The most skillful writers achieve their effects by using specific examples.

WHEN TO USE EXEMPLIFICATION

Assignments or exam essays like those below may be phrased in such a way that the need for specific illustrations is immediately apparent:

> Soap operas, whether shown during the day or in the evening, are among the most watched programs on television. Why is this so? Be sure to provide specific examples to support your position.

> Many observers claim that college students are interested less in learning than in getting ahead in their careers. Cite evidence to demonstrate the validity—or lack of validity—of this claim.

> A growing number of people feel that parents should not allow their children to participate in highly competitive, highly organized team sports. Basing your conclusion on your own experiences and observations, indicate whether you think these people have a reasonable point of view.

The wording of these assignments ("provide specific examples," "Cite evidence," "Basing your conclusion on your own experiences and observations") signals that each essay would be developed through examples, with the examples supporting the essay's purpose and viewpoint.

Usually, though, you will not be told to provide examples. Instead, the need for examples will emerge as you realize the essay requires supporting illustrations and concrete instances to achieve its purpose. You should therefore not be surprised to learn that examples are necessary in papers using the other patterns of development discussed in this book. Specific examples would be used, for instance, in an *argumentation-persuasion* essay on the need for national health insurance. To make its point, such a paper might cite a number of examples: people being bankrupted by medical bills; a poor person who died after being turned away by a hospital; individuals not getting the medical attention they needed because they didn't have the money to visit a doctor. Or consider a lightly satiric piece that pokes fun at cat-lovers. Insisting that cat-people are themselves strange creatures, the essay might make its point through a series of examples *contrasting* dog-lovers and cat-lovers: the qualities admired by each group (loyalty in dogs versus independence in cats) and the different expectations each group has for its pets (dog-lovers want Fido to be obedient and lovable, while cat-lovers are grateful for Felix's spurts of docility and affection). Similarly, examples would be needed in a *causal analysis* examining the impact on college students of a proposed tuition hike: reports about students who would have to leave school before receiving their degrees; interviews with students who would have to take full-time jobs to finance their education; statistics on the number of students who would have to abandon altogether the idea of higher education.

Whether you use examples as a primary or supplemental method of development, specific illustrations serve a number of important purposes. For one thing, examples make writing *interesting*. Assume you have decided to write an essay about sexism in TV commercials. If you merely repeat this frequently agreed-upon point in a general way and fail to cite examples of commercials that present stereotyped views of men and women, your essay will be lifeless and boring:

> Sexism is rampant in television commercials. It is very much alive, and most viewers seem to take it all in stride. Few people protest the obviously sexist characters and statements on such commercials. Surely, these commercials misrepresent the way most of us live.

Without interesting particulars, readers will be apt to think, "Who cares?" and remain uninvolved in what you have to say. By way of contrast, if specific examples are provided, readers will be pulled into the essay, and their attention will be drawn to the point being made:

> Sexism is rampant in television commercials. Although millions of women hold responsible jobs outside the home, commercials continue to portray women as simple creatures who spend most of their time thinking about wax build-up, cottony-soft bathroom tissue, and static-free clothes. Men, apparently, have better things to do than to fret over such mundane household matters. How many commercials can you recall that depict men proclaiming the virtues of squeaky-clean dishes or sparkling bathrooms? Not many.

Examples also make writing *persuasive*. Most writing involves an attempt to make a point. But many of us are reluctant to accept someone else's point of view without solid evidence that demonstrates the validity of that position. Imagine that you are writing an essay showing that latchkey children are more self-sufficient and emotionally secure than children who return from school to a home where a parent awaits them. Your thesis is obviously controversial. Without specific examples — from your own experience, from personal observations, or from research studies — you would not be able to convince readers that your point is valid. The lack of specific supporting examples would seriously weaken your thesis.

Moreover, examples *help explain* difficult, abstract, or unusual ideas. Suppose you have been assigned an essay on a complex subject such as inflation, zero population growth, or radiation exposure. As a writer, it is your responsibility to make these difficult concepts concrete and easily understandable. If you were writing an essay on radiation exposure in everyday life, you might start by providing specific examples of home appliances that emit radiation — color televisions, computers, and microwave ovens — and tell exactly how much radiation we absorb in a typical day from this equipment. To illustrate further the extent of our radiation exposure, you could also provide specifics about unavoidable sources of natural radiation (the sun, for instance) and details about the widespread use of radiation in medicine (x-rays, radiation therapy). These specific examples ground your discussion, making it immediate and concrete, preventing it from flying off into a vague and theoretical realm.

Finally, examples *help ensure clear communication*. All of us have experienced the frustration of not being understood, of having someone misinterpret what we said. In face-to-face communication, we often can detect when someone doesn't understand what we're saying and can provide on-the-spot clarification. Because instantaneous feedback is not available to you when writing, it's crucial that you do everything you can to make your meaning as clear as possible. Examples will help.

Let's assume that you are writing an essay developing the point that ineffective teaching is on the rise in today's high schools. In the paper, you would have to provide specific examples to clarify what you mean by "ineffective." You might mention the following: the teacher who spent so much time disciplining unruly students that he never got around to teaching an assigned lesson; the moonlighting teacher who was so tired in class that she regularly took naps during tests; the teacher who accepted obviously plagiarized reports simply because he was grateful that students handed in something.

Without these concrete examples, your readers will supply or fill in their own ideas — and these may not be what you had in mind. You may consider computerized instruction an ineffective teaching method, while the reader may believe that computers are precisely what more schools need to be effective. Specific examples help prevent this kind of misunderstanding and imprecise communication.

SUGGESTIONS FOR USING EXEMPLIFICATION IN AN ESSAY

The following suggestions will be helpful whether you use examples as a dominant or supportive pattern of development.

1. Generate examples. Where do you get the examples to develop your essay? The first batch of examples is generated during the prewriting stage. With your audience and thesis in mind, you should brainstorm and freewrite, making a broad sweep for examples. Search your own experience; recall or ask about other people's experience; visit the library.

Examples can take several forms, including specific names (people, places, products, for instance), anecdotes, events, and factual details gathered through research. But be sure to exercise caution with any statistics you come across. An old saying warns that there are lies, damn lies, and statistics — meaning that statistics can be misleading; they can be manipulated easily to suit varying ends. A commercial may claim that "in a test taste, eighty percent of those questioned indicated that they preferred Fizzy Cola." Impressed? Don't be — at least, not until you find out how the test was conducted. Perhaps the subjects had to choose between Fizzy Cola and battery acid, or perhaps there were only five subjects, including Fizzy Cola's four vice presidents and a hapless stranger.

During the prewriting stage, try to generate more examples than you think you can use. Starting with abundance — and then picking out the strongest examples — will give you a firm base on which to construct the essay. If you have a great deal of trouble finding examples to support your thesis, you may need to revise the thesis; you may be trying to support an idea that has little validity. On the other hand, while prewriting, you may unearth numerous examples but may find that many of them contradict the point you started out to support. If that happens, don't hesitate to recast your central point, always remembering that your thesis and examples must fit.

2. Select the examples to include.   If you have generated as many specifics as possible, you are now ready to narrow down your examples to the strongest items. At this point, keeping your thesis and audience in mind, you should ask yourself several key questions: "How many examples do I need? Should the examples be brief? Should they be extended?"

You may decide to include several brief examples within a single sentence:

> The French people's fascination with some American literary figures, such as Poe and Hawthorne, is understandable. But their great respect for "artists" like comedian Jerry Lewis is a mystery.

Or, you may elect to develop a paragraph with a number of "for instances":

A uniquely American style of movie-acting reached its peak in the 1950s. Certain charismatic actors completely abandoned the stage techniques and tradition that had been the foundation of acting up to that time. Instead of articulating their lines clearly, the actors mumbled; instead of making firm eye contact with their colleagues, they hung their heads, shifted their eyes, even talked with their eyes closed. Marlon Brando, and then James Dean, were two actors who exemplified this new trend.

Generally, you will need to provide *more than one example*. An essay with the thesis "Rock videos are dangerously violent" would not be convincing if only one example of a video were given. Several strong examples would be needed before anyone felt that enough support had been provided to illustrate the point. Occasionally, one *extended example*, fully developed with many details, can support an essay. It might be possible, for example, to support the thesis that "Federal legislation should be passed which raises the legal drinking age to twenty-one" with one compelling, highly detailed example describing the effects of one teenager's drunken driving spree.

You want to be sure your examples are *relevant* and develop the points they are intended to support. This may sound obvious, but writers sometimes use weak or inappropriate examples to support their positions. You would have a hard time convincing readers that Americans have callous attitudes toward the elderly if you described the wide range of new programs, all staffed by volunteers, at a well-financed center for senior citizens. Similarly, you would not convince your reader that pollution from landfills poses a serious health risk if you discussed legislation needed to control automobile emissions. Because these examples do not support their respective thesis statements, the logic of the essay would collapse, and your credibility would be compromised.

Finally, you need to select *representative* examples. Picking the oddball or one-in-a-million example to support a point — and passing it off as typical or usual — is dishonest. For instance, since the 1960s, some people have tagged feminists with the label "bra-burner." But how many liberationists actually burned bras? If such an incident happened only once, it is unfair to use it as proof that the women's movement is frivolous or destructive.

3. Develop examples with sufficient detail. To ensure that readers grasp the significance of the examples you include, you should develop key examples in enough detail. If you were asked to write an essay on the types of heroes that reappear in American movies, you could not string together a series of paragraphs, each of them like the one below.

> Heroes in American movies usually fall into types. One kind of hero is the tight-lipped loner, men like Clint Eastwood or Humphrey Bogart. Another movie hero is the quiet, shy, or fumbling type who has appeared in movies since the beginning. The main characteristic of this hero is lovableness, as seen in actors like Jimmy Stewart. Perhaps the most one-dimensional and predictable hero is the super-man who battles tough odds. This kind of hero is best illustrated by Sylvester Stallone as Rocky and Rambo.

If the essay were developed this way — if you moved quickly from one undeveloped example to another, without providing supporting specifics — you would not be writing an essay; you would be doing little more than making a list. To be effective, key examples must be expanded in sufficient detail. You could, for instance, develop the first example this way:

> Heroes can be tight-lipped loners who appear out of nowhere, form no permanent attachments, and walk, drive, or ride off into the sunset. In many of his Westerns, from the low-budget "spaghetti Westerns" of the 1960s to <u>Pale Rider</u> in 1985, Clint Eastwood personifies this kind of hero. He is remote, mysterious, and has few lines of dialogue. Yet he cleans the villains out of town, helps a little crippled girl, and shoots down an evil sheriff--acts that cement his heroic status. The loner might also be Humphrey Bogart as Sam Spade, a man with few true friends and no meaningful romantic attachments. Spade solves the crime and sends the guilty off to jail in a clearly heroic way, yet he holds his emotions in check and has no permanent ties beyond his faithful secretary and shabby office. One gets the feeling that he could walk away from these, too, if necessary. Even in <u>The Right Stuff</u>, a fairly factual account of America's early astronauts, the scriptwriters mold Chuck Yeager, the man who broke the sound barrier, into a classic loner. Yeager has a wife. But, as played by lanky, aloof Sam Shepard, the astronaut is insular. Depending only on himself, he rarely confides in anyone, taking mute pride in the knowledge that he is the best at what he does.

4. Organize the examples. If, as is usually the case, several examples are provided to support a point, you should be sure there is a reason for presenting the examples in the order you do. The examples cannot be presented randomly, without design. Instead, you should select a sequence that most effectively illustrates your thesis. Imagine you are writing an essay about the period of adjustment many students experience during the first months of college. The supporting examples could be arranged *chronologically*. You might start by providing examples of the ambivalence students feel the first day of college when their parents leave to go home; you might then offer an anecdote or two about students' frequent calls to Mom and Dad during the opening weeks of the semester; the essay might end with an account that details students' reluctance to leave campus at the mid-year break. An essay demonstrating that the furnishings in a room often reflect the character of its occupant might be organized *spatially*: from the empty soda cans on the floor to the spitballs on the ceiling. The *emphatic sequence* — in which you lead steadily from your first example to your final, most significant or dramatic example — is also an effective way to organize an essay containing many examples. A paper about Americans' characteristic impatience might progress from minor examples (dependence on fast food, obsession with ever-faster mail delivery services) to more disturbing manifestations of impatience (using drugs as quick solutions to problems, advocating simple answers to complex international problems: "Bomb them!").

Without appropriate and dynamic examples, an essay is a dry, bloodless thing. Even provocative and intriguing ideas lose their power — or may be misunderstood — if writers do not provide the specific details needed to explain and develop their central points. It's also important to remember that most readers will not take seriously a writer who has been too lazy to do anything but spout off a series of vague generalities. If you examine a stirring speech, a riveting newspaper article, an informative book, you are sure to find clear, well-developed examples. These specifics engage the reader and provide the writing with its distinctive energy.

STUDENT ESSAY AND COMMENTARY

The student essay that follows was written by Michael Pagano in response to this assignment:

> Anne Morrow Lindbergh states in "Channelled Whelk" that Americans impose unnecessary complications on their lives. Observe closely the way you and others conduct your daily lives. Use your observations to generate evidence for an essay that supports or refutes Lindbergh's point of view.

While reading the paper, try to determine how effectively it applies the principles concerning the use of exemplification. The commentary following the paper will help you look at Michael's essay more closely.

Pursuit of Possessions

In the essay, "Channelled Whelk," Anne Morrow Lindbergh states that Americans "who could choose simplicity, choose complication." Lindbergh herself is a prime example of the phenomenon she discusses. A wife and a mother as well as a writer, Lindbergh has many obligations which make for a complicated life. Even so, Lindbergh attempts to simplify her life by escaping to a beach cottage that is bare except for driftwood and shells for decoration; there she is happy. But very few of us would be willing to simplify our lives as Lindbergh does. Instead, we choose to clutter our lives with a stream of material possessions. And what is the result of this mania for possessions? Much of our time goes to buying new things, dealing with the complications they create, and working madly to buy more things or pay for the things we already have.

We devote a great deal of our lives to acquiring the material goods we imagine are essential to our well-being. Hours are spent planning and thinking about our future purchases. We windowshop for designer jogging shoes; we leaf through magazines looking at ads for elaborate stereo equipment; we research back issues of <u>Consumer Reports</u> to find out about recent developments in exercise equipment. Moreover, once we find what we are looking for, more time is taken up when we decide to actually buy the purchases. How do we find this time? That's easy. We turn evening, weekends, and holidays--time that used to be set aside for family and friends--into shopping expeditions. No wonder that family life is deteriorating and that children spend so much time in front of television sets. Their parents are seldom around.

As soon as we take our new purchases home, they begin to complicate our lives. A sleek new sports car has to be washed, waxed, and vacuumed. A fashionable pair of skintight jeans can't be thrown in the washing machine but has to be taken to the dry cleaners. New stereo equipment has to be connected with a tangled network of cables to the TV, radio, and cassette deck. Eventually, of course, the inevitable happens. Our indispensable possessions break down and need to be repaired. The home computer starts to lose data, the microwave has to have its temperature controls adjusted, and the videotape recorder has to be serviced when a cassette becomes jammed in the machine.

After more time has gone by, we sometimes discover that our purchases don't suit us anymore, and so we decide to replace them. Before making our replacement purchases, though, we have to find ways to get rid of the old items. If we want to replace our black-and-white 19-inch television set with a 25-inch color set, we have to find time to put an ad in the classified section of the paper. Then we have to handle phone calls and set up times people can come to look at the TV. We could store the set in the basement--if we are lucky enough to find a spot that isn't already filled with other discarded purchases.

Worst of all, this mania for possessions often influences our approach to work. It is not unusual for people to take a second or even a third job to pay off the debt they fall into because they have overbought. After paying for food, clothing, and shelter, many people see the rest of their paycheck go to Visa, MasterCard, department store charge accounts, and time payments. Panic sets in when they realize there simply is not enough money to cover all their expenses. Just to stay afloat, people may have to work overtime or take on additional jobs.

It is clear that many of us have allowed the pursuit of possessions to dominate our lives. We are so busy buying, maintaining, and paying for our worldly goods that we do not have much time to think about what is really important. We should try to step back from our compulsive need for more of everything and get in touch with the basic values that are the real point of our lives.

In his essay, "Pursuit of Possessions," Michael analyzes the mania in American society for acquiring material goods. He begins with a quotation from Anne Morrow Lindbergh's "Channelled Whelk" and briefly explains Lindbergh's strategy for uncomplicating her life. The reference to Lindbergh gives Michael a chance to contrast the way she tries to lead her life with the acquisitive and frenzied way many of us lead ours. This contrast leads logically to the essay's *thesis*: "We choose to clutter our lives with a stream of material possessions."

In the last sentence of the introductory paragraph, Michael provides a *plan of development* that reveals the paper's major supporting points and the order in which they will be discussed: (1) we spend a good deal of time buying things, (2) our possessions create complications, and (3) we have to work hard to pay for all our possessions. Essays of this length often do not need a plan of development. But Michael's paper is supported mainly through *exemplification* and thus is filled with many specific illustrations; the plan of development presents readers with the paper's overall structure, making it easier for them to see how all the details relate to the essay's central points. The plan of development also helps readers see that Michael's paper contains an element of *causal analysis*: the examples illustrate that our pursuit of possessions adversely affects our lives.

The *support* for the thesis consists of examples organized around the three major points. Michael uses one paragraph to develop his first and third points and two paragraphs to develop his second point. Each of the four supporting paragraphs is focused by a *topic sentence* which appears at the start of the paragraph: "We devote a great deal of our lives to acquiring the material goods we imagine are essential to our well-being" (paragraph 2); "As soon as we take our new purchases home, they begin to complicate our lives" (3); "After more time has gone by, we sometimes discover that our purchases don't suit us anymore, and so we decide to replace them" (4); and "Worst of all, this mania for possessions often influences our approach to work" (6). The transitional phrase "Worst of all" signals that Michael has sequenced his major points *emphatically*, saving for last the issue he considers most significant.

Now let's look more closely at some of the other techniques Michael uses to organize the essay. When reading the paper, you probably felt that there was an easy flow from one supporting paragraph to the next. How does Michael achieve such a graceful progression? Take a moment to reread the topic sentences that introduce the third and fourth paragraphs. Note the way the beginning of each sentence (in italics) *links back* to the preceding paragraph: "*As soon as we take our new purchases home*, they . . . complicate our lives," and "*After more time has gone by*, we . . . discover . . . our purchases don't suit us. . . .*"

Similar organizing strategies are used within the paragraphs to link material. For instance, the details in the supporting paragraphs are sequenced *chronologically*. Thus, the third paragraph starts by describing purchases that have just been brought home and then moves to what happens to the purchases after they have been home for a while. To help readers follow the chronological progression of points within the supporting paragraphs, Michael uses strong *transitional signals*: "*Moreover, once* we find what we are looking for, more time is taken up . . . " (2); "*Eventually*, of course, the inevitable happens" (3); "*Then* we have to handle phone calls . . . " (4).

As you read Michael's essay, you might have noticed that his paragraph development is not always consistent. You probably recall that an essay developed primarily through examples must include illustrative material that is *interesting, relevant, convincing*, and *sufficiently detailed*. On the whole, Michael's specifics are fairly successful in meeting these requirements. The third and fourth paragraphs especially include vigorous details that show how our mania for buying things can govern our lives. We may even laugh with self-recognition when reading about "skintight jeans that can't be thrown in the washing machine" or a "basement . . . filled with . . . discarded purchases."

But in other spots, Michael runs into trouble preparing well-developed paragraphs. Consider the second paragraph. The sentences "No wonder children spend so much time in front of the television set. Their parents are seldom around" disrupt the unity of the paragraph by introducing an issue unrelated to the paragraph's controlling idea. And once these two sentences are deleted, it becomes apparent that the paragraph is not very substantial. Indeed, the fact that the paragraph is now shorter than the introduction signals that more material is needed. To give the paragraph more solidity, Michael could go into more detail about a typical weekend shopping spree or an elaborate ritual preceding the purchase of some nonessential item.

The fifth paragraph is similarly underdeveloped. We know that this paragraph presents what Michael considers his most significant point, but the details in the paragraph are flat and unconvincing. When compared to the energetic specifics found in the third and fourth paragraphs, this section of the paper seems anticlimactic. More support and vigorous details are needed to round out this final supporting section. Michael could, for instance, mention specific people he knows who overspend, revealing how much they are in debt and how much they have to work to become solvent again. Or he could cite a television documentary or magazine article dealing with the issue of consumer debt. Such specifics would give the paragraph the solidity it now lacks.

The fifth paragraph has a second, more subtle problem; it presents an abrupt shift in tone. Although critical of our possession-mad culture, up to now Michael has poked fun at our obsession, keeping his tone conversational and gently satiric. But in this paragraph, Michael suddenly adopts a serious tone. And he assumes a preachy, somewhat moralistic stance in the next paragraph. It is, of course, legitimate to have a serious message in a lightly satiric piece. In fact, most satiric pieces have such an additional layer of meaning. But because Michael has trouble blending these two moods, there is a jarring shift in the feeling of the essay.

Although the essay needs work in some spots, it is much improved over the first draft. To see the kind of rethinking Michael did when editing the paper, it is helpful to compare the second and third supporting paragraphs above with what he originally wrote.

Unrevised Version

Our lives are spent not only buying things but in dealing with the inevitable complications that are created by our newly acquired possessions. First, we have to find places to put all the objects we bring home. More clothes demand more closets; a second car demands more garage space; a home entertainment center requires elaborate shelving. We shouldn't be surprised that the average American family moves once every three years. A good many families move simply because they need more space to store all the things they buy. In addition, our possessions demand maintenance time. A person who gets a new car will spend hours washing it, waxing it, and vacuuming it. A new pair of jeans has to go to the dry cleaners. New stereo systems have to be connected to already existing equipment. Eventually, of course, the inevitable happens. Our new items need to be repaired. Or we get sick of them and decide to replace them. Before making our replacement purchases, though, we have to get rid of the old items. That can be a real inconvenience.

When Michael looked more closely at this paragraph, he realized it rambled and lacked energy. He started to edit the paragraph by tightening the first sentence, making it more focused and less awkward. Certainly, the revised sentence ("As soon as we take our new purchases home, they begin to complicate our lives") is crisper than the original. Next, he decided to omit the discussion about finding places to put new possessions; these sentences about inadequate closet, garage, and shelf space were so exaggerated that they undercut the valid point he wanted to make. He also chose to eliminate the sentences about the mobility of American families. This was, he felt, an interesting point, but it introduced an issue too complex to be included in the paragraph.

Next, Michael strengthened the rest of the paragraph by making the details more specific. A "new car" became a "sleek new sports car," and a "pair of jeans" became a "fashionable pair of skintight jeans." Michael also realized he had to do more than merely write, "Eventually, . . . our new items need to be repaired." This point had to be dramatized by sharp, convincing details. And so, for the revision, he generated lively specifics describing how things — microwaves, home computers, VCRs — break down. Similarly, Michael realized it wasn't enough simply to say, as he had in the original, that we run into problems when we try to replace out-of-favor purchases. Vigorous details were again needed to make such a point. Michael thus used a typical "replaceable," an old black-and-white TV, as his key example, showing the nuisance involved in handling phone calls and setting up appointments so people can see the TV.

After adding these specifics, Michael realized he had enough material to devote a separate paragraph to the problems associated with replacing old purchases. By dividing his original paragraph in two, Michael ended up with two well-focused paragraphs, neither of which has the rambling quality found in the draft version.

In short, Michael's revisions show that he understands how to make writing stronger through rigorous editing. One more round of attentive editing would have made his essay considerably stronger. But even without this additional work, Michael has prepared an interesting essay that provides a helpful perspective on one of our cultural preoccupations.

The selections that follow use abundant examples as supporting evidence. Vance Packard, in "Children at Risk," demonstrates that youngsters today live in a hostile world. Betty Rollin's "Allene Talmey" uses lively anecdotes about a hard-to-please supervisor to sketch a memorable character study. In "Channelled Whelk," Anne Morrow Lindbergh provides examples of two kinds of lives, one that is busy and chaotic and one that is stripped to essential simplicity. "Sexism and Language," by Alleen Pace Nilsen, presents many instances of the way our language discriminates against women. Last, Malcolm Cowley's "The View from 80" presents examples of the positive as well as the negative sides of growing old.

Vance Packard

Over the last twenty-five years, Vance Packard (1914–   )
has written many bestselling books about American society.
The recipient of a master's degree in journalism from Colum-
bia University, Packard worked for many years as a newspa-
per reporter, magazine writer, and editor. His most well-
known books include The Hidden Persuaders *(1957),* The
Naked Society *(1964),* A Nation of Strangers *(1972), and*
The People Shapers *(1977). The following essay is the intro-*
duction to his most recent book, Our Endangered Children
(1983).

Children at Risk

We think of ourselves as a child-centered society. Yet in our
country children are sometimes banned from apartment com-
plexes and neighborhoods. Many are abused, victimized by
child pornographers, or exposed to alcohol, drugs, and sexually
explicit images at an early age. In this selection, Vance Pack-
ard examines such contradictions in our treatment of chil-
dren and warns us about turning into an anti-child culture.

Mismanagement in raising children did not begin in the late   1
twentieth century — only a new and dangerous kind of mismanagement. Other societies have been harsh, neglectful or misguided
with children, particularly when they, like us, were facing novel
difficulties under turbulent social conditions or new ideologies.

It wasn't until recent times that the concept of childhood, as a   2
state different from adulthood, even existed. Previously, children
in Western societies were treated as miniature adults.

In medieval societies as well as primitive ones, by the age of   3
seven children began sharing the work and play of adults. Philip
Aries, a leading historian of children, said that soon after weaning
"the child became the natural companion of the adult." Even when
adult play got a little voluptuous under the influence of drink, as

depicted in some of Brueghel's sixteenth-century paintings, the children were right there having their own kind of fun.

The lack of distinction between child and adult also applied to 4 clothing. Whether at work or play or at dress-up parties the children dressed pretty much as adults did. I have before me six American folk paintings of children or children with adults. All the children are dressed as adults. A painting of a "Schoolmaster and Two Boys" painted around 1815 shows all three in identical garb.

Only in nineteenth-century America did a general trend de- 5 velop to dress adults and children differently. Boys were put in short pants or sailor suits; girls in pigtails. In short, childhood came to be recognized as something apart. It coincided with the growing separation of children from adults which was brought about primarily by the rise of schooling.

Still there was little celebration of children as the Western 6 World broke into modern times. This was particularly true from the mid-seventeenth century to the mid-nineteenth century. The upheavals created by the harsh beginnings of industrialism, the sweeping up of people into vast cities, and the stern notions of the hell-fire Calvinists all tended to be bad news for children.

In many European cities during the eighteenth century it was 7 then the vogue for mothers to "put out" their infants to live with some local wet nurse. Commonly the infant was sent to a wet nurse in the countryside. At one point the great majority of Paris-born infants were thus put out in the country.

Callous and selfish? In many cases yes, although the infant still 8 had the advantage of a single caretaker. But consider the circumstances. Rapid urbanization had undermined much of the sense of family and community life and had made life considerably more hazardous for small children.

Cities were exploding. London, for example, by 1700 had 9 swollen to a vast filthy metropolis of 750,000 people. Garbage and piles of horse manure attracted rats, fleas, and flies bearing germs that caused typhus and infantile diarrhea.

Most children born in new urban areas died before their sixth 10 birthday. Under such odds parents of newborn babies may well have held back from developing any intense attachment to their infants and toddlers. Historians suggest that a kind of "tenderness taboo" existed in the seventeenth century regarding small children.

Or consider child labor. Children in traditional societies are   11
given early responsibilities. Six-year-olds are given responsibility
for younger brothers or sisters and carry them around in slings.

Before Western societies began industralizing it was common   12
for families to send all but the oldest son out of the home to be
apprentices to other masters. This usually occurred when the children were between seven and nine years old. The masters trained
the child in a trade, often were obligated to teach the child reading
and writing, and could discipline the child. The practice had some
logic at the time. Free public schooling was rarely available.

Child labor in the early days of the Industrial Revolution,   13
however, was something quite brutally different. Some of the exploitation of children was more appalling than I ever imagined
before I began this exploration.

There were few regulations regarding employment. Factory   14
and mine owners exploited the cheap labor of children. They cited
the Puritan Ethic, which defended child labor as a natural blessing;
and they benefited from the then-popular economic theory exalt-
ing laissez-faire capitalism.

In New England cotton mills children often worked at ma-   15
chines fourteen hours a day. In a "reformation" of 1842 the working hours of a child under twelve were reduced to ten hours a day.

Apparently the worst exploitation was in the early-nineteenth-   16
century coal mines of England and Scotland. The meager laws
regarding child labor in factories did not apply to mines. The
evidence of what went on was laid out coolly with many specifics in
a presentation made to the House of Commons in 1842 by the
seventh earl of Shaftesbury.

The earl detailed the sending of young boys *and* girls into the   17
pits. In Derbyshire children could be sent down into the mines at
the age of five. Near Oldham they began work as young as four
years old.

The children worked in the mines fourteen to sixteen hours a   18
day. Most of the boys and girls were used as beasts of burden in the
narrow tunnels. They were down on their hands and knees hauling
carts. The boys were typically naked, the girls stripped to the waist.
In this character-building work they had a girdle strapped around
their waist. A chain led back between their legs to the cart and often
scraped the flesh in the crotch. They went for hours without being

able to straighten their backs. Their lungs were fouled by coal dust.
If they complained, the bosses usually would beat them.

A clergyman of Tranent complained that children who went   19
into the mines with amiable tempers soon developed "hellish dispositions."

Another cause of painful childhood experience during the   20
seventeenth and eighteenth centuries was religion. Many children
raised in the home of dedicated evangelical Protestants—
particularly Calvinists—were viewed as carrying the burden of
Original Sin. They had to be cured of their satanic will in order to
achieve salvation and escape Hell's fires.

It was the Christian duty of their parents—and the new breed   21
of schoolmasters—to do the purging of sin with sternness and
whippings when indicated. Playfulness in children was considered
ominous. Any signs that a child had erred by wetting his bed might
result in the child's being required to drink a pint of piss.

In evangelical homes it was held that children could learn to   22
obey God only by first learning to obey their parents. The noted
clergyman John Wesley admonished parents: "Break their wills
that you may save their souls."

The widely held view that young children were inherently evil   23
and needed stern treatment was challenged most effectively by two
of the leading philosophers of the era. The great naturalist Rousseau scorned the idea that children were inherently evil. He advo-
cated that children were intrinsically natural and the laws of Nature
would assure healthy growth. Childhood was an important time in
life. He urged affectionate ties between parent and child. And the
highly regarded humanist John Locke urged parents to love their
children. To gain the respect of a son, he said, the parent must
respect that son.

The notions of Rousseau and Locke were particularly well   24
received in America where members of families were dependent
upon one another for survival on the frontiers and where servants
were scarce. American youngsters were quicker than those in Europe to lose their awe of elders.

During the century leading up to 1965 Americans generally   25
experienced a pattern of family living combining affection and
discipline and community-centered living that was congenial for
the development of most of their children.

The notion still persists that America is a uniquely child-cen-   26
tered country. Look at some of the indicators:

* North Americans spend twice as much per inhabitant on
  educating their youngsters as Europeans do.
* The nation has more than three million teachers; and of
  these about 67,000 are public school guidance counselors.
* The American Medical Association reported that at the beginning of 1981 U.S. children were watched over by 3,271
  child psychiatrists and 28,342 pediatricians.
* Dozens of books and thousands of articles offering counsel
  on child care are published each year.

Still, a deep malaise has rather swiftly come over child-raising   27
in the U.S.A. To some extent it is also afflicting other technologi-
cally advanced societies. This condition is starting to be sensed in
America. In 1982 the findings of a survey by the noted polling firm
Louis Harris and Associates was released. About two thousand
persons were questioned. Three-quarters were family adults, but
there were also teenagers, corporate and labor leaders, leaders of
women's groups. The conclusion:

"Clearly, the perception of deterioration in the overall quality   28
of parenting is widespread."

What's happening?   29

To me it seems clear that our society is seriously malfunction-   30
ing in its role of preparing children for adulthood. The upheaval
and disarray we are seeing in child-rearing patterns are unprecedented in modern times.

We make pronouncements about building a better life, mak-   31
ing progress and meeting tomorrow's challenges. But those prospects for tomorrow will be crucially affected by how well we bring
up today's children. Insistently we should be asking: But what
about the children?

Our Western World has millions of marvelous, well-devel-   32
oped children. They are raised in supportive, stimulating communities by thoughtful, loving parents. I have met many of them and
have felt rewarded by the encounters. The larger fact, however, is
that the whole tilt of our society, our institutions and, yes, our
family functioning is toward blighting our youngsters and burdening them with pain, anxiety, and discouraging problems. Many of

these pains and problems threaten to create a permanent warping of a large segment of our coming generation. All this is occurring at a time when we are seeing a demographic upsurge of young couples moving into the normal child-rearing stage.

Child-raising is becoming a bigger puzzle for parents and po-   33
tential parents — and a greater challenge. Many feel less in command of their family prospects. Parents often feel, justifiably, that both our institutions and our social attitudes are stacked against them. Our basic social unit, the family, is under significant assault.

A few years ago one of America's leading authorities on child-   34
rearing, Urie Bronfenbrenner, Professor of Human Development and Family Studies, Cornell University, warned that the radical changes occurring in the family have consequences for the young that were "approaching the calamitous."

What are the radical changes?   35

I believe they relate particularly to three areas of change in our   36
society.

1. Unwittingly we have developed an anti-child culture that confronts children with a cool, hard world outside their home.
2. We have failed to come to grips with one of the more momentous phenomena of this century, the surge of married women — including millions of mothers — into jobs outside the home.
3. We are witnessing a very great increase in the splitting up of parents and are just starting to perceive the reverberating impact on the millions of children involved.

These factors, I believe, contribute greatly to the "modern   37
forms of damnation that confront our children," to use Professor William Kessen's marvelously perceptive phrase.

Questions for Close Reading

1. What is the thesis of the selection? Locate the sentence(s) in which Packard states his main idea. If he does not state the thesis explicitly, express it in your own words.
2. Throughout history, Packard says, children were treated as "miniature adults." What does he mean by this?

3. Why were children treated unsympathetically before 1900? What factors, according to Packard, helped bring about a change in this attitude?
4. What evidence does Packard present to show that the U.S. is more children-centered than Europe?
5. Refer to your dictionary as needed to define the following words used in the selection: *ideologies* (paragraph 1), *urbanization* (8), *laissez-faire* (14), *congenial* (25), *malaise* (27), and *demographic* (32).

Questions about the Writer's Craft

1. An essay developed primarily through exemplification requires strong evidence to support its main idea. Where does Packard use statistics to support his points? Where does he use specific historical examples? Are there places where he speaks generally about children's treatment, without providing any supporting illustrations?
2. This essay originally appeared as the introduction to a book entitled *Our Endangered Children.* How does Packard lead us into the book that follows? What does he make us want to know more about?
3. In paragraph 18, Packard refers to the children's work in the mines as "character-building." What tone is he using here? Are there other places where he adopts this tone?
4. What effect does the use of very short paragraphs, most without transitional devices, have on the style of the essay? What is the relationship between the essay's style and its purpose?

Questions for Further Thought

1. Packard claims our culture is "anti-child." Do you agree? What evidence can you point to that shows this is true or untrue?
2. Should children be treated differently from adults, or are they miniature adults who should be treated the same?
3. At what age should adults treat young people as grown up and expect adult behavior of them? Is eighteen or twenty-one the right age for considering a young person an adult?
4. What are the best ways to prepare children to enter today's adult world? To what extent should children be shielded from the threats that Packard describes?

Writing Assignments Using Exemplification as a Method of Development

1. Write an essay in the form of a pamphlet to parents about ways to raise children to feel valued, wanted, and secure. Make specific recommen-

dations about what parents should do, and provide examples of each behavior or attitude you recommend.

2. Write an essay addressing the desire many young children have to be grown-up. Explain that being a child is better than they think and that life for teenagers, for example, is not all it appears. Using either a light or serious tone, provide examples from your own life and those of your friends to convey the disadvantages of young adulthood and the advantages of staying a child.

Writing Assignments Using Other Methods of Development

3. Some experts say that adolescence is being prolonged unnaturally. These days, for instance, it's not unusual for college students to remain at home after graduation, waiting until their mid- or late-twenties to leave home and settle down. Write a causal analysis explaining why it is that some young adults nowadays find it difficult to take on adult responsibilities. The essay should clarify your attitude toward young people whose entry into full adulthood is delayed.

4. Packard claims that our "basic social unit, the family, is under significant assault." Read "The Faltering Family" by George Gallup (pages 375–384). Then write an essay of your own about the health of the family unit in the United States. Agree or disagree with these writers about the strength of the family, being sure that your argument presents the reasons for your position.

Betty Rollin

Betty Rollin has been a writer and editor at Vogue *and* Look *magazines. More recently, she has been a correspondent for ABC News. Her 1976 book describing her battle with breast cancer,* First You Cry, *attracted much praise and notoriety, as has her most recent book,* Last Wish *(1985), about her terminally ill mother's suicide. The following excerpt is taken from Rollin's second book,* Am I Getting Paid for This?, *written in 1982.*

Allene Talmey

Everyone has a horror story about a demanding boss or teacher. We complain to friends about unpaid overtime, twenty-page papers due in two weeks, impossible standards. Betty Rollin had this kind of tough boss when she was a writer for Vogue. *But Rollin does not write to criticize Miss Talmey. Instead, with a shiver and a touch of humor, she praises her boss and thanks her for the important lesson she taught: "good enough" is just not good enough.*

Vogue was tough. The fashion department was tough because   1
it was supposed to be the best — and, under Diana Vreeland, it was.
And the features department was tough because fashion, not features, sold the magazine, so the features department could afford
to be the best — which, among the women's magazines, under
Allene Talmey, *it* probably was. Operative words: Allene Talmey.
When she wanted to, Miss Talmey had a special ability to make
those who thought they were tough cower. And she wanted to a lot.
Those of us who did not think we were tough did not cower; we
crumbled. We shriveled. We dissolved. I know Joan Didion only
slightly, but we share a unique Pavlovian symptom: to this day
should we see or speak to or run into Allene Talmey — and Joan
says the same holds true on coast-to-coast telephone calls — our
knees give. And the funny thing is, we both love her.

195

Throughout my tenure at *Vogue*, mercifully brief though it 2
was, on an average of once or twice a week, something Miss Talmey
said — sometimes it was just a look — would lead me to close my
office door, lean against it, and cry. It wasn't that Miss Talmey
raised her voice, nor even that she got angry. It was simply her way
of making everyone who entered her office and stood on the other
side of her desk feel like a worm. Say, God forbid, you wrote a
convoluted sentence. She would call you into her office (you never
knew at those times what you had done, only that it was bad), you
would then lower yourself onto the straight-backed polished ma-
hogany chair that faced her desk, hoping, all the while, that your
beating heart would not rupture your chest wall. Whereupon she
would look at you and, with her eyes fixed on your face, she'd hold
up with two fingers — as if it were a soiled bedsheet — this execra-
ble thing you had written. Slowly, she would read the offending
sentence, lingering and slightly increasing the volume of her voice,
when she got to the (particularly) offensive passage. Then she
would place the paper down on her desk and look at you again.

"What is it you are trying to say, dear?" she would ask, pro- 3
nouncing the word *dear* in the same tone of voice that is normally
used for the word *moron*. Then, falteringly, you would say what you
were "trying to say." You always knew what would come next, but
it had the same sting as a surprise:

"Why didn't you *write* it that way, dear?" Unless you were so 4
stupid as to try to explain, you would then rise, bite your lip (or
your hand, whichever was nearer), take your paper back, and, as
rapidly as possible, leave the room.

Convolution, however, was not the greatest sin. Writing a 5
cliché was. In that event, the meeting would be shorter and less
cordial. Sometimes she would stand behind her desk and, as you
entered, spit the cliché at you: "*High as a kite?*" Then, again, louder
and slower, letting each syllable drip like slime: "*High — as — a —
KITE?*" Then she would thrust the article or caption or whatever it
was at you, as if it had been used to wrap a flounder, with a final,
deadly: "Change it."

There were two other women writers in the department and 6
two secretaries, clustered in a small suite of offices, which, except
for the bright green carpeting (leftovers from the fashion floor),
looked like an accounting firm. Each of us dealt with the Talmey

situation differently. The secretaries dealt with it by being perfect. The most senior other writer dealt with it by being cool (I never figured out if it was an act or if she had something surgical done to sever her nerve endings). The third woman, who was married to a French diplomat, handled it by being lah-dee-dah. "Really, how *boring* of her," she would say, swishing past me in the small office we shared, having just retrieved one of her pieces from the meat grinder.

Miss Talmey's reactions to pieces were not always delivered in 7 person. Sometimes she wrote down what she thought in the margin and sent it back.

Once I submitted an idea for a piece for the Beautiful People 8 series, which was in full swing then. Almost every issue of the magazine had a spread on the Beautiful People of Rome, the Beautiful People of Tangiers, the Beautiful People of Palm Beach, and so forth. The previous evening I had gone to a dinner party in Brooklyn Heights — a rather fancy section of Brooklyn — at which there were a number of social types who, it seemed to me, made the grade as Beautiful People. So, the next morning, I wrote a memo to Miss Talmey, suggesting *Vogue* do the Beautiful People in Brooklyn. I went to lunch before getting a reply. When I returned, I walked into my office and noticed that the memo had been placed back on my desk. I read the comment in the margin upside down: *"Good, Good!"* I was thrilled — and not too surprised. I *knew* I had a winner — an idea which was in keeping with the concept, yet it had a fresh twist. To think I had actually hesitated before submitting it! I shook my head and smiled to myself. Go with your instincts, I thought, go with your instincts. (I was at the stage where I liked to make lessons out of things.)

Then I walked around to the front of my desk and read the 9 comment right side up. "Good God!" it said.

One reason for Miss Talmey's power over people — aside from 10 the fact that she was the boss, aside from the fact that she knew how, and loved, to terrorize — was that Miss Talmey was always right. Also, she knew everything. She thought we writers should know everything, too. Now and then, probably to make sure that we *knew* that she thought we should know everything, she gave quizzes. The quizzes were not formal. They just felt formal. It wasn't so bad when they were given to the three of us, together. That way, at least, you could usually count on someone else besides yourself making a mistake. To be quizzed alone, however, was excruciating. Usually, a quiz followed a transgression. Once, for example, I spelled the choreographer George Balanchine's name wrong. Miss Talmey *hated* spelling errors. *Vogue* has a "checker" whose job it was to check spelling and punctuation, so there was little danger of an error going uncorrected (only the Lord could save her if she overlooked one) into the magazine; but Miss Talmey held that the writer should *never* depend on the checker and a writer who made a spelling error was simply and inexcusably *sloppy*. In addition to which, an error connoted *ignorance* and even more contemptible than *slop* was *ignorance*.

"How do you spell Balanchine, dear?" I was standing. She was   11
seated at her desk. Her eyes were on the paper.

"D-did I spell it wrong?" I said, trying to keep my voice in a   12
normal range.

"You spelled it B-a-l-*e*. There is only one *e*" — she was looking   13
at me now — "in Mr. Balanchine's name and that is at the end."

"Of course — I — I knew that — I don't know why I — "   14

"Do you ever go to the ballet, dear?" Oh, God, it was going to   15
be a ballet quiz. But maybe not: "Do you read newspapers, dear?"

"I read the *Times*," I said, confused now.   16

"Is that all?" she said.   17

I had no idea where this was leading — only that it was making   18
me feel faint. "S-sometimes I read the *Post* — and, occasionally, *The Wall Street Journal*." (That was a lie. I never read *The Wall Street Journal*.)

"Do you read all sections of the newspaper?" she asked.   19

"Well, I try to," I said. (Another lie.)   20

"Who is Willie Mays?" My mouth went dry and my toes curled   21
under in my shoes.

"He's a baseball player, I think."   22

"You *think*?" said Miss Talmey. "What team does he play   23
for?"

"I'm not sure," I whispered, knowing all was lost.   24

"He plays for the Giants, dear," she said, pronouncing each   25
word as if I were a lip-reader. "His batting average last year was three fourteen. You should know that. From now on, when you read the newspapers, dear, read every section. *Every* section of *every* newspaper." And then, as she was wont to do sometimes when the

beating was over, she moved the corners of her mouth sideways (her version of a smile). "Okay?"

"Yes, Miss Talmey," I said, backing out.   26

Questions for Close Reading

1. What is the thesis of the selection? Locate the sentence(s) in which Rollin states her main idea. If she does not state the thesis explicitly, express it in your own words.
2. What was Miss Talmey's function at *Vogue*? What department did she rule? Who worked in the department?
3. What were Talmey's standards for her staff? What things did she hate?
4. How did Talmey reveal her displeasure? What were the reactions of her staff?
5. Refer to your dictionary as needed to define the following words in the selection: *cower* (paragraph 1), *convoluted* (2), *cordial* (5), *excruciating* (10), and *transgression* (10).

Questions about the Writer's Craft

1. Rollin provides several examples of Talmey's treatment of her staff. Why does she put Talmey's reaction to the "sin" of convolution first in the essay? Why does she save the example of the "quiz" for last?
2. The author reveals Allene Talmey to us by showing her effect on her subordinates. Why does Rollin keep strictly to this external view of her subject, rather than, for example, report Talmey's point of view on editing or running a magazine?
3. What is striking about the sentence patterns in the first paragraph? Why do you think Rollin chose this style for her introduction to Allene Talmey? How do these sentences affect you?
4. Rollin uses strong images and comparisons to convey the effect that Talmey had on her subordinates. Find some of these images. Are any of them exaggerated or humorous? How do they affect the tone of the essay?

Questions for Further Thought

1. Why would a writer, or any employee, stay in a job with a boss like Talmey? What positive effects might there be?
2. Does Rollin's account of her editor challenge or confirm common stereotypes about "lady editors" and female bosses?

3. What is the best way to handle a boss who loves "to terrorize"? Would you use one of the techniques described in paragraph 6, or handle Talmey another way if you worked under her?

4. It has been said there are two types of authority figures, those we love and those we fear. Which type do you prefer? Which is more effective? When you become a parent, boss, or a leader, which type will you try to be?

Writing Assignments Using Exemplification as a Method of Development

1. On the basis of your past work and educational experiences, decide whether you prefer a tough, demanding boss or a kind, helpful one. Consider both your comfort on the job and the quality of your performance. Explain in an essay why you work best (or worst) for a terrorizing or supportive supervisor. Use examples drawn from your experience to support the essay's thesis.

2. For *Vogue* staffers under Allene Talmey, there were some mistakes that were just unforgivable — using a cliche, for example. Write an essay that gives examples of some "unforgivable mistakes" of another occupation or role. For example, you might describe what errors would be unforgivable for a parent, a driver, a roommate, a cashier, a salesperson, and so on. Provide specific examples and anecdotes drawn from your experiences.

Writing Assignments Using Other Methods of Development

3. Write a descriptive character sketch of the toughest boss, teacher, or leader you ever had to work under. Follow Rollin's example in providing examples, dialogue, anecdotes, and sharp images to make your subject come alive.

4. What is the best style for a boss or manager to use with his or her staff? Read in the library about leadership or management styles. There are a number of magazines that regularly discuss techniques helpful to supervisors. Decide what approach you would take if and when you found it necessary to manage people. Write an essay explaining how you would manage effectively. To back up your analysis, use the information, quotations, facts, and so on found in your reading.

Anne Morrow Lindbergh

Anne Morrow Lindbergh (1906–   ) has had a successful career as a novelist, diarist, essayist, poet. In 1962, she published her first novel, Dearly Beloved, *a book about the Apollo moon mission, to be followed in 1969 by* Earth Shine, *and several well-received volumes of collected letters and diaries. The following selection first appeared in* Gift from the Sea *(1955).*

Channelled Whelk

"The world is too much with us, late and soon/Getting and spending, we lay waste our powers." Poet William Wordsworth wrote these lines in the early nineteenth century, but they still characterize our lives today. Like human pinballs, many of us bounce from one set of responsibilities to another —from career to family life to school and community service. In this essay, Anne Morrow Lindbergh reflects on the longed-for goal of simplicity and explains why it often eludes us in everyday living.

The shell in my hand is deserted. It once housed a whelk, a snail-like creature, and then temporarily, after the death of the first occupant, a little hermit crab, who has run away, leaving his tracks behind him like a delicate vine on the sand. He ran away, and left me his shell. It was once a protection to him. I turn the shell in my hand, gazing into the wide open door from which he made his exit. Had it become an encumbrance? Why did he run away? Did he hope to find a better home, a better mode of living? I too have run away, I realize, I have shed the shell of my life, for these few weeks of vacation.

But his shell — it is simple; it is bare, it is beautiful. Small, only the size of my thumb, its architecture is perfect, down to the finest detail. Its shape, swelling like a pear in the center, winds in a gentle spiral to the pointed apex. Its color, dull gold, is whitened by a wash

1

2

201

of salt from the sea. Each whorl, each faint knob, each criss-cross vein in its egg-shell texture, is as clearly defined as on the day of creation. My eye follows with delight the outer circumference of that diminutive winding staircase up which this tenant used to travel.

My shell is not like this, I think. How untidy it has become! 3 Blurred with moss, knobby with barnacles, its shape is hardly recognizable any more. Surely, it had a shape once. It has a shape still in my mind. What is the shape of my life?

The shape of my life today starts with a family. I have a hus- 4 band, five children and a home just beyond the suburbs of New York. I have also a craft, writing, and therefore work I want to pursue. The shape of my life is, of course, determined by many other things; my background and childhood, my mind and its education, my conscience and its pressures, my heart and its desires. I want to give and take from my children and husband, to share with friends and community, to carry out my obligations to man and to the world as a women, as an artist, as a citizen.

But I want first of all — in fact, as an end to these other desires 5 — to be at peace with myself. I want a singleness of eye, a purity of intention, a central core to my life that will enable me to carry out these obligations and activities as well as I can. I want, in fact — to borrow from the language of the saints — to live "in grace" as much of the time as possible. I am not using this term in a strictly theological sense. By grace I mean an inner harmony, essentially spiritual, which can be translated into outward harmony. I am seeking perhaps what Socrates asked for in the prayer from the *Phaedrus* when he said, "May the outward and inward man be at one." I would like to achieve a state of inner spiritual grace from which I could function and give as I was meant to in the eye of God.

Vague as this definition may be, I believe most people are 6 aware of periods in their lives when they seem to be "in grace" and other periods when they feel "out of grace," even though they may use different words to describe these states. In the first happy condition, one seems to carry all one's tasks before one lightly, as if borne along on a great tide; and in the opposite state one can hardly tie a shoestring. It is true that a large part of life consists in learning a technique of tying the shoe-string, whether one is in grace or not. But there are techniques of living too; there are even techniques in the search for grace. And techniques can be cultivated. I have learned by some experience, by many examples, and by the writings of countless others before me, also occupied in the search, that certain environments, certain modes of life, certain rules of conduct are more conducive to inner and outer harmony than others. There are, in fact, certain roads that one may follow. Simplification of life is one of them.

I mean to lead a simple life, to choose a simple shell I can carry   7
easily — like a hermit crab. But I do not. I find that my frame of life does not foster simplicity. My husband and five children must make their way in the world. The life I have chosen as wife and mother entrains a whole caravan of complications. It involves a house in the suburbs and either household drudgery or household help which wavers between scarcity and non-existence for most of us. It involves food and shelter; meals, planning, marketing, bills, and making the ends meet in a thousand ways. It involves not only the butcher, the baker, the candlestickmaker but countless other experts to keep my modern house with its modern "simplifications" (electricity, plumbing, refrigerator, gas-stove, oil-burner, dish-washer, radios, car, and numerous other labor-saving devices) functioning properly. It involves health; doctors, dentists, appointments, medicine, cod-liver oil, vitamins, trips to the drugstore. It involves education, spiritual, intellectual, physical; schools, school conferences, carpools, extra trips for basket-ball or orchestra practice; tutoring; camps, camp equipment and transportation. It involves clothes, shopping, laundry, cleaning, mending, letting skirts down and sewing buttons on, or finding someone else to do it. It involves friends, my husband's, my children's, my own, and endless arrangements to get together; letters, invitations, telephone calls and transportation hither and yon.

For life today in America is based on the premise of ever-wid-   8
ening circles of contact and communication. It involves not only family demands, but community demands, national demands, international demands on the good citizen, through social and cultural pressures, through newspapers, magazines, radio programs, political drives, charitable appeals, and so on. My mind reels with it. What a circus act we women perform every day of our lives. It puts the trapeze artist to shame. Look at us. We run a tight rope daily, balancing a pile of books on the head. Baby-carriage, parasol, kitchen chair, still under control. Steady now!

This is not the life of simplicity but the life of multiplicity that   9
the wise men warn us of. It leads not to unification but to fragmentation. It does not bring grace; it destroys the soul. And this is not

only true of my life, I am forced to conclude; it is the life of millions of women in America. I stress America, because today, the American woman more than any other has the privilege of choosing such a life. Woman in large parts of the civilized world has been forced back by war, by poverty, by collapse, by the sheer struggle to survive, into a smaller circle of immediate time and space, immediate family life, immediate problems of existence. The American woman is still relatively free to choose the wider life. How long she will hold this enviable and precarious position no one knows. But her particular situation has a significance far above its apparent economic, national or even sex limitations.

For the problem of the multiplicity of life not only confronts   10
the American woman, but also the American man. And it is not merely the concern of the American as such, but of our whole modern civilization, since life in America today is held up as the ideal of a large part of the rest of the world. And finally, it is not limited to our present civilization, though we are faced with it now in an exaggerated form. It has always been one of the pitfalls of mankind. Plotinus was preaching the dangers of multiplicity of the world back in the third century. Yet, the problem is particularly and essentially woman's. Distraction is, always has been, and probably always will be, inherent in woman's life.

For to be a woman is to have interests and duties, raying out in   11
all directions from the central mother-core, like spokes from the hub of a wheel. The pattern of our lives is essentially circular. We must be open to all points of the compass; husband, children, friends, home, community; stretched out, exposed, sensitive like a spider's web to each breeze that blows, to each call that comes. How difficult for us, then, to achieve a balance in the midst of these contradictory tensions, and yet how necessary for the proper functioning of our lives. How much we need, and how arduous of attainment is that steadiness preached in all rules for holy living. How desirable and distant is the ideal of the contemplative, artist, or saint — the inner inviolable core, the single eye.

With a new awareness, both painful and humorous, I begin to   12
understand why the saints were rarely married women. I am convinced it has nothing inherently to do, as I once supposed, with chastity or children. It has to do primarily with distractions. The bearing, rearing, feeding and educating of children; the running of a house with its thousand details; human relationships with their

myriad pulls—woman's normal occupations in general run counter to creative life, or contemplative life, or saintly life. The problem is not merely one of *Woman and Career, Woman and the Home, Woman and Independence*. It is more basically: how to remain whole in the midst of the distractions of life; how to remain balanced, no matter what centrifugal forces tend to pull one off center; how to remain strong, no matter what shocks come in at the periphery and tend to crack the hub of the wheel.

What is the answer? There is no easy answer, no complete   13
answer. I have only clues, shells from the sea. The bare beauty of the channelled whelk tells me that one answer, and perhaps a first step, is in simplification of life, in cutting out some of the distractions. But how? Total retirement is not possible. I cannot shed my responsibilities. I cannot permanently inhabit a desert island. I cannot be a nun in the midst of family life. I would not want to be. The solution for me, surely, is neither in total renunciation of the world, nor in total acceptance of it. I must find a balance somewhere, or an alternating rhythm between these two extremes; a swinging of the pendulum between solitude and communion, between retreat and return. In my periods of retreat, perhaps I can learn something to carry back into my worldly life. I can at least practice for these two weeks the simplification of outward life, as a beginning. I can follow this superficial clue, and see where it leads. Here, in beach living, I can try.

One learns first of all in beach living the art of shedding; how   14
little one can get along with, not how much. Physical shedding to begin with, which then mysteriously spreads into other fields. Clothes, first. Of course, one needs less in the sun. But one needs less anyway, one finds suddenly. One needs not need a closet-full, only a small suitcase-full. And what a relief it is! Less taking up and down of hems, less mending, and—best of all—less worry about what to wear. One finds one is shedding not only clothes—but vanity.

Next, shelter. One does not need the airtight shelter one has in   15
winter in the North. Here I live in a bare sea-shell of a cottage. No heat, no telephone, no plumbing to speak of, no hot water, a two-burner oil stove, no gadgets to go wrong. No rugs. There were some, but I rolled them up the first day; it is easier to sweep the sand off a bare floor. But I find I don't bustle about with unnecessary

sweeping and cleaning here. I am no longer aware of the dust. I have shed my Puritan conscience about absolute tidiness and cleanliness. Is it possible that, too, is a material burden? No curtains. I do not need them for privacy; the pines around my house are enough protection. I want the windows open all the time, and I don't want to worry about rain. I begin to shed my Martha-like anxiety about many things. Washable slipcovers, faded and old — I hardly see them; I don't worry about the impression they make on other people. I am shedding pride. As little furniture as possible; I shall not need much. I shall ask into my shell only those friends with whom I can be completely honest. I find I am shedding hypocrisy in human relationships. What a rest that will be! The most exhausting thing in life, I have discovered, is being insincere. That is why so much of social life is exhausting; one is wearing a mask. I have shed my mask.

I find I live quite happily without those things I think neces-   16
sary in winter in the North. And as I write these words, I remember, with some shock at the disparity in our lives, a similar statement made by a friend of mine in France who spent three years in a German prison camp. Of course, he said, qualifying his remark, they did not get enough to eat, they were sometimes atrociously treated, they had little physical freedom. And yet, prison life taught him how little one can get along with, and what extraordinary spiritual freedom and peace such simplification can bring. I remember again, ironically, that today more of us in America than anywhere else in the world have the luxury of choice between simplicity and complication of life. And for the most part, we, who could choose simplicity, choose complication. War, prison, survival periods, enforce a form of simplicity on man. The monk and the nun choose it of their own free will. But if one accidentally finds it, as I have for a few days, one finds also the serenity it brings.

Is it not rather ugly, one may ask? One collects material posses-   17
sions not only for security, comfort or vanity, but for beauty as well. Is your sea-shell house not ugly and bare? No, it is beautiful, my house. It is bare, of course, but the wind, the sun, the smell of the pines blow through its bareness. The unfinished beams in the roof are veiled by cobwebs. They are lovely, I think, gazing up at them with new eyes; they soften the hard lines of the rafters as grey hairs soften the lines on a middle-aged face. I no longer pull out grey hairs or sweep down cobwebs. As for the walls, it is true they

looked forbidding at first. I felt cramped and enclosed by their blank faces. I wanted to knock holes in them, to give them another dimension with pictures or windows. So I dragged home from the beach grey arms of driftwood, worn satin-smooth by wind and sand. I gathered trailing green vines with floppy red-tipped leaves. I picked up the whitened skeletons of conchshells, their curious hollowed-out shapes faintly reminiscent of abstract sculpture. With these tacked to walls and propped up in corners, I am satisfied. I have a periscope out to the world. I have a window, a view, a point of flight from my sedentary base.

I am content. I sit down at my desk, a bare kitchen table with a   18
blotter, a bottle of ink, a sand dollar to weight down one corner, a clam shell for a pen tray, the broken tip of a conch, pink-tinged, to finger, and a row of shells to set my thoughts spinning.

I love my sea-shell of a house. I wish I could live in it always. I   19
wish I could transport it home. But I cannot. It will not hold a husband, five children and the necessities and trappings of daily life. I can only carry back my little channelled whelk. It will sit on my desk in Connecticut, to remind me of the ideal of a simplified life, to encourage me in the game I played on the beach. To ask how little, not how much, can I get along with. To say — is it necessary? — when I am tempted to add one more accumulation to my life, when I am pulled toward one more centrifugal activity.

Simplification of outward life is not enough. It is merely the   20
outside. But I am starting with the outside. I am looking at the outside of a shell, the outside of my life — the shell. The complete answer is not to be found on the outside, in an outward mode of living. This is only a technique, a road to grace. The final answer, I know, is always inside. But the outside can give a clue, can help one to find the inside answer. One is free, like the hermit crab, to change one's shell.

Channelled whelk, I put you down again, but you have set my   21
mind on a journey, up an inwardly winding spiral staircase of thought.

Questions for Close Reading

1. What is the thesis of the selection? Locate the sentence(s) in which Lindbergh states her main idea. If she does not state the thesis explicitly, express it in your own words.

2. What appeals to Lindbergh about the shell of the channelled whelk?
3. Why are distraction and "multiplicity" so much a problem for women, in particular? Why are they less of a problem for men, according to the author?
4. Since Lindbergh prefers the life at the beach house, why doesn't she remain there? Why does she take the shell away with her?
5. Refer to your dictionary as needed to define the following words used in the selection: *apex* (paragraph 2), *conducive* (6), *myriad* (12), *periphery* (12), and *sedentary* (17).

Questions about the Writer's Craft

1. Essays developed through exemplification often provide extended illustrations to develop key points. In what paragraphs does Lindbergh include extended illustrations to clarify what she means by "simplification"?
2. Why does Lindbergh begin her essay about the distractions of women's lives with a few paragraphs about a whelk shell? Where does she return to discussing the shell? What does the shell come to represent?
3. In paragraph 6, the author uses the image of "tying a shoe-string." What aspects of life is she referring to through this image? At what point do you recognize that she is using "tying a shoe-string" as a metaphor for a larger part of life?
4. Why does Lindbergh end the essay with a short "speech" or address to the whelk shell? How does this last paragraph extend an idea suggested in the paragraph before it?

Questions for Further Thought

1. Lindbergh writes, "I want first of all . . . to be at peace with myself." Besides her method of simplification, how else could she achieve this inner peace?
2. Could we ever eliminate all the distractions from our lives? Do you think this would be desirable?
3. Lindbergh says the problems she has with distractions is particularly a woman's problem. Do you agree? Have women's lives — and men's — changed much since she wrote this essay?
4. How would *you* simplify your life, if you were given the opportunity? What would you shed? What would you be unable to shed? What might you be able to shed . . . but only after agonizing over it or getting help?

Writing Assignments Using Exemplification as a Method of Development

1. Write an essay about the excess of possessions in people's lives today. Give examples of people you know or have heard about. Alternately, you may use fictional characters (from books or TV shows) whose lives are obsessed with possessions.
2. Lindbergh writes that she often feels fragmented into a series of selves because of the numerous demands — family, community, and political — made on her. Analyze your own life to identify the different roles you play. Write an essay detailing the "balancing act" you perform in your life. When describing each of your roles, be sure to provide specific examples of the demands claiming your attention. In the conclusion, point briefly to some things you could do to make your life less fragmented and more harmonious.

Writing Assignments Using Other Methods of Development

3. Imagine simplifying your own life to achieve greater inner harmony. How would you go about it? Write an essay describing the process by which you would make your life simpler. For each step, include specific examples of activities, objects, relationships, and the like that you would eliminate.
4. Take a position opposed to Lindbergh's — that the multiplicity of our lives is beneficial to us. Argue that material possessions and our numerous "circles of contact" are necessary and advantageous. Use either a serious or a humorous tone.

Alleen Pace Nilsen

A specialist in children's literature, Alleen Pace Nilsen teaches at Arizona State University and edits a newsletter on adolescent literature. Nilsen's doctoral dissertation concerned sexism in the language of books written for children. The following selection is from Sexism and Language *(1977), a collection of essays by various authors published by the National Council of Teachers of English.*

Sexism and Language

Is there anything wrong in calling a woman a "fox" or a "chick"? Why is it embarrassing for a man to perform a job labeled "women's work," while it is a compliment for a woman to do "a man's job"? Would you rather be a female named "Sam" or a man called "Carol"? Your response to these questions most likely results from the attitudes you have acquired as a speaker of American English. In the following selection, Alleen Pace Nilsen will make you look more closely at the language you use, showing how seemingly innocent words and phrases reflect society's attitudes toward the roles — and worth — of men and women.

Over the last hundred years, American anthropologists have   1
travelled to the corners of the earth to study primitive cultures. They either became linguists themselves or they took linguists with them to help in learning and analyzing languages. Even if the culture was one that no longer existed, they were interested in learning its language because besides being tools of communication, the vocabulary and structure of a language tell much about the values held by its speakers.

However, the culture need not be primitive, nor do the people   2
making observations need to be anthropologists and linguists. Anyone living in the United States who listens with a keen ear or reads with a perceptive eye can come up with startling new insights about the way American English reflects our values.

Animal Terms for People — Mirrors of the Double Standard

If we look at just one semantic area of English, that of animal   3
terms in relation to people, we can uncover some interesting insights into how our culture views males and females. References to
identical animals can have negative connotations when related to a
female, but positive or neutral connotations when related to a
male. For example, a *shrew* has come to mean "a scolding, nagging,
evil-tempered woman," while *shrewd* means "keen-witted, clever,
or sharp in practical affairs; astute . . . businessman, etc." (*Webster's New World Dictionary of the American Language*, 1964).

A *lucky dog* or a *gay dog* may be a very interesting fellow, but   4
when a woman is a *dog*, she is unattractive, and when she's a *bitch*
she's the personification of whatever is undesirable in the mind of
the speaker. When a man is self-confident, he may be described as
cocksure or even *cocky*, but in a woman this same self-confidence is
likely to result in her being called a *cocky bitch*, which is not only a
mixed metaphor, but also probably the most insulting animal
metaphor we have. *Bitch* has taken on such negative connotations
— children are taught it is a swear word — that in everyday American English, speakers are hesitant to call a female dog a *bitch*. Most
of us feel that we would be insulting the dog. When we want to
insult a man by comparing him to a dog, we call him a *son of a bitch*,
which quite literally is an insult to his mother rather than to him.

If the female is called a *vixen* (a female fox), the dictionary says   5
this means she is "an ill-tempered, shrewish, or malicious woman."
The female seems both to attract and to hold on longer to animal
metaphors with negative connotations. A *vampire* was originally a
corpse that came alive to suck the blood of living persons. The
word acquired the general meaning of an unscrupulous person
such as a blackmailer and then, the specialized meaning of "a
beautiful but unscrupulous woman who seduces men and leads
them to their ruin." From this latter meaning we get the word
vamp. The popularity of this term and of the name *vampire bat* may
contribute to the idea that a female being is referred to in a phrase
such as *the old bat*.

Other animal metaphors do not have definitely derogatory   6
connotations for the female, but they do seem to indicate frivolity
or unimportance, as in *social butterfly* and *flapper*. Look at the

differences between the connotations of participating in a *hen party* and in a *bull session*. Male metaphors, even when they are negative in connotation, still relate to strength and conquest. Metaphors related to aggressive sex roles, for example, *buck, stag, wolf,* and *stud,* will undoubtedly remain attached to males. Perhaps one of the reasons that in the late sixties it was so shocking to hear policemen called *pigs* was that the connotations of *pig* are very different from the other animal metaphors we usually apply to males.

When I was living in Afghanistan, I was surprised at the cruelty   7 and unfairness of a proverb that said, "When you see an old man, sit down and take a lesson; when you see an old woman, throw a stone." In looking at Afghan folk literature. I found that young girls were pictured as delightful and enticing, middle-aged women were sometimes interesting but more often just tolerable, while old women were always grotesque and villainous. Probably the reason for the negative connotation of old age in women is that women are valued for their bodies while men are valued for their accomplishments and their wisdom. Bodies deteriorate with age but wisdom and accomplishments grow greater.

When we returned home from Afghanistan, I was shocked to   8 discover that we have remnants of this same attitude in America. We see it in our animal metaphors. If both the animal and the woman are young, the connotation is positive, but if the animal and the woman are old, the connotation is negative. Hugh Hefner might never have made it to the big time if he had called his girls *rabbits* instead of *bunnies.* He probably chose *bunny* because he wanted something close to, but not quite so obvious as *kitten* or *cat*—the all-time winners for connotating female sexuality. Also *bunny,* as in the skiers' *snow bunny,* already had some of the connotations Hefner wanted. Compare the connotations of *filly* to *old nag; bird* to *old crow* or *old bat*; and *lamb* to *crone* (apparently related to the early modern Dutch *kronje, old ewe* but now *withered old woman*).

Probably the most striking examples of the contrast between   9 young and old women are animal metaphors relating to cats and chickens. A young girl is encouraged to be *kittenish,* but not *catty.* And though most of us wouldn't mind living next door to a *sex kitten,* we wouldn't want to live next door to a *cat house.* Parents might name their daughter *Kitty* but not *Puss* or *Pussy,* which used to be a fairly common nickname for girls. It has now developed such sexual connotations that it is used mostly for humor, as in the James Bond movie featuring Pussy Galore and her flying felines. In the chicken metaphors, a young girl is a *chick*. When she gets 10 old enough she marries and soon begins feeling *cooped up*. To relieve the boredom she goes to *hen parties* and *cackles* with her friends. Eventually she has her *brood*, begins to *henpeck* her husband, and finally turns into an *old biddy*.

How English Glorifies Maleness

Throughout the ages physical strength has been very impor- 11 tant, and because men are physically stronger than women, they have been valued more. Only now in the machine age, when the difference in strength between males and females pales into insignificance in comparison to the strength of earth-moving machinery, airplanes, and guns, males no longer have such an inherent advantage. Today a man of intellect is more valued than a physical laborer, and since women can compete intellectually with men, their value is on the rise. But language lags far behind cultural changes, so the language still reflects this emphasis on the importance of being male. For example, when we want to compliment a male, all we need to do is stress the fact that he is male by saying he is a *he-man*, or he is *manly*, or he is *virile*. Both *virile* and *virtuous* come from the Latin *vir*, meaning *man*.

The command or encouragement that males receive in sen- 12 tences like "Be a man!" implies that *to be a man* is to be honorable, strong, righteous, and whatever else the speaker thinks desirable. But in contrast to this, a girl is never told to be a *woman*. And when she is told to be a *lady*, she is simply being encouraged to "act feminine," which means sitting with her knees together, walking gracefully, and talking softly.

The armed forces, particularly the Marines, use the positive 13 masculine connotation as part of their recruitment psychology. They promote the idea that to join the Marines (or the Army, Navy, or Air Force) guarantees that you will become a man. But this brings up a problem, because much of the work that is necessary to keep a large organization running is what is traditionally thought of as *women's work*. Now, how can the Marines ask someone who has signed up for a *man-sized job* to do *women's work*? Since they can't, they euphemize and give the jobs titles that either are more

prestigious or, at least, don't make people think of females. Waitresses are called *orderlies*, secretaries are called *clerk-typists*, nurses
are called *medics*, assistants are called *adjutants*, and cleaning up an
area is called *policing* the area. The same kind of word glorification
is used in civilian life to bolster a man's ego when he is doing such
tasks as cooking and sewing. For example, a *chef* has higher prestige
than a *cook* and a *tailor* has higher prestige than a *seamstress*.   14

Little girls learn early in life that the boy's role is one to be
envied and emulated. Child psychologists have pointed out that
experimenting with the role of the opposite sex is much more
acceptable for little girls than it is for little boys. For example, girls
are free to dress in boys' clothes, but certainly not the other way
around. Most parents are amused if they have a daughter who is a
tomboy, but they are genuinely distressed if they have a son who is a
sissy. The names we give to young children reflect this same attitude. It is all right for girls to have boys' names, but pity the boy
who has a girl's name! Because parents keep giving boys' names to
girls, the number of acceptable boys' names keeps shrinking. Currently popular names for girls include *Jo, Kelly, Teri, Chris, Pat,
Shawn, Toni,* and *Sam* (short for *Samantha*). *Evelyn, Carroll, Gayle,
Hazel, Lynn, Beverley, Marion, Francis,* and *Shirley* once were acceptable names for males. But as they were given to females, they
became less and less acceptable. Today, men who are stuck with
them self-consciously go by their initials or by abbreviated forms
such as *Haze, Shirl, Frank,* or *Ev.* And they seldom pass these
names on to their sons.

Many common words have come into the language from peo-   15
ple's names. These lexical items again show the importance of
maleness compared to the triviality of the feminine activities being
described. Words derived from the names of women include *Melba
toast,* named for the Australian singer Dame Nellie Melba; *Sally
Lunn cakes,* named after an eighteenth-century woman who first
made them; *pompadour,* a hair style named after Madame Pompadour; and the word *maudlin,* as in *maudlin sentiment,* from Mary
Magdalene, who was often portrayed by artists as displaying exaggerated sorrow.

There are trivial items named after men—*teddy bear* after   16
Theodore Roosevelt and *sideburns* after General Burnside—but
most words that come from men's names relate to significant in-

ventions or developments. These include *pasteurization* after Louis Pasteur, *sousaphone* after John Philip Sousa, *mason jar* after John L. Mason, *boysenberry* after Rudolph Boysen, *pullman car* after George M. Pullman, *braille* after Louis Braille, *franklin stove* after Benjamin Franklin, *diesel engine* after Rudolf Diesel, *ferris wheel* after George W. G. Ferris, and the verb *to lynch* after William Lynch, who was a vigilante captain in Virginia in 1780.

The latter is an example of a whole set of English words deal- 17 ing with violence. These words have strongly negative connotations. From research using free association and semantic differentials, with university students as subjects, James Ney concluded that English reflects both an anti-male and an anti-female bias because these biases exist in the culture (*Etc.: A Review of General Semantics*, March 1976, pp. 67–76). The students consistently marked as masculine such words as *killer, murderer, robber, attacker, fighter, stabber, rapist, assassin, gang, hood, arsonist, criminal, hijacker, villain,* and *bully,* even though most of these words contain nothing to specify that they are masculine. An example of bias against males, Ney observed, is the absence in English of a pejorative term for women equivalent to *rapist.* Outcomes of his free association test indicated that if "English speakers want to call a man something bad, there seems to be a large vocabulary available to them but if they want to use a term which is good to describe a male, there is a small vocabulary available. The reverse is true for women."

Certainly we do not always think positively about males; wit- 18 ness such words as *jerk, creep, crumb, slob, fink,* and *jackass.* But much of what determines our positive and negative feelings relates to the roles people play. We have very negative feelings toward someone who is hurting us or threatening us or in some way making our lives miserable. To be able to do this, the person has to have power over us and this power usually belongs to males.

On the other hand, when someone helps us or makes our life 19 more pleasant, we have positive feelings toward that person or that role. *Mother* is one of the positive female terms in English, and we see such extensions of it as *Mother Nature, Mother Earth, mother lode, mother superior,* etc. But even though a word like *mother* is positive it is still not a word of power. In the minds of English speakers being female and being powerless or passive are so closely related that we use the terms *feminine* and *lady* either to mean female or to describe a certain kind of quiet and unobtrusive behavior.

Words Labelling Women as Things

Because of our expectations of passivity, we like to compare   20
females to items that people acquire for their pleasure. For example, in a recent commercial for the television show "Happy Days," one of the characters announced that in the coming season they were going to have not only "cars, motorcycles, and girls," but also a band. Another example of this kind of thinking is the comparison of females to food since food is something we all enjoy, even though it is extremely passive. We describe females as such delectable morsels as a *dish*, a *cookie*, a *tart, cheesecake, sugar and spice*, a *cute tomato, honey*, a *sharp cookie*, and *sweetie pie*. We say a particular girl has a *peaches and cream complexion* or "she looks good enough to eat." And parents give their daughters such names as *Candy* and *Cherry*.

Other pleasurable items that we compare females to are toys.   21
Young girls are called *little dolls* or *China dolls*, while older girls — if they are attractive — are simply called *dolls*. We might say about a woman, "She's pretty as a picture," or "She's a fashion plate." And we might compare a girl to a plant by saying she is a *clinging vine*, a *shrinking violet*, or a *wallflower*. And we might name our daughters after plants such as *Rose, Lily, Ivy, Daisy, Iris*, and *Petunia*. Compare these names to boys' names such as *Martin* which means warlike. *Ernest* which means resolute fighter, *Nicholas* which means victory, *Val* which means strong or valiant, and *Leo* which means lion. We would be very hesitant to give a boy the name of something as passive as a flower although we might say about a man that he is a *late-bloomer*. This is making a comparison between a man and the most active thing a plant can do, which is to bloom. The only other familiar plant metaphor used for a man is the insulting *pansy*, implying that he is like a woman.

Questions for Close Reading

1. What is the thesis of the selection? Locate the sentence(s) in which Nilsen states her main idea. If she does not state the thesis explicitly, express it in your own words.

2. According to Nilsen, when animal metaphors are used for human females, what do they usually imply? What do male animal metaphors imply?
3. Why, according to Nilsen, do some professions or jobs have different names depending on whether a male or female is performing them? What is implied by the existence of two different terms for the same job?
4. When positive terms are used for women, what personality characteristics do they suggest? Why are there so many words connoting violence that are most often applied to men?
5. Refer to your dictionary as needed to define the following words used in the selection: *unscrupulous* (paragraph 5), *enticing* (7), *connotation* (8), *virile* (11), *lexical* (15), *maudlin* (15), and *vigilante* (16).

Questions about the Writer's Craft

1. Why does Nilsen use so many examples to illustrate each type of sexism in the English language? What point of view is she trying to anticipate and counteract?
2. What are the three main sexist motifs in English that Nilsen examines? How does she signal to us that she is moving from one to another?
3. Why do you think Nilsen begins by discussing animal terms for humans? What effect does placing this section first have on you as a reader?
4. What is Nilsen's tone in this essay? What terms and expressions reveal her personal viewpoint on sexism in our language?

Questions for Further Thought

1. Do you think most users of English are aware of the sexism of many of our everyday expressions? Were you surprised by any of Nilsen's examples? Why or why not?
2. Nilsen writes that "American English reflects our values." Do you agree that phrases like "man-sized jobs" and "women's work" or "cocky" and "old biddy" mean we are a sexist nation? Should we watch what we say to guard against biased terms and images for males and females?
3. The names for many professions and positions have been gender-identified: consider *policeman, chairman, actor/actress, master* and *journeyman,* and so on. Is it better to change these terms to uniform, nonsexual ones like *police officer, chairperson, actor,* and so on? Do these terms really affect our thinking about people's worth or the decisions young people make about their futures?
4. Can our language ever be made completely nonsexist? What changes would have to occur?

Writing Assignments Using Exemplification as a Method of Development

1. The author claims that our language glorifies maleness and denigrates femaleness. Are there other areas of our lives where typical male behavior and attitudes are considered superior to the typical female roles or characteristics? Consider sports, occupations, hobbies, authority figures, and other areas of life. Write an essay showing that our culture either glorifies males or denigrates females. Use examples from sports, occupations, and so on to support your thesis.
2. Our language embodies many prejudices besides sexism. There are many words and expressions that are based on or imply prejudice against skin colors, old age, youth, left-handedness, shortness, fatness, and so on. Explore one of these areas in an essay, using specific examples of prejudicial language to show how the words we use reflect our stereotypes and biases.

Writing Assignments Using Other Methods of Development

3. Gender-based stereotyping exists in many areas of our culture besides language. Pretend you are a visitor to the U.S. who knows nothing about the culture — perhaps you are a visitor from Mars. You watch TV for a week or study several issues of a popular general interest magazine, such as *People, Time,* or *Newsweek*, and then write a report back to your home about the differences in the United States between males and females. Use the comparison-contrast format to develop your paper's thesis, and cover at least three of the following areas: jobs, interests, and hobbies; intelligence (decision making, problem solving, etc.); emotionalism; relations to children; physical strength and fitness; and power. Use specific examples from your research in TV or magazines to back up your observations.
4. Imagine that you are the opposite sex. How would your life so far have been different? Would you have been treated differently by your parents, teachers, and friends? Are there any specific experiences or events that would have turned out differently had you been a different sex? Write an essay persuading readers that your life would have been essentially the same *or* very different had you been born exactly as you are except for your sex.

Malcolm Cowley

In the book The View from 80 *(1984), from which the following excerpt comes, Malcolm Cowley looks back over a long and productive life. Educated at Harvard, Cowley moved to New York and Paris during the 1920s and '30s, the years of the so-called "lost generation" of American writers. He produced important work as a poet, literary historian, critic, and editor. Among his books are* Exile's Return *(1934), about American expatriate writers, and* I Worked at the Writer's Trade *(1979).*

The View from 80

Young people often look at the old as if they were members of a different species. Perhaps this is a way of denying to themselves that they, too, will one day find themselves inside a body that is rapidly running down while the person inside remains young. In this essay, Malcolm Cowley examines what it is to be old but still personally vital. He describes the temptations of the aged and somewhat surprisingly, the pleasures one can take in being old.

Even before he or she is 80, the aging person may undergo   1
another identity crisis like that of adolescence. Perhaps there had
also been a middle-aged crisis, the male or the female menopause,
but for the rest of adult life he had taken himself for granted, with
his capabilities and failings. Now, when he looks in the mirror, he
asks himself, "Is this really me?" — or he avoids the mirror out of
distress at what it reveals, those bags and wrinkles. In his new
makeup he is called upon to play a new role in a play that must be
improvised. André Gide, that long-lived man of letters, wrote in his
journal, "My heart has remained so young that I have the continual
feeling of playing a part, the part of the 70-year-old that I certainly
am; and the infirmities and weaknesses that remind me of my age
act like a prompter, reminding me of my lines when I tend to stray.

219

Then, like the good actor I want to be, I go back into my role, and I pride myself on playing it well."

In his new role the old person will find that he is tempted by   2
new vices, that he receives new compensations (not so widely known), and that he may possibly achieve new virtues. Chief among these is the heroic or merely obstinate refusal to surrender in the face of time. One admires the ships that go down with all flags flying and the captain on the bridge.

Among the vices of age are avarice, untidiness, and vanity,   3
which last takes the form of a craving to be loved or simply admired. Avarice is the worst of those three. Why do so many old persons, men and women alike, insist on hoarding money when they have no prospect of using it and even when they have no heirs? They eat the cheapest food, buy no clothes, and live in a single room when they could afford better lodging. It may be that they regard money as a form of power; there is a comfort in watching it accumulate while other powers are dwindling away. How often we read of an old person found dead on a hovel, on a mattress partly stuffed with bankbooks and stock certificates! The bankbook syndrome, we call it in our family, which has never succumbed.

Untidiness we call the Langley Collyer syndrome. To explain,   4
Langley Collyer was a former concert pianist who lived alone with his 70-year-old brother in a brownstone house on upper Fifth Avenue. The once fashionable neighborhood had become part of Harlem. Homer, the brother, had been an admiralty laywer, but was now blind and partly paralyzed; Langley played for him and fed him on buns and oranges, which he thought would restore Homer's sight. He never threw away a daily paper because Homer, he said, might want to read them all. He saved other things as well and the house became filled with rubbish from roof to basement. The halls were lined on both sides with bundled newspapers, leaving narrow passageways in which Langley had devised booby traps to catch intruders.

On March 21, 1947, some unnamed person telephoned the   5
police to report that there was a dead body in the Collyer house. The police broke down the front door and found the hall impassable, then they hoisted a ladder to a second-story window. Behind it Homer was lying on the floor in a bathrobe; he had starved to death. Langley had disappeared. After some delay, the police broke into the basement, chopped a hole in the roof, and began throwing junk out of the house, top and bottom. It was 18 days before they

found Langley's body, gnawed by rats. Caught in one of his own booby traps, he had died in a hallway just outside Homer's door. By that time the police had collected, and the Department of Sanitation had hauled away, 120 tons of rubbish, including besides the newspapers, 14 grand pianos and the parts of a dismantled Model T Ford.

Why do so many old people accumulate junk, not on the scale   6
of Langley Collyer, but still in a dismaying fashion? Their tables are piled high with it, their bureau drawers are stuffed with it, their closet rods bend with the weight of clothes not worn for years. I suppose that the piling up is partly from lethargy and partly from the feeling that everything once useful, including their own bodies, should be preserved. Others, though not so many, have such a fear of becoming Langley Collyers that they strive to be painfully neat. Every tool they own is in its place, though it will never be used again; every scrap of paper is filed away in alphabetical order. At last their immoderate neatness becomes another vice of age, if a milder one.

.   The vanity of older people is an easier weakness to explain, and   7
to condone. With less to look forward to, they yearn for recognition of what they have been: the reigning beauty, the athlete, the soldier, the scholar. It is the beauties who have the hardest time. A portrait of themselves at twenty hangs on the wall, and they try to resemble it by making an extravagant use of creams, powders, and dyes. Being young at heart, they think they are merely revealing their essential persons. The athletes find shelves for their silver trophies, which are polished once a year. Perhaps a letter sweater lies wrapped in a bureau drawer. I remember one evening when a no-longer athlete had guests for dinner and tried to find his sweater. "Oh, that old thing," his wife said. "The moths got into it and I threw it away." The athlete sulked and his guests went home early.

Often the yearning to be recognized appears in conversation as   8
an innocent boast. Thus, a distinguished physician, retired at 94, remarks casually that a disease was named after him. A former judge bursts into chuckles as he repeats bright things that he said on the bench. Aging scholars complain in letters (or one of them does), "As I approach 70 I'm becoming avid of honors, and such things — medals, honorary degrees, etc. — are only passed around among academics on a *quid pro quo* basis (one hood capping another)." Or they say querulously, "Bill Underwood has ten honor-

ary doctorates and I have only three. Why didn't they elect me
to . . . ?" and they mention the name of some learned society.
That search for honors is a harmless passion, though it may lead to
jealousies and deformations of character, as with Robert Frost in
his later years. Still, honors cost little. Why shouldn't the very old
have more than their share of them?

To be admired and praised, especially by the young, is an   9
autumnal pleasure enjoyed by the lucky ones (who are not always
the most deserving). "What is more charming," Cicero observes in
his famous essay *De Senectute*, "than an old age surrounded by the
enthusiasm of youth! . . . Attentions which seem trivial and conventional are marks of honor — the morning call, being sought
after, precedence, having people rise for you, being escorted to and
from the forum. . . . What pleasures of the body can be compared
to the prerogatives of influence?" But there are also pleasures of the
body, or the mind, that are enjoyed by a greater number of older
persons.

Those pleasures include some that younger people find hard   10
to appreciate. One of them is simply sitting still, like a snake on a
sun-warmed stone, with a delicious feeling of indolence that was
seldom attained in earlier years. A leaf flutters down; a cloud moves
by inches across the horizon. At such moments the older person,
completely relaxed, has become a part of nature — and a living
part, with blood coursing through his veins. The future does not
exist for him. He thinks, if he thinks at all, that life for younger
persons is still a battle royal of each against each, but that now he
has nothing more to win or lose. He is not so much above as
outside the battle, as if he had assumed the uniform of some small
neutral country, perhaps Liechtenstein or Andorra. From a distance he notes that some of the combatants, men or women, are
jostling ahead — but why do they fight so hard when the most they
can hope for is a longer obituary? He can watch the scrounging and
gouging, he can hear the shouts of exultation, the moans of the
gravely wounded, and meanwhile he feels secure; nobody will attack him from ambush.

Age has other physical compensations besides the nirvana of   11
dozing in the sun. A few of the simplest needs become a pleasure to
satisfy. When an old woman in a nursing home was asked what she
really liked to do, she answered in one word: "Eat." She might have
been speaking for many of her fellows. Meals in a nursing home,
however badly cooked, serve as climactic moments of the day. The

physical essence of the pensioners is being renewed at an appointed hour; now they can go back to meditating or to watching TV while looking forward to the next meal. They can also look forward to sleep, which has become a definite pleasure, not the mere interruption it once had been.

Here I am thinking of old persons under nursing care. Others 12 ferociously guard their independence, and some of them suffer less than one might expect from being lonely and impoverished. They can be rejoiced by visits and meetings, but they also have company inside their heads. Some of them are busiest when their hands are still. What passes through the minds of many is a stream of persons, images, phrases, and familiar tunes. For some that stream has continued since childhood, but now it is deeper; it is their present and their past combined. At times they conduct silent dialogues with a vanished friend, and these are less tiring — often more rewarding — than spoken conversations. If inner resources are lacking, old persons living alone may seek comfort and a kind of companionship in the bottle. I should judge from the gossip of various neighborhoods that the outer suburbs from Boston to San Diego are full of secretly alcoholic widows. One of those widows, an old friend, was moved from her apartment into a retirement home. She left behind her a closet in which the floor was covered wall to wall with whiskey bottles. "Oh, those empty bottles!" she explained. "They were left by a former tenant."

Not whiskey or cooking sherry but simply giving up is the 13 greatest temptation of age. It is something different from a stoical acceptance of infirmities, which is something to be admired. At 63, when he first recognized that his powers were failing, Emerson wrote one of his best poems, "Terminus":

It is time to be old,
To take in sail: —
The god of bounds,
Who sets to seas a shore,
Came to me in his fatal rounds,
And said: "No more!
No farther shoot
Thy broad ambitious branches, and thy root.
Fancy departs: no more invent;
Contract thy firmament
To compass of a tent."

Emerson lived in good health to the age of 79. Within his   14
narrowed firmament, he continued working until his memory
failed; then he consented to having younger editors and collabora-
tors. The givers-up see no reason for working. Sometimes they lie in
bed all day when moving about would still be possible, if difficult. I
had a friend, a distinguished poet, who surrendered in that fashion.
The doctors tried to stir him to action, but he refused to leave his
room. Another friend, once a successful artist, stopped painting
when his eyes began to fail. His doctor made the mistake of telling
him that he suffered from a fatal disease. He then lost interest in
everything except the splendid Rolls-Royce, acquired in his prosperous days, that stood in the garage. Daily he wiped the dust from
its hood. He couldn't drive it on the road any longer, but he used to
sit in the driver's seat, start the motor, then back the Rolls out of the
garage and drive it in again, back twenty feet and forward twenty
feet; that was his only distraction.

I haven't the right to blame those who surrender, not being   15
able to put myself inside their minds or bodies. Often they must
have compelling reasons, physical or moral. Not only do they suffer from a variety of ailments, but also they are made to feel that
they no longer have a function in the community. Their families
and neighbors don't ask them for advice, don't really listen when
they speak, don't call on them for efforts. One notes that there are
not a few recoveries from apparent senility when that situation
changes. If it doesn't change, old persons may decide that efforts
are useless. I sympathize with their problems, but the men and
women I envy are those who accept old age as a series of challenges.

For such persons, every new infirmity is an enemy to be outwit-   16
ted, an obstacle to be overcome by force of will. They enjoy each
little victory over themselves, and sometimes they win a major
success. Renoir was one of them. He continued painting, and mag-
nificently, for years after he was crippled by arthritis; the brush had
to be strapped to his arm. "You don't need your hand to paint," he
said. Goya was another of the unvanquished. At 72 he retired as an
official painter of the Spanish court and decided to work only for
himself. His later years were those of the famous "black paintings"
in which he let his imagination run (and also of the lithographs,
then a new technique). At 78 he escaped a reign of terror in Spain
by fleeing to Bordeaux. He was deaf and his eyes were failing; in
order to work he had to wear several pairs of spectacles, one over

another, and then use a magnifying glass; but he was producing splendid work in a totally new style. At 80 he drew an ancient man propped on two sticks, with a mass of white hair and beard hiding his face and with the inscription "I am still learning."

Giovanni Papini said when he was nearly blind, "I prefer mar-   17
tyrdom to imbecility." After writing sixty books, including his famous *Life of Christ*, he was at work on two huge projects when he was stricken with a form of muscular atrophy. He lost the use of his left leg, then of his fingers, so that he couldn't hold a pen. The two big books, though never to be finished, moved forward slowly by dictation; that in itself was a triumph. Toward the end, when his voice had become incomprehensible, he spelled out a word, tapping on the table to indicate letters of the alphabet. One hopes never to be faced with the need for such heroic measures.

"Eighty years old!" the great Catholic poet Paul Claudel   18
wrote in his journal. "No eyes left, no ears, no teeth, no legs, no wind! And when all is said and done, how astonishingly well one does without them!"

Questions for Close Reading

1. What is the thesis of the selection? Locate the sentence(s) in which Cowley states his main idea. If he does not state the thesis explicitly, express it in your own words.
2. What, according to Cowley, are the "vices" of old age? Why are old people particularly prone to each of these weaknesses?
3. What pleasures do the old enjoy? Why are these pleasures hard for the young to understand?
4. What kind of old person does Cowley say he envies? Why?
5. Refer to your dictionary as needed to define the following words used in the selection: *menopause* (paragraph 1), *obstinate* (2), *lethargy* (6), *nirvana* (11), *infirmity* (16), and *atrophy* (17).

Questions about the Writer's Craft

1. Which of Cowley's examples do you find most striking or memorable? Why does he use comments about aging made by other writers and artists?
2. Cowley introduces his essay by establishing an imaginative comparison, or analogy, between old age and playing a role. Why is this comparison effective in conveying what old age feels like?

3. What organization underlies this essay? Where does the author provide a brief preview of what his organizational plan will be? Where does he discuss his most significant point?
4. Overall, what is the tone throughout the essay? For whom do you think Cowley was writing this essay, on the basis of the tone he adopts?

Questions for Further Thought

1. In his first sentence, the author suggests that the elderly may undergo an "identity crisis" like that of adolescence. Can you think of other similarities between the problems confronting a teenager and an old person?
2. What stereotypes about the elderly do we often hold? Does Cowley's essay combat any of these? Which of the stereotypes does the author find accurate?
3. Cowley's examples of those who live a vital old age are people who were able to continue their careers — Goya, Renoir, Emerson. Should older people continue to work? If they are forced to retire, in what ways might they still be productive?
4. What does it take to live to a happy old age? What inner and outer resources are necessary?

Writing Assignments Using Exemplification as a Method of Development

1. The author notes that the elderly "are made to feel they no longer have a function in the community." Write an essay in the form of a proposal to your town or to the elderly of your community. In this essay, explain what three functions you believe the elderly could be encouraged to play in your community. Give specific examples of the activities, duties, or roles you recommend.
2. Write an essay supporting the thesis that people can cope well and remain productive beyond conventional retirement age. You might focus on people you know or have heard about through family or friends. Or you could discuss such well-known individuals as athletes, politicians, entertainers, or the like.

Writing Assignments Using Other Methods of Development

3. Our youth-oriented culture tends to provide a distorted image of the old — or eliminates them altogether from TV, advertising, and so on. Write a letter to a TV network president or to a major advertiser (Pepsi,

for example, the choice of a "new generation") arguing that old people should be more fairly represented in TV shows and advertising. Develop your essay by explaining the reasons for your position.

4. We have all heard the phrase, "growing old gracefully." Write an essay outlining the steps one should follow to age into a "graceful" and happy older person.

Additional Writing Topics

EXEMPLIFICATION

General Assignments

Use examples to develop any of the following topics into a well-organized essay. When writing the paper, choose enough relevant examples to support your thesis. Organize the material into a sequence that most effectively illustrates the thesis, keeping in mind that emphatic order is often the most compelling way to present specifics.

1. Many of today's drivers have dangerous habits.
2. Drug and alcohol abuse is (or is not) a serious problem among many young people.
3. One rule of restaurant dining is, "Management often seems oblivious to problems that are perfectly obvious to customers."
4. Children today are not encouraged to use their imaginations.
5. The worst kind of hypocrite is a religious hypocrite.
6. The best things in life are definitely not free.
7. A part-time job is an important learning experience every student should have.
8. Many TV and magazine ads use sexual allusions to sell their products.
9. _____ (name someone you know well) is a _____ (use a quality: open-minded, dishonest, compulsive, reliable, gentle, and so on) person.
10. Television commercials stereotype the elderly (or another minority group).
11. Today, salespeople act as if they are doing you a favor by taking your money.
12. Most people behave very decently in their daily interactions with each other.
13. Pettiness, jealousy, and selfishness abound in our daily interactions with each other.
14. You can tell a lot about people by observing what they wear and eat.
15. Too many Americans are overly concerned with material things.
16. There are several study techniques that will help a student learn more efficiently.
17. Some teachers seem to enjoy turning tests into ordeals.

18. "Learning bad eating habits" is one course all college students take.
19. More needs to be done to eliminate obstacles faced by the physically handicapped.
20. Some of the best presents are those that cost the least.

Assignments with a Specific Audience and Purpose

1. A friend of yours has taken a job in a big city or moved to a small town. You want to warn your friend about what he or she can expect in this new environment. Give examples of what life in a big city or small town is like. You might focus on the benefits, or dangers, of both.
2. You are shopping for a new car. You become annoyed at how expensive the available options are. Or you become angry because the options available *should* be standard equipment. Write a letter of complaint to the auto manufacturer citing at least three examples of options that are too expensive, or options that should be standard, or options that should be required on all models.
3. Many people at your college or workplace have been experiencing stress lately. You have been asked to help them. Write a brochure that will be distributed by the counseling department on the subject of ways to reduce anxiety. Focus on how people can reduce stress, giving examples of each strategy you describe.
4. Assume that you teach in an elementary school. The school principal has asked you to make a speech to parents about the adverse effects of television on children. You decide to focus on just one aspect of this topic: how TV distorts reality. Write out the speech, giving examples to prove your point.
5. A pet food company is having an annual contest to choose a new animal to feature in its advertising and on packages of its product. In addition to appealing pictures of the animal, the company requires contestants to submit an essay proving that the animal of their choice is personable, playful, unique. Write an essay giving examples of your pet's special qualities. Your aim is to win the contest.
6. You have been asked to write a light article on the "three best consumer products of the last twenty-five years." You know that in a magazine article published several years ago, a prominent businessperson mentioned disposable diapers, pens, and lighters as examples of such products. What products do you feel are most worthy of this designation? Write an essay for your college humor magazine giving examples of at least three such products.

PROCESS
ANALYSIS

WHAT IS PROCESS ANALYSIS?

You have probably watched and admired at one time or another the dogged determination of small children. When learning to do something like tie their shoelaces or tell time, little children struggle along, creating knotted tangles, confusing the hour with the minute hand. But they don't give up. Mastering such basic skills empowers them and makes them feel less dependent on the adults of the world — all of whom, in the children's eyes, seem to know how to do everything. Actually, none of us is born knowing how to do very much. We depend not on inborn instinct for survival, but on our great capacity for learning. We spend a good deal of our lives learning — everything from speaking our first word to balancing our first bank statement. In short, many of the milestones of our lives are linked to the processes we master: how to cross the street alone; how to drive a car; how to make a speech without being paralyzed by fear.

Process analysis, a writing technique that explains the steps or sequence involved in doing something, fascinates us because it

231

satisfies our need to learn as well as our curiosity about how the world works. All the self-help books flooding the market today (*Managing Stress, How to Make a Million in Real Estate, Ten Days to a Perfect Body*) are examples of process analysis. The instructions on the federal tax form and the recipes in a cookbook are also process analyses. Not surprisingly, several television classics, now seen in reruns, capitalize on our desire to learn how things happen: "The Wild Kingdom" shows how animals survive in faraway lands, and "Mission Impossible" has great fun detailing elaborate plans for preventing the triumph of evil. But process analysis can deal with more than the merely interesting or entertaining. Process analysis can also focus on critical matters. Consider a waiter hurriedly skimming the "Choking Aid" instructions posted on the restaurant wall or an air traffic controller following emergency procedures in an effort to prevent a mid-air collision. In these last examples, the consequences could be fatal if the process analyses were slipshod, inaccurate, or confusing.

Undoubtedly, all of us have experienced less dramatic effects of poorly written process analyses. Perhaps you have tried to assemble a bicycle and spent hours sorting through a stack of parts, only to end up with one or two extra pieces never mentioned in the instructions. Or maybe you were baffled when putting up a set of wall shelves because the instructions insisted on using such unfamiliar terms as "mitered cleat," "wing nut," and "dowel pin." It's not surprising that many people stay clear of anything that actually admits "assembly required."

WHEN TO USE PROCESS ANALYSIS

You will write a process analysis in one of two situations: either you want to give step-by-step instructions to readers showing them how they can do something, or you want readers to understand how something happens even though they will not actually follow the steps outlined. The first kind of process analysis is called *directional process analysis*; the second is called *informational process analysis*. When you look at the instructions on a package of frozen vegetables or when you follow the instructions for completing a job application, you are reading directional process analysis. A letter to out-of-town friends telling them how to get to your new apartment and a note to your roommates advising them how to avoid getting scalded by a temperamental shower are also examples of directional process analysis. Informational process can range over an equally wide variety of topics: how the core of a nuclear power plant melts down; how dinosaurs became extinct; how television became so important in political campaigns.

College assignments frequently lead to process essays. Take a moment to consider the following examples.

The officials of this community have been accused of mismanaging the recent unrest over the public housing ordinance. Describe the steps the officials took, indicating whether you think they acted wisely. If not, how do you think the situation should have been handled?

Many colleges and universities have changed the eligibility guidelines for financial aid, with the result that fewer students can depend on student loans or scholarships to help finance their education. How can students and their families cope with the increasing educational costs they now have to incur? How can they ease the financial burden involved in obtaining a higher education?

There have been many reports recently citing the abuse of small children in day care centers. What can parents using day care do to guard against the mistreatment of their children?

Genius has been defined as ten percent inspiration and ninety percent perspiration. Do you consider this an apt description of the creative process? Support your point by showing how you or someone you know achieved a goal that required both hard work and imagination.

You will note that, with the exception of the last example, none of these assignments states explicitly that the essay response should use process analysis. Instead, the wording of the assignments ("Describe the steps . . . ," "How can they ease . . . ," and "What can parents do . . . ") signals that process analysis would be an appropriate strategy for developing the papers.

It's important to realize that assignments do not always contain such clear signals to use process analysis. But during the prewriting stage, as material is generated to support your thesis, you will often realize that you can best achieve your purpose by developing the essay—or part of it—using process analysis. Sometimes process analysis will end up being the primary strategy for organizing an essay; other times it will be used to help make a point in an essay organized according to another pattern of development. Let's take a moment to illustrate this second use.

Assume that you are writing a *causal analysis* examining the impact of television commercials on people's buying behavior. To make the point that commercials create a need where none exists, you might describe the various stages in an advertising campaign to pitch a new, completely frivolous product. In an essay *defining* a good boss, you could get across the point that effective managers must be skilled at settling disputes by explaining the steps your boss took to resolve a heated disagreement between two employees. If you wrote an *argumentation-persuasion* paper urging the funding of programs to ease the plight of the homeless, the tragedy of these people's lives would have to be dramatized. To achieve your purpose, you could devote part of the paper to an explanation of how the typical street person goes about finding a place to sleep and getting food to eat.

SUGGESTIONS FOR USING PROCESS ANALYSIS IN AN ESSAY

The suggestions that follow will be helpful whether you use process analysis as a predominant or supportive pattern of development.

1. Identify the desired outcome of the process analysis. Many papers developed primarily through process analysis have a clear-cut purpose: simply to tell readers as objectively as possible about a process: "Here is a way of making french fries at home that will surpass the best served in your favorite fast-food restaurant." But process essays may also have a persuasive edge, with the writer advocating a point of view about the process, perhaps even urging a course of action: "If you do not want your arguments to deteriorate into ugly battles, you should follow a

series of foolproof steps for having disagreements that leave friendships intact." Before starting to write, you need to decide if the
essay is to be purely factual or if it will include this kind of persuasive dimension.

**2. Decide whether the process analysis will be primarily direc-
tional or informational.** It's important to realize that directional and informational processes are not always distinct. In fact,
they may be complementary. Background information about a
process often has to be provided before the steps for performing the
process can be outlined. A paper might explain how the body burns
calories before describing a step-by-step approach for losing
weight. Or you could provide some theory about how organic
fertilizer works before detailing a plan for growing your own vegetables. Although both approaches may be needed in a paper using
process analysis as its predominant pattern, only one approach will
provide the focus of the essay.

The kind of process analysis chosen will have important implications for your paper. When the process analysis is *directional*, the
reader is addressed in the *second person*: "You should first rinse the
residue from the radiator by . . . ," or "Wrap the injured person
in a blanket and then. . . ." (In the second example, the pronoun
"you" is implied or understood.)

If the process analysis has an *informational* purpose, you do
not address the reader directly but have available a number of other
options. For example, the *first person* might be used. In a humorous
essay explaining how to study for finals, you could cite your own
study habits as a perfect example of what *not* to do: "Filled with
good intentions, I sit on my bed, pick up a pencil, open my note-
book, and fall promptly asleep." The *third person singular or plural*
could also be used: "The door-to-door salesperson walks up the
front walk, heart pounding, more than a bit nervous, but also
challenged by the prospect of striking a deal," or "The new recruits
next underwent a series of important balance tests in what they
referred to as the 'horror chamber.'" You might have noticed that
in the third person examples, the present tense was used in one
sentence, the past tense in the other. Past tense is appropriate for
events already completed, while present tense is used for habitual
or ongoing actions ("A dominant male goose usually flies at the
head of the V-wedge during migration"). The present tense is also

effective when you want to lend a sense of dramatic immediacy to a process, even if the steps were performed in the past ("The surgeon gently separates the facial skin and muscle from the underlying bony skull").

3. Identify the steps in the process. Before detailing a sequence for your readers, you need to think through the process, exploring it thoroughly, identifying its major parts and subparts, locating possible missteps or trouble spots. With your purpose and audience in mind, use the appropriate prewriting techniques to break the process down into its component parts. When prewriting, it's a good idea to start by generating more material than you expect to use. Then the raw material can be shaped and pruned to fit your purpose and the needs of your audience. The amount of work done during the prewriting stage will have a direct bearing on the clarity of your presentation.

4. Explain the process, one step at a time. Once the key stages in the process have been determined, you are ready to present the process in an easy-to-follow sequence. At times you will write about a process which follows a fairly fixed chronological sequence, consisting of a series of steps agreed upon by most people: how to make pizza, how to pot a plant, how to change a tire. In such cases, it's critical that you include all necessary steps, putting them in the correct chronological order, being sure not to omit any steps. Other times you will write about a process with no commonly accepted steps or sequence. If you prepare an essay explaining how to discipline a child or how to pull yourself out of a blue mood, you have to come up with your own definition of the key steps and then put those steps into a logical order. Since process analyses are not limited to describing a given progression of steps, you may use a process essay to reject or reformulate a traditional sequence. An interesting process analysis, for example, could be written based on the following thesis: "Our system for electing congressional representatives is inefficient and even undemocratic. It must be reformed."

Whether the essay describes a generally agreed upon or a not commonly accepted process, you must provide all the details needed to explain the process. Readers should be able to understand, even visualize, the process. There should be no fuzzy patches or confusing cuts from one scene to another. Be careful, however, not to overreact to this advice by going into obsessive detail about minor stages or steps. If you dwell for several hundred words on how to butter the pan, your readers will never stay with you long enough to learn how to make the omelet.

It is not unusual, especially in less defined sequences, if some steps occur simultaneously and overlap. When that occurs, you should present the steps in the most logical order, being sure to tell your readers that several steps are not perfectly distinct and may even merge. For example, if explaining how a species becomes extinct, you would have to indicate that overpopulation of hardy strains and destruction of endangered breeds are often simultaneous events. You would also need to clarify that the depletion of food sources both precedes and follows the demise of a species. Moreover, if a strict chronological ordering of steps means that a particularly important part of the sequence gets buried in the middle, the sequence probably should be juggled so that the crucial step receives the attention it deserves.

5. Provide the readers with the help needed to follow the sequence. Like all essays, a process analysis should be written with a specific audience in mind; otherwise, you cannot be certain about how much information to provide and how much knowledge can be assumed. Imagine you are writing an article advising students about the best way to use the university's computer center. The article will be published in a newsletter for computer science majors. You would seriously misjudge your audience — and probably put them to sleep — if you explained in detail how to transfer material from disk to disk or how to delete information from a file. But if the article were prepared for a general audience (your composition class, for instance), such detailed instructions would be appropriate.

If writing a directional analysis, you should tell your readers, either in the introduction or at the appropriate spot in the sequence, what material or equipment they will need. Don't assume they will know what is needed to perform the process. Also, at some points in a process analysis, warnings may be needed to head off possible mistakes or misinterpretations. When writing a paper on the artistry involved in butterflying a shrimp, you might say something like this:

Next, make a shallow cut with your sharpened knife along the convex curve of the shrimp's intestinal tract. The tract, usually a faint black line along the outside curve of the shrimp, is faintly visible beneath the translucent flesh. But some shrimp have a thick orange, blue, or gray line instead of a thin black one. In all cases, be careful not to slice too deeply, or you will end up with two shrimp halves instead of one butterflied shrimp.

You have told readers what to look for, citing the exceptions, and have warned them against making too deep a cut. Anticipating spots where communication might break down is a key part of writing an effective process analysis.

Transition words are also critical in helping readers understand the order of the steps being described. Time signals such as *first, next, now, while, after, before,* and *finally* provide the reader with a clear sense of the sequence as it unfolds. Entire sentences can also be used to link parts of the process, reminding the audience of what has already been discussed and indicating what will now be explained: "Once the panel of experts finishes its evaluation of the exam questions, randomly selected items are field-tested in schools throughout the country."

6. Decide what tone you want the process essay to project.   When writing a process essay, you want to be certain that your tone — your attitude toward your subject — suits your purpose. Will the essay be serious and straightforward? Will it be ironic, satiric, or humorous? Whatever mood you choose, you should try to make your essay seamless in tone. If your essay is a serious discussion of the best way to interview for a job, you don't want to veer off into humorous details about employers who are themselves terrified of interviews. Or in a light piece on the way computers are taking over our lives, it would not be appropriate to include a serious discussion about the abuse of computerized medical records.

7. Open and close the process analysis effectively.   A paper developed primarily through process analysis should make a strong beginning. Your introduction should state the process to be described and clarify whether the essay has an informational or directional intent. Once readers have that information, they should be able to follow your analysis with ease because they have a clear idea of your destination.

If you suspect your readers are indifferent to your subject, the introduction can be used to motivate them, telling them how important the subject is:

> Do you enjoy the salad bars found in many restaurants? If you do, you probably have noticed that the vegetables are always crisp and fresh--no matter how many hours they have been exposed to the air. What are the restaurants doing to make the vegetables look so inviting? There's a simple answer. Many restaurants dip and spray the vegetables with potent chemicals to make them appetizing.

Moreover, if you think the audience might feel intimidated by your subject, the introduction is a perfect spot to reassure them that the process being described is not beyond their grasp:

> Studies show that many people willingly accept a defective product just so they won't have to deal with the uncomfortable process of making a complaint. But once a few easy-to-learn basics are mastered, anyone can register a complaint that gets results.

Most process essays do not end as soon as the last step in the sequence has been explained. Instead, they usually include some brief closing comments that round out the piece and bring it to a satisfying close. This final section of the essay may summarize the main steps in the process — not repeating the steps verbatim but rephrasing and condensing them in several concise sentences. The conclusion can also be an effective spot to underscore the significance of the process, recalling what may have been said in the introduction about the importance of the subject. Or the essay could end by echoing the note of reassurance that may have been included at the start of the piece.

Despite the glut of "how-to" books on the market, effective process writing is not as easy to do as it might appear. Explaining how to do something is often as difficult as responding to the proverbial "How do I get there from here?" And explaining how something happened means recreating often complex events, restructuring the world so that logic and clarity take precedence over cloudiness and confusion. If after reading your piece the reader thinks or says, "I understand. I see what you mean," you can be confident that your process analysis has been successful. That is no mean accomplishment.

STUDENT ESSAY AND COMMENTARY

The student essay that follows was written by Robert Berry in response to this assignment:

> Steven Leacock's "How to Live to Be 200" pokes fun at our obsessive concern with physical fitness. Look around and observe people, identifying another example of an obsessive behavior which borders on the addictive. Then write a light-spirited essay explaining the various stages in the addiction. Since the essay is humorous in tone, it is important that you describe an addiction that does not have serious consequences.

While reading the paper, try to determine how effectively it applies the principles concerning the use of process analysis. The commentary following the paper will help you look at Robert's essay more closely.

Becoming a Videoholic

In the last several years, videocassette recorders have become   1
popular additions in many American homes. A recent newspaper article notes that one in three households has a VCR, with sales continuing to climb every day. VCRs seem to be the most popular technological breakthrough since television itself. No consumer warning labels are attached to these rapidly multiplying VCRs, but there should be. VCRs can be dangerous. Barely aware of what is happening, a person can turn into a compulsive videotaper. The descent from innocent hobby to full-blown addiction takes place in several stages.

In the first innocent stage, the unsuspecting person buys a VCR   2
for occasional use. I was at this stage when I asked my parents if they would buy me a VCR as a combined birthday and high school graduation gift. With the VCR, I could tape Star Trek and Miami Vice, shows I

would otherwise miss on nights I was at work. The VCR was perfect. I hooked it up to the old TV in my bedroom, recorded the intergalactic adventures of Captain Kirk and the high voltage escapades of Sonny Crockett, then watched the tapes the next day. Occasionally, I taped a movie which my friends and I watched over the weekend. I had just one cassette but that was all I needed since I watched every show I recorded and simply taped over the preceding show when I recorded another. In these early days, my VCR was the equivalent of light social drinking.

In the second phase on the road to videoholism, an individual 3 uses the VCR more frequently and begins to stockpile tapes rather than watch them. My troubles began in July when my family went to the shore for a week's vacation. I programmed the VCR to tape all five episodes of <u>Star</u> <u>Trek</u> while I was at the beach perfecting my tan. Since I used the VCR's long-play mode, I could get all five <u>Star</u> <u>Treks</u> on one cassette. But that ended up creating a problem. Even I, an avid Trekkie, didn't want to watch five shows in one sitting. I viewed two shows, but the three unwatched shows tied up my tape, making it impossible to record other shows. How did I resolve this dilemma? Very easily. I went out and bought several more cassettes. Once I had these additional tapes, I was free to record as many <u>Star</u> <u>Treks</u> as I wanted, plus I could tape reruns of classics like <u>The</u> <u>Honeymooners</u> and <u>Mission</u> <u>Impossible</u>. Very quickly, I accumulated six <u>Star</u> <u>Treks</u>, four <u>Honeymooners</u>, and three <u>Mission</u> <u>Impossibles</u>. Then a friend-- who shall go nameless--told me that only eighty-two episodes of <u>Star</u> <u>Trek</u> were ever made. Excited by the thought that I could acquire as impressive a collection of tapes as a Hollywood executive, I continued recording <u>Star</u> <u>Trek</u>, even taping shows while I watched them. Clearly, my once innocent hobby was getting out of control. I was now using the VCR on a regular basis--the equivalent of several stiff drinks a day.

In the third stage of videoholism, the amount of taping increases 4 significantly, leading to an even more irrational stockpiling of cassettes. The catalyst that propelled me into this third stage was my parents' decision to get cable TV. Selfless guy that I am, I volunteered to move my VCR and hook it up to the TV in the living room where the cable outlet was located. Now I could tape all the most recent movies and cable specials. With that delightful possibility in mind, I went out and bought two six-packs of blank tapes. Then, in addition to my regulars, I began to record a couple of additional shows every day. I taped <u>Rocky</u> III, <u>Magnum</u> <u>Force</u>, a James Bond movie, an HBO comedy special with Eddie Murphy, and an MTV concert featuring Mick Jagger. Where did I get time to watch all these tapes? I didn't. Taping at this point was more satisfying than watching. Reason and common sense were abandoned. Getting things on tape had become an obsession, and I was taping all the time.

In the fourth stage, videoholism creeps into other parts of the   5 addict's life, influencing behavior in strange ways. Secrecy becomes commonplace. One day, my mother came into my room and saw my bookcase filled with tapes--rather than with the paperbacks that used to be there. "Robert," she exclaimed, "isn't this getting a bit out of hand?" I assured her it was just a hobby, but I started hiding my tapes, putting them in a suitcase stored in my closet. I also taped at night, slipping downstairs to turn on the VCR after my parents had gone to bed and getting down first thing in the morning to turn off the VCR and remove the cassette before my parents noticed. Also, denial is not unusual during this stage of VCR addiction. At the dinner table, when my younger sister commented, "Robert tapes all the time," I laughingly told everyone--including myself--that the taping was no big deal. I was getting bored with it and was going to stop any day, I assured my family. Obsessive behavior also characterizes the fourth stage of videoholism. Each week, I pulled out the TV magazine from the Sunday paper and went through it carefully, circling in red all the shows I wanted to tape. Another sign of addiction was my compulsive organization of all the tapes I had stockpiled. Working more diligently than I ever had for any term paper, I typed up labels and attached them to each cassette. I also created an elaborate list that showed my tapes broken down into categories such as westerns, horror movies, and comedies.

In the final stage of an addiction, the individual either succumbs   6 completely to the addiction or is able to tear away from the habit. I broke my addiction, and I broke it cold turkey. This total withdrawal occurred when I went off to college. There was no point in taking my VCR to school because TVs were not allowed in the freshman dorms. Even though there were many things to occupy my time during the school week, cold sweats overcame me whenever I thought about everything on TV I was not taping. I even considered calling home and asking members of my family to tape things for me, but I knew they would think I was crazy. At the beginning of the semester, I also had to resist the overwhelming desire to travel the three hours home every weekend so I could get my fix. But after a while, the urgent need to tape subsided. Now, months later, as I write this, I feel detached and sober.

I have no illusions, though. I know that once a videoholic, always   7 a videoholic. Soon I will return home for the holidays, which, as everyone knows, can be a time for excess eating--and taping. But I will cope with the pressure. I will take each day one at a time. I will ask my little sister to hide my blank tapes. And if I feel myself succumbing to the temptations of taping. I will pick up the telephone and dial the video-holics' hotline: (800) VCR-TAPE. I will win the battle.

Robert's essay is an example of *informational process analysis*, his purpose being to describe — rather than teach — the process of becoming a "videoholic." The title, with its coined term "video-holic," tips us off that the essay is going to be entertaining. And the introductory paragraph clearly establishes the essay's playful, mock-serious tone with the words "No consumer warning labels are attached to these rapidly multiplying VCRs, but there should be. VCRs can be dangerous." The tone established, Robert briefly defines the term "videoholic" as a "compulsive videotaper," and then moves to the essay's *thesis*: "The descent from innocent hobby to full-blown addiction takes place in several stages." The thesis lets us know that the paper is going to explain how videoholism develops.

Robert sustains the humor of the introduction throughout the essay, poking fun at his quirks and mocking his own motivations: "Even I, an avid Trekkie, didn't want to watch five shows in one sitting" (paragraph 3); "Selfless guy that I am, I volunteered to move my VCR . . . " (4); "Working more diligently than I ever had for any term paper, I typed up labels. . . . " (5) In addition to the consistent tone underlying the essay, Robert's paper is unified by an *analogy*, the sustained comparison between Robert's video addiction and the obviously more serious addiction to alcohol. Handled incorrectly, the analogy could have been offensive, but Robert makes the comparison work to his advantage. The analogy is used in several spots: "In these early days, my VCR was the equivalent of light social drinking" (2); "I was now using the VCR on a regular basis — the equivalent of several stiff drinks a day" (3). Another place where Robert touches wittily on the analogy occurs in the middle of the fourth paragraph: "I went out and bought two six-packs of blank tapes" (4).

To meet the requirements of the assignment, Robert's major responsibility is to provide a *step-by-step* explanation of the process he has chosen to describe. And because he invented the term "videoholism," Robert likewise must invent the stages in the progression of the addiction. During his prewriting, Robert discovered five stages in his videoholism. These stages provide the organizing focus for his paper. Specifically, each supporting paragraph in the essay is devoted to one of the stages, with the *topic sentence* for each paragraph indicating the stage's distinctive characteristics: "In the first innocent stage, the unsuspecting person buys a VCR for occasional use" (2); "In the second phase on the road to videoholism, an individual uses the VCR more frequently and begins to stockpile tapes rather than watch them" (3); "In the third stage of videoholism, the amount of taping increases significantly, leading to an even more irrational stockpiling of cassettes" (4); "In the fourth stage, videoholism creeps into other parts of the addict's life, influencing behavior in strange ways" (5); and "In the final stage of any addiction, an individual either succumbs completely or is able to tear away from the habit" (6).

Although Robert's essay is playful, it is nonetheless a process analysis and so must have an organizational structure that is easy to follow. Keeping this in mind, Robert wisely includes *transitions* to signal what happened at each stage of his videoholism: "*Once* I had these additional tapes, I was free to record . . . "(3); "*Then*, in addition to my regulars, I began to tape . . . " (4); "*One day*, my mother came into my room . . . " (5); "*But after a while*, the urgent need . . . subsided" (6). In addition to such transitions, crisp questions are also used to move from idea to idea within a paragraph: "How did I resolve this dilemma? Very easily. I . . . bought several more cassettes" (3) and "Where did I get time to watch all these tapes? I didn't" (4). The conversational feel of these questions suits the entertaining tone of Robert's essay.

Robert generates lively details to illustrate the stages in his uncontrollable progression toward videoholism. You might have been amused, for instance, by the image of Robert's sneaking downstairs to tape shows during the night. Robert probably uses a bit of *dramatic license* when reporting some of these details, and we, as readers, understand that he is exaggerating for comic effect. Most likely he didn't break out in a cold sweat at the thought of the TV shows he was unable to tape, and he probably didn't hide his tapes in a suitcase. Nevertheless, this tinkering with the truth is legitimate because it allows Robert to create material that fits the essay's lightly satiric tone.

Even though Robert's specifics are — on the whole — vigorous and appropriate, he runs into a minor problem at the end of the fourth paragraph. Starting with the sentence "Reason and common sense were abandoned . . . ," he begins to ramble. These last two sentences fail to add anything substantial to what has already been said. Take a moment to read this paragraph aloud, omitting the last two sentences. Note how much sharper the new conclusion is: "Where did I get time to watch all these tapes? I didn't. Taping at this point was more satisfying than watching." This new ending says all that needs to be said in a punctuated, upbeat way.

When it was time to revise, Robert decided, in spite of his apprehension, to show his paper to his roommate, asking his roommate to read aloud to him what he had written. Robert knew this strategy would provide an objective perspective on his work. His roommate, at first an unwilling recruit, nonetheless laughed as he read the essay. That was just the response Robert wanted. But when his roommate got to the conclusion, Robert heard that the closing paragraph was flat and anticlimactic. Here is the original version of Robert's conclusion.

Unrevised Version

I have no illusions, though, that I am over my videoholism. Soon I will be returning home for the holidays, which can be a time for excess taping. All I can do is ask my little sister to hide my blank tapes. After that, I will hope for the best.

Robert and his roommate brainstormed ways to make the conclusion livelier and more consistent in spirit with the rest of the essay. They decided that the best approach would be to continue the playful, mock-serious tone that characterized earlier parts of the essay. Robert thus made three major changes. First, he tightened the first sentence of the paragraph ("I have no illusions, though, that I am over my videoholism"), making it crisper and more dramatic: "I have no illusions, though." Second, he added a few sentences to sustain the light, self-deprecating tone he had used earlier: "I know that once a videoholic, always a videoholic"; "But I will cope with the pressure"; "I will win the battle." Third, and perhaps most important, he returned to the alcoholism analogy: "I will take each day one at a time. . . . And if I feel myself succumbing to the temptations of taping, I will pick up the telephone and dial the videoholics' hotline. . . . "

These were not the only changes Robert made while reworking his paper, but they give you some sense of how sensitive he was to the effect he wanted to achieve. Certainly, the recasting of the conclusion was critical to the overall success of this amusing essay.

Process analysis is the heart of each of the following essays. In "How to Live to Be 200," Stephen Leacock gives some light-hearted instructions for those who believe exercise is the key to immortality. Sue Hubbell's "The Beekeeper," part narration and part description, centers on the surprising technique that bee-keepers use to develop resistance to bee venom. Jessica Mitford's "The American Way of Death" is a look at a process most of us will never perform but will, instead, have done *to* us. "How to Say Nothing in 500 Words," by Paul Roberts, shows students the way to write essays that will make their professors want to leave teaching. Finally, Peter McWilliams' "Selecting a Word Processing Computer" offers encouragement to would-be computer owners who are nervous about taking the plunge.

Stephen Leacock

Stephen Leacock (1869 – 1944) was born in Great Britain but spent most of his life in Canada. Educated at the University of Toronto, Leacock became a professor of economics at McGill University. In later life, he began to write humorous essays which brought him great popularity. Leacock's work was collected in such books as Literary Lapses *(1910) and* Winnowed Wisdom *(1926). The following essay is from* Literary Lapses.

How to Live to Be 200

Are you tired of being urged to exercise by talk show hosts and sleek TV celebrities? Are you annoyed by friends who brag about how often they work out or how many miles they run? Do you enjoy a good fast-food meal packed with preservatives, salt, and calories? If so, you have an ally in Stephen Leacock, who many years ago chided the Health Maniacs of his day. Health fanaticism, you see, is not new; there were health nuts even in the early 1900s. But as Leacock points out, they didn't live long enough to enjoy the current health craze.

Twenty years ago I knew a man called Jiggins, who had the 1 Health Habit.

He used to take a cold plunge every morning. He said it 2 opened his pores. After it he took a hot sponge. He said it closed the pores. He got so that he could open and shut his pores at will.

Jiggins used to stand and breathe at an open window for half 3 an hour before dressing. He said it expanded his lungs. He might, of course, have had it done in a shoe-store with a boot-stretcher, but after all it cost him nothing this way, and what is half an hour?

After he had got his undershirt on, Jiggins used to hitch him- 4 self up like a dog in harness and do Sandow exercises. He did them forwards, backwards, and hind-side up.

He could have got a job as a dog anywhere. He spent all his 5 time at this kind of thing. In his spare time at the office, he used to

247

lie on his stomach on the floor and see if he could lift himself up
with his knuckles. If he could, then he tried some other way until he
found one that he couldn't do. Then he would spend the rest of his
lunch hour on his stomach, perfectly happy.

In the evenings in his room he used to lift iron bars, cannon-   6
balls, heave dumb-bells, and haul himself up to the ceiling with his
teeth. You could hear the thumps half a mile.

He liked it.   7

He spent half the night slinging himself around his room. He   8
said it made his brain clear. When he got his brain perfectly clear, he
went to bed and slept. As soon as he woke, he began clearing it
again.

Jiggins is dead. He was, of course, a pioneer, but the fact that   9
he dumb-belled himself to death at an early age does not prevent a
whole generation of young men from following in his path.

They are ridden by the Health Mania.   10

They make themselves a nuisance.   11

They get up at impossible hours. They go out in silly little suits   12
and run Marathon heats before breakfast. They chase around bare-
foot to get the dew on their feet. They hunt for ozone. They bother
about pepsin. They won't eat meat because it has too much nitrogen. They won't eat fruit because it hasn't any. They prefer albumen and starch and nitrogen to huckleberry pie and doughnuts.
They won't drink water out of a tap. They won't eat sardines out of
a can. They won't use oysters out of a pail. They won't drink milk
out of a glass. They are afraid of alcohol in any shape. Yes, sir,
afraid. "Cowards."

And after all their fuss they presently incur some simple old-   13
fashioned illness and die like anybody else.

Now people of this sort have no chance to attain any great age.   14
They are on the wrong track.

Listen. Do you want to live to be really old, to enjoy a grand,   15
green, exuberant, boastful old age and to make yourself a nuisance
to your whole neighbourhood with your reminiscences?

Then cut out all this nonsense. Cut it out. Get up in the   16
morning at a sensible hour. The time to get up is when you have to,
not before. If your office opens at eleven, get up at ten-thirty. Take
your chance on ozone. There isn't any such thing anyway. Or, if
there is, you can buy a thermos bottle full for five cents, and put it
on a shelf in your cupboard. If your work begins at seven in the

morning, get up at ten minutes to, but don't be liar enough to say that you like it. It isn't exhilarating, and you know it.

Also, drop all that cold-bath nonsense. You never did it when   17
you were a boy. Don't be a fool now. If you must take a bath (you don't really need to), take it warm. The pleasure of getting out of a cold bed and creeping into a hot bath beats a cold plunge to death. In any case, stop gassing about your tub and your "shower," as if you were the only man who ever washed.

So much for that point.   18

Next, take the question of germs and bacilli. Don't be scared of   19
them. That's all. That's the whole thing, and if you once get on to that you never need to worry again.

If you see a bacilli, walk right up to it, and look it in the eye. If   20
one flies into your room, strike at it with your hat or with a towel. Hit it as hard as you can between the neck and the thorax. It will soon get sick of that.

But as a matter of fact, a bacilli is perfectly quiet and harmless   21
if you are not afraid of it. Speak to it. Call out to it to "lie down." It will understand. I had a bacilli once, called Fido, that would come and lie at my feet while I was working. I never knew a more affectionate companion, and when it was run over by an automobile, I buried it in the garden with genuine sorrow.

(I admit this is an exaggeration. I don't really remember its   22
name; it may have been Robert.)

Understand that it is only a fad of modern medicine to say that   23
cholera and typhoid and diphtheria are caused by bacilli and germs; nonsense. Cholera is caused by a frightful pain in the stomach, and diphtheria is caused by trying to cure a sore throat.

Now take the question of food.   24

Eat what you want. Eat lots of it. Yes, eat too much of it. Eat   25
till you can just stagger across the room with it and prop it up against a sofa cushion. Eat everything that you like until you can't eat any more. The only test is, can you pay for it? If you can't pay for it, don't eat it. And listen — don't worry as to whether your food contains starch, or albumen, or gluten, or nitrogen. If you are damn fool enough to want these things, go and buy them and eat all you want of them. Go to a laundry and get a bag of starch, and eat your fill of it. Eat it, and take a good long drink of glue after it, and a spoonful of Portland cement. That will gluten you, good and solid.

If you like nitrogen, go and get a druggist to give you a canful 26 of it at the soda counter, and let you sip it with a straw. Only don't think that you can mix all these things up with your food. There isn't any nitrogen or phosphorus or albumen in ordinary things to eat. In any decent household all that sort of stuff is washed out in the kitchen sink before the food is put on the table.

And just one word about fresh air and exercise. Don't bother 27 with either of them. Get your room full of good air, then shut up the windows and keep it. It will keep for years. Anyway, don't keep using your lungs all the time. Let them rest. As for exercise, if you have to take it, take it and put up with it. But as long as you have the price of a hack and can hire other people to play baseball for you and run races and do gymnastics when you sit in the shade and smoke and watch them — great heavens, what more do you want?

Questions for Close Reading

1. What is the thesis of the selection? Locate the sentence(s) in which Leacock states his main idea. If he does not state the thesis explicitly, express it in your own words.
2. What is the "Health Habit"? What does it include?
3. Why does Leacock call people who try to eat right "cowards"?
4. Instead of good health, what goals does the author imply should guide a person's daily behavior?
5. Refer to your dictionary as needed to define the following words used in the selection: *ozone* (paragraph 12), *pepsin* (12), and *cholera* (23).

Questions about the Writer's Craft

1. Why does Leacock use the imperative in the essay? What effect does this have on the tone of the piece?
2. What two processes does the author explain in this essay? How are these processes related?
3. Leacock uses exaggeration in the title of his essay. Where else does he use exaggeration? Why?
4. What are the characteristics of Leacock's typical sentences? Why does he use this sentence style? How does it add to the comedy of the essay?

Questions for Further Thought

1. What kind of person does Leacock reveal himself to be? How serious do you take his objections to health consciousness to be? Do you think he goes overboard into intolerance?

2. Leacock describes a health maniac as an obsessed person, How do people become obsessed? Are obsessions always bad?
3. We are presently in the midst of a health and fitness boom. To what extent has this trend affected our culture in general, and your life in particular?
4. Which is more important, to enjoy life's pleasures or to sacrifice some of them to keep physically fit? Are these two goals necessarily incompatible?

Writing Assignments Using Process Analysis as a Method of Development

1. Write a humorous essay showing how to conquer an addiction to some food, activity, or object that is not normally considered addictive. Since the paper is light in tone, you should choose a topic that can be discussed in a playful manner. You might find it helpful to look at the student essay on pages 240–243.
2. Imagine you are Jiggins, and that Leacock has just "passed on" as a result of his Unhealthy Habit. Write an essay similar to Leacock's, deploring the daily habits of people like Leacock. Describe as specifically as possible how such people live, generating lively details to support your point. Then explain the steps these people should follow if they want to be healthy and live to be 200.

Writing Assignments Using Other Methods of Development

3. Write an essay classifying people's attitudes toward food. In each section, use specific facts and examples to convey how people in each category shop, cook, eat, and talk or think about food. You might choose such types as junk-food addicts, vegetarians, food snobs, health-food fanatics, "chocoholics," finicky eaters, compulsive eaters or dieters, and so on. To make the essay more than a random collection of categories, you should provide a unifying point for your analysis.
4. Leacock presents Jiggins, the health nut, as motivated by a concern for his health. However, in your experience, do people often have other, perhaps less legitimate motives for going to the gym or running? Write an essay about the "real" reasons why people try to keep fit. Provide specific examples of people you know to illustrate each reason you discuss.

Sue Hubbell

Sue Hubbell keeps bees on her ninety-acre farm in Missouri. Born and raised in Kalamazoo, Michigan, she holds a journalism degree from the University of Southern California and a library science degree from Drexel University in Philadelphia. Hubbell's freelance writing has appeared in such publications as Time, Sports Illustrated, Country Journal, *and* Harper's. *Her latest work is entitled* A Country Year: Living the Question *(1986). The following selection first appeared as one of the "Hers" columns in* The New York Times.

The Beekeeper

One of nature's miracles is the ability of bees to transform the nectar of flowers into honey. In the following essay, Sue Hubbell describes the removal of honey from the hives so it can be processed. Accomplishing this task means confronting thousands of angry bees. So Hubbell and her co-workers follow a series of unusual steps to protect themselves against the inevitable stings that await them. The interesting process described by Hubbell implies something important about humans' tolerance of stressful situations.

For the past week I've been spending my afternoons out in the honey house getting things ready for the harvest. I'm making sure the screens are all tight because once I get started clouds of bees will surround the place and try to get in, lured by the scent of honey. I've been checking the machinery, repairing what isn't running properly, and I've been scrubbing everything down so that the health inspector will be proud.

My honey house contains a shiny array of stainless-steel tanks, a power uncapper for slicing honeycomb open, an extractor for spinning the honey out of the comb and a pump to move it— machinery that whirs, whomps, hums and looks very special. My neighbors call it the honey factory, and I'm not above insinuating slyly that what I'm really running back here in the woods is a still.

The bees have been working since early spring, gathering nec- 3 tar, first from wild plum, peach, and cherry blossoms, later from blackberries, sweet clover, water willow and other wildflowers as they bloomed. As they have gathered it, their enzymes have changed the complex plant sugars in the nectar to the simple ones of honey. In the hive young bees have formed into work crews to fan the droplets of nectar with their wings, evaporating its water until it is thick and heavy. Summertime heat has helped them, and now the honey is ripe and finished. The bees have capped over each cell of honeycomb with snowy white wax from their bodies, so the honey is ready for my harvest.

The honey that I take from the bees is the extra that they will 4 not need for the winter; they store it above their hives in wooden boxes called supers. When I take it from them I stand behind the hives with a gasoline-powered machine called a bee blower and blow the bees out of the supers while the strong young men that I hire to help me carry the supers, weighing 60 pounds each, and stack them on pallets in the truck. There may be 30 to 50 supers in every one of my bee yards, and we have about half an hour to get them off the hives and stacked before the bees realize what we are up to and begin getting cross about it.

The time to harvest honey is summer's end, when it is hot. The 5 temper of the bees requires that we wear protective clothing: a full set of coveralls, a zippered bee veil and leather gloves. Even a very strong young man works up a sweat wrapped in a bee suit in the heat, hustling 60-pound supers while being harassed by angry bees. It is a hard job, harder even than haying, but jobs are scarce here and I've always been able to hire help.

This year David, the son of friends of mine, is working for me. 6 He is big and strong and used to labor, but he was nervous about bees. After we had made the job arrangement I set about desensitizing him to bee stings. I put a piece of ice on his arm to numb it and then, holding a bee carefully by its head, I put it on the numbed spot and let it sting him. A bee stinger is barbed and stays in the flesh, pulling loose from the body of the bee as it struggles to free itself. The bulbous poison sac at the top of the stinger continues to pulsate after the bee has left, pumping the venom and forcing the stinger deeper into the flesh.

That first day I wanted David to have only a partial dose of venom, so after a minute I scraped the stinger out. A few people are seriously sensitive to bee venom; each sting they receive can cause a more severe reaction than the one before — reactions ranging from hives, breathing difficulties, accelerated heart beat and choking to anaphylactic shock and death. I didn't think David would be allergic in that way, but I wanted to make sure. 7

We sat down and had a cup of coffee and I watched him. The spot where the stinger went in grew red and began to swell. That was a normal reaction, and so was the itching that he felt later on. 8

The next day I coaxed a bee into stinging him again, repeating the procedure, but I left the stinger in place for 10 minutes, until the venom sac was empty. Again the spot was red, swollen and itchy but had disappeared in 24 hours. By that time David was ready to catch a bee himself and administer his own sting. He also decided that the ice cube was a bother and gave it up. I told him to keep to one sting a day until he had no redness or swelling and then to increase to two stings. He was ready for them the next day. The greater amount of venom caused redness and swelling for a few days, but soon his body could tolerate it without reaction and he increased the number of stings once again. 9

Today he told me he was up to six stings. His arms look as though they have track marks on them, but the fresh stings are having little effect. I'll keep him at it until he can tolerate 10 a day with no reaction and then I'll not worry about taking him out to the bee yard. 10

I know what will happen to him there. For the first few days his movements will be nervous and quick and he will be stung without mercy. After that he will relax and the bees, in turn, will calm down. 11

The reason I am hiring David this year is that a young man I have used in the past has moved away. We worked well together and he liked bees though even he was stung royally at first. I admired his courage the first day we were out together, for he stood holding a super from which I was blowing bees while his arm was fast turning into a pin cushion from stings. 12

When we carried the stacked supers to the honey house's load- 13
ing dock, he would scorn the hot bee veil as he wheeled the supers
on the handtruck despite the cross bees flying around the dock.
One time, as I opened the door for him to bring in the load, I
noticed that his face was contorted in what I took to be the effort of
getting the handtruck down the ramp. We quickly wheeled the load
of supers up to the scale, where we weigh each load. He was going
too fast, so that when he stopped at the scale he fell backward and
350 pounds of supers dropped on him. Pinned down, he loyally
balanced himself on one fist so that he didn't harm the honey pump
against which he had fallen. The reason for his knotted face and his
speed was obvious for the first time: He was being stung on the
forehead by three bees.

Good boss that I am, I did not choose that moment to go to 14
the cabin and make myself a cup of coffee; I picked the supers off his
chest, scraped off the stingers and helped him to his feet. It became
one of our shared legends of working together. This year I miss
him.

Now it is David, still shy about working for a friend of his 15
parents, still a little nervous about bees. He is 19 and eager to
please. But he is going to be fine. In a month we will have finished
and he will be easy and relaxed, and he and I will have our own set of
shared legends.

Questions for Close Reading

1. What is the thesis of the selection? Locate the sentence(s) in which
   Hubbell states her main idea. If she does not state the thesis explicitly,
   express it in your own words.
2. Why does the author hire David to harvest the honey? What qualities
   does David have that make him a good choice?
3. What is desensitization? What role does it play in the honey harvesting
   process?
4. What are the supers, and what role do they play in the harvesting
   process? How do the bees use them? How do the people use them?
5. Refer to your dictionary as needed to define the following words used
   in the selection: *enzymes* (paragraph 3), *desensitize* (6), *bulbous* (6),
   pulsate (6), and *anaphylactic* (7).

Questions about the Writer's Craft

1. How many steps are there in the process of making and gathering honey? Does Hubbell provide sufficient detail for you to understand this process?
2. What technical terms of the honey-making trade does the author take time to define? Where in the essay does she provide her definitions? What technical terms does she leave undefined? Why?
3. Where does Hubbell break out of the chronological process description? Why does she include this material in the essay? What does it add?
4. What is the author's attitude toward the subject of the essay? Is the job of harvesting just another job, just in the day's work, or is it something more? Find places where this attitude is revealed.

Questions for Further Thought

1. Hubbell says that she has little trouble finding helpers because "jobs are scarce around here." Would you have to be desperate for a job to become a beekeeper's assistant? What other satisfactions might this job offer?
2. Is Hubbell a good boss? How would you describe her treatment of her employees?
3. Would you deliberately allow yourself to be stung by bees so you could work on a bee farm? Can you think of other jobs that require desensitization to pain? What are some of them? What kinds of pain are involved?
4. Is becoming "hardened" to physical or mental pain a good thing? A necessary thing?

Writing Assignments Using Process Analysis as a Method of Development

1. Write an essay describing a process that you know well, but that most people would consider unusual. You may have learned the process in school, on a job, from a relative or friend, or on your own. As Hubbell does, explain the steps clearly enough that a wide audience of people could understand the sequence. Make sure you define any special terms. Possible subjects could be milking a cow, moving a piano, carving a decoy, making pretzels from scratch, or the like.
2. Many jobs require becoming hardened to pain or discomfort. House-painters must work with their arms held up, waiters and waitresses feel pain from being on their feet all day, journalists have to become toughened to interview victims and survivors. Write an essay about an experience you have had which desensitized you to physical pain or

discomfort, or to mental pain or fear. Describe the process of becoming used to the pain and growing able to perform the task or job without being unduly distressed.

Writing Assignments Using Other Methods of Development

3. Hubbell clearly finds pleasure and satisfaction in her work. Write an essay exploring the three most important satisfactions you hope for in your future career. Be specific about what you want and why you want it. As part of the paper, explain how you became interested in this kind of work.

4. Hubbell's essay concludes with a "shared legend" — a story of a crisis in which the author and her employee helped each other, survived, and became closer. Write a narrative about an experience that became the basis for a shared legend between you and someone else. Explore what it was about the event that made it legendary, showing how your bond with the other person changed or deepened as a result of the experience.

Jessica Mitford

English-born Jessica Mitford came to the United States in 1939 at the age of twenty-one and received her American citizenship during the war. Mitford worked as a bartender and salesperson before becoming an investigator for the Office of Price Administration in Washington. She did not begin her writing career until the age of thirty-eight. Her books include an autobiography, Daughters and Rebels *(1960), and* Kind and Unusual Punishment *(1974), which is a critique of the American penal system. The following selection is from the book that gave Mitford a national reputation as an investigative writer,* The American Way of Death *(1963). A scathing attack on the American funeral industry, this book shocked readers and enraged morticians.*

The American Way of Death

If you were in charge of the funeral arrangements for a loved one, would you ask to have that person's lips sewed, eyes glued, blood drained, and face painted? If you answered "No," you probably don't know much about the world of mortuary science. In this world, the appearance of death is to be avoided, and the goal is to make people look as if they are asleep. In the following selection, Jessica Mitford parts the "formaldehyde curtain" to reveal our funeral practices. Such practices, she implies, reflect our deep-seated fear of death.

Embalming is indeed a most extraordinary procedure, and one 1 must wonder at the docility of Americans who each year pay hundreds of millions of dollars for its perpetuation, blissfully ignorant of what it is all about, what is done, how it is done. Not one in ten thousand has any idea of what actually takes place. Books on the subject are extremely hard to come by. They are not to be found in most libraries or bookshops.

In an era when huge television audiences watch surgical oper- 2 ations in the comfort of their living rooms, when, thanks to the animated cartoon, the geography of the digestive system has become familiar territory even to the nursery school set, in a land where the satisfaction of curiosity about almost all matters is a national pastime, the secrecy surrounding embalming can, surely, hardly be attributed to the inherent gruesomeness of the subject. Custom in this regard has within this century suffered a complete reversal. In the early days of American embalming, when it was performed in the home of the deceased, it was almost mandatory for some relative to stay by the embalmer's side and witness the procedure. Today, family members who might wish to be in attendance would certainly be dissuaded by the funeral director. All others, except apprentices, are excluded by law from the preparation room.

A close look at what does actually take place may explain in 3 large measure the undertaker's intractable reticence concerning a procedure that has become his major *raison d'être*. Is it possible he fears that public information about embalming might lead patrons to wonder if they really want this service? If the funeral men are loath to discuss the subject outside the trade, the reader may, understandably, be equally loath to go on reading at this point. For those who have the stomach for it, let us part the formaldehyde curtain . . .

The body is first laid out in the undertaker's morgue — or 4 rather, Mr. Jones is reposing in the preparation room — to be readied to bid the world farewell.

The preparation room in any of the better funeral establish- 5 ments has the tiled and sterile look of a surgery, and indeed the embalmer – restorative artist who does his chores there is beginning to adopt the term "dermasurgeon" (appropriately corrupted by some mortician-writers as "demisurgeon") to describe his calling. His equipment, consisting of scalpels, scissors, augers, forceps, clamps, needles, pumps, tubes, bowls and basins, is crudely imitative of the surgeon's, as is his technique, acquired in a nine- or twelve-month post-high-school course in an embalming school. He is supplied by an advanced chemical industry with a bewildering array of fluids, sprays, pastes, oils, powders, creams, to fix or soften tissue, shrink or distend it as needed, dry it here, restore the moisture there. There are cosmetics, waxes and paints to fill and cover features, even plaster of Paris to replace entire limbs. There are ingenious aids to prop and stabilize the cadaver: a Vari-Pose

Head Rest, the Edwards Arm and Hand Positioner, the Repose Block (to support the shoulders during the embalming), and the Throop Foot Positioner, which resembles an old-fashioned stocks.

Mr. John H. Eckels, president of the Eckels College of Mortu- 6
ary Science, thus describes the first part of the embalming procedure: "In the hands of a skilled practitioner, this work may be done
in a comparatively short time and without mutilating the body
other than by slight incision — so slight that it scarcely would cause
serious inconvenience if made upon a living person. It is necessary
to remove the blood, and doing this not only helps in the disinfect-
ing, but removes the principal cause of disfigurements due to discoloration."

Another textbook discusses the all-important time element: 7
"The earlier this is done, the better, for every hour that elapses
between death and embalming will add to the problems and complications encountered. . . . " Just how soon should one get
going on the embalming? The author tells us, "On the basis of such
scanty information made available to this profession through its
rudimentary and haphazard system of technical research, we must
conclude that the best results are to be obtained if the subject is
embalmed before life is completely extinct — that is, before cellular
death has occurred. In the average case, this would mean within an
hour after somatic death." For those who feel that there is something a little rudimentary, not to say haphazard, about this advice, a
comforting thought is offered by another writer. Speaking of fears
entertained in early days of premature burial, he points out, "One
of the effects of embalming by chemical injection, however, has
been to dispel fears of live burial." How true; once the blood is
removed, chances of live burial are indeed remote.

To return to Mr. Jones, the blood is drained out through the 8
veins and replaced by embalming fluid pumped in through the
arteries. As noted in *The Principles and Practices of Embalming*,
"every operator has a favorite injection and drainage point — a fact
which becomes a handicap only if he fails or refuses to forsake his
favorites when conditions demand it." Typical favorites are the
carotid artery, femoral artery, jugular vein, subclavian vein. There
are various choices of embalming fluid. If Flextone is used, it will
produce a "mild, flexible rigidity. The skin retains a velvety soft-
ness, the tissues are rubbery and pliable. Ideal for women and

children." It may be blended with B. and G. Products Company's Lyf-Lyk tint, which is guaranteed to reproduce "nature's own skin texture . . . the velvety appearance of living tissue." Suntone comes in three separate tints: Suntan; Special Cosmetic Tint, a pink shade "especially indicated for young female subjects"; and Regular Cosmetic Tint, moderately pink.

About three to six gallons of a dyed and perfumed solution of   9
formaldehyde, glycerin, borax, phenol, alcohol, and water is soon circulating through Mr. Jones, whose mouth has been sewn together with a "needle directed upward between the upper lip and gum and brought out through the left nostril," with the corners raised slightly "for a more pleasant expression." If he should be bucktoothed, his teeth are cleaned with Bon Ami and coated with colorless nail polish. His eyes, meanwhile, are closed with flesh-tinted eye caps and eye cement.

The next step is to have at Mr Jones with a thing called a trocar.   10
This is a long, hollow needle attached to a tube. It is jabbed into the abdomen, poked around the entrails and chest cavity, the contents of which are pumped out and replaced with "cavity fluid." This done, and the hole in the abdomen sewn up, Mr. Jones's face is heavily creamed (to protect the skin from burns which may be caused by leakage of the chemicals), and he is covered with a sheet and left unmolested for a while. But not for long — there is more, much more, in store for him. He has been embalmed, but not yet restored, and the best time to start the restorative work is eight to ten hours after embalming, when the tissues have become firm and dry.

The object of all this attention to the corpse, it must be re-   11
membered, is to make it presentable for viewing in an attitude of healthy repose. "Our customs require the presentation of our dead in the semblance of normality . . . unmarred by the ravages of illness, disease or mutilation," says Mr. J. Sheridan Mayer in his *Restorative Art*. This is rather a large order since few people die in the full bloom of health, unravaged by illness and unmarked by some disfigurement. The funeral industry is equal to the challenge: "In some cases the gruesome appearance of a mutilated or disease-ridden subject may be quite discouraging. The task of restoration may seem impossible and shake the confidence of the embalmer. This is the time for intestinal fortitude and determination. Once

the formative work is begun and affected tissues are cleaned or removed, all doubts of success vanish. It is surprising and gratifying to discover the results which may be obtained."

The embalmer, having allowed an appropriate interval to   12
elapse, returns to the attack, but now he brings into play the skill and equipment of sculptor and cosmetician. Is a hand missing? Casting one in plaster of Paris is a simple matter. "For replacement purposes, only a cast of the back of the hand is necessary; this is within the ability of the average operator and is quite adequate." If a lip or two, a nose or an ear should be missing, the embalmer has at hand a variety of restorative waxes with which to model replacements. Pores and skin texture are simulated by stippling with a little brush, and over this cosmetics are laid on. Head off? Decapitation cases are rather routinely handled. Ragged edges are trimmed, and head joined to torso with a series of splints, wires and sutures. It is a good idea to have a little something at the neck — a scarf or high collar — when time for viewing comes. Swollen mouth? Cut out tissue as needed from inside the lips. If too much is removed, the surface contour can easily be restored by padding with cotton. Swollen necks and cheeks are reduced by removing tissue through vertical incisions made down each side of the neck. "When the deceased is casketed, the pillow will hide the suture incisions . . . as an extra precaution against leakage, the suture may be painted with liquid sealer."

The opposite condition is more likely to present itself — that   13
of emaciation. His hypodermic syringe now loaded with massage cream, the embalmer seeks out and fills the hollowed and sunken areas by injection. In this procedure the backs of the hands and fingers and the under-chin area should not be neglected.

Positioning the lips is a problem that recurrently challenges   14
the ingenuity of the embalmer. Closed too tightly they tend to give a stern, even disapproving expression. Ideally, embalmers feel, the lips should give the impression of being ever so slightly parted, the upper lip protruding slightly for a more youthful appearance. This takes some engineering, however, as the lips tend to drift apart. Lip drift can sometimes be remedied by pushing one or two straight pins through the inner margin of the lower lip and then inserting them between the two front upper teeth. If Mr. Jones happens to have no teeth, the pins can just as easily be anchored in his Arm-

strong Face Former and Denture Replacer. Another method to maintain lip closure is to dislocate the lower jaw, which is then held in its new position by a wire run through holes which have been drilled through the upper and lower jaws at the midline. As the French are fond of saying, *il faut souffrir pour être belle*.

If Mr. Jones has died of jaundice, the embalming fluid will very   15
likely turn him green. Does this deter the embalmer? Not if he has intestinal fortitude. Masking pastes and cosmetics are heavily laid on, burial garments and casket interiors are color-correlated with particular care, and Jones is displayed beneath rose-colored lights. Friends will say, "How *well* he looks." Death by carbon monoxide, on the other hand, can be rather a good thing from the embalmer's viewpoint: "One advantage is the fact that this type of discolor-ation is an exaggerated form of a natural pink coloration." This is nice because the healthy glow is already present and needs but little attention.

The patching and filling completed, Mr. Jones is now shaved,   16
washed and dressed. Cream-based cosmetic, available in pink, flesh, suntan, brunette, and blond, is applied to his hands and face, his hair is shampooed and combed (and, in the case of Mrs. Jones, set), his hands manicured. For the horny-handed son of toil special care must be taken; cream should be applied to remove ingrained grime, and the nails cleaned. "If he were not in the habit of having them manicured in life, trimming and shaping is advised for better appearance — never questioned by kin."

Jones is now ready for casketing (this is the present participle   17
of the verb "to casket"). In this operation his right shoulder should be depressed slightly "to turn the body a bit to the right and soften the appearance of lying flat on the back," Positioning the hands is a matter of importance, and special rubber positioning blocks may be used. The hands should be cupped slightly for a more lifelike, relaxed appearance. Proper placement of the body requires a deli-cate sense of balance. It should lie as high as possible in the casket, yet not so high that the lid, when lowered, will hit the nose. On the other hand, we are cautioned, placing the body too low "creates the impression that the body is in a box."

Jones is next wheeled into the appointed slumber room where   18
a few last touches may be added — his favorite pipe placed in his hand or, if he was a great reader, a book propped into position. (In

the case of little Master Jones a Teddy bear may be clutched.) Here he will hold open house for a few days, visiting hours 10 A.M. to 9 P.M.

Questions for Close Reading

1. What is the thesis of the selection? Locate the sentence(s) in which Mitford states her main idea. If she does not state the thesis explicitly, express it in your own words.
2. Why, according to Mitford, do Americans know so little about the embalming process?
3. Mitford quotes from a textbook on embalming practices (paragraph 11). What does the passage reveal about the goals of mortuary science?
4. In what ways is the body made to look even better than it did when alive?
5. Refer to your dictionary as needed to define the following words used in the selection: *docility* (paragraph 1), *intractable* (3), *reticence* (3), *augers* (5), *distend* (5), *stippling* (12), and *jaundice* (15).

Questions about the Writer's Craft

1. What are the main stages of the mortician's craft? What happens in each step? What words and phrases does Mitford use to indicate she is moving from one step to the next?
2. Why does Mitford refer to the body being embalmed as Mr. Jones? What effect does this naming have on the reader?
3. Mitford interweaves her description of the embalming and restoring process with many quotations from mortuary science texts. Why does she do this? What do you notice about the writing style of the authors of these texts?
4. What is Mitford's tone in this essay? Do you feel she is being objective in her description of the funeral industry? Why or why not?

Questions for Further Thought

1. Does embalming strike you as a worthwhile process now that you know more about it? Do you feel it is the proper way to treat the dead?
2. One embalmers' manual states that cleaning and trimming the nails of a working man is "never questioned by kin." Are kin prevented from questioning embalmers' techniques? Do you think the funeral industry

as a whole takes advantage of grief and disorientation to sell its products?

3. Mitford describes a method of preparation for burial that is undignified and, at times, ludicrous. How does this practice help confirm the statement that funerals are for the living, not for the dead? What kinds of final rites would show more respect for the dead—and for the process of dying?

4. Once, Mitford says, relatives prepared a body for burial, and death was thus blended into ordinary life. Today, the process of burial is given over to specialists. Do you think this change has harmed the survivors? Have any other natural aspects of life been turned over to "specialists" and thus separated from daily life?

Writing Assignments Using Process Analysis as a Method of Development

1. Write a paper telling your survivors how you wish to be treated after death. Explain how they should conduct your funeral, whether they should embalm you, where they should put your remains and what you would like said in your eulogy. Be as specific as possible as you outline the steps to be taken.

2. Many important events or changes in our lives are marked by celebrations or rituals. Often, the basic outlines of these rituals are established by tradition, but we can personalize these traditions by making some changes or additions to fit our special occasion. Select an important change or event that you will celebrate in the future. Explain how you would like to experience the event. Your choice could include any of the following: your marriage, the birth of a child, your graduation, your parent's retirement, or some other notable time.

Writing Assignments Using Other Methods of Development

3. Write an essay describing a funeral or viewing which you have attended. Focus on what seems to you the most important scene. Your thesis should express a dominant feeling about the scene: depression, grief, discomfort, fear, disbelief, anger, or some other emotion. Alternatively, write a similar essay about any other ceremony or ritual you have experienced (for example, a wedding, bar/bat mitzvah, or graduation). Your dominant feeling may be positive or negative.

4. Write an essay showing that Americans often pretend that death does not exist or is not really happening. Give examples drawn from your

own life, your family's, or from public events. You might consider such typical situations as the following: the expressions we use with children ("Grandpa's gone away"; "Kitty is sleeping"); the euphemistic language we have for death ("passed away"; "no longer with us"); our obsession with looking young and keeping fit; our beliefs about "eternal life"; people's resistance to making a will; our refusal to discuss the implications of aging, even with close relatives.

Paul Roberts

*Paul Roberts (1917–1967) was a scholar of linguistics and
a respected teacher whose textbooks helped scores of high school
and college students become better writers. Roberts' works
include* English Syntax *(1954) and* Patterns of English
*(1956). The following selection is from his most well-known
book,* Understanding English *(1958).*

How to Say Nothing
in 500 Words

*Student essays are written on the bus, in the cafeteria, during
television shows, and after midnight. Not surprisingly, many
are uninspired last-ditch attempts to fulfill an assignment.
Paul Roberts, who spent many bleary-eyed hours reading such
papers, has great fun presenting a typical freshman essay for
analysis. He then provides students with lively and helpful
advice on ways to write essays that are worth something.*

Nothing About Something

It's Friday afternoon, and you have almost survived another   1
week of classes. You are just looking forward dreamily to the week
end when the English instructor says: "For Monday you will turn
in a five-hundred word composition on college football."

Well, that puts a good big hole in the week end. You don't have   2
any strong views on college football one way or the other. You get
rather excited during the season and go to all the home games and
find it rather more fun than not. On the other hand, the class has
been reading Robert Hutchins in the anthology and perhaps
Shaw's "Eighty-Yard Run," and from the class discussion you have
got the idea that the instructor thinks college football is for the
birds. You are no fool, you. You can figure out what side to take.

After dinner you get out the portable typewriter that you got   3
for high school graduation. You might as well get it over with and

267

enjoy Saturday and Sunday. Five hundred words is about two dou-
ble-spaced pages with normal margins. You put in a sheet of paper,
think up a title, and you're off:

Why College Football Should Be Abolished

College football should be abolished because it's bad   4
for the school and also bad for the players. The players are
so busy practicing that they don't have any time for their
studies.

This, you feel, is a mighty good start. The only trouble is that   5
it's only thirty-two words. You still have four hundred and sixty-
eight to go, and you've pretty well exhausted the subject. It comes
to you that you do your best thinking in the morning, so you put
away the typewriter and go to the movies. But the next morning
you have to do your washing and some math problems, and in the
afternoon you go to the game. The English instructor turns up too,
and you wonder if you've taken the right side after all. Saturday
night you have a date, and Sunday morning you have to go to
church. (You shouldn't let English assignments interfere with your
religion.) What with one thing and another, it's ten o'clock Sunday
night before you get out the typewriter again. You make a pot of
coffee and start to fill out your views on college football. Put a little
meat on the bones.

Why College Football Should be Abolished

In my opinion, it seems to me that college football   6
should be abolished. The reason why I think this to be true
is because I feel that football is bad for the colleges in
nearly every respect. As Robert Hutchins says in his article
in our anthology in which he discusses college football, it
would be better if the colleges had race horses and had
races with one another, because then the horses would not
have to attend classes. I firmly agree with Mr. Hutchins
on this point, and I am sure that many other students
would agree too.

One reason why it seems to me that college football is   7
bad is that it has become too commercial. In the olden

times when people played football just for the fun of it, maybe college football was all right, but they do not play football just for the fun of it now as they used to in the old days. Nowadays college football is what you might call a big business. Maybe this is not true at all schools, and I don't think it is especially true here at State, but certainly this is the case at most colleges and universities in America nowadays, as Mr. Hutchins points out in his very interesting article. Actually the coaches and alumni go around to the high schools and offer the high school stars large salaries to come to their colleges and play football for them. There was one case where a high school star was offered a convertible if he would play football for a certain college.

Another reason for abolishing college football is that   8
it is bad for the players. They do not have time to get a college education, because they are so busy playing football. A football player has to practice every afternoon from three to six, and then he is so tired that he can't concentrate on his studies. He just feels like dropping off to sleep after dinner, and then the next day he goes to his classes without having studied and maybe he fails the test.

(Good ripe stuff so far, but you're still a hundred and fifty-one words from home. One more push.)

Also I think college football is bad for the colleges   9
and the universities because not very many students get to participate in it. Out of a college of ten thousand students only seventy-five or a hundred play football, if that many. Football is what you might call a spectator sport. That means that most people go to watch it but do not play it themselves.

(Four hundred and fifteen. Well, you still have the conclusion, and when you retype it, you can make the margins a little wider.)

These are the reasons why I agree with Mr. Hutchins   10
that college football should be abolished in American colleges and universities.

On Monday you turn it in, moderately hopeful, and on Friday   11
it comes back marked "weak in content" and sporting a big "D."

This essay is exaggerated a little, not much. The English in-   12
structor will recognize it as reasonably typical of what an assignment on college football will bring in. He knows that nearly half of
the class will contrive in five hundred words to say that college
football is too commercial and bad for the players. Most of the
other half will inform him that college football builds character
and prepares one for life and brings prestige to the school. As he
reads paper after paper all saying the same thing in almost the same
words, all bloodless, five hundred words dripping out of nothing,
he wonders how he allowed himself to get trapped into teaching
English when he might have had a happy and interesting life as an
electrician or a confidence man.

Well, you may ask, what can you do about it? The subject is   13
one on which you have few convictions and little information. Can
you be expected to make a dull subject interesting? As a matter of
fact, this is precisely what you are expected to do. This is the writer's
essential task. All subjects, except sex, are dull until somebody
makes them interesting. The writer's job is to find the argument,
the approach, the angle, the wording that will take the reader with
him. This is seldom easy, and it is particularly hard in subjects that
have been much discussed: College Football, Fraternities, Popular
Music, Is Chivalry Dead?, and the like. You will feel that there is
nothing you can do with such subjects except repeat the old bromides. But there are some things you can do which will make your
papers, if not throbbingly alive, at least less insufferably tedious
than they might otherwise be.

Avoid the Obvious Content

Say the assignment is college football. Say that you've decided   14
to be against it. Begin by putting down the arguments that come to
your mind: it is too commercial, it takes the students' minds off
their studies, it is hard on the players, it makes the university a kind
of circus instead of an intellectual center, for most schools it is
financially ruinous. Can you think of any more arguments just off
hand? All right. Now when you write your paper, *make sure that you
don't use any of the material on this list.* If these are the points that
leap to your mind, they will leap to everyone else's too, and

whether you get a "C" or a "D" may depend on whether the instructor reads your paper early when he is fresh and tolerant or late, when the sentence "In my opinion, college football has become too commercial," inexorably repeated, has brought him to the brink of lunacy.

Be against college football for some reason or reasons of your own. If they are keen and perceptive ones, that's splendid. But even if they are trivial or foolish or indefensible, you are still ahead so long as they are not everybody else's reasons too. Be against it because the colleges don't spend enough money on it to make it worth while, because it is bad for the characters of the spectators, because the players are forced to attend classes, because the football stars hog all the beautiful women, because it competes with baseball and is therefore un-American and possibly Communist inspired. There are lots of more or less unused reasons for being against college football.   15

Sometimes it is a good idea to sum up and dispose of the trite and conventional points before going on to your own. This has the advantage of indicating to the reader that you are going to be neither trite nor conventional. Something like this: 16

> We are often told that college football should be abolished because it has become too commercial or because it is bad for the players. These arguments are no doubt very cogent, but they don't really go to the heart of the matter.   17

Then you go to the heart of the matter.

Take the Less Usual Side

One rather simple way of getting interest into your paper is to take the side of the argument that most of the citizens will want to avoid. If the assignment is an essay on dogs, you can, if you choose, explain that dogs are faithful and lovable companions, intelligent, useful as guardians of the house and protectors of children, indispensable in police work—in short, when all is said and done, man's best friends. Or you can suggest that those big brown eyes conceal, more often than not, a vacuity of mind and an inconstancy of purpose; that the dogs you have known most intimately have   18 been mangy, ill-tempered brutes, incapable of instruction; and that only your nobility of mind and fear of arrest prevent you from kicking the flea-ridden animals when you pass them on the street.

Naturally, personal convictions will sometimes dictate your approach. If the assigned subject is "Is Methodism Rewarding to the Individual?" and you are a pious Methodist, you have really no choice. But few assigned subjects, if any, will fall in this category. Most of them will lie in broad areas of discussion with much to be said on both sides. They are intellectual exercises and it is legitimate to argue now one way and now another, as debaters do in similar circumstances. Always take the side that looks to you hardest, least defensible. It will almost always turn out to be easier to write interestingly on that side.   19

This general advice applies where you have a choice of subjects. If you are to choose among "The Value of Fraternities" and "My Favorite High School Teacher" and "What I Think About Beetles," by all means plump for the beetles. By the time the instructor gets to your paper, he will be up to his ears in tedious tales about the French teacher at Bloombury High and assertions about how fraternities build character and prepare one for life. Your views on beetles, whatever they are, are bound to be a refreshing change.   20

Don't worry too much about figuring out what the instructor thinks about the subject so that you can cuddle up with him. Chances are his views are no stronger than yours. If he does have convictions and you oppose them, his problem is to keep from grading you higher than you deserve in order to show he is not biased. This doesn't mean that you should always cantankerously dissent from what the instructor says; that gets tiresome too. And if the subject assigned is "My Pet Peeve," do not begin, "My pet peeve is the English instructor who assigns papers on 'my pet peeve.'" This was still funny during the War of 1812, but it has sort of lost its edge since then. It is in general good manners to avoid personalities.   21

Slip Out of Abstraction

If you will study the essay on college football . . . you will perceive that one reason for its appalling dullness is that it never gets down to particulars. It is just a series of not very glittering generalities: "football is bad for the colleges," "it has become too   22 commercial," "football is a big business," "it is bad for the players," and so on. Such round phrases thudding against the reader's brain are unlikely to convince him, though they may well render him unconscious.

If you want the reader to believe that college football is bad for 23 the players, you have to do more than say so. You have to display the evil. Take your roommate, Alfred Simkins, the second-string center. Picture poor old Alfy coming home from football practice every evening, bruised and aching, agonizingly tired, scarcely able to shovel the mashed potatoes into his mouth. Let us se him staggering up to the room, getting out his econ textbook, peering desperately at it with his good eye, falling asleep and failing the test in the morning. Let us share his unbearable tension as Saturday draws near. Will he fail, be demoted, lose his monthly allowance, be forced to return to the coal mines? And if he succeeds, what will be his reward? Perhaps a slight ripple of applause when the third-string center replaces him, a moment of elation in the locker room if the team wins, of despair if it loses. What will he look back on when he graduates from college? Toil and torn ligaments. And what will be his future? He is not good enough for pro football, and he is too obscure and weak in econ to succeed in stocks and bonds. College football is tearing the heart from Alfy Simkins and, when it finishes with him, will callously toss aside the shattered hulk.

This is no doubt a weak enough argument for the abolition of 24 college football, but it is a sight better than saying, in three or four variations, that college football (in your opinion) is bad for the players.

Look at the work of any professional writer and notice how 25 constantly he is moving from the generality, the abstract statement, to the concrete example, the facts and figures, the illustration. If he is writing on juvenile delinquency, he does not just tell you that juveniles are (it seems to him) delinquent and that (in his opinion) something should be done about it. He shows you juveniles being delinquent, tearing up movie theatres in Buffalo, stabbing high school principals in Dallas, smoking marijuana in Palo Alto. And more than likely he is moving toward some specific remedy, not just a general wringing of the hands.

It is no doubt possible to be *too* concrete, too illustrative or 26 anecdotal, but few inexperienced writers err this way. For most the soundest advice is to be seeking always for the picture, to be always

turning general remarks into seeable examples. Don't say, "Sororities teach girls the social graces." Say "Sorority life teaches a girl
how to carry on a conversation while pouring tea, without sloshing
the tea into the saucer." Don't say, "I like certain kinds of popular
music very much." Say, "Whenever I hear Gerber Spinklittle play
'Mississippi Man' on the trombone, my socks creep up my ankles."

Get Rid of Obvious Padding

The student toiling away at his weekly English theme is too   27
often tormented by a figure: five hundred words. How, he asks
himself, is he to achieve this staggering total? Obviously by never
using one word when he can somehow work in ten.

He is therefore seldom content with a plain statement like   28
"Fast driving is dangerous." This has only four words in it. He
takes thought, and the sentence becomes:

In my opinion, fast driving is dangerous.

Better, but he can do better still:

In my opinion, fast driving would seem to be rather
dangerous.

If he is really adept, it may come out:

In my humble opinion, though I do not claim to be
an expert on this complicated subject, fast driving, in
most circumstances, would seem to be rather dangerous
in many respects, or at least so it would seem to me.

Thus four words have been turned into forty, and not an iota of
content has been added.

Now this is a way to go about reaching five hundred words,   29
and if you are content with a "D" grade, it is as good a way as any.
But if you aim higher, you must work differently. Instead of stuffing your sentences with straw, you must try steadily to get rid of the
padding, to make your sentences lean and tough. If you are really
working at it, your first draft will greatly exceed the required total,
and then you will work it down, thus:

It is thought in some quarters that fraternities do not contribute as much as might be expected to campus life.

Some people think that fraternities contribute little to campus life.

The average doctor who practices in small towns or in the country must toil night and day to heal the sick.

Most country doctors work long hours.

When I was a little girl, I suffered from shyness and embarrassment in the presence of others.

I was a shy little girl.

It is absolutely necessary for the person employed as a marine fireman to give the matter of steam pressure his undivided attention at all times.

The fireman has to keep his eye on the steam gauge.

You may ask how you can arrive a five hundred words at this rate. Simply. You dig up more real content. Instead of taking a couple of obvious points off the surface of the topic and then circling warily around them for six paragraphs, you work in and explore, figure out the details. You illustrate. You say that fast driving is dangerous, and then you prove it. How long does it take to stop a car at forty and at eighty? How far can you see at night? What happens when a tire blows? What happens in a head-on collision at fifty miles an hour? Pretty soon your paper will be full of broken glass and blood and headless torsos, and reaching five hundred words will not really be a problem. | 30

Call a Fool a Fool

Some of the padding in freshman themes is to be blamed not on anxiety about the word minimum but on excessive timidity. The student writes, "In my opinion, the principal of my high school acted in ways that I believe every unbiased person would have to call foolish." This isn't exactly what he means. What he means is, "My high school principal was a fool." If he was a fool, call him a | 31 fool. Hedging the thing about with "in-my-opinion's" and "it-seems-to-me's" and "as-I-see-it's" and "at-least-from-my-point-of-view's" gains you nothing. Delete these phrases whenever they creep into your paper.

The student's tendency to hedge stems from a modesty that in   32
other circumstances would be commendable. He is, he realizes, young and inexperienced, and he half suspects that he is dopey and fuzzy-minded beyond the average. Probably only too true. But it doesn't help to announce your incompetence six times in every paragraph. Decide what you want to say and say it as vigorously as possible, without apology and in plain words.

Linguistic diffidence can take various forms. One is what we   33
call *euphemism*. This is the tendency to call a spade "a certain garden implement" or women's underwear "unmentionables." It is stronger in some eras than others and in some people than others but it always operates more or less in subjects that are touchy or taboo: death, sex, madness, and so on. Thus we shrink from saying "He died last night" but say instead "passed away," "left us," "joined his Maker," "went to his reward." Or we try to take off the tension with a lighter cliché: "kicked the bucket," "cashed in his chips," "handed in his dinner pail." We have found all sorts of ways to avoid saying *mad*: "mentally ill," "touched," "not quite right upstairs," "feeble-minded," "innocent," "simple," "off his trolley," "not in his right mind." Even such a now plain word as *insane* began as a euphemism with the meaning "not healthy."

Modern science, particularly psychology, contributes many   34
polysyllables in which we can wrap our thoughts and blunt their force. To many writers there is no such thing as a bad schoolboy. Schoolboys are maladjusted or unoriented or misunderstood or in need of guidance or lacking in continued success toward satisfactory integration of the personality as a social unit, but they are never bad. Psychology no doubt makes us better men or women, more sympathetic and tolerant, but it doesn't make writing any easier. Had Shakespeare been confronted with psychology, "To be or not to be" might have come out, "To continue as a social unit or not to do so. That is the personality problem. Whether 'tis a better sign of integration at the conscious level to display a psychic tolerance toward the maladjustments and repressions induced by one's lack of orientation in one's environment or—"But Hamlet would never have finished the soliloquy.

Writing in the modern world, you cannot altogether avoid   35 modern jargon. Nor, in an effort to get away from euphemism, should you salt your paper with four-letter words. But you can do much if you will mount guard against those roundabout phrases, those echoing polysyllables that tend to slip into your writing to rob it of its crispness and force.

Beware of the Pat Expression

Other things being equal, avoid phrases like "other things 36 being equal." Those sentences that come to you whole, or in two or three doughy lumps, are sure to be bad sentences. They are no creation of yours but pieces of common thought floating in the community soup.

Pat expressions are hard, often impossible, to avoid, because 37 they come too easily to be noticed and seem too necessary to be dispensed with. No writer avoids them altogether, but good writers avoid them more often than poor writers.

By "pat expressions" we mean such tags as "to all practical 38 intents and purposes," "the pure and simple truth," "from where I sit," "the time of his life," "to the ends of the earth," "in the twinkling of an eye," "as sure as you're born," "over my dead body," "under cover of darkness," "took the easy way out," "when all is said and done," "told him time and time again," "parted the best of friends," "stand up and be counted," "gave him the best years of her life," "worked her fingers to the bone." Like other clichés, these expressions were once forceful. Now we should use them only when we can't possibly think of anything else.

Some pat expressions stand like a wall between the writer and 39 thought. Such a one is "the American way of life." Many student writers feel that when they have said that something accords with the American way of life or does not they have exhausted the subject. Actually, they have stopped at the highest level of abstraction. The American way of life is the complicated set of bonds between a hundred and eighty million ways. All of us know this when we think about it, but the tag phrase too often keeps us from thinking about it.

So with many another phrase dear to the politician: "this great 40 land of ours," "the man in the street," "our national heritage." These may prove our patriotism or give a clue to our political beliefs, but otherwise they add nothing to the paper except words.

Colorful Words

The writer builds with words, and no builder uses a raw mate-   41
rial more slippery and elusive and treacherous. A writer's work is a
constant struggle to get the right word in the right place, to find
that particular word that will convey his meaning exactly, that will
persuade the reader or soothe him or startle or amuse him. He
never succeeds altogether — sometimes he feels that he scarcely
succeeds at all — but such successes as he has are what make the
thing worth doing.

There is no book of rules for this game. One progresses   42
through everlasting experiment on the basis of ever-widening experience. There are few useful generalizations that one can make
about words as words, but there are perhaps a few.

Some words are what we call "colorful." By this we mean that   43
they are calculated to produce a picture or induce an emotion. They
are dressy instead of plain, specific instead of general, loud instead
of soft. Thus, in place of "Her heart beat," we may write "Her heart
pounded, throbbed, fluttered, danced." Instead of "He sat in his
chair," we may say, "He *lounged, sprawled, coiled.*" Instead of "It
was hot," we may say, "It was *blistering, sultry, muggy, suffocating,
steamy, wilting.*"

However, it should not be supposed that the fancy word is   44
always better. Often it is as well to write "Her heart beat" or "It was
hot" if that is all it did or all it was. Ages differ in how they like their
prose. The nineteenth century liked it rich and smoky. The twentieth has usually preferred it lean and cool. The twentieth century
writer, like all writers, is forever seeking the exact word, but he is
wary of sounding feverish. He tends to pitch it low, to understate
it, to throw it away. He knows that if he gets too colorful, the
audience is likely to giggle.

See how this strikes you: "As the rich, golden glow of the   45
sunset died away along the eternal western hills, Angela's limpid
blue eyes looked softly and trustingly into Montague's flashing
brown ones, and her heart pounded like a drum in time with the
joyous song surging in her soul." Some people like that sort of
thing, but most modern readers would say, "Good grief," and turn
on the television.

Colored Words

Some words we would call not so much colorful as colored —   46
that is, loaded with associations, good or bad. All words — except

perhaps structure words — have associations of some sort. We have said that the meaning of a word is the sum of the contexts in which it occurs. When we hear a word, we hear with it an echo of all the situations in which we have heard it before.

In some words, these echoes are obvious and discussable. The 47 word *mother*, for example, has, for most people, agreeable associations. When you hear *mother* you probably think of home, safety, love, food, and various other pleasant things. If one writes, "She was like a mother to me," he gets an effect which he would not get in "She was like an aunt to me." The advertiser makes use of the associations of *mother* by working it in when he talks about his product. The politician works it in when he talks about himself.

So also with such words as *home, liberty, fireside, contentment,* 48 *patriot, tenderness, sacrifice, childlike, manly, bluff, limpid.* All of these words are loaded with favorable associations that would be rather hard to indicate in a straightforward definition. There is more than a literal difference between "They sat around the fireside" and "They sat around the stove." They might have been equally warm and happy around the stove, but *fireside* suggests leisure, grace, quiet tradition, congenial company, and *stove* does not.

Conversely, some words have bad associations. *Mother* sug- 49 gests pleasant things, but *mother-in-law* does not. Many mothers-in-law are heroically lovable and some mothers drink gin all day and beat their children insensible, but these facts of life are beside the point. The thing is that *mother* sounds good and *mother-in-law* does not.

Or consider the word *intellectual*. This would seem to be a 50 complimentary term, but in point of fact it is not, for it has picked up associations of impracticality and ineffectuality and general dopiness. So also with such words as *liberal, reactionary, Communist, socialist, capitalist, radical, schoolteacher, truck driver, undertaker, operator, salesman, huckster, speculator.* These convey meanings on the literal level, but beyond that — sometimes, in some places — they convey contempt on the part of the speaker.

The question of whether to use loaded words or not depends 51 on what is being written. The scientist, the scholar, try to avoid them; for the poet, the advertising writer, the public speaker, they are standard equipment. But every writer should take care that they do not substitute for thought. If you write, "Anyone who thinks that is nothing but a Socialist (or Communist or capitalist)" you have said nothing except that you don't like people who think that, and such remarks are effective only with the most naïve readers. It is always a bad mistake to think your readers more naïve than they really are.

Colorless Words

But probably most student writers come to grief not with   52
words that are colorful or those that are colored but with those that
have no color at all. A pet example is *nice*, a word we would find it
hard to dispense with in casual conversation but which is no longer
capable of adding much to a description. Colorless words are those
of such general meaning that in a particular sentence they mean
nothing. Slang adjectives, like *cool* ("That's real cool") tend to
explode all over the language. They are applied to everything, lose
their original force, and quickly die.

Beware also of nouns of very general meaning, like *circum-*   53
stances, cases, instances, aspects, factors, relationships, attitudes, even-
tualities, etc. In most circumstances you will find that those cases of
writing which contain too many instances of words like these will
in this and other aspects have factors leading to unsatisfactory
relationships with the reader resulting in unfavorable attitudes on
his part and perhaps other eventualities, like a grade of "D." Notice
also what "etc." means. It means "I'd like to make this list longer,
but I can't think of any more examples."

Questions for Close Reading

1. What is the thesis of the selection? Locate the sentence(s) in which
   Roberts states his main idea. If he does not state the thesis explicitly,
   express it in your own words.
2. According to Roberts, what do students assume they have to do to get a
   good grade on an English composition?
3. What is the difference between "colorful words," "colored words,"
   and "colorless words"? Which are preferred in essay writing?
4. What are Roberts' most important pieces of advice for the student
   writer?
5. Refer to the dictionary as needed to define the following words used in
   the selection: *bromides* (paragraph 13), *insufferably* (13), *inexorably*
   (14), *dissent* (21), *abolition* (24), *adept* (28), *euphemism* (33), and *insen-*
   sible (49).

Questions about the Writer's Craft

1. What two processes does Roberts analyze in this essay? Is each process informational, directional, or a combination of the two?
2. Why does Roberts use the second person "you" throughout the essay? How does this choice of point of view affect your response to the essay?
3. What is Roberts' tone in this essay? Find some typical examples of this tone. What does Roberts do to achieve this tone? Considering his intended audience, is this tone a good choice?
4. Does Roberts "practice what he preaches" about writing? Review the section headings of the essay and find examples of each piece of advice in the essay.

Questions for Further Thought

1. Roberts writes that making "a dull subject interesting . . . is precisely what you are expected to do" in college English. Do you agree most writing subjects are dull? If so, do you think assignments could be made more interesting? And how could instructors get students to write honestly, instead of writing what they think the instructor wants to read?
2. Is Roberts' suggestion to write about the least obvious topic always appropriate? Would you follow this advice yourself?
3. In paragraph 17, Roberts says the difference between a "C" or a "D" may depend on when the teacher grades the paper. Do you think instructors' grades are usually fair, objective, and appropriate? Or do they often seem arbitrary and subjective?
4. Do you think students on your campus are preoccupied with things like word-counting and guessing the instructor's opinion on a topic? Are you? Why do some students handle writing assignments this way? What could professors do to encourage students to focus more on the challenge of writing?

Writing Assignments Using Process Analysis as a Method of Development

1. Write a humorous essay showing how to avoid doing schoolwork, household chores, or anything else most people tend to put off. You may use the second person as Roberts does. Or you may use the first person and describe your typical method of avoidance.
2. Borrowing some of Roberts' lively techniques, make a routine, predictable process interesting to read about. You might choose an activity such as how to register to vote, apply for a driver's license, sign up for college courses, take care of laundry, play a simple game, study for an exam, or some other familiar process.

Writing Assignments Using Other Methods
of Development

3. Is freshman writing a beneficial and valuable experience? Or should the course be scrapped? Write an essay arguing the value — or lack of value — of freshman writing courses. Follow Roberts' advice for writing a lively composition on a time-worn subject: avoid obvious padding, choose unusual points, avoid abstractions, go to the heart of the matter, use colorful words.

4. Write a paper detailing your experiences as a student in English classes — from elementary school up to now. Using several examples, describe how successfully or unsuccessfully English has been taught, and recommend any specific reforms or changes you feel are needed.

Peter McWilliams

Peter McWilliams was born in 1949 in Detroit, Michigan, and educated at Eastern Michigan University and Maharishi International University. Although his primary interest has been writing poetry, McWilliams has also written books on such diverse topics as transcendental meditation, coping with the loss of a loved one, and computers. Formerly a teacher of transcendental meditation, he is the cofounder and owner of several publishing companies. The following essay is taken from his The Word Processing Book *(1984).*

Selecting a Word Processing Computer

Buying a word processor — or a comparable piece of sophisticated technology — can be downright intimidating. How is it possible to make a good decision in a high-tech market where new products appear almost daily? Leavening his advice with wry humor, Peter McWilliams provides several practical suggestions for searching out the right computer.

How does one go about purchasing a word processing computer? The same way porcupines and Catholics make love: very carefully. Pretend you were about to buy your first car and you knew something about cars, but you'd never driven one; you did not, in fact, even know quite what they look like. You would have many automobile showrooms to visit, each full of bright-to-surly salespersons, each claiming that his or her car was *the* car. 1

The analogy of buying-a-computer-is-like-buying-a-car breaks down at a certain point. The fact is, more often than not, buying a computer is like joining a religion. If you ask people what they think about their computer it's a lot like asking people what they think about God. Expect emotionally charged and not necessarily 2 coherent replies. Some will proselytize; others will find discussing It "too personal." Some are wide-eyed with enthusiasm; others are silent with serene Knowing. Some believe their computer is the One Way, the Right Way, and the Only Way; others accept that there are many paths to RAM.

You'll find this attitude among friends who own computers   3 (the "converts"), the people who sell them (the "preachers"), and those of us who write about them (the "Biblical scholars"). Every so often, much to my amazement and amusement, I find myself responding negatively to positive comments about the direct competitor of the computer I own. In actuality I know that there is not one whit of difference between these two machines, but I note the wave of resentment passes over me as I see an advertisement for that "other" machine.

In selecting a computer and selecting a religion I would give   4 you the same advice: Take your time, investigate all claims carefully, don't make any hasty decisions, and remember that it must work for *you*. Take the histrionics of the zealots with more than a few grains of salt. And save some salt for the journey; the road may well be slippery ahead.

When shopping for a word processing computer, visit not   5 only the popular stores (they'll usually have the word "computer" cleverly used in their name), but investigate, too, computerized office machine stores.

Don't expect too much from computer salespeople. The computer world is growing so quickly that truly knowledgeable people   6 can make several hundred dollars a day as consultants; why on earth should they hang around a computer store at minimum wage in the hope of an occasional commission?

The Peter Principle is rife in computer stores as well: If Tom   7 knows a great deal about computers and how to sell them, he soon becomes the store manager. Tom knows nothing about scheduling personnel or ordering hardware or hiring or supervising, so he spends most of his time doing what he doesn't know how to do. Meanwhile, the bad salespeople never get promoted because they're not very good, but they never get fired for Tom is afraid to make any changes. There certainly are some glowing exceptions to this scenario, but on the whole, visit computer stores to look at computers, not stellar sales techniques.

In all fairness, computerdom is in the midst of an information   8 explosion, one that will be increasing in geometric proportions for some time to come. An ordinary human being, even one dedicated to learning all he or she can, simply cannot keep up. I can't keep up with the rather narrow field of word processing — and I don't have to wait on customers all day. I can imagine the difficulty someone might have if, in addition to word processing, they were asked to know all about four or five different computers and thirty or forty software programs ranging from general ledger to electronic pinball.

Here are ten suggestions you might want to keep in mind   9
while shopping for your word processing computer.

1. Make an appointment. Most computer stores have their   10
games expert, their accounting expert, their programming expert, etc. Telephone and ask to speak to their word processing expert. Make an appointment with that person. If you walk in cold off the street, the first available salesperson will glom onto you, and if he or she is working on a commission, he or she will not be very willing to unglom, even if his or her total knowledge of word processing can be put on the underside of a caraway seed. You'll find this salesperson running to the salesperson who knows about word processing with your questions and returning with broadly interpretive answers. Every time you walk into that store you will "belong" to that unknowing salesperson.

2. Do not be intimidated by jargon. Salespeople who use exces-   11
sive jargon either know everything about computers and nothing about communication, or they know very little about computers and are trying to conceal that fact. When in doubt about what a word or phrase means, ask. Asking may not do you any good, but don't be afraid to give it a try.

3. See if you can spend some time alone with the computer. This   12
usually isn't too hard to arrange. When you think you know enough to attempt a solo flight all you have to say is, "Why don't you take care of some of your other customers and come back to me later?" There are almost always other customers to be taken care of.

4. Ask for print-outs. It's a good idea to have two or three   13
paragraphs that are the same (Gettysburg Address, Pledge of Allegiance, "Casey At The Bat," anything) so that you can have print-outs from several printers of the same material. It's easier to compare print quality when the text is the same.

5. When trying a computer, do the work that you'll be using the   14
computer for. If you're going to use it for creative writing, write something creative. If you're going to use it for correspondence,

write letters. (My friends never got more letters than when I was shopping for a computer.) If you'll be using it to transcribe dictation, bring some dictation.

6. *Make notes.* Write down model numbers, prices, salespeople's names, everything. After leaving the store, debrief yourself and note the pros and the cons of the machines you just evaluated. The things that are clear in your mind upon leaving a store will be hopelessly muddled a few weeks and a dozen computers later. Ask, too, for any printed literature the store can part with.   15

7. *Trust your intuition.* It's important that you feel good about the computer you purchase — especially the keyboard and the video screen. Include your emotional reactions in your notes and in your decision. Just as cars are more than how many MPG they get, computers are more than how much RAM they have.   16

8. *What happens if it breaks?* Be sure to investigate what you'll have to do if the computer does not compute either in or out of warranty. Can you bring it back to the store or will you have to pack it up and ship it to California? How much time will repairs take? Are loaners available for free or at a reasonable cost? Will the store put all its promises in writing? Think about the unthinkable before you buy.   17

9. *Take your time.* Don't try to look at everything in a week. You might experience a personal Systems Overload. Take it easy. If you must travel to The Big City to do your investigations, it's better to plan several shorter trips rather than one long one. Gather all the information you can, let it digest, and make your decision from a calm, neutral frame of mind.   18

10. *Enjoy yourself.* Keep in mind that it's hard to lose. Whatever personal computer with word processing capabilities you eventually own will be light years ahead of whatever you're using now, even if it's the finest of electric typewriters. You might not buy the very best computer that fills your every need for the very best price, but so what? Whatever you do buy will serve you faithfully and brilliantly for years to come. Knowing there's no way to lose, enjoy playing one of the most intricate computer games around: buying a computer.   19

Questions for Close Reading

1. What is the thesis of the selection? Locate the sentence(s) in which McWilliams states his main idea. If he does not state the thesis explicitly, express it in your own words.
2. According to the author, buying a computer is more like joining a religion than buying a car. What are his reasons for this claim?
3. Why does McWilliams feel that computer salespeople are not reliable as experts on the computers they sell?
4. What factors make buying a computer so difficult and time-consuming?
5. Refer to your dictionary as needed to define the following words used in the selection: *analogy* (paragraph 2), *proselytize* (2), *histrionics* (4), *rife* (7), *jargon* (11), and *debrief* (15).

Questions about the Writer's Craft

1. McWilliams suggests a series of steps to follow when buying a computer. Are these suggestions in any particular order? What changes would have to be made to shape the steps into a more conventional sequence?
2. Why, in paragraph 2, does McWilliams capitalize the initial letter of certain words and phrases (for example, "Knowing" and "One Way")?
3. Find word choices and phrases that indicate the lighthearted tone that McWilliams has used in presenting his information. Since purchasing a word processor is a serious investment, why might McWilliams have used such a tone?
4. Examine McWilliams' development of each of his ten suggestions. What are some of the different techniques that he uses to clarify each suggestion?

Questions for Further Thought

1. Have you ever made a major purchase like a computer or some other very expensive product? What factors did you consider before you made your first decision?
2. Many people who write by hand or use a typewriter resist the idea of using a computer to compose. Why might they be so reluctant to change to a new technology? Do you yourself feel open to new products and inventions, or do you avoid learning about them and using them? Why?
3. Do you think that most salespeople are well informed about the products they sell, or are most of them basically too overwhelmed with their day-to-day jobs to keep up with the product information? Whose re-

sponsibility is it to be knowledgeable about a product, the seller's or the buyer's?

4. Word processing is one example of a practical use to which a home computer can be put. Do you think computers will have other uses in the home, or have they been overrated as forces that will soon reshape our personal lives?

Writing Assignments Using Process Analysis as a Method of Development

1. Think of a major purchase that you or your family would like to make (for example, a car, television, stereo equipment, or a major appliance). What steps would you go through to buy this item? Write an essay describing the process of purchasing this major item. Use chronological order to explain the steps in the process.

2. "Computerdom" is experiencing an information explosion, making it difficult for anyone to keep up with new developments. You may feel the same way about a field you are interested in, such as current events, music, sports, and so on. Write a process essay explaining the best ways for fans or buffs in this field to keep abreast of new ideas, products, data, and the like.

Writing Assignments Using Other Methods of Development

3. McWilliams claims that buying a computer is like joining a religion. Write an essay comparing a certain kind of purchase to some other significant process. For instance, you could write a humorous piece showing that "Buying a car is like getting married."

4. Write an essay relating the "religious" feeling that you or someone you know has had for a particular material possession. Develop your essay by examples or by narrating how the person worshipped the possession and held it in irrational esteem.

Additional Writing Topics
PROCESS ANALYSIS

General Assignments

Develop one of the following topics through process analysis. Explain the process one step at a time, organizing the steps chronologically. If there is no set, agreed-upon sequence, design your own series of steps. Use transitions to ease the audience through the steps in the process. You may, of course, use any tone you wish, from serious to light.

Directional: How To Do Something

1. How to improve a course you have taken
2. How to drive defensively
3. How to get away with ＿＿＿＿＿＿＿＿
4. How to succeed at a job interview
5. How to relax
6. How to show appreciation to others
7. How to get through school despite personal problems
8. How to be a responsible pet owner
9. How to conduct a garage or yard sale
10. How to look fashionable on a limited budget
11. How to protect a home from burglars
12. How to meet more people
13. How to improve the place where you work
14. How to gain or lose weight
15. How to complain effectively

Informational: How Something Happens

1. How a student becomes burned-out
2. How a library card catalog organizes books
3. How a dead thing decays (or some other natural process)
4. How the college registration process works
5. How *Homo sapiens* chooses a mate
6. How a VCR (or some other machine) works
7. How a bad habit develops
8. How people fall into debt

290 Process Analysis

Assignments with a Specific Audience and Purpose

1. As a kindergarten teacher or day care center worker, you want to show a young child how to do something simple—put on boots, water a plant, or any other task. Explain the process in terms a young child would understand.
2. You've been asked to write part of a driver's education textbook that deals with one of the following: making a three-point turn, parallel parking, handling a skid, or any other driving maneuver. Explain the process one step at a time. Remember, your audience consists of sixteen-year-olds who are just learning how to drive and who lack self-confidence and experience.
3. Write an article for *Consumer Reports* on how to shop for a certain product or service. Give specific steps explaining how to save money, get your money's worth, and so on.
4. Write a process analysis showing how to save a life in a specific way. The paper might be on CPR or rescue breathing or the Heimlich maneuver or any other life-saving method. Your audience will be people from your neighborhood who are taking a first-aid class.
5. Your best friend plans to move into his/her own apartment and doesn't know the first thing about how to choose one. Explain the process of selecting an apartment—where to look, what to investigate, what questions to ask before signing a lease.
6. You write an "advice to the lovelorn" column for the campus paper. A correspondent writes saying that he or she wants to break up with a steady boyfriend/girlfriend but doesn't know how to do it without hurting the person. Advise the writer on the process of ending a meaningful relationship with a minimal amount of pain.

COMPARISON-
CONTRAST

WHAT IS COMPARISON-CONTRAST?

As reasoning creatures, we frequently try to make sense of the world by finding similarities and differences in the experiences we encounter. Seeing how things are alike (comparing) and seeing how they are different (contrasting) helps us impose meaning on experiences that otherwise might remain fragmented and disconnected. We may think to ourselves — barely aware of the fact that we are comparing and contrasting — "I woke up in a great mood this morning, but now I feel uneasy and anxious. I wonder why I don't feel the same way. I wonder why I feel so different." This inner questioning, which often occurs in a flash, is just one example of the way we use comparison and contrast to understand ourselves and the world around us.

Comparing and contrasting also helps us make choices in everyday life. We compare and contrast everything from two brands of soap we might buy to two possible colleges we might attend. We listen to a favorite radio station, watch a preferred nightly news show, select a particular dessert from a menu—all because we have done some degree of comparing and contrasting. We often weigh these alternatives in an unstudied, casual manner, as when we flip from one radio station to another. But if we have to make important decisions, we tend to think rigorously about how things are alike or different: Should I live in a dorm or rent an apartment? Should I accept the higher-paying job or the lower-paying job that offers more challenges? Such a deliberate approach to comparison-contrast may also provide us with needed insight into significant social issues: Do recent events in South America parallel what happened earlier in Vietnam? What are the merits of the various positions on abortion?

WHEN TO USE COMPARISON-CONTRAST

When writing an essay, you must be careful to use the comparison-contrast format in a structured, conscious way. For one thing, you need to develop a sure sense of when it is appropriate to use the comparison-contrast method of development. Often the wording of an assignment, as in those that follow, will signal that comparison-contrast is called for:

> Compare the way male and female relationships are depicted in *Cosmopolitan, Ms., Playboy,* and *Esquire.* Which publication has the most limited view of men and women? Which has the broadest perspective?

> Many social commentators have observed that college students and their parents share the same view about the purpose of a college education: both expect young people to be equipped with immediately marketable skills. Indicate whether you think this is an accurate assessment by comparing your and your parents' beliefs about the value of a college degree.

> One has only to watch a few football, basketball, or baseball games to realize that each sport has a special appeal to its fans. Contrast the unique drawing power of each sport, being sure to arrive at some conclusions about the nature of each sport's following.

> The issue of prayer in public school has received a good deal of attention lately. Take a position on the controversy by contrasting the views of those who believe prayer should be allowed in public schools with those who believe it should be prohibited.

Comparison-contrast assignments like these are common in college writing classes because they demand logical thinking and sound organizational skills.

Other times, assignments will, with a little thought, lend themselves to the comparison-contrast format. For instance, although the following assignments do not use the words *compare* or *contrast* specifically, they could nevertheless be organized around a comparison-contrast theme.

> People's definition of the term "vigilantism" often determines whether they think it is an appropriate strategy for dealing with crime. Clarify your stance by discussing what you think vigilantism is and what it is not.

> The emergence of the two-career family is one of the major phenomena of our culture. Discuss the advantages and disadvantages of having both parents work, showing how you feel about such two-career households.

> There has been considerable criticism recently of the news coverage in the city's two leading newspapers, the *Herald* and the *Beacon*. Indicate whether you think the criticism is valid by discussing the similarities and differences in the two papers' news coverage.

Assume you were writing a paper based on the last assignment above. Although not worded in strict comparison-contrast terms, the assignment leads logically to a comparison-contrast essay. Moreover, the assignment also shows that a comparison-contrast essay is not always limited to explaining the similarities *or* the differences between subjects. The essay may focus on both.

As you have seen, comparison-contrast can be the key strategy for achieving an essay's purpose. But comparison-contrast can also be a supplemental method used to help make a point in an essay organized chiefly around another pattern of development. A paper *defining* common sense, for example, might include a section contrasting common sense with book learning. Or a paper analyzing the *effects* of reinstating the draft might spend some time comparing different views toward compulsory military service. Or if you were writing an *argumentation-persuasion* essay urging stricter controls over drug abuse in the workplace, you might compare several companies' approaches for dealing with drug-related work problems.

SUGGESTIONS FOR USING COMPARISON-CONTRAST IN AN ESSAY

The following suggestions will be helpful whether you use comparison-contrast as a dominant or supportive pattern of development.

1. Clarify your purpose.   It is important to keep in mind that comparison-contrast is not an end in itself. As with all the patterns discussed in this book, comparison-contrast should be viewed as a technique for meeting broader objectives. Otherwise, a comparison-contrast essay may turn into a mechanical, useless listing of "how *A* differs from *B*" or "how *A* is like *B*."

Sometimes, your purpose will be to *present information* about your subjects as objectively as possible: "This is what the *Herald*'s news coverage is like. This is what the *Beacon*'s news coverage is like." The purpose of comparison-contrast here is purely *informative*.

More frequently, you will use comparison-contrast to *evaluate* your subjects. In such a case, your goal will be to reach a conclusion so that you can make a judgment. ("The *Herald* and the *Beacon* spend too much time reporting local news," or "Neither the *Herald* nor the *Beacon* provided complete, accurate coverage of the recent hostage crisis.") Comparison-contrast can also *persuade* the audience to act in a certain way. ("The reader interested in comprehensive coverage of international events should read the *Herald*.")

Comparing and contrasting also make it possible to draw an *analogy* between two seemingly unrelated subjects. An analogy is an imaginative comparison that delves beneath the surface differences of the subjects in order to expose their unsuspected similarities or significant differences. Your purpose may be to show that singles bars and zoos share a number of striking similarities. Or you may want to illustrate that wolves and humans raise their young in much the same way, but that wolves go about the process in a more civilized manner. The analogical approach can also make a complex subject easier to understand — as when the national deficit is compared to a household budget gone awry. Analogies are often dramatic and instructive, challenging you and your audience to consider subjects in a new light. But analogies do not speak for themselves. It must be clear to the reader how the analogy demonstrates your purpose.

2. Select subjects that are at least somewhat alike. Unless you plan to develop an analogy, the subjects you choose to compare or contrast should have in common somewhat obvious characteristics or qualities. It makes sense to compare different parts of the country, two situation comedies, or several college teachers. But an interesting and reasonable paper would probably not result from, let's say, a comparison of a situation comedy with a detective show. Your subjects must belong to the same general group so that your comparison-contrast stays within logical bounds and does not veer off into pointlessness.

3. Present a clear thesis. An essay developed primarily through comparison-contrast should be focused by a strong thesis. This controlling idea will often do the following:

- Name the subjects being compared and contrasted.
- Indicate whether the essay focuses on the subjects' similarities *or* differences, or whether the essay focuses on the subjects' similarities *and* differences.
- State the main point of comparison or contrast covered in the essay.

Here are several examples of well-written thesis statements for comparison-contrast essays. The first thesis statement signals similarities, the second indicates differences, and the last shows similarities and differences:

The confusion many people feel as they approach middle age is much like the upheavals they experienced as adolescents.

Most retired people have different priorities than people in their forties and fifties who are still working.

Nontraditional students struggle with the same problems most students do, but they also have to deal with a special set of pressures.

Not all comparison-contrast essays will contain thesis statements as structured as those above. Moreover, the thesis in a comparison-contrast essay does not have to be placed at the start of an essay; it may appear as a judgment or persuasive statement at the conclusion of the paper. In all cases, though, the thesis should state what you will show or what you have shown about your subjects.

4. Select the points to be discussed.   Once the purpose, subject, and thesis of your essay have been determined, you need to decide which points of similarity or difference to discuss. This means you have to identify which aspects of the subjects to compare or contrast. College professors, for instance, could be compared and contrasted on the basis of their testing methods, ability to motivate students, confidence in front of a classroom, personalities, level of enthusiasm, or a number of other qualities.

Brainstorming is invaluable for generating possible points to cover. When brainstorming, try to produce more raw material than you think you will need, so that you then have the luxury of narrowing the list down to its most significant points. When you select the points to cover, be sure to consider your readers. Ask yourself: "Will they be familiar with this item? Will I need this item to get my message across? Will my audience find this item interesting or convincing?" What the audience knows, what they do not know, and what you can project about their reactions should influence your choices. And, of course, you need to select points that provide strong support for your thesis. If you want your essay to show the differences between healthy, sensible diets and dangerous crash diets, there would be no need to talk about aerobic exercise. Finally, the points discussed must introduce important and interesting issues. It does not make much sense to focus on points of comparison or contrast that are obvious and require little or no thought from you or your reader. Imagine you want to write an essay making the point that, despite their differences, hard rock of the 1960s and punk rock of the 1970s both reflected young people's disillusionment with society. You would produce little of value if you contrasted brand names of the guitars used by several groups or variations in the groups' hair styles. On the other hand, contrasting song lyrics (protest lyrics and nihilistic messages) would lead to insights of interest and significance.

5. Organize the points to be discussed. After selecting the points to include in the essay, you should use a systematic, logical plan for presenting the points of comparison and contrast. If the points are not organized, your essay will be little more than a confusing maze of ideas. There are two common ways to organize an essay developed wholly or in part by comparison-contrast: the *one-side-at-a-time* method and the *point-by-point* method. Although both strategies may be used in a paper, one method usually predominates.

One-side-at-a-time method. In the one-side-at-a-time method, you discuss everything relevant about one subject first and then switch, in turn, to the other subjects. For example, in the assignment that asked you to discuss the news coverage in two local papers, you might first discuss the *Herald*'s coverage of international, national, and local news; then you would discuss the *Beacon*'s coverage of international, national, and local news. Note that the areas being compared or contrasted should be discussed in the same order. Moreover, the areas discussed should be the same for both newspapers. It would not be logical to discuss the *Herald*'s coverage of international, national, and local news and then to discuss the *Beacon*'s magazine supplements, modern living section, and comics page.

This is how you would organize an essay using the one-side-at-a-time method:

Everything about *A*	*Herald*'s news coverage: • international • national • local
Everything about *B*	*Beacon*'s news coverage: • international • national • local

Point-by-point method. In the point-by-point method of development, you alternate from one aspect of the first subject to the same aspect in your other subject(s). For example, if this method were used when comparing or contrasting the *Herald* and the *Beacon*, you would first discuss the *Herald*'s international coverage and then the *Beacon*'s international coverage; next the *Herald*'s national coverage and then the *Beacon*'s national coverage; and finally, the *Herald*'s local coverage and then the *Beacon*'s local coverage.

An essay using the point-by-point method would be organized like this:

First Aspect of *A* and *B*   *Beacon*: international coverage
    Herald: international coverage

Second Aspect of *A* and *B*   *Beacon*: national coverage
    Herald: national coverage

Third Aspect of *A* and *B*   *Beacon*: local coverage
    Herald: local coverage

Deciding which of these two methods of organization to use is a personal choice, but there are a number of factors to consider. The one-side-at-a-time method tends to convey a more unified feeling since it highlights broad similarities and differences. It is, therefore, an effective pattern to use when your subjects are fairly uncomplicated. This strategy also works well when essays are brief; the reader won't find it difficult to remember what has been said about *A* when reading about *B*.

The point-by-point method, because it permits more extensive coverage of similarities and differences, is a wise choice when subjects are complex. Similarly, this pattern is useful when an essay is lengthy since the reader would probably find it difficult to remember ten pages of information about *A* while reading the next ten pages of *B*. But keep in mind that the depth of coverage made possible by this approach may cause the reader to lose sight of the broader picture.

6. Supply the reader with clear organizational cues. Although an organized comparison-contrast format is important, it does not guarantee that the reader will be able to follow your line of thought easily. Organizational cues — especially cues that signal similarities or differences — are needed to show readers where they have been and where they are going.

Such organizational cues are essential in all writing, but they are especially crucial when you write a paper using comparison-contrast. By indicating clearly when subjects are being compared or contrasted, the cues help weave the discussion into a coherent, seamless whole.

The linking cues in boldface below could be used to *signal similarities* in an essay discussing the news coverage in the *Herald* and the *Beacon*:

- The *Beacon* **also** allots only a small portion of the front page to global news.
- **In the same way,** the *Herald* tries to include at least three local stories on the first page.
- **Likewise,** the *Beacon* emphasizes the importance of up-to-date reporting of town meetings.
- The *Herald* is **similarly** committed to extensive coverage of high school and college sports.

The following linking cues in boldface could be used to *signal differences* in the same essay:

- **By way of contrast,** the *Herald*'s editorial page deals with national matters on the average of three times a week.
- **On the other hand,** the *Beacon* does not share the *Herald*'s enthusiasm for interviews with national figures.
- The *Beacon*, **however,** does not encourage its reporters to tackle national stories the way the *Herald* does.
- **But** the *Herald*'s coverage of the Washington scene is much more comprehensive than its competitor's.

When using comparison-contrast, you need to guard against the tendency to pay obsessive attention to the mechanics of organizing the essay. Although you want to prepare a logically structured paper, you do not want the essay to deteriorate into a rote listing of how things are alike or different. Nor do you want to become a slave to the format you have settled upon, forcing points into an artificial or uncomfortable fit, rather like Cinderella's sisters hacking off their toes in order to squeeze into the glass slipper. Remember that comparison-contrast is a means to an end, and that your end is always to open up a subject for exploration, providing readers with new ways to think about your subject.

STUDENT ESSAY AND COMMENTARY

The following student essay was written by Carol Siskin in response to this assignment:

> In "High Noon," Art Spikol contrasts youthful innocence with mature sophistication, suggesting that he misses "the wonder and the awe" of youth. Given your choice, which would you rather be, younger or older? Your essay should explain why you prefer one time of life to another.

While reading Carol's paper, try to determine how well it applies the principles concerning the use of comparison-contrast. The commentary following the paper will help you look at Carol's essay more closely.

The Virtues of Growing Older

Our society worships youth. Advertisements convince us to buy   1
Grecian Formula and Oil of Olay so we can hide the gray in our hair
and smooth the lines on our face. Television shows feature attractive
young stars with firm bodies, perfect complexions, and thick manes of
hair. Middle-aged folks work out in gyms and jog down the street,
trying to delay the effects of age.

Wouldn't any person over thirty gladly sign with the devil just to   2
be young again? Isn't aging an experience to be dreaded? Perhaps it
is un-American to say so, but I believe the answer is "No." Being
young is often pleasant, but being older has distinct advantages.

When young, you are apt to be obsessed with your outward   3
appearance. When my brother Dave and I were teens, we worked
feverishly to perfect the bodies we had. Dave lifted weights, took
megadoses of vitamins, and drank a half-dozen milk shakes a day in
order to turn his wiry adolescent frame into some muscular ideal. And

as a teenager, I dieted constantly. No matter what I weighed, though, I was never satisfied with the way I looked. My legs were too heavy, my shoulders too broad, my waist too big. When Dave and I were young, we begged and pleaded for the "right" clothes. If our parents didn't get them for us, we felt our world would fall apart. How could we go to school wearing loose-fitting blazers when everyone else would be wearing smartly tailored leather jackets? We would be considered freaks. I often wonder how my parents, and parents in general, manage to tolerate their children during the adolescent years. Now, however, Dave and I are beyond such adolescent agonies. My rounded figure seems fine, and I don't deny myself a slice of pecan pie if I feel in the mood. Dave still works out, but he has actually become fond of his tall lanky frame. The two of us enjoy wearing fashionable clothes, but we are no longer slaves to style. And women, I'm embarrassed to admit, even more than men, have always seemed to be at the mercy of fashion. Now my clothes--and my brother's--are attractive yet easy to wear. We no longer feel anxious about what others will think. As long as we feel good about how we look, we are happy.

Being older is preferable to being younger in another way. Obviously, I still have important choices to make about my life, but I have already made many of the critical decisions that confront those just starting out. I chose the man I wanted to marry. I decided to have children. I elected to return to college to complete my education. But when you are young, major decisions await you at every turn. "What college should I attend?" "What career should I pursue?" "Should I get married?" "Should I have children?" These are just a few of the issues facing young people. It's no wonder that, despite their carefree facade, they are often confused, uncertain, and troubled by all the unknowns in their future.

But the greatest benefit of being forty is knowing who I am. The most unsettling aspect of youth is the uncertainty you feel about your values, goals, and dreams. Being young means wondering what is worth working for. Being young means feeling happy with yourself one day and wishing you were never born the next. It means trying on new selves by taking up with different crowds. It means resenting your parents and their way of life one minute and then feeling you will never be as good or as accomplished as they are. By way of contrast, forty is sanity. I have a surer self-identity now. I don't laugh at jokes I don't think are funny. I can make a speech in front of a town meeting or complain in a store because I am no longer terrified that people will laugh at me; I am no longer anxious that everyone must like me. I no longer blame my parents for my every personality quirk or keep a running score of everything they did wrong raising me. Life has taught me that I, not they, am responsible for who I am. We are all human beings--neither saints nor devils.

Most Americans blindly accept the idea that newer is automati-   6
cally better. But a human life contradicts this premise. There is a
great deal of happiness to be found as we grow older. My own parents,
now in their sixties, recently told me that they are happier now than
they have ever been. They would not want to be my age. Did this
surprise me? At first, yes. Then it gladdened me. Their contentment
holds out great promise for me as I move into the next--perhaps even
better--phase of my life.

In response to the assignment, Carol decided to disprove the
widespread belief that being young is preferable to being old. The
comparison-contrast pattern allows her to analyze the drawbacks of
one and the merits of the other, thus providing the essay with an
evaluative purpose. Using the title to indicate her point of view,
Carol places the *thesis* at the end of her two-paragraph introduction: "Being young is often pleasant, but being older has distinct
advantages." Note that the thesis accomplishes several things. It
names the two subjects to be discussed and clarifies Carol's point of
view about her subjects. The thesis also implies that the essay will
focus on the contrasts between these two periods of life.

To support her assertion that older is better, Carol supplies
examples from her own life, organizing the examples around three
main points: attitudes about appearance, decisions about life
choices, and questions of self-concept. These key points are explored in separate supporting paragraphs, with each paragraph focused by a topic sentence: "When young, you are apt to be obsessed
with your outward appearance" (paragraph 3); "Being older is
preferable to being younger in another way" (4); and "But the
greatest benefit of being forty is knowing who I am" (5).

Now let's look more closely at the way these three central
points are presented. Carol obviously considers appearances the
least important of a person's worries, life choices more important,
and self-concept the most critical. And so she uses *emphatic order* to
sequence the supporting paragraphs, with the phrase "But the
greatest benefit" signaling the special significance of the last issue.
Carol is also careful throughout the essay to use *transitions* to help
readers follow her line of thinking: "*Now, however,* Dave and I are
beyond such adolescent agonies" (3); "*But* when you are young,
major decisions await you at every turn" (4); and "*By way of contrast,* forty is sanity" (5).

Although Carol has worked hard to write a well-organized paper—and has on the whole been successful—she does not feel compelled to make the paper fit a rigid format. She does not, for example, use the identical structure in each supporting paragraph. All three supporting paragraphs do use the *one-side-at-a-time format*—that is, everything about one age group is discussed before there is a shift to the other age group. But notice that the third and fifth paragraphs start with young people and then move to adults, whereas the fourth paragraph reverses the sequence by starting with older people.

As you read the third paragraph, you might have observed that Carol ran into a problem. Two sentences in the paragraph disrupt the *unity* of Carol's discussion: "I often wonder how my parents, and parents in general, tolerate their children during the adolescent years," and "Women, I'm embarrassed to admit . . . have always seemed to be at the mercy of fashion." These sentences should be deleted because they do not develop the idea that adolescents are overly concerned with appearances.

Carol's final paragraph brings the essay to a pleasing and interesting close. The conclusion recalls the point made in the introduction; that is, Americans overvalue youth. Carol also uses the conclusion to broaden the scope of her discussion. Rather than continuing to focus on herself, she briefly mentions her parents and the pleasure they take in life. By bringing her parents into the essay, Carol is able to make a gently philosophical observation about the promise that awaits her as she grows older. The implication is that a similarly positive future awaits us, too.

Carol made a number of changes when reworking her essay, but it is especially interesting to see the way she revised the introduction. The original draft of the introduction is reprinted here.

Unrevised Version

America is a land filled with people who worship youth. We admire dynamic young achievers; our middle-aged citizens work out in gyms; all of us wear tight tops and colorful sneakers--clothes that look fine on the young but ridiculous on aging bodies. Television shows revolve around perfect-looking young stars, while commercials entice us with products that will keep us young.

Wouldn't every older person want to be young again? Isn't aging to be avoided? It may be slightly unpatriotic to say so, but I believe the answer is "No." Being young may be pleasant at times, but I would rather be my forty-year-old self. I no longer have to agonize about my physical appearance, I have already made many of my crucial life decisions, and I am much less confused about who I am.

After looking closely at her original two-paragraph introduction, Carol was dissatisfied with what she had written. Although not quite sure what bothered her, she knew the paragraphs were flat and failed to start the essay on a strong note. She decided to begin her revision by whittling down the wordy opening sentence, making it crisper and more powerful: "Our society worships youth." That done, she next eliminated two bland sentences ("We admire dynamic young achievers," and "all of us wear tight tops and colorful sneakers"), and she made several vague references more concrete and interesting. "Commercials entice us with products that will keep us young" became "Grecian Formula and Oil of Olay . . . hide the gray in our hair and smooth the lines on our face"; "perfect-looking young stars" became "attractive young stars with firm bodies, perfect complexions, and thick manes of hair." With the addition of these specifics, the first paragraph became more vigorous and interesting.

Carol next made some subtle changes in the two questions that opened the second paragraph of the original introduction. Certainly, the revised sentences ("Wouldn't any person over thirty gladly sign with the devil just to be young again?" and "Isn't aging an experience to be dreaded?") are more emphatic than the originals. Moreover, these rephrased, attention-getting questions convey our national obsession with youth, a point that had to be made dramatically if the essay were to achieve its purpose. Carol also revised the end of the original version of her second paragraph. Because the paper is relatively short, and the subject matter easy to understand, Carol decided to omit her somewhat awkward *plan of development* ("I no longer have to agonize about my physical appearance, I have already made many of my crucial life decisions, and I am much less confused about who I am"). This change made it possible to end the introduction with a strong statement of the essay's thesis.

Once these revisions were made, Carol was able to get her essay off to a solid start. And, on the whole, she maintains this strength to the end, producing an interesting piece that offers valuable food for thought.

The essays that follow use comparison and contrast to explore a wide range of subjects. Michael LeBoeuf's "Japan: The Productivity Challenge" contrasts American and Japanese styles of management. In "Male and Female," Alison Lurie reaches some interesting conclusions about the politics of sex while analyzing the differences between male and female clothing. In "High Noon," Art Spikol compares the magical movie matinees of years past with the current crop of films that attract youngsters. Richard Rodriguez's "Workers" is a highly personal account of different work situations. And Loren Eiseley, in "The Brown Wasps," compares the deep yearning that can be found in both the animal and the human world for a permanence in life.

Michael LeBoeuf

*At the University of New Orleans, Michael LeBoeuf teaches
management theory, organizational behavior, and communication. In addition to his academic duties, LeBoeuf also
works as a management consultant in business and industry.
LeBoeuf has also authored several books, including* Working
Smart *(1980) and* The Greatest Management Principle in
the World *(1985). This excerpt is from his 1982 book,* The
Productivity Challenge.

Japan: The
Productivity Challenge

*Not very long ago, the label "Made in Japan" meant shoddy,
cheap, second-rate. Now, however, many people seek out Japanese brand names because they want to buy the highest quality
products. How has Japan come so far in one generation? In
the following selection, Michael LeBoeuf identifies the factors
that have propelled Toyota, Mitsubishi, Sony, and other Japanese firms to the top of the business world.*

Incredible! It's the only way to describe Japanese productivity 1
when you consider the circumstances. Here is a nation with half as
many people as the U.S. has crowded onto a land area the size of
Montana. Japan imports 100 percent of its aluminum, 99.8 percent of its oil, 98.4 percent of its iron ore, 66.4 percent of its
lumber, and only 15 percent of its land area is arable. In 1945,
Japan's industrial capacity was totally destroyed and years later
"Made in Japan" was a catch phrase for shoddy, second-rate mer-
chandise. Things have changed.

In the 1970s, while the U.S. earned the poorest productivity 2
improvement record of major free-world nations, Japan set the
pace. Consider these facts:

- Japanese steel outcompetes American steel.
- Japanese motorcycles have eliminated the British motorcycle industry.
- The German camera and lens industry and the Swiss watch industry have given way to Japanese superiority.
- Japan is the leading developer, producer, and user of robots.
- In 1980, Japan surpassed the U.S. as the world's leading producer of automobiles.
- If subsidized housing is included, Japanese wages surpassed American wages in 1978 and are growing at a faster rate.
- Due to successful energy conservation, Japan can produce a unit of gross national product at one-third the energy cost of the U.S. unit.
- Illiteracy is virtually nonexistent in Japan.
- Japanese crime rates are a fraction of those in the U.S. and declining.
- In 1977, Japanese longevity surpassed Sweden's to become first in the world.

Additionally, Japan has for years been a leader in consumer 3
electronics, has played havoc with the American photocopy industry, and is now mounting a serious challenge in the world computer industry. Good grief, Charlie Brown! How did they do it?

Today, American executives and consultants are journeying to 4
Japan and treating it with the reverence of an industrial Mecca. Everyone is eager to learn the secrets of Japanese productivity that enabled an industrially destroyed nation to rebuild itself into the world's second largest free-world power in less than thirty-five years.

Actually, there aren't any secrets. The Japanese have simply 5
learned to get maximum productivity from people because people are their only resource. Japanese executives are among the best in the world and their approach to human resources is one of unparalleled excellence. If there's one lesson we can learn from Japan, it's that productivity improvement begins with people improvement. Once you have a trained, organized, and committed workforce pulling together, productivity takes care of itself.

In this essay we will look at some of the reasons Japan has 6 enjoyed such phenomenal success. We will also look at what we are learning from the Japanese that can be applied to solve our own productivity problems.

Economic insecurity is the driving force behind Japan's   7
booming success. Does that surprise you? It would be reasonable to assume that the Japanese should be very smug about their economic success, but just the opposite is true. Japan may be a very affluent country but the Japanese don't see it that way.

From parents, teachers, the media, and every other informa-   8
tive source, young Japanese are told again and again that Japan must cram 115 million people onto a small island and depend on foreign sources for everything from food to oil. As a result, if you ask a Japanese citizen about Japan's prosperity you're likely to hear a real hardship story, like "We are a very poor nation with no natural resources. All of us must work very, very hard."

And very, very hard is how they work. Japanese managers have   9
little trouble motivating employees to work hard because most of them come to the job believing that they, in part, shoulder the burden for Japan's survival. To paraphrase the Datsun slogan, they are driven.

Most Americans are surprised to learn that the Japanese are   10
rather uneasy about their lot. After all, most of us hear and read success stories and predictions of how Japan will surpass the U.S. in per capita GNP by 1990. But the insecurity is very real and understandable. Imagine, if you would:

- Crowding the U.S. population into two states the size of Montana.
- Removing all of our oil and mineral resources and just about all of our agricultural resources.
- Putting the gigantic defense umbrella that protects the U.S. into the hands of a foreign power.
- Having experienced total destruction of the U.S. in your lifetime through conventional and nuclear war.

Would these conditions and experiences increase your con-   11
cern about America's future? Now you're beginning to understand the Japanese pangs of insecurity. A fifty-year-old Japanese citizen has experienced all of these things in his nation in his lifetime.

In addition to explaining the Japanese capacity for hard work, insecurity also explains their superior capacity for self-denial. Personal consumption in Japan takes a smaller percentage of total income than in most developed countries. The Japanese save 20 percent of their income and government policies stress the need for investment and productivity. Japan, compared to other advanced countries, lags in such areas as highways, hospitals, housing, schools (not education), and recreational facilities.

Other indicators of self-denial in the name of economic growth abound. Cities are overcrowded, lengthy commutes are common, and Tokyo is the world's most polluted city. In one sense, Japan is a nation of workaholics. Perhaps Carnegie-Mellon president Richard Cyert summed it up best when he remarked, "It's the old syndrome, when you're number two, you have to work harder. I wish we Americans would get a little of that 'We're number two' spirit. If we don't we're going to be." In fact, if current trends continue, Japan will lead the world in gross national product by the year 2000.

Insecurity may be the driving force behind Japan's success, but it's hardly a sufficient explanation. Many other resource-poor, hard-working, insecure nations remain destitute. Obviously, Japan works smarter.

The following are some of the major contributors to Japan's superproductivity. As you read each of these factors, ask yourself, "What lessons are here that we can learn and profit from?" For years, Japanese executives and government officials have let America teach them to work better. Now it's the students' turn to teach and our turn to sit back, listen, and learn.

The most striking factor about the Japanese is their strong sense of national purpose and clear-cut goals for every person, group, organization, and industry. Everyone's role is related to helping achieve the ultimate goal of a more prosperous Japan. In a sense, Japan is one gigantic program of management by objectives. Each worker works for the company who, in turn, works for the industry, who, in turn, works for Japan. Japan, Inc. (as Japan's triumvirate of government, banking, and industry has been enviously labeled) gives the impression of being one gigantic team.

And teamwork has been a major key to Japan's success. Management, government, labor, and the banks have all worked together in a rather simple, straightforward plan to build a better Japan. Here's how the plan was set up:

1. In the government, Japan's Ministry of International Trade and Industry (MITI) worked with businesses and developed policies to guide industrial growth.
2. Japan's banks and the Ministry of Finance saw to it that the capital was supplied to the businesses to enable them to grow.
3. Business and labor were given a relatively free hand to develop without government intervention in a free-enterprise, capitalistic environment. Social programs and governmental regulations were minimized or deferred.
4. Top priority was given to building first-class modern industries with the best technology available.

Management, labor, and the government all pulled together   18
with a common plan. And the plan worked.

Capital formation is an essential ingredient to increasing pro-   19
ductivity. And the Japanese have come up with a great way to assure
that banks have a ready supply of capital to lead to businesses.
Japanese workers receive approximately 40 percent of their   20
yearly income in two bonuses. The size of the bonus is based on
how well the company does, which gives everyone an incentive to
work better. But the real national advantage is that workers become
accustomed to living at a level less than their income. Consequently, the average citizen saves 20 percent of his income, which
supplies a ready source of capital for banks to lend to businesses.
The result is that Japanese firms rely more heavily on bank   21
loans than on selling stocks and bonds for raising capital. And bank
loans put far less pressure on businesses to look good today at the
expense of ignoring long-term investments. The average Japanese
company raises only one-sixth of its capital needs by selling securi-
ties compared to one-half in the United States.
The growth of Japanese capital has been a key factor in their   22
success. Available capital has made investing in new plants, retool-
ing old ones, new industries, and basic research all possible. In fact,
one study by the New York Stock Exchange attributes Japan's eco-

nomic growth between 1973 and 1979 to the fact that capital stock increased at a rate of 7.2 percent. The study also claims that the U.S. growth rate would have equaled Japan's during that period had our capital stock increased at an equal rate.

The pursuit of knowledge is a near-obsession with the Japa- 23
nese. They realize that a high-technology, industrial nation needs information like a car needs gasoline. Consequently the Japanese are the most avid learners in the world. This unending thirst for knowledge exhibits itself in many ways.

Most important, Japan is the world's best educated nation. In 24
addition to having a thorough grounding in Japanese, millions of Japanese are fluent in English and many speak three and four languages. In international testing programs Japanese youth score higher than American youth, whose scores continue to decline. On a per capita basis. Japan graduates over twice as many scientists and engineers as the U.S. and the level of mathematical and scientific instruction in Japan is reputed to be the highest in the world.

Japanese education is rigorous and tightly controlled by the 25
Japanese Ministry of Education. A premium is placed on academic achievement, and the environment (like Japanese business) is extremely competitive. In addition to mastering the very difficult Japanese language (which involves memorizing almost 2000 characters), math, and science, Japanese children must take courses in ethics that stress proper social behavior, work, and community obligations. Unlike the U.S., Japan sees nothing inconsistent about teaching moral values in public schools and the constitutional separation of church and state.

But the Japanese appetite for information doesn't end with 26
their formal education. Training is a regular part of every employee's job until he retires. Japanese workers are always on the lookout for new ideas, new techniques, new books, or any type of information that will enable them to increase productivity and improve themselves. Japanese executives will be the first to tell you that much of their success has come from applying knowledge that was learned from Western nations, most notably the U.S.

The ability to listen and learn also pays off handsomely for 27
Japan in the area of international trade. No other country equals the Japanese in defining what the world will buy. Instead of developing new products and then trying to sell them, the Japanese

listen very carefully to the customer and then give him the product that *he* wants.

Although the spirit of teamwork permeates the Japanese cul-   28
ture, it should be pointed out that fierce competition is also a part
of Japan. Competition for entrance into top schools and colleges is
very rigorous. And competition between firms and industries is
extremely heavy. Those that emerge as winners are encouraged and
supported in their efforts to expand internationally.

What happens to the losers? I can assure you the government   29
doesn't bail them out. Japanese banks take a merciless approach to
dying products and industries and refuse to finance them. Weak
companies make better use of their resources or go out of business.
Japanese competition is a battle where the strong survive. And this
internal competition helps Japan decide which products, companies, and industries are most likely to succeed in the world market
place.

Large Japanese corporations offer employees much more than   30
wages. They offer a way of life and a large dose of paternalism.

About 35 percent of Japan's labor force enjoys the security of   31
guaranteed employment until age fifty-five. When business is poor
everyone receives lower salaries or bonuses instead of being fired or
furloughed. Most workers are employed directly out of school and
remain with the company for the length of their careers. Such a
practice offers several advantages:

1. The workers develop strong company loyalty because of
   job security and the fact that salary increases are based on
   seniority.
2. Companies can invest in the continuous training and development of workers with the confidence that it will pay
   off.
3. Workers are eager to learn and accept new ways to increase
   productivity. A new robot or computer won't put them out
   of work and will likely increase their income.
4. Employees can be evaluated over a long period of time to
   discover their strengths and how the company can best use
   them.

Decisions by consensus and extensive participation are an-   32
other major component of the Japanese work culture. It's a long,
tedious process that may involve scores of individuals and would
drive many American managers up the wall. Everyone affected by a
decision is given the opportunity to have a voice in making the
decision. The goal is to find an alternative that everyone can agree
on and live with. Once agreement is reached, decisions are much
more readily accepted and implemented because everyone is in
agreement. No one attempts to slow down or sabotage the plan.
The willingness to achieve consensus through compromising is
one of the most important native characteristics of the Japanese.

This isn't to say that Japanese management is soft and permis-   33
sive. In a Japanese organization there's no doubt about who's boss
and bosses demand large amounts of work, loyalty, and discipline
from employees. But every worker's opinion is regarded as important and he is consulted on decisions that will affect him.

To the Japanese, a corporation's most important role isn't to   34
make a profit but to provide for the wellbeing of its workers and
society as a whole. Japanese managers place much more emphasis
on providing a work environment that most of us would think of as
one big family. Japanese organizations downplay the status distinctions between managers and workers, which helps to promote a
team atmosphere rather than one of "us versus them." Typically,
Japanese managers don't have private offices. They feel that the
open offices nurture a feeling of togetherness.

Company identity is very strong. It's common for employees   35
at all levels to wear company uniforms and workers often begin
their days by singing the company song and doing exercises. Most
companies have a ceremony to welcome new employees and the
ritual is attended by the new recruit's parents and other relatives.
Lifetime employee training stresses the importance of individual
growth and improvement through self-discipline. New employees
are often housed in company dormitories and company financing
is frequently provided for workers wanting to buy their own
homes. Company social clubs provide for off-the-job needs, offering everything from short courses in the tea ceremony to wedding
arrangements. In short, the employee's life revolves around the
company.

It should be pointed out that all of these characteristics are   36
descriptive of large Japanese corporations and that not everyone in

Japan works in such an environment. Japanese society also consists of a large number of persons who are self-employed as farmers, shopkeepers, scholars, writers, lawyers, artists, and the like. Japan is an essentially free society and anyone who works for a large, paternalistic corporation does so by choice.

The extensive training given to Japanese managers is one reason they are so good. Young trainees take part in a lengthy program that may last up to one year and places a heavy emphasis on learning coupled with a healthy dose of hands-on experience.   37

New trainees typically begin learning about their company by attending a series of lectures given by company executives. For a one- or two-week period, new recruits are schooled in such areas as company background, products, production, sales, and basic business skills.   38

Realizing that lectures can often be boring and ineffective, many companies require employees to compile a company handbook after hearing the lectures. This forces them to assimilate the knowledge and express it themselves. Another orientation exercise is to distribute employee handbooks to trainees and tell them the company is dissatisfied and wants it revised. Teams of five or six employees are then asked to write a revised handbook by the next morning. In addition to providing the company with fresh ideas, this gives the trainees experience in working as a team against a tight deadline.   39

Following the orientation period, management trainees usually spend several months involved in practical work experience. Manufacturing-oriented companies require trainees to work various production jobs to enable them to understand the inner workings of the company. Thus, a new trainee may work around-the-clock shifts alongside regular production workers as part of his training. Later he may be transferred to sales and service and asked to work in these areas. Still later he may be assigned to a financial job, inventory control, purchasing, personnel, or some other division. Rotating future managers through a number of training assignments gives them broad experience in understanding how the pieces of the organization fit together and the problems associated with each department. The experience also teaches them how to communicate, work, and empathize with people from all areas of   40 the company. Later on as managers they will probably settle into one functional area and stay there throughout their career.

Live-in training is also another important aspect of most Japa- 41
nese training programs. During the training period, new employees live together in company residences or external training centers. In addition to making a successful transition from student life to company life, trainees are expected to learn and experience teamwork, punctuality, human relations, and social rules. Through live-in training future managers are also expected to learn self-sufficiency, a positive attitude, and consideration for others. Live-in training lasts from a few days to several months, depending on the company.

Most companies require new employees to keep a diary of their 42
experiences and impressions throughout the entire training program. At the end of the program, participants are asked to submit a written report based on the diary.

By the end of the training period, the company and the future 43
manager both know a lot more about each other than at the start. The trainee has been observed in various work situations and management can use this information to identify which work area would be best for the new manager. And the new manager has been indoctrinated, has experienced the company from many different viewpoints and been absorbed into the corporate culture. He hasn't had the specialized training of his American counterpart. But why should he worry? Once he is assigned to a functional area he will continue learning about it for the rest of his career.

One quality that the Japanese have an abundance of is pa- 44
tience. Unlike the Americans, they haven't been crippled by wanting everything now. Japanese executives and governmental officials aren't interested in the quick payoff or the fast yen. Rather, they think in terms of five, ten, and twenty years ahead, and their ultimate aim is to build a solid prosperity and stability that will serve Japan for generations to come. And they are realistic and pragmatic enough to realize that the future belongs to those who plan for it, work hard, and invest in it. The seeds of today's Japanese success story were sowed more than thirty years ago.

Unlike American firms, Japanese firms don't suffer from 45
short-term pressures from Wall Street. As pointed out earlier, most

of the businesses are invested in or partly owned by banks and banks are much more interested in solid, long-term growth than in inflated stock prices and fast dividends. This, coupled with the savings of the Japanese people, has contributed immensely to Japan's success by making long-range investments possible. And those investments are paying off handsomely today.

Questions for Close Reading

1. What is the thesis of the selection? Locate the sentence(s) in which LeBoeuf states his main idea. If he does not state the thesis explicitly, express it in your own words.
2. How many factors leading to Japan's great productivity does LeBoeuf identify? What are they?
3. What handicaps has Japan had to overcome to be the free world's second largest power?
4. How does the Japanese work culture foster a positive attitude among workers about their jobs, their companies, and themselves?
5. Refer to your dictionary as needed to define the following words used in the selection: *longevity* (paragraph 2), *phenomenal* (6), *destitute* (14), *triumvirate* (16), *furloughed* (31), *consensus* (32), *compile* (39), and *counterpart* (43).

Questions about the Writer's Craft

1. Generally, writers using the comparison-contrast format devote equal time to each side of their subject. But LeBoeuf spends very little time telling his readers about the United States' side of his analysis. Why? Who is his intended audience?
2. An essay on economics could be very dry, but the author has made this essay quite readable. What tone has he used? What does he do to keep you interested?
3. What contrast does LeBoeuf develop in paragraphs 1, 2, and 3? What other techniques does he use in this introduction to draw you into the essay?
4. LeBoeuf provides much information about the Japanese in order to support his idea that we have much to learn from them. Which points are supported by facts and statistics? By general information? Are there places where the support is weak or lacking?

Questions for Further Thought

1. Would you work for a Japanese company? Why or why not?
2. Do you think that American education should be directed by the fed-

eral government? Should other changes be instituted to make our graduates as educated as Japanese students? Would you be willing, for example, to learn one or two foreign languages fluently?
3. American business operates on the profit motive: whatever leads to the biggest profit becomes policy. What is the main goal of Japanese corporations? Should the U.S. copy this attitude? Are there any Japanese-style motivations you would like to see brought to the American workplace?
4. Would you want to work for the same company for thirty-five years? Does our system of changing jobs, competing for promotions, and so on have any advantages for workers, workers' families, or the economy as a whole?

Writing Assignments Using Comparison-Contrast as a Method of Development

1. Write an essay for Japanese readers comparing and/or contrasting some aspect of our work or educational environment with that found in Japan. Just as LeBoeuf includes little material about the United States because he assumes his readers are from this country, you should provide only minimal background about the Japanese side of your subject. Use the information in LeBoeuf's essay to develop any needed material on Japan. Possible subjects for your essay include types of courses taught in the school, management styles in the business world, attitudes toward saving wages, and sources of motivation in the world of work.
2. The U.S. is a diverse place with many different kinds of schools and workplaces. Write an essay in which you compare and contrast the conditions in two schools you have attended (high school and college, for example) or at two jobs you have held. Make sure your paper's thesis signals the main point of the comparison as well as your attitude toward your subject.

Writing Assignments Using Other Methods of Development

3. Do Americans still value hard work and ingenuity as much as we used to? Or have other ways of gaining wealth and prestige become more important than "good old-fashioned hard work?" Develop the argument that Americans still do (or do not any longer) value hard work as a source of life's rewards.
4. Imagine how some aspect of your life — such as a task, decision, project, or conflict situation — would have turned out if you had used

one of the Japanese productivity techniques. For instance, you might focus on teamwork, productivity, participative decision making, or the ability to listen and learn. Write an essay outlining the effects of such a technique on one aspect of your life. Your thesis could be something like, "If my family had used participative decision-making, I would not have found our recent relocation to a new state so traumatic," or "If I could save even ten percent of my income, my life would be much easier."

Alison Lurie

Alison Lurie is the author of seven novels, including The War
Between the Tates *(1974),* Only Children *(1979), and*
Foreign Affairs, *which won the 1985 Pulitzer Prize for fiction. Born in 1926, Lurie grew up in New York City and
graduated from Radcliffe College. Before publishing her first
book, she worked as a librarian and a ghostwriter and currently teaches English at Cornell University. The following
selection from her 1981 book,* The Language of Clothes, *is
an analysis of the symbolic meaning of fashion.*

Male and Female

*How would a Martian newly arrived on earth figure out
which humans were male and female? Are the creatures in the
two-legged garments male? Are the humans with long hair
female? Are earrings worn by one sex, or both? Despite such
ambiguities, the alien would be able to draw one sound conclusion: clothes are important — far beyond their ability to
warm and protect our bodies. In the following selection, Alison
Lurie explores the values and messages implicit in the clothing
we wear.*

In the past sexual modesty was often proposed as the purpose   1
of dress. The Bible tells us that this was the original reason for
wearing clothes: Adam and Eve, once they realized that they were
naked, "sewed fig leaves together, and made themselves aprons."
Historically, however, shame seems to have played very little part
in the development of costume. In ancient Egypt, Crete and Greece
the naked body was not considered immodest; slaves and athletes
habitually went without clothing, while people of high rank wore
garments that were cut and draped so as to show a good deal when
in motion.

Some modern writers believe that the deliberate concealment   2
of certain parts of the body originated not as a way of discouraging
sexual interest, but as a clever device for arousing it. According to

this view, clothes are the physical equivalent of remarks like "I've got a secret"; they are a tease, a come-on. It is certainly true that parts of the human form considered sexually arousing are often covered in such a way as to exaggerate and draw attention to them. People done up in shiny colored wrappings and bows affect us just as a birthday present does: we're curious, turned on; we want to undo the package.

The naked unadorned body, by contrast, is not intrinsically   3
very exciting, especially en masse. Ingres' *Le Bain turc (The Turkish Bath)*, in which twenty plump nudes are crammed into a circular frame that repeats their generous curves, can seem — as Kenneth Clark says — "almost suffocating." Without the large figure in the foreground, he adds, "the whole composition might have made us feel slightly seasick." Too much nakedness in real life can have the same effect. Many visitors to nudist camps report that the sight of all that uncovered flesh brings fatigue and a sense of being slightly unwell. Later, after one gets used to it as the ancients were, it seems merely banal. Even in isolation an unadorned human body is often less exciting than a clothed one, and the most stimulating costumes of all are those which simultaneously conceal and reveal, like a suggestively wrapped gift hinting at delights beneath.

Whether it was the first cause or not, from the earliest times   4
one important function of clothing has been to promote erotic activity: to attract men and women to one another, thus ensuring the survival of the species. If maximum fertility is to be achieved, we must select members of the opposite sex rather than our own to make love to. One basic purpose of costume, therefore, is to distinguish men from women. In some periods this separation is absolute: what is properly worn by a man cannot be worn by a woman, and vice versa. As might be expected, at such times the birth rate is usually high. In other periods, such as our own, many items of clothing are sexually interchangeable, and the birth rate is lower. Even today, however, most garments are recognizably male or female — as anyone who has sorted rummage for a charity sale will recall.

Pink Kittens and Blue Spaceships

Sex-typing in dress begins at birth with the assignment of pale-pink   5
layettes, toys, bedding and furniture to girl babies, and pale-blue ones to boy babies. Pink, in this culture, is associated with senti-

ment; blue with service. The implication is that the little girl's future concern will be the life of the affections; the boy's, earning a living. As they grow older, light blue becomes a popular color for girls' clothes — after all, women must work as well as weep — but pink is rare on boys: the emotional life is never quite manly.

In early childhood girls' and boys' clothes are often identical   6 in cut and fabric, as if in recognition of the fact that their bodies are much alike. But the T-shirts, pull-on slacks and zip jackets intended for boys are usually made in darker colors (especially forest green, navy, red and brown) and printed with designs involving sports, transportation and cute wild animals. Girls' clothes are made in paler colors (especially pink, yellow and green) and decorated with flowers and cute domestic animals. The suggestion is that the boy will play vigorously and travel over long distances; the girl will stay home and nurture plants and small mammals. Alternatively, these designs may symbolize their wearers: the boy is a cuddly bear or a smiling tiger, the girl a flower or a kitten. There is also a tendency for boys' clothes to be fullest at the shoulders and girls' at the hips, anticipating their adult figures. Boys' and men's garments also emphasize the shoulders with horizontal stripes, epaulets or yokes of contrasting color. Girls' and women's garments emphasize the hips and rear through the strategic placement of gathers and trimmings.

Rectangular Men and Rounded Women

Even for children dress-up clothing tends to be sex-typed in shape   7 as well as in color and decoration. By adolescence most of what we wear incorporates traditional male or female indicators: among them, for men, the garment that fastens to the right and the classic jacket, shirt and tie; for women the garment that fastens to the left, ruffles and bows, high-heeled shoes and the skirt in all its forms.

Male clothing has always been designed to suggest physical   8 and/or social dominance. Traditionally, the qualities that make a man attractive are size and muscular strength. In the past this preference was practical: most men were farmers, hunters or warriors, and the women who attached herself to a big, strong man had a better chance of survival. Men's garments therefore tended to enlarge the body through the use of strong colors and bulky materials, and to emphasize angularity with rectangular shapes and sharp points. They suggested or called attention to well-developed leg, shoulder and arm muscles by means of tight hose, trousers and jackets; and they increased the width of shoulders and chest with padding.

The modern sack suit, on the other hand, though often dark   9 and always rectangular in cut, suppresses or conceals all the features that are supposed to constitute male beauty: broad shoulders, slim waist and hips, flat stomach and well-muscled legs. But, as pointed out earlier, for a man who lacks these attributes the sack suit is flattering. If it is well cut it can hide a sunken chest or a small pot. And whether a man is athletically built or not, it diverts attention from his physical qualifications and focuses attention on his economic and social status. The sack suit is a middle-class indicator, and in a world in which class membership is a safer guarantee of prosperity than pure brawn, an expensive version may have considerable erotic charm, especially for women who are looking for husbands rather than lovers.

Female costume, during most of modern European history,   10 was designed to suggest successful maternity. It emphasized rounded contours and rich, soft materials, and tended to center interest on the breasts and stomach. Energy, strength and health were regarded as attractive, and they were expressed through bright, glowing colors and full-cut gowns with strong, sweeping curves that often accommodated and flattered the pregnant woman. Such clothes can be seen in many paintings of the Renaissance and Baroque period, and (in a somewhat more refined form) in those of the Rococo.

Romantic Frailty

In the early nineteenth century, however, a new feminine ideal   11 appeared. Women were redefined as something between children and angels: weak, timid, innocent creatures of sensitive nerves and easily alarmed modesty who could only be truly safe and happy under the protection of some man. Physical slightness and fragility were admired, and what was now called "rude health" was considered coarse and lower-class. To be pale and delicate, to blush and faint readily and lie about on sofas was ladylike; strength and vigor were the characteristics of vulgar, red-cheeked, thick-waisted servants and factory girls. The more useless and helpless a woman looked, the higher her presumed social status, and the more elegant and beautiful she was perceived as being.

Early nineteenth-century fashions were designed to give a look 12 of fragile immaturity. They emphasized weakness of both structure and substance through the use of pale colors and delicate, easily damaged materials. More ominously, these clothes ensured the charming ill-health of their wearers by putting them into thin-soled slippers and short-sleeved, low-necked dresses or semitransparent muslin. When worn in the drafty ballrooms and along the icy, muddy lanes of a British or North American winter, such clothes were almost a guarantee of the feverish colds and sore throats that are so common in the novels of Jane Austen and the Brontës; looking at portraits of the period, it seems no surprise that consumption was the most dreaded disease of the time.

Fashionable Debility: The Corset

By the 1830s, female fashions offered somewhat more protection 13 from the climate, but they continued to suggest — and to promote — physical frailty. Early-Victorian costume not only made women *look* weak and helpless, it made them weak and helpless. The main agent of this debility, as many writers have pointed out, was the corset, which at the time was thought of not as a mere fashion but as a medical necessity. Ladies' "frames," it was believed, were extremely delicate; their muscles could not hold them up without assistance. Like many such beliefs, this one was self-fulfilling. Well-brought-up little girls, from the best motives, were laced into juvenile versions of the corset as early as three or four. Gradually, but relentlessly, their stays were lengthened, stiffened and tightened. By the time they reached late adolescence they were wearing cages of heavy canvas reinforced with whalebone or steel, and their back muscles had often atrophied to the point where they could not sit or stand for long unsupported. The corset also deformed the internal organs and made it impossible to draw a deep breath. As a result the fashionably dressed lady blushed and fainted easily, suffered from lack of appetite and from digestive complaints, and felt weak and exhausted after any strenuous exertion. When she took off her corset her back soon began to ache; and sometimes she still could not breathe properly because her ribs had been permanently compressed inward.

Over this debilitating foundation garment the Victorian 14
woman wore several layers of shifts and chemises, three or more
petticoats, a hoop skirt or crinoline and a long dress that might
contain twenty yards of heavy wool or silk and was often also boned
in the bodice and trimmed with additional fabric, ribbon and
beads. When she left the house she added a heavy woolen shawl and
a large bonnet or hat decorated with feathers, flowers, ribbons and
veiling. Altogether she might carry from ten to thirty pounds of
clothing; a contemporary writer, feeling this to be a bit of a burden,
suggested seven pounds as the minimum for a respectable woman.
Yet even with all this weight on her back the Victorian lady was not
protected from the climate, since fashion (especially evening fashion) often demanded that her neck, shoulders and chest be exposed.

In this costume it was difficult to move about or walk vigor- 15
ously, and almost impossible to run. But then, ladies did not
"walk," since in polite discourse they had no legs — rather they
"glided" or "swept" across the floor like carpet sweepers — and
they certainly did not run. In an emergency the proper thing to do
was to faint, relying on the protection of the nearest gentleman.

Even more important than the medical justification of the 16
corset was its social justification. Women were considered the
frailer sex not only physically but morally: their minds and their
wills as well as their backs were weak. A lady might be pure and
innocent, of course, but this purity and innocence could be preserved only by constant vigilance. Therefore she must not attend a
university or follow a profession; she must not travel without a
chaperone; she must not visit a man's rooms; and she must not see
any play or read any book that might inflame her imagination —
even Shakespeare was dangerous except in the expurgated version
of Thomas Bowdler. Even thus guarded, the early-Victorian
woman was in constant danger of becoming the victim of man's
lust and her own weakness. She needed to be at once supported and
confined, in a many-layered, heavily reinforced costume that
would make undressing a difficult and lengthy process. . . .

The Lady as a Luxury Item

Why did the early-Victorian woman put up with early-Victorian 17
fashions? Partly, no doubt, because they were admired by men and

described everywhere as beautiful, elegant and charming. But also, certainly, because she believed the current propaganda: she thought of the clothes that imprisoned and deformed her as medically necessary and morally respectable. Tight lacing was associated in the popular mind with virtue: a well-dressed woman whose stays were loose, however rich her costume, was probably a loose woman. A girl of relatively modest means, however, if her shoes and gloves were tight enough, her dress properly fragile and her corset laced so that she could scarcely breathe, might hope to be admired. She might even, if lucky, become the petted and indulged and confined wife of a man of means.

In a patriarchal society a helpless, foolish, pretty woman is the 18 ultimate object of Conspicuous Consumption. Rich men chose to purchase and maintain such a woman as a sign of their own economic and sexual power. What she looks like physically is not important; she may be a plump odalisque, a proper Victorian lady, or a twentieth-century Dumb Blonde of the Petty Girl type (now a vanishing species). For maximum status gain, however, such a woman must be of no practical use. She must be unable to type, cook, clean, care for children, manage an estate or keep track of your investments—all these things must be done by paid employees. Ideally, the clothes this woman wears will identify her as a luxury item. The Dumb Blonde is supposed to be in bouncy good health and to have a Florida tan, but her tight satin sheath, spike heels and long, brittle, varnished nails—like the Victorian lady's corset and crinoline—make her prestigious uselessness obvious.

The costumes of the Victorian lady and the expense-account 19 blonde are examples of the principle still in force, that clothes which make a woman's life difficult and handicap her in competition with men are always felt to be sexually attractive. This is true not only of tight, figure-revealing garments, but also of heavy, clumsy fashions such as platform shoes and the trailing skirt. As Thorstein Veblen pointed out over a hundred years ago, "The substantial reason for our tenacious attachment to the skirt is just this: it is expensive and it hampers the wearer at every turn and incapacitates her for all useful exertion." The women who chooses to wear such clothes announces to everyone that she is willing to be handicapped in life in relation to men; men reward her for this by finding both her and her clothes attractive.

Questions for Close Reading

1. What is the thesis of the selection? Locate the sentence(s) in which Lurie states her main idea. If she does not state the thesis explicitly, express it in your own words.
2. How does children's clothing often imitate the sex-typed styles of adult dress?
3. What male characteristics does the modern man's "sack suit" suppress? What male characteristics does it emphasize?
4. In what ways did the corset reflect the social status of women during the nineteenth century? How did the corset help contribute to a particular image of femaleness?
5. Refer to your dictionary as needed to define the following words used in the selection: *en masse* (paragraph 3), *banal* (3), *atrophied* (13), *debilitating* (14), and *tenacious* (19).

Questions about the Writer's Craft

1. Does Lurie use the point-by-point or one-side-at-a-time method to develop her essay?
2. Lurie begins this selection with an *epigraph*—a quotation from another writer. How does this quotation about fashion help her make her point?
3. The author analyzes clothing through history to point out certain trends and themes. What support does she supply for her interpretations of the meaning of human dress?
4. What is the writer's tone in this selection? Are there places where she directly or indirectly reveals her own opinion about women's dress?

Questions for Further Thought

1. Should women dress differently than men? Why or why not? Should extreme, and often painful, styles of women's (as of men's) clothing be eliminated?
2. Of the many functions performed by clothing, what purpose is uppermost in your mind as you shop or get dressed? Do you follow fashion trends or dress to project an image? Do you see your friends or family dressing for comfort or to impress?
3. To what extent do we judge other people by their clothing? When you meet someone, how important are such clothing characteristics as neatness, trendiness, individuality, luxury, and so on, as you form an impression of the person?
4. Does Lurie persuade you that clothing is designed primarily to entice, not promote modesty or protect our bodies as we are usually taught? Should people continue to dress to attract, or should we try to play down this function, and dress for comfort and protection?

Writing Assignments Using Comparison-Contrast as a Method of Development

1. Lurie analyzes the meaning of clothing to show how our culture's expectations for males and females are very different. Pick another area of life where you see different priorities for males and females. You might choose one of the following or any other area of life:

   Styles of hair or accessories.
   Styles of decorating homes or dorm rooms.
   Leisure pursuits.
   Use of cosmetics and toiletries.

   Using the comparison-contrast format to analyze the area of life selected, discuss what you observe about male and female attitudes and behavior. Your analysis should help explain the role of societal expectations in defining these characteristic patterns.

2. Clothes are not the only area of life where fashions change. Choose another realm where there have been changes over the years, such as

cars	rock music
houses	leisure pursuits
furniture	preferred careers

   Write an essay comparing and/or contrasting what these things were like years ago to the way they are today. Be sure to discuss what the changes indicate about our society, its attitudes and values.

Writing Assignments Using Other Methods of Development

3. Lurie writes as if all members of the same sex in a society dress the same. Actually, there are many subgroups that adopt a particular style of clothing. Examples are some religious groups (the Amish or strict Muslims), some economic and occupational groups (business people, rock stars, crafts and trades people), and rebels (beatniks, hippies, and punks). Choose one subgroup that is characterized by a particular style of attire. Describe the typical dress for people in this subgroup and explain the symbolic meaning of the clothing worn.

4. Write an essay arguing against a typical or common form of contemporary dress. For example, you might take the position that women should not wear high heels, bras, pocketbooks, lace, and ruffles, or that men should not wear earrings, ties, or three-piece suits. Provide at least three reasons for your point of view. Your essay may be light or serious in tone.

Art Spikol

Art Spikol has used his writing talents in many ways. He was editor of Philadelphia Magazine, *one of the country's most successful city publications; author of* Magazine Writing: The Inside Angle; *founder of The Philadelphia Writer's School. He has lectured widely on the subject of writing, but is probably best known for his "Nonfiction" column, a staple of* Writer's Digest *for over a decade. Today, a self-employed writer, editor, and graphic designer, he divides his time between advertising and his "real love," writing; his first novel recently sold to a major publisher. This selection originally appeared in* Philadelphia Magazine.

High Noon

In some ways, life is a series of losses. Loved ones leave, pets die, neighborhoods are left behind. Yet the things we lose can endure — if we work at remembering them. In the following selection, Art Spikol recreates an experience that was a highlight of his childhood: the Saturday movie matinee. Discovering the extent of his loss when he takes his daughter to a modern-day matinee, Spikol reminisces about the vanished world of cliffhanger serials, newsreels, and cartoons. And behind this nostalgia lies a sense of loss for the world that disappeared along with the Saturday matinee.

The Saturday matinee, for those of you who ever chafed while 1 waiting for the weekend to arrive, is dead. I learned this only recently when I took my seven-year-old daughter, Elizabeth, to one; first I consulted the neighborhood movie guide in the paper, expecting to find dozens of kiddie matinees, and found maybe four or five in the city. The movies I attended as a kid — the Lindley, the Logan and the Rockland in the Logan section of the city — are no longer there. The ones I attended as a teenager — the Benner, the Castor and the Tyson, all on Castor Avenue in the Northeast — were showing R-rated films and had no matinees listed.

328

I finally ended up at a theater called the Parkwood Manor in a   2
small shopping center at Academy and Byberry Roads in the
Northeast, dragging my daughter, who would rather have gone to a
friend's house anyway, behind me.

Driving out there, we talked. I told Elizabeth about the old   3
Saturday matinees, the ones that I grew up with. I told her about
the time I was ejected from the Lindley on 5th Street because I ran
up on the stage to avoid capture by a neighborhood bully, and how
I sat and wept on the steps of the theater, not knowing where to go
or what to do. I told her about the harmonica contest I entered at
the Logan Theater on Broad Street with what would have seemed a
pretty good chance of winning—there was only one other
contestant—and how I played "Oh Susannah" and "Old Black
Joe" and how nobody recognized either song, and how I turned red
and stared at my shoes while the other kid played "The Flight of the
Bumble Bee." I told her about the drawings they used to have—
they'd give away a bicycle to the lucky kid whose ticket stub number
matched the one they called—and how it was always a rich kid who
won. The more I told her about these things and other things like
the candy boxes that used to honk and popcorn that came out of
machines, the more excited and curious she became to arrive at the
Parkwood Manor—not so much to see *The Wonders of Aladdin*
and the two cartoons, but to relive something of her daddy's world.

The Parkwood Manor, it turned out, is a large theater by   4
today's standards and a good-sized one by yesterday's, not yet
having been twinned. It shows signs of wear—many of the seats
have been cut or torn and are held intact by wide strips of tape, and
some of the wall decorations have seen better days, but overall the
theater is pleasant and so are the people who work there: a cheerful
ticket-seller who smiled and said hello; an older, gray-haired ticket-
taker who chatted amiably about how bad business is these days,
and a young woman behind the candy counter who told me that
she'd be on duty throughout the picture if I wanted anything else.

We bought our popcorn and Raisinets and Jujyfruits and soda   5
and took our seats, and waited.

I will tell you what I learned at the Parkwood Manor. But first,   6
let me tell you about 1944 and a woman, a gorgeous, smooth-
skinned brunette goddess who managed to move unencumbered

despite her tight khaki pants, despite the sleek boots and the pure white, tight, button-down-the-front blouse which barely restrained a chest yearning for release. I loved her for things she had and which I did not understand: her breasts, her buttocks. I loved the way she moved through the jungle, graceful and sure of herself, like the ladies in today's deodorant commercials, and I loved it when she moved over rough terrain and what happened to her hips when she did so. The camera spent a lot of time following her, as did the native bearers who never thought to take advantage of their position at the rear, as did I, from the audience. But while those on the screen were worried about mean-looking men with too-perfect mustaches, used-car-salesmen types transplanted, somehow, to darkest Africa, I was worried about her buttons.

I was eight and in love with Nyoka the Jungle Girl.   7

I had her for only a few minutes each week, but after they were   8
over I took her memory home and thought about her in the privacy of my bed, in that little tent theater under my covers. I was old enough to get a tickly feeling in my loins, too young to know what it was all about: I simply wished she could have been my mother.

This was the stuff of which the serials were made: 9

Scene: a cavern   Nyoka has been lured there, and now she   10
stands alone, vulnerable and trapped. Suddenly there is a sound like pistol fire — it is the floor of the cavern cracking beneath her feet. The whole screen trembles, the theater vibrates from the noise. And then, with a rip and a gasp, the cavern floor opens — it is like watching an earthquake — and bubbling up from under it is molten lava. A thousand little kids are bouncing up and down, screaming; one of them spills his candy on me.

Nyoka leaps for a hanging vine — and the cavern floor col-   11
lapses. I am, at this point, transfixed; my heart is thumping and I have forgotten the wad of candy in my cheek. I sit there watching her hang from the vine (she even *hangs* beautifully), kicking her wonderful legs, and as the lava bubbles up, almost touching her, I am wondering about what happens if she falls: will those breasts and hips and buttocks boil away and become vapor? The vine begins to tear [*closeup of vine*] thread by thread, each thread snapping like the crack of a whip. When there is only enough left to floss Nyoka's beautiful white teeth, the screen disintegrates into a crescendo of organ music and gives way to a title something like:

NEXT WEEK
LAIR OF EVIL

If that were all there'd been to it — the few minutes of Nyoka   12
or Flash Gordon or Secret Agent X-9 — the serials alone would
have been worth the three-block walk to the Lindley. The Saturday
matinee was the high point of every kid's week back then; it was the
long-awaited moment, like a particularly good dessert after a
dreadful meal, filling enough to have been the meal itself. Today
you can see some of it on television — the Dead End Kids, Our
Gang, the Bowery Boys, the Three Stooges — but watching on a
small screen, interrupted by commercials for overpriced games and
toys, is not anything like seeing it giant-sized and experiencing it as
a member of a concerned multitude.

To relieve the tension, cartoons usually followed the serials.   13
The Second World War was being fought, and it was probably
fought nowhere as bravely and as brilliantly as in neighborhood
theaters: Bugs Bunny, for instance, was pitted against Hitler, and
won. Or there was more serious stuff, some of it outright propaganda, subtly indoctrinating us, and we would laugh and cheer in
all the right parts, patriotic little bastards that we were. There was a
sense of total participation in that war that has never since been
duplicated, and the louder we cheered, the surer victory.

This was all before television — which made the movies not   14
only the sole visual treat of the week, but the only place to see film
coverage of the events that shaped the world, and so the newsreel
was an important part of any theater fare, Saturday matinees included. Warner-Pathé News opened with a burst of Sousa-like band
music and the crowing of the famous rooster, and it was the
Warner-Pathé rooster which told us it was time to go to the
bathroom: do it now or you'll miss something important. For me,
the rooster was part of a conditioned response. Even if I didn't *have*
to go, the rooster made me *want* to go. And when I got back, there
was still time to boo the enemy, cheer American advances and
FDR, and whistle at the beauty contest queens without knowing
why.

Then the coming attractions — small, magic glimpses of our   15
movie future — and then the main feature.

The main feature! You'd almost forgotten there *was* one, and a   16 sort of excitement filled you when you realized that the show was just *starting*. It was at the Lindley that I saw *Cat People*, a film which so terrified me that I sat up in bed for three nights straight, afraid to lie down or close my eyes. I saw *The Purple Heart* at the Lindley, and *Bataan*, and *Guadalcanal Diary*. I saw Frank Sinatra sing *The House I Live In*, a very moving short about brotherhood and working together, things that seemed very possible in those days. I saw every adventure that ever unfolded on the Spanish Main or the Barbary Coast or in Sherwood Forest. It was the fighting we wanted to see, the tales of bravery, although we knew that we had to put up with a little mush when Errol Flynn would have to stop swinging on curtain sashes occasionally to make love to somebody — but in those soft, tender moments we would boo and throw candy at girls. When the action came back on again, the theater fell silent once more until the hero came to the rescue and the good guys attacked the bad guys.

When it was over we ran from the theater and continued the   17
action in the streets on the way home, and what part you took would depend upon how much influence you had with your peers, which usually depended upon how big you were. For us smaller guys, it was a *fait accompli*: I was a Japanese soldier, or the Sheriff of Nottingham, and I was doomed to die soon and in agony. But I was glad to do it for the cause.

I would arrive home soaked with sweat, and my mother, who   18
thought of perspiration of any kind as the first sign of yellow fever, would run her hand through my hair with disapproval and tell me I would probably get sick and miss school, not as bad a fate as she imagined, and then she would ask me how the movie had been. I would always say the same thing: "Great!"

And it was. There was nothing like it, and I guess there will be   19
nothing like it ever again. There was something unrestrained about Saturday matinees, and whatever it was, it's dead now. To remember it is to mourn.

I had hoped to find it alive and well at the Parkwood Manor, a   20
theater which can seat about 1,000 people. But when we went to our seats, we had the theater to ourselves. There were no more than 20 to 25 people there, and that was all there was going to be. There is no question that such a matinee loses money, despite the fact that

there is no newsreel, no serial, no coming attractions, no shorts, and only two old and not-very-good cartoons.

But—almost as if they knew what I was there for—they   21 showed as their "main feature" *The Wonders of Aladdin*, with Donald O'Connor, a color extravaganza produced at no small cost back when it was made—about 15 years ago, I would guess. The fact that it was out of another era was not hard to substantiate: in one scene, the Prince, one of the heroes, tells a wounded soldier to chew a little hashish to relieve the pain: in another, the heroine is running across the desert trying to escape from the baddies, and—because she is wearing a very short dress—she is running with one hand holding the dress down over her crotch. Take my word for it, it was an old movie, and I even vaguely remembered seeing it once, long ago. The kids who were there seemed to like it, but it was hard to tell. No one would have dared to cheer; it would have been hollow and presumptuous, like the noise made when a book is dropped in a library.

I remember one whispered comment, from a little boy a few   22 rows behind us. Donald O'Connor races in to rescue the lady in distress, in this case a voluptuous brunette hanging by her wrists, apparently stark naked. She has been tortured. She is also hidden from the viewer's eyes by a large gong, and when she sees O'Connor she twists frantically to turn her body around so that he can't see her private parts. It is one of the movie's funniest moments, this maiden suddenly getting modesty, and one of the kids behind me says wistfully, "If only that thing wasn't in the way, we could see *everything*." He was about seven years old.

Kids haven't changed much, but the world around them has.   23 The Saturday matinee may be alive and well under certain circumstances—like when a film ballyhooed on TV comes to town for a limited engagement—but then it is simply an event, not *the* event. The circus is over.

Movies used to open with "The Star Spangled Banner." The   24 audience, kids and grownups alike, would rise as one to the music and sing the words, watching the screen as the flag whipped slowly in the wind. I don't think the flag is particularly beautiful, but when I remember myself at eight, I know that it was beautiful once. Occasionally there'd be a serviceman in the audience home on furlough, and he'd salute while other adults would place their hands over their hearts, and we kids, identifying much more strongly with the guys at the front than with our parents at home, would salute, too. We didn't question the flag. We didn't know that it could be used to cover things up as well as to liberate. It may not have been the best of times back then, but it was certainly the easiest of times; we knew all we had to know, and we knew what we had to do.

Sophistication killed the Saturday matinee, and the kid who   25
watches *Kojak* and *All in the Family* and *Police Woman* and the uncountable news and talk shows gets sophisticated early. There is no Aladdin's lamp, no genie. The wonder and the awe and the innocence are gone.

And what's left? What is an appropriate way to say goodbye to   26
an era that meant so much to so many, an era in which you could always tell the good guys from the bad, the right causes from the wrong? Maybe to do it like the old cartoons did — not say *The End*, but have a happy little pig stick his head out through a multicolored circle, wave his white glove across our vanished childhoods, and say, to joyful, upbeat music, "Th-th-tha-that's all, folks!"

Questions for Close Reading

1. What is the thesis of the selection? Locate the sentence(s) in which Spikol states his main idea. If he does not state the thesis explicitly, express it in your own words.
2. Why did Spikol enjoy the Saturday matinees he attended as a child? What needs does he say these matinees filled for him?
3. According to Spikol, what factors contributed to the death of the Saturday matinee? Do you agree with his conclusions?
4. The matinees of Spikol's childhood occurred during wartime. What evidence is there in the essay that Spikol's nostalgia for matinees is connected with his nostalgia for a particular era?
5. Refer to your dictionary as needed to define the following words used in the selection: *chafed* (paragraph 1), *transfixed* (11), *crescendo* (11), *indoctrinating* (13), *substantiate* (21), and *furlough* (24).

Questions about the Writer's Craft

1. Find where Spikol moves from the present movie theater to the past, and where he moves back into the present, thus completing his compar-

ison-contrast. How does Spikol signal that these shifts in time are going to occur?

2. The title "High Noon" is taken from a classic Western movie — filmed in black and white — about a duel between a hero and a villain. Why do you think Spikol chose this title for his essay?

3. In a typical comparison-contrast essay, a writer balances the time given to each side. Why do you think Spikol devotes most of "High Noon" to the Saturday matinees he saw as a child and so little to the show to which he took his daughter?

4. Why does Spikol end his essay with the image of the "happy little pig" waving goodbye? What things have come to an end?

Questions for Further Thought

1. How might Spikol's experience prove the maxim, "You can't go home again"? What experiences have you had that exemplify this saying?

2. Movies tend to reflect the values of contemporary society. What messages do today's movies convey to children? Consider closely specific films and movie characters.

3. If the Saturday matinee is dead, what has replaced it? How do today's children amuse themselves on weekends? Are the new forms of recreation any better — or are they worse?

4. There has been a growing trend toward watching movies at home rather than going out to theaters. What has been gained or lost by this change?

Writing Assignments Using Comparison-Contrast as a Method of Development

1. The adult Art Spikol can now understand and articulate the meaning of his childhood experiences at the Saturday matinee. Spikol obviously did not have this kind of insight at the time. Write an essay about a past experience, contrasting your understanding and feelings about it then with your understanding now. Some possibilities to consider might be a divorce in the family, an argument, an embarrassing event, a frightening moment, or some other experience.

2. Write an essay comparing and/or contrasting a place as it was in the past with that same place today. Some possibilities to consider might be a house, a school, a playground, a rural area, a neighborhood, or some other place you know well. Use vivid details to make the contrasting images of this place as sharp and clear as a pair of photographs.

Writing Assignments Using Other Methods of Development

3. Spikol believes that today's Saturday matinees are not as good as they once were. He could be right about other things as well. In an essay, describe something you believe has changed for the worse. Some possible topics for the essay might be television shows, restaurants, parties, fashions, sports, music, or food. In your introduction, you should mention briefly what you liked about yesterday's version of your subject.

4. Conduct one or more personal interviews (with a teacher, parent, older brother or sister, or other person), so you can write an essay describing a vanished activity or thing as it was before your time. You might interview people about an era they lived through or an activity they participated in. Your essay should indicate clearly whether you are pleased or regretful that things have changed. Be sure to include only those details that support your dominant impression.

Richard Rodriguez

In Hunger of Memory *(1981), from which the following selection is taken, Richard Rodriguez describes his experiences growing up in America as a first-generation Mexican-American. Born in 1944 in San Francisco, Rodriguez spoke only Spanish for the first six years of his life. After winning a scholarship to a private high school, Rodriguez attended Stanford, Columbia, and the University of California at Berkeley where he earned a Ph.D. in English Literature. Rodriguez now writes, lectures, and serves as an educational consultant from his home base in San Francisco.*

Workers

As a college student, you probably look forward to a working world where individuals feel a sense of accomplishment and prestige, where personal growth is as much a consideration as monetary rewards. Richard Rodriguez discovered a very different world of work during a summer spent as a laborer, a world in which work is survival and the boss is god. For such workers, there are no alternatives, no exits, no chances for fulfillment.

It was at Stanford, one day near the end of my senior year, that 1 a friend told me about a summer construction job he knew was available. I was quickly alert. Desire uncoiled within me. My friend said that he knew I had been looking for summer employment. He knew I needed some money. Almost apologetically he explained: It was something I probably wouldn't be interested in, but a friend of his, a contractor, needed someone for the summer to do menial jobs. There would be lots of shoveling and raking and sweeping. Nothing too hard. But nothing more interesting either. Still, the pay would be good. Did I want it? Or did I know someone who did?

I did. Yes, I said, surprised to hear myself say it. 2

In the weeks following, friends cautioned that I had no idea 3 how hard physical labor really is. ('You only *think* you know what it

337

is like to shovel for eight hours straight.') Their objections seemed to me challenges. They resolved the issue. I became happy with my plan. I decided, however, not to tell my parents. I wouldn't tell my mother because I could guess her worried reaction. I would tell my father only after the summer was over, when I could announce that, after all, I did know what 'real work' is like.

The day I met the contractor (a Princeton graduate, it turned out), he asked me whether I had done any physical labor before. 'In high school, during the summer,' I lied. And although he seemed to regard me with skepticism, he decided to give me a try. Several days later, expectant, I arrived at my first construction site. I would take off my shirt to the sun. And at last grasp desired sensation. No longer afraid. At last become like a *bracero*. 'We need those tree stumps out of here by tomorrow,' the contractor said. I started to work.   4

I labored with excitement that first morning — and all the days after. The work was harder than I could have expected. But it was never as tedious as my friends had warned me it would be. There was too much physical pleasure in the labor. Especially early in the day, I would be most alert to the sensations of movement and straining. Beginning around seven each morning (when the air was still damp but the scent of weeds and dry earth anticipated the heat of the sun), I would feel my body resist the first thrusts of the shovel. My arms, tightened by sleep, would gradually loosen; after only several minutes, sweat would gather in beads on my forehead and then — a short while later — I would feel my chest silky with sweat in the breeze. I would return to my work. A nervous spark of pain would fly up my arm and settle to burn like an ember in the thick of my shoulder. An hour, two passed. Three. My whole body would assume regular movements; my shoveling would be described by identical, even movements. Even later in the day, my enthusiasm for primitive sensation would survive the heat and the dust and the insects pricking my back. I would strain wildly for sensation as the day came to a close. At three-thirty, quitting time, I would stand upright and slowly let my head fall back, luxuriating in the feeling of tightness relieved.   5

Some of the men working nearby would watch me and laugh. Two or three of the older men took the trouble to teach me the right way to use a pick, the correct way to shovel. 'You're doing it wrong, too fucking hard,' one man scolded. Then proceeded to   6 show me—what persons who work with their bodies all their lives quickly learn—the most economical way to use one's body in labor.

'Don't make your back do so much work,' he instructed. I 7
stood impatiently listening, half listening, vaguely watching, then noticed his work-thickened fingers clutching the shovel. I was annoyed. I wanted to tell him that I enjoyed shoveling the wrong way. And I didn't want to learn the right way. I wasn't afraid of back pain. I liked the way my body felt sore at the end of the day.

I was about to, but, as it turned out, I didn't say a thing. Rather 8
it was at that moment I realized that I was fooling myself if I expected a few weeks of labor to gain me admission to the world of the laborer. I would not learn in three months what my father had meant by 'real work.' I was not bound to this job; I could imagine its rapid conclusion. For me the sensations of exertion and fatigue could be savored. For my father or uncle, working at comparable jobs when they were my age, such sensations were to be feared. Fatigue took a different toll on their bodies—and minds.

It was, I know, a simple insight. But it was with this realization 9
that I took my first step that summer toward realizing something even more important about the 'worker.' In the company of carpenters, electricians, plumbers, and painters at lunch, I would often sit quietly, observant. I was not shy in such company. I felt easy, pleased by the knowledge that I was casually accepted, my presence taken for granted by men (exotics) who worked with their hands. Some days the younger men would talk and talk about sex, and they would howl at women who drove by in cars. Other days the talk at lunchtime was subdued; men gathered in separate groups. It depended on who was around. There were rough, good-natured workers. Others were quiet. The more I remember that summer, the more I realize that there was no single *type* of worker. I am embarrassed to say I had not expected such diversity. I certainly had not expected to meet, for example, a plumber who was an abstract painter in his off hours and admired the work of Mark Rothko. Nor did I expect to meet so many workers with college diplomas. (They were the ones who were not surprised that I intended to enter graduate school in the fall.) I suppose what I really want to say here is painfully obvious, but I must say it nevertheless: The men of that summer were middle-class Americans. They certainly didn't constitute an oppressed society. Carefully completing

their work sheets; talking about the fortunes of local football teams; planning Las Vegas vacations; comparing the gas mileage of various makes of campers — they were not *los pobres* my mother had spoken about.

On two occasions, the contractor hired a group of Mexican   10 aliens. They were employed to cut down some trees and haul off debris. In all, there were six men of varying age. The youngest in his late twenties; the oldest (his father?) perhaps sixty years old. They came and they left in a single old truck. Anonymous men. They were never introduced to the other men at the site. Immediately upon their arrival, they would follow the contractor's directions, start working — rarely resting — seemingly driven by a fatalistic sense that work which had to be done was best done as quickly as possible.

I watched them sometimes. Perhaps they watched me. The   11 only time I saw them pay me much notice was one day at lunchtime when I was laughing with the other men. The Mexicans sat apart when they ate, just as they worked by themselves. Quiet. I rarely heard them say much to each other. All I could hear were their voices calling out sharply to one another, giving directions. Otherwise, when they stood briefly resting, they talked among themselves in voices too hard to overhear.

The contractor knew enough Spanish, and the Mexicans — or   12 at least the oldest of them, their spokesman — seemed to know enough English to communicate. But because I was around, the contractor decided one day to make me his translator. (He assumed I could speak Spanish.) I did what I was told. Shyly I went over to tell the Mexicans that the *patrón* wanted them to do something else before they left for the day. As I started to speak, I was afraid with my old fear that I would be unable to pronounce the Spanish words. But it was a simple instruction I had to convey. I could say it in phrases.

The dark sweating faces turned toward me as I spoke. They   13 stopped their work to hear me. Each nodded in response. I stood there. I wanted to say something more. But what could I say in Spanish, even if I could have pronounced the words right? Perhaps I just wanted to engage them in small talk, to be assured of their confidence, our familiarity. I thought for a moment to ask them where in Mexico they were from. Something like that. And maybe I wanted to tell them (a lie, if need be) that my parents were from the same part of Mexico.

I stood there. 14

Their faces watched me. The eyes of the man directly in front 15
of me moved slowly over my shoulder, and I turned to follow his
glance toward *el patrón* some distance away. For a moment I felt
swept up by that glance into the Mexicans' company. But then I
heard one of them returning to work. And then the others went
back to work. I left them without saying anything more.

When they had finished, the contractor went over to pay them 16
in cash. (He later told me that he paid them collectively — 'for the
job,' though he wouldn't tell me their wages. He said something
quickly about the good rate of exchange 'in their own country.') I
can still hear the loudly confident voice he used with the Mexicans.
It was the sound of the *gringo* I had heard as a very young boy. And I
can still hear the quiet, indistinct sounds of the Mexican, the oldest, who replied. At hearing that voice I was sad for the Mexicans.
Depressed by their vulnerability. Angry at myself. The adventure of
the summer seemed suddenly ludicrous. I would not shorten the
distance I felt from *los pobres* with a few weeks of physical labor. I
would not become like them. They were different from me.

After that summer, a great deal — and not very much really — 17
changed in my life. The curse of physical shame was broken by the
sun; I was no longer ashamed of my body. No longer would I deny
myself the pleasing sensations of my maleness. During those years
when middle-class black Americans began to assert with pride,
'Black is beautiful,' I was able to regard my complexion without
shame. I am today darker than I ever was as a boy. I have taken up
the middle-class sport of long-distance running. Nearly every day
now I run ten or fifteen miles, barely clothed, my skin exposed to
the California winter rain and wind or the summer sun of late
afternoon. The torso, the soccer player's calves and thighs, the arms
of the twenty-year-old I never was, I possess now in my thirties. I
study the youthful parody shape in the mirror: the stomach lipped
tight by muscle; the shoulders rounded by chin-ups; the arms
veined strong. This man. A man. I meet him. He laughs to see me,
what I have become.

The dandy. I wear double-breasted Italian suits and custom- 18
made English shoes. I resemble no one so much as my father — the
man pictured in those honeymoon photos. At that point in life
when he abandoned the dandy's posture, I assume it. At the point
when my parents would not consider going on vacation, I register

at the Hotel Carlyle in New York and the Plaza Athenée in Paris. I am as taken by the symbols of leisure and wealth as they were. For my parents, however, those symbols became taunts, reminders of all they could not achieve in one lifetime. For me those same symbols are reassuring reminders of public success. I tempt vulgarity to be reassured. I am filled with the gaudy delight, the monstrous grace of the nouveau riche.

In recent years I have had occasion to lecture in ghetto high 19 schools. There I see students of remarkable style and physical grace. (One can see more dandies in such schools than one ever will find in middle-class high schools.) There is not the look of casual assurance I saw students at Stanford display. Ghetto girls mimic high-fashion models. Their dresses are of bold, forceful color; their figures elegant, long; the stance theatrical. Boys wear shirts that grip at their overdeveloped muscular bodies. (Against a powerless future, they engage images of strength.) Bad nutrition does not yet tell. Great disappointment, fatal to youth, awaits them still. For the moment, movements in school hallways are dancelike, a procession of postures in a sexual masque. Watching them, I feel a kind of envy. I wonder how different my adolescence would have been had I been free. . . . But no, it is my parents I see — their optimism during those years when they were entertained by Italian grand opera.

The registration clerk in London wonders if I have just been to 20 Switzerland. And the man who carries my luggage in New York guesses the Caribbean. My complexion becomes a mark of my leisure. Yet no one would regard my complexion the same way if I entered such hotels through the service entrance. That is only to say that my complexion assumes its significance from the context of my life. My skin, in itself, means nothing. I stress the point because I know there are people who would label me 'disadvantaged' because of my color. They make the same mistake I made as a boy, when I thought a disadvantaged life was circumscribed by particular occupations. That summer I worked in the sun may have made me physically indistinguishable from the Mexicans working nearby. (My skin was actually darker because, unlike them, I worked without wearing a shirt. By late August my hands were probably as tough as theirs.) But I was not one of *los pobres*. What made me different from them was an attitude of *mind*, my imagination of myself.

I do not blame my mother for warning me away from the sun 21
when I was young. In a world where her brother had become an old
man in his twenties because he was dark, my complexion was something to worry about. 'Don't run in the sun,' she warns me today. I
run. In the end, my father was right—though perhaps he did not
know how right or why—to say that I would never know what real
work is. I will never know what he felt at his last factory job. If
tomorrow I worked at some kind of factory, it would go differently
for me. My long education would favor me. I could act as a public
person—able to defend my interests, to unionize, to petition, to
speak up—to challenge and demand. (I will never know what real
work is.) I will never know what the Mexicans knew, gathering
their shovels and ladders and saws.

Their silence stays with me now. The wages those Mexicans 22
received for their labor were only a measure of their disadvantaged
condition. Their silence is more telling. They lack a public identity.
They remain profoundly alien. Persons apart. People lacking a
union obviously, people without grounds. They depend upon the
relative good will or fairness of their employers each day. For such
people, lacking a better alternative, it is not such an unreasonable
risk.

Their silence stays with me. I have taken these many words to 23
describe its impact. Only: the quiet. Something uncanny about it.
Its compliance. Vulnerability. Pathos. As I heard their truck rum-
bling away, I shuddered, my face mirrored with sweat. I had finally
come face to face with *los pobres*.

Questions for Close Reading

1. What is the thesis of the selection? Locate the sentence(s) in which
   Rodriguez states his main idea. If he does not state the thesis explicitly,
   express it in your own words.
2. What appealed to Rodriguez about the construction job when his
   friend first offered it to him?
3. Once on the job, how long does it take Rodriguez to realize he will
   never be a "laborer"? Why does he feel this way?
4. According to the author, what makes him different from *los pobres*? Is
   poverty the only thing that makes them distinctive?
5. Refer to your dictionary as needed to define the following words in the
   selection: *menial* (paragraph 1), *skepticism* (4), *luxuriating* (5), *diversity*
   (9), *ludicrous* (16), *nouveav riche* (18), and *pathos* (23).

Questions about the Writer's Craft

1. One way Rodriguez develops his essay is by comparing and contrasting himself to the two groups of workers. Which group is he most like? What specifics does Rodriguez provide to show his similarity to this group and his dissimilarity to the other?
2. Rodriguez's main support for his comparison of the two other groups of workers is narrative. How many narrative segments appear in the essay? Why does Rodriguez put the story about the Mexican workers last?
3. Why does the author include some Spanish words in his essay? How is the use of these words related to the overall theme?
4. Rodriguez uses especially vivid language to describe the sun, his sweat, and the sensation of digging. Locate some examples of these descriptions. Which ones particularly stand out?

Questions for Further Thought

1. Why does Rodriguez decide not to tell his parents about his summer job? What do you think his mother's fears would have been? How would your parents and friends react if you went to work in construction after graduating from college?
2. Rodriguez discovers that "there was no single *type* of worker" on the construction job. What do you think his preconceptions about construction workers were? What other kinds of workers are often stereotyped?
3. What does Rodriguez desire to gain from this job that he could not, presumably, learn at Stanford or in graduate school? Have you ever felt a similar need to learn outside the classroom?
4. What are the characteristics of "real work" for Rodriguez at the start of his summer? How would you say his definition of "real work" has changed by the end of the job? Would you agree with his perception that a college-educated person can never know the meaning of "real work"?

Writing Assignments Using Comparison-Contrast as a Method of Development

1. Write an essay comparing and/or contrasting a part-time or summer job you've had with your (or someone else's) full-time or "real" job. Use examples, description, anecdotes, and illustrations to clarify the points of comparison or contrast.
2. Compare and/or contrast the job you hope to have after graduation

with a job you now have or have had in the past. Your analysis should reach conclusions about your interests, skills, and values.

Writing Assignments Using Other Methods of Development

3. In an essay, define what you mean by the term "real work." Support your definition by citing experiences you have had and/or have heard about.
4. Phil Donahue once did a show on people who had "terrible jobs." Guests included a garbage man, toll collector, car repossessor, IRS auditor, and diaper-service truck driver. Write an essay describing what would be terrible work for you, work that you could never do. It might be one or more of the jobs held by a Donahue guest or some other type of jobs.

Loren Eiseley

Loren Eiseley, born in 1907, was one of those rare individuals who managed to bridge the gap between science and poetry, between the esoteric concerns of specialized knowledge and the common matters of daily life. At the time of his death in 1977, Loren Eiseley was Benjamin Franklin Professor of Anthropology and the History of Science at the University of Pennsylvania. Among his many books are The Immense Journey *(1957),* The Firmament of Time *(1960), and* The Night Country *(1971), where "The Brown Wasps" first appeared.*

The Brown Wasps

A mouse tunnels into a potted farm. An old impoverished man props himself against a train station bench, the only home he has. A flock of pigeons returns to a demolished train station, searching for crumbs from long-removed vending machines. A man thinks with longing of a tree that is alive only in his imagination. To Loren Eiseley, all these images are profoundly connected; all are instances of creatures clinging to places they consider home.

There is a corner in the waiting room of one of the great 1
Eastern stations where women never sit. It is always in the shadow
and overhung by rows of lockers. It is, however, always frequented
— not so much by genuine travelers as by the dying. It is here that a
certain element of the abandoned poor seeks a refuge out of the
weather, clinging for a few hours longer to the city that has fathered
them. In a precisely similar manner I have seen, on a sunny day in
midwinter, a few old brown wasps creep slowly over an abandoned
wasp nest in a thicket. Numbed and forgetful and frost-blackened,
the hum of the spring hive still resounded faintly in their sodden
tissues. Then the temperature would fall and they would drop away
into the white oblivion of the snow. Here in the station it is in no
way different save that the city is busy in its snows. But the old ones
cling to their seats as though these were symbolic and could not be

346

given up. Now and then they sleep, their gray old heads resting with painful awkwardness on the backs of the benches.

Also they are not at rest. For an hour they may sleep in the gasping exhaustion of the ill-nourished and aged who have to walk in the night. Then a policeman comes by on his round and nudges them upright. 2

"You can't sleep here," he growls. 3

A strange ritual then begins. An old man is difficult to waken. After a muttered conversation the policeman presses a coin into his hand and passes fiercely along the benches prodding and gesturing toward the door. In his wake, like birds rising and settling behind the passage of a farmer through a cornfield, the men totter up, move a few paces, and subside once more upon the benches. 4

One man, after a slight, apologetic lurch, does not move at all. Tubercularly thin, he sleeps on steadily. The policeman does not look back. To him, too, this has become a ritual. He will not have to notice it again officially for another hour. 5

Once in a while one of the sleepers will not awake. Like the brown wasps, he will have had his wish to die in the great droning center of the hive rather than in some lonely room. It is not so bad here with the shuffle of footsteps and the knowledge that there are others who share the bad luck of the world. There are also the whistles and the sounds of everyone, everyone in the world, starting on journeys. Amidst too many journeys somebody is bound to come out all right. Somebody. 6

Maybe it was on a like thought that the brown wasps fell away from the old paper nest in the thicket. You hold till the last, even if it is only to a public seat in a railroad station. You want your place in the hive more than you want a room or a place where the aged can be eased gently out of the way. It is the place that matters, the place at the heart of things. It is life that you want, that bruises your gray old head with the hard chairs; a man has a right to his place. 7

But sometimes the place is lost in the years behind us. Or sometimes it is a thing of air, a kind of vaporous distortion above a heap of rubble. We cling to a time and a place because without them man is lost, not only man but life. This is why the voices, real or unreal, which speak from the floating trumpets at spiritualist seances are so unnerving. They are voices out of nowhere whose only reality lies in their ability to stir the memory of a living person with some fragment of the past. Before the medium's cabinet both 8 the dead and the living revolve endlessly about an episode, a place, an event that has already been engulfed by time.

This feeling runs deep in life; it brings stray cats running over   9
endless miles, and birds homing from the ends of the earth. It is as though all living creatures, and particularly the more intelligent, can survive only by fixing or transforming a bit of time into space or by securing a bit of space with its objects immortalized and made permanent in time. For example, I once saw, on a flower pot in my own living room, the efforts of a field mouse to build a remembered field. I have lived to see this episode repeated in a thousand guises, and since I have spent a large portion of my life in the shade of a nonexistent tree I think I am entitled to speak for the field mouse.

One day as I cut across the field which at that time extended on   10
one side of our suburban shopping center, I found a giant slug feeding from a runnel of pink ice cream in an abandoned Dixie cup. I could see his eyes telescope and protrude in a kind of dim uncertain ecstasy as his dark body bunched and elongated in the curve of the cup. Then, as I stood there at the edge of the concrete, contemplating the slug, I began to realize it was like standing on a shore where a different type of life creeps up and fumbles tentatively among the rocks and sea wrack. It knows its place and will only creep so far until something changes. Little by little as I stood there I began to see more of this shore that surrounds the place of man. I looked with sudden care and attention at things I had been running over thoughtlessly for years. I even waded out a short way into the grass and the wild-rose thickets to see more. A huge blackbelted bee went droning by and there were some indistinct scurryings in the underbrush.

Then I came to a sign which informed me that this field was to   11
be the site of a new Wanamaker suburban store. Thousands of obscure lives were about to perish, the spores of puffballs would go smoking off to new fields, and the bodies of little white-footed mice would be crunched under the inexorable wheels of the bulldozers. Life disappears or modifies its appearances so fast that everything takes on an aspect of illusion — a momentary fizzing and boiling with smoke rings, like pouring dissident chemicals into a retort. Here a man was advancing, but in a few years his plaster and bricks would be disappearing once more into the insatiable maw of the clover. Being of an archaeological cast of mind, I

thought of this fact with an obscure sense of satisfaction and waded back through the rose thickets to the concrete parking lot. As I did so, a mouse scurried ahead of me, frightened of my steps if not of that ominous Wanamaker sign. I saw him vanish in the general direction of my apartment house, his little body quivering with fear in the great open sun on the blazing concrete. Blinded and confused, he was running straight away from his field. In another week scores would follow him.

I forgot the episode then and went home to the quiet of my   12 living room. It was not until a week later, letting myself into the apartment, that I realized I had a visitor. I am fond of plants and had several ferns standing on the floor in pots to avoid the noon glare by the south window.

As I snapped on the light and glanced carelessly around the   13 room, I saw a little heap of earth on the carpet and a scrabble of pebbles that had been kicked merrily over the edge of one of the flower pots. To my astonishment I discovered a full-fledged burrow delving downward among the fern roots. I waited silently. The creature who had made the burrow did not appear. I remembered the wild field then, and the flight of the mice. No house mouse, no *Mus domesticus*, had kicked up this little heap of earth or sought refuge under a fern root in a flower pot. I thought of the desperate little creature I had seen fleeing from the wild-rose thicket. Through intricacies of pipes and attics, he, or one of his fellows, had climbed to his high green solitary room. I could visualize what had occurred. He had an image in his head, a world of seed pods and quiet, of green sheltering leaves in the dim light among the weed stems. It was the only world he knew and it was gone.

Somehow in his flight he had found his way to this room with   14 drawn shades where no one would come till nightfall. And here he had smelled green leaves and run quickly up the flower pot to dabble his paws in common earth. He had even struggled half the afternoon to carry his burrow deeper and had failed. I examined the hole, but no whiskered twitching face appeared. He was gone. I gathered up the earth and refilled the burrow. I did not expect to find traces of him again.

Yet for three nights thereafter I came home to the darkened   15 room and my ferns to find the dirt kicked gaily about the rug and the burrow reopened, though I was never able to catch the field mouse within it. I dropped a little food about the mouth of the burrow, but it was never touched. I looked under beds or sat reading with one ear cocked for rustlings in the ferns. It was all in vain; I never saw him. Probably he ended in a trap in some other tenant's room.

But before he disappeared I had come to look hopefully for his 16 evening burrow. About my ferns there had begun to linger the insubstantial vapor of an autumn field, the distilled essence, as it were, of a mouse brain in exile from its home. It was a small dream, like our dreams, carried a long and weary journey along pipes and through spider webs, past holes over which loomed the shadows of waiting cats, and finally, desperately, into this room where he had played in the shuttered daylight for an hour among the green ferns on the floor. Every day these invisible dreams pass us on the street, or rise from beneath our feet, or look upon us from beneath a bush.

Some years ago the old elevated railway in Philadelphia was 17 torn down and replaced by a subway system. This ancient El with its barnlike stations containing nut-vending machines and scattered food scraps had, for generations, been the favorite feeding ground of flocks of pigeons, generally one flock to a station along the route of the El. Hundreds of pigeons were dependent upon the system. They flapped in and out of its stanchions and steel work or gathered in watchful little audiences about the feet of anyone who rattled the peanut-vending machines. They even watched people who jingled change in their hands, and prospected for food under the feet of the crowds, who gathered between trains. Probably very few among the waiting people who tossed a crumb to an eager pigeon realized that this El was like a food-bearing river, and that the life which haunted its banks was dependent upon the running of the trains with their human freight.

I saw the river stop. 18

The time came when the underground tubes were ready; the 19 traffic was transferred to a realm unreachable by pigeons. It was like a great river subsiding suddenly into desert sands. For a day, for two days, pigeons continued to circle over the El or stand close to the red vending machines. They were patient birds, and surely this great river which had flowed through the lives of unnumbered generations was merely suffering from some momentary drought.

They listened for the familiar vibrations that had always her- 20 alded an approaching train; they flapped hopefully about the head of an occasional workman walking along the steel runways. They passed from one empty station to another, all the while growing hungrier. Finally they flew away.

I thought I had seen the last of them about the El, but there 21 was a revival and it provided a curious instance of the memory of living things for a way of life or a locality that has long been cherished. Some weeks after the El was abandoned workmen began to tear it down. I went to work every morning by one particular station, and the time came when the demolition crews reached this spot. Acetylene torches showered passers-by with sparks, pneumatic drills hammered at the base of the structure, and a blind man who, like the pigeons, had clung with his cup to a stairway leading to the change booth, was forced to give up his place.

It was then, strangely, momentarily, one morning that I wit- 22 nessed the return of a little band of the familiar pigeons. I even recognized one or two members of the flock that had lived around this particular station before they were dispersed into the streets. They flew bravely in and out among the sparks and the hammers and the shouting workmen. They had returned — and they had returned because the hubbub of the wreckers had convinced them that the river was about to flow once more. For several hours they flapped in and out through the empty windows, nodding their heads and watching the fall of girders with attentive little eyes. By the following morning the station was reduced to some burned-off stanchions in the street. My bird friends had gone. It was plain, however, that they retained a memory for an insubstantial structure now compounded of air and time. Even the blind man clung to it. Someone had provided him with a chair, and he sat at the same corner staring sightlessly at an invisible stairway where, so far as he was concerned, the crowds were still ascending to the trains.

I have said my life has been passed in the shade of a nonexistent 23 tree, so that such sights do not offend me. Prematurely I am one of the brown wasps and I often sit with them in the great droning hive of the station, dreaming sometimes of a certain tree. It was planted sixty years ago by a boy with a bucket and a toy spade in a little Nebraska town. That boy was myself. It was a cottonwood sapling and the boy remembered it because of some words spoken by his father and because everyone died or moved away who was supposed to wait and grow old under its shade. The boy was passed from hand to hand, but the tree for some intangible reason had taken root in his mind. It was under its branches that he sheltered; it was from this tree that his memories, which are my memories, led away into the world.

After sixty years the mood of the brown wasps grows heavier upon one. During a long inward struggle I thought it would do me good to go and look upon that actual tree. I found a rational excuse in which to clothe this madness. I purchased a ticket and at the end of two thousand miles I walked another mile to an address that was still the same. The house had not been altered. 24

I came close to the white picket fence and reluctantly, with great effort, looked down the long vista of the yard. There was nothing there to see. For sixty years that cottonwood had been growing in my mind. Season by season its seeds had been floating farther on the hot prairie winds. We had planted it lovingly there, my father and I, because he had a great hunger for soil and live things growing, and because none of these things had long been ours to protect. We had planted the little sapling and watered it faithfully, and I remembered that I had run out with my small bucket to drench its roots the day we moved away. And all the years since it had been growing in my mind, a huge tree that somehow stood for my father and the love I bore him. I took a grasp on the picket fence and forced myself to look again. 25

A boy with the hard bird eye of youth pedaled a tricycle slowly up beside me. 26

"What'cha lookin at?" he asked curiously. 27

"A tree," I said. 28

"What for?" he said. 29

"It isn't there," I said, to myself mostly, and began to walk away at a pace just slow enough not to seem to be running. 30

"What isn't there?" the boy asked. I didn't answer. It was obvious I was attached by a thread to a thing that had never been there, or certainly not for long. Something that had to be held in the air, or sustained in the mind, because it was part of my orientation in the universe and I could not survive without it. There was more than an animal's attachment to a place. There was something else, the attachment of the spirit to a grouping of events in time; it was part of our mortality. 31

So I had come home at last, driven by a memory in the brain as surely as the field mouse who had delved long ago into my flower pot or the pigeons flying forever amidst the rattle of nut-vending machines. These, the burrow under the greenery in my living room 32 and the red-bellied bowls of peanuts now hovering in midair in the minds of pigeons, were all part of an elusive world that existed nowhere and yet everywhere. I looked once at the real world about me while the persistent boy pedaled at my heels.

It was without meaning, though my feet took a remembered 33 path. In sixty years the house and street had rotted out of my mind. But the tree, the tree that no longer was, that had perished in its first season, bloomed on in my individual mind, unblemished as my father's words. "We'll plant a tree here, son, and we're not going to move any more. And when you're an old, old man you can sit under it and think how we planted it here, you and me, together."

I began to outpace the boy on the tricycle. 34

"Do you live here, Mister?" he shouted after me suspiciously. I 35 took a firm grasp on airy nothing — to be precise, on the bole of a great tree. "I do," I said. I spoke for myself, one field mouse, and several pigeons. We were all out of touch but somehow permanent. It was the world that had changed.

Questions for Close Reading

1. What is the thesis of the selection? Locate the sentence(s) in which Eiseley states his main idea. If he does not state the thesis explicitly, express it in your own words.
2. What is the connection between brown wasps and old men? Why does Eiseley call himself "one of the brown wasps" in paragraph 23?
3. What is Eiseley's attitude toward the imminent construction of the new Wanamaker store? In what way is the new store symbolic?
4. Why does Eiseley answer, "I do," when the small boy asks if he lives in the old house? How does this answer reinforce the main idea of the essay?
5. Refer to your dictionary as needed to define the following words used in the selection: *oblivion* (paragraph 1), *vaporous* (8), *guises* (9), *tentatively* (10), *essence* (16), *stanchions* (17), *pneumatic* (21), and *vista* (25).

Questions about the Writer's Craft

1. To what extent does Eiseley develop an analogy between humans and animals such as the wasps? What is his purpose in discovering similarities in such a variety of creatures?
2. Eiseley is a science writer who is noted for his attention to details. For example, in paragraph 1, he describes the wasps as "numbed and for-

getful and frost-blackened." Locate other examples of sharp descriptive details. How do these evocative details strengthen Eiseley's essay?
3. Some natural objects in this essay take on symbolic significance. One example is the "nonexistent tree." What does this tree represent, to Eiseley's father at the time of planting, to Eiseley then and now? Find at least two other symbols in "The Brown Wasps" and discuss what they represent.
4. How do you normally feel about creatures such as wasps, slugs, mice, and pigeons? Why do you think Eiseley chose to make his point using these animals rather than ones we feel more affinity with?

Questions for Further Thought

1. When Eiseley and his father planted the cottonweed sapling, his father made some promises. How realistic were these promises? In what sense did his father's words come true?
2. One quarter of all Americans move each year. What might be the psychological cost of such rootlessness? On the basis of Eiseley's essay, what do we do to protect ourselves psychologically from such losses?
3. Do you have any childhood memories as strong as Eiseley's? How might such memories help you to survive change and loss?
4. What should be our attitude toward changes that dislocate people and other creatures? Some of the changes, especially those caused by humans, could be stopped. Should they be? Is it possible or desirable to eliminate from our lives changes that result in loss?

Writing Assignments Using Comparison-Contrast as a Method of Development

1. Pet owners often notice that their animals become very personlike. Sometimes people even train pets to imitate human behavior — to "speak," shake hands, and so on. Using the comparison-contrast format, write an essay showing three ways a pet — owned by you or someone you know — was very "human." Your thesis might be, for example, "Pets and their owners are often alike," or "My two cats reflect the two sides of my personality."
2. Think of a place you knew well that has changed dramatically. It could be a town, a particular house, a garden, a park, a natural place, or even a favorite shop, public building, or street corner. Write an essay comparing and/or contrasting the old place and what it has become. Use details that recreate the feeling the place held for you as well as details that describe the specific changes which have occurred.

Writing Assignments Using Other Methods
of Development

3. Loren Eiseley was a scientist with the rare ability to relate his scientific knowledge to the realms of feeling, human experiences, and ordinary life. He was also a powerful writer, a product of an educational system that stressed being well read in the great works of Western culture. Write an essay arguing that students in college today should or should not be required to study widely in areas that are unrelated to their majors or their career fields.

4. In the library, look up some information on the psychological problems of relocation, both for children and adults. On the basis of your reading, write an essay outlining three or four steps people can take to ease the stress involved in having to move away from home. Before writing, determine a specific audience for your paper: young children going away to summer camp, college students leaving home to live in a dorm, older people having to sell their home and move into more manageable quarters, and so on.

Additional Writing Topics
COMPARISON-CONTRAST

General Assignments

Using comparison-contrast, write an essay on any of the following topics. Your thesis should indicate whether the two subjects are being compared, contrasted, or both. Organize the paper by arranging the details in a one-side-at-a-time or point-by-point pattern. Remember to use organizational cues to help the audience follow your analysis of the subjects.

1. Two-career family versus one-career family
2. Two approaches for dealing with problems
3. Children's pastimes today and yesterday
4. Two rooms where you spend a good deal of time
5. Neighborhood stores versus shopping malls
6. Two characters in a novel or other literary work
7. Living at home versus living in an apartment or dorm
8. Two attitudes toward money
9. A sports team then and now
10. Watching a movie on television versus going out to a theater
11. Two attitudes about a controversial subject
12. Two approaches to parenting
13. Walking or biking versus driving a car
14. Marriage versus living together
15. The atmosphere in two classes
16. Two approaches to studying
17. The place where you live and the place where you would like to live
18. Two comedians
19. The coverage of an event on TV versus the coverage in a newspaper
20. Significant trend versus passing fad
21. Two horror or adventure movies
22. Typewriter versus word processor
23. Two candidates for an office
24. Your attitude before and after getting to know someone
25. Two friends with different lifestyles

Assignments with a Specific Audience and Purpose

1. You have decided you want to change your campus living arrangements next year: you want to switch from a dorm room to an off-campus apartment, or you want to move from home onto campus, or any other change. You will first have to convince your parents, who are paying most of your college costs, that the move will be beneficial. Write your parents a letter contrasting your current situation with your proposed one, explaining why the new arrangement will be better.

2. You have managed a retail store for several years and done a good job—sales are up. Your regional manager has asked you to write a memo to your fellow store managers, explaining how you are able to attract so many customers. Feeling that the key to success lies in the ability to lure all kinds of customers to the store, you write a memo using the comparison-contrast format: you compare/contrast the needs and shopping habits of several different consumer groups (by age, or spending ability, or sex, and so on) and show why each feels comfortable in your store.

3. Some of the students in your school are putting together an alternative/underground booklet called "The Real Guide to College Life," intended primarily for entering freshmen. You are going to write the section on "Taking Exams" and have decided to contrast the right and wrong ways to prepare for and take exams. You have decided that your purpose is basically serious, but that you will leaven the section on how *not* to take exams with a little humor.

4. You work part-time in a medical office and have been asked to write an informational brochure to be placed in the patients' waiting room. The brochure is intended to show people how to avoid stress by changing their behavior patterns. You decide to center the brochure on the contrast between "Type A" and "Type B" personalities: the former is nervous, hard-driving, competitive, while the latter is relaxed and non-competitive. Give specific examples of how each "type" tends to act in a stressful situation, such as waiting in line, dealing with frustration or failure, coping with job or family crises.

5. Congratulations! You have been tapped to be one of the President's key advisers. Your first assignment is to draft a recommendation for the President on a specific issue: for example, whether to tighten quotas on imported cars or whether to allow the vehicles to come into the country unrestricted. To prepare your analysis, you contrast the advantages and disadvantages of the courses of action available, ending the document with a recommendation about which position the President should take.

6. Your old high school has invited you back to make a speech before an

audience of seniors; you will discuss "how to choose the college that is right for you." Write your speech in the form of a comparison-contrast analysis. Focus on the choices available (two-year and four-year, large school and small, local school and faraway one, and so on), showing the advantages and/or disadvantages of each.

CAUSE-EFFECT

WHAT IS CAUSE-EFFECT?

Superstition has it that curiosity killed the cat. Maybe so. But our science, technology, storytelling abilities, and fascination with the past and the future all spring from our determination to know "why" and "what if." Young children seeking explanations barrage adults with endless questions ("Why is the sky blue?" "Why doesn't the sun shine at night?"). And as they grow older, children become fascinated with possibilities ("If the coach had let me play, would my team have won?" "If Mom and Dad hadn't gotten married, would I still be me?").

This elemental need to make connections is at the heart of cause-effect writing, often called *causal analysis*. Because the drive to understand reasons and results is so fundamental, causal analysis is a common kind of writing. An article analyzing the unexpected outcome of an election, a report linking poor nutrition to children's academic achievement, an editorial predicting the impact of a proposed tax cut — all are examples of cause-effect writing.

359

Cause-effect pieces, if done well, can uncover the subtle and often surprising connections that link events and phenomena. By discovering causes and predicting effects, causal analysis enables us to make sense of our experiences, revealing a universe that is at least somewhat less arbitrary and chaotic.

WHEN TO USE CAUSE-EFFECT

Many assignments and exam questions in college involve writing essays that analyze causes, effects, or both. Sometimes, as in the following examples, you will be told to write an essay developed primarily through the cause-effect pattern.

> Although divorces have leveled off the last few years, the number of marriages ending in divorce is still greater than it was a generation ago. What do you think are the causes of this phenomenon?

> Political commentators were surprised that so few people voted in the last election. Discuss the causes of this unexpectedly weak voter turnout.

> Americans never seem to tire of gossip about the rich and famous. What effect has this fascination with celebrities had on American culture?

> The federal government is expected to pass legislation which will reduce significantly the funding of student loans. Analyze the possible effects of such a cutback on your life.

Other assignments or exam questions may not specify causes or effects but will use words that suggest causal analysis would be appropriate. Consider these examples, paying special attention to the italicized words.

> In contrast to the socially involved youth of the 1960s, many young people today tend to remove themselves from political issues. What do you think are the *sources* of the political apathy found among eighteen- to twenty-five-year-olds? (cause)

A number of experts predict that drug abuse will be the most significant factor affecting American productivity in the coming decade. Evaluate the validity of this observation by discussing the *impact* of drugs in the workplace. (effect)

According to school officials, a predictable percentage of entering students drop out of college at some point during their first year. What *motivates* students to drop out? What *happens* to them once they leave? (cause and effect)

By now, it's apparent that causal analysis can be the primary technique for achieving an essay's purpose. But causal analysis can also be a supplemental method used to help make a point in an essay organized chiefly around another pattern of development. For instance, assume you want to write an essay *defining* the term "the homeless." To make the point that most of the homeless are not faceless derelicts but people very much like the rest of us, you might discuss some of the unavoidable, everyday factors leading to homelessness. In an *argumentation-persuasion* paper advocating the elimination of letter grade evaluations, you would probably spend some time analyzing the impact of such a system on students and faculty.

As you can see, causal analysis pushes you to do some serious thinking, challenging you to explore often unfamiliar terrain. It is important to remember, though, that few cause-effect relationships are definitive. Causes and effects generally extend backward and forward in time, existing in multileveled layers so that final truth is often difficult to determine. This does not mean that cause-effect writing is fruitless. On the contrary, causal analysis frequently reveals new insights and dispels confusion.

SUGGESTIONS FOR USING CAUSE-EFFECT IN AN ESSAY

The following suggestions will be helpful whether you use causal analysis as a dominant or supportive pattern of development.

1. Determine the purpose of a paper developed mainly through causal analysis. You should always clarify to yourself the purpose for writing a cause-effect essay. Do you wish to inform?

Persuade? Speculate about possibilities? Or do you want to achieve some combination of these purposes? Consider, for example, a paper on the causes of widespread child abuse. Concerned primarily with explaining the problem to your readers, you might take a purely *informative* approach.

> Although parental stress is the immediate cause of child abuse, the more compelling reason for such behavior lies in the way parents were themselves mistreated in their own families.

Or you might want to *persuade* the audience about some point or idea concerning child abuse:

> The tragic consequences of child abuse provide strong support for more aggressive handling of such cases by social workers and judges.

Then again, you could choose a *speculative* approach, your main purpose being to suggest possibilities:

> Psychologists disagree about the potential effect on youngsters of all the media attention to child abuse. Will the children grow up assertive, self-confident, and able to protect themselves, or will they become fearful and distrustful?

These examples illustrate that causal analysis may have more than one purpose. For instance, although the last paper has a primarily speculative purpose, it would have to start by informing the reader about the experts' conflicting views regarding the media's impact on children. Similarly, the paper could even have a persuasive slant if it urged parents to take specific steps to offset the media's influence.

The purpose of a cause-effect essay determines what supporting material to select as well as what language to use. If you were writing a primarily informative paper on child abuse, you would —in a straightforward, objective way—present information, facts, and statistics to show that the parents' own upbringing influenced how they treated their children. On the other hand, if you were writing a persuasive paper taking a stand against the way judges and social workers deal with the child abuse problem, a more emotional and impassioned approach would be appropriate.

You might cite case histories that dramatize in a vivid way what happens when suspected child abuse is not taken seriously.

2. Think logically about causes and effects.   Cause-effect relationships are complex. To write a well-conceived paper, you should do some careful thinking about these relationships. Causes and effects are seldom simple or obvious — as suggested by the ongoing nature of scientific debates (How did humans evolve?), historical analyses (What happened in Vietnam?), and literary criticism (What were Hamlet's motivations?). Children tend to oversimplify causes and effects ("Mommy and Daddy are getting divorced because I was bad the other day"), and barroom arguments are also characterized by hasty, often slipshod thinking ("All these immigrants willing to work cheaply have made us lose our jobs"). But imprecise thinking has no place in essay writing. You should be willing to dig for causes, to think creatively about effects. You should examine your subject in depth, looking beyond the obvious and superficial.

Brainstorming is one way to explore causes and effects thoroughly. When brainstorming, generate as many explanations as possible by asking yourself a battery of questions: *What happened? Why did it happen? What other reasons were there for its happening? What will most likely happen now? What else might happen? How could it be prevented from happening again?*

If you remain open and do not let yourself settle for the obvious, you will discover that a cause may have many effects. Imagine you are writing a paper on the effects of smoking. There are a number of consequences that might be discussed, some more apparent than others: increased risk of lung cancer, increased risk of heart disease, shortening of breath, lower birth weights in babies of mothers who smoke, nicotine stains on teeth leading to various dental problems, conflicts between smoking and nonsmoking members of the same family, and legal battles regarding the rights of smokers and nonsmokers in public places.

In the same way, brainstorming will help you see that an effect may have multiple causes. An essay analyzing the reasons for world hunger could discuss many causes, again some more evident than others: overpopulation, climatic changes, poor farming techniques, internal political disruptions, lack of long-range planning by governments, cultural predispositions for large families, and international rivalries that turn the feeding of hungry people into a political rather than an ethical issue.

Brainstorming may also uncover a causal chain in which one cause brings about another, which brings about another, and so on. Here is an example of a causal chain: prohibition went into effect; bootleggers and organized crime stepped in to supply public demand for alcohol; ordinary citizens began breaking the law by buying illegal alcohol and patronizing speakeasies; disrespect for legal authority became widespread and acceptable. You can see that a causal chain often leads to interesting results. In this case, the subject of prohibition led not just to the obvious (illegal consumption of alcohol) but to a more complex issue: a significant change in society, characterized by decreasing respect for legal authority.

When determining the validity of the causes and effects generated during brainstorming, you should be careful to avoid the logical fallacy called *post hoc* thinking — from a Latin phrase that means "After this, therefore because of this." This kind of faulty thinking occurs when you assume that simply because one event followed another, the first event *caused* the second. For example, if the Republicans win a majority of seats in Congress and, several months later, the economy collapses, can you conclude that the Republicans caused the collapse? A quick assumption of "Yes" fails the test of logic, for the timing of events could be coincidental and not indicative of any cause-effect relationship. The collapse may have been triggered by uncontrolled inflation that began well before the Congressional elections.

After evaluating the brainstormed material, you need to identify which causes and effects are primary and which are secondary. How extensively you cover secondary causes and effects will depend on your purpose and the audience for whom you are writing. In an essay intended to inform a general audience of the harmful effects of pesticides, you would most likely concentrate on the effects that are immediately damaging to humans — polluted water, hazardous waste, residues in food. Given your purpose and audience, you would probably decide not to include a full discussion of more scientific and long-range effects (evolution of resistant insects, disruption of ecosystems).

Finally, keep in mind that a rigorous causal analysis involves more than loose talk about causes and effects. Creating plausible connections may require research, interviewing, or a combination of both. Often you will need to provide facts, statistics, details, personal observations, or other corroborative material if readers are going to accept the reasoning behind your analysis.

3. Write a thesis that focuses the paper on causes, effects, or both. The thesis in a paper developed through causal analysis often indicates whether the essay will deal mostly with causes, effects, or both. Here, for example, are three thesis statements for causal analyses dealing with the public school system. You will see that each thesis indicates the particular emphasis for that essay:

Our school system has been weakened by paltry teaching salaries, an overemphasis on trendy electives, and decreasing parental support. (causes)

An ineffectual public school system has led to high illiteracy rates, crippling teachers' strikes, and widespread disrespect for education. (effects)

Societal neglect and bureaucratic inefficiency have created a school system unresponsive to the emotional and intellectual needs of children. (causes and effects)

Note that each thesis statement — in addition to signaling whether the paper will discuss causes or effects or both — also points to the plan of development for the essay. Consider the first thesis statement. The thesis makes clear that the paper will discuss poor salaries first, then gimmicky electives, and last, parental indifference.

The thesis statement in a causal analysis does not have to specify whether the essay will discuss causes, effects, or both. Nor does the thesis have to be worded in such a way that the essay's plan of development is apparent. But when first writing cause-effect essays, you may find that a highly focused thesis will keep your analysis on track.

4. Choose an organizational pattern. When presenting your cause-effect discussion, you have two basic ways to organize your points. You may select a *chronological* order, discussing causes and effects in the order in which they occur or will occur. Suppose you were writing an essay on the causes for the growing popularity of imported cars. Causes might be discussed in chronological sequence: American plant workers became frustrated and dissatisfied on the job; some workers got careless while others deliberately sabotaged the product; a growing number of defective cars hit the market; consumers grew dissatisfied with American cars and switched to imports.

Chronology might also be used to organize a discussion about effects. Imagine that you were writing an essay about the need to guard against disrupting the delicate balances in the country's wildlife population. You might start the essay by discussing the disturbance that occurred when the starling, a nonnative bird, was introduced into the American environment. Because the starling had few natural predators, the starling population soared out of control; the starlings took over food sources and habitats of native species; the bluebird, a native species, declined and is now threatened with extinction.

Although a chronological pattern can be an effective way to organize material, a strict time sequence can present a problem if your primary cause or effect ends up buried in the middle of the sequence. In such a case, you might want to use *emphatic order*, reserving the most significant cause/effect for the end of the essay. For example, an exact time sequence for an essay detailing the reasons behind a candidate's unexpected victory might include the following: Less than a month after the candidate's earlier defeat, a full-scale fundraising campaign for the next election was started; the candidate spoke to many crucial power groups early in the campaign; the candidate did exceptionally well in the pre-election debates; good weather and large voter turnout on election day favored the candidate. But if you believe that the candidate's appearance before influential groups was the key factor in the victory, you would emphasize that point by saving it for the end. This is what is meant by emphatic order—saving for last the point you want to stress.

Emphatic order is an especially effective way to sequence cause-effect points when readers seem to hold mistaken or narrow views about your subject. If your readers need to be encouraged to look more closely at the real issues, you can present the erroneous or obvious views first, show why they are unsound or limited, and then present your analysis of the real causes and effects. Such a sequence nudges the audience into giving further thought to the causes and effects you have discovered. Here are brief outlines for two causal analyses using this approach.

Subject: The causes of the riot at a rock concert
1. Some commentators blame the excessively hot weather.
2. Others cite drug use among the concert-goers.
3. Still others blame the liquor sold at the concessions.
4. But the real cause of the disaster was poor planning by the concert promoters.

Subject: The effects of campus crime
1. Immediate problems
   a. Students feel insecure and fearful.
   b. Many night-time campus activities have been curtailed.
2. More significant long-term problems
   a. Unfavorable publicity about campus crime will affect future student enrollments.
   b. Hiring faculty will become more difficult.

If emphatic order is used in the causal analysis, you might want to word the thesis in such a way that it signals which point your essay will stress. Consider the following thesis statements:

Many recent immigrants lack marketable skills and often are forced to contend with prejudice once they arrive in America. But the most pressing problem is the difficulty they have dealing with an unfamiliar language.

The space program has led to dramatic advances in computer technology and medical science. Even more important, though, the program has helped change many people's attitudes toward the planet we live on.

These statements reflect an awareness of the complex nature of cause-effect relationships. While not dismissing secondary issues, the statements establish the points that are considered most note-worthy. The second paper, for instance, would touch upon the technological and medical advances made possible by the space program but would emphasize the way the program has changed people's attitudes toward the earth.

5. Use language that hints at the complexity of cause-effect relationships. Because it is difficult—if not impossible—to determine that the causes and effects you discuss are the only possible ones, you want to use language that reflects this element of uncertainty. Instead of writing, "There is no doubt that . . . ," you might say, "It is probable that . . . " or "One likely cause/ effect of. . . . " Using such language is not indecisive; it is reasonable and reflects your understanding of the often tangled nature of causes and effects. Be careful, though, of going to the other extreme and being reluctant to take a stand on the issues. If you have thought long and hard about causes and effects, you have a right to state your analysis with conviction. Don't undercut the hard work you have done by writing as if your ideas were unworthy of your reader's attention.

Cause-effect writing is gratifying for both writer and audience. As a writer, you experience the pleasure of stretching your mind, confident that your exploration of causes and effects has gone beyond the obvious. Readers feel a comparable satisfaction, knowing that they have a clearer understanding of an event or phenomenon. Causal analysis also has the potential for generating vigorous discussion and honest disagreement about important concerns. Determining why things happen and predicting consequences can lead to changes on issues ranging from political unrest to international terrorism to environmental pollution. Cause-effect writing is certainly one of the most critical ways we have for thinking about matters that concern us.

STUDENT ESSAY AND COMMENTARY

The following student essay was written by Carl Novack in response to this assignment:

> In "The Faltering Family," George Gallup, Jr. points to a number of factors that have caused the decline of the American family. Think of another institution, process, or practice that has changed recently and discuss several factors you believe are responsible for the change.

While reading Carl's paper, try to determine how well it applies the principles concerning the use of causal analysis. The commentary following the paper will help you look at Carl's essay more closely.

Americans and Food

An offbeat but timely cartoon recently appeared in the local 1
newspaper. The single panel showed a gravel-pit operation with piles
of raw earth and large cranes. Next to one of the cranes stood the
owner of the gravel pit--a grizzled, tough-looking character, hammer
in hand, pointing proudly to the new sign he had just tacked up. The
sign read, "Fred's Fill Dirt and Croissants." The cartoon illustrates an
interesting phenomenon: the changing food habits of Americans. Our
meals used to consist of something like home-cooked pot roast,
mashed potatoes laced with butter and salt, a thick slice of apple pie
topped with a healthy scoop of vanilla ice cream--plain, heavy
meals, cooked from scratch, and eaten leisurely at home. But America
has changed, and as it has, so has what we Americans eat and how
we eat it.

We used to have simple, unsophisticated tastes and looked with 2
suspicion at anything more exotic than hamburger. Admittedly, we
did adopt some foods from the various immigrant groups who flocked
to our shores. We learned to eat Chinese food, pizza, and bagels. But in
the last few years, the international character of our diet has grown
tremendously. We can walk into any mall in Middle America and buy
pita bread, quiche, and tacos. Such foods are often changed on their
journey from exotic imports to ordinary "American" meals (no Pakis-
tani, for example, eats frozen-on-a-stick boysenberry-flavored yogurt), but the imports are still a long way from hamburger on a bun.

Why have we become more worldly in our tastes? For one thing, 3
television blankets the country with information about new food
products and trends. Viewers in rural Montana know that the latest
craving in Washington, D.C. is Cajun cooking or that something called
tofu is now available in the local supermarket. Another reason for the
growing international flavor of our food is that many young Americans have traveled abroad and gotten hooked on new tastes and
flavors. Backpacking students and young professionals vacationing
in Europe come home with cravings for authentic French bread or
German beer. Finally, continuing waves of immigrants settle in the
cities where many of us live, causing significant changes in what we
eat. Vietnamese, Haitians, and Thais, for instance, bring their native

foods and cooking styles with them and eventually open small markets or restaurants. In time, the new food will become Americanized enough to take its place in our national diet.

Our growing concern with health has also affected the way we   4
eat. For the last few years, the media have warned us about the dangers of our traditional diet, high in salt and fat, low in fiber. The media also began to educate us about the dangers of processed foods pumped full of chemical additives. As a result, consumers began to demand healthier foods, and manufacturers started to change some of their products. Many foods, such as lunch meat, canned vegetables, and soups were made available in low-fat, low-sodium versions. Whole grain cereals and high fiber breads also began to appear on the grocery shelves. Moreover, the food industry started to produce all-natural products--everything from potato chips to ice cream--without additives and preservatives. Not surprisingly, the restaurant industry responded to this switch to healthier foods, luring customers with salad bars, broiled fish, and steamed vegetables.

Our food habits are being affected, too, by the rapid increase in   5
the number of women working outside the home. Sociologists and other experts believe that two important factors triggered this phenomenon: the women's movement and a changing economic climate. Women were assured that it was acceptable, even rewarding, to work outside the home; many women also discovered that they had to work just to keep up with the cost of living. As the traditional role of the homemaker changed, so did the way families ate. With Mom working, there wasn't time for her to prepare the traditional three square meals a day. Instead, families began looking for alternatives to provide quick meals. What was the result? For one thing, there was a boom in fast-food restaurants. The suburban or downtown strip that once contained a lone McDonald's now features Wendy's, Roy Rogers, Taco Bell, Burger King, and Pizza Hut. Families also began to depend on frozen foods as another time-saving alternative. Once again, though, demand changed the kind of frozen food available. Frozen foods no longer consist of foil trays divided into greasy fried chicken, watery corn niblets, and lumpy mashed potatoes. Supermarkets now stock a range of supposedly gourmet frozen dinners--from fettucini in cream sauce to braised beef en brochette.

It may not be possible to pick up a ton of fill dirt and a half-dozen   6
croissants at the same place, but America's food habits are definitely changing. If it is true that "you are what you eat," then America's identity is evolving along with its diet.

Asked to prepare a paper analyzing the reasons behind a change in our lives, Carl decided to write about a shift he had noticed in Americans' eating habits. The title of Carl's essay, "Americans and Food," does identify his subject but needs to be reworked so it is livelier and more interesting.

Despite his uninspired title, Carl starts his *causal analysis* with a sharp, attention-getting opener — the vivid description of a cartoon. He then connects the cartoon to his subject with the following sentence: "The cartoon illustrates an interesting phenomenon: the changing food habits of Americans." To back up his belief that there has been a revolution in our eating habits, Carl uses the first paragraph to provide a capsule summary of the kind of meal that people used to eat, suggesting that such a meal is pretty much a thing of the past. At that point, Carl moves into his thesis: "But America has changed, and as it has, so has what we Americans eat and how we eat it." Note that the thesis implies that Carl's paper will focus on both causes and effects.

Carl's purpose is to write an *informative* causal analysis. But he realizes that before presenting the causes of the change, he must provide additional evidence to show that we do in fact eat differently from the way we used to. He therefore spends the second paragraph documenting one aspect of this change — the internationalization of our eating habits. Now that the validity of the phenomenon is established, Carl is ready to explore the reasons behind the change.

At the start of the third paragraph, Carl uses a question ("Why have we become more worldly in our tastes?") to signal that his discussion of causes is about to begin. This question also serves as the paragraph's *topic sentence*, indicating that the paragraph will focus on reasons for the increasingly international flavor of our food. The next two paragraphs, also focused by topic sentences, identify two other major reasons for the change in eating habits: "Our growing concern with health has also affected the way we eat" (paragraph 4) and "Our food habits are being affected, too, by the rapid increase in the number of women working outside the home" (5).

Since Carl's essay has an informational intent, he must support the point expressed in each topic sentence. Without convincing specifics, he will not be able to demonstrate the validity of his analysis. Consider for a moment the essay's third paragraph. In this section, Carl asserts that one reason for our new eating habits is our growing exposure to international foods. To illustrate the aptness of his analysis, Carl provides evidence showing that we have indeed become more familiar with international cuisine. Television exposes rural Montana to Cajun cooking; students traveling abroad take a liking to hard-crusted French bread; urban folks enjoy the exotic fare served by numerous immigrant groups settled in the cities.

The fourth and fifth paragraphs use similarly convincing specifics to demonstrate the soundness of the points made by the topic sentences. Let's look more closely at the evidence Carl uses to develop these points. As you know, causal analyses rely on clear thinking and logic. And Carl, not satisfied with obvious explanations, thought about his essay carefully, even brainstorming with friends to arrive at as comprehensive an analysis as possible. Not surprisingly, much of the evidence Carl uncovered took the form of *causal chains*. In the fourth paragraph, Carl writes, "The media also began to educate us about the dangers of processed foods pumped full of chemical additives. As a result, consumers began to demand healthier food . . . and manufacturers started to change some of their products." And the next paragraph shows how the changing role of American women caused families to look for alternative ways of eating. This shift, in turn, caused the restaurant and food industries to respond with a staggering range of food alternatives.

Although Carl's analysis digs beneath the surface and reveals complex cause-effect relationships, he wisely limits his pursuit of causal chains. He does not let the complexities distract him from his main purpose: to show why and how the American diet is changing. He knows his analysis must focus on key cause-effect relationships. Carl is also careful to provide his essay with abundant *connecting devices*, making it easy for readers to see the links between the points in his analysis. Consider the use of *transitions* (signaled by italics) in the following sentences: "*Another* reason for the growing international flavor of our food is that many young Americans have traveled abroad . . . " (3); "*As a result*, consumers began to demand healthier foods . . . " (4); and "*As* the traditional role of homemaker changed, *so* did the way families ate" (5).

When reading the essay, you probably noticed that Carl's conclusion is a bit weak. Although his reference to the cartoon works well, the rest of the paragraph limps to a tired close. Ending an otherwise vigorous essay with such a slight conclusion undercuts the effectiveness of the whole paper. Carl spent so much energy developing the body of his essay that he ran out of the stamina needed to conclude the piece more forcefully. Careful budgeting of his time would have allowed him to prepare a stronger concluding paragraph.

When Carl revised his paper, he realized that his fourth paragraph needed extensive work. Here is the original version of that paragraph.

Unrevised Version

A growing concern with health has also affected the way we eat, especially because the media has sent us warnings the last few years about the dangers of salt, sugar, food additives, high-fat and low-fiber diets. We have started to worry that our traditional meals may have been shortening our lives. As a result, consumers demanded healthier foods and manufacturers started taking some of the salt and sugar out of canned foods. "All-natural" became an effective selling point, leading to many preservative-free products. Restaurants, too, adapted their menus, luring customers with light meals. Because we now know about the link between overweight and a variety of health problems, including heart attacks, we are counting calories. In turn, food companies made fortunes on diet beer and diet cola. Sometimes, though, we seem a bit confused about the health issue; we drink soda that is sugar-free but loaded with chemical sweeteners. Still, we believe we are lengthening our lives through changing our diets.

Carl's editing of this paragraph started with a reworking of the awkward first sentence. The sentence contained too much material and thus did not function as an effective topic sentence for the paragraph. Carl corrected the problem by breaking the overlong sentence into two separate sentences: "Our growing concern with health has also affected the way we eat. For the last few years, the media have warned us about the dangers of our traditional diet, high in salt and fat, low in fiber." The first of these sentences serves as a crisp topic sentence that focuses the rest of the paragraph.

In addition, Carl decided to omit all references to the way our concern with weight has affected our eating habits. It's true, of course, that calorie-counting has changed how we eat. But as soon as Carl started to discuss this point, he got involved in a causal chain that undercut the unity of the paragraph. He ended up describing the paradoxical situation in which we find ourselves. In an attempt to eat healthily, we stay away from sugar, using instead artificial sweetners that probably aren't very good for us. This is an interesting issue, but it detracts from the point Carl wants to make: that our concern with health has affected our eating habits in a positive way.

Finally, while revising the paragraph, Carl made many of his details more concrete. He changed " . . . manufacturers started taking some of the salt and sugar out of canned foods" to the more specific "Many foods, such as lunch meats, canned vegetables, and soups, were made available in low-fat, low-sodium versions." Similarly, the allusions to restaurants' light meals and the popularity of all-natural products were made more vigorous: " . . . the restaurant industry responded to this switch to healthier foods, luring customers with salad bars, broiled fish, and steamed vegetables" and " . . . the food industry started to produce all-natural products — everything from potato chips to ice cream — without additives and preservatives."

Carl did an equally fine job revising other sections of his paper. With the exception of the weak spots already discussed, he made the changes needed to craft a well-reasoned essay which demonstrated his ability to analyze a complex phenomenon.

The essays in this chapter analyze some of the important cause-effect relationships that exist in the world today. In "The Faltering Family," George Gallup, Jr. studies why the American family is changing and makes some disturbing predictions about future changes. Peter Farb, in "In Other Words," describes a rather surprising cause of some children's poor school performance. In "O Rotten Gotham — Sliding Down into the Behavioral Sink," Tom Wolfe uses black humor to show how overpopulation leads to human aggression. "Communication in the Year 2000," by Tony Schwartz, describes future developments in communications and speculates on how these extraordinary changes will affect our lives. Finally, Lewis Thomas, in "The Health Care System," traces our obsession with fitness and concludes by explaining why our preoccupation can be unhealthy.

George Gallup, Jr.

*Born in Illinois in 1930, George Gallup, Jr. is president of the
Gallup Poll, the well-known research firm that measures
public opinion. Gallup still resides in Princeton, where he
graduated from the University, and has served as executive
director of the Princeton Religion Research Center. He has
published articles about religion, politics, and other current
issues. His books include* America's Search for Faith *(1980)
with David Poling,* My Kid on Drugs? *(1981) with Art
Linkletter,* Adventures in Immortality (1982) *and* Forecast 2000 *(1985), both with William Proctor. The following
essay is from* Forecast 2000.

The Faltering Family

*For better or worse, the American family — one of society's
most important structures — is changing in response to a variety of cultural forces. Based on the results of several national
opinion polls, the following selection presents George Gallup's
conclusions about the future of the family. According to Gallup, if current trends continue, the traditional family will
fade into a mere memory.*

In a recent Sunday school class in a United Methodist Church   1
in the Northeast, a group of eight- to ten-year-olds were in a deep
discussion with their two teachers. When asked to choose which of
ten stated possibilities they most feared happening, their response
was unanimous. All the children most dreaded a divorce between
their parents.

Later, as the teachers, a man and a woman in their late thirties,   2
reflected on the lesson, they both agreed they'd been shocked at the
response. When they were the same age as their students, they said,
the possibility of their parents' being divorced never entered their
heads. Yet in just one generation, children seemed to feel much less
security in their family ties.

Nor is the experience of these two Sunday school teachers an   3
isolated one. Psychiatrists revealed in one recent newspaper investigation that the fears of children definitely do change in different
periods; and in recent times, divorce has become one of the most
frequently mentioned anxieties. In one case, for example, a four-
year-old insisted that his father rather than his mother walk him to
nursery school each day. The reason? He said many of his friends
had "no daddy living at home, and I'm scared that will happen to
me" (*The New York Times*, May 2, 1983).

In line with such reports, our opinion leaders expressed great   4
concern about the present and future status of the American family. In the poll 33 percent of the responses listed decline in family
structure, divorce, and other family-oriented concerns as one of the
five major problems facing the nation today. And 26 percent of the
responses included such family difficulties as one of the five major
problems for the United States in the year 2000.

Historical and sociological trends add strong support to these   5
expressions of concern. For example, today about one marriage in
every two ends in divorce. Moreover, the situation seems to be
getting worse, rather than better. In 1962, the number of divorces
was 2.2 per 1,000 people, according to the National Center for
Health Statistics. By 1982, the figure had jumped to 5.1 divorces
per 1,000 people — a rate that had more than doubled in two
decades.

One common concern expressed about the rise in divorces and   6
decline in stability of the family is that the family unit has traditionally been a key factor in transmitting stable cultural and moral
values from generation to generation. Various studies have shown
that educational and religious institutions often can have only a
limited impact on children without strong family support.

Even grandparents are contributing to the divorce statistics.   7
One recent study revealed that about 100,000 people over the age
of fifty-five get divorced in the United States each year. These
divorces are usually initiated by men who face retirement, and the
relationships being ended are those that have endured for thirty
years or more (*The New York Times Magazine*, December 19,
1982).

What are the pressures that have emerged in the past twenty   8
years that cause long-standing family bonds to be broken?

Many now agree that the sexual revolution of the 1960s   9
worked a profound change on our society's family values and personal relationships. Certainly, the seeds of upheaval were present
before that critical decade. But a major change that occurred in the
mid-sixties was an explicit widespread rejection of the common
values about sexual and family relationships that most Americans
in the past had held up as an ideal.

We're just beginning to sort through all the changes in social   10
standards that have occurred. Here are some of the major pressures
that have contributed to those changes:

Pressure One: Alternative Lifestyles

Twenty years ago, the typical American family was depicted as   11
a man and woman who were married to each other and who produced children (usually two) and lived happily ever after. This was
the pattern that young people expected to follow in order to become "full" or "normal" members of society. Of course, some
people have always chosen a different route — remaining single,
taking many partners, or living with a member of their own sex. But
they were always considered somewhat odd, and outside the social
order of the traditional family.

In the last two decades, this picture has changed dramatically.   12
In addition to the proliferation of single people through divorce,
we also have these developments:

- Gay men and women have petitioned the courts for the right   13
  to marry each other and to adopt children. These demands
  are being given serious consideration, and there may even be
  a trend of sorts in this direction. For example, the National
  Association of Social Workers is increasingly supporting full
  adoption rights for gay people (*The New York Times*, January
  10, 1983).
- Many heterosexual single adults have been permitted to   14
  adopt children and set up single-parent families. So being
  unattached no longer excludes people from the joys of parenthood.
- Some women have deliberately chosen to bear children out   15
  of wedlock and raise them alone. In the past, many of these

children would have been given up for adoption, but no longer.

A most unusual case involved an unmarried psycholo-   16
gist, Dr. Afton Blake, who recently gave birth after being
artificially inseminated with sperm from a sperm bank to
which Nobel Prize winners had contributed (*The New York
Times*, September 6, 1983).

• In a recent Gallup Youth Poll, 64 percent of the teenagers   17
questioned said that they hoped their lives would be different from those of their parents. This included having more
money, pursuing a different kind of profession, living in a
different area, having more free time — and staying single
longer.

Most surveys show increasing numbers of unmarried   18
couples living together. Also, there are periodic reports of
experiments in communal living, "open marriages," and
other such arrangements. Although the more radical approaches to relationships tend to come and go and never
seem to attract large numbers of people, the practice of living together without getting married seems to be something
that's here to stay. The law is beginning to respond to these
arrangements with awards for "palimony" — compensation
for long-term unmarried partners in a relationship. But the
legal and social status of unmarried people who live together
is still quite uncertain — especially as far as any children of
the union are concerned.

• Increasing numbers of married couples are choosing to re-   19
main childless. Planned Parenthood has even established
workshops for couples to assist them in making this decision
(*Los Angeles Herald-Examiner*, November 27, 1979).

So clearly, a situation has arisen during the last twenty years in   20
which traditional values are no longer as important. Also, a wide
variety of alternatives to the traditional family have arisen. Individuals may feel that old-fashioned marriage is just one of many options.

Pressure Two: Sexual Morality

The changes in attitudes toward sexual morality have changed   21
as dramatically in the last two decades as the alternatives to tradi-

tional marriage. Hear what a widely used college textbook, published in 1953, said about premarital sex:

> The arguments against premarital coitus outweigh   22
> those in its favor. Except for the matter of temporary
> physical pleasure, all arguments about gains tend to be
> highly theoretical, while the risks and unpleasant conse-
> quences tend to be in equal degree highly practical. . . .
>   The promiscuity of young men is certainly poor prep-   23
> aration for marital fidelity and successful family life. For
> girls it is certainly no better and sometimes leads still
> further to the physical and psychological shock of abor-
> tion or the more prolonged suffering of bearing an illegit-
> imate child and giving it up to others. From the viewpoint
> of ethical and religious leaders, the spread of disease
> through unrestrained sex activities is far more than a
> health problem. They see it as undermining the depend-
> able standards of character and the spiritual values that
> raise life to the level of the "good society."

(This comes from *Marriage and the Family* by Professor Ray E. Baber of Pomona College, California, which was part of the McGraw-Hill Series in Sociology and Anthropology and required reading for some college courses.)

Clearly, attitudes have changed a great deal in just three dec-   24
ades. Teenagers have accepted the idea of premarital sex as the norm. In one recent national poll, 52 percent of girls and 66 percent of boys favored having sexual relations in their teens. Ironically, however, 46 percent of the teenagers thought that virginity in their future marital partner was fairly important. Youngsters, in other words, display some confusion about what they want to do sexually, and what they expect from a future mate.

But of course, only part of the problem of defining sexual   25
standards lies with young people and premarital sex. The strong emphasis on achieving an active and rewarding sex life has probably played some role in encouraging many husbands and wives into rejecting monogamy. Here's some of the evidence that's been accumulating:

• Half of the men in a recent nationwide study admitted   26
  cheating on their wives (*Pensacola Journal*, May 30, 1978).

- Psychiatrists today say they see more patients who are think-   27
ing about having an extramarital affair and who wonder if it
would harm their marriage (*New York Post*, November 18,
1976).
- A psychiatrist at the Albert Einstein College of Medicine   28
says, "In my practice I have been particularly struck by how
many women have been able to use an affair to raise their
consciousness and their confidence."

So the desire for unrestrained sex now tends to take a place   29
among other more traditional priorities, and this can be expected
to continue to exert strong pressure on marriage relationships.

Pressure Three: The Economy

The number of married women working outside the home has   30
been increasing steadily, and most of these women are working out
of economic necessity. As a result, neither spouse may have time to
concentrate on the nurturing of the children or of the marriage
relationship.

One mother we interviewed in New Jersey told us about her   31
feelings when she was forced to work full time in a library after her
husband lost his job.

"It's the idea that I have no choice that really bothers me," she   32
said. "I have to work, or we won't eat or have a roof over our heads.
I didn't mind working part-time just to have extra money. I suppose that it's selfish, but I hate having to work every day and then to
come home, fix dinner, and have to start doing housework. Both
my husband and I were raised in traditional families, where the
father went to work and the mother stayed home and took care of
the house and children. [My husband] would never think of cooking or doing housework. I've raised my boys the same way, and now
I'm paying for it. Sometimes, I almost hate my husband, even
though I know it's not his fault."

Unfortunately, such pressures probably won't ease in the fu-   33
ture. Even if the economy improves and the number of unemployed workers decreases, few women are likely to give up their
jobs. Economists agree that working-class women who have be-

come breadwinners during a recession can be expected to remain in the work force. One reason is that many unemployed men aren't going to get their old jobs back, even when the economy improves.

"To the extent that [the men] may have to take lower-paying   34
service jobs, their families will need a second income," says Michelle Brandman, associate economist at Chase Econometrics. "The trend to two paycheck families as a means of maintaining family income is going to continue" (*The Wall Street Journal*, December 8, 1982).

In addition to the pressures of unemployment, the cost of   35
having, rearing, and educating children is steadily going up. Researchers have found that middle-class families with two children *think* they're spending only about 15 percent of their income on their children. Usually, though, they *actually* spend about 40 percent of their money on them. To put the cost in dollars and cents, if you had a baby in 1977, the estimated cost of raising that child to the age of eighteen will be $85,000, and that figure has of course been on the rise for babies born since then (*New York Daily News*, July 24, 1977).

Another important factor that promises to keep both spouses   36
working full time in the future is the attitude of today's teenagers toward these issues. They're not so much concerned about global issues like overpopulation as they are about the high cost of living. Both boys and girls place a lot of emphasis on having enough money so that they can go out and do things. Consequently, most teenage girls surveyed say they expect to pursue careers, even after they get married.

So it would seem that by the year 2000 we can expect to see   37
more working mothers in the United States. The woman who doesn't hold down any sort of outside job but stays at home to care for her children represents a small percentage of wives today. By the end of the century, with a few exceptions here and there, she may well have become a part of America's quaint past.

As women have joined the work force in response to economic   38
needs, one result has been increased emotional strains on the marriage and family relationships. But there's another set of pressures that has encouraged women to pursue careers. That's the power of feminist philosophy to permeate attitudes in grassroots America during the past couple of decades.

Pressure Four: Grassroots
Feminist Philosophy

Many women may not agree with the most radical expressions   39
of feminist philosophy that have arisen in the past decade or so. But
most younger women — and indeed, a majority of women in the
United States — tend to agree with most of the objectives that even
the radical feminist groups have been trying to achieve. The basic
feminist philosophy has filtered down to the grass roots, and young
boys and girls are growing up with feminist assumptions that may
have been foreign to their parents and grandparents.

For example, child care and housework are no longer regarded   40
strictly as "women's work" by the young people we've polled.
Also, according to the Gallup Youth Poll, most teenage girls want
to go to college and pursue a career. Moreover, they expect to
marry later in life and to continue working after they're married.
Another poll, conducted by *The New York Times* and CBS News,
revealed that only 2 percent of the youngest age group interviewed
— that is, those eighteen to twenty-nine years old — preferred
"traditional marriage." By this, they meant a marriage in which the
husband is exclusively a provider and the wife is exclusively a homemaker and mother.

If these young people continue to hold views similar to these   41
into later life, it's likely that the changes that are occurring today in
the traditional family structure will continue. For one thing, more
day-care centers for children will have to be established. Consequently, the rearing of children will no longer be regarded as solely
the responsibility of the family, but will become a community or
institutional responsibility.

But while such developments may lessen the strain on mothers   42
and fathers, they may also weaken the bonds that hold families
together. Among other things, it may become psychologically easier to get a divorce if a person is not getting along with a spouse,
because the divorcing spouses will believe it's less likely that the
lives of the children will be disrupted.

So the concept of broadening the rights of women vis-à-vis   43
their husbands and families has certainly encouraged women to
enter the working world in greater numbers. They're also more
inclined to seek a personal identity that isn't tied up so much in
their homelife.

These grassroots feminist forces have brought greater benefits   44
to many, but at the same time they've often worked against traditional family ties, and we remain uncertain about what is going to
replace them. Feminists may argue that the traditional family
caused its own demise — or else why would supposedly content
wives and daughters have worked so hard to transform it? Whatever its theories, though, feminism is still a factor that, in its present
form, appears to exert a destabilizing influence on many traditional familial relationships among husbands, wives, and children.

As things stand now, our family lives are in a state of flux and   45
will probably continue to be out of balance until the year 2000. The
pressures we've discussed will continue to have an impact on our
family lives in future years. But at the same time, counterforces,
which tend to drive families back together again, are also at work.
One of these factors is a traditionalist strain in the large major-   46
ity of American women. The vast majority of women in this
country — 74 percent — continue to view marriage with children
as the most interesting and satisfying life for them personally,
according to a Gallup Poll for the White House Conference on
Families released in June, 1980.
Another force supporting family life is the attitude of Ameri-   47
can teenagers toward divorce. According to a recent Gallup Youth
Poll, 55 percent feel that divorces are too easy to get today. Also,
they're concerned about the high rate of divorce, and they want to
have enduring marriages themselves. But at the same time — in a
response that reflects the confusion of many adult Americans on
this subject — 67 percent of the teens in this same poll say it's right
to get a divorce if a couple doesn't get along together. In other
words, they place little importance on trying to improve or salvage
a relationship that has run into serious trouble.
There's a similar ambivalence in the experts we polled. As   48
we've seen, 33 percent of them consider family problems as a top
concern today, and 26 percent think these problems will be a big
difficulty in the year 2000. But ironically, less than 3 percent suggest that strengthening family relationships is an important consideration in planning for the future! It's obvious, then, that we're
confused and ambivalent in our feelings about marriage and the
family. Most people know instinctively, without having to read a
poll or a book, that happiness and satisfaction in life are rooted

largely in the quality of our personal relationships. Furthermore, the most important of those relationships usually begin at home. So one of the greatest challenges we face before the year 2000, both as a nation and as individuals, is how to make our all-important family ties strong and healthy. It's only upon such a firm personal foundation that we can hope to venture forth and grapple effectively with more public problems.

Questions for Close Reading

1. What is the thesis of the selection? Locate the sentence(s) in which Gallup states his main idea. If he does not state the thesis explicitly, express it in your own words.
2. According to Gallup, what are the major pressures that have caused the change in American attitudes to marriage and the family?
3. What new styles of pairing up and parenting have entered the American mainstream and now compete with traditional marriage?
4. Why are more and more women choosing to work outside the home? Why does the author believe that this is a permanent lifestyle change for American women?
5. Refer to your dictionary as needed to define the following words in the selection: *explicit* (paragraph 9), *proliferation* (12), *inseminated* (16), *salvage* (47), and *ambivalence* (48).

Questions about the Writer's Craft

1. In this selection, Gallup tries to account for the changes in the American ideals of marriage and family. Why does he use the term *pressures* rather than *causes*? Does he intend the list of pressures to be complete?
2. What techniques does the author use to introduce the selection? What feeling does this introduction create in you toward marriage and the family? How is the introduction related to the data covered in the article?
3. Examine the supporting evidence for each "pressure." For which ones does the author provide facts or statistics? What other kinds of evidence does he provide for the remaining pressures?
4. How does the author create a sense of objectivity about the report? Are there any clues in the author's word choices that reveal his actual opinions about the transformation of American family values?

Questions for Further Thought

1. Are there any forces in our society acting to preserve the traditional American family? Do you think these forces are outweighed by the pressures mentioned in the selection?
2. The author concludes that "most people know instinctively . . . that happiness and satisfaction in life are rooted largely in the quality of our personal relationships." Do you agree? Do you know people whose major satisfaction comes from other areas of life?
3. Do American TV and the other media put pressure on our personal lifestyles? Is the image of family and relationships in the media a reflection of our changing personal values, or an influence on them?
4. How widespread are the alternative lifestyles in the lives of people you know and go to school with?

Writing Assignments Using Cause-Effect as a Method of Development

1. Consider the forces that lead people to adopt the same lifestyles as their parents. Write an essay analyzing the pressures your generation feels to conform to the same standards as generations past. Maintain an objective reporting tone, if you wish, or choose a tone that indicates your position on the issue.
2. Write an essay explaining how people are affected when those close to them choose an alternative lifestyle. For example, think of someone you know who has chosen divorce, single parenthood, a gay lifestyle, cohabitation, or some other nontraditional way of life. Decide what positive and/or negative effects resulted from this choice and write an essay outlining these effects. You may wish to evaluate the choice on the basis of how it turned out, but be careful of generalizing from one case to universal rules of behavior.

Writing Assignments Using Other Methods of Development

3. When a family breaks apart, many lives are disrupted. Parents, children, grandparents, relatives, friends, even neighbors must cope with disorder and confusion. Write an essay illustrating the kinds of turmoil that may be felt by one of these groups. Develop the paper by drawing on your own and/or other people's experience. The essay should include some brief recommendations about ways the group under discussion can learn to cope with the dislocations that occur.

4. Watch prime-time TV for a week and keep a numerical record of how often alternative lifestyles (extramarital affairs, divorce, single parenthood, and so on) appear in the plots of TV dramas. Write up your findings in the form of a letter to *TV Guide*, either criticizing or praising the TV networks for their presentation of these life choices. Support your argument with specific references to the shows you watched.

Peter Farb

*Peter Farb (1929 – 1980) was born in New York and at-
tended Vanderbilt University. Farb served as a consultant to
the Smithsonian Institution and as a visiting lecturer at Yale
University. A deep interest in language and human cultures
led Farb to write* Face of North America *(1963),* Man's
Rise to Civilization as Shown by the Indians of North
America *(1968), and* Word Play: What Happens When
People Talk *(1973). This selection is from* Word Play.

In Other Words

*How can Clever Hans, a horse that solved mathematical
problems, provide insight into a serious problem in public education? Surprisingly, there is a strong connection. In the following essay, Peter Farb uses the story of Clever Hans to show
how subtly a teacher's body language can affect children's
performance in the classroom.*

Early in this century, a horse named Hans amazed the people   1
of Berlin by his extraordinary ability to perform rapid calculations
in mathematics. After a problem was written on a blackboard
placed in front of him, he promptly counted out the answer by
tapping the low numbers with his right forefoot and multiples of
ten with his left. Trickery was ruled out because Hans's owner,
unlike owners of other performing animals, did not profit
financially — and Hans even performed his feats whether or not
the owner was present. The psychologist O. Pfungst witnessed one
of these performances and became convinced that there had to be a
more logical explanation than the uncanny intelligence of a horse.

Because Hans performed only in the presence of an audience   2
that could see the blackboard and therefore knew the correct answer, Pfungst reasoned that the secret lay in observation of the
audience rather than of the horse. He finally discovered that as
soon as the problem was written on the blackboard, the audience

387

bent forward very slightly in anticipation to watch Hans's forefeet. As slight as that movement was, Hans perceived it and took it as his signal to begin tapping. As his taps approached the correct number, the audience became tense with excitement and made almost imperceptible movements of the head — which signaled Hans to stop counting. The audience, simply by expecting Hans to stop when the correct number was reached, had actually told the animal when to stop. Pfungst clearly demonstrated that Hans's intelligence was nothing but a mechanical response to his audience, which unwittingly communicated the answer by its body language.

The "Clever Hans Phenomenon," as it has come to be known, raises an interesting question. If a mere horse can detect unintentional and extraordinarily subtle body signals, might they not also be detected by human beings? Professional gamblers and con men have long been known for their skill in observing the body-language cues of their victims, but only recently has it been shown scientifically that all speakers constantly detect and interpret such cues also, even though they do not realize it. 3

An examination of television word games several years ago revealed that contestants inadvertently gave their partners body-language signals that led to correct answers. In one such game, contestants had to elicit certain words from their partners, but they were permitted to give only brief verbal clues as to what the words might be. It turned out that sometimes the contestants also gave body signals that were much more informative than the verbal clues. In one case, a contestant was supposed to answer *sad* in response to his partner's verbal clue of *happy* — that is, the correct answer was a word opposite to the verbal clue. The partner giving the *happy* clue unconsciously used his body to indicate to his fellow contestant that an opposite word was needed. He did that by shifting his body and head very slightly to one side as he said *happy*, then to the other side in expectation of an opposite word. 4

Contestants on a television program are usually unsophisticated about psychology and linguistics, but trained psychological experimenters also unintentionally flash body signals which are sometimes detected by the test subjects — and which may distort the results of experiments. Hidden cameras have revealed that the sex of the experimenter, for example, can influence the responses of subjects. Even though the films showed that both male and female experimenters carried out the experiments in the same way and 5 asked the same questions, the experimenters were very much aware of their own sex in relation to the sex of the subjects. Male experimenters spent 16 per cent more time carrying out experiments with female subjects than they did with male subjects; similarly, female experimenters took 13 per cent longer to go through experiments with male subjects than they did with female subjects. The cameras also revealed that chivalry is not dead in the psychological experiment; male experimenters smiled about six times as often with female subjects as they did with male subjects.

The important question, of course, is whether or not such   6
nonverbal communication influences the results of experiments. The answer is that it often does. Psychologists who have watched films made without the knowledge of either the experimenters or the subjects could predict almost immediately which experimenters would obtain results from their subjects that were in the direction of the experimenters' own biases. Those experimenters who seemed more dominant, personal, and relaxed during the first moments of conversation with their subjects usually obtained the results that they secretly hoped the experiments would yield. And they somehow communicated their secret hopes in a completely visual way, regardless of what they said or their paralanguage when they spoke. That was made clear when these films were shown to two groups, one of which saw the films without hearing the sound track while the other heard only the sound track without seeing the films. The group that heard only the voices could not accurately predict the experimenters' biases — but those who saw the films without hearing the words immediately sensed whether or not the experimenters were communicating their biases.

A person who signals his expectations about a certain kind of   7
behavior is not aware that he is doing so — and usually he is indignant when told that his experiment was biased — but the subjects themselves confirm his bias by their performances. Such bias in experiments has been shown to represent self-fulfilling prophecies. In other words, the experimenters' expectations about the results of the experiment actually result in those expectations coming true. That was demonstrated when each of twelve experimenters was given five rats bred from an identical strain of laboratory animals. Half of the experimenters were told that their rats could be expected to perform brilliantly because they had been bred especially for high intelligence and quickness in running through a

maze. The others were told that their rats could be expected to perform very poorly because they had been bred for low intelligence. All the experimenters were then asked to teach their rats to run a maze.

Almost as soon as the rats were put into the maze it became   8
clear that those for which the experimenters had high expectations would prove to be the better performers. And the rats which were expected to perform badly did in fact perform very badly, even though they were bred from the identical strain as the excellent performers. Some of these poor performers did not even budge from their starting positions in the maze. The misleading prophecy about the behavior of the two groups of rats was fulfilled — simply because the two groups of experimenters unconsciously communicated their expectations to the animals. Those experimenters who anticipated high performance were friendlier to their animals than those who expected low performance; they handled their animals more, and they did so more gently. Clearly, the predictions of the experimenters were communicated to the rats in subtle and unintended ways — and the rats behaved accordingly.

Since animals such as laboratory rats and Clever Hans can   9
detect body-language cues, it is not surprising that human beings are just as perceptive in detecting visual signals about expectations for performance. It is a psychological truth that we are likely to speak to a person whom we expect to be unpleasant in such a way that we force him to act unpleasantly. But it has only recently become apparent that poor children — often black or Spanish-speaking — perform badly in school because that is what their teachers expect of them, and because the teachers manage to convey that expectation by both verbal and nonverbal channels. True to the teachers' prediction, the black and brown children probably will do poorly — not necessarily because children from minority groups are capable only of poor performance, but because poor performance has been expected of them. The first grade may be the place where teachers anticipate poor performances by children of certain racial, economic, and cultural backgrounds — and where the teachers actually teach these children how to fail.

Evidence of the way the "Clever Hans Phenomenon" works in   10
many schools comes from a careful series of experiments by psychologist Robert Rosenthal and his co-workers at Harvard University. They received permission from a school south of San Francisco

to give a series of tests to the children in the lower grades. The teachers were blatantly lied to. They were told that the test was a newly developed tool that could predict which children would be "spurters" and achieve high performance in the coming year. Actually, the experimenters administered a new kind of IQ test that the teachers were unlikely to have seen previously. After IQ scores were obtained, the experimenters selected the names of 20 percent of the children completely at random. Some of the selected children scored very high on the IQ test and others scored low, some were from middle-class families and others from lower-class. Then the teachers were lied to again. The experimenters said that the tests singled out this 20 per cent as the children who could be expected to make unusual intellectual gains in the coming year. The teachers were also cautioned not to discuss the test results with the pupils or their parents. Since the names of these children had been selected completely at random, any difference between them and the 80 per cent not designated as "spurters" was completely in the minds of the teachers.

All the children were given IQ tests again during that school   11
year and once more the following year. The 20 per cent who had been called to the attention of their teachers did indeed turn in the high performances expected of them — in some cases dramatic increases of 25 points in IQ. The teachers' comments about these children also were revealing. The teachers considered them more happy, curious, and interesting than the other 80 per cent — and they predicted that they would be successes in life, a prophecy they had already started to fulfill. The experiment plainly showed that children who are expected to gain intellectually do gain and that their behavior improves as well.

The results of the experiment are clear — but the explanation   12
for the results is not. It might be imagined that the teachers simply devoted more time to the children singled out for high expectations, but the study showed that was not so. Instead, the influence of the teachers upon these children apparently was much more subtle. What the teachers said to them, how and when it was said, the facial expressions, gestures, posture, perhaps even touch that accompanied their speech — some or all of these things must have communicated that the teachers expected improved performance from them. And when these children responded correctly, the teachers were quicker to praise them and also more lavish in their

praise. Whatever the exact mechanism was, the effect upon the children who had been singled out was dramatic. They changed their ideas about themselves, their behavior, their motivation, and their learning capacities.

The lesson of the California experiment is that pupil perform-   13
ance does not depend so much upon a school's audio-visual equipment or new textbooks or enriching trips to museums as it does upon teachers whose body language communicates high expectations for the pupils — even if the teacher thinks she "knows" that a black, a Puerto Rican, a Mexican-American, or any other disadvantaged child is fated to do poorly in school. Apparently, remedial instruction in our schools is misdirected. It is needed more by the middle-class teachers than by the disadvantaged children.

Questions for Close Reading

1. What is the thesis of the selection? Locate the sentence(s) in which Farb states his main idea. If he does not state the thesis explicitly, express it in your own words.
2. Does Farb consider the "Clever Hans Phenomenon" a true phenomenon, or does he give reasons for it? What kinds of people and animals are likely to detect and interpret body language clues?
3. The author refers to an experiment which used rats in a maze. Who was really the subject of that experiment, the rats, or someone else?
4. What did the Harvard experiment in the San Francisco schools prove? In this experiment, who were the "rats"?
5. Refer to your dictionary as needed to define the following words in the selection: *unwittingly* (paragraph 2), *linguistics* (5), and *blatantly* (10).

Questions about the Writer's Craft

1. Scientific experiments are set up to limit the possible causes of an effect. In describing the "Clever Hans Phenomenon," Farb reveals that naive viewers thought that the cause of the phenomenon was one thing (Hans doing math in his head), while the psychologist Pfungst determined that the cause was something else (Hans reacting to body movements of the audience). Locate this pattern of an effect and two possible causes — one simple, one subtle — in Farb's other examples of the "Clever Hans Phenomenon."
2. This essay begins with a detailed description of a clever horse in Berlin in the early 1900s and follows with an example of game show contes-

tants. Why do you think these examples precede the discussion of modern scientific experiments? Why does Farb save the research on school children for last?

3. A qualifier is a word that moderates or "tones down" the certainty of a statement. *Often, usually, almost,* and *sometimes* are common qualifiers. Their absence and the use of terms like *always* and *never* produce "unqualified" statements. Look for qualifiers in "In Other Words"—especially at places where Farb interprets research for us. Does he qualify his statements more or less as the essay goes on?

4. Is Farb serious in his closing remarks about who really needs remedial work? Why does he make his final point this way?

Questions for Further Thought

1. What are the "other words" Farb refers to in the title? How are they different from the words we use when we speak aloud?

2. Are you aware of the subtle (and sometimes not-so-subtle) distinctions made by teachers and expressed in their treatment of students? What are some examples from your own experience of these subtle signals?

3. In at least two of the research projects Farb discusses, the scientists lied to their subjects. In the grade school experiment, a direct result of this was that teachers favored some students, and, presumably, looked on others with disfavor. Do you think it was ethical for researchers to set up an experiment on the basis of lies?

4. In our dealings with each other, are we sufficiently careful of our body language? What could we do to make our nonverbal communication more positive?

Writing Assignments Using Cause-Effect as a Method of Development

1. As Farb implies, many game shows test the ability of contestants to guess or "mind-read" the responses of others. Sometimes in our own lives we have the feeling that people have read our minds, or that we have read theirs. Brainstorm a short list of such experiences you have had. Then, pick one or two and write an essay in which you examine the experience(s). Analyze the factors that contributed to the effect of "mind reading." These could include detecting someone's body language cues, knowing another person's habits or opinions, being familiar with his or her schedule, sharing a common or similar past experience.

2. Write an essay discussing the effects of a lie you or someone else told. Did the lie have positive or negative effects on the behavior, events, or lives of people? Some examples could be a lie told to "save face," lies

told to protect children from "grown-up realities," or lies told to soften the pain of a tragedy. Decide whether you think the lie was a good or a bad idea.

Writing Assignment Using Other Methods of Development

3. Imagine that you are the principal of a high school attended by disadvantaged students. Write a letter to your faculty briefly explaining the gist of the Rosenthal experiment. Then make three recommendations to your staff about techniques they can use to encourage high achievement in students. When making your recommendations, keep in mind that the students have been in school for many years; they are already suffering the effects of teachers' biases. Take this into account in making your recommendations. Choose your tone and words carefully, for you want to avoid offending the faculty or implying that they are not already doing their best.

4. Write an essay on an interesting person you know or have heard about who surpassed the restricted expectations held by other people. Citing the Rosenthal study in your introduction, prepare a strong argument refuting Rosenthal's research. Support your proposition with dramatic evidence showing how the person overcame the obstacles imposed by others.

Tom Wolfe

Born in Richmond, Virginia, in 1931, Tom Wolfe has worked as a reporter for the Washington Post *and other newspapers. In his articles for* Esquire *and* The New Yorker, *Wolfe pioneered a prose style known as the "new journalism," which blends the subjective awareness of the writer with objective reportage. Wolfe's books focus on subcultures of American society and include such works as* The Kandy-Kolored, Tangerine-Flake Streamline Baby *(1965),* The Electric Kool-Aid Acid Test *(1968),* The Pump-House Gang *(1968), and* The Right Stuff *(1979). This selection is from* The Pump-House Gang.

O Rotten Gotham — Sliding Down into the Behavioral Sink

Have you ever looked down from the top of a tall building and thought, "They all look like ants down there?" We may not like it, but humans do indeed resemble ants, or any other kind of communal, social animal. In the following selection, Tom Wolfe leads a lively tour through overcrowded New York City, pointing at how we humans react to the pressures of city life. He then links his observations to the findings of scientists who have examined how other animals handle the stresses created by competition and overcrowding. Overall, Wolfe concludes, the prospects for human life look pretty grim.

I just spent two days with Edward T. Hall, an anthropologist, 1 watching thousands of my fellow New Yorkers short-circuiting themselves into hot little twitching death balls with jolts of their own adrenalin. Dr. Hall says it is overcrowding that does it. Overcrowding gets the adrenalin going, and the adrenalin gets them queer, autistic, sadistic, barren, batty, sloppy, hot-in-the-pants,

395

chancred-on-the-flankers, leering, puling, numb—the usual in New York, in other words, and God knows what else. Dr. Hall has the theory that overcrowding has already thrown New York into a state of behavioral sink. Behavioral sink is a term from ethology, which is the study of how animals relate to their environment. Among animals, the sink winds up with a "population collapse" or "massive die-off." O rotten Gotham.

It got to be easy to look at New Yorkers as animals, especially looking down from some place like a balcony at Grand Central at the rush hour Friday afternoon. The floor was filled with the poor white humans, running around, dodging, blinking their eyes, making a sound like a pen full of starlings or rats or something.   2

"Listen to them skid," says Dr. Hall.   3

He was right. The poor old etiolate animals were out there skidding on their rubber soles. You could hear it once he pointed it out. They stop short to keep from hitting somebody or because they are disoriented and they suddenly stop and look around, and they skid on their rubber-soled shoes, and a screech goes up. They pour out onto the floor down the escalators from the Pan-Am Building, from 42nd Street, from Lexington Avenue, up out of subways, down into subways, railroad trains, up into helicopters—   4

"You can also hear the helicopters all the way down here," says Dr. Hall. The sound of the helicopters using the roof of the Pan-Am Building nearly fifty stories up beats right through. "If it weren't for this ceiling"—he is referring to the very high ceiling in Grand Central—"this place would be unbearable with this kind of crowding. And yet they'll probably never 'waste' space like this again."   5

They screech! And the adrenal glands in all those poor white animals enlarge, micrometer by micrometer, to the size of cantaloupes. Dr. Hall pulls a Minox camera out of a holster he has on his belt and starts shooting away at the human scurry. The Sink!   6

Dr. Hall has the Minox up to his eye—he is a slender man, calm, 52 years old, young-looking, an anthropologist who has worked with Navajos, Hopis, Spanish-Americans, Negroes, Trukese. He was the most important anthropologist in the government during the crucial years of the foreign aid program, the 1950's. He directed both the Point Four training program and the   7

Human Relations Area Files. He wrote *The Silent Language* and *The Hidden Dimension*, two books that are picking up the kind of "underground" following his friend Marshall McLuhan started picking up about five years ago. He teaches at the Illinois Institute of Technology, lives with his wife, Mildred, in a high-ceilinged town house on one of the last great residential streets in downtown Chicago, Astor Street; he has a grown son and daughter, loves good food, good wine, the relaxed, civilized life — but comes to New York with a Minox at his eye to record! — perfect — The Sink.

We really got down in there by walking down into the Lexington Avenue line subway stop under Grand Central. We inhaled those nice big fluffy fumes of human sweat, urine, effluvia, and sebaceous secretions. One old female human was already stroked out on the upper level, on a stretcher, with two policemen standing by. The other humans barely looked at her. They rushed into line. They bellied each other, haunch to paunch, down the stairs. Human heads shone through the gratings. The species North European tried to create bubbles of space around themselves, about a foot and a half in diameter — 8

"See, he's reacting against the line," says Dr. Hall. 9

— but the species Mediterranean presses on in. The hell 10 with bubbles of space. The species North European resents that, this male human behind him presses forward toward the booth . . . *breathing* on him, he's disgusted, he pulls out of the line entirely, the species Mediterranean resents him for resenting it, and neither of them realizes what the hell they are getting irritable about exactly. And in all of them the old adrenals grow another micrometer.

Dr. Hall whips out the Minox. Too perfect! The bottom of 11 The Sink.

It is the sheer overcrowding, such as occurs in the business 12 sections of Manhattan five days a week and in Harlem, Bedford-Stuyvesant, southeast Bronx every day — sheer overcrowding is converting New Yorkers into animals in a sink pen. Dr. Hall's argument runs as follows: all animals, including birds, seem to have a built-in inherited requirement to have a certain amount of territory, space, to lead their lives in. Even if they have all the food they need, and there are no predatory animals threatening them, they cannot tolerate crowding beyond a certain point. No more

than two hundred wild Norway rats can survive on a quarter acre of
ground, for example, even when they are given all the food they can
eat. They just die off.

But why? To find out, ethologists have run experiments on all   13
sorts of animals, from stickleback crabs to Sika deer. In one major
experiment, an ethologist named John Calhoun put some domes-
ticated white Norway rats in a pen with four sections to it, connected by ramps. Calhoun knew from previous experiments that
the rats tend to split up into groups of ten to twelve and that the
pen, therefore, would hold forty to forty-eight rats comfortably,
assuming they formed four equal groups. He allowed them to
reproduce until there were eighty rats, balanced between male and
female, but did not let it get any more crowded. He kept them
supplied with plenty of food, water, and nesting materials, In other
words, all their more obvious needs were taken care of. A less
obvious need — space — was not. To the human eye, the pen did
not even look especially crowded. But to the rats, it was crowded
beyond endurance.

The entire colony was soon plunged into a profound behav-   14
ioral sink. "The sink," said Calhoun, "is the outcome of any behavioral process that collects animals together in unusually great numbers. The unhealthy connotations of the term are not accidental: a
behavioral sink does act to aggravate all forms of pathology that
can be found within a group."

For a start, long before the rat population reached eighty, a   15
status hierarchy had developed in the pen. Two dominant male rats
took over the two end sections, acquired harems of eight to ten
females each, and forced the rest of the rats into the two middle
pens. All the overcrowding took place in the middle pens. That was
where the "sink" hit. The aristocrat rats at the end grew bigger,
sleeker, healthier, and more secure the whole time.

In The Sink, meanwhile, nest building, courting, sex behavior,   16
reproduction, social organization, health — all of it went to pieces.
Normally, Norway rats have a mating ritual in which the male
chases the female, the female ducks down into a burrow and sticks
her head up to watch the male. He performs a little dance outside
the burrow, then she comes out, and he mounts her, usually for a
few seconds. When The Sink set in, however, no more than three
males — the dominant males in the middle sections — kept up the
old customs. The rest tried everything from satyrism to homosexu-

ality or else gave up on sex altogether. Some of the subordinate males spent all their time chasing females. Three or four might chase one female at the same time, and instead of stopping at the burrow entrance for the ritual, they would charge right in. Once mounted, they would hold on for minutes instead of the usual seconds.

Homosexuality rose sharply. So did bisexuality. Some males   17 would mount anything—males, females, babies, senescent rats, anything. Still other males dropped sexual activity altogether, wouldn't fight and, in fact, would hardly move except when the other rats slept. Occasionally, a female from the aristocrat rats' harems would come over the ramps and into the middle sections to sample life in The Sink. When she had had enough, she would run back up the ramp. Sink males would give chase up to the top of the ramp, which is to say, to the very edge of the aristocratic preserve. But one glance from one of the king rats would stop them cold and they would return to The Sink.

The slumming females from the harems had their adventures   18 and then returned to a placid, healthy life. Females in The Sink, however, were ravaged, physically and psychologically. Pregnant rats had trouble continuing pregnancy. The rate of miscarriages increased significantly, and females started dying from tumors and other disorders of the mammary glands, sex organs, uterus, ovaries, and Fallopian tubes. Typically, their kidneys, livers, and adrenals were also enlarged or diseased or showed other signs associated with stress.

Child-rearing became totally disorganized. The females lost   19 the interest or the stamina to build nests and did not keep them up if they did build them. In the general filth and confusion, they would not put themselves out to save offspring they were momentarily separated from. Frantic, even sadistic competition among the males was going on all around them and rendering their lives chaotic. The males began unprovoked and senseless assaults upon one another, often in the form of tail-biting. Ordinarily, rats will suppress this kind of behavior when it crops up. In The Sink, male rats gave up all policing and just looked out for themselves. The "pecking order" among males in The Sink was never stable. Normally, male rats set up a three-class structure. Under the pressure of overcrowding, however, they broke up into all sorts of unstable subclasses, cliques, packs—and constantly pushed, probed, explored, tested one another's power. Anyone was fair game, except for the aristocrats in the end pens.

Calhoun kept the population down to eighty, so that the next 20 stage, "population collapse" or "massive die-off," did not occur. But the autopsies showed that the pattern—as in the diseases among the female rats—was already there.

The classic study of die-off was John J. Christian's study of Sika 21 deer on James Island in the Chesapeake Bay, west of Cambridge, Maryland. Four or five of the deer had been released on the island, which was 280 acres and uninhabited, in 1916. By 1955 they had bred freely into a herd of 280 to 300. The population density was only about one deer per acre at this point, but Christian knew that this was already too high for the Sikas' inborn space requirements, and something would give before long. For two years the number of deer remained 280 to 300. But suddenly, in 1958, over half the deer died; 161 carcasses were recovered. In 1959 more deer died and the population steadied at about 80.

In two years, two-thirds of the herd had died. Why? It was not 22 starvation. In fact, all the deer collected were in excellent condition, with well-developed muscles, shining coats, and fat deposits between the muscles. In practically all the deer, however, the adrenal glands had enlarged by 50 percent. Christian concluded that the die-off was due to "shock following severe metabolic disturbance, probably as a result of prolonged adrenocortical hyperactivity. . . . There was no evidence of infection, starvation, or other obvious cause to explain the mass mortality." In other words, the constant stress of overpopulation, plus the normal stress of the cold of the winter, had kept the adrenalin flowing so constantly in the deer that their systems were depleted of blood sugar and they died of shock.

Well, the white humans are still skidding and darting across 23 the floor of Grand Central. Dr. Hall listens a moment longer to the skidding and the darting noises, and then says, "You know, I've been on commuter trains here after everyone has been through one of these rushes, and I'll tell you, there is enough acid flowing in the stomachs in every car to dissolve the rails underneath."

Just a little invisible acid bath for the linings to round off the 24 day. The ulcers the acids cause, of course, are the one disease people have already been taught to associate with the stress of city life. But overcrowding, as Dr. Hall sees it, raises a lot more hell with the body than just ulcers. In everyday life in New York—just the usual, getting to work, working in massively congested areas like 42nd Street between Fifth Avenue and Lexington, especially now that the Pan-Am Building is set in there, working in cubicles such as those in the editorial offices at Time-Life, Inc., which Dr. Hall cites as typical of New York's poor handling of space, working in cubicles with low ceilings and, often, no access to a window, while construction crews all over Manhattan drive everybody up the Masonite wall with air-pressure generators with noises up to the boil-a-brain decibel level, then rushing to get home, piling into subways and trains, fighting for time and for space, the usual day in New York — the whole now-normal thing keeps shooting jolts of adrenalin into the body, breaking down the body's defenses and winding up with the work-a-daddy human animal stroked out at the breakfast table with his head apoplexed like a cauliflower out of his $6.95 semi-spread Pima-cotton shirt, and nosed over into a plate of No-Kloresto egg substitute, signing off with the black thrombosis, cancer, kidney, liver, or stomach failure, and the adrenals ooze to a halt, the size of eggplants in July.

One of the people whose work Dr. Hall is interested in on this score is Rene Dubos at the Rockefeller Institute. Dubos's work indicates that specific organisms, such as the tuberculosis bacillus or a pneumonia virus, can seldom be considered "the cause" of a disease. The germ or virus, apparently, has to work in combination with other things that have already broken the body down in some way — such as the old adrenal hyperactivity. Dr. Hall would like to see some autopsy studies made to record the size of adrenal glands in New York, especially of people crowded into slums and people who go through the full rush-hour-work-rush-hour cycle every day. He is afraid that until there is some clinical, statistical data on how overcrowding actually ravages the human body, no one will be willing to do anything about it. Even in so obvious a thing as air pollution, the pattern is familiar. Until people can actually see the smoke or smell the sulphur or feel the sting in their eyes, politicians will not get excited about it, even though it is well known that many of the lethal substances polluting the air are invisible and odorless. For one thing, most politicians are like the aristocrat rats. They are insulated from The Sink by practically sultanic buffers — limousines, chauffeurs, secretaries, aides-de-camp, doormen, shuttered houses, high-floor apartments. They almost never ride subways, fight rush hours, much less live in the slums or work in the Pan-Am Building.

25

Questions for Close Reading

1. What is the thesis of the selection? Locate the sentence(s) in which Wolfe states his main idea. If he does not state the thesis explicitly, express it in your own words.
2. In paragraph 5, Dr. Hall comments on the high ceiling of Grand Central Station: "They'll probably never 'waste' space like this again." Why is the word "waste" emphasized? Why does Wolfe include this remark in the essay?
3. Why does Dr. Hall come to New York? Who is John Calhoun, and what does he have to do with "rotten Gotham"?
4. How do the male and female rats respond to overcrowding? Are Dr. Hall's observations in Grand Central pertinent to both human sexes? To all races and classes of people in New York?
5. Refer to your dictionary as needed to define the following words used in the selection: *autistic* (paragraph 1), *chancred* (1), *etiolate* (4), *effluvia* (8), *sebaceous* (8), *ethologist* (13), *satyrism* (16), and *adrenocortical* (22).

Questions about the Writer's Craft

1. What is the causal chain of behaviors established in the essay? How does the author organize the results of scientific research to suggest this chain?
2. Locate the points where Wolfe shifts from a discussion of one researcher's work and moves to another's. How does Wolfe achieve these transitions? How much space does he devote to them?
3. Wolfe uses gross exaggeration in the essay: adrenal glands "the size of cantaloupes," for example. What are some other examples of hyperbole in the essay? Is this technique appropriate for an essay on a scientific subject?
4. Dr. Hall seems almost lighthearted as he snaps photos of New Yorkers "short-circuiting themselves" at Grand Central Station. "Listen to them skid," Wolfe reports him saying. What is the tone of the essay? Is the tone an appropriate one for Wolfe's subject?

Questions for Further Thought

1. In what ways do big cities resemble the rat colonies in Calhoun's lab? Is your opinion based on experience or hearsay?
2. How do you react to crowding when you commute, study, shop, attend classes, or engage in other activities? What reactions do you notice in others? Are there any situations in which crowding is *fun*?
3. Are humans able to rise above the level of viciousness exhibited by the

rats — or do we behave in the same manner? What remedies, short- and long-term, can you imagine to prevent humans from becoming mired in a "sink"?

4. Survivalists are people who are preparing for a national disaster — war, riots, economic collapse — by stockpiling weapons, food, and other supplies. Are survivalists being sensible? Are they admirable?

Writing Assignments Using Cause-Effect as a Method of Development

1. Examine the effects of overcrowding, or excessive competition, or a frenzied pace on a particular aspect of American life. You might choose to focus on any of the following: student life, life in cities, life in a large corporation, life in the suburbs, or vacations in crowded resorts or national parks. Choose at least three important effects and write an essay warning readers of the dangers involved in allowing such conditions to continue.

2. Assume you have been assigned to write a guest editorial for your college newspaper. You decide to recommend a small change in student behavior or in college administrative policy, showing how such a change could make a significant difference on campus. Establish a causal chain that demonstrates the value of your proposed change. For example, "If students would bus their own trays in the cafeteria," or "If the college library would allow book renewal by phone. . . . "

Writing Assignments Using Other Methods of Development

3. If you have visited a large city, you probably have some first-hand knowledge of the conditions Wolfe writes about in "O Rotten Gotham. . . . " Write a narrative of your experience, referring to specific urban problems. Show the reader the low points of human behavior in the city you visited. Make it vivid by using a style similar to Wolfe's: full of hyperbole, slang, and vivid imagery.

4. Write an essay arguing that architecture can influence people. Discuss the reasons why people are attracted to or feel distaste for certain styles or structures — for example, why people flock to comfortable courtyards in cities or on campus; why they feel threatened by low-ceilinged or windowless offices or rooms; why they are repelled by monolithic industrial buildings and may even become prone to vandalism when forced to live, work, or go to school in such buildings.

Tony Schwartz

Now a professor of telecommunications at New York University, Tony Schwartz worked for many years in the field of media production and advertising. He has written and produced television commercials for corporations and political candidates, hosted a weekly radio show, "Around New York," designed the sound for Broadway shows, and produced records. Schwartz's books are The Responsive Chord *(1974) and* Media: The Second God *(1983), from which this selection is taken.*

Communication in the
Year 2000

Within the memories of people living today is the image of the telephone as a screechy, temperamental communications tool used only by a small elite. Now, communications satellites transmit television shows to billions of people around the globe, computers call each other with information, and electronic mail delivers letters in seconds, rather than in days. According to Tony Schwartz, even greater wonders are on the way. And such wonders have broad implications for the future of our society — from the values we espouse to the form of government we choose.

During these last two decades of the century, a broad range of communication technologies will develop and change how many of us work, learn, and use leisure time. We will send and receive electronic mail, talk back to our television sets and be heard by our program host, and participate in electronic business meetings with colleagues who are scattered around the globe. The technological means are not science-fiction dreams; each exists today. However, it will take a number of years for them to be implemented on a large scale.

The new communication systems are fascinating hybrids which mix together technological developments in cable television, telephone-line transmission, computer science, and satellites. This creates a regulatory nightmare for government agencies which operate under laws designed to separate the computer, telephone, and television industries. These developments may be hindered if control of the new communication systems is in the hands of the moguls at the major networks and their counterparts in existing industries such as the telephone and data-processing companies. In the standard grabbing for money and monopolistic control, such companies might want to use these developments for private ends and prevent them from reaching the public. The potential of the new communication technology does not guarantee that these companies will make exciting new services generally available. For years, people were enjoined from using any but telephone company equipment on telephone company lines. Now that the law allows the use of other equipment, we have seen a proliferation of products designed for use with telephone lines: automatic dialing, answering machines, Teletext equipment, telephone amplifiers, wireless phones that can be used anyplace in the home or office, data-servicing equipment, and many more.

However, three characteristics of the new communication systems suggest that they may indeed arrive in our homes and offices. 3 First, they have bucked the inflationary trend of the past decade and will probably continue bucking it through the mid-1980s. Thus, while the cost of roast beef and potatoes has risen and will continue to rise, the cost of large-scale integrated circuits and memory chips (the meat and potatoes of our new technology) has declined and will continue to decline for a few more years, following the pattern established by digital watches and pocket calculators, which began as very expensive items and then plummeted in price as they became mass-produced. Digital watches that used to cost several hundred dollars are now available for eight or ten dollars. Computers costing ten or twelve thousand dollars do the work of earlier computers that cost several hundred thousand dollars. Second, the new communication systems do not require audiences in the millions to make them economically viable or socially appealing. They will find their audience through narrowcasting, rather than broadcasting, and they will serve special-interest groups. Third, most of the new communication services are two-way. People can participate in these media, not merely receive them. In the past, a relatively small group of people created the movies, television programs, and other forms of mass entertainment for the public. With the new services, many more people (in a way, everyone) will create communications for others.

Perhaps the best way to think about these new communication 4 services is to begin with the telephone, that inexpensive, two-way, narrowcast medium which has been with us for so long. In audio, conferencing microphones and speakers can replace telephones, so ten, twenty, or more people in one room can talk freely to similar groups at other locations. A range of equipment exists which can transmit simple writing or graphics over ordinary phone lines. The "electronic blackboard" is one such device. With it, people at separate locations can talk to each other and write information which everyone can see. Another technology, called slow-scan television and facsimile transfer equipment, can send still photographs, X rays, charts, etc., over telephone lines. These systems are currently operating in some business, medical, and educational settings. A key element in their growth is the use of the telephone lines for transmission. Equipment can be plugged in wherever a phone line exists, and the cost of sending the information is the cost of a phone call.

Electronic mail also uses the telephone system. In this case, a 5 central computer with phone lines attached acts as a postal service. A person with a modified electronic typewriter calls the central computer, then types a message for another person, who also needs a modified electronic typewriter to receive it. He or she gets the message by going to the electronic mailbox, i.e., calling the central computer. The computer then prints out the message. Electronic mail is an adaptable and growing service in business. Some expect that when the cost of a first-class letter reaches twenty-five cents, people will turn to electronic mail as an economically feasible alternative for private correspondence.

The growth of cable television is bringing about another new 6 range of services. First, cable television has the capacity for many channels. Thus we have already witnessed the growth of several new channels of special-interest programming: all movies (Home Box Office), all sports, all news (Cable News Network). This trend will likely continue as additional narrowcast audiences are defined. Just as magazines are geared to skiers, chess players, teenage women, and other groups, cable television programming will probably pursue select non-mass audiences.

However, this is only the beginning of the changes ahead. A   7
television cable, like a telephone line, can be used for two-way
communication. The home viewer can communicate back to the
program or to other viewers through the cable. The development
of interactive cable television has already begun in a number of
communities. The most widely known of these is the Qube two-
way cable system, which was first used in Columbus, Ohio. The
Qube system provides the viewer with a special box that has several
buttons. These buttons communicate back to the cable studio.
Viewers can answer polling questions, express their views about the
program or performer they are watching, and direct how the program should proceed. The ways in which viewers "vote" can be
calculated instantly and displayed on the screen for all to see.
Elsewhere (Spartanburg, South Carolina), systems like Qube have
been used to bring together and facilitate the work of people in
educational and social services. In Rockford, Illinois, a similar
system provides advanced training for teachers and firemen.

Even more exciting is a model interactive cable television sys-   8
tem in Reading, Pennsylvania. Some twenty locations around
Reading are wired as neighborhood communication centers. The
interaction among the centers as the people talk to one another
creates a new type of television involvement. People at home participate by calling in and speaking over a telephone connection that
everyone can hear. Curiously, the interactive cable programming
they create competes successfully with network programming.

A cable television channel may also be used to deliver special-   9
ized information to individual viewers. This makes use of a technology developed in Britain which allows many pages of print and
graphic information to be multiplexed and combined electronically, then sent over the lines in a television signal. Using one cable
television channel, it is possible to transmit eight hundred pages of
print information in three seconds. Thus, a cable television channel can be used to transmit an electronic newspaper into the home,
either printed on paper or projected onto a screen, or the cable
channel can be connected to an electronic library and the user can
go through an index and select information to be transmitted over
the cable.

The problem with all of this new technology is not the equip-   10
ment, which exists and works, but what to do with it now that we
have it. What kinds of services, entertainment, and information do

people want, and what will they buy, watch, and listen to? A few of the services and projects which have already succeeded may provide some clues about the future.

Alaska recently experimented with electronic town meetings.   11 Via the combination of television and telephone, people were able to see the moderator and speakers, ask questions, and vote from their homes by telephone or electronic buttons. The success of the experiment may well be a sign of the future. More people watched the television town meetings than have participated in all town meetings since the founding of the state of Alaska. While voting in regular elections ran to 23 percent of the population, voting in the electronic town meetings ran to 66 percent of the population. Voters participated by voting yes or no on certain topics. Politicians who took part in the town meetings were reluctant to commit themselves early on any issue. This revealed their awareness of its political effects. Answers to research questions could be tabulated and exhibited before the next question was asked. Questionnaires could be adjusted and perfected in the course of asking the questions. Although the politicians were divided in their acceptance of this electronic concept, the program had a 90-percent share of the television audience during the broadcast.

In Philadelphia, Pennsylvania, and Phoenix, Arizona, the po-   12 lice departments have developed the use of two-way television to cut transportation costs and speed up the flow of communication. Some react instinctively against the use of advanced technology by a police department, but the results are impressive. In Phoenix, for example, public defenders meet with prisoner-clients over two-way picture telephones. (The prisoner-client must agree to use the system, and not all meetings are conducted over picture telephones.) This has resulted in more "meetings" between the public defenders and the prisoner-clients. At the same time, the system has reduced costs, because the public defenders can handle more clients.

In Philadelphia, witnesses to a crime can view color-slide mug   13 shots over a two-way cable television system. The slides are centralized, but the witness can view them from any precinct house. Similarly, using this two-way cable television system, detectives can retrieve centralized information (films, fingerprints, case records) from a data bank and view it at the local precinct. In addition, video conferences and prearrayment hearings are conducted over the cable. This highly sophisticated private cable television system has significantly reduced paper and transportation costs and freed police officers to spend more time on field work.

In southern Arizona, NASA and the Indian Health Service 14 have set up a fascinating application of advanced space technology to provide health care. A central hospital which serves the Papago Indians is linked via two-way microwave to a specially equipped truck which travels throughout the reservation (hundreds of square miles). Paramedics in the truck can conduct sophisticated tests on patients. The results are communicated telemetrically to a doctor in the central hospital. In addition, the doctor and the patient many miles away can see and hear each other. Further, the paramedic and the doctor both have instant access to computerized medical histories which are stored one hundred miles away, in northern Arizona. The NASA system is quite expensive. However, it has paved the way for other, more cost-efficient medical services between a central hospital and remote health stations or clinics. We have already seen a form of medical telemetry between individuals at home and a doctor in the hospital, via telephone lines.

In Britain, two forms of electronic print services are well under 15 way, although neither can be classified as a success yet, because a number of gremlins need elimination. In one system, called Viewdata, a central computer contains many thousands of pages of information, from current sports results to recipes to airline schedules. Using a special decoder, a person calls the computer, and an ordinary television set displays the requested information that the computer transmits. Users can also obtain a computer printout of the information. In the other service, Broadcast Teletext, a computer at the television station contains a few hundred pages of information, e.g., television listings, movie schedules, weather, and news headlines. These pages are electronically "piggybacked" on the regular television signal. A viewer who wants to read the pages must have a special decoder that can pull them out and display them on the television screen. It is also possible to obtain a hard copy of Broadcast Teletext pages.

Viewdata, which transmits printed matter, is particularly interesting to many business interests, since it can be used for electronic shopping. Viewdata transmits information over telephone lines and is, therefore, interactive. The person in the home can not 16 only request information, e.g., airline schedules, but also purchase services. Viewdata can be used to make an airline reservation, do catalog shopping, and reserve a table at a restaurant.

If the new communication services (or a significant portion of 17 them) make their way into the average home and office, the social effects may be quite far-reaching. First, television network programming will lose some of its control over the mass audience. People will still watch television, but they will have access to a wider range of programs. They will also use the television set as a display screen for some information and entertainment services other than programs. They will be able to receive weather reports, traffic reports, local sports, shopping news, and the like. They can have access to any section of their newspapers and magazines, or follow the activities of local and national government. They can also use television as a ticket-purchasing service. One need neither weep over nor applaud the demise of the television networks, as they are likely to be financially involved in the new communication services which prove successful.

A significant shift in work patterns may occur. The new com- 18 munication services can substitute for a portion of the business travel which now occurs. Moreover, a greater number of people will work out of their homes, using the new technology to conduct business and link them to central offices. Before locating a corporate headquarters, industries will pay greater heed to available telephone network switching, cable systems, and satellite linkups.

The potential implications of the new communication ser- 19 vices are dramatic. Technology will mediate more and more of the communication that now takes place between individuals. This technology and the services which it does or doesn't offer will affect the quality and character of our communication with others. It may develop as the telephone did, with content determined by users. Indeed, one hopes that the new services will supplement, rather than supplant, interpersonal contact, creating new kinds of interactions among people. Developments could go either way.

The new technology could allow more sources of information 20 to reach the public. This may break up the common information environment which television has created. In the sixties and seventies, most people received most of their information from one source: television.

The new communication technologies provide a means for 21

instantaneous feedback from the public. Each person in his home will be able to push a button to vote or express an opinion on public issues. This may lead to more participation in politics but also to even less voting in elections than exists today. If this occurs, the logical response might be to incorporate the new communication process formally into government. People could vote directly on many laws and policy issues. In such circumstances, many elected officials might be replaced by administrators whose job would be to present issues for public voting. This might also lead to a speedup in government. Politics and laws could change more quickly. Cycles of recession and recovery might be reduced from many months to a few weeks. As information flow increases, so does social and political change.

Undoubtedly a number of problems will accompany the use of   22
the new communication technologies in governing a country. It might be valuable to consider them in much greater depth, because technology can lead to important social and political effects which are unforeseen but inevitable. These technologies can lead to a restructuring of government. The basic reason for having a representative government is that all the people cannot themselves be at the seat of government. Therefore we call on others to be there and to speak for us. But with the new technologies, for all practical purposes we *can* be there, and we may not need representatives, because we now represent ourselves.

No one chose to give the President twenty minutes to decide   23
the fate of the world. The design of missile technology chose it. And as we perfect our mastery of the second god, we must realize that we have given the god we created the power to change us and our ways.

Questions for Close Reading

1. What is the thesis of the selection? Locate the sentence(s) in which Schwartz states his main idea. If he does not state the thesis explicitly, express it in your own words.
2. Why, according to Schwartz, will new communication systems create "a regulatory nightmare?"
3. What factors make Schwartz sure that these new communication systems will soon arrive in our homes and offices?

4. If two-day communication becomes commonplace in America, what effects will it have on our lives, according to Schwartz?
5. Refer to your dictionary as needed to define the following words used in the selection: *hybrids* (paragraph 2), *moguls* (2), *viable* (3), *feasible* (5), and *telemetry* (14).

Questions about the Writer's Craft

1. What combination of purposes does Schwartz have in this cause-effect essay?
2. How many sections are there in the body of the essay? What paragraphs contain the transitions from section to section?
3. How would you characterize the tone of this essay? Why might the author have chosen to present the material in this fashion?
4. Why does the author wait until the conclusion to mention any problems with this new technology? Why does he use such phrases as "the fate of the world" and "the second god"? What effect do these phrases have on you?

Questions for Further Thought

1. Have any of the communications advances discussed in the essay become realities in your life or the lives of friends? In your hometown or college locale? Do you believe that these advances will come as soon as the year 2000?
2. Would you prefer shopping by computer at home, voting from your living room, and reading the newspaper on a video monitor? Do you feel that these innovations would improve the quality of your life? Would they make your life more interesting or more efficient?
3. Television is often accused of causing its viewers to become unimaginative, passive, and accepting of the most ludicrous programming. If the new communication technology becomes a reality, do you think this will change? Will TV become a means of action and creativity?
4. Schwartz' essay deals primarily with speeded-up communications. In what other ways have our lives become faster-paced?

Writing Assignments Using Cause-Effect as a Method of Development

1. Choose another technological advance besides those Schwartz covers in his article, and write an essay explaining its effects on people's lives. You may wish to focus on the lives of a particular group of people or on Americans' lives in general. The effects you discuss may be political,

psychological, behavioral, ecological, or social. Some suggestions include the following: nuclear power, mass transit, copiers, audio (video) tape recorders, robots, and computers. Before writing, be sure to decide what your attitude is toward these effects.

2. To some extent, electronic mail is already a part of the American workplace. Write an essay outlining the effects, positive or negative, of electronic mail becoming the major mail carrier for us all. Write your essay as an attempt to persuade or dissuade your college or town from adopting an electronic mail system.

Writing Assignments Using Other Methods of Development

3. Americans seem obsessed with doing things faster. But many other countries do not share our obsessive concern. As one Irish saying proclaims, "When God made time, He made plenty of it." Perhaps we are more concerned with how much time we *save* than with how we *spend* our time. Write an essay illustrating several ways we hurry — perhaps unnecessarily — to complete our everyday tasks. At appropriate spots in the paper, discuss what we lose in our haste to get through our days quickly.

4. Write an essay warning readers of the dangers to our privacy, to our relationships, or to our sense of community if we rely on interactive TV and computers as much as Schwartz suggests we will. Focus on one or two dangers, supporting your claims with descriptions of how our lives will change.

Lewis Thomas

*Lewis Thomas (1913–   ) attended Princeton University
and earned his M.D. at Harvard. He has worked as a research pathologist and has held several positions in medical
administration. Thomas is a gifted writer whose lucid prose
makes accessible to ordinary people specialized information as
well as his own acute personal observations. He has written
columns for* The New England Journal of Medicine *and*
Discover *magazine. His books include* The Lives of a Cell, *a
1974 collection of essays that won the National Book Award;*
The Medusa and the Snail *(1979) — which is the source of
the following essay — and* Late Night Thoughts on Listening to Mahler's Ninth Symphony *(1984).*

The Health Care System

*According to Lewis Thomas, we are turning into a nation
obsessed with health and disease — and the media are largely
responsible. Made-for-TV movies and nightly newscasts
dramatize precarious new operations, rare birth defects, and
unusual epidemics. Every few minutes, we are assaulted by
commercials for pills and potions. Instead of celebrating our
freedom from such killers of the past as polio and tuberculosis
we brood on misleading images of fragility and vulnerability.*

The health-care system of this country is a staggering enter-   1
prise, in any sense of the adjective. Whatever the failures of distribution and lack of coordination, it is the gigantic scale and scope of
the total collective effort that first catches the breath, and its cost.
The dollar figures are almost beyond grasping. They vary from year
to year, always upward, ranging from something like $10 billion in
1950 to an estimated $140 billion in 1978, with much more to
come in the years just ahead, whenever a national health-insurance
program is installed. The official guess is that we are now investing
a round 8 percent of the GNP in Health; it could soon rise to 10 or
12 percent.

414

Those are the official numbers, and only for the dollars that   2
flow in an authorized way — for hospital charges, physician's fees,
prescribed drugs, insurance premiums, the construction of facilities, research, and the like.

But these dollars are only part of it. Why limit the estimates to   3
the strictly professional costs? There is another huge marketplace,
in which vast sums are exchanged for items designed for the improvement of Health.

The television and radio industry, no small part of the national   4
economy, feeds on Health, or, more precisely, on disease, for a
large part of its sustenance. Not just the primarily medical dramas
and the illness or surgical episodes threaded through many of the
nonmedical stories, in which the central human dilemma is illness;
almost all the commercial announcements, in an average evening,
are pitches for items to restore failed health: things for stomach gas,
constipation, headaches, nervousness, sleeplessness or sleepiness,
arthritis, anemia, disquiet, and the despair of malodorousness,
sweat, yellowed teeth, dandruff, furuncles, piles. The food industry
plays the role of surrogate physician, advertising breakfast cereals
as though they were tonics, vitamins, restoratives; they are now
out-hawked by the specialized Health-food industry itself, with its
nonpolluted, organic, "naturally" vitalizing products. Chewing
gum is sold as a tooth cleanser. Vitamins have taken the place of
prayer.

The publishing industry, hardcover, paperbacks, magazines,   5
and all, seems to be kept alive by Health, new techniques for achieving mental health, cures for arthritis, and diets mostly for the
improvement of everything.

The transformation of our environment has itself become an   6
immense industry, costing rather more than the moon, in aid of
Health. Pollution is supposed to be primarily a medical problem;
when the television weatherman tells whether New York's air is
"acceptable" or not that day, he is talking about human lungs, he
believes. Pollutants which may be impairing photosynthesis by
algae in the world's oceans, or destroying all the life in topsoil, or
killing all the birds are being worried about lest they cause cancer in
us, for heaven's sake.

Tennis has become more than the national sport; it is a rigor-   7
ous discipline, a form of collective physiotherapy. Jogging is done
by swarms of people, out onto the streets each day in underpants,

moving in a stolid sort of rapid trudge, hoping by this to stay alive. Bicycles are cures. Meditation may be good for the soul but it is even better for the blood pressure.

As a people, we have become obsessed with Health.   8

There is something fundamentally, radically unhealthy about   9 all this. We do not seem to be seeking more exuberance in living as much as staving off failure, putting off dying. We have lost all confidence in the human body.

The new consensus is that we are badly designed, intrinsically   10 fallible, vulnerable to a host of hostile influences inside and around us, and only precariously alive. We live in danger of falling apart at any moment, and are therefore always in need of surveillance and propping up. Without the professional attention of a health-care system, we would fall in our tracks.

This is a new way of looking at things, and perhaps it can only   11 be accounted for as a manifestation of spontaneous, undirected, societal *propaganda*. We keep telling each other this sort of thing, and back it comes on television or in the weekly newsmagazines, confirming all the fears, instructing us, as in the usual final paragraph of the personal-advice columns in the daily paper, to "seek professional help." Get a checkup. Go on a diet. Meditate. Jog. Have some surgery. Take two tablets, with water. *Spring* water. If pain persists, if anomie persists, if boredom persists, see your doctor.

It is extraordinary that we have just now become convinced of   12 our bad health, our constant jeopardy of disease and death, at the very time when the facts should be telling us the opposite. In a more rational world, you'd think we would be staging bicentennial ceremonies for the celebration of our general good shape. In the year 1976, out of a population of around 220 million, only 1.9 million died, or just under 1 percent, not at all a discouraging record once you accept the fact of mortality itself. The life expectancy for the whole population rose to seventy-two years, the longest stretch ever achieved in this country. Despite the persisting roster of still-unsolved major diseases — cancer, heart disease, stroke, arthritis, and the rest — most of us have a clear, unimpeded run at a longer and healthier lifetime than could have been foreseen by any earlier generation. The illnesses that plague us the most, when you count up the numbers in the U.S. Vital Statistics reports, are respiratory and gastrointestinal infections, which are, by and large, transient, reversible affairs needing not much more than Grandmother's advice for getting through safely. Thanks in great part to the improved sanitary engineering, nutrition, and housing of the past century, and in real but less part to contemporary immunization and antibiotics, we are free of the great infectious diseases, especially tuberculosis and lobar pneumonia, which used to cut us down long before our time. We are even beginning to make progress in our understanding of the mechanisms underlying the chronic illnesses still with us, and sooner or later, depending on the quality and energy of biomedical research, we will learn to cope effectively with most of these, maybe all. We will still age away and die, but the aging, and even the dying, can become a healthy process. On balance, we ought to be more pleased with ourselves than we are, and more optimistic for the future.

The trouble is, we are being taken in by the propaganda, and it   13
is bad not only for the spirit of society; it will make any health-care system, no matter how large and efficient, unworkable. If people are educated to believe that they are fundamentally fragile, always on the verge of mortal disease, perpetually in the need of support by health-care professionals at every side, always dependent on an imagined discipline of "preventive" medicine, there can be no limit to the numbers of doctors' offices, clinics, and hospitals required to meet the demand. In the end, we would all become doctors, spending our days screening each other for disease.

We are, in real life, a reasonably healthy people. Far from being   14
ineptly put together, we are amazingly tough, durable organisms, full of health, ready for most contingencies. The new danger to our well-being, if we continue to listen to all the talk, is in becoming a nation of healthy hypochrondriacs, living gingerly, worrying ourselves half to death.

And we do not have time for this sort of thing anymore, nor   15
can we afford such a distraction from our other, considerably more urgent problems. Indeed, we should by worrying that our preoccupation with personal health may be a symptom of copping out, an excuse for running upstairs to recline on a couch, sniffing the air for contaminants, spraying the room with deodorants, while just outside, the whole of society is coming undone.

Questions for Close Reading

1. What is the thesis of the selection? Locate the sentence(s) in which Thomas states his main idea. If he does not state the thesis explicitly, express it in your own words.
2. Why does Thomas consider radio and TV to be part of our health care system? Does he consider the media a positive or negative force in America's health?
3. What support does Thomas give for his statement that Americans "have become obsessed with health"?
4. What evidence does Thomas present that we are healthier than ever before?
5. Refer to your dictionary as needed to define the following words in the selection: *malodorousness* (paragraph 4), *furuncles* (4), *surrogate* (4), *anomie* (11), and *contingencies* (14).

Questions about the Writer's Craft

1. In which paragraph does he discuss causes, and in which, effects? What is the cause-effect relationship that Thomas defines in this essay? Is his analysis of our health care system logical and well supported?
2. Why is paragraph 12 so long? What is Thomas's purpose in using statistics in this paragraph?
3. The author uses overstatement frequently in this essay. For example, he writes, "Vitamins have taken the place of prayer," in paragraph 4. Find some other examples of overstatement. What is his tone in these places? What effect do these exaggerations have on you?
4. Why does Thomas capitalize the "H" in *health* throughout the essay?

Questions for Further Thought

1. Americans spend a tremendous amount on health care. Is our money well spent? Would you say our health care system is fair and adequate?
2. Do you agree that Americans are concerned with health in a "radically unhealthy way"? Or is the new emphasis on health foods, exercise, and so on a positive development?
3. What does Thomas mean by saying in paragraph 12 that "the aging, and even the dying, can become a healthy process"? Under what conditions could this occur?
4. What, according to Thomas, are more important concerns than our health? What should we be worrying about? Do you agree our concern with health is "bad . . . for the spirit of society"?

Writing Assignments Using Other Methods of Development

1. One aspect of our concern with health is our desire to be thin. Write an essay analyzing the positive and/or negative effects of this desire on the behavior, habits, and overall sense of wellbeing of one segment of the population: teenagers, college women or men, your co-workers, or another distinctive group.
2. Why are health-related industries in the country booming? Choose either the health-food industry or the health spa phenomenon and discuss several possible causes for its present success. Your thesis should signal how you feel about the causes you identify.

Writing Assignments Using Other Methods of Development

3. Prepare an essay arguing against Thomas's point of view. In your essay, provide examples that show that Americans don't take very good care of themselves and are even self-destructive in their behavior.
4. Write a paper describing a balanced, intelligent approach to health. You might contend that it is possible to be neither hypochondriacal nor overly casual about one's own health. Make specific recommendations to people who wish to be health-conscious but not health-obsessed. Explain the steps they should take to lead such a balanced life.

Additional Writing Topics
CAUSE-EFFECT

General Assignments

Write an essay that analyzes the causes and/or effects of any of the following topics. Determine your purpose before beginning to write: Will the essay be informative, persuasive, or speculative? As you prewrite, think rigorously about causes and effects; try to identify causal chains. Provide solid evidence for the thesis and use either chronological or emphatic order to organize your supporting points.

1. Having the parents you have
2. Sleep deprivation
3. Lack of communication in a relationship
4. Overexercising or not exercising
5. A particular TV or rock star's popularity
6. Skill or ineptitude in sports
7. A major life decision
8. Stiffer legal penalties for drunken driving
9. Changing attitudes toward protecting the environment
10. A particular national crisis
11. The mass movement of women into the work force
12. Choosing to attend this college
13. "Back to basics" movement in schools
14. Headaches
15. An act of violence
16. A natural event: leaves turning, birds migrating, animals hibernating, an eclipse occurring
17. Pesticide use
18. Use of computers in the classroom
19. Banning disposable cans and bottles
20. A bad habit
21. A fear of _____
22. Legalizing prostitution or marijuana
23. Abolishing the F grade
24. Joining a particular organization
25. Owning a pet

Assignments with a Specific Audience and Purpose

1. The athletic program on your campus is in a state of crisis. The college has been accused of placing sports above studies (there have been several grade-fixing and recruiting scandals). You do not believe, as some people have suggested, that your school should abandon "big-time athletics." You have been designated to appear on the local TV news show to reply to an anti-sports editorial. Write a script for your brief on-air reply, explaining why it would be disastrous for the university to curtail its involvement with sports.

2. Why do students "flunk out" of college? Write an article for the opening-day issue of the campus newspaper outlining the main causes of failure. Your goal is to warn incoming students so they don't fall into the dangerous patterns that lead to poor grades or dropping out.

3. You probably have read many articles in the paper recently about the current "trash crisis" in America, especially in crowded Eastern states. Dumps are overflowing, garbage is piling up, people protest waste incinerators in their neighborhoods. Write a letter to the editor, analyzing the causes of this crisis. Be sure to mention the nationwide love affair with disposable items and the general abandonment of the idea of thrift.

4. As a part-time employee of the college employment/work-study office, you have been given the task of drafting a brief pamphlet: "Things to Keep in Mind if You Plan to Work While Attending College." The pamphlet will be given to your fellow students and it will focus on the effects — both negative and positive — of combining a part-time job with college studies.

5. Teenage suicide has been on the rise. Why might this be so? Write a fact sheet to be given to parents of teenagers and to high school guidance counselors, describing the factors that could make a student desperate enough to attempt suicide.

6. Some communities have conducted campaigns encouraging residents to give up television for a fixed period of time. The communities believe that such a move would change life for the better. You feel your community should participate in such an experiment. Write a letter to the PTA or the mayor encouraging a public relations effort in favor of "Turn Off the TV Month." Cite specifically the positive effects such a program would have on parents, children, and the community in general.

DEFINITION 🌿

WHAT IS DEFINITION?

In Lewis Carroll's wise and whimsical tale, *Through the Looking Glass*, Humpty Dumpty proclaims, "When *I* use a word . . . , it means just what I choose it to mean — neither more nor less." If the world were filled with characters like Humpty Dumpty, all of them bending words to their own purposes and accepting no challenges to their personal definitions, communication would be an exercise in frustration. You would say a word, and it would mean one thing to you but perhaps something completely different to a close friend. Without a common understanding, the two of you would be talking at cross-purposes, missing each other's meanings as you blundered through a conversation.

In order for language to work as a means of communication, words must have accepted definitions. Dictionaries, the sourcebooks for accepted definitions, are compilations of current word-meanings, enabling speakers of a language to understand each other. But as you might suspect, things are not as simple as they first appear. We all know that a word like *discipline* has a standard

423

dictionary definition. We also know, though, that parents argue every day over the meaning of "discipline" and that controversies about the meaning of "discipline" rage within school systems year after year.

Words *are* graspable, yet they also can be slippery. Each of us has our own unique experiences, attitudes, and values, providing us with personal filters which color the way we use words and the way we interpret the words of others. Lewis Carroll may have been exaggerating, but Humpty Dumpty's attitude exists — in a very real way — within all of us.

In addition to the idiosyncratic interpretations that may attach to words, words may also shift in meaning over time. The word *pedagogue*, for instance, used to mean "a teacher or leader of children." Over the last several years, though, *pedagogue* has come to mean "a dogmatic, pedantic teacher." And, of course, some words (*modem, byte*) are simply new and unfamiliar to many people. It is not surprising that formulating definitions is such a common practice for writers.

When writing a definition, you try to answer the basic question: What does _____ mean? What is the special or true nature of _____? The word to be defined may be an object, a complex or abstract concept, a person, a place, or a phenomenon. Potential subjects for definition might be a computer, animal rights, a respected teacher, your hometown, cabin fever. As you will see, there are various strategies for expanding definitions far beyond the single-word synonyms or brief phrases that dictionaries use to clarify meanings.

WHEN TO USE DEFINITION

Many times, short-answer questions on exams are worded in such a way that a definition is clearly required. Consider the following:

> Define the term *mob psychology*.

> Clarify the difference between a metaphor and a simile.

> How would you characterize a religious cult? Explain what it is and what it is not.

In such cases, a good response might involve a definition of several sentences or several paragraphs.

Other times definition may be used in part of a longer essay that is organized mainly around another pattern of development. When this situation occurs, all that is needed is a brief formal definition or a short definition in your own words. For instance, a *process analysis* showing how computers have revolutionized the typical business office might start with a textbook definition of "artificial intelligence." In an *argumentation-persuasion* paper urging the elimination of fraternities and sororities, you could refer to the definitions of "blackballing" and "hazing" found in the university handbook. Or your personal definition of "hero" could be the starting point for a *causal analysis* that examines why there are so few real heroes in today's world.

But the most complex use of definition, and the one we are primarily concerned with in this chapter, involves exploring a subject through an *extended definition*. Extended definition allows you to apply a personal interpretation to a word, to make a case for a revisionist view of a commonly accepted meaning, to analyze words representing complex or controversial issues. "Pornography," "gun control," "secular humanism," and "right-to-life" would be excellent subjects for extended definition — each is multifaceted, often misunderstood, and fraught with emotional meaning. "Junk food," "anger," "leadership," "anxiety" could make interesting subjects, especially if the extended definition helped readers develop a new understanding of the word. You might, for example, write a paper on "anxiety," defining it not as a negative state to be avoided but as a positive force propelling us to significant action.

Although the extended definitions you write will most likely run several paragraphs or several pages, you might keep in mind that extended definitions can be developed over a number of chapters; even a whole book is possible. If this seems unlikely, remember that you can find whole books defining "excellence" and that theologians, philosophers, and pop psychologists have devoted entire books to such concepts as "death" and "love."

SUGGESTIONS FOR USING DEFINITION IN AN ESSAY

The following suggestions will be helpful whether you use definition as a dominant or supportive pattern of development.

1. Decide on the essay's purpose and tone. Since your purpose for writing an extended definition will shape the entire paper, it is important to clarify to yourself the essay's goal. A definition essay with a purely *informative* purpose seeks only to explain or make meaning clear. But a definition essay with a *persuasive* slant also wants to convince the reader about a particular point of view. Suppose for a moment that you decide to write an essay defining "jazz." The paper might lend itself to an informative or persuasive approach. The essay could be purely factual and straightforward, discussing the origins of jazz, its characteristic tonal patterns, some of the great jazz musicians of the past. Or the essay could move beyond the purely informative and take on a persuasive edge. The essay might, for example, take the position that jazz is the only contemporary form of music worth considering seriously.

Just as your purpose in writing a definition essay will vary, so will the tone you use. Most often, a strictly informative definition will assume an objective, serious tone ("Apathy is an emotional state characterized by listlessness and indifference"). A definition essay with a persuasive bent could be serious ("Student apathy can be combated through a series of programs designed to engage students in campus life"), or it might take a light — even satiric — approach ("An apathetic stance is a wise choice for any thinking student").

When deciding on the purpose and tone of the essay, you must remember to consider your audience. Not only does the audience determine what terms have to be defined (and how detailed the definition should be), but the audience also helps you focus on the most appropriate purpose and tone to select. You probably would not, for instance, write a strictly informative, serious piece for the college newspaper about the "mystery meat" served in the campus cafeteria. Instead, you would adopt a light tone as you defined the culinary horror and might even make a persuasive pitch about what could be done to improve the quality of food prepared on campus.

2. Formulate an effective definition. Most definition essays start with a brief *formal definition* — either the dictionary's, a textbook's, or your own — and then go on to expand that initial definition with supporting details. Formal definitions are traditionally worded as three-part statements which consist of the following: the *term*, the *class* to which the term belongs, and the *characteristics* that distinguish the term from other members of its class.

Term	Class	Characteristics
The peregrine falcon,	an endangered bird,	is the world's fastest flyer.
A bodice-ripper	is a paperback book,	usually read by women, that deals with highly charged romance in exotic places and faraway times.
Back to basics	is a trend in education	that emphasizes skill mastery through rote learning.

A definition that meets these guidelines will clarify what your subject *is* and what it *is not*. These guidelines also establish the boundaries of your definition, removing unlike items from consideration in your (and your reader's) mind.

For example, defining "back to basics" as a trend that emphasizes rote learning signals a certain boundary; other educational trends, such as those that emphasize children's social or emotional development, would not be part of the essay's definition.

One pitfall to avoid in writing such three-part definitions is *circularity*, or saying virtually identical things in different words and therefore defining neither. Here is a circular definition: "A campus tribunal is a tribunal composed of various members of the university community." We learn nothing from such a definition about what a campus tribunal is, for the writer has said only that "X is X." When writing a definition, you also want to avoid another potential trouble spot: depending on the old-hat "the dictionary says" or "according to Webster" approach. Such weak starts are just plain boring and often herald an unimaginative essay. You should also keep in mind that a strict dictionary definition may actually confuse readers. Suppose you were writing a paper on the way all of us absorb ideas and values from the media. Likening this automatic response to the scientific process of osmosis, you decide to open the paper with a dictionary definition. But if you write, "According to the dictionary, osmosis is the tendency of a solvent to disperse through a porous membrane into a more concentrated solution," readers are apt to be baffled, even hostile. Remember that the purpose of a definition is to clarify, not obscure, meaning.

3. Develop the extended definition. You can choose from a variety of patterns when developing an extended definition. Description, narration, process, comparison, or any of the other patterns discussed in the book can be used. To illustrate, imagine that you are planning to write an extended definition of "robotics." You might choose to develop the term using any of the following patterns (or combination of patterns): by providing *examples* of the ways robots are currently being used in scientific research; by *comparing* and *contrasting* human and robot capabilities; by *classifying* robots, starting with the most basic and moving to the most advanced or futuristic models.

The patterns of development to use will often become apparent during the prewriting stage. Here is a list of prewriting questions as well as the pattern of development implied by each brainstorming question.

Question	Pattern of Development
What does it look like?	Description
What happened?	Narration
What are some typical instances of it?	Examples
How does it work?	Process
What things is it like or not like?	Comparison-contrast
Why did it happen? What will its impact be?	Cause-effect
What are its subparts? How can it be categorized?	Division-classification

Those questions yielding the most material often suggest effective pattern(s) for developing an extended definition.

4. Organize the material that supports the definition. If you use a single method to develop the extended definition, apply the principles of organization suited to that method, as described in the appropriate chapter of this book. Assume that you are defining "fad" by means of *process analysis*. You might organize your paragraphs according to the steps in the process: a fad's slow start as something avant-garde or eccentric; a fad's wildfire acceptance by the general public; a fad's demise as it becomes familiar or tiresome. If "character" is going to be defined by means of a single *narration*, paragraphs would be organized chronologically.

In a definition essay using several methods of development, you should devote separate paragraphs to each pattern. A definition of "relaxation," for instance, might start with a paragraph that *narrates* a particularly relaxing day; then it might move to several *examples* of people who find it difficult to unwind; finally, it might end by explaining a *process* for relaxing the mind and body.

5. Write an effective introduction. As you might guess, it's a good idea to provide — near the start of a definition essay — a brief formal definition of the term you are going to develop in the rest of the paper. Beyond this basic element, the introduction may include a number of other features. You may explain the *origin* of the term being defined: "Acid rock is a term first coined in the 1960s to describe music that was written or listened to under the influence of the drug LSD." Similarly, you may explain the *etymology*, or linguistic origin, of the key word that focuses the paper. "The term *vigilantism* is derived from the Latin word meaning 'to watch and be awake.'"

Second, the introduction may clarify what the subject is *not*. This *definition by negation* can be an effective strategy at the beginning of a paper, especially if readers do not share your particular view of the subject. In such a case, you would write something like this: "The gorilla, far from being the vicious killer of jungle movies and popular imagination, is a sedentary, gentle creature living in a closely knit family group." Such a statement provides the special focus for your essay and signals some of the misconceptions or fallacies soon to be discussed.

You may also decide to include in the introduction a *stipulative definition*, a definition that puts special restrictions on a term: "Strictly defined, a mall refers to a one- or two-story enclosed building containing a variety of retail shops and at least two large anchor stores. Highway-strip shopping centers or downtown centers cannot be considered true malls." When a term has multiple meanings, or when its meaning has become fuzzy through misuse, a stipulative definition sets the record straight right at the start, so that writer and audience know exactly what is, and is not, being defined.

Finally, the introduction may end with *a plan of development* which implies how the definition essay will unfold. A student who returned to school after having raised a family decided to write a paper defining the midlife crisis that had led to her enrollment in college. After providing a brief formal definition of midlife crisis, the student rounded off her introduction with this sentence. "Such a midlife crisis starts with inklings of doubt, turns into depression, and concludes with a significant change in lifestyle."

Semanticists, those who study the nature of language, have noted that meaning lies in people, not in words. Because words are symbols—and therefore open to multiple interpretations—dictionaries can only be starting points, never ultimate authorities. The complex nature of language makes the formulation of definitions an important part of writing. Extended definitions are one way we can sort out for ourselves the confusing nature of a word or term. Similarly, extended definitions are an effective way to clear up confusion that others may have about a word's meaning. We see the importance of definition every day. The courts define "right to privacy"; the campus handbook explains what "plagiarism" is; international negotiators try to forge an agreement on the meaning of "arms parity." Because definition essays are so flexible in the ways they can be developed and in the freedom they give the writer, they make demands quite different from most other assignments. Definition essays are, in short, a challenge worth mastering.

STUDENT ESSAY AND COMMENTARY

The following student essay was written by Laura Chen in response to this assignment:

In "Entropy," K. C. Cole takes a scientific term from physics and gives it a broader definition and a wider application. Choose another specialized term and define it in such a way that you reveal something significant about contemporary life.

While reading Laura's paper, try to determine how well it applies the principles concerning the use of definition. The commentary following the paper will help you look at Laura's essay more closely.

Physics in Everyday Life

A boulder sits on a mountain side for a thousand years. The boulder will remain there forever unless an outside force intervenes. Suppose a force does affect the boulder--an earthquake, for instance. Once the boulder begins to thunder down the mountain, it will remain in motion and head in one direction only--downhill--until another force interrupts its progress. If the boulder tumbles into a gorge, it will finally come to rest as gravity anchors it to the earth once more. In both cases, the boulder is exhibiting the physical principle of inertia: the tendency of matter to remain at rest or, if moving, to keep moving in one direction unless affected by an outside force. Inertia, an important factor in the world of physics, also plays a crucial role in the human world. Inertia affects our individual lives as well as the direction taken by society as a whole. 1

Inertia often influences our value systems and personal growth. Inertia is at work, for example, when people cling to certain behaviors and views. Like the boulder firmly fixed to the mountain, most people are set in their ways. Without thinking, they vote Republican or Democratic because they have always voted that way. They regard with suspicion a couple having no children, simply because everyone else in the neighborhood has a large family. It is only when an outside force--a jolt of some sort--occurs that people change their views. A white American couple may think little about racial discrimination, for instance, until they adopt an Asian child and must comfort her when classmates tease her because she looks different. Parents may consider promiscuous any unmarried teenage girl who has a baby until their 17-year-old honors-student daughter confesses that she is pregnant. Personal jolts like these force people to think, perhaps for the first time, about issues that now affect them directly. 2

To illustrate how inertia governs our lives, it is helpful to compare the world of television with real life. On TV, inertia does not exist. Television shows and commercials show people making all kinds of drastic changes. They switch brands of coffee or try a new 3 haircolor with no hesitation. In one car commercial, an ambitious young accountant abandons her career with a flourish and is seen driving off into the sunset as she heads for a small cabin by the sea to write poetry. In a soap opera, a character may progress from home-maker to hooker to nun in a single year. But in real life, inertia rules. People tend to stay where they are, to keep their jobs, to be loyal to products. A second major difference between television and real life is that, on television, everyone takes prompt and dramatic action to solve problems. The construction worker with a thudding headache is pain-free at the end of the sixty-second commercial; the police catch the murderer within an hour; the family learns to cope with their son's life-threatening drug addiction by the time the made-for-TV movie ends at eleven. But in the real world, inertia persists, so that few problems are solved neatly or quickly. Illnesses drag on, few crimes are solved, and family conflicts last for years.

Inertia is, most importantly, a force at work in the life of our nation. Again, inertia is two-sided. It keeps us from moving and, once we move, it keeps us pointed in one direction. We find ourselves mired in a certain path, accepting the inferior, even the dangerous. We settle for toys that break, winter coats with no warmth, and rivers clogged with pollution. Inertia also compels our nation to keep mov-ing in one direction--despite the uncomfortable suspicion that it is the wrong direction. We are not sure if manipulating genes is a good idea, yet we continue to fund scientific projects in genetic engineering. More than forty years ago, we were shaken when we saw the devasta-tion caused by an atomic bomb. But we went on to develop weapons hundreds of times more destructive. Although warned that excessive television viewing may be harmful, we continue to watch hours of television each day. 4

We have learned to defy gravity, one of the basic laws of physics; we fly high above the earth, even float in outer space. But most of us have not learned to defy inertia. Those special individuals who are able to act when everyone else seems paralyzed are rare. But the fact that such people do exist means that inertia is not all-powerful. If we use our reasoning ability and our creativity, we can conquer inertia, just as we have conquered gravity. 5

As the title of her essay suggests, Laura — like the author of "Entropy" — has taken a scientific term from a specialized field and used the term to help explain some everyday phenomena. Laura opens her essay with a vivid *descriptive* example of "inertia," the term at the heart of the paper. This description is then followed by a *formal definition* of inertia: "the tendency of matter to remain at rest or, if moving, to keep moving in one direction unless affected by an outside force." Laura wisely begins the paper with the attention-getting description rather than with the scientific definition. Had the order been reversed, the essay would not have gotten off to nearly as effective a start. Laura then ends her introductory paragraph with a two-sentence *thesis*: "Inertia, an important factor in the world of physics, also plays a crucial role in the human world. Inertia affects our individual lives as well as the direction taken by society as a whole."

Like all effective *definition essays*, Laura's paper helps us look at ourselves and the world in a new light. And since Laura wants us to accept her definition of inertia and her view that it often governs human behavior, her essay also contains a distinct element of *argumentation-persuasion*.

To support her definition of inertia and her belief that it can rule our lives, Laura generates a number of compelling examples. She organizes these examples by grouping them into three major points, each point signaled by a *topic sentence* that appears at the start of the essay's three supporting paragraphs: "Inertia often influences our value systems and personal growth" (paragraph 2); "To illustrate how inertia governs our lives, it is helpful to compare the world of television with real life" (3); and "Inertia is, most importantly, a force at work in the life of our nation" (4).

Note that a definite organizational strategy underpins the sequence of Laura's three central points. The essay moves from the way inertia affects the individual to the way it shapes the life of the nation. And the words "most importantly" at the start of the fourth paragraph indicate that Laura has arranged her points emphatically, believing that inertia's impact on society is most critical.

In the body of the essay, Laura uses a number of writing patterns to show that inertia can be a powerful force. For instance, the third paragraph uses *comparison-contrast* to highlight the differences between television and real life. On television, people zoom into action, but in everyday life, people tend to stay put and muddle through. The two other supporting paragraphs use *causal analysis* to explain how people and nations can be paralyzed by inertia. In the second paragraph, Laura indicates that only "an outside force — a jolt of some kind" can motivate inert people to change. Then, to support this causal analysis, Laura provides two examples of parents who experience such jolts. In the beginning of the fourth paragraph, Laura contends that inertia causes the persistence of specific national problems: shoddy consumer goods, and environmental pollution.

You might have noticed when reading the rest of the fourth paragraph that Laura's examples are not sequenced as effectively as they could be. To show that we, as a nation, tend to keep moving in the same direction, Laura discusses our ongoing uneasiness about genetic engineering, nuclear arms, and excessive television viewing. The point about nuclear weapons is most significant, yet it gets lost because it is sandwiched in the middle. The paragraph would be stronger if it ended with the point about nuclear arms. Moreover, the idea about excessive television viewing does not belong in this paragraph since — at best — it has limited bearing in the issue being discussed.

Laura's *conclusion* rounds off the essay nicely and brings it to a satisfying close. Laura refers to another law of physics, one with which we are all familiar — gravity. Creating an *analogy* between gravity and inertia, she suggests that our ability to defy gravity should encourage us to try to defy inertia. The analogy enlarges the scope of the essay; it allows Laura to reach out to her readers by challenging them to action. Such a challenge is, of course, appropriate in a definition essay having a persuasive bent.

When it was time to rework her essay, Laura put her paper aside for a while before starting to revise in earnest. Once the editing process began, she made a number of changes but found that the original version of her third paragraph needed special attention. The preliminary draft of the paragraph is reprinted here.

Unrevised Version

The ordinary actions of daily life are, in part, determined by inertia. To understand this, it is helpful to compare the world of television with real life, for, in the TV-land of ads and entertainment, inertia does not exist. For example, on television, people are often shown making all kinds of drastic changes. They switch brands of coffee or try a new hair color with no hesitation. In one car commercial, a young accountant leaves her career and sets off for a cabin by the sea to write poetry. In a soap opera, a character may progress from homemaker to hooker to nun in a single year. In contrast, inertia rules in real life. People tend to stay where they are, to keep their jobs, to be loyal to products (wives get annoyed if a husband brings home the wrong brand or color of bathroom tissue from the market). Middle-aged people wear the hairstyles or makeup that suited them in high school. A second major difference between television and real life is that, on TV, everyone takes prompt and dramatic action to solve problems. A woman finds the solution to dull clothes at the end of a commercial; the police catch the murderer within an hour; the family learns to cope with a son's disturbing lifestyle by the time the movie is over. In contrast, the law of real-life inertia means that few problems are solved neatly or quickly. Things, once started, tend to stay as they are. Few crimes are actually solved. Medical problems are not easily diagnosed. Messy wars in foreign countries seem endless. National problems are identified, but Congress does not pass legislation to solve them.

After rereading what she had written, Laura realized that the paragraph rambled. To tighten and gain control over this section of the paper, Laura did a number of things. First, she eliminated two flat, unconvincing examples: the idea about wives who get annoyed when their husbands bring home the wrong brand of bathroom tissue and the references to hairstyles and makeup. In addition, she condensed the two disjointed sentences that originally opened the paragraph. Note how much more crisp and focused the revised sentences are: "To illustrate how inertia rules our lives, it is helpful to compare the world of television with real life. On TV, inertia does not exist."

Laura also worked to make the details and the language in the paragraph more specific and vigorous. The vague sentence "A woman finds the solution to dull clothes at the end of the commercial" is dropped for the more dramatic "The construction worker with a thudding headache is pain-free at the end of the sixty-second commercial." Similarly, Laura changed a "son's troublesome life-style" to a "son's life-threatening drug addiction," and "when the movie is over" to "when the made-for-TV movie ends at eleven." Moreover, the sentence " . . . a young accountant leaves her career and sets off for a cabin by the sea to write poetry" became " . . . an ambitious young accountant abandons her career with a flourish and is seen driving off into the sunset as she heads for a small cabin by the sea to write poetry."

Most important, Laura made some shrewd organizational changes in the paragraph. She removed the last two sentences because they referred to inertia in national affairs: "Messy wars in foreign countries seem endless" and "National problems are identified, but Congress does not pass legislation. . . . " Laura realized that these sentences did not belong in the paragraph because this section of the paper focused on inertia in the life of the individual. Once these sentences were eliminated, she decided to round off the paragraph by adding a powerful summary statement that implied the difference between real life and television: "Illnesses drag on, few crimes are solved, and family conflicts last for years."

These revisions in the third paragraph are similar to the kind Laura made in the other sections of her first draft. Such astute changes enabled her to turn her already effective paper into an especially thoughtful analysis of human behavior.

As the following selections show, definition essays generally use a variety of patterns to develop the concept that is at the heart of the essay. K. C. Cole uses facts, examples, and anecdotes while showing how a specialized concept — "Entropy" — applies to everyday life. Stuart Chase, in "A Very Private Utopia," uses comparison and contrast as he defines his own notion of a perfect world. In "Why I Want a Wife," Judy Syfers generates examples to clarify her definition of a traditional wife. H. L. Mencken employs examples, description, and brief narratives as he defines the essence of "The Politician." Finally, Marie Winn draws a compelling analogy to clarify her definition of "TV Addiction."

K. C. Cole

K. C. Cole's writings about science, especially physics, have made a great deal of specialized knowledge available to the general public. A graduate of Barnard College, she has contributed numerous articles to such publications as The New York Times, *the* Washington Post, *and* Newsday. *Most recently, Cole has written a regular column for* Discover *magazine. Her work with the Exploratorium, a San Francisco science museum, led her to write several books on the exhibits there. In 1985, Cole published a collection of essays,* Sympathetic Vibrations: Reflections on Physics as a Way of Life. *The following selection first appeared as a "Hers" column in* The New York Times.

Entropy

Scientific concepts often sound unintelligible to the layperson. Can any of us state Einstein's theory of relativity, for example? But the natural laws at work in the universe are not just for geniuses. Instead, they are the invisible strings that control all creatures on the planet, including ourselves. In her essay, K. C. Cole takes an odd-sounding, specialized concept from physics and shows how it is a factor in everyone's daily life.

It was about two months ago when I realized that entropy was getting the better of me. On the same day my car broke down (again), my refrigerator conked out and I learned that I needed root-canal work in my right rear tooth. The windows in the bedroom were still leaking every time it rained and my son's baby sitter was still failing to show up every time I really needed her. My hair was turning gray and my typewriter was wearing out. The house needed paint and I needed glasses. My son's sneakers were developing holes and I was developing a deep sense of futility.

After all, what was the point of spending half of Saturday at the Laundromat if the clothes were dirty all over again the following Friday?

Disorder, alas, is the natural order of things in the universe.   3
There is even a precise measure of the amount of disorder, called
entropy. Unlike almost every other physical property (motion,
gravity, energy), entropy does not work both ways. It can only
increase. Once it's created it can never be destroyed. The road to
disorder is a one-way street.

Because of its unnerving irreversibility, entropy has been   4
called the arrow of time. We all understand this instinctively. Children's rooms, left on their own, tend to get messy, not neat. Wood
rots, metal rusts, people wrinkle and flowers wither. Even mountains wear down; even the nuclei of atoms decay. In the city we see
entropy in the rundown subways and worn-out sidewalks and
torn-down buildings, in the increasing disorder of our lives. We
know, without asking, what is old. If we were suddenly to see the
paint jump back on an old building, we would know that something was wrong. If we saw an egg unscramble itself and jump back
into its shell, we would laugh in the same way we laugh at a movie
run backward.

Entropy is no laughing matter, however, because with every   5
increase in entropy energy is wasted and opportunity is lost. Water
flowing down a mountainside can be made to do some useful work
on its way. But once all the water is at the same level it can work no
more. That is entropy. When my refrigerator was working, it kept
all the cold air ordered in one part of the kitchen and warmer air in
another. Once it broke down the warm and cold mixed into a
lukewarm mess that allowed my butter to melt, my milk to rot and
my frozen vegetables to decay.

Of course the energy is not really lost, but it has defused and   6
dissipated into a chaotic caldron of randomness that can do us no
possible good. Entropy is chaos. It is loss of purpose.

People are often upset by the entropy they seem to see in the   7
haphazardness of their own lives. Buffeted about like so many
molecules in my tepid kitchen, they feel that they have lost their
sense of direction, that they are wasting youth and opportunity at
every turn. It is easy to see entropy in marriages, when the partners
are too preoccupied to patch small things up, almost guaranteeing
that they will fall apart. There is much entropy in the state of our
country, in the relationships between nations — lost opportunities
to stop the avalanche of disorders that seems ready to swallow us
all.

Entropy is not inevitable everywhere, however. Crystals and   8
snowflakes and galaxies are islands of incredibly ordered beauty in
the midst of random events. If it was not for exceptions to entropy,
the sky would be black and we would be able to see where the stars
spend their days; it is only because air molecules in the atmosphere
cluster in ordered groups that the sky is blue.

The most profound exception to entropy is the creation of life.   9
A seed soaks up some soil and some carbon and some sunshine and
some water and arranges it into a rose. A seed in the womb takes
some oxygen and pizza and milk and transforms it into a baby.

The catch is that it takes a lot of energy to produce a baby. It   10
also takes energy to make a tree. The road to disorder is all downhill
but the road to creation takes work. Though combating entropy is
possible, it also has its price. That's why it seems so hard to get
ourselves together, so easy to let ourselves fall apart.

Worse, creating order in one corner of the universe always   11
creates more disorder somewhere else. We create ordered energy
from oil and coal at the price of the entropy of smog.

I recently took up playing the flute again after an absence of   12
several months. As the uneven vibrations screeched through the
house, my son covered his ears and said, "Mom, what's wrong with
your flute?" Nothing was wrong with my flute, of course. It was my
ability to play it that had atrophied, or entropied, as the case may
be. The only way to stop that process was to practice every day, and
sure enough my tone improved, though only at the price of constant work. Like anything else, abilities deteriorate when we stop
applying our energies to them.

That's why entropy is depressing. It seems as if just breaking   13
even is an uphill fight. There's a good reason that this should be so.
The mechanics of entropy are a matter of chance. Take any ice-cold
air molecule milling around my kitchen. The chances that it will
wander in the direction of my refrigerator at any point are exactly
50-50. The chances that it will wander away from my refrigerator
are also 50-50. But take billions of warm and cold molecules mixed
together, and the chances that all the cold ones will wander toward
the refrigerator and all the warm ones will wander away from it are
virtually nil.

Entropy wins not because order is impossible but because   14
there are always so many more paths toward disorder than toward
order. There are so many more different ways to do a sloppy job

than a good one, so many more ways to make a mess than to clean it up. The obstacles and accidents in our lives almost guarantee that constant collisions will bounce us on to random paths, get us off the track. Disorder is the path of least resistance, the easy but not the inevitable road.

Like so many others, I am distressed by the entropy I see   15
around me today. I am afraid of the randomness of international events, of the lack of common purpose in the world; I am terrified that it will lead into the ultimate entropy of nuclear war. I am upset that I could not in the city where I live send my child to a public school; that people are unemployed and inflation is out of control; that tensions between sexes and races seem to be increasing again; that relationships everywhere seem to be falling apart.

Social institutions — like atoms and stars — decay if energy is   16
not added to keep them ordered. Friendships and families and economies all fall apart unless we constantly make an effort to keep them working and well oiled. And far too few people, it seems to me, are willing to contribute consistently to those efforts.

Of course, the more complex things are, the harder it is. If   17
there were only a dozen or so air molecules in my kitchen, it would be likely — if I waited a year or so — that at some point the six coldest ones would congregate inside the freezer. But the more factors in the equation — the more players in the game — the less likely it is that their paths will coincide in an orderly way. The more pieces in the puzzle, the harder it is to put back together once order is disturbed. "Irreversibility," said a physicist, "is the price we pay for complexity."

Questions for Close Reading

1. What is the thesis of the selection? Locate the sentence(s) in which Cole states her main idea. If she does not state the thesis explicitly, express it in your own words.
2. How does entropy differ from the other properties of the physical world? Is the image "the arrow of time" helpful in establishing this difference?
3. Why is the creation of life an exception to entropy? What is the relationship between entropy and energy?
4. Why does Cole say that entropy "is no laughing matter"? What is so depressing about the entropy she describes?

5. Refer to your dictionary as needed to define the following words in the selection: *futility* (paragraph 1), *dissipated* (6), *buffeted* (7), *tepid* (7), and *atrophied* (12).

Questions about the Writer's Craft

1. What is Cole's underlying purpose in defining the scientific term *entropy*? Is she being merely informative, or does her essay have a subtle persuasive edge as well?
2. What tone does the author adopt to break down our resistance to reading about a scientific concept? Find some examples where her tone is especially prominent.
3. Cole uses such words as *futility, loss,* and *depressing.* How do these words affect you? Why do you think the author chose such terms? Find other similar words in the essay.
4. Many of Cole's sentences follow a two-part pattern: "The road to disorder is all downhill, but the road to creation takes work." "There are so many more different ways to do a sloppy job than a good one. . . ." Find other examples of this sentence pattern. Why do you think Cole finds it useful to explain the effects of entropy by using this pattern?

Questions for Further Thought

1. Besides the examples provided by Cole, what instances of entropy do you see around you?
2. Is entropy in nature the same as entropy in society? In a marriage? In a city? In international relations? Do you accept Cole's application of the term *entropy* to these various realms?
3. Entropy means that paint peels, "people wrinkle, flowers wither." How does our society respond to these phenomena?
4. Cole writes that it's "so hard to get ourselves together, so easy to let ourselves fall apart." If so, why do we bother? Overall, would you say the author is optimistic or pessimistic about humans getting themselves together?

Writing Assignments Using Definition as a Method of Development

1. Define *order* or *disorder* by applying the term to an institution, organization, or system that you know well. You might focus on your school, dorm, family, workplace, or any other system. Develop your definition through any combination of writing patterns: by supplying examples and instances, by showing contrasts, by analyzing the process of the organization and so on.

2. Choose a technical term that might be unfamiliar to many people. Write a humorous or serious paper defining the term as it is used technically, and then show how the term can be used to explain some aspect of your life. For example, the concept in astronomy of a *supernova* could be used to explain your sudden emergence as a new star on the athletic field, in your schoolwork, on the social scene. Here are a few suggested terms:

Symbiosis	Volatility	Resonance
Velocity	Erosion	Catalyst
Neutralization	Equilibrium	Malleability

Writing Assignments Using Other Methods of Development

3. Can one person make much difference in the amount of entropy—disorder and decay—in the world? Explain your views in an essay. Use examples of people, past or present, who tried—successfully or not—to overcome the tendency of things to "fall apart."

4. How much control do people have over their own lives? Is our sense of self-determination an illusion, given what Cole says about entropy? She claims that "People are often upset by . . . the haphazardness of their own lives. Buffeted about like so many molecules . . . , they feel that they have lost their sense of direction, that they are wasting youth and opportunity at every turn." Write an essay arguing that people either do or do not control their own fates. Use specific examples of lives in or out of control.

Stuart Chase

Educated as an accountant at MIT and Harvard University, Stuart Chase (1888–1985) soon discovered he preferred being a writer. A frequent contributor to numerous magazines, Chase has written books on topics ranging from consumer rights to politics to language use. Among his best-known works are The Tragedy of Waste *(1925)*, Rich Land, Poor Land *(1936)*, Democracy Under Pressure *(1945)*, Guides to Straight Thinking *(1956)*, and* Some Things Worth Knowing *(1958). The selection below first appeared in* The Nation *magazine.*

A Very Private Utopia

Human beings have always imagined ideal worlds or utopias. Such civilizations would banish ugliness, evil, and suffering, allowing individuals to reach their highest potential. Visionaries have occasionally started utopian communities. In America, for example, utopias have ranged from the nineteenth-century Brook Farm to some of the communes of the 1960s. The essay below depicts the society that Stuart Chase would find perfect. Such a utopia would satisfy Chase's personal aspirations but would also provide for the need of others.

Lewis Mumford in *The Golden Day* has given us a brilliant   1
review of American culture as reflected in American literature from
Jonathan Edwards to John Dewey. It is on the whole an exceedingly critical review. He tells us frequently, passionately, and beautifully what he is against, but only rarely does he let it be known
what he is for. Modern industrial civilization has nourished a great
array of critics. Few of them are as competent or as penetrating as
Mr. Mumford, but all of them — save possibly the Utopians —
follow his general method. They are indefatigable in pointing out
the shortcomings of society, but they are vague as to the precise
nature of available substitutes. They seldom define their standards.
Yet standards they must have; otherwise it would be impossible to

criticize. They either take it for granted that the reader shares their inward knowledge, or else, and more probably, the standards have never been formulated in the critic's conscious processes at all. They have grown in the back of his mind, darkly.

From the artists, the dramatists, the socialists, the poets, the   2
uplifters of all varieties, has poured forth in never-ending flood the challenge that *homo sapiens* is only half alive.

What does he look like when he is alive?   3

The question would seem to be a fair one, but it is seldom   4
answered. The writers of Utopia have struggled with it, but their canvases are usually so great that we are seldom able to see ourselves or our neighbors living or behaving in that world. There is a strange chill about all Utopias; they are inhabited by gods, not men. Even when a critical play of modern manners, the "Beggar on Horseback," forsook its role of satire for a moment and gave us a picture of happiness about a sun-drenched breakfast table, we stared unconvinced at such very yellow bliss. The negatives stretch to the horizon, but the positives are either lacking entirely or, when focused before us, appear cold or a little absurd. Indeed to seek to describe with clearness and precision the specific target at which programs for ushering in the good life should aim can only be an adventure tinged with absurdity. But a possible approach may be to delimit the kind of life one personally would like to live. Will this remove the Utopian chill and at the same time furnish the beginnings of a standard? We can but test it.

I have thrown my arrows with the rest at the sweating corpus of   5
the world as it is. I have called it ugly, machine-minded, dull, ignorant, and cruel. I have said that the few live, and they precariously, while the many exist, half-dead in their frustrations and blind alleys. Before hurling another quiver it would seem only fair—however dubious the result—to define rather specifically what I mean, or think I mean, when I mark off the quick from the dead.

The hours roll into days, the days into years. Down this funnel   6
of time one drifts, now easily, now painfully. One is happy, one is miserable. There are days of the most intense blue; days of a terrible black; with perhaps the majority of days an all-pervading mauve-gray. The causes for the color of these days are far from clear; one takes life as it comes. Modern psychology is groping for causes, but it has not as yet brought much that is genuinely helpful into the

light. It cannot tell you where the good life has been competently analyzed or even adequately described. Science has perhaps even less to report than the poets and the critics. And so about all the data is oneself.

I note that the following things or conditions do, by and large, 7 kill the juices of zestful living, and reduce me to mere existing. I state the negative first, the positive to follow shortly:

Ill health.
Monotonous work with no discernible goal — such as auditing, indexing, dishwashing.
Eating poor food; eating in ugly places.
The sensation of living in ugly or uncomfortable houses.
All transit, whether by foot or on wheels, about New York City.
Being looked down upon, or laughed at (save for very minor foibles).
The bulk of all business interviews, conferences, talks — the juicelessness of the personal contact.
The defacement of natural beauty with billboards, pop stands, suburban lots, gas tanks, shacks, factories. (A factory can be made to respond to architecture as well as a sky-scraper.)
Reading newspapers — save for perhaps one one-hundredth of the surface of not more than three of them.
Going to formal entertainments — particularly dinners devoted to the raising of funds for worthy causes.
Treating relatives as preferred creditors.
Wearing ugly or uncomfortable clothes as decreed by the *mores*, e.g., coats and hats for men in summer.
Shopping — with rare exceptions.
Worrying about money.
Being bored with bad plays, concerts, lectures, radios, meetings, conversations — especially the last.
Being everlastingly hustled around.
Seeing other people bored, unhappy, or in pain. Looking down mean streets and into frowsy windows.

My notebooks show scores of other conditions which take the 8 joy out of life, but the above are the chief ones in the daily run of my activity. They consume, on the basis of a rough estimate, upwards of two thirds of my waking hours, though the ratio shifts with the seasons, being noticeably worse in winter. The average annual ratio, furthermore, is better when living in the country the year around than in the city. I am dead, I conclude, about two thirds of the time. I am alive, by and large, under the following conditions:

> On encountering a vivid awareness of health.
> In pursuing creative work, intellectual or manual. There are definite time limits to both.
> Eating good food, drinking good wine, in comfortable places.
> The sensation of living in well-designed and sunny houses.
> Being looked up to and praised — but the butter must not be spread too thick.
> Being with my friends.
> Looking at beautiful scenery, beautiful pictures, beautiful things.
> Reading great books; reading of new and stimulating ideas.
> Looking at Charlie Chaplin's feet.
> Swimming, diving, playing tennis, dancing, skiing, mountain climbing. Watching good sport at not too frequent intervals.
> Daydreaming.
> Going on spontaneous and amusing parties.
> Making love spontaneously.
> Wearing beautiful — not fashionable — clothes.
> Collecting things. For me, certain sorts of information.
> Listening to good music — especially Russian gypsy songs.
> The sensation of being some paces in front of the wolf.
> Home life — in fits and starts.
> Kindly casual contacts with strangers.
> Travel, other than for business reasons.
> Keen discussion.
> A good fight, not necessarily sanguinary, in what seems to be a decent cause.
> The sense of being in bodily danger.

So runs the major classification of what seem to constitute the 9 good life for me. To hold that the list is applicable to all is, of course, ridiculous. Yet it must serve as a starting-point for the thing we have set ourselves to define. I do not know how other people feel. Logic declares that, conditioned by the same forces that have conditioned me, other people would feel much the same, but logic is not an infallible guide in human affairs.

What kind of a community would I build to increase the count 10 of the hours that live as against the count of the hours that die? God knows. The difficulty is that the pluses and the minuses are never clean-cut emotional states, registering faithfully at every exposure to a given condition. When one is in abounding health, even fill-ing-station architecture is tolerable if not positively enjoyable. When one sits, like Mr. Polly, athwart a stile, with civil war in his interior, the sunset itself becomes a flat and overestimated specta-cle. There are times when the best of friends becomes a bore, when one wishes all printing presses would stop forever. Indeed, the whole concept is in the curved grip of relativity.

Nevertheless, I think that I would be appreciably more alive in 11 a community that deliberately fostered the sorts of things enumer-ated on the second list, of which good health is probably the most important single factor. If it be objected that the animals are mostly healthy, I would reply that they appear to get more out of life than the majority of human beings. Fortunately the laws underlying the promotion of health are beginning to be understood. We already have the technical knowledge available to increase immeasurably bodily well-being. Here and there it is being applied, as the declin-ing death-rate and the lengthening age span show.

Secondly, I would like to live in a community where beauty 12 abounded; where cities were nobly planned, industrial areas segre-gated; where great stretches of forest, lake, and mountain were left wild and free and close at hand; where houses and their furnishings were spare and fine and colorful, and there was not a single bill-board in a day's march. Cities and houses have been so built; nature over great (but distant) areas is still free; advertising is only a century old, despite the pious historical labors of Bruce Barton. Surely a community rich in natural beauty, rich in architecture, is no Utopia. It has been repeatedly achieved, and without the vast potential assistance of mechanical power.

Thirdly, I would like to live, and to have my neighbors live, 13 free from the fear of want. Such communities there have been, but not many of them. Peru under the Incas is said to have achieved this goal; Denmark is not far from it today. Not only is it the release of the individual which is desirable, but, vastly more important, the release of the whole group. As things are in America today I never know how far my own actions are ignoble by economic considerations, nor how far my neighbors and associates regard me on my own merits or as a means to a hopefully profitable end. All human relationships are poisoned with this suspicion; or cut and bruised with the frank brutality of elbowing one's way above the line of economic insecurity. This is the more lamentable in that the industrial arts have already demonstrated how utterly to abolish poverty, double — aye treble — the standard of living, produce more than enough to go around.

Fourthly, I would like to live in a community where I could do the kind of work that is the most fun. Fun for me is economic research and writing about it. If there should prove a plethora of better men in this field, I would have a lot of fun as an anthropologist, a psychologist, or a biologist. Or I might go back to my boyhood dreams of architecture. In exchange for the fun, the giving of an hour or two on the average day to the necessary manual work of the world would seem, in anticipation at least, the merest justice. Furthermore, digging ditches, painting walls, simple carpentry would both preserve the sense of reality and serve by contrast to heighten the fun of the chosen occupation.   14

I would like to be able to dress as I pleased, or indeed not to dress at all when the sun was high and the water blue. I should like to experiment with colors and combinations now rigidly proscribed for males by the folkways — save at fancy-dress balls. I should like to be able to dance more, sing more, let myself go more. Here New England dogs me like an iron shroud. I should like ampler and less hurried opportunities to play the games I enjoy. I should like to travel more; to visit the lost cities of which I dream; to climb in the Andes and the Himalayas. It does not do to turn one's back for long on the bright face of danger.   15

I should like to be a more compelling and less self-conscious lover, but just how a community would proceed to organize great lovers escapes me. (Here we hover at once on absurdity and on what, following health, is probably the most important factor in the good life — a balanced sexual rhythm.)   16

I would like to live in a world where many good books were being published — fiction, poetry, science, history, philosophy; where good plays and good music were just around the corner —   17 without too much standing in line and too little ventilation; where good pictures were being hung; where the arts and crafts were flourishing on indigenous rather than imitative material; and particularly and especially, where good conversation abounded, together with the leisure to pursue it. Of all the joys which life has to offer none, for me, can exceed that of keen stimulating talk; and nothing is rarer in America today.

Finally, I would like to live in a community that held a genuine sense of its uniqueness; where one could take pride in community achievements, match one's art and craftsmanship and sport against a neighbor group; where one could contribute in person to the local theater, the local schools; help to plan a beautiful region, and see that plan grow before one's eyes—and so take root in one's own soil, a part of the earth, earthy, as well as a dreamer in the clouds. So the Greeks must have looked back to the plains and hills and cedar trees of Attica and Laconia. Here one might have the leisure to play with children as they should be played with; here one might bring the carnival and the pageant—with color and wine and flowers—back to meaning and to life. 18

Above all, leisure, leisure, a break in the remorseless and meaningless urgencies of the twentieth-century pace. 19

This—if you will—Utopia may be cold to you, but it is not cold to me. I can see it, feel it, aye, long for it. How would you change it to include the things for which you long? Anthropologists, you say, have yet to find a people without a well-marked religion; that need is indigenous, cardinal, and necessary to you. Good. Let us have a church with a great nave and a great organ and the sound of vespers across the evening fields. You dislike my games and want other games. Again good. The more games the better so long as we play them ourselves. You want to paint or design or build bridges. Each to his own desire, so long as the necessary work is done. You do not want to do anything. There will be a nice, forest-circled, psychopathic hospital until sanity returns. You do not want roots, you want to keep on the move. Would you object to moving through communities which had abolished squalor and striven to individualize and beautify themselves? 20

Add what you please, so long as it does not make for ugliness or drabness or cruelty; so long as it does not quench life that the lives of a few may burn with a spurious brightness. I do not know what your desires may be, but if they make you happy and others 21 not too unhappy they are welcome. The question is not what is good for other people but good for you.

The preliminary definition of the good life which I have tried 22 to outline is crude enough, but it can be used. Swing it as a searchlight where you will — on Mr. Calvin Coolidge or on Mr. Bernard Shaw; on Miss Jane Addams or on Mrs. Peaches Browning; on a soap factory, a department store, an iron mine, an advertising campaign, a prize fight, a laboratory, a best seller; swing it upon Wall Street or Main Street or Downing Street; on Denmark or on Pittsburgh — it can give basis for judgment. Would this person, or thing, or area, be out of place in such a community? Would it clash, jar, disintegrate; or would it be welcomed and at home? The architecture of Beacon Hill would, the architecture of South Chicago would not; the Lincoln Memorial would, Park Avenue would not; Mr. Chaliapin would, Mr. Shubert would not; the Olympic games would, professional baseball would not; Mr. H. G. Wells would (very much at home he would be), Dr. Frank Crane would not. Mark for yourself the quick from the dead.

The question is not primarily what would make you happy, 23 but rather what would make you more alive. Perhaps complete Nirvana is the happiest conceivable state, but it remains at the opposite pole from vivid life. Pain, heartache, failure in achievement, failure in love, the shock of physical danger, even envy, must remain so long as we behave like human beings. Only the surplus of pain and confusion induced by stupidity would tend to disappear.

It would seem that the end of human effort upon this planet 24 should be to give a maximum of living and a minimum of existing — the life more abundant. Against such an end, those who regard life as a gateway of mortification to a Utopia beyond the grave make their sincere protest. But it is doubtful how far that protest can continue effective in an era of wide knowledge and unlimited possibilities for technical control over nature.

Even if we can win to life ourselves, the contemplation of the 25 existing of those over the brink about us takes, in a sensitive heart, most of the joy out of personal salvation here below. Even if democracy is not sound doctrine, and biological inferiority can be definitely established, there is no particular reason why those handicapped from the germ plasm — and who will perforce have to do most of the dirty work of the world — should not be given surroundings from which they can take the maximum of what life holds for them. Lafcadio Hearn can tell you about the ancient

Japanese communities and how extraordinarily high in the sense of beauty and appreciation it has been proved possible for the mass to go.

Granting for the time being—until coal is gone, and the Ice   26
Cap moves south again—granting that a beautiful life here and now should be the major goal of human effort, of what strands shall it be woven? How shall Mr. Mumford and his fellow-critics be appeased? The above is, if you will, a feeble and absurd beginning. But perhaps it will serve as a point of departure for the speculations of wise men and women.

Questions for Close Reading

1. What is the thesis of the selection? Locate the sentence(s) in which Chase states his main idea. If he does not state the thesis explicitly, express it in your own words.
2. Why did Chase decide to write a description of his Utopia? How does the Lewis Mumford book prompt this effort?
3. What are the broad subjects of Chase's two lists? After providing these lists, Chase moves on to a related subject—what is it?
4. How does Chase's list of what makes him "live" differ from his standards for Utopia?
5. Refer to your dictionary as needed to define the following words in the selection: *indefatigable* (paragraph 1), *corpus* (5), *foibles* (7), *sanguinary* (8), *infallible* (9), *plethora* (14), *indigenous* (17), *spurious* (21), and *Nirvana* (23).

Questions about the Writer's Craft

1. In defining what makes him "live," Chase lists the negative first, a technique knows as definition by negation. What effect does this strategy have on the reader?
2. Chase says, by his own estimation, that he is "dead . . . about two-thirds of the time." Where in the essay is his style that of a person who is "merely existing" and who has lost "the juices of zestful living"? Where in the essay does he seem truly alive?
3. How does the author clearly signal when he is moving from one phase of his extended definition to another? Locate three places where he accomplishes these transitions.
4. How does Chase attempt to defuse any objections his readers might have? Locate several of his disclaimers. What kind of audience does Chase feel he is addressing?

Questions for Further Thought

1. If Stuart Chase were running for President with this essay as his platform, would you vote for him? What features of his Utopia do you object to, if any? Are there omissions in his description of the perfect society? Do you accept his overall goals, as expressed in the closing paragraphs?
2. Chase provides this maxim: "The question is not primarily what would make you happy, but rather what would make you more alive." Do you find that people commonly make this distinction? Is it a useful one, in your opinion? Which would you rather be, happy or more alive?
3. Chase explains his proposed Utopia in detail, yet he calls it "a very private utopia." Is this a contradiction? What is so private about this perfect society?
4. Would living in one's ideal world ever become boring? Is there any value at all in life's negative experiences? Explain.

Writing Assignments Using Definition as a Method of Development

1. As Chase does in his essay, brainstorm a list of what makes you "exist" and a list of what makes you "live." Then, write your own personal definition of the Utopia that would best suit you, focusing the essay on the most crucial items from your list of pleasures and satisfactions.
2. Granted that a Utopian world is not likely to exist any time soon, how could a person live the fullest life possible? Write a definition essay on "the good life" as you *could* live it in the world as it now is. To develop the essay, you should think about your goals and values as well as about people who seem to be getting the most from life.

Writing Assignments Using Other Methods of Development

3. A society designed to be perfect but so extreme that it becomes nightmarish is called a *dystopia*. Aldous Huxley described a dystopia in *Brave New World*. How could Chase's ideas, taken to an extreme, create a dystopia? Use the items on his list of pleasures as the basis for an essay describing a Utopia gone wrong. The tone of your essay may be serious or light.
4. Write a character sketch of a person you know who is "really living" or, conversely, a person who is mired in "mere existence." Develop the essay by focusing on the person's pervasive attitudes and types of pursuits. You may also discuss the outside forces that have shaped the individual.

Judy Syfers

Judy Syfers was born in 1937 in San Francisco and was educated at the University of Iowa. She became a freelance writer during the 1960s and has written articles for a variety of publications. The provocative essay here first appeared in Ms. *magazine in 1971 and has become a classic of feminist satire.*

Why I Want a Wife

According to the dictionary, a wife is a "woman married to a man." But, as many women know, a wife is much more: cook, housekeeper, nutritionist, chauffeur, friend, sex partner, valet, nurse, social secretary, ego-builder, and more. Rather than complain about all the responsibilities she and other women assume, Judy Syfers explains why she herself would like to have a wife.

I belong to that classification of people known as wives. I am A 1
Wife. And, not altogether incidentally, I am a mother.

Not too long ago a male friend of mine appeared on the scene 2
from the Midwest fresh from a recent divorce. He had one child,
who is, of course, with his ex-wife. He is obviously looking for
another wife. As I thought about him while I was ironing one
evening, it suddenly occurred to me that I, too, would like to have a
wife. Why do I want a wife?

I would like to go back to school so that I can become econom- 3
ically independent, support myself, and, if need be, support those
dependent upon me. I want a wife who will work and send me to
school. And while I am going to school I want a wife to take care of
my children. I want a wife to keep track of the children's doctor and
dentist appointments. And to keep track of mine, too. I want a wife
to make sure my children eat properly and are kept clean. I want a
wife who will wash the children's clothes and keep them mended. I
want a wife who is a good nurturant attendant to my children,
arranges for their schooling, makes sure that they have an adequate

social life with their peers, takes them to the park, the zoo, etc. I want a wife who takes care of the children when they are sick, a wife who arranges to be around when the children need special care, because, of course, I cannot miss classes at school. My wife must arrange to lose time at work and not lose the job. It may mean a small cut in my wife's income from time to time, but I guess I can tolerate that. Needless to say, my wife will arrange and pay for the care of the children while my wife is working.

I want a wife who will take care of *my* physical needs. I want a   4
wife who will keep my house clean. A wife who will pick up after my children, a wife who will pick up after me. I want a wife who will keep my clothes clean, ironed, mended, replaced when need be, and who will see to it that my personal things are kept in their proper place so that I can find what I need the minute I need it. I want a wife who cooks the meals, a wife who is a *good* cook. I want a wife who will plan the menus, do the necessary grocery shopping, prepare the meals, serve them pleasantly, and then do the cleaning up while I do my studying. I want a wife who will care for me when I am sick and sympathize with my pain and loss of time from school. I want a wife to go along when our family takes a vacation so that someone can continue to care for me and my children when I need a rest and a change of scene.

I want a wife who will not bother me with rambling com-   5
plaints about a wife's duties. But I want a wife who will listen to me when I feel the need to explain a rather difficult point I have come across in my course of studies. And I want a wife who will type my papers for me when I have written them.

I want a wife who will take care of the details of my social life.   6
When my wife and I are invited out by my friends, I want a wife who will take care of the babysitting arrangements. When I meet people at school that I like and want to entertain, I want a wife who will have the house clean, will prepare a special meal, serve it to me and my friends, and not interrupt when I talk about the things that interest me and my friends. I want a wife who will have arranged that the children are fed and ready for bed before my guests arrive so that the children do not bother us. I want a wife who takes care of the needs of my guests so that they feel comfortable, who makes sure that they have an ashtray, that they are passed the hors d'oeuvres, that they are offered a second helping of the food, that their wine glasses are replenished when necessary, that their coffee

is served to them as they like it. And I want a wife who knows that sometimes I need a night out by myself.

I want a wife who is sensitive to my sexual needs, a wife who   7
makes love passionately and eagerly when I feel like it, a wife who makes sure that I am satisfied. And, of course, I want a wife who will not demand sexual attention when I am not in the mood for it. I want a wife who assumes the complete responsibility for birth control, because I do not want more children. I want a wife who will remain sexually faithful to me so that I do not have to clutter up my intellectual life with jealousies. And I want a wife who understands that *my* sexual needs may entail more than strict adherence to monogamy. I must, after all, be able to relate to people as fully as possible.

If, by chance, I find another person more suitable as a wife   8
than the wife I already have, I want the liberty to replace my present wife with another one. Naturally, I will expect a fresh, new life; my wife will take the children and be solely responsible for them so that I am left free.

When I am through with school and have acquired a job, I   9
want my wife to quit working and remain at home so that my wife can more fully and completely take care of a wife's duties.

My God, who *wouldn't* want a wife?   10

Questions for Close Reading

1. What is the thesis of the selection? Locate the sentence(s) in which Syfers states her main idea. If she does not state the thesis explicitly, express it in your own words.
2. What event sparked Syfers to think about why she would like to have a wife? How is this event related to her thesis?
3. What are the duties of a wife, according to Syfers?
4. How are a wife's duties different from her spouse's? Which roles apply to the wife and not her spouse?
5. Refer to your dictionary as needed to define the following words used in the selection: *nurturant* (paragraph 3), *replenished* (6), *entail* (7), and *adherence* (7).

Questions about the Writer's Craft

1. What is Syfers's tone in this essay? How does this tone help us understand her definition of what it is to be a "wife"?

2. Why does the author repeat "I want a wife" over and over? How does this repetition add to the essay's effectiveness?
3. Are the reasons why Syfers wants a wife listed in any particular order? Why does she save sexual needs and the right to divorce for last?
4. How does Syfers develop her definition of "wife"? Does she ever provide a direct summary statement of what a wife is?

Questions for Further Thought

1. This essay was first published in 1972, when the women's movement was still new. Have times changed? Or is Syfers's message still relevant today?
2. Syfers concludes, "My God, who wouldn't want a wife?" Would you? Why or why not?
3. Syfers casts herself in the role of a spouse of a certain kind of wife. What is your opinion of this spouse? How do you think most husbands would react to reading this essay?
4. Do you know any couples in which the woman is a "wife" such as Syfers describes? Are these people happy? Do you see any positive aspects to such a relationship?

Writing Assignments Using Definition as a Method of Development

1. Adopting either a positive or negative viewpoint, write an essay defining the idea of a husband. Use either "I want a husband" or "I don't want a husband" as your theme. Build your definition around numerous examples of the way husbands behave.
2. Define what you mean by the phrase "a good marriage" — that is, the kind of marriage you would like to have. Develop your definition in an essay that explains what the two partners should do to make a good marriage a reality.

Writing Assignments Using Other Methods of Development

3. Write an essay from the point of view of a traditional housewife defending such a lifestyle as fulfilling and important. Try to persuade your audience that it is a worthy lifestyle by giving reasons and examples of its benefits and advantages.

4. Syfers dwells a great deal on housework and home-related duties, once the sole responsibility of the wife. Write an essay, either serious or playful in tone, arguing that both partners in a marriage should or should not be responsible for the home-related tasks traditionally considered woman's work. Household duties could include such areas as cleaning, child care, laundry, entertaining, meal preparation, and shopping.

H. L. Mencken

With a cool eye and biting wit, H. L. Mencken (1880 – 1956) examined the mores and foibles of American culture. A prolific writer, Mencken founded the journal American Mercury, *edited the* Baltimore Sun, *and published dozens of books, including studies of American English and several volumes of autobiography. Known for his ability to puncture pretensions and skewer foolishness, Mencken invented the term "booboisie" to describe the middle class, and insisted that no one ever went broke underestimating the intelligence of the American people. The essay here was published in* A Mencken Chrestomathy *(1949).*

The Politician

Politicians are not, for the most part, highly respected. We seem to enjoy electing our public officials so that we can later claim, "They're all crooks." In the following selection, H. L. Mencken denounces the politicians of his day for being dealers in "hokum" and "hooey." Before deciding that Mencken exaggerates, take a long look at the many political scandals that Mencken didn't live long enough to see.

After damning politicians up hill and down dale for many 1
years, as rogues and vagabonds, frauds and scoundrels, I sometimes suspect that, like everyone else, I often expect too much of them. Though faith and confidence are surely more or less foreign to my nature, I not infrequently find myself looking to them to be able, diligent, candid, and even honest. Plainly enough, that is too large an order, as anyone must realize who reflects upon the manner in which they reach public office. They seldom if ever get there by merit alone, at least in democratic states. Sometimes, to be sure, it happens, but only by a kind of miracle. They are chosen normally for quite different reasons, the chief of which is simply their power to impress and enchant the intellectually underprivileged. It is a talent like any other, and when it is exercised by a radio crooner, a

458

movie actor or a bishop, it even takes on a certain austere and sorry respectability. But it is obviously not identical with a capacity for the intricate problems of statecraft.

Those problems demand for their solution — when they are 2 soluble at all, which is not often — a high degree of technical proficiency, and with it there should go an adamantine kind of integrity, for the temptations of a public official are almost as cruel as those of a glamor girl or a dipsomaniac. But we train a man for facing them, not by locking him up in a monastery and stuffing him with wisdom and virtue, but by turning him loose on the stump. If he is a smart and enterprising fellow, which he usually is, he quickly discovers there that hooey pleases the boobs a great deal more than sense. Indeed, he finds that sense really disquiets and alarms them — that it makes them, at best, intolerably uncomfortable, just as a tight collar makes them uncomfortable, or a speck of dust in the eye, or the thought of Hell. The truth, to the overwhelming majority of mankind, is indistinguishable from a headache. After trying a few shots of it on his customers, the larval statesman concludes sadly that it must hurt them, and after that he taps a more humane keg, and in a little while the whole audience is singing "Glory, glory, hallelujah," and when the returns come in the candidate is on his way to the White House.

I hope no one will mistake this brief account of the political 3 process under democracy for exaggeration. It is almost literally true. I do not mean to argue, remember, that all politicians are villains in the sense that a burglar, a child-stealer, or a Darwinian are villains. Far from it. Many of them, in their private characters, are very charming persons, and I have known plenty that I'd trust with my diamonds, my daughter or my liberty, if I had any such things. I happen to be acquainted to some extent with nearly all the gentlemen, both Democrats and Republicans, who are currently itching for the Presidency, including the present incumbent, and I testify freely that they are all pleasant fellows, with qualities above rather than below the common. The worst of them is a great deal better company than most generals in the army, or writers of murder mysteries, or astrophysicists, and the best is a really superior and wholly delightful man — full of sound knowledge, competent and prudent, frank and enterprising, and quite as honest as any American can be without being clapped into a madhouse. Don't ask me what his name is, for I am not in politics. I can only tell you that he has been in public life a long while, and has not been caught yet.

But will this prodigy, or any of his rivals, ever unload any   4
appreciable amount of sagacity on the stump? Will any of them venture to tell the plain truth, the whole truth and nothing but the truth about the situation of the country, foreign or domestic? Will any of them refrain from promises that he knows he can't fulfill — that no human being *could* fulfill? Will any of them utter a word, however obvious, that will alarm and alienate any of the huge packs of morons who now cluster at the public trough, wallowing in the pap that grows thinner and thinner, hoping against hope? Answer: maybe for a few weeks at the start. Maybe before the campaign really begins. Maybe behind the door. But not after the issue is fairly joined, and the struggle is on in earnest. From that moment they will all resort to demagogy, and by the middle of June of election year the only choice among them will be a choice between amateurs of that science and professionals.

They will all promise every man, woman and child in the   5
country whatever he, she or it wants. They'll all be roving the land looking for chances to make the rich poor, to remedy the irremediable, to succor the unsuccorable, to unscramble the unscrambleable, to dephlogisticate the undephlogisticable. They will all be curing warts by saying words over them, and paying off the national debt with money that no one will have to earn. When one of them demonstrates that twice two is five, another will prove that it is six, six and a half, ten, twenty, *n*. In brief, they will divest themselves of their character as sensible, candid and truthful men, and become simply candidates for office, bent only on collaring votes. They will all know by then, even supposing that some of them don't know it now, that votes are collared under democracy, not by talking sense but by talking nonsense, and they will apply themselves to the job with a hearty yo-heave-ho. Most of them, before the uproar is over, will actually convince themselves. The winner will be whoever promises the most with the least probability of delivering anything.

Some years ago I accompanied a candidate for the Presidency   6
on his campaign-tour. He was, like all such rascals, an amusing fellow, and I came to like him very much. His speeches, at the start, were full of fire. He was going to save the country from all the stupendous frauds and false pretenses of his rival. Every time that

rival offered to rescue another million of poor fish from the neglects and oversights of God he howled his derision from the back platform of his train. I noticed at once that these blasts of common sense got very little applause, and after a while the candidate began to notice it too. Worse, he began to get word from his spies on the train of his rival that the rival was wowing them, panicking them, laying them in the aisles. They threw flowers, hot dogs and five-cent cigars at him. In places where the times were especially hard they tried to unhook the locomotive from his train, so that he'd have to stay with them awhile longer, and promise them some more. There were no Gallup polls in those innocent days, but the local politicians had ways of their own for finding out how the cat was jumping, and they began to join my candidate's train in the middle of the night, and wake him up to tell him that all was lost, including honor. This had some effect upon him — in truth, an effect almost as powerful as that of sitting in the electric chair. He lost his intelligent manner, and became something you could hardly distinguish from an idealist. Instead of mocking he began to promise, and in a little while he was promising everything that his rival was promising, and a good deal more.

One night out in the Bible country, after the hullabaloo of the day was over, I went into his private car along with another newspaper reporter, and we sat down to gabble with him. This other reporter, a faithful member of the candidate's own party, began to upbraid him, at first very gently, for letting off so much hokum. What did he mean by making promises that no human being on this earth, and not many of the angels in Heaven, could ever hope to carry out? In particular, what was his idea in trying to work off all those preposterous bile-beans and snake-oils on the poor farmers, a class of men who had been fooled and rooked by every fresh wave of politicians since Apostolic times? Did he really believe that the Utopia he had begun so fervently to preach would ever come to pass? Did he honestly think that farmers, as a body, would ever see all their rosy dreams come true, or that the share-croppers in their lower ranks would ever be more than a hop, skip and jump from starvation? The candidate thought awhile, took a long swallow of the coffin-varnish he carried with him, and then replied that the answer in every case was no. He was well aware, he said, that the plight of the farmers was intrinsically hopeless, and would probably continue so, despite doles from the treasury, for centuries to

462   Definition

come. He had no notion that anything could be done about it by merely human means, and certainly not by political means: it would take a new Moses, and a whole series of miracles. "But you forget, Mr. Blank," he concluded sadly, "that our agreement in the premisses must remain purely personal. You are not a candidate for President of the United States. *I am*." As we left him his interlocutor, a gentleman grown gray in Washington and long ago lost to every decency, pointed the moral of the episode. "In politics," he said, "man must learn to rise above principle." Then he drove it in with another: "When the water reaches the upper deck," he said, "follow the rats."

Questions for Close Reading

1. What is the thesis of the selection? Locate the sentence(s) in which Mencken states his main idea. If he does not state the thesis explicitly, express it in your own words.
2. Mencken writes his essay as a political "insider." What are the characteristics of the politician, from this insider's perspective? What changes does a politician undergo once he or she begins campaigning?
3. Who is at fault for the deplorable political situation Mencken describes — the politicians themselves or the voters who elected them? Find evidence in the essay to support your answer.
4. Mencken is neither a politician nor a typical voter — he is a journalist. Why does Mencken say that he avoids "naming names"? How did journalists of Mencken's time view their responsibilities as reporters?
5. Refer to your dictionary as needed to define the following words used in the selection: *candid* (paragraph 1), *austere* (1), *adamantine* (2), *dipsomaniac* (2), *sagacity* (4), *demagogy* (4), *succor* (5), and *interlocutor* (7).

Questions about the Writer's Craft

1. Mencken uses a variety of patterns to convince the reader to accept his definition of a politician. Identify places where exemplification, process analysis, or other patterns of development appear in the essay. What hard evidence (facts, statistics, and so on) does Mencken use to support his ideas?
2. The humor of Mencken's essay results largely from the satiric technique known as invective, or insult. For instance, Mencken calls voters "boobs" and says they are more receptive to "hooey" than to sense. Find other examples of invective in the essay.

3. Note the things Mencken says about himself at the start of the essay and in occasional self-references. How does he create a sense of himself as a credible commentator on presidential politics? Does he consider himself to be addressing "packs of morons" or another type of audience?

4. One technique the author uses to achieve his satiric effects is to juxtapose ideas or items that are not normally related. In paragraph 2, he groups three things that make people uncomfortable: "a tight collar . . . or a speck of dust in the eye, or the thought of Hell." Find some other juxtapositions. In each case, what effect does the juxtaposition have on the point Mencken is making at the time?

Questions for Further Thought

1. This essay was written nearly fifty years ago. Is it valid now? Have our political process and our politicians changed? What similarities exist between the politicians Mencken describes and politicians today?

2. Satirists, by definition, exaggerate the vices of their targets and ignore the virtues, if any. Do you think Mencken is being unfair to those who run for office or to the American public? What good qualities of his targets is he deliberately omitting?

3. How do Americans decide whom to vote for? Do we look at the candidates' records, experience, or stands on various issues? Or are we largely swayed by physical appearance, public speaking skills, wit, and personality? How effective are advertising campaigns in determining voters' choices?

4. What constitutes the ideal training for a future politician? Mencken suggests (facetiously) "looking him up in a monastery and stuffing him with wisdom and virtue." Should a political candidate be scholarly, worldly wise, or some combination of the two?

Writing Assignments Using Definition as a Method of Development

1. Choose your favorite target: any group of people you feel is worthy of criticism. Write a satiric definition essay decrying the faults of this group. Use Mencken's techniques (insults, juxtapositions, disparaging comparisons, bold slang, and a peppering of fancy words). Some possible groups to consider include the following: a teenage "type" (jock, preppie, campus queen, and so on); the boss; the doctor, lawyer, or other professional person; the teacher; the rock star or fan; the professional _____ (name a sport) player.

2. After studying Mencken's essay and considering other examples of satire (*Saturday Night Live, SCTV, Monty Python, National Lampoon,* the "Doonesbury" comic strip, and so on), decide how you would

define satire. Write an extended definition, explaining what satire is, how it operates, and what it accomplishes. Use specific examples to support your ideas.

Writing Assignments Using Other Methods of Development

3. In *The Making of the President,* a series of books about American presidential campaigns, Theodore White attempted to show that Americans are greatly influenced by the mass-media marketing of political candidates. Do you think the increased availability of TV coverage has lessened or exacerbated the tendency of politicians to deliver "hokum" to the public? Write an essay arguing either that television helps to root out dishonesty in politics or that it makes "style" the determining factor in political success.

4. Write an essay explaining why you voted (or would have voted) for _____ in the most recent Presidential election. Clarify the factors that led to your choice. Be honest: were you swayed by personality, looks, the choices of friends and family, the candidate's previous record or stance on public issues? How much of your choice was based on solid information and how much on image or hearsay?

Marie Winn

Born in Czechoslovakia and brought by her family to New York, Marie Winn was educated at Radcliffe College. The author or editor of ten children's books, Winn developed a special interest in the effect of television on children. She has contributed numerous articles to such publications as The New York Times *and* The Village Voice. *Winn's provocative and influential study,* The Plug-In Drug: Television, Children and Family, *was originally published in 1977 and was revised in 1985. The selection that follows is from that book.*

TV Addiction

You arrive home from work or school. Is the TV on where you live? If not, do you automatically flick it on? You are probably aware that television has become an overwhelming presence in society. In the following selection, Marie Winn suggests that television resembles such addictive substances as alcohol and drugs. She warns us that the similarity is more than metaphorical since TV addiction has real, life-damaging consequences. It can cause people to lose jobs, families, and a normal perspective on life.

The word "addiction" is often used loosely and wryly in conversation. People will refer to themselves as "mystery book addicts" or "cookie addicts." E. B. White writes of his annual surge of interest in gardening: "We are hooked and are making an attempt to kick the habit." Yet nobody really believes that reading mysteries or ordering seeds by catalogue is serious enough to be compared with addictions to heroin or alcohol. The word "addiction" is here used jokingly to denote a tendency to overindulge in some pleasurable activity.

People often refer to being "hooked on TV." Does this, too, fall into the lighthearted category of cookie eating and other pleasures that people pursue with unusual intensity, or is there a kind of

465

television viewing that falls into the more serious category of destructive addiction?

When we think about addiction to drugs or alcohol, we frequently focus on negative aspects, ignoring the pleasures that accompany drinking or drug-taking. And yet the essence of any serious addiction is a pursuit of pleasure, a search for a "high" that normal life does not supply. It is only the inability to function without the addictive substance that is dismaying, the dependence of the organism upon a certain experience and an increasing inability to function normally without it. Thus a person will take two or three drinks at the end of the day not merely for the pleasure drinking provides, but also because he "doesn't feel normal" without them.

An addict does not merely pursue a pleasurable experience and need to experience it in order to function normally. He needs to *repeat* it again and again. Something about that particular experience makes life without it less than complete. Other potentially pleasurable experiences are no longer possible, for under the spell of the addictive experience, his life is peculiarly distorted. The addict craves an experience and yet he is never really satisfied. The organism may be temporarily sated, but soon it begins to crave again.

Finally a serious addiction is distinguished from a harmless pursuit of pleasure by its distinctly destructive elements. A heroin addict, for instance, leads a damaged life: his increasing need for heroin in increasing doses prevents him from working, from maintaining relationships, from developing in human ways. Similarly an alcoholic's life is narrowed and dehumanized by his dependence on alcohol.

Let us consider television viewing in the light of the conditions that define serious addictions.

Not unlike drugs or alcohol, the television experience allows the participant to blot out the real world and enter into a pleasurable and passive mental state. The worries and anxieties of reality are as effectively deferred by becoming absorbed in a television program as by going on a "trip" induced by drugs or alcohol. And just as alcoholics are only inchoately aware of their addiction, feeling that they control their drinking more than they really do ("I can cut it out any time I want — I just like to have three or four drinks before dinner"), people similarly overestimate their control over television watching. Even as they put off other activities to spend hour after hour watching television, they feel they could easily resume living in a different, less passive style. But somehow or other while the television set is present in their homes, the click doesn't sound. With television pleasures available, those other experiences seem less attractive, more difficult somehow.

A heavy viewer (a college English instructor) observes: "I find 8 television almost irresistible. When the set is on, I cannot ignore it. I can't turn it off. I feel sapped, will-less, enervated. As I reach out to turn off the set, the strength goes out of my arms. So I sit there for hours and hours."

The self-confessed television addict often feels he "ought" to 9 do other things — but the fact that he doesn't read and doesn't plant his garden or sew or crochet or play games or have conversations means that those activities are no longer as desirable as television viewing. In a way a heavy viewer's life is as imbalanced by his television "habit" as a drug addict's or an alcoholic's. He is living in a holding pattern, as it were, passing up the activities that lead to growth or development or a sense of accomplishment. This is one reason people talk about their television viewing so ruefully, so apologetically. They are aware that it is an unproductive experience, that almost any other endeavor is more worthwhile by any human measure.

Finally it is the adverse effect of television viewing on the lives 10 of so many people that defines it as a serious addiction. The television habit distorts the sense of time. It renders other experiences vague and curiously unreal while taking on a greater reality for itself. It weakens relationships by reducing and sometimes eliminating normal opportunities for talking, for communicating.

And yet television does not satisfy, else why would the viewer 11 continue to watch hour after hour, day after day? "The measure of health," writes Lawrence Kubie, "is flexibility . . . and especially the freedom to cease when sated." But the television viewer can never be sated with his television experiences — they do not provide the true nourishment that satiation requires — and thus he finds that he cannot stop watching.

Questions for Close Reading

1. What is the thesis of the selection? Locate the sentence(s) in which Winn states her main idea. If she does not state the thesis explicitly, express it in your own words.

2. Why, according to Winn, is a gardening addiction or a mystery book addiction a humorous kind of habit? What does she call "the essence of any serious addiction"?
3. In paragraph 7, the author says that television allows the viewer "to enter into a pleasurable . . . mental state," and later that "television does not satisfy." How does Winn prepare you earlier in the essay for this seeming contradiction?
4. Since television does "not provide the true nourishment that satiation requires," what activities does Winn suggest as truly nourishing alternatives?
5. Refer to your dictionary as needed to define the following words in the selection: *wryly* (paragraph 1), *inchoately* (7), *ruefully* (9), *adverse* (10), and *satiation* (11).

Questions about the Writer's Craft

1. At the beginning of the essay, Winn uses definition by negation to clarify her interpretation of the term *television addiction*. What kinds of things does Winn say are *not* the equivalents of TV addiction? Why does she use this strategy of definition by negation?
2. How does Winn organize the two extended definitions of addiction and TV addiction? How does this organization pattern help persuade us to accept her point that TV is addicting?
3. What does the quotation from the TV addict add to the author's argument? Why does she choose a quotation from this person?
4. Few of us would dispute Winn's discussion of serious addictions in paragraphs 3 to 5. How does this lengthy treatment of a term we already understand assist the author in convincing us that TV is addicting?

Questions for Further Thought

1. Do you agree with Winn that excess TV viewing is a problem of the same magnitude as an addiction? Or would you say instead that television viewing in excess is merely analogous to being addicted to a drug or chemical? Is using the medical idea of addiction a useful way for our society to go about understanding and solving the problem of "too much TV"?
2. Consider the characteristics of addiction as set out in paragraphs 3 to 5. Do you think all types of people are equally likely to become addicted to something? Are there any types of people who might be totally immune?
3. Do you or people you know watch too much TV? Or do you find

yourself addicted to some other electronic medium — or another non-drug activity? Is your addiction humorous or serious?

4. Reformed alcoholics and drug abusers are taught to avoid places where they might feel tempted. Few families would be willing to get rid of their televisions. What methods could parents or individuals use to prevent or lessen TV addiction?

Writing Assignments Using Definition as a Method of Development

1. In her introduction, Winn describes how people often use a very serious term — *addiction* — when referring to a light or harmless experience. Think of another term which you feel is serious, but which people use lightly and apply loosely. Your choice could be friendship, love, hate, or another word. Begin with an example that shows how the word is misused, and then provide an extended definition clarifying the proper use of the term.

2. TV addiction is only one of the forms of addiction in our society. Many other forms exist, such as addiction to gambling, baseball games, cars, bingo, chocolate, the latest clothing styles, or the like. Write an essay on another addiction, using one of the addictions listed or another of your own choice. Use Winn's essay as a model.

Writing Assignments Using Other Methods of Development

3. Many kinds of TV shows come in for criticism. Pick one type — sitcoms, detective shows, game shows, or whatever — and write an essay defending this type of show as having something to offer a thinking person. Use examples from the best shows of this type. If you feel very critical of TV, you may wish to adopt a humorous tone in the essay.

4. You have probably heard from older relatives (or may yourself know) what life was like before TV. Similarly, during your own life, new technologies have created items that are transforming the way we live. Write an essay for your future children or grandchildren describing what life was like before one or several of these new products: home computers and word processors, VCRs, cable TV, microwave ovens, bank cards, cassette players, laser discs. Persuade your descendants that life was better *or* worse before these items were invented.

Additional Writing Topics

DEFINITION

General Assignments

Use definition to develop any of the following topics. Once you fix on a limited subject, decide if the essay has an informative or persuasive purpose. The paper might begin with the etymology of the term, with a stipulative definition, or with a definition by negation. You may want to use a number of writing patterns — such as description, comparison, narration, process — to develop the definition. Remember, too, that the paper does not have to be scholarly and serious. There is no reason it can't be a lighthearted discussion of the meaning of a term.

1. Fads
2. A family fight
3. Helplessness
4. An epiphany
5. A workaholic
6. A Pollyanna
7. A con artist
8. A stingy person
9. A team player
10. A Yiddish term such as *mensch, klutz, chutzpah,* or *dreck,* or a term from some other ethnic group
11. Idiomatic expressions
12. Fast food
13. A perfect day
14. A do-nothing day
15. Inner peace
16. Obsession
17. Generosity
18. Exploitation
19. Depression
20. A double bind

Assignments with a Specific Audience and Purpose

1. *Newsweek* magazine runs a popular column called "My Turn," consisting of readers' opinions on subjects of general interest. You decide to

send in a column on today's college students, a subject on which you are knowledgeable. Your purpose is to define the college students of today, especially in light of all the generalizations made about them by the general public: "They're apathetic"; "They're not as bright as college students used to be"; "They're spoiled rich kids"; "They're interested only in making money."

2. You are an attorney arguing a case of sexual harassment—a charge your client has leveled against her boss, a business executive. If you are to win the case, you must present to the jury a clear definition of exactly what sexual harassment is and isn't. Write your definition for your opening remarks in court.

3. You have been asked to write a pamphlet to be distributed to students by the college health services clinic. In the pamphlet, you will warn students about a certain condition/ailment and detail the symptoms. Choose any of the following as your subject: depression; stress; burnout; anxiety (test or general); addiction (to alcohol, drugs, or TV); workaholic syndrome; excessive competitiveness.

4. A new position has opened in your company. You have been asked to write a job description that will then be sent to employment agencies who will do the actual screening of candidates. Select any occupational category or designation and write a job description that does the following: defines the job's purpose, states the duties or responsibilities the job entails, and outlines the position's essential qualifications.

5. Part of your job as a marriage counselor is helping troubled couples communicate better. For example, you have recently realized that when couples discuss what is missing from their marriage, each person often has a different concept of what _____ means. Choose your own term or one of these: respect; maturity; sharing; equality; fidelity; support. You decide to write a definition of this term for your clients, based on your years of counseling experience. Part of your definition employs definition by negation; you tell them what this quality is *not*.

6. You have worked for several summers at a hotel in a popular resort area. You have been so good at your job that the hotel manager has asked you to give a talk to this year's incoming summer employees. The manager wants you to define *courtesy* for the new workers. This is the factor that has made you so popular with guests, and the manager believes it is the one quality that will make or break the hotel's business. Write your speech for the new workers, using specific examples to define this term.

DIVISION- CLASSIFICATION

WHAT IS DIVISION-CLASSIFICATION?

Try to imagine what life would be like if this is how an average day might unfold:

> You have to stop at the supermarket for only five items. But your marketing takes over an hour because all the items in the store are jumbled together. Clerks put new shipments anywhere they please; the milk might be with the vegetables on Monday but with laundry detergent on Thursday. Next, you go to the drug store to pick up some photos you left to be developed. You don't have time, though, to wait while the cashier roots through the large carton into which all the pick-up envelopes have been thrown. You return to your car and decide to stop at the town hall to pay a parking ticket. But the town hall baffles you. The offices are unmarked, and there's not even a directory to tell you on what floor the Violations

Bureau can be found. Annoyed, you get back into your car and, minutes later, end up colliding with another car. When you wake up in the hospital, you find there are three other patients in your room: a man with a heart problem, a young boy ready to have his tonsils removed, and a woman about to go into labor.

Such a muddled world, lacking the most basic forms of organization, would make daily life chaotic. All of us instinctively look for ways to order our environment. Without systems, categories, or sorting mechanisms, we would be overwhelmed by life's complexity. An organization like a college or university, for example, is made more manageable by being divided into various schools (Liberal Arts, Performing Arts, Engineering, and so on). The schools are then separated into departments (English, History, Political Science), and each department's offerings are grouped into distinct categories — English, for instance, into Literature and Composition — before being further divided into specific courses. Now take a moment to consider how overwhelmed people often feel when buying expensive items like stereos and cars. The multitude of choices and considerations can be perplexing. One way to plow through the tangle of possibilities is to buy a magazine like *Consumer Reports*, examining the "Best Buy," "Recommended," and "Not Recommended" categories, thereby eliminating many items from consideration.

The kind of ordering system we have been discussing is called *division-classification*, a logical method of thinking that allows us to make sense of the world. Division and classification, though separate processes, are often used together as complementary techniques. *Division* involves taking a single unit or concept, breaking the unit down into its parts, and then analyzing the connection among the parts and between the parts and the whole. For instance, if we wanted to organize the chaotic hospital described at the start of the chapter, we might think about how the single concept "a hospital" could be broken down into its components. We might come up with the following kind of breakdown for a given hospital: pediatric wing, cardiac wing, maternity wing, and so on.

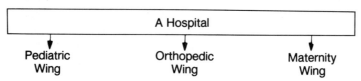

What we have just done involves division: we have taken a single entity (a hospital) and divided it into some of its component parts or wings, each with its own facilities and patients.

Classification, on the other hand, brings two or more related items together and categorizes them according to type or kind. If the disorganized supermarket described earlier were to be restructured, the clerks would have to classify the separate items arriving at the loading dock. Cartons of lettuce, tomatoes, cucumbers, butter, yogurt, milk, shampoo, conditioner, and setting lotion would be assigned to the appropriate categories:

Lettuce	Butter	Shampoo
Tomatoes	Yogurt	Conditioner
Cucumbers	Milk	Setting Lotion
↓	↓	↓
Produce	Dairy	Hair Products

WHEN TO USE DIVISION-CLASSIFICATION

The reorganized hospital and supermarket are concrete examples of the way division and classification work in everyday life. But it's important to realize that this analytic approach also comes into play during the writing process. Because division involves breaking a subject into parts, it can be a helpful strategy when exploring broad, complex subjects: the organization of the restaurant or store where you work; the structure of a film; the motivation of a character in a novel; the problem your community has with vandalism; the issue of school prayer; the controversy surrounding arms control. An editorial examining a recent hostage crisis, for example, might divide the crisis into three areas: how the hostages were treated by their captors, by the governments negotiating their release, and by the media. The purpose of the editorial might be to show that the governments' treatment of the hostages was particularly exploitative.

On the other hand, classification is useful when you want to understand how the subjects you are writing about — all of which share some common characteristics — are alike or different. Classification would, then, be a helpful strategy when you are analyzing such topics as the following: techniques for impressing teachers; comic styles of talk-show hosts; views on abortion; effects of federal budget cuts on the elderly; reasons for the current rise in volunteerism. For instance, classification might be used in an article explaining the way Americans are undermining their health through their obsessive pursuit of supposedly fail-safe diets. The article might begin by categorizing, according to type, the endless number of diets that have gained popularity in recent years: high fiber, low protein, high carbohydrate, and so on. Once the diets were grouped, the problems within each category could be discussed, demonstrating that none of the diets is safe or effective.

By now you may realize that division-classification can be a helpful approach to use when responding to college assignments. Consider the following:

> Analyze the components that go into being an effective parent. Indicate which components you feel are most critical for raising confident, well-adjusted children.

> Based on your observations, what kinds of appeals do television advertisers use when selling automobiles? In your view, do any of these appeals pose moral questions?

> Describe the hierarchy of the typical high school clique, identifying the various parts of the hierarchy. Use your analysis to support or refute the view that adolescents have a strong need to conform.

> Many social commentators have observed that rudeness and discourtesy are on the rise in America. Indicate whether you think this is a valid observation by characterizing the types of everyday encounters you have with people.

These assignments suggest division-classification through the use of such words as *components, kinds, parts, types*. But you generally will not receive such clear signals to write an essay using division-classification. Instead, the broad purpose of the essay — and the point you want to make — will lead you to the analytical thinking characteristic of division-classification. You will develop the essay, or part of the essay, using division-classification because the pattern allows you to meet your goal in writing.

Sometimes division-classification will be the dominant technique for structuring an essay; other times it will be used as a supplemental pattern in an essay organized mostly around another pattern of development. Here, for example, is how division-classification could be used in a number of essays. You may want to write a paper *explaining a process* (surviving adolescence; creating a hit record; shepherding a bill through Congress; using the Heimlich maneuver on people who are choking). In such a case, you would *divide* the process into parts or stages, demonstrating, let's say, that the Heimlich maneuver is an easily mastered technique that should be taught in all public schools. Or *classification* could be used in a light essay that analyzes the *effects* of changing sex roles on students' social lives. Assume you want to show that shifting gender roles make young men and women more uncertain around the opposite sex than ever before. To make your point, you might start by categorizing the places where students scout out each other: in class, at the library, at parties, or in dorms. Then you could show how students approach each other with almost comic tentativeness in these four environments.

Now imagine that you are writing an *argumentation-persuasion* essay advocating that the federal government prohibit the feeding of antibiotics to livestock to stimulate their growth. The paper could begin by *dividing* the antibiotics cycle into stages: the effects of antibiotics on animals; the short-term effects on humans who consume the livestock; the possible long-term effects of consuming such animals over a period of years. To strengthen your argument, you might decide to discuss the antibiotics controversy in terms of an even larger issue: the various ways our food is treated before consumption. In this case, you would consider the different procedures (use of additives, preservatives, artificial colors, and so on), *classifying* these treatments into several types — from least harmful (some additives or artificial colors, perhaps) to most harmful (you might decide to slot the antibiotics here). Such an essay would be developed using division and classification in tandem: first, the division of the antibiotics cycle and then the classification of the various food treatments. Frequently, this interdependence will be reversed, and classification will precede rather than follow division.

SUGGESTIONS FOR USING DIVISION-CLASSIFICATION IN AN ESSAY

The following suggestions will be helpful whether you use division-classification as a dominant or supportive pattern of development.

1. **Select the principle of division-classification that focuses the essay.** If your general purpose indicates the logic of using division-classification, you need to identify the principle of division-classification that will guide the paper. It's important to keep in mind that most subjects can be divided or classified any number of ways. An essay discussing the student senate on campus could be organized according to a number of different principles of division: the role of each senate officer; the growing dissatisfaction with students involved in campus government; the function of each senate committee; a plan for getting more students involved in the senate. The principle of division selected would depend on your purpose for writing the essay. Similarly, a paper on contemporary music groups could be classified according to various principles: the different ages that the groups appeal to (pre-teens, adolescents, people in their twenties); the various kinds of music played by the groups (hard rock, mainstream rock, jazz); the kinds of influence earlier musicians had on the contemporary groups. Again, your purpose for writing would determine which principle of classification you choose.

Essays may use more than one principle of division as they unfold. Consider the essay on student government. If you wanted to write a paper about the senate's lack of credibility, you might start by discussing pervasive dissatisfaction with many of the students involved in the senate (one principle of division). This point could be developed by focusing on disappointment with the following: students' meager qualifications for office; students' dubious campaign tactics; students' questionable actions once elected to the senate. Near the end, the paper might move to a second principle of division as it outlined a plan to get more students involved in campus government: editorials in the campus newspaper; announcements on the college radio station; articles in the college opinion magazine.

When writing an essay that uses classification as its primary method of development, you generally need to be careful about changing the principle of classification that focuses the paper. Imagine that you decided to write an essay showing that the success of contemporary music groups has less to do with musical talent than with the groups' ability to market themselves to a distinct segment of the listening audience. To develop your point, you might categorize several groups according to the age group they appeal to most, and then analyze the marketing strategies the groups use to gain the support of their fans. The logic of the essay would be undermined if you switched to another principle of classification — lets say, the influence of earlier groups of today's music scene. In others words, most papers developed through classification generally revolve around a single principle.

The principle of division-classification selected must meet one stringent requirement: it must lead to a point that has some significance. Suppose you want to write a paper explaining why you think several episodes of a new situation comedy are destined to become classics. As you organize the material generated during the prewriting stage, you conclude that an analysis based on division-classification would be the best way to explain why these episodes have such enduring quality. You settle upon a principle of classification: you decide to write about the characters in the shows according to the frequency with which they appear. Your categories include main characters (appearing in every show), supporting characters (appearing in most shows), and guests stars (appearing once or twice). You discuss each of the categories in detail, naming the characters and describing the parts they play. But is this principle of classification significant? Has it anything to do with why the shows will become classics? No, it hasn't. Such an essay would be little more than a meaningless exercise in classifying things just to classify them.

By way of contrast, a significant principle of classification might involve looking at a number of shows and categorizing them according to the distinct styles of comedy presented or the easily recognized human types portrayed. You might decide, for example, to write about the last principle and develop your point by showing how the selected episodes focus on the Pompous Know-It-All, the Boss Who's Out of Control, the Lovable Grouch, the Surprisingly Savvy Innocent.

2. Apply the principle of division-classification logically. In an essay using division-classification, you need to demonstrate to your readers that your analysis is the result of careful thought. This means, first of all, that your division-classification should be as *complete* as possible. Your analysis should include — within reason — all the parts into which you can divide your subject or all the types into which you categorize your subjects. Let's say you are writing an essay showing that where college students live is an important factor in determining how satisfied they are with college life. Keeping your purpose in mind, you classify students according to where they live: with parents, in dorms, in fraternity and sorority houses. But what about all the students who live in rented apartments, houses, or rooms off campus? If these places of residence are ignored, your classification will not be complete; you will lose credibility with your readers because they will probably realize that you have overlooked several important considerations.

Your division-classification should also be *consistent*, meaning that the parts into which you break your subject or the groups into which you place your subjects should be as mutually exclusive as possible; the parts or categories should not be mixed, nor should they overlap. Assume you are writing an essay describing the animals at the zoo in a nearby city. You decide to describe the zoo's mammals, reptiles, birds, and endangered species. But such a classification is inconsistent. You began by categorizing the animals according to scientific class (mammals, birds, reptiles), then switched to another principle when you classified some animals according to whether or not they are endangered. Because you drifted over to a different principle of classification, your categories are no longer mutually exclusive: endangered species could overlap with any of the other categories. In which section of the paper, for instance, would you describe an exotic parrot that is obviously a bird but is also nearly extinct? And how would you categorize the zoo's rare mountain gorilla? This impressive creature is a mammal, but it is also an endangered species. Such overlapping categories undercut the logic that gives an essay its integrity.

A helpful tip: a solid outline is invaluable when you write papers using division-classification. The outline encourages you to do the rigorous thinking needed to arrive at divisions and classifications that are logical, complete, and consistent.

3. Prepare an effective thesis. If your essay uses division-classification as its dominant method of development, it might be helpful to prepare a thesis that does more than signal the subject of the paper and suggest your attitude toward that general subject. You may want the thesis to state the principle of division-classification at the heart of the essay; you may also want it to express your view about the part or category you regard as most important. Consider the two thesis statements below:

As the observant beachcomber moves from the tidal area, to the upper beach, to the sandy dunes, rich variations in marine life become apparent.

Although most people focus on the dangers associated with the disposal of toxic waste in the land and ocean, the incineration of toxic matter may pose an even more serious threat to human life.

The first thesis statement makes clear that the writer will organize the paper by classifying the varieties of marine life according to the principle of location. The shore life being described could have been classified according to another principle — seasonal differences in the marine life found at the beach, for example. But the thesis indicates that location will be the focus of the paper. Since the purpose of the essay is to inform as objectively as possible, the thesis does not suggest the writer's opinion about which category is most significant.

The second thesis signals that the essay will evolve by dividing the issue of toxic waste according to the method of disposal. Another principle of division could have been used to focus the subject of toxic waste — for instance, local, state, and federal legislation needed to protect workers involved in the disposal of toxins. But the thesis indicates that the organizing principle of this essay will be the method of disposal. Moreover, because the paper takes an unusual stance on an already controversial subject, the thesis is worded in such a way that it reveals the writer's view about which aspect of the topic is most important. Such a clear statement of the writer's position is an effective strategy in an essay of this kind.

The thesis statements in papers developed primarily through division-classification do not have to be as structured as the two examples above. As long as the thesis indicates the subject of the

essay and implies your attitude toward the subject, you have prepared an effective thesis. If the paper is well written, the principle of
division-classification focusing the paper will become apparent as
the essay unfolds. Similarly, if you have an opinion about which
part or category is most significant, that viewpoint will emerge as
the essay develops.

4. Organize the paper logically.   You probably noticed that the
thesis statements on the previous page signal each paper's organizational plan. The first essay, for instance, would use specific facts,
examples, and details to describe the kinds of marine life in each of
the following areas: first, in the tidal area; next, in the upper beach;
finally, in the dunes.

Whether your paper has a structured thesis or is developed
wholly or in part by division-classification, the essay should always
have a logical structure. Within reason, you should try to discuss
comparable points in each subsection of the paper. For example, in
the essay on seashore life, you might describe life in the tidal area by
discussing the mollusks, crustaceans, birds, and amphibians that
live or feed there. You would then follow through, as much as
possible, with this arrangement in the other sections of the paper
(upper beach and dune). Forgetting to describe the birdlife thriv-
ing in the dunes, especially when you had discussed birdlife in the
tidal and upper-beach areas, would compromise the structure of
the paper. Of course, perfect parallelism is not always possible—
there are no mollusks in the dunes, for instance. But striving for
this sort of consistency gives the essay a solid integrity. Connecting
signals also link the various parts of the paper, making it come
together as an integrated whole ("Another characteristic of marine
life battered by the tides . . . "; "A final important trait of both
tidal and upper-beach crustaceans is . . . "; "Unlike the creatures
of the tidal area and the upper beach, the dune animals are . . . ").
Such cues make clear the connections among the ideas in the essay.

**5. State any conclusions or recommendations in the final sec-
tion of the paper.**   The analytic thinking that occurs during division-classification often leads to interesting conclusions or recommendations. A paper might categorize different kinds of coaches,

from unforgettably inspiring to incredibly incompetent, making the point that athletes learn a great deal about human relations simply by having to get along with their coaches — regardless of the coaches' skills. Such a paper might conclude that participating in a team sport teaches more about human nature than several courses in psychology. Or the essay might end with a proposal: new recruits and seasoned team members should be paired so that incoming players can get advice on dealing with coaching eccentricities. In either case, the final section of the paper is the logical spot for such conclusions or recommendations.

As products of Western culture, we consider order and exactness to be virtues, finding satisfaction in the process of dividing and classifying. Does our urge to divide and classify make us intolerant of that which cannot be pigeonholed? Do we lose sight of the whole by focusing on types and parts? Some cultures and philosophers believe we do and criticize our mania for dissecting and segregating. Yet dividing and classifying can be a way to understand the whole. Our achievements in science and technology are based on such analytic thinking. We use division-classification to understand everything from plants to animals, from the geologic history of earth to the mysteries of human evolution. Division-classification can, in short, be a powerful strategy for making sense of the complexities around us.

STUDENT ESSAY AND COMMENTARY

The following student essay was written by Gail Oremland in response to this assignment:

> In "Making Medical Mistakes," David Hilfiker discusses the kinds of errors made by a professional — in this case, a family physician. Choose another profession or distinct group of people and discuss the types of mistakes that can occur. Your analysis, which may be serious or humorous, should imply your attitude toward the people making the errors.

While reading the paper, try to determine how effectively it applies the principles concerning the use of division-classification. The commentary following the paper will help you look at Gail's essay more closely.

The Truth About College Teachers

A recent TV news story told about a group of college professors 1 from a nearby university who were hired by a local school system to help upgrade the teaching in the community's public schools. The professors were to visit classrooms, analyze teachers' skills, and then conduct workshops to help the teachers become more effective at their jobs. But after the first round of workshops, the superintendent of schools decided to cancel the whole project. He fired the learned professors and sent them packing back to their ivory tower. Why did the project fall apart? There was a simple reason. The college professors, who were supposedly going to show the public school teachers how to be more effective, were themselves poor teachers. Many college students could have predicted such a disastrous outcome. They know, firsthand, that college teachers are strange. They know that professors often exhibit bizarre behaviors, relating to students in ways that make it difficult for students to stay awake, or--if awake--to learn.

One type of professor assumes, legitimately enough, that her 2 function is to pass on to students the vast store of knowledge she has acquired. But because the "Knowledgeable One" regards herself as an expert and her students as the ignorant masses, she adopts an elitist approach that sabotages learning. The Knowledgeable One enters a lecture hall with a self-important air, walks to the podium, places her yellowed-with-age notes on the stand, and begins her lecture at the exact second the class is officially scheduled to begin. There can be a blizzard or hurricane raging outside the lecture hall; students can be running through freezing sleet and howling winds to get to class on time. Will the Knowledgeable One wait for them to arrive before beginning her lecture? Probably not. The Knowledgeable One's time is precious. She's there, set to begin, and that's what matters.

Once the monologue begins, the Knowledgeable One drones on 3 and on. The Knowledgeable One is a fact person. She may be the history prof who knows the death toll of every Civil War battle, the biology prof who can diagram all the common biological molecules, the accounting prof who enumerates every clause of the federal tax form. Oblivious to students' glazed eyes and stifled yawns, the

Knowledgeable One delivers her monologue, dispensing one dry fact after another. The only advantage to being on the receiving end of this boring monologue is that students do not have to worry about being called on to question a point or provide an opinion; the Knowledgeable One is not willing to relinquish one minute of her time by giving students a voice. Assume for one improbable moment that a student actually manages to stay awake during the monologue and is brave enough to ask a question. In such a case, the Knowledgeable One will address the questioning student as "Mr." or "Miss." This formality does not, as some students mistakenly suppose, indicate respect for the student as a fledgling member of the academic community. Not at all. This impersonality represents the Knowledgeable One's desire to keep as wide a distance as possible between her and her students.

The Knowledgeable One's monologue always comes to a close at   4
the precise second the class is scheduled to end. No sooner has she delivered her last forgettable word than the Knowledgeable One packs up her notes and shoots out the door, heading back to the privacy of her office where she can pursue her specialized academic interests--free of any possible interruption from students. The Knowledgeable One's hasty departure from the lecture hall makes it clear she has no desire to talk with students. In her eyes, she has met her obligations; she has taken time away from her research to transmit to students what she knows. Any closer contact might mean she would risk contagion from students, that great unwashed mass. Such a danger is to be avoided at all costs.

Unlike the Knowledgeable One, the "Leader of Intellectual Dis-   5
cussion" seems to respect students. Emphasizing class discussion, the Leader encourages students to confront ideas ("What is Twain's view of morality?" "Was our intervention in Vietnam justified?" "Should big business be given tax breaks?") and discover their own truths. Then about three weeks into the semester, it becomes clear that the Leader wants students to discover <u>his</u> version of the truth. Behind the Leader's democratic guise lurks a dictator. When a student voices an opinion which the Leader accepts, the student is rewarded by hearty nods of approval and "Good point, good point." But if a student is rash enough to advance a conflicting viewpoint, the Leader responds with killing politeness: "Well, yes, that's an interesting perspective. But don't you think that . . . ?" Grade-conscious students soon learn not to chime in with their viewpoint. They know that when the Leader, with seeming honesty, says, "I'd be interested in hearing what you think. Let's open this up for discussion," they had better figure out what the Leader wants to hear before advancing

their own theories. "Me-tooism" rather than independent thinking, they discover, guarantees good grades in the Leader's class.

Then there is the professor who comes across as the students' "Buddy." This kind of professor does not see himself as an imparter of knowledge or a leader of discussion but as a pal, just one in a community of equals. The Buddy may start his course this way: "All of us know that this college stuff--grades, degrees, exams, required reading--is a game. So let's not play it, OK?" Dressed in jeans, sweatshirt, and scuffed sneakers, the Buddy projects a relaxed, casual attitude. He arranges the class seats in a circle (he would never take a position in front of the room) and insists that students call him by his first name. He uses no syllabus and gives few tests, believing that such constraints keep students from directing their own learning. A free spirit, the Buddy often teaches courses like "The Psychology of Interpersonal Relations" or "The Social Dynamics of the Family." If students choose to use class time to discuss the course material, that's fine. If they want to discuss something else, that's fine, too. It's the self-expression, the honest dialogue, that counts. In fact, the Buddy seems especially fond of digressions from academic subjects. By talking about his political views, his marital problems, his tendency to drink one too many beers, the Buddy lets students see that he is a regular guy--just like them. At first, students look forward to classes with the Buddy. They enjoy the informality, the chitchat, the lack of pressure. But after a while, they wonder why they are paying for a course where they learn nothing. They might as well stay home and watch the soaps.

Obviously, some college professors are excellent. They are learned, hardworking, and imaginative; they enjoy their work and like being with students. On the whole, though, college professors are a strange lot. Despite their advanced degrees and their own exposure to many different kinds of teachers, they do not seem to understand how to relate to students. Rather than being hired as consultants to help others upgrade their teaching skills, college professors should themselves hire consultants to tell them what they are doing wrong and how they can improve. Who should these consultants be? That's easy: the people who know them best--their students.

After years of being graded by teachers, Gail took special pleasure in writing an essay that gave her a chance to evaluate her teachers — in this case, her college professors. Even her title, "The Truth About College Professors," implies that Gail is going to have fun knocking profs down from their ivory towers. To introduce her subject, she uses a timely news story. This brief anecdote leads directly to the essay's *thesis*: " . . . professors often exhibit bizarre behaviors, relating to students in ways that make it difficult for students to stay awake, or — if awake — to learn." You will note that Gail's thesis is not highly structured; it does not, for example, name the specific categories to be discussed. Still, the thesis suggests that the essay is going to *categorize* a range of teaching behaviors, using as a *principle of classification* the strange ways that college profs relate to students.

As with all papers developed through division-classification, Gail's essay does not use classification as an end in itself. Gail uses classification because it helps her achieve a broader *purpose*. She wants to *convince* readers — without moralizing or abandoning her humorous tone — that such teaching styles inhibit learning. In other words, there's a serious underside to her essay. This additional layer of meaning is characteristic of satiric writing.

The body of the essay, consisting of five paragraphs, presents the three categories that make up Gail's analysis. In Gail's view, college teachers can be categorized as the Knowledgeable One (paragraphs 2, 3, 4), the Leader of Intellectual Discussion (5), or the Buddy (6). Obviously, there are other ways teaching styles might be classified, but given Gail's purpose, audience, and lightly satiric tone, her categories are appropriate; they are reasonably *complete*, *consistent*, and *mutually exclusive*.

To make it easy for the reader to follow the progression of her analysis, Gail uses *topic sentences* to introduce the three kinds of professors: "But because the 'Knowledgeable One' regards herself as an expert and her students as the ignorant masses, she adopts an elitist approach that sabotages learning" (2); "Unlike the Knowledgeable One, the 'Leader of Intellectual Discussion' seems to respect students" (5); and "Then there is the professor who comes across as the students' 'Buddy.' This kind of professor does not see himself as an imparter of knowledge or a leader of discussion but as a pal . . . " (6).

When reading the essay, you probably were aware that Gail is able to shift smoothly and easily from one category to the next. How does she achieve such a graceful transition? Take a moment to reread the topic sentences that introduce her second and third categories. Look at the way the beginning of each sentence (in italics) links back to the preceding category or categories: *"Unlike the Knowledgeable One,* the 'Leader of Intellectual Discussion' seems to respect students" and the Buddy *"does not see himself as an imparter of knowledge or a leader of discussion* but as a pal. . . . "

Gail is equally careful about providing clear *organizational cues* within each section. For instance, she uses a chronological sequence to organize her three-paragraph discussion of the Knowledgeable One. The first paragraph deals with the beginning of the Knowledgeable One's lecture; the second paragraph, with the lecture itself; and the third paragraph, with the end of the lecture. In turn, topic sentences ("Once the monologue begins, the Knowledgeable One drones on and on" and "The Knowledgeable One's monologue always comes to a close at the precise second the class is scheduled to end") signal this passage of time. Similarly, *transitions* are used in the paragraphs on the Leader of Intellectual Discussion and the Buddy to insure a logical progression of points: *"Then* about three weeks into the semester, it becomes clear that the Leader wants students to discover his version of the truth" (5) and *"At first* students look forward to classes with the Buddy . . . But *after a while*, they wonder why they are paying for a course where they learn nothing" (6).

In addition to such organizational strategies, the essay's unity can also be traced to Gail's skill in sustaining the satiric mood of the piece. Throughout the essay, she selects details that fit her gently mocking attitude. The paragraph about the Knowledgeable One describes a teacher who lectures from "yellowed-with-age notes . . . oblivious to students' glazed eyes and stifled yawns," unwilling to wait for students who "run . . . through freezing sleet and howling winds to get to class on time." And Gail's tongue-in-cheek description of the Leader of Intellectual Discussion focuses on the way this second special breed of teacher sounds: "Good point, good point. . . . Well, yes, that's an interesting perspective. But don't you think that . . . ?" Finally, the Buddy, dressed in "jeans, sweatshirt, and scuffed sneakers," is portrayed with similar killing accuracy. It's interesting to note that Gail's satiric depiction of her three professional types depends on many of the techniques associated with *narrative* and *descriptive writing*: she uses vigorous images, highly connotative language, and dialogue.

Although Gail's essay is unified and organized, you may have felt that the first category is out of proportion to the other two. There is, of course, no need to balance the length of the categories exactly. But Gail's extended treatment of the first category sets up an expectation that the others will be treated as fully. One way to remedy this problem is to delete some material from the discussion of the Knowledgeable One. Gail might, for instance, omit the first five sentences in the third paragraph (about the professor who addresses students as Mr. or Miss). Such a change could be made without taking the bite out of her portrayal. Even better, Gail could simply switch the order of her paragraphs, putting the portrait of the Knowledgeable One at the end of the essay. If this section were placed at the end, the extended discussion would not seem out of proportion. Rather, it would look as though Gail has used *emphatic order* to sequence her categories, saving for last the category she had most to say about.

It's apparent that an essay as engaging as Gail's must have undergone a good deal of editing. That was in fact the case. Gail made many changes in the body of the essay, but it is particularly interesting to review what happened to the introduction as she revised the paper. Reprinted below is the original introduction Gail prepared.

Unrevised Version
Despite their high IQs, advanced degrees, and published papers, some college professors just don't know how to teach. Found in almost any department, in tenured and untenured positions, they prompt student apathy. They fail to convey ideas effectively and to challenge or inspire students. Students thus finish their courses having learned very little. Contrary to popular opinion, these professors' ineptitude is not simply a matter of delivering boring lectures or not caring about students. Many of them care a great deal. Their failure actually stems from their unrealistic perceptions of what a teacher should be. Specifically, they adopt teaching styles or roles that alienate students and undermine learning. Three of the most common ones are "The Knowledgeable One," "The Leader of Intellectual Discussion," and "The Buddy."

When Gail showed the first draft of the essay to her composition instructor, he laughed — and occasionally squirmed — when reading what she had prepared. On the whole, he was enthusiastic about the paper but felt that there was a problem with the tone of the introductory paragraph. It was too serious when compared to the playful and lightly satiric mood in the rest of the essay. When Gail reread the paragraph, she agreed with her instructor but was uncertain about the best way to remedy the problem. After making some changes in other parts of the essay, she decided to let the paper sit for a while before going back to rewrite the introduction. In the meantime, Gail wanted some time to relax, so she switched on the TV. The timing couldn't have been better; she had tuned into a news story about some learned professors who had been fired from a consulting job because they had proven to be such poor teachers. This was exactly the kind of item Gail needed to start her essay. Now she was able to prepare a completely new introduction, making it consistent in spirit with the rest of the paper.

Once the essay's opening had been reworked, Gail realized she should revise her conclusion so that it would reflect the changes made in the introduction. With the new introduction in mind, she decided to use the conclusion to recall the story about the fired consultants. By echoing the anecdote in the introduction, Gail was able to end the paper with a wonderful jibe at professors. The revised conclusion also gave Gail a chance to hint at a longed-for role reversal between students and teachers, with students — finally — having the upper hand. This was a perfect way for Gail to close her clever and insightful essay.

The selections in this chapter show how division and classification can be used to explore a variety of subjects. In "In Depth, but Shallowly," Dave Barry analyzes the components of a local news program — from smiling anchorperson to ghastly accident footage. William Zinsser describes the various kinds of "College Pressures" that students typically encounter, while David Hilfiker, in "Making Medical Mistakes," confesses to the types of errors he has committed as a doctor. Classifying "Propaganda Techniques in Today's Advertising" is the method Ann McClintock uses to demonstrate how pervasive and effective such techniques can be. And in "Individual and Group Identity," Desmond Morris organizes territorial zones into types to dramatize their subtle yet important influence on human behavior.

Dave Barry

A 1969 graduate of Haverford College, Dave Barry writes a syndicated humor column for the Miami Herald. *His droll observations about the ludicrous side of life appear in many newspapers across the country. Barry's books of collected essays and satires include* Babies and Other Hazards of Sex, The Taming of the Screw, *and* Stay Fit and Healthy Until You're Dead. *The following piece is from his 1985 book,* Bad Habits.

In Depth, but Shallowly

Local news once imitated the national networks: sober accounts of important events read by a distinguished male with a sonorous voice — local versions of Walter Cronkite or Eric Sevareid. Then, sometime in the mid-'70s, happy-talk news took over the local stations. Friendly, attractive newscasters traded wisecracks and reported photographable disasters and fluffy human-interest stories. In the following selection, Dave Barry skewers happy-talk news with needle-sharp wit. Beneath the humor lie some unpleasant messages about the numbing effects of televised news.

If you want to take your mind off the troubles of the real world, you should watch local TV news shows. I know of no better way to escape reality, except perhaps heavy drinking.

Local TV news programs have given a whole new definition to the word *news*. To most people, *news* means *information about events that affect a lot of people.* On local TV news shows, *news* means *anything that you can take a picture of, especially if a local TV News Personality can stand in front of it.* This is why they are so fond of car accidents, burning buildings, and crowds: these are good for standing in front of. On the other hand, local TV news shows tend to avoid stories about things that local TV News Personalities cannot stand in front of, such as budgets and taxes and the economy. If you want to get a local TV news show to do a story on the budget, your best bet is to involve it in a car crash.

I travel around the country a lot, and as far as I can tell, 3 virtually all local TV news shows follow the same format. First you hear some exciting music, the kind you hear in space movies, while the screen shows local TV News Personalities standing in front of various News Events. Then you hear the announcer:

Announcer: From the On-the-Spot Action Eyewitness News Stu- 4
dios, this is the On-the-Spot Action Eyewitness
News, featuring Anchorman Wilson Westbrook,
Co-Anchorperson Stella Snape, Minority-Group
Member James Edwards, Genial Sports Personality
Jim Johnson, Humorous Weatherperson Dr. Reed
Stevens, and Norm Perkins on drums. And now,
here's Wilson Westbrook.

Westbrook: Good evening. Tonight from the On-the-Spot Ac- 5
tion Eyewitness News Studios we have actual color
film of a burning building, actual color film of two
cars after they ran into each other, actual color film of
the front of a building in which one person shot
another person, actual color film of another burning
building, and special reports on roller-skating and
child abuse. But for the big story tonight, we go to
City Hall, where On-the-Spot reporter Reese Kernel
is standing live.

Kernel: I am standing here live in front of City Hall being 6
televised by the On-the-Spot Action Eyewitness
News minicam with Mayor Bryce Hallbread.

Mayor: That's "Hallwood." 7

Kernel: What? 8

Mayor: My name is "Hallwood." You said "Hallbread." 9

Kernel: Look, Hallbread, do you want to be on the news or 10
don't you?

Mayor: Yes, of course, it's just that my name is — 11

Kernel: Listen, this is the top-rated news show in the three- 12
county area, and if you think I have time to memorize
every stupid detail, you'd better think again.

Mayor: I'm sorry. "Hallbread" is fine, really. 13

Kernel: Thank you, Mayor Hallbread. And now back to Wil- 14 son Westbrook in the On-the-Spot Action Eyewitness News Studios.

Westbrook: Thank you, Reese; keep us posted if anything further 15 develops on that important story. And now, as I promised earlier, we have actual color film of various objects that either burned or crashed, which we will project on the screen behind me while I talk about them. Here is a building on fire. Here is another building on fire. Here is a car crash. This film was shot years ago, but you can safely assume that objects just like these crashed or burned in the three-county area today. And now we go to my Co-Anchorperson, Stella Snape, for a Special Report on her exhaustive three-week investigation into the problem of child abuse in the three-county area. Well, Stella, what did you find?

Snape: Wilson, I found that child abuse is very sad. What 16 happens is that people abuse children. It's just awful. Here you see some actual color film of me standing in front of a house. Most of your child abuse occurs in houses. Note that I am wearing subdued colors.

Westbrook (reading from a script): Are any efforts under way here in 17 the three-county area to combat child abuse?

Snape: Yes. 18

Westbrook: Thank you, Stella, for that informative report. On the 19 lighter side, On-the-Spot Action Eyewitness Reporter Terri Tompkins has prepared a three-part series on roller-skating in the three-county area.

Tompkins: Roller-skating has become a major craze in California 20 and the three-county area, as you can see by this actual color film of me on roller skates outside the On-the-Spot Action Eyewitness News Studio. This certainly is a fun craze. Tomorrow, in Part Two of this series, we'll see actual color film of me falling down. On Wednesday we'll see me getting up.

Westbrook: We'll look forward to those reports. Our next story is 21 from Minority-Group Reporter James Edwards, who, as he has for the last 324 consecutive broadcasts, spent the day in the minority-group sector of the three-county area finding out what minorities think.

Edwards:	Wilson, I'm standing in front of a crowd of minority-group members, and as you can see, their mood is troubled. *(The crowd smiles and waves at the camera.)*	22
Westbrook:	Good report, James. Well, we certainly had a sunny day here in the three-county area, didn't we, Humorous Weatherperson Dr. Reed Stevens?	23
Stevens:	Ha ha. We sure did, though I'm certainly troubled by that very troubling report Stella did on child abuse. But we should see continued warm weather through Wednesday. Here are a bunch of charts showing the relative humidity and stuff like that. Ha ha.	24
Westbrook:	Ha ha. Well, things weren't nearly as bright on the sports scene, were they, Genial Sports Personality Jim Johnson?	25
Johnson:	No, Wilson, they certainly weren't. The Three-County Community College Cutlasses lost their fourth consecutive game today. Here you see actual color footage of me watching the game from the sidelines. The disgust is evident on my face. I intended to have actual color film of me interviewing the coach after the game, but the team bus crashed and everyone was killed.	26
Westbrook:	Thank you, Jim. And now, here is Basil Holp, the General Manager of KUSP-TV, to present an Editorial Viewpoint:	27
Holp:	The management of KUSP-TV firmly believes that something ought to be done about earthquakes. From time to time we read in the papers that an earthquake has hit some wretched little country and knocked houses down and killed people. This should not be allowed to continue. Maybe we should have a tax or something. What the heck, we can afford it. The management of KUSP-TV is rolling in money.	28
Announcer:	The preceding was the opinion of the management of KUSP-TV. People with opposing points of view are probably in the vast majority.	29
Westbrook:	Well, that wraps up tonight's version of the On-the-Spot Action Eyewitness News. Tune in tomorrow to see essentially the same stories.	30

Questions for Close Reading

1. What is the thesis of the selection? Locate the sentence(s) in which Barry states his main idea. If he does not state the thesis explicitly, express it in your own words.
2. According to Barry, what are the typical "news personality" types on a local TV news show? Why does Barry include the drummer in his list?
3. What kinds of news items are most likely to receive coverage on local news shows? What news items don't fit in well with the formats of local news?
4. What are the subjects of the two special reports on the news show Barry describes? What information is provided in these segments?

Questions about the Writer's Craft

1. In this satiric piece, Barry uses division to identify the typical elements making up the format of a local TV news program. How does Barry's presentation of a scene from each division help him achieve his purpose? What needed changes are implied by this spoof?
2. Most of this essay is an imaginary local news show. How does this fictional show script help Barry make his point? Is the script more effective than an analytic critique of a news show?
3. Barry suggests that watching the local news is as good a way to escape reality as heavy drinking. What is the effect of putting this comparison at the start of the essay? How does it affect your expectations of what is to follow?
4. Why does Barry have the news staff repeat such phrases as "actual color film"? What do you think he means to say about local news by using these repetitions? Find other examples of repeated phrases.

Questions for Further Thought

1. The title of Barry's essay, "In Depth, but Shallowly," is a paradox, that is, a statement that seems to contradict itself. How can local news be both "in depth" and "shallow"? Why do you think Barry chose this title?
2. Besides making us laugh, Barry's essay identifies several flaws he finds in most local newscasts. What other things does he find wrong with local news shows?
3. "Happy talk" local news shows are often the highest rated newscasts in their marketing area. Do you think the public really wants chatty, fun news shows? Why do people watch such shows?
4. Do you think the national news shows are more serious and thought-

provoking than local news shows, or are they just as "shallowly in depth" in their own way? If so, how can one become better informed about the world we live in?

Writing Assignments Using Division-Classification as a Method of Development

1. Analyze a top TV show to reveal what makes it popular. Identify the elements that make the show so appealing: believable acting, audience identification, interesting themes, expensive or unusual sets or costumes, and so on. Use the division-classification format to develop your analysis of the show's popularity.
2. Select a type of TV show, other than local news, and give it "the Barry treatment." That is, write an essay using division-classification to analyze the types of people usually found in this kind of show. Develop the analysis by creating a humorous script for these stereotypical characters. You might choose daytime or nighttime soaps, doctor shows, magazine shows, or whatever type seems to you most worthy of such satire.

Writing Assignments Using Other Methods of Development

3. Watch one TV news program, preferably local, and jot down all the stories covered. Then compare this list with the local newspaper. Write an essay comparing and contrasting the two media in terms of stories covered, importance given to stories, depth of coverage, and so on. Use the analysis to make a judgment about the way news is treated by the two media.
4. Argue against Barry's essay, using the thesis that local news does an effective job providing the public with what it wants. You might consider the point that people do not turn to local news for insightful coverage of national and international stories. Instead, they look to local news for updates on what is happening in their immediate community. Provide a series of strong examples to support your argument. The essay should make clear how you feel about the expectations people have for local television.

William Zinsser

William Zinsser has written news journalism, drama criticism, magazine columns, and several books on American culture. Born in 1922 in New York, Zinsser attended Princeton University and worked for the New York Herald Tribune, Life, *and* Look. *In 1970, Zinsser designed a course in nonfiction writing for Yale University; from his teaching experience at Yale came his popular guide,* On Writing Well *(1976). His other books include* The City Dwellers *(1962),* Pop Goes America *(1966),* The Lunacy Boom *(1970), and* Writing with a Word Processor *(1982). The following essay first appeared in the magazine* Country Journal *in 1979.*

College Pressures

Campuses today are flooded with business majors and budding computer scientists. Many students' primary goal is to go where the money is — to transform themselves into marketable commodities who will, by the age of thirty, have luxurious homes, expensive cars, and profitable investment portfolios. William Zinsser sympathizes with the pressures that cause students' obsession with material success, yet he doubts that such a single-minded concern with a lucrative career is the surest route to happiness.

Dear Carlos: I desperately need a dean's excuse for my chem midterm which will begin in about 1 hour. All I can say is that I totally blew it this week. I've fallen incredibly, inconceivably behind.

Carlos: Help! I'm anxious to hear from you. I'll be in my room and won't leave it until I hear from you. Tomorrow is the last day for . . .

Carlos: I left town because I started bugging out again. I stayed up all night to finish a take-home make-up exam & am typing it to hand in on the 10th. It was due on the 5th. P.S. I'm going to the dentist. Pain is pretty bad.

Carlos: Probably by Friday I'll be able to get back to my studies. Right now I'm going to take a long walk. This whole thing has taken a lot out of me.

Carlos: I'm really up the proverbial creek. The problem is I really *bombed* the history final. Since I need that course for my major I . . .

Carlos: Here follows a tale of woe. I went home this weekend, had to help my Mom, & caught a fever so didn't have much time to study. My professor . . .

Carlos: Aargh! Trouble. Nothing original but everything's piling up at once. To be brief, my job interview . . .

Hey Carlos, good news! I've got mononucleosis.

Who are these wretched supplicants, scribbling notes so laden with anxiety, seeking such miracles of postponement and balm? They are men and women who belong to Branford College, one of the twelve residential colleges at Yale University, and the messages are just a few of the hundreds that they left for their dean, Carlos Hortas — often slipped under his door at 4 A.M. — last year. 1

But students like the ones who wrote those notes can also be found on campuses from coast to coast — especially in New England and at many other private colleges across the country that have high academic standards and highly motivated students. Nobody could doubt that the notes are real. In their urgency and their gallows humor they are authentic voices of a generation that is panicky to succeed. 2

My own connection with the message writers is that I am master of Branford College. I live in its Gothic quadrangle and know the students well. (We have 485 of them.) I am privy to their hopes and fears — and also to their stereo music and their piercing 3 cries in the dead of night ("Does anybody *ca-a-are?*"). If they went to Carlos to ask how to get through tomorrow, they come to me to ask how to get through the rest of their lives.

Mainly I try to remind them that the road ahead is a long one 4 and that it will have more unexpected turns than they think. There will be plenty of time to change jobs, change careers, change whole attitudes and approaches. They don't want to hear such liberating news. They want a map — right now — that they can follow unswervingly to career security, financial security, Social Security and, presumably, a prepaid grave.

What I wish for all students is some release from the clammy 5 grip of the future. I wish them a chance to savor each segment of their education as an experience in itself and not as a grim preparation for the next step. I wish them the right to experiment, to trip and fall, to learn that defeat is as instructive as victory and is not the end of the world.

My wish, of course, is naïve. One of the few rights that America 6 does not proclaim is the right to fail. Achievement is the national god, venerated in our media — the million-dollar athlete, the wealthy executive — and glorified in our praise of possessions. In the presence of such a potent state religion, the young are growing up old.

I see four kinds of pressure working on college students today: 7 economic pressure, parental pressure, peer pressure, and self-induced pressure. It is easy to look around for villains — to blame the colleges for charging too much money, the professors for assigning too much work, the parents for pushing their children too far, the students for driving themselves too hard. But there are no villains; only victims.

"In the late 1960s," one dean told me, "the typical question 8 that I got from students was 'Why is there so much suffering in the world?' or 'How can I make a contribution?' Today it's 'Do you think it would look better for getting into law school if I did a double major in history and political science, or just majored in one of them?'" Many other deans confirmed this pattern. One said: "They're trying to find an edge — the intangible something that will look better on paper if two students are about equal."

Note the emphasis on looking better. The transcript has be- 9 come a sacred document, the passport to security. How one appears on paper is more important than how one appears in person. *A* is for Admirable and *B* is for Borderline, even though, in Yale's official system of grading, *A* means "excellent" and *B* means "very good." Today, looking very good is no longer good enough, especially for students who hope to go on to law school or medical school. They know that entrance into the better schools will be an entrance into the better law firms and better medical practices where they will make a lot of money. They also know that the odds are harsh. Yale Law School, for instance, matriculates 170 students from an applicant pool of 3,700; Harvard enrolls 550 from a pool of 7,000.

It's all very well for those of us who write letters of recommen- 10
dation for our students to stress the qualities of humanity that will make them good lawyers or doctors. And it's nice to think that admission officers are really reading our letters and looking for the extra dimension of commitment or concern. Still, it would be hard for a student not to visualize these officers shuffling so many transcripts studded with *A*s that they regard a *B* as positively shameful.

The pressure is almost as heavy on students who just want to 11
graduate and get a job. Long gone are the days of the "gentleman's *C*," when students journeyed through college with a certain relaxation, sampling a wide variety of courses — music, art, philosophy, classics, anthropology, poetry, religion — that would send them out as liberally educated men and women. If I were an employer I would rather employ graduates who have this range and curiosity than those who narrowly pursued safe subjects and high grades. I know countless students whose inquiring minds exhilarate me. I like to hear the play of their ideas. I don't know if they are getting *A*s or *C*s, and I don't care. I also like them as people. The country needs them, and they will find satisfying jobs. I tell them to relax. They can't.

Nor can I blame them. They live in a brutal economy. Tuition, 12
room, and board at most private colleges now comes to at least $7,000, not counting books and fees. This might seem to suggest that the colleges are getting rich. But they are equally battered by inflation. Tuition covers only 60 percent of what it costs to educate a student, and ordinarily the remainder comes from what colleges receive in endowments, grants, and gifts. Now the remainder keeps being swallowed by the cruel costs — higher every year — of just opening the doors. Heating oil is up. Insurance is up. Postage is up.

Health-premium costs are up. Everything is up. Deficits are up. We are witnessing in America the creation of a brotherhood of paupers — colleges, parents, and students, joined by the common bond of debt.

Today it is not unusual for a student, even if he works part time 13 at college and full time during the summer, to accrue $5,000 in loans after four years — loans that he must start to repay within one year after graduation. Exhorted at commencement to go forth into the world, he is already behind as he goes forth. How could he not feel under pressure throughout college to prepare for this day of reckoning? I have used "he," incidentally, only for brevity. Women at Yale are under no less pressure to justify their expensive education to themselves, their parents, and society. In fact, they are probably under more pressure. For although they leave college superbly equipped to bring fresh leadership to traditionally male jobs, society hasn't yet caught up with this fact.

Along with economic pressure goes parental pressure. Inevita- 14 bly, the two are deeply intertwined.

I see many students taking pre-medical courses with joyless 15 tenacity. They go off to their labs as if they were going to the dentist. It saddens me because I know them in other corners of their life as cheerful people.

"Do you want to go to medical school?" I ask them. 16

"I guess so," they say, without conviction, or "Not really." 17

"Then why are you going?" 18

"Well, my parents want me to be a doctor. They're paying all 19 this money and . . . "

Poor students, poor parents. They are caught in one of the 20 oldest webs of love and duty and guilt. The parents mean well; they are trying to steer their sons and daughters toward a secure future. But the sons and daughters want to major in history or classics or philosophy — subjects with no "practical" value. Where's the payoff on the humanities? It's not easy to persuade such loving parents that the humanities do indeed pay off. The intellectual faculties developed by studying subjects like history and classics — an ability to synthesize and relate, to weigh cause and effect, to see events in perspective — are just the faculties that make creative leaders in business or almost any general field. Still, many fathers would rather put their money on courses that point toward a specific profession — courses that are pre-law, pre-medical, pre-business, or, as I sometimes heard it put, "pre-rich."

But the pressure on students is severe. They are truly torn. One 21
part of them feels obligated to fulfill their parents' expectations;
after all, their parents are older and presumably wiser. Another part
tells them that the expectations that are right for their parents are
not right for them.

I know a student who wants to be an artist. She is very ob- 22
viously an artist and will be a good one — she has already had
several modest local exhibits. Meanwhile she is growing as a well-
rounded person and taking humanistic subjects that will enrich the
inner resources out of which her art will grow. But her father is
strongly opposed. He thinks that an artist is a "dumb" thing to be.
The student vacillates and tries to please everybody. She keeps up
with her art somewhat furtively and takes some of the "dumb"
courses her father wants her to take — at least they are dumb
courses for her. She is a free spirit on a campus of tense students —
no small achievement in itself — and she deserves to follow her
muse.

Peer pressure and self-induced pressure are also intertwined, 23
and they begin almost at the beginning of freshman year.

"I had a freshman student I'll call Linda," one dean told me, 24
"who came in and said she was under terrible pressure because her
roommate, Barbara, was much brighter and studied all the time. I
couldn't tell her that Barbara had come in two hours earlier to say
the same thing about Linda."

The story is almost funny — except that it's not. It's sympto- 25
matic of all the pressures put together. When every student thinks
every other student is working harder and doing better, the only
solution is to study harder still. I see students going off to the
library every night after dinner and coming back when it closes at
midnight. I wish they would sometimes forget about their peers
and go to a movie. I hear the clacking of typewriters in the hours
before dawn. I see the tension in their eyes when exams are approaching and papers are due: *Will I get everything done?*"

Probably they won't. They will get sick. They will get 26
"blocked." They will sleep. They will oversleep. They will bug out.
Hey Carlos, help!

Part of the problem is that they do more than they are expected 27 to do. A professor will assign five-page papers. Several students will start writing ten-page papers to impress him. Then more students will write ten-page papers, and a few will raise the ante to fifteen. Pity the poor student who is still just doing the assignment.

Once you have twenty or thirty percent of the student popula- 28 tion deliberately overexerting," one dean points out, "it's bad for everybody. When a teacher gets more and more effort from his class, the student who is doing normal work can be perceived as not doing well. The tactic works, psychologically."

Why can't the professor just cut back and not accept longer 29 papers? He can, and he probably will. But by then the term will be half over and the damage done. Grade fever is highly contagious and not easily reversed. Besides, the professor's main concern is with his course. He knows his students only in relation to the course and doesn't know that they are also overexerting in their other courses. Nor is it really his business. He didn't sign up for dealing with the student as a whole person and with all the emotional baggage the student brought along from home. That's what deans, masters, chaplains, and psychiatrists are for.

To some extent this is nothing new: a certain number of pro- 30 fessors have always been self-contained islands of scholarship and shyness, more comfortable with books than with people. But the new pauperism has widened the gap still further, for professors who actually like to spend time with students don't have as much time to spend. They also are overexerting. If they are young, they are busy trying to publish in order not to perish, hanging by their finger nails onto a shrinking profession. If they are old and tenured, they are buried under the duties of administering departments — as departmental chairmen or members of committees — that have been thinned out by the budgetary axe.

Ultimately it will be the students' own business to break the 31 circles in which they are trapped. They are too young to be prisoners of their parents' dreams and their classmates' fears. They must be jolted into believing in themselves as unique men and women who have the power to shape their own future.

"Violence is being done to the undergraduate experience," 32 says Carlos Hortas. "College should be open-ended: at the end it should open many, many roads. Instead, students are choosing their goal in advance, and their choices narrow as they go along. It's

almost as if they think that the country has been codified in the type
of jobs that exist — that they've got to fit into certain slots. Therefore, fit into the best-paying slot.

"They ought to take chances. Not taking chances will lead to a   33
life of colorless mediocrity. They'll be comfortable. But something
in the spirit will be missing."

I have painted too drab a portrait of today's students, making   34
them seem a solemn lot. That is only half of their story; if they were
so dreary I wouldn't so thoroughly enjoy their company. The other
half is that they are easy to like. They are quick to laugh and to offer
friendship. They are not introverts. They are unusually kind and are
more considerate of one another than any student generation I
have known.

Nor are they so obsessed with their studies that they avoid   35
sports and extracurricular activities. On the contrary, they juggle
their crowded hours to play on a variety of teams, perform with
musical and dramatic groups, and write for campus publications.
But this in turn is one more cause of anxiety. There are too many
choices. Academically, they have 1,300 courses to select from;
outside class they have to decide how much spare time they can
spare and how to spend it.

This means that they engage in fewer extracurricular pursuits   36
than their predecessors did. If they want to row on the crew and
play in the symphony they will eliminate one; in the '60s they
would have done both. They also tend to choose activities that are
self-limiting. Drama, for instance, is flourishing in all twelve of
Yale's residential colleges as it never has before. Students hurl
themselves into these productions — as actors, directors, carpenters, and technicians — with a dedication to create the best possible
play, knowing that the day will come when the run will end and
they can get back to their studies.

They also can't afford to be the willing slave of organizations   37
like the *Yale Daily News*. Last spring at the one-hundredth anniver-
sary banquet of that paper — whose past chairmen include such
once and future kings as Potter Stewart, Kingman Brewster, and
William F. Buckley, Jr. — much was made of the fact that the editorial staff used to be small and totally committed and that "newsies"
routinely worked fifty hours a week. In effect they belonged to a
club; Newsies is how they defined themselves at Yale. Today's
student will write one or two articles a week, when he can, and he

defines himself as a student. I've never heard the word Newsie
except at the banquet.

 If I have described the modern undergraduate primarily as a   38
driven creature who is largely ignoring the blithe spirit inside who
keeps trying to come out and play, it's because that's where the
crunch is, not only at Yale but throughout American education.
It's why I think we should all be worried about the values that are
nurturing a generation so fearful of risk and so goal-obsessed at
such an early age.

 I tell students that there is no one "right" way to get ahead—   39
that each of them is a different person, starting from a different
point and bound for a different destination. I tell them that change
is a tonic and that all the slots are not codified nor the frontiers
closed. One of my ways of telling them is to invite men and women
who have achieved success outside the academic world to come and
talk informally with my students during the year. They are heads of
companies or ad agencies, editors of magazines, politicians, public
officials, television magnates, labor leaders, business executives,
Broadway producers, artists, writers, economists, photographers,
scientists, historians—a mixed bag of achievers.

 I ask them to say a few words about how they got started. The   40
students assume that they started in their present profession and
knew all along that it was what they wanted to do. Luckily for me,
most of them got into their field by a circuitous route, to their
surprise, after many detours. The students are startled. They can
hardly conceive of a career that was not pre-planned. They can
hardly imagine allowing the hand of God or chance to nudge them
down some unforeseen trail.

Questions for Close Reading

1. What is the thesis of the selection? Locate the sentence(s) in which
   Zinsser states his main idea. If he does not state the thesis explicitly,
   express it in your own words.
2. According to Zinsser, why are the pressures on college students today
   so harmful?
3. Zinsser says that some of the pressures are "intertwined." What does he
   mean? Give examples from the essay.

4. What actions or attitudes on the part of students can help free them from these pressures?
5. Refer to your dictionary as needed to define the following words used in the selection: *privy* (paragraph 3), *venerated* (6), *exhorted* (13), *tenacity* (15), *vacillates* (22), *furtively* (22), and *circuitous* (40).

Questions about the Writer's Craft

1. When analyzing a subject, writers usually try to identify divisions and classifications that are—within reason—mutually exclusive. But Zinsser acknowledges that the four pressures he discusses can be seen as two distinct pairs, with each pair consisting of two "deeply intertwined" pressures. How does this overlapping of categories help Zinsser make his point?
2. In addition to using classification in this essay, what other mode of development does Zinsser use?
3. Why did the author use the notes to Carlos as his introduction? What profile of college students do you get from these notes?
4. In paragraph 4, the author writes that students want a map "they can follow unswervingly to career security, financial security, Social Security and, presumably, a prepaid grave." What tone is Zinsser using here? Where else does he uses this tone?

Questions for Further Thought

1. Zinsser is a college professor at Yale. Do you think he is well qualified to advise students about career choices? Do you think he knows enough about the real world to advise students to "relax" and take a wide range of courses, instead of focusing on a practical "pre-rich" major?
2. Is it possible to both major in something "safe" and practical, and take electives to become liberally educated? Is is desirable?
3. Zinsser states that today's students "engage in fewer extracurricular pursuits than their predecessors." Do you agree that students are focusing more on their majors? Are extracurricular activities at your college suffering low membership and lack of interest?
4. What does the author mean by saying that "One of the few rights that America does not proclaim is the right to fail"? Do you agree that students should take more risks? If so, what kinds of risks should they take?

Writing Assignments Using Division-Classification as a Method of Development

1. Zinsser writes as if all students are the same—panicky, overwrought, and materialistic. Take a position counter to his and write an essay

explaining that campuses contain many students different from those Zinsser writes about. To support your point, categorize students into types, giving examples of what each type is like. Be sure that the categories you identify refute Zinsser's analysis of the typical student body.

2. Is economic security the only kind of satisfaction that students should pursue? Write an essay classifying the various kinds of satisfactions that students could aim for. At the end of the paper, include brief recommendations about ways students could best spend their time preparing for these different kinds of satisfactions.

Writing Assignments Using Other Methods of Development

3. Using Zinsser's analysis of the pressures on college students, write an essay explaining how these pressures can be reduced or eliminated. Give practical suggestions as to how students can avoid or get around the pressures. Also, indicate what society, parents, and college staff can do to help ease the situation.

4. Zinsser's essay indicates that today's students are "slotting" themselves into preordained careers and not leaving themselves open to later opportunities that may present themselves. Write an essay arguing that this inclination to specialize is either beneficial or disastrous for students. Consider such issues as individual freedom, career confusion, changing job markets, changes in society, and the like.

David Hilfiker

Dr. David Hilfiker (1945–) spent his childhood years in Buffalo, New York, graduated from Yale University, then earned his medical degree from the University of Minnesota Medical School. He now works in two Washington, D.C. clinics caring for disadvantaged patients. In Healing Wounds: A Physician Looks at His Work *(1985), Hilfiker reveals the pressures, doubts, and anxieties endured by the ordinary family doctor. The following excerpt is taken from this book.*

Making Medical Mistakes

We want our doctors to be human: sympathetic and generous-spirited. We also want them to be godlike: all-knowing and infallible. But physicians do make mistakes, no matter how much we — and they — don't like to recognize this fact. In this selection, Hilfiker confesses that he has made several errors in medical judgment. By breaking the usual code of silence, Hilfiker explores what society can do to ease the burden of perfection imposed on doctors.

A warm July morning. I finish my rounds at our small country 1 hospital around nine o'clock and walk across the parking lot to the clinic. I am a primary-care practitioner, a family doctor; my partners and I work together in a small office building. After greeting the receptionist, I look through the list of my day's appointments and notice that Barb Daily will be in for her first prenatal examination. "Wonderful," I think, recalling the joy of helping her deliver her first child two years ago. Barb and her husband, Russ, had been friends of mine before Heather was born, but we grew much closer with the shared experience of her birth. In a rural family practice such as mine, much of every workday is taken up with disease; I look forward to the prenatal visit with Barb, to the continuing relationship with her over the next months, to the prospect of birth.

At her appointment that afternoon, Barb seems to be in good   2
health, with all the signs and symptoms of pregnancy: slight nausea, some soreness in her breasts, a little weight gain. But when the
nurse tests Barb's urine to determine if she is pregnant, the result is
negative. The test measures the level of a hormone that is produced
by a woman and shows up in her urine when she is pregnant. But
occasionally it fails to detect the low levels of the hormone during
early pregnancy. I reassure Barb that she is fine and schedule another test for the following week.

Barb leaves a urine sample at the clinic a week later, but the test   3
is negative again. I am troubled. Perhaps she isn't pregnant. Her
missed menstrual period and her other symptoms could be a result
of a minor hormonal imbalance. Maybe the embryo has died within
the uterus and a miscarriage is soon to take place. I could find out
by ordering an ultrasound examination. This procedure would
give me a "picture" of the uterus and of the embryo. But Barb
would have to go to Duluth, 110 miles from our village in northern
Minnesota, for the examination. The procedure is also expensive. I
know the Dailys well enough to know they have a modest income.
Besides, by waiting a few weeks, I should be able to find out for sure
without the ultrasound: Either the urine test will be positive or
Barb will have a miscarriage. I call her and tell her about the negative test result, about the possibility of a miscarriage, and about the
necessity of seeing me again if she misses her next menstrual period.

I work in a summer resort area, and it is, as usual, a hectic   4
summer; I think no more about Barb's troubling state until a
month later, when she returns to my office. Nothing has changed:
still no menstrual period, still no miscarriage. She is confused and
upset. "I feel so pregnant," she tells me. I am bothered, too. Her
uterus, upon examination, is slightly enlarged, as it was on the
previous visit. But it hasn't grown any larger. Her urine test remains negative. I can think of several possible explanations for her
condition, including a hormonal imbalance or even a tumor. But
the most likely explanation is that she is carrying a dead embryo. I
decide it is time to break the bad news to her.

"I think you have what doctors call a 'missed abortion,'" I tell   5
her. "You were probably pregnant, but the baby appears to have
died some weeks ago, before your first examination. Unfortunately, you didn't have a miscarriage to get rid of the dead tissue

from the baby and the placenta. If a miscarriage doesn't occur within a few weeks, I'd recommend a re-examination, another pregnancy test, and, if nothing shows up, a dilation and curettage procedure to clean out the uterus."

Barb is disappointed; there are tears. She is college educated, 6
and she understands the scientific and technical aspects of her situation; but that doesn't alleviate the sorrow. We talk at some length and make an appointment for two weeks later.

When Barb returns, Russ is with her. Still no menstrual period; 7
still no miscarriage; still another negative pregnancy test, the fourth. I explain to them what has happened. The dead embryo must be removed or there could be serious complications. Barb could become sterile. The conversation is emotionally difficult for all three of us. We schedule the dilation and curettage for later in the week.

Friday morning, Barb is wheeled into the operating room of 8
the sixteen-bed county hospital. Barb, the nurses, and I all know one another — small-town life. The atmosphere is warm and re-laxed; we chat before the operation. After Barb is anesthetized, I examine her pelvis again. Her muscles are now completely relaxed, and it is possible to perform a more reliable examination. Her uterus feels bigger than it did two days previously; it is perhaps the size of a small grapefruit. But since all the pregnancy tests were negative and I'm so sure of the diagnosis, I ignore the information from my fingertips and begin the operation.

Dilation and curettage, or D & C, is a relatively simple surgical 9
procedure performed thousands of times each day in this country. First, the cervix is stretched by pushing smooth metal rods of in-creasing diameter in and out of it. After about five minutes of this, the cervix has expanded enough so that a curette can be inserted through it into the uterus. The curette is another metal rod, at the end of which is an oval ring about an inch at its widest diameter. It is used to scrape the walls of the uterus. The operation is done completely by feel after the cervix has been stretched, since it is still too narrow to see through.

Things do not go easily this morning. There is considerably 10
more blood than usual, and it is only with great difficulty that I am able to extract anything. What should take ten or fifteen minutes stretches out into a half-hour. The body parts I remove are much

larger than I expected, considering when the embryo died. They are not bits of decomposing tissue. These are parts of a body that was recently alive!

I do my best to suppress my rising panic and try to complete 11 the procedure. Working blindly, I am unable to evacuate the uterus completely; I can feel more parts inside but cannot remove them. Finally I stop, telling myself that the uterus will expel the rest within a few days.

Russ is waiting outside the operating room. I tell him that 12 Barb is fine but that there were some problems with the operation. Since I don't completely understand what happened, I can't be very helpful in answering his questions. I promise to return to the hospital later in the day after Barb has awakened from the anesthesia.

In between seeing other patients that morning I place several 13 almost frantic phone calls, trying to piece together what happened. Despite reasurances from a pathologist that it is "impossible" for a pregnant woman to have four consecutive negative pregnancy tests, the realization is growing that I have aborted Barb's living child. I won't know for sure until the pathologist has examined the fetal parts and determined the baby's age and the cause of death. In a daze, I walk over to the hospital and tell Russ and Barb as much as I know for sure without letting them know all I suspect. I tell them that more tissue may be expelled. I can't face my own suspicions.

Two days later, on Sunday morning, I receive a tearful call 14 from Barb. She has just passed some recognizable body parts; what is she to do? She tells me that the bleeding has stopped and that she now feels better. The abortion I began on Friday is apparently over. I set up an appointment to meet with her and Russ to review the entire situation.

The pathologist's report confirms my worst fears: I aborted a 15 living fetus. It was about eleven weeks old. I can find no one who can explain why Barb had four negative pregnancy tests. My meeting with Barb and Russ later in the week is one of the hardest things I have ever been through. I describe in some detail what I did and what my rationale had been. Nothing can obscure the hard reality: I killed their baby.

Politely, almost meekly, Russ asks whether the ultrasound 16 examination would have shown that Barb was carrying a live baby. It almost seems that he is trying to protect my feelings, trying to absolve me of some of the responsibility. "Yes," I answer, "if I had ordered the ultrasound, we would have known the baby was alive." I cannot explain why I didn't recommend it.

Mistakes are an inevitable part of everyone's life. They happen; 17
they hurt — ourselves and others. They demonstrate our fallibility. Shown our mistakes and forgiven them, we can grow, perhaps in some small way become better people. Mistakes, understood this way, are a process, a way we connect with one another and with our deepest selves.

But mistakes seem different for doctors. This has to do with 18
the very nature of our work. A mistake in the intensive care unit, in the emergency room, in the surgery suite, or at the sickbed is different from a mistake on the dock or at the typewriter. A doctor's miscalculation or oversight can prolong an illness, or cause a permanent disability, or kill a patient. Few other mistakes are more costly.

Developments in modern medicine have provided doctors 19
with more knowledge of the human body, more accurate methods of diagnosis, more sophisticated technology to help in examining and monitoring the sick. All of that means more power to intervene in the disease process. But modern medicine — with its invasive tests and potentially lethal drugs — has also given doctors the power to do more harm.

Yet precisely because of its technological wonders and near- 20
miraculous drugs, modern medicine has created for the physician an expectation of perfection. The technology seems so exact that error becomes almost unthinkable. We are not prepared for our mistakes and we don't know how to cope with them when they occur.

Doctors are not alone in harboring expectations of perfection. 21
Patients expect doctors to be perfect, too. Perhaps patients have to consider their doctors less prone to error than other people: How else can a sick or injured person, already afraid, come to trust the doctor? Further, modern medicine has taken much of the treatment of illness out of the realm of common sense; a patient must trust a physician to make decisions that he, the patient, only vaguely understands. But the degree of perfection expected by patients is no doubt also a result of what we doctors have come to

believe about ourselves, or, better, have tried to convince ourselves about ourselves.

This perfection is a grand illusion, of course, a game of mirrors   22
that everyone plays. Doctors hide their mistakes from patients, from other doctors, even from themselves. Open discussion of mistakes is banished from the consultation room, from the operating room, from physicians' meetings. Mistakes become gossip, and are spoken of openly only in court.

Unable to admit our mistakes, we physicians are cut off from   23
healing. We cannot ask for forgiveness, and we get none. We are thwarted, stunted; we do not grow.

During the days, and weeks, and months after I aborted Barb's   24
baby, my guilt and anger grew. I did discuss what had happened with my partners, with the pathologist, with obstetric specialists. Some of my mistakes were obvious: I had relied too heavily on one test; I had not been skillful in determining the size of the uterus by pelvic examination; I should have ordered the ultrasound before proceeding to the D & C. There was no way I could justify what I had done. To make matters worse, there were complications following the D & C, and Barb was unable to become pregnant again for two years.

Although I was as honest with the Dailys as I could be, and   25
although I told them everything they wanted to know, I never shared with them my own agony. I felt they had enough sorrow without having to bear my burden as well. I decided it was my responsibility to deal with my guilt alone. I never asked for their forgiveness.

When I began at the age of thirty to practice medicine, I was   26
certainly not prepared for the reality of my mistakes or my emotional responses to them. Like many other physicians, I had entered medical school out of a deep desire to serve people and to relieve suffering. I chose to practice in a remote rural area because it desperately needed physicians, because it seemed to offer the opportunity to establish a practice with the kind of personal care I wanted to provide, and because it seemed to be a good place for me and my family to live.

Along with three other doctors also committed to personal   27
medical care, I practiced for seven years in that small Minnesota town. Marja and I raised our family, entered into the life of our

community, and tried to live out our dreams. Finally, however, I could no longer tolerate the stresses, and I chose to leave. Dealing with my mistakes was among the stresses.

Doctors' mistakes come in a variety of packages and stem from   28
a variety of causes. For primary-care practitioners, who see every kind of problem, from cold sores to cancer, the mistakes are often simply a result of not knowing enough. One evening during my years in Minnesota a local boy was brought into the emergency room after a drunken driver had knocked him off his bicycle. I examined him right away. Aside from swelling and bruising of the left leg and foot, he seemed fine. An X-ray showed what appeared to be a discoloration of the foot from the ankle. I consulted by telephone with an orthopedic specialist in Duluth, and we decided that I could operate on the boy. As was my usual practice, I offered the patient and his mother a choice: I could do the operation or they could travel to Duluth to see the specialist. My pride was hurt when she decided to take her son to Duluth.

My feelings changed considerably when the specialist called   29
the next morning to thank me for the referral. He reported that the boy had actually suffered an unusual muscle injury, a posterior compartment syndrome, which had twisted his foot and caused it to appear to be dislocated. I had never even heard of such a syndrome, much less seen or treated it. The boy had required immediate surgery to save the muscles of his lower leg. Had his mother not decided to take him to Duluth, he would have been permanently disabled.

Sometimes a lack of technical skill leads to a mistake. After I   30
had been in town a few years, the doctor who had done most of the surgery at the clinic left to teach at a medical school. Since the clinic was more than a hundred miles from the nearest surgical center, my partners and I decided that I should get some additional training in order to be able to perform emergency surgery. One of my first cases was a young man with appendicitis. The surgery proceeded smoothly enough, but the patient did not recover as quickly as he should have, and his hemoglobin level (a measure of the amount of blood in the system) dropped slowly. I referred him to a surgeon in Duluth, who, during a second operation, found a significant amount of old blood in his abdomen. Apparently I had left a small

blood vessel leaking into the abdominal cavity. Perhaps I hadn't noticed the oozing blood during surgery; perhaps it had begun to leak only after I had finished. Although the young man was never in serious danger, although the blood vessel would probably have sealed itself without the second surgery, my mistake had caused considerable discomfort and added expense.

Often, I am sure, mistakes are a result of simple carelessness. 31 There was the young girl I treated for what I thought was a minor ankle injury. After looking at her X-rays, I sent her home with what I diagnosed as a sprain. A radiologist did a routine follow-up review of the X-rays and sent me a report. I failed to read it carefully and did not notice that her ankle had been broken. I learned about my mistake five years later when I was summoned to a court hearing. The fracture I had missed had not healed properly, and the patient had required extensive treatment and difficult surgery. By that time I couldn't even remember her original visit and had to piece together what had happened from my records.

Some mistakes are purely technical; most involve a failure of 32 judgment. Perhaps the worst kind involve what another physician has described to me as a "failure of will." She was referring to those situations in which a doctor knows the right thing to do but doesn't do it because he is distracted, or pressured, or exhausted.

Several years ago I was rushing down the hall of the hospital to 33 the delivery room. A young woman stopped me. Her mother had been having chest pains all night. Should she be brought to the emergency room? I knew the mother well, had examined her the previous week, and knew of her recurring bouts of chest pains. She suffered from angina; I presumed she was having another attack.

Some part of me knew that anyone with all-night chest pains 34 should be seen right away. But I was under pressure. The delivery would make me an hour late to the office, and I was frayed from a weekend on call, spent mostly in the emergency room. This new demand would mean additional pressure. "No," I said, "take her over to the office, and I'll see her as soon as I'm done here." About twenty minutes later, as I was finishing the delivery, the clinic nurse rushed into the room. Her face was pale. "Come quick!" she told me. "Mrs. Helgeson just collapsed." I sprinted the hundred yards to the office, where I found Mrs. Helgeson in cardiac arrest. Like many doctors' offices at the time, ours did not have the advanced life-support equipment that helps keep patients alive long enough to get them to a hospital. Despite everything we did, Mrs. Helgeson died.

Would she have survived if I had agreed to see her in the   35
emergency room, where the requisite staff and equipment were available? No one will ever know for sure. But I have to live with the possibility that she might not have died if I had not had a "failure of will." There was no way to rationalize: I had been irresponsible, and a patient had died.

Many situations do not lend themselves to a simple determina-   36
tion of whether a mistake has been made. Seriously ill, hospitalized patients, for instance, require of doctors almost continuous decision-making. Although in most cases no single mistake is obvious, there always seem to be things that could have been done differently or better: administering more of this medication, starting that treatment a little sooner . . . The fact is that when a patient dies, the physician is left wondering whether the care he provided was adequate. There is no way to be certain, for it is impossible to determine what would have happened if things had been done differently. In the end, the physician has to suppress the guilt and move on to the next patient.

Maiya Martinen first came to see me halfway through her   37
pregnancy. I did not know her or her husband well, but I knew that they were solid, hard-working people. This was to be their first child. When I examined Maiya, it seemed to me that the fetus was unusually small, and I was uncertain about her due date. I sent her to Duluth for an ultrasound examination and an evaluation by an obstetrician. The obstetrician thought the baby would be small, but he thought it could be safely delivered in the local hospital.

Maiya's labor was quite uneventful, except it took her longer   38
than usual to push the baby through to delivery. Her baby boy was born blue and floppy, but he responded well to routine newborn resuscitation measures. Fifteen minutes after birth, however, he had a short seizure. We checked his blood-sugar level and found it to be low, a common cause of seizures in small babies who take longer than usual to emerge from the birth canal. We immediately administered intravenous glucose, and baby Marko seemed to improve. He and his mother were discharged from the hospital several days later.

It was about two months later, a few days after I had given him   39 his first set of immunizations, that Marko began having short spells. Not long after that he started to have full-blown seizures. Once again the Martinens made the trip to Duluth, and Marko was hospitalized for three days of tests. No cause for the seizures was found, and he was placed on medication. Marko continued to have seizures, however. When he returned for his second set of immunizations, it was clear to me that he was not doing well.

The remainder of Marko's short life was a tribute to the faith 40
and courage of his parents. He was severely retarded, and the seizures became harder and harder to control. Maiya eventually went east for a few months so Marko could be treated at the National Institutes of Health. But nothing seemed to help, and Maiya and her baby returned home. Marko had to be admitted frequently to the local hospital in order to control his seizures. At two o'clock one morning I was called to the hospital; the baby had had a respiratory arrest. Despite our efforts, Marko died, ending a year and a half struggle with life.

No cause for Marko's condition was ever determined. Did 41
something happen during the birth that briefly cut off oxygen to his brain? Should Maiya have delivered at the high-risk obstetric center in Duluth, where sophisticated fetal monitoring is available? Should I have sent Marko to the neonatal intensive care unit in Duluth immediately after his first seizure in the delivery room? I subsequently learned that children who have seizures should not routinely be immunized. Would it have made any difference if I had never given Marko the shots? There were many such questions in my mind and, I am sure, in the minds of the Martinens. There was no way to know the answers, no way for me to handle the guilt I experienced, perhaps irrationally, whenever I saw Maiya.

The emotional consequences of mistakes are difficult enough 42
to handle. But soon after I started practicing I realized I had to face another anxiety as well: It is not only in the emergency room, the operating room, the intensive care unit, or the delivery room that I can blunder into tragedy. Medicine is not an exact science; errors are always possible, even in the midst of the humdrum routine of daily care. Was that baby I just sent home with a diagnosis of mild viral fever actually in the early stage of serious meningitis? Will that nine-year-old with stomach cramps whose mother I just lectured about psychosomatic illness end up in the hospital tomorrow with a ruptured appendix? Did that Vietnamese refugee have a problem

I didn't understand because of the language barrier? A doctor has to confront the possibility of a mistake with every patient visit.

My initial response to the mistakes I did make was to question   43
my competence. Perhaps I just didn't have the necessary intelligence, judgment, and discipline to be a physician. But was I really incompetent? My University of Minnesota Medical School class had voted me one of the two "best clinicians." My diploma from the National Board of Medical Examiners showed scores well above average. I knew that the townspeople considered me a good physician; I knew that my partners, with whom I worked daily, and the consultants to whom I referred patients considered me a good physician, too. When I looked at it objectively, my competence was not the issue. I would have to learn to live with my mistakes.

A physician is even less prepared to deal with his mistakes than   44
is the average person. Nothing in our training prepares us to respond appropriately to the mistakes we will inevitably make. Medical school is a competitive place, discouraging any sharing of feelings. And resident doctors are typically so overburdened with work that there is literally no time to reflect. An atmosphere of precision pervades the teaching hospital; there is little opportunity to confront the emotional consequences of making mistakes.

Physicians in private practice are no more likely to find errors   45
openly acknowledged or discussed, even though they occur regularly. My own mistakes represent only some of those of which I am aware. I know of one physician who administered a potent drug in a dose ten times that recommended; his patient almost died. Another doctor examined a child in an emergency room late one night and told the parents the problem was only a mild viral infection. Only because the parents did not believe the doctor, only because they consulted another doctor the following morning, did the child survive a life-threatening infection. Still another physician killed a patient while administering a routine test: a needle slipped and lacerated a vital artery. Whether the physician is a rural general practitioner with years of experience but only basic training or a recently graduated, highly trained neurosurgeon working in a sophisticated technological environment, the basic problem is the same.

Because doctors do not discuss their mistakes, I do not know   46
how other physicians come to terms with theirs. But I suspect that

many cannot bear to face their mistakes directly. We either deny the misfortune altogether or blame the patient, the nurse, the laboratory, other physicians, the System, Fate — anything to avoid our own guilt.

The medical profession seems to have no place for its mistakes.   47
Indeed, one would almost think that mistakes were sins. If the medical profession has no room for doctors' mistakes, neither does society. The number of malpractice suits filed each year is symptomatic of this. In what other profession are practitioners regularly sued for hundreds of thousands of dollars because of misjudgments? I am sure the Dailys could have successfully sued me for a large amount of money had they chosen to do so.

The drastic consequences of our mistakes, the repeated oppor-   48
tunities to make them, the uncertainty about our culpability, and the professional denial that mistakes happen all work together to create an intolerable dilemma for the physician. We see the horror of our mistakes, yet we cannot deal with their enormous emotional impact.

Perhaps the only way to face our guilt is through confession,   49
restitution, and absolution. Yet within the structure of modern medicine there is no place for such spiritual healing. Although the emotionally mature physician may be able to give the patient or family a full description of what happened, the technical details are often so difficult for the layperson to understand that the nature of the mistake is hidden. If an error is clearly described, it is frequently presented as "natural," "understandable," or "unavoidable" (which, indeed, it often is). But there is seldom a real confession: "This is the mistake I made; I'm sorry." How can one say that to a grieving parent? to a woman who has lost her mother?

If confession is difficult, what are we to say about restitution?   50
The very nature of a physician's work means that there are things that cannot be restored in any meaningful way.

What can I do to make good the Dailys' loss? . . .   51

Questions for Close Reading

1. What is the thesis of the selection? Locate the sentence(s) in which Hilfiker states his main idea. If he does not state the thesis explicitly, express it in your own words.

2. What led Hilfiker to believe that Mrs. Daily was no longer pregnant? Why didn't he order an ultrasound test?
3. What does the author mean by a mistake caused by a "failure of will"? Why is this the worst kind of mistake?
4. What was Hilfiker's reaction to his own medical errors? How does the medical profession in general deal with the issue of diagnostic and treatment mistakes?
5. Refer to your dictionary as needed to define the following words in the selection: *alleviate* (paragraph 6), *rationale* (15), *thwarted* (23), *angina* (33), *rationalize* (35), *culpability* (48), and *absolution* (49).

Questions about the Writer's Craft

1. How does the author classify the typical mistakes of doctors? What is the principle of classification that he uses to establish these categories?
2. Why does Hilfiker begin with a narrative? What tone does it set for the rest of the essay? What image of the author does it create in your mind?
3. In addition to division and classification, what other modes of development does the author use?
4. Locate places where Hilfiker uses questions. What is the effect of these questions? Are they merely rhetorical, or are they questions with answers?

Questions for Further Thought

1. If you had been Mr. or Mrs. Daily, would you have sued Dr. Hilfiker for his mistake? Why or why not? Is legal action a solution to errors in medicine?
2. The author writes, " . . . mistakes seem different for doctors." Is this true? How should doctors deal with their mistakes?
3. Why does Hilfiker reveal so many of his own mistakes — and such serious ones? Does this essay serve a personal purpose for him, as well as act as a place for him to communicate his message about how all doctors make mistakes?
4. "Mistakes . . . are a process, a way we connect with one another and with our deepest selves." What do you think Hilfiker means by this statement? How do we in our everyday lives come to terms with mistakes we make?

Writing Assignments Using Division-Classification as a Method of Development

1. Hilfiker writes, "Mistakes are an inevitable part of everyone's life." Using Hilfiker's statement as your point of departure, write a paper

that classifies three or four typical kinds of mistakes all of us tend to make. So that you prepare an essay unified by a common theme, make sure your categories are based on the same principle of classification. You might, for instance, use as a principle of classification the kinds of errors you think many parents make relating to their teenage children: they are overly critical; they are suspicious; they are insensitive. Your essay may be serious or light. In either case, the paper should indicate clearly your attitude toward the mistakes described.

2. Classify the types of stress experienced by people in a particular occupation. This occupation may be one you know about through friends, relatives, your reading, or your own experience. For example, an essay on waitressing might discuss the stresses of close supervision, physical exertion, and customers' demands. Develop your essay by providing examples of the kinds of incidents that cause these stresses. End the essay with some recommendations about ways to ease the stresses you have identified.

Writing Assignments Using Other Methods of Development

3. Physicians are high-status professionals in this country. In other countries, such as Russia, this is not so — there physicians are more like technicians and are not highly paid. Write an essay arguing that the high status and pay of physicians in the United States is or is not a good thing for American health care.

4. Research the training involved in becoming a doctor in the United States. You'll probably narrow your research to a particular kind of physician: a family practice doctor, a cardiologist, a pediatrician, and so on. Write an essay explaining the process involved in becoming a doctor. The concluding section of your paper should evaluate this process and explain why it is or is not adequate for producing competent, ethical, and responsible physicians.

Ann McClintock

Ann McClintock (1946–) was educated at Temple University in Philadelphia and later earned an advanced degree from the University of Pennsylvania. Currently Director of Occupational Therapy at Ancora State Hospital in New Jersey, she has also worked as a freelance editor and writer. A frequent speaker before community groups, McClintock is especially interested in the effects of advertising on American life. This essay is part of a work in progress on the way propaganda techniques are used to sell products and political candidates.

Propaganda Techniques in Today's Advertising

Propaganda is not just the tool of totalitarian governments and dictators. Rather, propaganda is all around us — in the form of commercials and advertisements. The author of this selection shows how Madison Avenue uses many of the techniques typical of political propaganda to convince us that we need certain products and services. After reading the essay, you may regard in a different light the jingles, endorsements, and slogans characteristic of today's commercials.

Americans, adults and children alike, are being seduced. They are being brainwashed. And no one protests. Why? Because the seducers and the brainwashers are the advertisers we willingly invite into our homes. We are victims, content — even eager — to be victimized. We read advertisers' propaganda messages in newspapers and magazines; we watch their alluring images for hours at a time on television. We absorb their messages and images into our subconscious. We all do it — even those who claim to see through advertisers' tricks and therefore feel immune to advertising's charm. Advertisers lean heavily on propaganda to sell their products, whether the "products" are a brand of toothpaste, a candidate for office, or a particular political viewpoint.

Propaganda is a systematic effort to influence people's opin- 2
ions, to win them over to a certain view or side. Propaganda is not necessarily concerned with what is true or false, good or bad. Propagandists simply want people to believe the messages being sent. Often, propagandists will use outright lies or more subtle techniques to sway people's opinions. In a propaganda war, any tactic is considered fair.

When we hear the word "propaganda," we usually think of it 3
as some kind of foreign menace: anti-American radio programs broadcast by the Soviets or brainwashing tactics practiced on helpless G. I. prisoners-of-war. But the vast majority of us are, right this minute, targets in the advertisers' propaganda war. Every day, we are bombarded with slogans, print ads, commercials, packaging claims, billboards, trademarks, logos, and designer brands — all forms of propaganda. One study claims that each of us, during an average day, is exposed to over *five hundred* advertising claims of various types. This intensive saturation may even increase in the future, for current trends include showing ads on movie screens, shopping carts, pay-cable TV services, even public television.

What kind of propaganda techniques do advertisers use? 4
There are seven basic types:

1. *Name Calling* Name calling is a propaganda tactic in 5
which negatively-charged names are hurled against the opposing side or competitor. By using such names, propagandists try to arouse feelings of hate, fear, and mistrust in their audiences. For example, political advertisements may label opposing candidates as "losers," "fence-sitters," and "back-room politicians"; or ads may state that rival candidates are "inconsistent," "dishonest," "radical," or "warmongers." Depending on the advertiser's target market, labels such as "big government," "big business," or "the old politics" can be the epithets that damage an opponent. Ads for products may also use name calling. An American manufacturer may refer, for instance, to a "foreign car" in its commercial — not an "imported" one. The label of foreignness clearly has unpleasant connotations in many people's minds. Unlike the childhood

rhyme which states that "names can never hurt me," name calling is an effective way to damage the opposition, whether it is another car maker or a Congressional candidate.

2. *Glittering Generalities*   Using glittering generalities is the   6
opposite of name calling; in this case, advertisers surround their products with attractive—and slippery—words and phrases. They use vague terms that are difficult to define and that may have different meanings to different people: "freedom," "democratic," "all-American," "progressive," "Christian," and "justice." As you can see, many of these words also have patriotic echoes. This kind of language stirs positive feelings in people, feelings that may spill over to the product or idea being pitched. As with name calling, the emotional response may overwhelm logic. Target audiences accept the product without thinking very much about what the glittering generalities mean—or whether they even apply to that product. After all, how can anyone oppose "truth, justice, and the American way"?

The ads for politicians and political issues often use glittering   7
generalities because such "buzz words" can influence votes. For example, election slogans include high-sounding but basically empty phrases like the following:

"He cares about people." (That's nice, but is he a better candidate than his opponent?)
"Vote for progress." (What kind of progress? And is progress automatically good?)
"Vote for the future." (What kind of future?)
"If you love America, vote for Phyllis Smith." (If I don't vote for Smith, does that mean I don't love America?)
"He'll make this country great again." (What does "great" mean? Does "great" mean the same thing to others as it does to me?)

Ads for consumer goods are also sprinkled with glittering   8
generalities. Product names, for instance, are supposed to evoke good feelings: Luvs diapers, New Freedom feminine hygiene products, Joy, Futura, Home Pride, Loving Care, Almost Home, Yankee Doodles. Product slogans lean heavily on vague but comforting phrases: Kinney is "The Great American Shoe Store," General

Electric "brings good things to light," and for years, Westinghouse claimed that "progress" was their most important product. Old Grand-Dad bourbon portrays pastoral scenes labeled "The Spirit of America," and Chrysler calls the Dodge 600 "The American Dream: Built by Americans for Americans." Chevrolet used a jingle about "baseball, hot dogs, apple pie, and Chevrolet," probably the most obvious string of glittering generalities ever assembled to support a product. And it worked.

3. *Transfer* In transfer, advertisers try to improve the image 9 of a product by associating it with a symbol many people respect or admire, such as the cross, the American flag or Uncle Sam. In this way, the advertisers hope to carry over the same feelings of respect and prestige to the product. Many companies use transfer devices to identify their products: Lincoln Insurance shows a profile of the President; Continental Insurance portrays a Revolutionary War minuteman; Amtrak's logo is red, white, and blue; Liberty Mutual's corporate symbol is the Statue of Liberty; Allstate's name is cradled by a pair of protective, fatherly hands; IBM creates a friendly image by featuring a Charlie Chaplin double in its ads.

Corporations also use the transfer technique when they spon- 10 sor prestigious shows on radio and television; these shows function as symbols of dignity and class. Kraft Corporation, for instance, sponsored a "Leonard Bernstein Conducts Beethoven" concert, while Gulf Oil is the sponsor of *National Geographic* specials and Mobil supports public television's *Masterpiece Theater*. In this way, corporations can reach an educated, influential audience and, perhaps, improve their public image by associating themselves with quality programming.

Political ads, of course, practically wrap themselves in the flag. 11 Ads for a political candidate often show either the Washington Monument, a Fourth of July parade, the Stars and Stripes, a bald eagle soaring over the mountains, or a little white-steepled church on the village green. The National Anthem or "America the Beautiful" may play softly on the soundtrack. Such appeals to Americans' patriotism and love of country can surround the candidate with an aura of respectability and integrity.

4. *Testimonial* The testimonial is one of the advertisers' 12 most-loved and most-used propaganda techniques. Similar to the

transfer device, the testimonial uses the admiration people have for a celebrity to make the product shine more brightly — even though the celebrity is not an expert on the product being sold.

Print and television ads offer a nonstop parade of testimonials: 13 here's Cher for Holiday Spas; then Bruce Jenner touts orange juice; Cliff Robertson, Joan Rivers, and Burt Lancaster appear for various telephone services; Michael Jackson sings about Pepsi; American Express features a slew of well-known people with lesser-known faces who ask "Do you know me?" and then assure us that they never go anywhere without their American Express card. Testimonials can sell movies — read the movie reviewers' comments in the newspaper ads. They can sell books — see the blurbs by celebrities and critics on the backs of paperbacks.

Political candidates — as well as their ad agencies — know the 14 value of testimonials. Carroll O'Connor endorses Senator Ted Kennedy, and Robert Redford lends his star appeal to Gary Hart's campaign. Even controversial social issues are debated by celebrities. The nuclear freeze, for instance, stars Paul Newman for the pro side and Charlton Heston for the con.

As illogical as testimonials sometimes are (Michael Jackson, 15 for instance, is a Jehovah's Witness who does not drink Pepsi), they are effective propaganda. We like the *person* so much that we like the *product* too.

5. *Plain Folks*   The plain folks approach says, in effect, "Buy 16 me or vote for me. I'm just like you." Regular folks will surely like Bob Evans' Down on the Farm Country sausage or good old-fashioned Countrytime Lemonade. Some ads emphasize the idea that "we're all in this boat together." We see people making long-distance calls for just the reasons we do — to put the baby on the phone to grandma or to tell Mom we love her. And how do these folksy, warmhearted (usually saccharine) scenes affect us? They're supposed to make us feel that A T & T — the multinational corporate giant — has the same values we do. Similarly, we are introduced to the little people at Ford, the ordinary folks who work on the assembly line, not to the bigwigs in their exclusive offices. What's the purpose of such an approach? That's easy. It's to encourage us to buy a car built by these honest, hardworking "everyday Joes" who care about quality as much as we do.

Political advertisements make almost as much use of the "just 17 folks" appeal as they do of transfer devices. Candidates wear hard hats, farmers' caps, jeans, lab smocks, butchers' aprons, and T-shirts; they jog around the block and carry their own luggage through the airport. The idea is to convince voters that the candidates are real people, not wealthy lawyers and executives (as they often are) who might otherwise appear too elitist or out of touch with the common man.

6. *Card Stacking* When people say that "the cards were 18
stacked against me," they mean that they were never given a fair chance. Applied to propaganda, card stacking means that one side may suppress or distort evidence, tell half-truths, oversimplify the facts, or set up a "straw man" — a false target — to be attacked while the main issue is overlooked. Card stacking is a difficult form of propaganda both to detect and dispute. When a candidate claims that an opponent has "changed his mind five times on this important issue," we must do some research into — or already know about — the subject in order to be objective. Did the candidate, for instance, have good reasons for changing his mind? What is his side of the story? But many people do not investigate before making up their minds; instead, they are swayed by what may be one-sided or distorted evidence.

Advertisers often stack the cards in favor of the products they 19
are pushing. They may, for instance, use what are called "weasel words." These are small words that usually slip right past us, but that make the difference between reality and illusion. The weasel words are underlined in the following claims:

> "Helps control dandruff symptoms." (The audience usually
>   interprets this as stops dandruff.)
> "Most dentists surveyed recommend sugarless gum for their
>   patients who chew gum." (We hear the "most dentists"
>   and "for their patients," but we don't think about how
>   many were surveyed or whether or not the dentists first
>   recommended that the patients not chew gum at all.)
> "Sticker price $1000 lower than most comparable cars."
>   (How many is "most"? What cars does the advertiser
>   consider "comparable"?)

Advertisers also use a card stacking trick when they make an 20
unfinished claim. For example, they will say that their product has

"twice as much pain reliever." We are left with a favorable impression; we don't usually ask, "Twice as much pain reliever as what?" Or advertisers may make extremely vague claims that sound alluring on the surface, but that have no substance: Toyota's "Oh, what a feeling!"; Vantage cigarette's "the taste of success"; "the spirit of Marlboro"; "the real thing"; "the right stuff," for example. Another way to stack the cards in favor of a certain product is to use scientific-sounding claims that are not supported by sound research. Ford, for example, claimed that the LTD model was "400% quieter." Consumers believed that the car was quieter than all other cars but, when taken to court, Ford admitted they meant that it was 400% quieter inside the car than outside. Other scientific-sounding claims use mysterious ingredients that are never explained as selling points: "Retsyn," "special whitening ingredients," "the ingredient doctors recommend," "cleaning agents."

7. Bandwagon In the bandwagon technique, advertisers 21 urge, "Everyone's doing it. Why don't you?" This kind of propaganda often succeeds because people have a deep desire not to be different. Political ads tell us to vote for the "winning candidate"; the advertisers know we want to do what the majority is doing; we want to be on the winning team. Or ads show a series of people proclaiming, "I'm voting for the Senator. I don't know why anyone wouldn't." Again, the audience feels under pressure to conform to what everyone else is doing.

In the marketplace, the bandwagon approach lures buyers. 22 Ads tell us that "nobody doesn't like Sara Lee" (the message is that you must be weird if you don't). They tell us that "most people prefer Brand X two-to-one over other leading brands" (to be like the majority, we should buy Brand X). If we don't drink Pepsi, we're left out of "the Pepsi generation." We are told to "join the switch to Burger King." We are even treated to a tour around the country intended to prove that most American women wear Underalls: "Come on, America! Show us your Underalls!" In other words, join the crowd and wear Underalls. Honda motorcycle ads sing to us of the virtues of being a follower and tell us to hop on the bandwagon: "Follow the leader. He's on a Honda."

Why do these propaganda techniques work? Why do we buy 23 the products, viewpoints, and candidates urged on us by propaganda messages? They work, first of all, because some of them appeal to prejudices and biases we already have. For example, if we are convinced that environmentalists are radicals who want to destroy America's record of growth and progress, then we will agree with the candidate who uses a name calling approach — "treehugger" — against an opponent. The main reason propaganda techniques work, however, is that they appeal to our emotions, not to our minds. Clear thinking requires hard work: analyzing a claim, researching the facts, examining both sides of an issue, using logic to see the flaws in an argument. Many of us would rather let the propagandists do our thinking for us. We are content to sit back and let out emotions be manipulated by others.

Because propaganda is so effective, it is important to track it   24
down and understand how it is used. We may eventually agree with what the propandist says because all propaganda isn't necessarily bad; some advertising, for instance, urges us not to drive drunk, to have regular dental checkups, to contribute to the United Way. Even so, we must be aware that propaganda is being used. Otherwise, we will have consented to handing over our independence, our decision-making ability, and our brains.

Questions for Close Reading

1. What is the thesis of the selection? Locate the sentence(s) in which McClintock states her main idea. If she does not state the thesis explicitly, express it in your own words.
2. What is propaganda? What mistaken associations do people often have with this term?
3. What are "weasel words"? How do they trick listeners?
4. Why does McClintock believe we should be better informed about propaganda techniques?
5. Refer to your dictionary as needed to define the following words in the selection: *seduced* (paragraph 1), *warmongers* (5), and *elitist* (17).

Questions about the Writer's Craft

1. Before explaining the categories into which propaganda techniques can be grouped, McClintock provides a definition of propaganda. Is the definition purely informative, or does it have a larger objective? If you think the latter, what is the definition's broader purpose?

2. In her introduction, McClintock uses loaded words like *seduced* and *brainwashed*. What effects do these words have on the reader?
3. Locate places where McClintock uses questions. Which ones are rhetorical, and which ones are real questions?
4. What kind of conclusion does McClintock provide for the essay?

Questions for Further Thought

1. Do you agree with McClintock that not only is propaganda political, but we are subjected to commercial propaganda every day? Is *propaganda* the right term to use for today's advertising techniques?
2. Which of these advertising techniques are easiest to identify in an ad? Which are the least obvious? Can you recall examples of ads that make use of these techniques?
3. Do you suspect that advertising really influences you? Or do you think that you are relatively immune to it? What factors influence your decision to purchase a particular brand or product?
4. Since propaganda is so effective, is it ethical for advertisers and politicians to use it? Is awareness enough to protect us from the effects of such propaganda — or do we need stronger protection? What other means could we use to protect ourselves?

Writing Assignments Using Division-Classification as a Method of Development

1. Develop an essay around the point that popular TV shows can be categorized into three types. Avoid the obvious system of classifying according to game shows, sitcoms, detective shows, and so on. Instead, categorize the shows according to your own original principle of classification. For example, you could classify shows according to any one of the following: how family life is depicted; the way the world of work is presented; how male and female relationships are portrayed. Refer to specific shows to support your classification system, and be sure to make clear your attitude toward the shows being discussed.
2. McClintock cautions us to be sensitive to propaganda in advertising, but of course young children aren't capable of this kind of awareness. Watch some commercials aimed at children, such as those for toys, cereals, and fast food. Take notes, and then analyze the use of propaganda techniques in these commercials. Using division-classification, write an essay describing the main propaganda techniques you observe. Support your analysis with examples and illustrations drawn from the commercials studied. Remember to organize the categories around a thesis that signals your opinion of the advertising techniques.

Writing Assignments Using Other Methods of Development

3. Consider three purchases, minor or major, you or your family made recently. What role did advertising play in these purchases? Write an essay exploring how propaganda — in the form of advertising — did or did not influence your behavior in purchasing these items.

4. To increase your sensitivity to the moral dimensions of propaganda, write a proposal describing an ad campaign for a real or imaginary product or politician. The introduction to your proposal should identify the product being promoted, and the thesis or plan of development should indicate the specific propaganda techniques you propose. Use the paper's supporting paragraphs to explain how these techniques will be utilized to promote your product or candidate.

Desmond Morris

Zoologist Desmond Morris was born in England in 1928 and studied at Birmingham and Oxford Universities. At Oxford and the London Zoo, Morris conducted scholarly research on animals, often using his findings to arrive at controversial explanations of human behavior. Morris has reached a large popular audience through his books The Naked Ape *(1967),* The Human Zoo *(1970),* Manwatching *(1977), and* Bodywatching *(1985). The following excerpt is from* Manwatching.

Individual and Group Identity

Like other animals, we humans are territorial beings. Each of us has visible and invisible boundaries that define our personal space, our family units, and our social and national allegiances. When our boundaries are crossed, we may react with discomfort or even aggression. In the following selection, Morris explains how territorial claims dictate people's behavior on elevators and cause nations to go to war.

A territory is a defended space. In the broadest sense, there are   1
three kinds of human territory: tribal, family and personal.

It is rare for people to be driven to physical fighting in defense   2
of these "owned" spaces, but fight they will, if pushed to the limit.
The invading army encroaching on national territory, the gang
moving into a rival district, the trespasser climbing into an orchard, the burglar breaking into a house, the bully pushing to the
front of a queue, the driver trying to steal a parking space, all of
these intruders are liable to be met with resistance varying from the
vigorous to the savagely violent. Even if the law is on the side of the
intruder, the urge to protect a territory may be so strong that
otherwise peaceful citizens abandon all their usual controls and
inhibitions. Attempts to evict families from their homes, no matter

how socially valid the reasons, can lead to siege conditions reminiscent of the defense of a medieval fortress.

The fact that these upheavals are so rare is a measure of the success of Territorial Signals as a system of dispute prevention. It is sometimes cynically stated that "all property is theft," but in reality it is the opposite. Property, as owned space which is *displayed* as owned space, is a special kind of sharing system which reduces fighting much more than it causes it. Man is a co-operative species, but he is also competitive, and his struggle for dominance has to be structured in some way if chaos is to be avoided. The establishment of territorial rights is one such structure. It limits dominance geographically. I am dominant in my territory and you are dominant in yours. In other words, dominance is shared out spatially, and we all have some. Even if I am weak and unintelligent and you can dominate me when we meet on neutral ground, I can still enjoy a thoroughly dominant role as soon as I retreat to my private base. Be it ever so humble, there is no place like a home territory.

Of course, I can still be intimidated by a particularly dominant individual who enters my home base, but his encroachment will be dangerous for him and he will think twice about it, because he will know that here my urge to resist will be dramatically magnified and my usual subservience banished. Insulted at the heart of my own territory, I may easily explode into battle — either symbolic or real — with a result that may be damaging to both of us.

In order for this to work, each territory has to be plainly advertised as such. Just as a dog cocks its leg to deposit its personal scent on the trees in its locality, so the human animal cocks its leg symbolically all over his home base. But because we are predominantly visual animals we employ mostly visual signals, and it is worth asking how we do this at the three levels: tribal, family, and personal.

First: the Tribal Territory. We evolved as tribal animals, living in comparatively small groups, probably of less than a hundred, and we existed like that for millions of years. It is our basic social unit, a group in which everyone knows everyone else. Essentially, the tribal territory consisted of a home base surrounded by extended hunting grounds. Any neighboring tribe intruding on our social space would be repelled and driven away. As these early tribes swelled into agricultural supertribes, and eventually into industrial nations, their territorial defense systems became increasingly elaborate. The tiny, ancient home base of the hunting tribe became the great capital city, the primitive warpaint became the flags, emblems, uniforms, and regalia of the specialized military, and the war-chants became national anthems, marching songs and bugle calls. Territorial boundary-lines hardened into fixed borders, often conspicuously patrolled and punctuated with defensive structures — forts and lookout posts, checkpoints and great walls, and, today, customs barriers.

Today each nation flies its own flag, a symbolic embodiment 7 of its territorial status. But patriotism is not enough. The ancient tribal hunter lurking inside each citizen finds himself unsatisfied by membership in such a vast conglomeration of individuals, most of whom are totally unknown to him personally. He does his best to feel that he shares a common territorial defense with them all, but the scale of the operation has become inhuman. It is hard to feel a sense of belonging with a tribe of fifty million or more. His answer is to form sub-groups, nearer to his ancient pattern, smaller and more personally known to him — the local club, the teenage gang, the union, the specialist society, the sports association, the political party, the college fraternity, the social clique, the protest group, and the rest. Rare indeed is the individual who does not belong to at least one of these splinter groups, and take from it a sense of tribal allegiance and brotherhood. Typical of all these groups is the development of Territorial Signals — badges, costumes, headquarters, banners, slogans, and all the other displays of group identity. This is where the action is, in terms of tribal territorialism, and only when a major war breaks out does the emphasis shift upwards to the higher group level of the nation.

Each of these modern pseudo-tribes sets up its own special 8 kind of home base. In extreme cases non-members are totally excluded, in others they are allowed in as visitors with limited rights and under a control system of special rules. In many ways they are like miniature nations, with their own flags and emblems and their own border guards. The exclusive club has its own "customs barrier": the doorman who checks your "passport" (your membership card) and prevents strangers from passing in unchallenged. There is a government: the club committee; and often special displays of the tribal elders: the photographs or portraits of previous officials on the walls. At the heart of the specialized territories there is a powerful feeling of security and importance, a sense of shared defense against the outside world. Much of the club chatter, both serious and joking, directs itself against the rottenness of everything outside the club boundaries — in that "other world" beyond the protected portals.

In social organizations which embody a strong class system, 9 such as military units and large business concerns, there are many territorial rules, often unspoken, which interfere with the official hierarchy. High-status individuals, such as officers or managers, could in theory enter any of the regions occupied by the lower levels in the pecking order, but they limit this power in a striking way. An officer seldom enters a sergeant's mess or a barrack room unless it is for a formal inspection. He respects those regions as alien territories even though he has the power to go there by virtue of his dominant role. And in businesses, part of the appeal of unions, over and above their obvious functions, is that with their officials, headquarters, and meetings they add a sense of territorial power for the staff workers. It is almost as if each military organization and business concern consists of two warring tribes: the officers versus the other ranks, and the management versus the workers. Each has its special home base within the system, and the territorial defense pattern thrusts itself into what, on the surface, is a pure social hierarchy. Negotiations between managements and unions are tribal battles fought out over the neutral ground of a boardroom table, and are as much concerned with territorial display as they are with resolving problems of wages and conditions. Indeed, if one side gives in too quickly and accepts the other's demands, the victors feel strangely cheated and deeply suspicious that it may be a trick. What they are missing is the protracted sequence of ritual and counter-ritual that keeps alive their group territorial identity.

Likewise, many of the hostile displays of sports fans and teen- 10 age gangs are primarily concerned with displaying their group image to rival fan-clubs and gangs. Except in rare cases, they do not attack one another's headquarters, drive out the occupants, and reduce them to a submissive, subordinate condition. It is enough to have scuffles on the borderlands between the two rival territories. This is particularly clear at football matches, where the fan-club headquarters becomes temporarily shifted from the club-house to a section of the stands and where minor fighting breaks out at the unofficial boundary line between the massed groups of rival supporters. Newspaper reports play up the few accidents and injuries which do occur on such occasions, but when these are studied in relation to the total numbers of displaying fans involved it is clear that the serious incidents represent only a tiny fraction of the overall group behavior. For every actual punch or kick there are a thousand war-cries, war-dances, chants, and gestures.

Second: the Family Territory. Essentially, the family is a breeding unit and the family territory is a breeding ground. At the center of this space, there is the nest — the bedroom — where, tucked up in bed, we feel at our most territorially secure. In a typical house the bedroom is upstairs, where a safe nest should be. This puts it farther away from the entrance hall, the area where contact is made, intermittently, with the outside world. The less private reception rooms, where intruders are allowed access, are the next line of defense. Beyond them, outside the walls of the building, there is often a symbolic remnant of the ancient feeding grounds — a garden. Its symbolism often extends to the plants and animals it contains, which cease to be nutritional and become merely decorative — flowers and pets. But like a true territorial space it has a conspicuously displayed boundary-line, the garden fence, wall, or railings. Often no more than a token barrier, this is the outer territorial demarcation, separating the private world of the family from the public world beyond. To cross it puts any visitor or intruder at an immediate disadvantage. As he crosses the threshold, his dominance wanes, slightly but unmistakably. He is entering an area where he senses that he must ask permission to do simple things that he would consider a right elsewhere. Without lifting a finger, the territorial owners exert their dominance. This is done by all the hundreds of small ownership "markers" they have deposited on their family territory: the ornaments, the "possessed" objects positioned in the rooms and on the walls; the furnishings, the furniture, the colors, the patterns, all owner-chosen and all making this particular home base unique to them.   11

It is one of the tragedies of modern architecture that there has been a standardization of these vital territorial living units. One of the most important aspects of a home is that it should be similar to other homes only in a general way, and that in detail it should have many differences, making it a *particular* home. Unfortunately, it is cheaper to build a row of houses, or a block of flats, so that all the family living-units are identical, but the territorial urge rebels   12 against this trend and house-owners struggle as best they can to make their mark on their mass-produced properties. They do this with garden-design, with front-door colors, with curtain patterns, with wallpaper and all the other decorative elements that together create a unique and different family environment. Only when they have completed this nest-building do they feel truly "at home" and secure.

When they venture forth as a family unit they repeat the pro- 13 cess in a minor way. On a day-trip to the seaside, they load the car with personal belongings and it becomes their temporary, portable territory. Arriving at the beach they stake out a small territorial claim, marking it with rugs, towels, baskets, and other belongings to which they can return from their seaboard wanderings. Even if they all leave it at once to bathe, it retains a characteristic territorial quality and other family groups arriving will recognize this by setting up their own "home" bases at a respectful distance. Only when the whole beach has filled up with these marked spaces will newcomers start to position themselves in such a way that the inter-base distance becomes reduced. Forced to pitch between several existing beach territories they will feel a momentary sensation of intrusion, and the established "owners" will feel a similar sensation of invasion, even though they are not being directly inconvenienced.

The same territorial scene is being played out in parks and 14 fields and on riverbanks, wherever family groups gather in their clustered units. But if rivalry for spaces creates mild feelings of hostility, it is true to say that, without the territorial system of sharing and space-limited dominance, there would be chaotic disorder.

Third: the Personal Space. If a man enters a waiting-room and 15 sits at one end of a long row of empty chairs, it is possible to predict where the next man to enter will seat himself. He will not sit next to the first man, nor will he sit at the far end, right away from him. He will choose a position about halfway between these two points. The next man to enter will take the largest gap left, and sit roughly in the middle of that, and so on, until eventually the latest newcomer will be forced to select a seat that places him right next to one of the already seated men. Similar patterns can be observed in cinemas, public urinals, airplanes, trains, and buses. This is a reflection of the fact that we all carry with us, everywhere we go, a portable territory

called a Personal Space. If people move inside this space, we feel
threatened. If they keep too far outside it, we feel rejected. The
result is a subtle series of spatial adjustments, usually operating
quite unconsciously and producing ideal compromises as far as this
is possible. If a situation becomes too crowded, then we adjust our
reactions accordingly and allow our personal space to shrink.
Jammed into an elevator, a rush-hour compartment, or a packed
room, we give up altogether and allow body-to-body contact, but
when we relinquish our Personal Space in this way, we adopt certain special techniques. In essence, what we do is to convert these
other bodies into "nonpersons." We studiously ignore them, and
they us. We try not to face them if we can possibly avoid it. We wipe
all expressiveness from our faces, letting them go blank. We may
look up at the ceiling or down at the floor, and we reduce body
movements to a minimum. Packed together like sardines in a tin,
we stand dumbly still, sending out as few social signals as possible.

Even if the crowding is less severe, we still tend to cut down   16
our social interactions in the presence of large numbers. Careful
observations of children in play groups revealed that if they are
high-density groupings there is less social interaction between the
individual children, even though there is theoretically more opportunity for such contacts. At the same time, the high-density groups
show a higher frequency of aggressive and destructive behavior
patterns in their play. Personal Space — "elbow room" — is a vital
commodity for the human animal, and one that cannot be ignored
without risking serious trouble.

Of course, we all enjoy the excitement of being in a crowd, and   17
this reaction cannot be ignored. But there are crowds and crowds.
It is pleasant enough to be in a "spectator crowd," but not so
appealing to find yourself in the middle of a rush-hour crush. The
difference between the two is that the spectator crowd is all facing
in the same direction and concentrating on a distant point of
interest. Attending a theatre, there are twinges of rising hostility
toward the stranger who sits down immediately in front of you or
the one who squeezes into the seat next to you. The shared armrest
can become a polite, but distinct, territorial boundary-dispute region. However, as soon as the show begins, these invasions of
Personal Space are forgotten and the attention is focused beyond
the small space where the crowding is taking place. Now, each
member of the audience feels himself spatially related, not to his

cramped neighbors, but to the actor on the stage, and this distance is, if anything, too great. In the rush-hour crowd, by contrast, each member of the pushing throng is competing with his neighbors all the time. There is no escape to a spatial relation with a distant actor, only the pushing, shoving bodies all around.

Those of us who have to spend a great deal of time in crowded   18
conditions become gradually better able to adjust, but no one can ever become completely immune to invasions of Personal Space. This is because they remain forever associated with either powerful hostile or equally powerful loving feelings. All through our childhood we will have been held to be loved and held to be hurt, and anyone who invades our Personal Space when we are adults is, in effect, threatening to extend his behavior into one of these two highly charged areas of human interaction. Even if his motives are clearly neither hostile nor sexual, we still find it hard to suppress our reactions to his close approach. Unfortunately, different countries have different ideas about exactly how close is close. It is easy enough to test your own "space reaction": when you are talking to someone in the street or in any open space, reach out with your arm and see where the nearest point on his body comes. If you hail from western Europe, you will find that he is at roughly fingertip distance from you. In other words, as you reach out, your fingertips will just about make contact with his shoulder. If you come from eastern Europe you will find you are standing at "wrist distance." If you come from the Mediterranean region you will find that you are much closer to your companion, at little more than "elbow distance."

Trouble begins when a member of one of these cultures meets   19
and talks to one from another. Say a British diplomat meets an Italian or an Arab diplomat at an embassy function. They start talking in a friendly way, but soon the fingertips man begins to feel uneasy. Without knowing quite why, he starts to back away gently from his companion. The companion edges forward again. Each tries in his way to set up a Personal Space relationship that suits his own background. But it is impossible to do. Every time the Mediterranean diplomat advances to a distance that feels comfortable for him, the British diplomat feels threatened. Every time the Briton moves back, the other feels rejected. Attempts to adjust this situation often lead to a talking pair shifting slowly across a room, and many an embassy reception is dotted with western-European

fingertip-distance men pinned against the walls by eager elbow-distance men. Until such differences are fully understood and allowances made, these minor differences in "body territories" will continue to act as an alienation factor which may interfere in a subtle way with diplomatic harmony and other forms of international transaction.

If there are distance problems when engaged in conversation, then there are clearly going to be even bigger difficulties where people must work privately in a shared space. Close proximity of others, pressing against the invisible boundaries of our personal body-territory, makes it difficult to concentrate on non-social matters. Flat-mates, students sharing a study, sailors in the cramped quarters of a ship, and office staff in crowded work-places, all have to face this problem. They solve it by "cocooning." They use a variety of devices to shut themselves off from the others present. The best possible cocoon, of course, is a small private room — a den, a private office, a study, or a studio — which physically obscures the presence of other nearby territory-owners. This is the ideal situation for non-social work, but the space-sharers cannot enjoy this luxury. Their cocooning must be symbolic. They may, in certain cases, be able to erect small physical barriers, such as screens and partitions, which give substance to their invisible Personal Space boundaries, but when this cannot be done, other means must be sought. One of these is the "favored object." Each space-sharer develops a preference, repeatedly expressed until it becomes a fixed pattern, for a particular chair, or table or alcove. Others come to respect this, and friction is reduced. This system is often formally arranged (this is my desk, that is yours), but even where it is not, favored places soon develop. Professor Smith has a favorite chair in the library. It is not formally his, but he always uses it and others avoid it. Seats around a mess-room table, or a boardroom table, become almost personal property for specific individuals. Even in the home, father has his favorite chair for reading the newspaper or watching television. Another device is the blinkers-posture. Just as a horse that over-reacts to other horses and the distractions of the noisy race-course is given a pair of blinkers to shield its eyes, so people studying privately in a public place put on pseudo-blinkers in the form of shielding hands. Resting their elbows on the table, they sit with their hands screening their eyes from the scene on either side.

20

A third method of reinforcing the body-territory is to use   21
personal markers. Books, papers, and other personal belongings
are scattered around the favored site to render it more privately
owned in the eyes of companions. Spreading out one's belongings
is a well-known trick in public-transport situations, where a travel-
ler tries to give the impression that seats next to him are taken. In
many contexts carefully arranged personal markers can act as an
effective territorial display, even in the absence of the territory
owner. Experiments in a library revealed that placing a pile of
magazines on the table in one seating position successfully reserved that place for an average of 77 minutes. If a sports-jacket was
added, draped over the chair, then the "reservation effect" lasted
for over two hours.

In these ways, we strengthen the defenses of our Personal   22
Spaces, keeping out intruders with the minimum of open hostility.
As with all territorial behavior, the object is to defend space with
signals rather than with fists and at all three levels — the tribal, the
family, and the personal — it is a remarkably efficient system of
space-sharing. It does not always seem so, because newspapers and
newcasts inevitably magnify the exceptions and dwell on those
cases where the signals have failed and wars have broken out, gangs
have fought, neighboring families have feuded, or colleagues have
clashed, but for every territorial signal that has failed, there are
millions of others that have not. They do not rate a mention in the
news, but they nevertheless constitute a dominant feature of
human society — the society of a remarkably territorial animal.

Questions for Close Reading

1. What is the thesis of the selection? Locate the sentence(s) in which
   Morris states his main idea. If he does not state the thesis explicitly,
   express it in your own words.
2. Why do territories prevent disputes, according to Morris? How do
   humans signal the existence of their territories?
3. Why, according to Morris, aren't people's needs to be part of a tribe
   satisfied by citizenship in a nation? What other ways do people find to
   satisfy their tribal needs?
4. What do we do when we cannot avoid having our personal space invaded?

5. Refer to your dictionary as needed to define the following words in the selection: *encroaching* (paragraph 2), *regalia* (5), *portals* (9), *protracted* (9), *demarcation* (11), *proximity* (20).

Questions about the Writer's Craft

1. What three types of territory does Morris describe? What is the basis for this classification? What subcategories does Morris develop within each kind of territory? How does he use these classifications and sub-classifications to illustrate his thesis?
2. Examine Morris's introduction. Why is it so lengthy? What mode of development does he use in this introduction?
3. How does Morris signal he is moving from the discussion of one type of territoriality to another? What kind of transitional signals does he provide within each section?
4. Who do you think is the intended audience for this essay? Consider such stylistic and content features as sentence and paragraph length, types of support, and vocabulary.

Questions for Further Thought

1. Of the three types of territoriality, which is most important to you? Which would you be willing to fight to defend?
2. What signs of territoriality do you see in the classroom on the part of students and teachers? In the light of this article, would you say a professor who holds classes at his or her home is being casual and friendly, or is the professor moving the class from a neutral to a personal territory?
3. Do people act differently on their home base than out in public or in another's space? Think of examples of your friends at home, at parties, at restaurants.
4. Morris portrays territoriality as a positive force, one that "prevents" disputes rather than causes them. Do you agree? Or is territoriality really the cause of most human conflicts? Should civilization be working to eliminate or limit the importance of territory in our lives?

Writing Assignments Using Division-Classification as a Method of Development

1. Analyze the shared space you currently occupy; this could be your dorm room, group apartment, family home, or work space. Write an essay explaining how the space really consists of three territories: public, shared intimate, and solitary space. Characterize fully the nature of each subdivision, giving, for instance, examples of who is or is not

admitted to each level of space. Use your analysis to make a point about the nature of human interaction.

2. Write an essay categorizing several organizations on campus. Think of a logical principle of classification — membership or function, for example. Show how each type of organization satisfies one of the tribal needs that Morris describes.

Writing Assignments Using Other Methods of Development

3. Write a narrative essay about a time your space was invaded by someone else — or about a time you accidentally or deliberately invaded someone else's space. Describe what happened — whether, for example, a covert or overt conflict occurred — and explain what lessons about territorial conflict could be learned from this incident.

4. Write the copy for a brochure about the significance of personal space in the working environment. Persuade office managers that high morale and productivity require that workers "own" some space and have some privacy. Include suggestions for turning work stations into personal territory.

Additional Writing Topics
DIVISION-CLASSIFICATION

General Assignments

Choose one of the following subjects and write an essay developed wholly or in part through division-classification. Start by determining the purpose of the essay. Do you want to inform, compare and contrast, or persuade? Apply a single, significant principle of division or classification to your subject. Do not switch the principle midway through your analysis. Also, be sure that the types or categories you create are as complete and mutually exclusive as possible.

Division

1. A shopping mall
2. A video and/or stereo system
3. A fruit such as a pineapple, an orange, or a banana
4. A tax dollar
5. A particular kind of team
6. A word-processing system
7. A human hand
8. A meal
9. A meeting
10. A favorite poem, story, or play
11. A favorite restaurant
12. A school library
13. A basement
14. A playground, gym, or other recreational area
15. A church service
16. A wedding or funeral
17. An eventful week in your life
18. A college campus
19. A TV show or movie
20. A homecoming or other special weekend

Classification

1. People in a waiting room
2. Holidays
3. Closets

4. Roommates
5. Salad bars
6. Divorces
7. Beds
8. Students in a class
9. Shoes
10. Summer movies
11. Teachers
12. Neighbors
13. College courses
14. Bosses
15. TV watchers
16. Mothers or fathers
17. Commercials
18. Vacations
19. Trash
20. Friends

Assignments with a Specific Audience and Purpose

1. You are a dorm counselor. During orientation week, you will be talking to students on your floor about "what to expect in college." As part of the talk, you plan to tell them about the different types of instructors they are likely to encounter. Write your talk, labeling each "kind" of instructor and describing the behaviors and/or attitudes of each.
2. You are a driving instructor. As part of the classroom work you do with neophyte drivers, you give a lecture on the types of drivers your students are likely to encounter on the road. Write your lecture, categorizing drivers according to a specific principle and showing the behaviors of each type.
3. You have been asked to write a booklet for "new recruits" — new workers on your job, new students in your college class, new members of the team, and so on. The title of the booklet is "How to Succeed Now That You're Here." In the booklet, identify at least three general qualities needed for success in this organization.
4. A seasoned camp counselor, you have been assigned to orient new counselors to their jobs. You prepare an informational sheet on the kinds of emotional needs that children have. Decide exactly what those needs are and give examples of what the counselors should do to make the summer psychologically rewarding for the youngsters in their care.
5. You are the television critic for *People* magazine, reviewing the new fall shows. You are upset by the fact that the networks show little originality in the shows they televise. The problem is especially apparent in the comedies and crime-drama shows on the air. In order to show how

stereotypical the programs are, you divide one of these two kinds of shows into subtypes, based on a specific principle (which could be "level of reality on the show," "appeal of the leading character(s)," or any other principle). Remember that your goal is to prove how poor *all* the current programs are.

6. You have been asked to write an editorial for the campus paper. You decide to do a semi-serious piece on taking "mental health" days off from classes. Your essay is structured around three kinds of occasions when "playing hooky" is an absolute necessity for one's sanity.

ARGUMENTATION-
PERSUASION

WHAT IS ARGUMENTATION-
PERSUASION?

"You can't possibly believe what you're saying."
"Look, I know what I'm talking about, and that's that."

When most of us hear the word *argument*, we think about a heated situation with one person pitted against another. We may even picture a verbal battle that deteriorates into hostile accusations or worse. All of us have been involved in arguments which were propelled more by stubbornness and irrational thinking than by reason and logic. When caught up in the heat of an argument — whether it is about which candidate to vote for or which baseball team will win the World Series — we often assume that our perspective is the only valid one. Or we may become so emotionally involved in a contest of wills that we end up forgetting the point we're trying to make and get sidetracked by unrelated and often personal issues. That's how unreasonable we can be.

Argumentation in writing, though, is a different matter. *Argumentation* attempts to demonstrate — in a focused, thoughtful way — the soundness of the writer's position on a complex, often controversial issue. Using reason and logic, argumentation tries to convince readers of the validity of the viewpoint being advanced. If, while trying to convince, the writer uses strong emotional appeals to the readers' concerns, beliefs, and values, then the piece is called *persuasion*. But persuasion frequently tries to do more than get the audience to accept a particular position. Persuasion often urges the audience to take a specific course of action. Assume for a moment that you are writing an essay for English class about the controversial use of animals in medical research. If your purpose is to document, coolly and objectively, how animals are mistreated in medical experiments, you would prepare an argumentation essay. But if your purpose is to shake up your instructor and the other students in the class, perhaps even encourage them to write letters to their congressional representatives urging stricter controls over the use of animals in medical research, your essay would have a persuasive intent.

Because all of us respond rationally *and* emotionally to situations, most writing combines elements of argumentation *and* persuasion. Suppose you decided to write an article for the campus newspaper advocating a pre-Labor Day start for the school year. You know that your readers will include the college administration, students, and faculty. The article might begin by *arguing* that several schools have discovered that starting the academic year earlier allows them to close for the month of January, thus reducing costly heating expenses. Such an argument, supported by specific examples and figures, would obviously appeal to the college officials. Realizing that you also have to gain student and faculty commitment to your idea, you might next use emotional appeals or *persuasion* to encourage students and faculty to endorse this suggested change. You could demonstrate the value of the proposed schedule by appealing to students' desires to complete exams before Christmas break and to professors' wishes to leave campus without a pile of exams and reports to read over the winter vacation. In other words, your article would combine elements of argumentation *and* persuasion. Throughout this chapter, we will use the term *argumentation-persuasion* to refer to writing which advances a position through an appeal to both the readers' reason and emotions.

WHEN TO USE ARGUMENTATION-PERSUASION

At this point, you are probably thinking to yourself that much of the writing you do involves argumentation-persuasion. You're right, it does. When you prepare a *causal analysis*, a *descriptive piece*, a *narrative*, or a *definition essay*, you are advancing a specific point of view: MTV has a negative influence on young teens' view of sex; Cape Cod in winter is imbued with a special kind of magic; a disillusioning experience can teach people much about themselves; character can be defined as the willingness to take unpopular positions on difficult issues. Moreover, an essay taking a position may even have a persuasive intent. You may, for example, encourage readers to try out for themselves a *process* you have explained, or you could urge them to see one of two movies you have *compared*. In short, many of the essays you prepare contain elements of argumentation-persuasion.

But argumentation-persuasion is a separate form of writing with its own special demands. As in most writing, you present your view and provide evidence to support your position. When preparing an argumentation-persuasion essay, though, you must also keep in mind that the issue under discussion is complex and often debatable; opposing views are a certainty. Effective argumentation-persuasion requires attention to these facts. Take a moment to consider the following assignments. All of them, requiring the writer to take a position on a complex, controversial issue, would lead to argumentation-persuasion essays:

> In various parts of the country, communities established for older citizens or childless couples have refused to rent to families with children. How do you feel about this situation? What do you think are the rights of the parties involved?

> Citing the fact that the highest percentage of automobile accidents involve young men, insurance companies con-

sistently charge their highest rates to young males. Is this fair? Why or why not?

For years, debate raged over the registration of young men for the draft. Now there is a controversy regarding the registration of women to serve in the armed services. Should women as well as men be compelled to register for the draft?

It is impossible to predict with 100 percent certainty what will make readers accept the view you advance or the course of action you propose. But the ancient Greeks, who formulated our basic concepts of logic, isolated three factors that help determine the effectiveness of argumentation-persuasion messages. Although the Greeks were concerned with public speaking, the factors they identified play an equally significant role in writing. The key factors they discussed were *logos, pathos*, and *ethos.*

Most important, you have to be concerned with the *logos* — the soundness — of your argument. *Logos* involves the information you have marshalled to support your viewpoint: facts, statistics, examples, statements from authoritative sources. Imagine that you want to write a piece convincing people that a popular charity misappropriates the money it receives from the public. Your readers, inclined to believe in the good works of the charity, are apt to dismiss your argument unless you can substantiate your claim with well-documented evidence. Without that solid evidence, your argument will be flimsy and unconvincing. Later on, this chapter offers suggestions for selecting evidence and structuring an essay to enhance its logic. The important point here is that clear thinking or *logos* is at the heart of effective argumentation-persuasion.

Sensitivity to the *pathos*, to the emotional power of the written piece, is another key consideration when writing argumentation-persuasion essays. *Pathos* involves readers by appealing to their needs, values, and attitudes; it encourages readers to commit themselves to a viewpoint or course of action. *Pathos* is an especially crucial element in pieces having a persuasive edge.

The *pathos* of a piece derives partly from the language the writer uses. *Connotative* language — words with strong emotional overtones — can convince readers to accept a point of view and may even spur them to action. Propaganda is perhaps the most dramatic example of the way *pathos* can be used to influence and even manipulate people. And we see every day the way *pathos* is used in advertisements, another kind of persuasive writing that relies heavily on connotative language. Take a moment to compare the following pitches for a man's cologne and a woman's perfume; the language — and the attitudes to which the language appeals — are different in each case.

> Brawn: Experience the power. Bold. Yet subtle. Clean, masculine. The scent for the man who's in charge.

> Black Lace is for you — the woman who dresses for success but who dares to be provocative, slightly naughty. Black Lace. Perfect with pearls by day and with diamonds by night.

The appeal to men plays on the impact that words such as *Brawn*, *bold*, *power*, and *in charge* have for some males. By way of contrast, the charged words *Black Lace*, *provocative*, *naughty*, and *diamonds* are intended to appeal to high-powered business women who — in the advertiser's mind, at least — are looking for ways to reconcile sensuality and professionalism.

When writing an argumentation-persuasion piece, you have to pay almost as much attention to the emotional content of words as advertising copywriters do. The language used must reinforce your viewpoint. In a paper urging support of an expanded immigration policy, you might use such charged phrases as "land of liberty," "a nation of immigrants," "America's open-door policy," and "hardworking freedom-seekers." On the other hand, if you were arguing that strict immigration quotas should be imposed, you might use language like "save jobs for unemployed Americans," "flood of unskilled labor," and "illegal aliens."

Finally, whenever you write an argumentation-persuasion essay, you should establish your *ethos* or your credibility and reliability. If readers are going to accept and even act on your point of view, you have to convince them you know what you are talking about and that you are worth listening to. But how is *ethos* achieved? How do you establish your credibility? You will seem knowledgeable and trustworthy if you present a logical, reasoned argument that takes opposing views into account. You should also be careful that your appeals to emotion are not excessive. Overwrought emotionalism undercuts credibility.

It's important to keep in mind that *ethos* is not constant; it is not a given. Because *ethos* is closely linked with subject matter, you may have credibility on one subject but not on another. An Army general might be a reliable source for information on military preparedness but not for information on federal funding of day care.

Writing an effective argumentation-persuasion essay involves an interplay among *logos, pathos, and ethos*. Deciding how to balance these three factors is determined by your purpose — whether you want your audience simply to agree with you or whether you want them to act — and, most important, by the people who make up your audience. A clear sense of the audience is essential because the essay should be tailored specifically for your readers. When analyzing your audience, you should think carefully about these points: how your readers feel about the subject; how they feel about you; how much they know or don't know about the issue to be discussed; what values and attitudes they hold; what needs and concerns motivate them.

Your readers will probably fall into one of three broad categories. The audience will be supportive, wavering, or hostile.

1. A supportive audience.   You may be fortunate and have an audience who agrees with your position and trusts your credibility. When that is the situation, a highly reasoned argument dense with facts, examples, and statistics is not needed. Instead, you should concentrate on *pathos*, on a strong emotional appeal, to reinforce the audience's commitment to your viewpoint. Let's assume you belong to the local chapter of the National Rifle Association (NRA) and have volunteered to write an article encouraging members to contribute to efforts to preserve hunting rights in specific areas. Because the audience already supports the NRA's hunting programs, your best bet would be an appeal to the readers' emotions. You might remind readers of the quiet camaraderie among hunters, the exhilarating confrontation between humans and wildlife, the special beauty of the outdoors, and conclude: "If you want to continue enjoying these pleasures, I urge you to make a generous contribution to our fund."

2. A wavering audience. At times readers may be interested in what you have to say but may not have committed themselves fully to your view. Or perhaps they are not as informed about the subject as they should be. In either case, because the audience needs to be encouraged to give their complete support, you should concentrate on *ethos* and *logos*, bolstering your reputation as a reliable source and providing the final evidence needed to advance your position. If you want to convince an audience of high school seniors that taking a year off to work between high school and college is a good idea, you might establish your authority by recounting the year you spent working, being sure to show the positive effects it had on your life *(ethos)*. In addition, you might try to win your audience by citing two studies which show that delayed entry into college often leads to higher grade-point averages. Why is this so? The year's cushion of savings helps ease the financial strain that students frequently experience, freeing them to study rather than worry about their ability to pay tuition *(logos)*.

3. A hostile audience. It should come as no surprise that an apathetic, skeptical, or downright hostile audience is most difficult to convince. With such an audience, you should be careful to avoid emotional appeals and instead weigh your argument heavily in favor of reliable, incontrovertible facts *(logos)*. Assume that you plan to submit to the college newspaper an open letter to the student body, supporting the administration's unpopular attempt to ban alcohol from the student pub. To support your view, you cite some important facts. Many college pubs across the country have gone dry and have found their revenues actually increase because all students — not just those of drinking age — can now support the pub. With the increased revenues, a number of schools have been able to upgrade the food served in their pubs and hire disk jockeys or musical groups to provide entertainment. You could also point out that many of these schools have seen a sharp reduction in alcohol-related vandalism. Finally, you might show that colleges making this move have found that they have significantly improved their relationship with the town police and local residents. By giving your readers a hard dose of facts, you encourage them to reconsider their position. They may not be totally convinced, but they may soften or reshape their views when brought face to face with your logical, authoritative argument.

SUGGESTIONS FOR USING ARGUMENTATION-PERSUASION IN AN ESSAY

1. At the beginning of the paper, state the issue being discussed and your position on the issue.   The introduction to an argumentation-persuasion essay should present the issue to be developed in the paper. Your knowledge of the audience will determine how much background to supply. Even if only minimal background information is needed, you should be sure the introduction clarifies in a general way the focus of the controversy.

The thesis in an argumentation-persuasion paper is often called the *assertion* or *proposition*. Occasionally an argumentation-persuasion essay will save the proposition for the end of the paper. But usually the proposition is stated at the beginning of the piece. If you present the thesis at the start, your audience will know where you stand and will be better able to evaluate the evidence for your position.

The thesis should also demonstrate that argumentation-persuasion tackles complex issues involving more than one viewpoint. Keeping that in mind, you should avoid a proposition that is merely a factual statement; a fact is demonstrably true and allows little room for discussion. Instead, your proposition should focus on a controversial matter, and it should signal your view on the issue. To see the difference between a factual statement and an effective thesis, contrast the two statements below:

Fact: The economic crisis in the farm belt has led to serious problems for the nation's small farmers.

Thesis: The small farmer's inability to manage efficiently is largely responsible for the economic crisis in the nation's farm belt.

The first statement is a statement of inarguable fact. It would be difficult to find anyone who believed that these are easy times for the farming community. Because the statement invites little opposition, it cannot serve as the focal point of an argumentation-persuasion essay. The second statement, though, takes a controversial

stance on a complex issue. Such a proposition can be a valid starting point for a paper.

The first statement also points to another potential difficulty
associated with propositions. In addition to being obvious and
factual, the statement is also too general. A vague, overly general
proposition does not provide the boundaries needed to write a
focused essay. When framing the essay's proposition, remember to
keep the assertion narrow and specific. Having such clarity of purpose allows you to collect your thoughts in a purposeful way. Take
a moment to consider the following statements:

Broad thesis: The welfare system has been abused over the
years.

Narrow thesis: No one except the handicapped and
mothers of pre-school-age children should be eligible to
receive welfare payments.

If you tried to write a paper based on the first statement, you would
face an unmanageable task — showing all the ways that welfare has
been abused. Your readers would also be confused about what to
expect in the paper. Will you discuss unscrupulous bureaucrats,
fraudulent bookkeeping, dishonest recipients? By way of contrast,
the revised thesis is limited and specific. It signals that the paper
will propose limiting welfare payments to two groups. Such a proposal will surely have its opponents and is thus an appropriate
subject for an argumentation-persuasion essay.

The thesis in an argumentation-persuasion essay can simply
state your opinion about the issue in question, or it can go a step
further and call for some action to be taken.

Opinion: The lack of affordable day care centers discriminates against lower-income families.

Call for action: The federal government should help un-
derwrite corporations' efforts to establish on-site day care
centers.

In either case, your stand on the issue being discussed must be clear
to your readers.

2. Generate strong support for the thesis.   Finding convincing evidence is a crucial part of writing an argumentation-persuasion essay. A good deal of support will be accumulated during the prewriting stage. As in any effective essay, the evidence included must be unified, adequate, and specific. The evidence might consist of personal experience or observation. Or it could be gathered from outside sources — statistics, facts, examples, expert authority. A paper arguing that elderly Americans are better off than they used to be might incorporate the following pieces of evidence:

- A description of the writer's grandparents who are living comfortably on Social Security and pensions (personal observation or experience)
- A statement that the per capita after-tax income of older Americans is $335 greater than the national average (statistic)
- The point that the majority of elderly Americans do not live in nursing homes or on the street; they have their own houses or apartments (fact)
- Accounts of several elderly couples living in retirement villages in Florida (example)
- A statement by Dr. Marie Sanchez, a specialist in geriatrics: "An over-65 American today is likely to be healthier, and have a longer life expectancy, than a 50-year-old living only a decade ago." (expert authority)

Always keep in mind, of course, that the evidence you collect must be accurate; otherwise, your argument and credibility will be undermined.

Because facts, statistics, examples, and expert testimony are often needed to support your position, you may have to turn to such outside sources as books, articles, reports, interviews, and television documentaries. When an essay includes such information, you should be sure to *document* or give credit to your sources. If these sources are not acknowledged, readers may dismiss your evidence because they consider it nothing more than your subjective opinion; they have no way of knowing that your evidence actually comes from authoritative sources. On the other hand, if your audience is aware that you have drawn on outside information, they will regard as dishonest your failure to cite your indebtedness. Your instructor can provide information about ways to document sources.

3. Organize the supporting evidence. The support for an argumentation paper can be organized in a variety of ways. Any of the patterns described in this book—description, narration, definition, causal analysis, and so on—may be used to develop the essay's proposition. Imagine that you are writing a paper arguing that car racing should be banned from television. The essay might contain a *description* of a horrifying accident that was televised in graphic detail; you might devote part of the paper to a *causal analysis*, showing that the broadcast of such races encourages teens to drive carelessly; you could include a *process analysis*, explaining how young drivers "soup up" their own cars in a dangerous attempt to imitate the racers seen on television.

When presenting evidence to support your argument, you should arrange the details so they create a strong, convincing effect. That means you often will end with your most compelling point, leaving readers with dramatic evidence that underscores the validity of your proposition.

4. Acknowledge and perhaps refute the opposition. If your essay has a clear thesis and strong support, you have taken important steps toward winning readers over to your way of thinking. But most argumentation-persuasion essays do more than state a position and marshal evidence to support that viewpoint. Because such essays tend to focus on controversial issues, they generally spend some time taking opposing points of view into account. You should, of course, feel a strong commitment to your proposition, but as you think and read about the subject, it is important to seek out arguments on the other side. A good argument does not ignore the opposition; it admits that the opposition exists, perhaps even acknowledging that the other side has a viewpoint worthy of consideration. Dealing with the opposition in this way helps strengthen your argument because it identifies you as a reasonable person, not a hardheaded fanatic. Researching and acknowledging the opposition sharpens your position in another way, too. Because you have investigated arguments on the other side, you will be more sensitive to weaknesses and flaws in your own position.

As you will see in the professional essays in this chapter, there are a number of techniques that writers can use to deal with the opposition. Here are three particularly effective strategies.

First, you can simply acknowledge the competing viewpoint in your proposition, granting the opposition its opinion, and then stating your own. With such an approach, you may not have to spend time discussing the opposing position. The thesis below illustrates this strategy (the opposing viewpoint is underlined once and the writer's position is underlined twice):

<u>Although moderate exercise is essential for good health</u>, the current fitness craze has lead to an obsessive attitude towards physical well-being.

At times, though, it may be necessary to do more than merely recognize the opposition in the thesis. You may have to summarize the opposition, admit the validity of its points, and then go on to present the thinking behind your position.

Finally, you need to keep in mind that citing the opposition in your thesis or even summarizing the opposing argument won't always be enough to satisfy your readers. They may demand more than your simple acknowledgment of differing viewpoints; they will not be satisfied with your simply saying, "I grant you A, but my point is B." In such cases, part of the essay should be devoted to a *refutation* of the competing view. Refutation means pointing out problems with the opposition's point of view, thus demonstrating the superiority of your own position. To refute the opposition, you may focus on the inadequacies or inaccuracies in the evidence the opposition uses to support its argument. Or you may point to illogical spots in the opposition's thinking. (Pages 562–567 identify some common examples of illogical thinking.)

Here is how the opposition could be refuted in an essay arguing in favor of sex education in public schools. You might start by acknowledging the prominent opposition view: "Sex education should be the prerogative of parents." Then, while granting the validity of this view in an ideal world, you might continue by showing that many parents do not meet their responsibilities in this area. You could provide statistics showing the number of parents who are uncomfortable talking about sex with their children and therefore avoid doing so; you could cite studies revealing that children in single-parent homes are apt to receive even less parental guidance about sex; you could describe several young people whose parents provided sketchy, even misleading, information about sex.

There are various ways to present and develop the refutation section of your paper. The method used will depend on the length of the paper and the complexity of the issue in question. Two possible sequences are outlined below:

First Strategy

State your proposition.

Cite the opposition's viewpoint and the evidence for its position.

Refute the opposition by presenting counterarguments to its evidence.

Second Strategy

State your proposition.

Present primary evidence for your proposition.

Cite the opposition's viewpoint and the evidence for its position.

Refute the opposition by presenting additional evidence to counter its arguments.

Within these two general patterns, a number of additional options are open. You may, for instance, decide to refute the opposition *in toto*, or you may present and refute the opposing argument one point at a time.

One last suggestion for dealing with the opposition: Always keep in mind that your refutation should lean toward logic and reason rather than charged emotion. Emotional appeals are often suspect, whereas strong evidence is difficult to dispute.

5. Think logically about your argument. The chain of reasoning used to develop an argument is the surest indicator of how rigorously you have thought through your position. There are two basic ways to think about a subject: inductive and deductive reasoning. Though the following discussion treats induction and deduction as separate processes, the two often overlap and complement one another.

Inductive reasoning examines an issue or problem by looking closely at specific cases, facts, or examples. Based on these specifics, you then draw a conclusion or make a generalization. This is the kind of thinking scientists use when they examine the evidence or facts (the results of many experiments, for example) and then draw a *conclusion*: Smoking causes cancer. All of us use inductive thinking in everyday life. We might think the following: My head is aching (evidence). My nose is stuffy (evidence). I'm coming down with a cold (conclusion). Based on the conclusion, we might go a step further and decide to take some action: I think I'll take an aspirin.

When inductive reasoning is used in an essay, the conclusion reached serves as the proposition for an argumentation essay. (Of course, the essay will most likely include elements of persuasion since strict argumentation — with no appeal to emotions — is uncommon.) If the paper advances a course of action, the proposition often states the action proposed, thus signaling that the essay has a distinctly persuasive purpose.

Let's suppose that you are writing a paper about the current crime wave in the small town where you live. You might use inductive thinking to structure the argument for the essay:

Several people were mugged last week while shopping in the center of town. (evidence)

A number of homes and apartments were burglarized the past few weeks. (evidence)

A growing number of cars have been stolen from people's driveways. (evidence)

The police force has been negligent about protecting town residents. (proposition for an argumentation essay with probable elements of persuasion)

The police force needs to take definite steps to upgrade its ability to protect town residents. (proposition for an argumentation essay with a clearly persuasive intent)

This inductive sequence helps point the way to a possible structure for the essay. For example, after providing a clear statement of your proposition, you might detail the recent mugging, burglary, and stolen car incidents. Then you could move to the opposition viewpoint: a description of the steps the police say they have taken to protect town members. At that point, you would refute the police's claim, citing additional evidence that shows the measures taken have not been sufficient. Finally, if you wanted your essay to have a decidedly persuasive purpose, the paper could end with specific steps the police should take to improve their ability to protect the community.

As in all essays, your evidence should be specific, unified, and adequate. This last characteristic is critical when you think inductively. You want to be certain your conclusion is based on enough evidence, guaranteeing that the conclusion would be equally valid even if other evidence were presented. Insufficient evidence often leads to hasty generalizations which mar the logic of an essay. Here is an example of a hasty generalization. You might think the following: Some elderly people are very wealthy and do not need Social Security checks (evidence), and some Social Security recipients illegally collect several checks (evidence). On the basis of this limited evidence, you could conclude, "The Social Security system is a waste of the taxpayers' money." But your conclusion is invalid and hasty because it is based on only a few examples. Millions of Social Security recipients are not wealthy and do not abuse the system. Because you failed to consider the full range of evidence, any action you propose ("The Social Security system should be disbanded") will probably be considered suspect by thoughtful readers. It is possible, of course, that Social Security should be disbanded. But the evidence leading to such an argument must be sufficient and representative. Such is not the case in this situation.

When reasoning inductively, you should also be careful that the evidence you collect is accurate. No valid conclusion can result from erroneous evidence. To ensure that your evidence is sound, you need to evaluate the reliability of your sources. Gossip, hearsay, and biased opinions are not authoritative sources. When a person who is legally drunk claims to have seen a flying saucer, the evidence is shaky, to say the least. But if two respected scientists, both with 20-20 vision, saw the saucer, their evidence is worth considering.

Finally, it's important to realize that there is always an element of uncertainty in inductive reasoning. The conclusion can never be more than an *inference*, involving what logicians call an *inductive leap*. There could be other explanations for the evidence cited and thus other positions to take and persuasive actions to urge. For example, from the evidence above concerning a crime wave in a small town, you might conclude not so much that the police force has been remiss, but that people in the town do not know how to protect themselves. In turn, you might call for a different kind of action: the police force should conduct workshops for the public in self-defense and home security. In an inductive argument, your task is to weigh the evidence, consider alternative explanations, and then choose the conclusion and course of action that seem most valid.

With inductive reasoning, you start with specific cases and move toward a generalization or conclusion. In *deduction*, you begin with a generalization, then apply that generalization to a specific case so a conclusion can be drawn. This movement from general to specific involves a three-step form of reasoning called a *syllogism*. The first part of a syllogism is called the *major premise*. The major premise is a general statement about a large group. The second part of a syllogism is a *minor premise*, a statement about an individual within that group. The syllogism ends with a *conclusion* about that individual.

Just as we use inductive thinking in everyday life, so we use deductive thinking — often without being aware of it — to sort out our experiences. For instance, when trying to make a decision about which car to buy, you might think as follows:

Major premise: In an accident, large cars are safer than small cars.

Minor premise: The Chevy Cruiser is a large car.

Conclusion: In an accident, the Chevy Cruiser will be safer than a small car.

Based on your conclusion, you could decide to take a specific action, buying the Cruiser rather than the smaller car you had first considered.

In order to create a valid syllogism and thus a sound conclusion, you should be aware of two major pitfalls when reasoning deductively. First, you want to be sure not to start with a *sweeping* or *hasty generalization* as your *major premise*. Second, you need to be careful about accepting as truth a *minor premise* that is *inaccurate* or *incomplete*. Let's look at each of these problems in turn.

Perhaps you are concerned about a trash-to-steam incinerator that is scheduled to open near your home. Although not fully conscious of your reasoning, your thinking about the situation might follow along these lines:

Major premise:	Trash-to-steam incinerators have had serious problems and pose significant threats to the well-being of people living near the plants.
Minor premise:	The proposed incinerator in my neighborhood will be a trash-to-steam plant.
Conclusion:	The proposed trash-to-steam incinerator in my neighborhood will have serious problems and pose significant threats to the well-being of people living near the plant.

Having arrived at this conclusion, you might decide to join organized protests against the opening of the incinerator. But your thinking is somewhat illogical. Your *major premise* is a *sweeping* one that indiscriminately groups all trash-to-steam plants into a single category. It is unlikely that you are familiar with the operations of all the trash-to-steam incinerators in this country and abroad. Moreover, it is probably not true that all the plants have had serious difficulties that endangered the public safety. For your argument to reach a valid conclusion, the major premise must be based on repeated observations or verifiable fact. You would have a better argument, and thus reach a more valid conclusion, if the major premise were restricted or qualified — if it were applied to some, not all, of the group. The qualified syllogism would more likely be valid.

Major premise:	A number of trash-to-steam incinerators have had serious problems and posed significant threats to the well-being of people living near the plants.
Minor premise:	The proposed incinerator in my neighborhood will be a trash-to-steam plant.

Conclusion: It is possible that the proposed trash-to-steam incinerator in my neighborhood will run into serious problems and pose significant threats to the well-being of people living near the plant.

This new conclusion, the result of more careful reasoning, would probably encourage you to learn more about trash-to-steam incinerators in general and about the proposed plant in particular. If further research still left you feeling uncomfortable about the plant, you would probably decide to join the protest. On the other hand, your research might convince you that the plant has incorporated into its design a number of safeguards that have been used with great success at other plants. This added information could reassure you that your original fears were unfounded. In either case, the revised deductive process would lead to a more informed conclusion and course of action.

Similarly, your syllogism — and thus your reasoning — will be invalid if your *minor premise* is *inaccurate* or *incomplete*. Assume that you plan to write a letter to the college newspaper urging the resignation of the president of the student government. Perhaps without being aware of it, you pursued a line of reasoning that went like this:

Major premise: Students who plagiarize term papers must appear before the Faculty Committee on Academic Policies and Procedures.

Minor premise: Yesterday, Jennifer Kramer, president of the student government, appeared before the Faculty Committee on Academic Policies and Procedures.

Conclusion: Jennifer must have plagiarized her term paper.

Action: Jennifer should resign her position as president of the student government.

Such a chain of reasoning is illogical and unfair. Why? A conclusion was reached and a course of action proposed, both based on an invalid syllogism. You failed to consider that there could be a number of reasons why Jennifer appeared before the committee. She could have been speaking on behalf of another student; she could have been protesting some action that the committee took; she could have been seeking the committee's help on an article she plans to write about academic honesty. The oversimplified minor premise fails to take into account these other possible explanations.

Now that you have a clear sense of the problems that can occur when thinking deductively, let's look more closely at the way syllogistic reasoning might be used to structure an argumentation-persuasion essay. Suppose you decide to write a paper advocating support for a projected space mission. You are aware that a good deal of controversy surrounds the space program, especially since seven astronauts died in a 1986 launch. Confident that the tragedy has led to more rigorous controls, you want to urge support of an upcoming mission, arguing that the mission's benefits outweigh its risks. An essentially deductive pattern could be used to develop your argument. In fact, outlining your thinking as a syllogism might help you formulate a proposition, organize your evidence, deal with the opposition, and — if appropriate — propose a course of action.

Major premise:	Space programs in the past have led to important developments in technology, especially in medical science.
Minor premise:	The Cosmos Mission is the newest space program.
Proposition (essay might be persuasive):	The Cosmos Mission will lead to important developments in technology, especially in medical science.
Proposition (essay clearly persuasive):	Congress should continue its funding of the Cosmos Mission.

Having outlined the deductive pattern of your thinking, you might begin by stating your proposition and then discuss some of the new procedures that have been developed to protect the safety of the astronauts and the structural integrity of the rocket system. With that background established, you could detail the opposition's claim that little of value has been produced by the space programs of the past. You could then move to your refutation, citing the significant medical advances emerging from former space missions. Finally, the paper might conclude on a persuasive note, with a plea to Congress to take the steps necessary to ensure the continued funding of the latest space mission.

6. Recognize logical fallacies in your own and other people's thinking.   In addition to being aware of the illogical thinking that can occur when reasoning inductively or deductively, you need to avoid several other pitfalls when writing an argumentation-persuasion essay. The *logical fallacies* described here can defeat an argument, revealing serious flaws in your thinking. Logicians have identified many logical fallacies — including the kinds of hasty generalizations and inaccurate minor premises discussed earlier — but there are three other fallacies to be especially wary of when preparing an essay. The ability to detect these fallacies also enables you to identify weaknesses in the opposition's view, providing a solid basis for the refutation portion of your essay.

Post hoc thinking (from a Latin phrase which means, "After this, therefore because of this") occurs when you conclude that a cause-effect relationship necessarily exists simply because one event preceded another. For example, it would be illogical to develop an essay arguing that recently arrived immigrants are the sole cause of the economic slump in a nearby city. To support your argument, you cite two pieces of evidence: the growing number of immigrants who have settled in the city and the city's economic decline. Such a chain of thinking is faulty because it assumes a cause-effect relationship based purely on the coincidence of time. Perhaps the immigrants' arrival was a factor, but there could also be several other reasons for the situation: the lack of financial incentives to attract business to the city, restrictions on the size of the manufacturing facilities built in the city, citywide labor disputes that make companies leery of settling in the area. Your argument should also consider these possibilities.

Ad hominem argument (from the Latin meaning "to the man") occurs when you attack a person rather than an issue. Suppose you want to write a letter to the school newspaper, arguing against the college's plan to sponsor a symposium on the abortion controversy. The symposium would be attended by physicians on both sides of this complex issue. The letter starts with your reasons for protesting the proposed symposium. But soon you get sidetracked and take swipes at the doctors who support the right to abortion. You mention that one physician has serious marital difficulties and had just filed for divorce; you indicate that the other doctor is alleged to have a drinking problem. By hurling personal invective at the doctors, you avoid discussing the loopholes in their position and the merits of your stance. Mudslinging is a poor substitute for reasoned argument.

Begging the question involves reasoning that never establishes proof for a debatable point. Instead, the writer starts with an arguable premise and expects readers to accept as given a premise that is actually controversial. You would have trouble convincing readers that prayer in public schools should be banned if you based your argument on the premise that school prayer violates the Constitution. Perhaps the Constitution does, either explicitly or implicitly, prohibit the use of prayer in public education. But your essay must demonstrate that fact. You cannot build a sound argument if you stick your head in the sand and pretend there is no controversy surrounding your premise.

Few of today's critical problems — for example, arms control, terrorism, care for the homeless — lend themselves to quick solutions. Overwhelmed by endless facts and speculations, many of us look to the experts to help us arrive at personally meaningful positions on these complex issues. We may read one article and conclude, "Yes, this position makes sense," only to read another article that advances an opposing but equally compelling viewpoint. Perhaps the key to finding answers is to rely on ourselves — not on the experts — to sort out information and ideas. Writing an argumentation-persuasion essay is the perfect vehicle for such an investigation. The very act of writing helps us discover how we feel and what we think. Weighing fact against fact, stipulation against stipulation, we use reason to draw conclusions that make sense. Argumentation-persuasion also gives us a chance to share that point of view with others, perhaps even convincing readers of the soundness of our view. Indeed, as average people with limited political clout or recognized expertise, we may find that argumentation-persuasion provides us with one of our strongest sources of personal power.

STUDENT ESSAY AND COMMENTARY

The following student essay was written by Mark Simons in response to this assignment:

> In "My Pistol-Packing Kids," Jean Marzollo refutes the popular notion that parents should prohibit their children's aggressive games and use of warlike toys. Select a controversial issue you feel strongly about and, using logic and solid evidence, convince your readers of the validity of your viewpoint.

While reading Mark's paper, try to determine how effectively it applies the principles concerning the use of argumentation-persuasion. The commentary following the paper will help you look at Mark's essay more closely.

Compulsory National Service

Our high school history class spent several weeks studying the   1
events of the 1960s. The most intriguing thing about that decade was the spirit of service and social commitment in young people. In the Sixties, young people thought about issues beyond themselves; they joined the Peace Corps and participated in freedom marches against segregation. They accepted President Kennedy's urging to "Ask not what your country can do for you; ask what you can do for your country." Most young people today, despite their obvious concern with careers and getting ahead, would also like an opportunity to make a worthwhile contribution to society. By instituting a program of compulsory national service, our country could tap this desire in young people. Such a system would yield significant benefits.

Compulsory national service means that everyone between the   2
ages of 17 and 25 would serve their country for two years. Young people could choose between two major options: military service or a public-service corps. They could serve their time at any point within

the eight-year span. The unemployed or the uncertain could join immediately after high school; college-bound students could complete their education before joining the national service.

The idea of compulsory national service has been discussed for 3 many years, and some nations such as Israel have embraced it wholeheartedly. The idea could also be workable in this country. Unfortunately, detractors have prevented the idea from taking hold. Opponents contend, first of all, that the program would cost too much; they argue that a great deal of money would have to be spent administering the program. In addition, young people would have to receive at least a minimum wage for their work, and some of them would need housing--both costly items. Another argument against compulsory national service is that it would demoralize young people; the plan would prevent the young from getting on with their careers and would make them feel as though they were engaged in work that had no personal reward. A final argument is that compulsory service would lay the groundwork for a military state. The picture is painted of an army of young robots totally at the mercy of the government, like the Hitler Youth of the Second World War.

Despite opponents' claims that compulsory national service 4 would involve exorbitant costs, the program would not have to be that expensive to run. The program might use as a model the Peace Corps, which has achieved great benefits even while being administered on a fairly modest budget. Also, the sums required for wages and housing could be reduced considerably through payments made by the towns, cities, and states using the corps' services. And the economic benefits of the program could be significant. The public-service corps could repair deteriorating bridges, highways, public buildings, and inner-city neighborhoods. The corps could organize recycling projects; it could staff public health clinics, day care centers, legal aid centers, and homes for the handicapped. The corps could also monitor pollution, clean up litter, and help care for the country's growing elderly population. All of these projects would help solve many of the problems that plague our nation, and they would probably cost much less than if they were handled by traditional government bureaucracies or the private sector.

Also, rather than undermining the spirit of young people, as 5 opponents contend, the program would be likely to boost their morale. Many young people feel enormous pressure and uncertainty. They are not sure what they want to do, or they have trouble finding a way to begin their careers. Compulsory national service could give young people a much-needed breathing space and could even equip them with the skills needed to start a career. Moreover, participating in compulsory national service could provide an emotional boost for the young; all of them would experience the pride that comes from working hard, reaching goals, acquiring skills, and handling responsibilities. A positive mind-set would also result from the sense of community that would be created by serving in the national service. All young people — rich or poor, educated or not, regardless of sex or social class — would come together during this time. Young people would grow to understand one another and learn that every person has an ability to aid the welfare of the whole group. Each young person would have the satisfaction of knowing that he or she has made a real contribution to the nation.

Finally, contrary to what opponents claim, compulsory national service would not signal the start of a dictatorship. Although the service would be required, young people could have complete freedom to choose any two years between the ages of 17 and 25. They would also have complete freedom to choose the branch of the military or public-service corps which suits them best. Nor would there be any need to outfit the public-service corps in military uniforms or to keep the corps confined to barrack-like camps. The corps could be set up like a regular job, with young people living at home as much as possible, following a nine-to-five schedule, enjoying all the personal freedoms that would ordinarily be theirs. Also, a dictatorship would no more likely emerge from a program of compulsory national service than it has from our present military system. We would still have a series of checks and balances to prohibit the taking of power by one group or individual. We should also keep in mind that our system is different from that of fascist regimes; our long tradition of personal liberty makes improbable the seizing of absolute power by one person or faction. A related but even more important point to remember is that freedom does not mean people are guaranteed the right to pursue only their individual needs. That is mistaking selfishness for freedom. And, as everyone knows, selfishness leads only to misery. It cannot lead to a happy life. The national service would not take away freedom. On the contrary, it would help young people grasp this larger concept of freedom, a concept that is badly needed to counteract the deadly "look out for number one" attitude that is spreading like a poison across the nation.

Perhaps there will never be a time like the 1960s when so many young people were concerned with remaking the world. Still, a good many of today's young people want meaningful work. They want to feel that what they do makes a difference. A program of compulsory national service would tap this willingness in young people, helping them realize the best in themselves. Such a program would also allow us as a nation to make substantial headway against the social problems that haunt the country. It is apparent that compulsory national service is an idea whose time has come.

In his *argumentation-persuasion* essay, Mark tackles — as the assignment required — a complex and controversial social issue. He takes the position that compulsory national service would benefit both the country and its young people. Mark's essay is a good example of the way argumentation and persuasion often mix; although the paper presents Mark's position in a focused, thoughtful manner, it also appeals to readers' personal value systems and suggests a course of action to be taken.

When planning the essay, Mark realized that most of his audience — his composition class — would consist of two kinds of readers. Some people would be wavering but inclined to agree with him if he presented his case well. Others would probably be reluctant to accept his view. Because of this mixed audience, Mark knew he could not depend on *pathos* (an appeal to emotion) to convince his readers of the soundness of his position. Rather, his argument had to be based on *logos* (reason) and *ethos* (his own credibility). Thus, after carefully thinking through the pros and cons of the issue, Mark decided to present a series of logical arguments. He also decided to evoke his own authority, drawing on his "inside" knowledge of young people as well as his knowledge of history.

Mark introduces his subject by discussing an earlier decade when large numbers of young people worked for societal change. This historical reference establishes a context for Mark's point of view. The specifics about the Peace Corps and freedom marches as well as the inclusion of Kennedy's famous statement help reinforce Mark's credibility and the validity of the position he will take. All this leads logically to the two-sentence *thesis* at the end of the introduction: "By instituting a system of compulsory national service, our country could tap this desire in young people to serve. Such a system would yield significant benefits."

The next paragraph is developed around a *definition* which clarifies exactly what is meant by compulsory national service. The definition guarantees that Mark and his readers have a common base of understanding. Without this paragraph, readers might be unprepared to grasp the concept at the heart of the essay.

Mark is now in a good position to launch his argument. Like most argumentation-persuasion essays, the paper addresses a controversial issue, and, as we have seen, Mark wisely recognizes that some people will not agree with him. Rather than ignoring the opposition's point of view, he acknowledges its existence in the *topic sentence* of the essay's third paragraph: "Unfortunately, detractors have prevented the idea from taking hold in America." He then summarizes the main points the opposition might make: compulsory national service would be expensive, demoralizing to young people, and dangerously authoritarian. Mark uses the rest of the essay to argue against these three criticisms.

You probably realized that Mark's summary of the opposition's criticisms is not grounded in research. Since the assignment did not require outside sources, Mark brainstormed with friends to discover some of the reservations people might have about compulsory national service. If he had been writing a longer paper, or if the assignment had required library research, Mark would have been obligated to read what critics of compulsory national service say about such a program. Indeed, such research would have strengthened Mark's argument. By investigating the opposition viewpoint, he would have become more aware of possible weaknesses in his own position. Moreover, research would have enabled him to quote the opposition directly, thus appearing even more authoritative to his audience. But in an essay of this kind, it is acceptable not to conduct such outside research.

The next three paragraphs *refute* the opposition's stance and represent Mark's evidence for his position. Mark structures the essay so that readers can follow his *counterargument* with ease. Each paragraph argues against one of the opposition's points and begins with a *topic sentence* that serves as Mark's response to his opponents. In fact, note the way the italicized portion of each topic sentence recalls an opposition point cited earlier: "Despite opponents' claims that *compulsory national service would involve exorbitant costs*, the program would not have to be that expensive to run" (paragraph 4); "Also, rather than *undermining the spirit of young people*, as opponents contend, the program world be likely to boost their morale" (5); "Finally, contrary to what opponents claim, *compulsory national service would* not *signal the start of a dictatorship*" (6). Mark also guides the reader through the various points in the refutation by using *transitions* within paragraphs: "*And* the economic benefits . . . could be significant" (4); "*Moreover*, participating in compulsory national service would provide an emotional boost . . . "(5); "*Also*, a dictatorship would no more likely emerge . . . " (6).

As we have seen, Mark's essay is not based on researched facts, statistics, or other hard evidence. Just as he used brainstorming to generate material on the opposition's view, Mark brainstormed his counterarguments, arriving at his position *inductively* — through an *inference* or *inductive leap*. Starting with a number of specific observations, Mark moved to a general *conclusion* that compulsory national service would be both workable and beneficial. In other words, Mark's support, as thoughtful and convincing as it may be, takes the form of reasonable speculation. The evidence for his argument constitutes a kind of *causal analysis* which assumes that certain things will happen if compulsory national service is implemented. Of course, Mark cannot be sure that the consequences he envisions will actually occur, but he has worked hard to show the logic behind his thinking. Moreover, since Mark's projected consequences cannot be proven, he seeks to reinforce his position by infusing the essay with several *persuasive* or emotional appeals. For example, he points to consequences that most people would endorse with enthusiasm: If the program were in operation, pollution would be reduced, the nation's elderly would be cared for, deteriorating highways would be repaired. Such attractive prospects make Mark's argument all the more compelling.

When reading the essay, you may have felt that Mark loses some control over his argument in the last part of the sixth paragraph. Beginning with "And as everyone knows . . . ," Mark falls into the *logical fallacy* called *begging the question*. He also indulges in charged emotionalism. For one thing, he shouldn't assume that everyone agrees that a selfish life inevitably brings misery. Also, when he refers — somewhat melodramatically — to the "deadly 'look out for number one' attitude that is spreading like a poison across the nation," he assumes that readers agree with his assessment; he presents his view as truth when actually it needs to be proven. These presumptions, especially when combined with the overwrought language, undercut somewhat Mark's credibility and the effectiveness of his argument.

Despite this problem, Mark recovers and comes up with a solid concluding paragraph. This final section echoes the point Mark made in the introduction about the Sixties and also restates the essay's thesis. The essay then ends with a crisp assertion which suggests a course of action to be taken.

Given the complex nature of his argument, it is not surprising that Mark revised his essay several times. One way to illustrate some of the changes he made is to compare his final introduction with the original draft reprinted here:

Unrevised Version

"There's no free lunch." "You can't get something for nothing." "You have to earn your way." In America, these sayings are not really true. In America, we gladly take but give back little. In America, we receive economic opportunity, legal protection, the right to vote, and, most of all, a personal freedom unequaled throughout the world. How do we repay our country for such gifts? In most cases, we don't. This unfair relationship must be changed. The best way to make a start is to institute a system of national compulsory service for young people. This system would be of real benefit to the country and its citizens.

When Mark met with his editing partner for a feedback session, he found that his partner had a number of helpful suggestions for revising various sections of the essay. But Mark's partner focused most of her comments on the essay's introduction because she felt it needed special attention. Mark read the paragraph aloud and agreed that the opening was weak. For one thing, it was choppy and awkward. More important, though, Mark's partner helped him see that the introduction did not provide an effective lead-in to the essay's thesis. The original introduction referred in a general way to the one-sided relationship between America and Americans. The paragraph did not help readers see that Mark was concerned specifically with young people. Mark reconsidered his opening paragraph and decided to focus it exclusively on American youth. When revising the paragraph, he also decided to mention the social commitment characteristic of young people in the Sixties. This reference to an earlier period provided the discussion with an important historical perspective and lent a note of authority to Mark's argument.

These are just a few of the many changes Mark made while reworking his essay. Because he budgeted his time carefully, he was able to do a thorough job of revising. Thus, with the exception of the problem mentioned in the sixth paragraph, Mark was able to prepare a well-reasoned, convincing essay.

The selections ahead demonstrate that argumentation-persuasion can stimulate thinking on numerous compelling issues. In "My Pistol-Packing Kids," Jean Marzollo argues that children's violent play does not lead to violent lives. Paul Fussell draws upon extensive comparisons, examples, and quotations to support his view that the much-maligned "The Boy Scout Handbook" offers solid advice for living with grace and integrity. Harold Krents uses several examples in "Darkness at Noon" to make a point about the treatment of the handicapped. Loudon Wainwright also depends on examples to support the position he advocates in "A Little Banning Is a Dangerous Thing." Roger Rosenblatt's "The Man in the Water" argues that humans can be noble and self-sacrificing, while Mark Twain ("The Damned Human Race"), Thomas Tutko and William Bruns ("To Win or Not to Win: That Is the Question"), and Frank Trippett ("A Red Light for Scofflaws") make strong points about some of the flaws in human nature. Finally, Margaret Mead's "One Vote for This Age of Anxiety" argues that unease and conflict can have a positive impact on our lives.

Jean Marzollo

A Connecticut native, Jean Marzollo received her B.A. in English from the University of Connecticut and her M.A. from Harvard University. Before becoming a freelance writer, Marzollo taught high school and directed educational programs for disadvantaged children. Her articles have appeared in many popular magazines, including Redbook, Parents, Mademoiselle, *and* Working Mother. *The author of several books for children and teenagers, she has recently started an adult novel. The following selection was first published in* Parents *magazine.*

My Pistol-Packing Kids

Marbles, hopscotch, and hide-and-seek are all old, familiar childhood games. But the most favorite of all may be "Bang, bang, you're dead." All children seem to enjoy games of make-believe violence, played with sticks, pointed fingers, or toy weapons that shoot plastic darts, "laser" beams, or rubber projectiles. Parents debate whether such games are healthy or damaging to young minds. Jean Marzollo maintains that such shoot-'em-up games have hidden dimensions that parents may not at first appreciate.

One day as I was loading the dishwasher, I glanced over at my two boys, Danny and David, ages seven and five, respectively, and thought how sweet and quiet they are. I wonder what they are drawing so intently; I think I'll go see. I went over to the kitchen table and found, rather to my dismay, two lurid pictures of outer space battles. Blood and destruction was everywhere. 1

These frail little babes I held in my arms, what made them grow up and want to create things like this? Repeatedly? Given clay, they make monsters and destroy them limb by limb with home-made clay bombs. Given yarn, they devise tarantula traps behind the couch. Given board and blocks they rig ramps to crash their cars into each other at high speed. 2

576

Outdoors, straight sticks are knives and bent ones are guns.   3
Danny and David stick them into their belts and swagger around
on the grass like John Wayne and Burt Reynolds.

Oh, sure, they also like to roll out cookie dough, play the   4
piano, build sand castles, and pet cats, but nothing, I have noticed,
quite catches their fancy as does violence.

With their friends they are superheroes or spacemen, and, as I   5
watch them run around shooting each other, I sometimes feel
guilty that it was I who took them to (and enjoyed) the movies
Superman, Star Wars, and *The Empire Strikes Back.* Adding to this
guilt is the fact that my husband and I let them watch Saturday
morning cartoons so we can sleep late.

On a slow, regular basis their innocent little minds have been   6
contaminated with kiddie media culture. It's excessively violent,
which is why Danny and David, at the ripe old ages of five and
seven, like it so much. They are at the ages when they know what
they see on television is not real. Instead of worrying about reality
as they did when they were three or four, they now spend their
energy memorizing the exact order in which their favorite cartoons
appear.

What About the Kids of Parents Who Say "No"?

Good and stalwart friends of ours, wishing to protect their   7
children's minds from nefarious influences, do not buy TVs, do
not permit guns, and do not take their children to ungentle movies.
But when their children come to visit, they dive into the box in the
entryway that contains two squirt guns, a plastic laser gun, an
orange pistol that shoots rubber darts (all of which have been lost),
and a homemade wooden machine gun. Although these kids have
never watched morning TV, they know exactly how to play with
toy weapons, and they do so with the passion of converts.

Secretly, wickedly, I feel better. Why? Because I'm haunted by   8
the idea that our actions, or the lack of them, may be bringing out
in our children a natural tendency toward aggressive violence that
should be suppressed. In a time of assassinations, political terrorism, nuclear buildup, and much publicized violence in people's
daily lives, we desire more consciously than ever peace and safety in

the world. It is out of this concern that we worry about the place and legitimacy of toy guns in the lives of our children.

What if, we wonder, all parents kept all children from toy weapons and the media that glorifies them; wouldn't the world be better off? We could take the TV and the laser guns to the dump. But what about the sticks, yarns, and crayons? Should we take them, too? 9

We could also lay down the law: no more torpedoes in the bathtub. Play only with rubber ducks. No more bows and arrows may be made out of construction toys. Make houses instead. No more clay bombs. Make bowls. Our laws would require rigid surveillance and strict discipline, but the means (our dictatorship) would be justified by the end (their innocence). Childhood, after all, should be a time of kittens, mittens, gingerbread, and yo-yo's. 10

Think positive. Be happy. Play nice, our laws would say. 11

But our children don't want to play nice. They want to have fun. And they have so much fun *pretending* to wipe each other out. 12

Kids Want Both Sides

It seems kids want to learn about *both* sides of childhood, not just the mittens and kittens side, full of discovery and nurturing, but also the ghosts and ghouls side, full of dread and helplessness. Watching our children and their friends at play, it is clear to me that the mock violence in their play has a great deal to do with their need to *do* something about the underside of their lives. In order to fight back the witches, giants, and werewolves that menace them in the night, they run around in the daytime with toy pistols, toy knives, and toy swords. When I stop to think about their play in these terms, I find I can accept it. 13

I'm not talking about condoning real violence, nor am I suggesting we avoid the responsibilities to teach morals and ethics to our children. As a matter of course, we teach them that no matter how mad they are at someone else, they must not hit, bite, pull hair, and pinch. We teach them to protest verbally, to negotiate a deal if they can, or simply to say, "I'm not going to play with you anymore if you do that." We teach them basically not to hurt others to get their own way. And just as we teach our children safety precautions about cars, roads, matches, broken glass, and electrical outlets, we caution them about real knives and guns. We tell them how very 14 dangerous these things are, how they must be used correctly, and that the use of guns is prohibited for young children.

"Your Thing, Not Mine"

Guns are a particularly sensitive topic for parents, and many of   15
us feel uncomfortable when our children lust for plastic ones. Although I do not prohibit my children from playing with them, I try to make it clear that such activity is their thing, not mine. I say, "Don't point that rifle at me because it reminds me of a real gun and I don't like real guns." I also insist that gunplay take place outside.

Some friends of mine won't buy toy guns but permit their   16
children to do so with their own money. Others will not allow any toy guns in their homes but do not interfere if their children play guns with sticks or their fingers. Still other parents own real guns, go hunting, and bring home carcasses on the top of the car. Their children, we hope, learn the ethic of the hunter: one must be a good shot, one must kill only for food.

But the use of real guns is not really the point here. Danny and   17
David do not use real guns nor would they want to. *They are using toys and they are only pretending.* While I admit that it can be unsettling to see how truly inspired they can be at their games, I am impressed by their powers of invention and the fact that what they are doing is not only fun, but refined, effective, and safe.

It is refined in the sense that the children organize themselves   18
to take the different parts involved. They also know how to act out all the parts and how to cooperate with each other to enhance the overall drama. They have a remarkable ability to improvise scenes and an almost professional attitude about giving and taking directions. Listening to them play with their little men dolls, it is almost as if I were listening to puppeteers or movie directors.

"All right," says Danny. "You land your guy behind the   19
mountain, and I'll find him and blast him out of the water."

"Okay, here goes." (Realistic landing sounds.) "Let's set up   20
camp here. Oh no! They found us. Watch out!" (Explosion sounds. Swimming sounds.) "Look, here's an underwater cave! Let's go in!" (Aside) "Let's pretend the cave is really a giant shark."

"Yeah, and I'll kill it and save you."   21

"Okay. Oh no! It's a giant shark! Look at those teeth!"   22

Their Own Play Therapy

It seems to me that fantasy play is effective in the sense that it 23 allows children to blow off a lot of steam. Let's face it, on some level every child lives with tyrants (us) on whom he or she is absolutely dependent. We may be benevolent tyrants, but we are tyrants nonetheless, and the whole thrust of our children's growing up is to liberate themselves from us.

By playing out fantasies, children release frustrations and ex- 24 perience illusory control over things, such as big people's power and the threat of death, over which, in fact, they have no control at all. Day after day, they take turns acting out scene after scene in which they as good guys heroically defend themselves against horrible bad guys. Every child I have watched can play both roles.

In a way children are their own play therapists, helping each 25 other cope with pent-up rage. They seem to know how long each session should last. The game is over when the kids are bored, or tired, or someone thinks of something else to do and everyone agrees; in short, when enough steam has been blown off.

As far as I can see, violent fantasies are safe precisely because 26 they are not real. They are thrilling for the same reason. Children don't want to get hurt. From my observation, the kids who enjoy playing with toy guns in the yard are those who have already learned to be cautious around cars, ovens, and climbing equipment. *They don't want to get hurt and they know how not to.* Just because they crash toy cars now does not mean they will drive real ones over cliffs when they are twenty. And just because they love to shoot each other with imaginary guns now does not mean they will abuse guns when they grow up.

It takes more than toy guns to make a killer. Conversely, many 27 peace-loving grown-ups I know tell me they played war with a vengeance when they were little.

No Winners, No Losers?

Another important point: Have you ever noticed that in mock 28 violent play no one ever wins or loses? You get shot, you fall down, you get up, you shoot someone else. A five-year-old can play as skillfully as an eight-year-old. The weakest child is on par with the strongest. The game is safe emotionally as well as physically.

Paradoxically, games that involve less violent imagination but   29
more real jeopardy are harder for children to play, and one has to be
mature enough to handle them. To play baseball, for example, you
have to be able to strike out without bursting into tears. In Monop-
oly you have to be able to land on Park Place when someone else
owns it and lose all your money. In a class play you have to be able
to keep going even though some kid in the back row whistles.

I don't want to see my kids strike out or forget their lines, but I   30
know they may, that they have to, and that they will put up with
such discomfort in order to participate in the next stage of life. On
their own, I suspect, they will realize eventually that fantasy violence is for little kids. What's for big kids? Real violence? No, at
least not for kids who have learned about love and respect for
others.

Graduating into Life

For older kids there is a stage of activity that moves closer to   31
real life. Sports, science projects, model making, music lessons,
dancing, arts and crafts — all these activities help children sharpen
their skills, develop their imagination, and explore their interests.
The toy guns, toy dolls, and toy cars will be given away or collect
dust on a shelf in the basement. Real tools and real equipment will
have replaced them.

Eventually, Danny and David will move on to real life with its   32
possibilities for real jeopardy, real success, real independence, and
satisfaction. By then I hope they will have gained whatever skills
and strength of character they need to play this last, and hardest,
and most rewarding game of all. I trust that part of their maturity
will be based upon the ability they gained at an early age to distinguish between fantasy and reality.

Questions for Close Reading

1. What is the thesis of the selection? Locate the sentence(s) in which
   Marzollo states her main idea. If she does not state the thesis explicitly,
   express it in your own words.
2. Why, according to the author, do kids want to play at violence?

3. Marzollo suggests children progress through different stages of maturity. What are these? In which stages do children focus on reality and in which on fantasy?
4. What does Marzollo mean by saying that play with toy guns is "refined"? How is it "effective" and safe?
5. Refer to your dictionary as needed to define the following words used in the selection: *stalwart* (paragraph 7), *legitimacy* (8), *condoning* (14), *improvise* (18), and *vengeance* (27).

Questions about the Writer's Craft

1. Why do you think the author chooses the first person point of view to develop her argument? How does the first person affect the persuasiveness of the essay?
2. What contrast makes the introduction dramatic? How does this contrast underlie the theme of the essay?
3. Examine the places where Marzollo uses direct quotations as opposed to reporting conversation indirectly. What is gained by using exact words at these points?
4. Marzollo asks rhetorical questions at several points in the essay. How do these questions help focus her argument? How do these questions function as transitional devices?

Questions for Further Thought

1. What kinds of games involving pretended violence, destruction, and death did you play as a child? What was your parents' reaction? Were you aware of playing with something adults considered very serious?
2. From your experience, do you think all children (both male and female, from all ethnic groups and backgrounds) play games of pretended violence? Would you say such play is normal?
3. It has been said that play is "the child's work," in that through play children try on new behaviors and skills and test their abilities. Would Marzollo agree? What things specifically can children learn through play?
4. What might be some of the reasons for the popularity with adults of violent action movies (such as the Rambo and Dirty Harry series)? Do you see any connection between child's fantasy play and the popularity of these films? Are these films beneficial, harmless, or dangerous for people to view?

Writing Assignments Using Argumentation-Persuasion as a Method of Development

1. In paragraphs 15 and 16, Marzollo mentions four different parental attitudes toward guns. Write an essay that makes a case for parents'

adopting one of these attitudes. After citing possible counterarguments, support your proposition with reason and emotional appeals. Draw, as Marzollo does, on your own experience as a child, babysitter, neighbor, parent, and so on.

2. One of Marzollo's points is that physical play and fantasy have important, healing roles in the lives of children. Write an essay defending the role of physical activity and/or fantasy in adults' lives as ways to release pent-up rage about things adults cannot control. Make your proposition as specific as possible, supporting it with examples from your own life and with references to films, TV, and books. At some point in the essay, you should acknowledge briefly the opposing view that escaping from reality can have negative repercussions.

Writing Assignments Using Other Methods of Development

3. Write an essay about the games (physical, fantasy, or other) that helped you grow up. These may have been games that taught you about yourself, others, feelings, or life in general. Describe the games that absorbed you and explain their benefits.

4. Marzollo contends that childhood play with weapons is not a cause of violence among adults. What, then, are the causes of the violence in our world? Write an essay explaining the causes of a particular kind of violence in your town or city, the United States, or the world. Be specific. Focus on only one type of violence and account for its existence.

Paul Fussell

Long a professor at Rutgers University, Paul Fussell now holds the Donald T. Regan Chair of English Literature at the University of Pennsylvania. Born in California in 1924, Fussell took his Ph.D. at Harvard after serving in World War II. His book, The Great War and Modern Memory, *a study of the British experience of World War I, won the National Book Award in 1976. Other works by Fussell include a 1982 collection of essays,* The Boy Scout Handbook and Other Observations, *and* Class: A Guide Through the American Status System *(1983), a wry look at social class in America. The following selection is taken from Fussell's 1982 collection.*

The Boy Scout Handbook

Isn't The Boy Scout Handbook *a remnant of a simpler time when bracing outdoor activities and the Victorian virtues of bravery and reverence were all a boy needed? Not so, argues author Paul Fussell. The* Handbook *has not only been updated through the decades, but it has managed to hold on to some values of real worth to society. We might all benefit, maintains Fussell, from heeding the advice in this "book about goodness."*

It's amazing how many interesting books humanistic criticism 1
manages not to notice. Staring fixedly at its handful of teachable
masterpieces, it seems content not to recognize that a vigorous
literary-moral life constantly takes place just below (sometimes
above) its vision. What a pity Lionel Trilling or Kenneth Burke
never paused to examine the intersection of rhetoric and social
motive among, say, the Knights of Columbus or the Elks. That
these are their fellow citizens is less important than that the desires
and rituals of these groups are desires and rituals, and thus of

584

permanent social and psychological consequence. The culture of the Boy Scouts deserves this sort of look-in, especially since the right sort of people don't know much about it.

The right sort consists, of course, of liberal intellectuals. They 2 have often gazed uneasily at the Boy Scout movement. After all, a general, the scourge of the Boers, invented it; Kipling admired it; the Hitlerjugend (and the Soviet Pioneers) aped it. If its insistence that there is a God has not sufficed to alienate the enlightened, its khaki uniforms, lanyards, salutes, badges, and flag-worship have seemed to argue incipient militarism, if not outright fascism. The movement has often seemed its own worst enemy. Its appropriation of Norman Rockwell as its official Apelles has not endeared it to those of exquisite taste. Nor has its cause been promoted by events like the TV appearance a couple of years ago of the Chief Pardoner, Gerald Ford, rigged out in scout neckerchief, assuring us from the teleprompter that a Scout is Reverent. Then there are the leers and giggles triggered by the very word "scoutmaster," which in knowing circles is alone sufficient to promise comic pederastic narrative. "*All* scoutmasters are homosexuals," asserted George Orwell, who also insisted that "*All* tobacconists are Fascists."

But anyone who imagines that the scouting movement is ei- 3 ther sinister or stupid or funny should spend a few hours with the latest edition of *The Official Boy Scout Handbook* (1979). Social, cultural, and literary historians could attend to it profitably as well, for after *The Red Cross First Aid Manual*, *The World Almanac*, and the Gideon Bible, it is probably the best-known book in this country. Since the first edition in 1910, twenty-nine million copies have been read in bed by flashlight. The first printing of this ninth edition is 600,000. We needn't take too seriously the ascription of authorship to William ("Green Bar Bill") Hillcourt, depicted on the title page as an elderly gentleman bare-kneed in scout uniform and identified as Author, Naturalist, and World Scouter. He is clearly the Ann Page or Reddy Kilowatt of the movement, and although he's doubtless contributed to this handbook (by the same author is *Baden-Powell: The Two Lives of a Hero* [1965]), it bears all the marks of composition by committee, or "task force," as it's called here. But for all that, it's admirably written. And although a complex sentence is as rare as a reference to girls, the rhetoric of this new edition has made no compromise with what we are told is the new illiteracy of the young. The book assumes an audience pre-

pared by a very good high-school education, undaunted by terms   4
like *biosphere, ideology,* and *ecosystem.*

The pliability and adaptability of the scout movement explains
its remarkable longevity, its capacity to flourish in a world dramatically different from its founder's. Like the Roman Catholic
Church, the scout movement knows the difference between cosmetic and real change, and it happily embraces the one to avoid any
truck with the other. Witness the new American flag patch, now
worn at the top of the right sleeve. It betokens no excess of jingoism
or threat to a civilized internationalism. It simply conduces to
dignity by imitating a similar affectation of police and fire departments in anarchic towns like New York City. The message of the
flag patch is not "I am a fascist, straining to become old enough to
purchase and wield guns." It is, rather, "I can be put to quasi-offi-
cial use, and like a fireman or policeman I am trained in first aid and
ready to help."

There are other innovations, none of them essential. The   5
breeches of thirty years ago have yielded to trousers, although
shorts are still in. The wide-brimmed army field hat of the First
World War is a fixture still occasionally seen, but it is now aug-
mented by headwear deriving from succeeding mass patriotic exercises: overseas caps and berets from World War II, and visor caps of
the sort worn by General Westmoreland and sunbelt retirees. The
scout handclasp has been changed, perhaps because it was discovered in the context of the new internationalism that the former one,
in which the little finger was separated from the other three on the
right hand, transmitted inappropriate suggestions in the Third
World. The handclasp is now the normal civilian one, but given
with the left hand. There's now much less emphasis on knots than
formerly; as if to signal this change, the neckerchief is no longer
religiously knotted at the tips. What used to be known as artificial
respiration ("Out goes the bad air, in comes the good") has given
way to "rescue breathing." The young are now being familiarized
with the metric system. Some bright empiric has discovered that a
paste made of meat tenderizer is the best remedy for painful insect
stings. Constipation is not the bugbear it was a generation ago.
And throughout there is a striking new lyricism. "Feel the wind
blowing through your hair," the scout is adjured, just as he is
exhorted to perceive that Being Prepared for life means learning
"to live happy" and — equally important — "to die happy."

There's more emphasis now on fun and less on duty; or rather, duty is validated because, properly viewed, it is a pleasure. (If that sounds like advice useful to grown-ups as well as to sprouts, you're beginning to get the point.)

There are only two possible causes of complaint. The term "free world" surfaces too often, although the phrase is mercifully uncapitalized. And the Deism is a bit insistent. The United States is defined as a country "whose people believe in a supreme being." The words "In God We Trust" on the coinage and currency are taken almost as a constitutional injunction. The camper is told to carry along the "Bible, Testament, or prayer book of your faith," even though, for light backpacking, he is advised to leave behind air mattress, knife and fork, and pancake turner. When the scout finds himself lost in the woods, he is to "stay put and have faith that someone will find you." In aid of this end, "Prayer will help." But the religiosity is so broad that it's harmless. The words "your church" are followed always by the phrase "or synagogue." The writers have done as well as they can considering that they're saddled with the immutable twelve points of Baden-Powell's Scout Law, stating unambiguously that "A Scout is Reverent" and "faithful to his religious duties." But if "You have the right to worship God in your own way," you must see to it that "others retain their right to worship God in their way." Likewise, if "you have the right to speak your mind without fear of prison or punishment," you must "ensure that right for others, even when you do not agree with them." If the book adheres to any politics, they can hardly be described as conservative; they are better described as slightly archaic liberal. It is broadly hinted that industrial corporations are prime threats to clean air and conservation. In every illustration depicting more than three boys, one is black. The section introducing the reader to some Great Americans pays respects not only to Franklin and Edison and John D. Rockefeller and Einstein; it also makes much of Walter Reuther and Samuel Gompers, as well as Harriet Tubman, Martin Luther King, and Whitney Young. There is a post-Watergate awareness that public officials must be watched closely. One's civic duties include the obligation to "keep up on what is going on around you" in order to "get involved" and "help change things that are not good."   6

Few books these days could be called compendia of good sense. This is one such, and its good sense is not merely about   7 swimming safely and putting campfires "cold out." The good sense is psychological and ethical as well. Indeed, this handbook is among the very few remaining popular repositories of something like classical ethics, deriving from Aristole and Cicero. Except for the handbook's adhesions to the motif of scenic beauty, it reads as if the Romantic movement had never taken place. The constant moral theme is the inestimable benefits of looking objectively outward and losing consciousness of self in the work to be done. To its young audience vulnerable to invitations to "trips" and trances and anxious self-absorption, the book calmly says: "Forget yourself." What a shame the psychobabblers of Marin County will never read it.

There is other invaluable advice, applicable to adults as well as to scouts. Some is practical, like "Never use flammable fluids to start a charcoal fire. They burn off fast, lighting only a little of the charcoal." Some is civic-moral: "Take a 2-hour walk where you live. Make a list of things that please you, another of things that should be improved." And then the kicker: "Set out to improve them." Some advice is even intellectual, and pleasantly uncompromising: "Reading trash all the time makes it impossible for anyone to be anything but a second-rate person." But the best advice is ethical: "Learn to think." "Gather knowledge." "Have initiative." "Respect the rights of others." Actually, there's hardly a better gauge for measuring the gross official misbehavior of the seventies than the ethics enshrined in this handbook. From its explicit ethics you can infer such propositions as "A scout does not tap his acquaintances' telephones," or "A scout does not bomb and invade a neutral country, and then lie about it," or "A scout does not prosecute war unless, as the Constitution provides, it has been declared by the Congress." Not to mention that because a scout is clean in thought, word, and deed, he does not, like Richard Nixon, designate his fellow citizens "shits" and then both record his filth and lie about the recordings ("A scout tells the truth").

Responding to Orwell's satiric analysis of "Boys' Weeklies" forty years ago, the boys' author Frank Richards, stigmatized by Orwell as a manufacturer of excessively optimistic and falsely wholesome stories, observed that "The writer for young people should . . . endeavor to give his young readers a sense of stability and solid security, because it is good for them, and makes for happiness and peace of mind." Even if it is true, as Orwell objects, that the happiness of youth is a cruel delusion, then, says Richards, "Let youth be happy, or as happy as possible. Happiness is the best preparation for misery, if misery must come. At least the poor kid will have had something." In the current world of Making It and Getting Away with It, there are not many books devoted to associating happiness with virtue. The shelves of the CIA and the State Department must be bare of them. "Horror swells around us like an oil spill," Terrence Des Pres said recently. "Not a day passes without more savagery and harm." He was commenting on Philip Hallie's *Lest Innocent Blood Be Shed*, an account of a whole French village's trustworthiness, loyalty, helpfulness, friendliness, courtesy, kindness, cheerfulness, and bravery in hiding scores of Jews during the Occupation. Des Pres concludes: "*Goodness*. When was the last time anyone used that word in earnest, without irony, as anything more than a doubtful cliché?" *The Official Boy Scout Handbook*, for all its focus on Axmanship, Backpacking, Cooking, First Aid, Flowers, Hiking, Map and Compass, Semaphore, Trees, and Weather, is another book about goodness. No home, and certainly no government office, should be without a copy. The generously low price of $3.50 is enticing and so is the place on the back cover where you're invited to inscribe your name.

Questions for Close Reading

1. What is the thesis of the selection? Locate the sentence(s) in which Fussell states his main idea. If he does not state the thesis explicitly, express it in your own words.
2. What changes in scouting are reflected in the new edition of *The Boy Scout Handbook*? How are these the results of "changing times"?
3. In what sense is *The Boy Scout Handbook* a "compendium of good sense"?
4. What criticisms does Fussell himself have about *The Boy Scout Handbook*? Does he consider these flaws serious ones? Why or why not?
5. Refer to your dictionary as needed to define the following words in the selection: *humanistic* (paragraph 1), *incipient* (2), *fascism* (2), *ascription* (3), *empiric* (5), *unambiguously* (6), and *compendia* (7).

Questions about the Writer's Craft

1. Like most writers discussing a controversial issue, Fussell does not disregard the opposing viewpoint. Instead, he wisely mentions it a

number of times. Where in the essay does Fussell cite objections to the Boy Scout movement and its handbook? How does this acknowledgment strengthen his argument?

2. The author admires the handbook because it "assumes an audience prepared by a very good high-school education," one "undaunted" by sophisticated words. On the basis of Fussell's word choice and sentence length, what audience would you say he "assumes" for his essay? In terms of the essay's content, who are its intended readers?

3. Wit has been defined as "finding similarities in dissimilar things." What examples of surprising comparisons do you find in this essay?

4. Fussell occasionally pokes fun at *The Boy Scout Handbook*. Find some places where he does this. Does this light ribbing injure his main point? Why or why not?

Questions for Further Thought

1. Were you among those who thought scouting was "either sinister or stupid or funny" before you read this essay? Has your opinion changed because of reading Fussell's analysis?

2. On the basis of what Fussell tells us about scouting, do you think being a boy or girl scout would prepare you well for adult life? Why or why not?

3. Is there any book that is, to you, a "compedium of good sense," a book to live by? What books have influenced your philosophy of life and your moral code?

4. What does the quote from Terrence Des Pres in paragraph 9 imply about our present-day attitudes to "goodness"? Do you feel we undervalue "goodness" today?

Writing Assignments Using Argumentation-Persuasion as a Method of Development

1. Fussell comments that former president Richard Nixon would not have made a good boy scout because of his conduct in Watergate. Write an essay arguing that a person you know, a person in public life, or a fictional character would or would not make a good scout.

2. Write an argumentation-persuasion essay recommending either that parents should or should not enroll their children in a scout troop. Assume that your audience is a group of parents who are somewhat opposed to your idea. Follow Fussell's organizational pattern in a general way: counter criticisms; show that the problems associated with joining are minor; save for the end of the essay an emphatic statement of the main benefit of your recommendation.

Writing Assignments Using Other Methods of Development

3. If you have ever been a scout, do you feel you benefited from the experience? How? Write a narrative or descriptive essay revealing the experiences that did or did not make scouting worthwhile. If you have not been a scout, use your membership in some other youth organization or your experiences at camp as the topic of your essay.

4. Some employees and professionals are required to wear uniforms, although a few professions in recent years have made uniforms optional (nursing, some clergy). Write an essay comparing the benefits and disadvantages of uniforms in the workplace. You may choose a specific profession or workplace (fast-food restaurants, airlines, gas stations). Or you may write in a more general way about uniforms, using examples drawn from particular jobs. Use your comparison of advantages and disadvantages to support a thesis that uniforms either should or should not be required of employees.

Harold Krents

In spite of lifelong blindness, Harold Krents graduated from Harvard University and received law degrees from Harvard Law School and Oxford University. He is a practicing attorney whose special interest in the rights of the handicapped has led him to work for several organizations devoted to fair treatment for the disabled. The following essay originally appeared on the Op-Ed page of The New York Times.

Darkness at Noon

At some point, most of us have thought, "What would it be like to be blind?" Then, with a slight shudder and unspoken gratitude for our sight, we return to our daily routine. For some people, of course, this "what if" is a reality. While we may think of the disabled solely in terms of their physical impairment, Harold Krents argues that being disabled is not the sum total of his or any handicapped person's life.

Blind from birth, I have never had the opportunity to see myself and have been completely dependent on the image I create in the eye of the observer. To date it has not been narcissistic. 1

There are those who assume that since I can't see, I obviously also cannot hear. Very often people will converse with me at the top of their lungs, enunciating each word very carefully. Conversely, people will also often whisper, assuming that since my eyes don't work, my ears don't either. 2

For example, when I go to the airport and ask the ticket agent for assistance to the plane, he or she will invariably pick up the phone, call a ground hostess and whisper: "Hi, Jane, we've got a 76 here." I have concluded that the word "blind" is not used for one of two reasons: Either they fear that if the dread word is spoken, the ticket agent's retina will immediately detach, or they are reluctant to inform me of my condition of which I may not have been previously aware. 3

On the other hand, others know that of course I can hear, but 4 believe that I can't talk. Often, therefore, when my wife and I go out to dinner, a waiter or waitress will ask Kit if "*he* would like a drink" to which I respond that "indeed *he* would."

This point was graphically driven home to me while we were in   5
England. I had been given a year's leave of absence from my Washington law firm to study for a diploma in law degree at Oxford University. During the year I became ill and was hospitalized. Immediately after admission, I was wheeled down to the X-ray room. Just at the door sat an elderly woman — elderly I would judge from the sound of her voice. "What is his name?" the woman asked the orderly who had been wheeling me.

"What's your name?" the orderly repeated to me.   6
"Harold Krents," I replied.   7
"Harold Krents," he repeated.   8
"When was he born?"   9
"When were you born?"   10
"November 5, 1944," I responded.   11
"November 5, 1944," the orderly intoned.   12
This procedure continued for approximately five minutes at   13
which point even my saint-like disposition deserted me. "Look," I finally blurted out, "this is absolutely ridiculous. Okay, granted I can't see, but it's got to have become pretty clear to both of you that I don't need an interpreter."

"He says he doesn't need an interpreter," the orderly reported   14
to the woman.

The toughest misconception of all is the view that because I   15
can't see, I can't work. I was turned down by over forty law firms because of my blindness, even though my qualifications included a cum laude degree from Harvard College and a good ranking in my Harvard Law School class.

The attempt to find employment, the continuous frustration   16
of being told that it was impossible for a blind person to practice law, the rejection letters, not based on my lack of ability but rather on my disability, will always remain one of the most disillusioning experiences of my life.

Fortunately, this view of limitation and exclusion is beginning   17
to change. On April 16, [1976,] the Department of Labor issued regulations that mandate equal-employment opportunities for the handicapped. By and large, the business community's response to offering employment to the disabled has been enthusiastic.

I therefore look forward to the day, with the expectation that it 18 is certain to come, when employers will view their handicapped workers as a little child did me years ago when my family still lived in Scarsdale.

I was playing basketball with my father in our backyard ac- 19 cording to procedures we had developed. My father would stand beneath the hoop, shout, and I would shoot over his head at the basket attached to our garage. Our next-door neighbor, aged five, wandered over into our yard with a playmate. "He's blind," our neighbor whispered to her friend in a voice that could be heard distinctly by Dad and me. Dad shot and missed; I did the same. Dad hit the rim: I missed entirely: Dad shot and missed the garage entirely. "Which one is blind?" whispered back the little friend.

I would hope that in the near future when a plant manager is 20 touring the factory with the foreman and comes upon a handi-capped and nonhandicapped person working together, his comment after watching them work will be, "Which one is disabled?"

Questions for Close Reading

1. What is the thesis of the selection? Locate the sentence(s) in which Krents states his main idea. If he does not state the thesis explicitly, express it in your own words.
2. Krents describes three ways people react to meeting him, a blind man. What are they?
3. When Krents quotes the child's question, "Which one is blind?," what inference does he want his readers to make?
4. In what ways does the author's handicap limit him? In what ways is he not handicapped?
5. Refer to your dictionary as needed to define the following words used in the selection: *narcissistic* (paragraph 1), *conversely* (2), *cum laude* (15), and *mandate* (17).

Questions about the Writer's Craft

1. How does Krents organize the three misconceptions people have about him as a blind person? In what way does this sequence reinforce the persuasiveness of his argument?
2. In what places does the author use humor? How is this humor impor-tant to your acceptance of his points?

3. Most of the paragraphs in "Darkness at Noon" are very short. What effect does this have on you as a reader? Does it make the essay more or less convincing?

4. Paragraph 17 indicates that employment opportunities for the handicapped are improving, but does not supply any supporting details. Why doesn't Krents develop this idea further?

Questions for Further Thought

1. Why do people react to a person with a handicap as if he or she were totally helpless? How do you feel and act when you meet a handicapped person?

2. If you were arrested, would you hire a blind or disabled lawyer to represent you? Would you hire a disabled lawyer to write your will or bring a suit for damages after an accident? Why or why not?

3. As a child, what were you taught about handicapped people? Do you think the ideas you learned were valid or not?

4. Do you feel the disabled, as a minority group, will ever be treated equally in the employment marketplace? Why or why not?

Writing Assignments Using Argumentation-Persuasion as a Method of Development

1. Many physically disabled people feel that the structural barriers found in buildings, rest rooms, sidewalks, and public buses limit their access to the world. Observe your most frequented places to determine how accessible they would be to you if you broke both legs and were temporarily confined to a wheelchair. Based on your observations, write an essay arguing that the physically handicapped do indeed encounter difficulties gaining access to facilities on campus or in your hometown. Be sure, though, to acknowledge what has been done to make places more accessible to the physically disabled. In the essay's concluding paragraph, propose what should be done to improve the situation.

2. Write an essay presenting an able-bodied person's view of the way to treat the handicapped. Remembering to consider the opposing viewpoint, argue one of the following:

   - Able-bodied people should assume that a handicapped person is as functional as anyone else and treat him or her no differently.
   - Able-bodied people should reach out and help handicapped people any way they can without being asked.
   - It is extremely difficult for a stranger to know what is appropriate when meeting a handicapped individual.

Writing Assignments Using Other Methods of Development

3. Krents tells us about his adjustment under trying circumstances. Write an essay describing injustices, slights, or hurts you experience during a difficult time. You might focus on your first days at college or a new job, the break-up of a relationship, being accused of something you didn't do, or any other situation. In the essay, tell how you were treated and show how inappropriate this treatment was. At the end of the paper, discuss what you learned from this stressful situation.

4. Write an essay that compares and/or contrasts the discrimination faced by the handicapped with the discrimination faced by another group. The group could be women, the elderly, or a racial or ethnic minority. To develop the comparison/contrast, focus on one key area of discrimination such as the following: how the groups are denied certain rights; how the groups are stereotyped; how the groups react to others' distorted perceptions.

Loudon Wainwright

A native New Yorker, Loudon Wainwright graduated from the University of North Carolina. After leaving the Marine Corps in 1945, Wainwright began his career at Life *magazine, where he worked as a writer, assistant picture editor, articles editor, and assistant managing editor. Now retired, he nonetheless continues to write "A View From Here,"* Life's *first and longest-running column. Focusing on a wide range of personal and social issues, Wainwright has written essays dealing with such subjects as the parent–child relationship, drug abuse, and—as in the selection reprinted here—censorship.*

A Little Banning Is a Dangerous Thing

Which books should children in school be allowed to read? Should a book with a character called "Nigger Jim" be banned because it appears racist? Should a book about a woman who bears an illegitimate child be prohibited because it deals with a touchy subject? But what if the books in question are two masterpieces of American writing, Huckleberry Finn *and* The Scarlet Letter? *In the following selection, Loudon Wainwright argues that book banners understand neither the material they want to censor nor the needs and good sense of children.*

My own introduction to sex in reading took place about 1935, 1
I think, just when the fertile soil of my young mind was ripe for
planting. The exact place it happened (so I've discovered from
checking the source in my local library) was the middle of page 249,
in a chapter titled "Apples and Ashes," soon after the beginning of
Book III of a mildly picaresque novel called *Anthony Adverse.* The
boy Anthony, 16, and a well-constructed character named Faith
Paleologus ("Her shoulders if one looked carefully were too wide.

But so superb was the bosom that rose up to support them. . . . ")
made it right there in her apartment where he'd gone to take a quick
bath, thinking (ho-ho) that she was out.

Faith was Anthony's sitter, sort of, and if author Hervey Allen   2
was just a touch obscure about the details of their moon-drenched
meeting, I filled in the gaps. "He was just in time," Allen wrote,
"to see the folds of her dress rustle down from her knees into coils
at her feet. . . . He stood still, rooted. The faint aroma of her body
floated to him. A sudden tide of passion dragged at his legs. . . .
He was half blind, and speechless now. All his senses had merged
into one feeling. . . . To be supported and yet possessed by an
ocean of unknown blue depths below you and to cease to think!
Yes, it was something like swimming on a transcendent summer
night."

Wow! Praying that my parents wouldn't come home and   3
catch me reading this terrific stuff, I splashed ahead, line after
vaguely lubricious line, exhilarated out of my mind at Anthony's
good fortune. "After a while he was just drifting in a continuous
current of ecstasy that penetrated him as if he were part of the
current in which he lay." I still don't understand *that* line, but I
sure feel the old surge of depravity. And reading it again, I thank
God there was no righteous book banner around at the time to
snatch it from me. *Anthony Adverse* doesn't rank as literature, or
even required reading, but I'm convinced it served a useful, even
educational, purpose for me at the time.

Alert vigilantes of the printed word worked hard to suppress   4
the novel then. The wretched little war to keep the minds of children clean is always going on. In fact, it has heated up considerably
since President Reagan came to power, with libraries around the
country reporting a threefold increase in demands that various
volumes even less ruinous than *Anthony Adverse* be withdrawn.
School boards, too, are feeling the cleansing fire of assorted cru-
saders against dirty words and irreverent expressions of one sort or
another. Protesters range from outraged individual parents to
teachers to local ministers to such well-organized watchdog outfits
as the Gabler family of Texas, Washington's Heritage Foundation
and, of course, the Moral Majority.

The victims are fighting back. Writers are leading public   5
"read-ins" of their banned works. One school board case, which
actually dates to 1976, has gone all the way to the U.S. Supreme

Court. Before the end of the current term, the court is expected to rule on whether or not the First Amendment rights (to free expression) of five students in Island Trees, N.Y., were denied when the board took nine books out of circulation. A far more personal thrust against censorship was made recently by author Studs Terkel. At the news that his book *Working* was in danger of being banned in Girard, Pa., Terkel went there and standing before the whole school in assembly made his own eloquent case for the book, for the so-called bad language in it and for reading in general. Six weeks later the school board voted unanimously to keep *Working* in the reading program where it had initially been challenged. Presumably they were persuaded, in part at least, that Terkel was *not*, as Kurt Vonnegut wrote in a furious and funny defense of his own *Slaughterhouse-Five*, one of those "sort of ratlike people who enjoy making money from poisoning the minds of young people."

What gets me is the weird presumption that the book banners   6
actually know something about the minds of young people. Vonnegut, among others, suspects that a lot of censors never even get around to reading the books they suppress. And just the briefest scanning of the list of titles currently banned or under threat in various communities calls the banners' credentials to rude question. *The Scarlet Letter, The Great Gatsby, A Farewell to Arms, Huckleberry Finn, The Grapes of Wrath* are a few of the variously seminal works challenged as somehow being dangerous to the stability of impressionable young minds. *Mary Poppins* and *The American Heritage Dictionary* have been under attack, too, the former after protests that its black characters were stereotypes, the latter presumably as a storehouse of words that shouldn't be viewed by innocent eyes, much less defined.

More critically, the censors forget, if they ever knew, many of   7
the needs of childhood. One, obviously, is the need for privacy, for a place to get away from the real world, a place where one is safe from — among other things — difficult or boring adult demands. The world that a reader makes is a perfect secret world. But if its topography is shaped by adults pushing their own hardened views of life, the secret world is spoiled.

Yet the world of the young human mind is by no means a   8
comfy habitat, as much as a lot of interfering adults would like to shape it that way. In *The Uses of Enchantment*, Bruno Bettelheim's book about the great importance of folk and fairy tales to child

development, the author writes: "There is a widespread refusal to let children know that the source of much that goes wrong in life is due to our very own natures — the propensity of all men for acting aggressively, asocially, selfishly, out of anger and anxiety. Instead, we want our children to believe that, inherently, all men are good. But children know that *they* are not always good; and often, even when they are, they would prefer not to be." In the fantasies commonly churned out in the mind of a normal child, whatever that is, bloody acts of revenge and conquest, daredevil assaults and outlandish wooings are common currency. To achieve the bleak, cramped, sanitized, fear-ridden state of many adults takes years of pruning and repression.

Books, as everyone but the censors knows, stimulate growth   9
better than anything — better than sit-coms, better than *Raiders of the Lost Ark*, better than video games. Many books, to be sure, are dreadful heaps of trash. But most of these die quickly in the marketplace or become best-sellers incapable of harming the adults who buy them.

It's often the best books that draw the beadiest attention of the   10
censors. These are the books that really have the most to offer, the news that life is rich and complicated and difficult. Where else, for example, could a young male reader see the isolation of his painful adolescence reflected the way it is in *The Catcher in the Rye*, one of the *most* banned books in American letters. In the guise of fiction, books offer opportunities, choices and plausible models. They light up the whole range of human character and emotion. Each, in its own way, tells the truth and prepares its eager readers for the unknown and unpredictable events of their own lives.

Anthony Adverse, my first banned book, was just a huge pot-   11
boiler of the period. Still, it tickled my fantasy. And it sharpened my appetite for better stuff, like *Lady Chatterley's Lover*. Actually I didn't read that tender and wonderful book until I was almost 50. I wish I'd read it much sooner while we were both still hot.

Questions for Close Reading

1. What is the thesis of the selection? Locate the sentence(s) in which Wainwright states his main idea. If he does not state the thesis explicitly, express it in your own words.

2. What was Wainwright's initial reaction to *Anthony Adverse?* Why does he say it served a "useful, even educational" purpose in his childhood?
3. Who are the book banners, according to the author? What kind of people are they—and what motivates them?
4. According to Wainwright, what benefits do children get from reading books, even ones with "bannable" characteristics? Are these the same benefits of reading that educators stress?
5. Refer to your dictionary as needed to define the following words in the selection: *lubricious* (paragraph 3), *ecstasy* (3), *depravity* (3), *vigilantes* (4), and *potboiler* (11).

Questions about the Writer's Craft

1. In describing those who would ban books, Wainwright uses negatively charged words. For example, he calls them "vigilantes" in paragraph 4. Find other examples of vivid words and phrases that contain negative connotations. What effect do these loaded words have on the argument against banning?
2. You probably have heard the expression, "A little learning is a dangerous thing." Why does Wainwright use a variant of this saying as his title? How is a little banning "dangerous"?
3. Why does the author use the agricultural metaphor "the fertile soil of my young mind was ripe for planting" in the first sentence? What does this farming image have to do with reading a sexy passage in a book?
4. What is Wainwright's tone in the final paragraph? Why do you think he chose to conclude with this reference to a renowned banned book rather than present a conventional summary or concluding argument?

Questions for Further Thought

1. Should any books be banned? If so, which ones, and why? Should the reading of children and young people be closely monitored?
2. Does it really matter what children read, see, listen to, in books and the media? Is their moral development determined by their homelife and upbringing, their community environment, their formal education, or by such cultural experiences as books and TV?
3. The quotation from psychologist Bruno Bettelheim suggests that children are aware they are capable of wrong, yet adults often try to shelter them from life's realities. Should children be kept innocent, or should they be taught about all aspects of life?
4. Are books the best way of educating children, or are TV, films and video better for stimulating children intellectually? Is Wainwright old-fashioned in his preference for books?

Writing Assignments Using Argumentation-Persuasion as a Method of Development

1. Wainwright is concerned about attempts to ban literary works and middle-brow books, those that make the bestseller list. But what about books and magazines that cater to the basest parts of human nature — for example, publications that feature sadism, child pornography, and racism? Should society censor these publications? Or should we have total freedom of the press? Write an essay arguing for or against control of such material.

2. As a moral majority member, you have read Wainwright's essay and have decided to respond. Write an essay rebutting three of Wainwright's statements. Or base the essay on three reasons why the reading of young people should be controlled by responsible adults. In either case, your argument should take the opposition into account.

Writing Assignments Using Other Methods of Development

3. Choose three books and/or magazines you read as a child that would have upset your parents (or grandparents) if they had known. Write an essay showing that the materials you read are precisely the kinds of publications that children should be allowed *or* forbidden to read. Support your point of view with convincing examples.

4. Discuss the amount of explicit sexual content in one of the following:

Movies	Popular song lyrics	TV miniseries
Soap operas	Magazine ads	Billboards

Your working thesis might be that there is *or* there is not too much explicit sexual content in today's ⸺⸺⸺⸺⸺⸺⸺⸺ .

Roger Rosenblatt

Time *magazine publishes a one-page essay each week, and its author is often Roger Rosenblatt, senior writer for the magazine. Born in 1940, Rosenblatt earned his doctorate at Harvard University and directed the university's expository writing program for several years. Later, he served as the literary editor of* The New Republic *and joined the editorial board of the* Washington Post. *The following selection first appeared in* Time.

The Man in the Water

During a crisis, people often go to extremes. Some panic, fall apart, or flee. Others display utter calm, great physical courage, and extraordinary stamina. In "The Man in the Water," Roger Rosenblatt describes a plane crash and its aftermath. He focuses especially on the heroism of one person, a person whose instincts represent the best qualities in human nature.

As disasters go, this one was terrible, but not unique, certainly 1 not among the worst on the roster of U.S. air crashes. There was the unusual element of the bridge, of course, and the fact that the plane clipped it at a moment of high traffic, one routine thus intersecting another and disrupting both. Then, too, there was the location of the event. Washington, the city of form and regulations, turned chaotic, deregulated, by a blast of real winter and a single slap of metal on metal. The jets from Washington National Airport that normally swoop around the presidential monuments like famished gulls are, for the moment, emblemized by the one that fell; so there is that detail. And there was the aesthetic clash as well — blue-and-green Air Florida, the name a flying garden, sunk down among gray chunks in a black river. All that was worth noticing, to be sure. Still, there was nothing very special in any of it, except death, which, while always special, does not necessarily bring millions to tears or to attention. Why, then, the shock here?

Perhaps because the nation saw in this disaster something   2
more than a mechanical failure. Perhaps because people saw in it no
failure at all, but rather something successful about their makeup.
Here, after all, were two forms of nature in collision: the elements
and human character. Last Wednesday, the elements, indifferent as
ever, brought down Flight 90. And on that same afternoon, human
nature — groping and flailing in mysteries of its own — rose to the
occasion.

Of the four acknowledged heroes of the event, three are able to   3
account for their behavior. Donald Usher and Eugene Windsor, a
park police helicopter team, risked their lives every time they
dipped the skids into the water to pick up survivors. On television,
side by side in bright blue jumpsuits, they described their courage
as all in the line of duty. Lenny Skutnik, a 28-year-old employee of
the Congressional Budget Office, said: "It's something I never
thought I would do" — referring to his jumping into the water to
drag an injured woman to shore. Skutnik added that "somebody
had to go in the water," delivering every hero's line that is no less
admirable for its repetitions. In fact, nobody had to go into the
water. That somebody actually did so is part of the reason this
particular tragedy sticks in the mind.

But the person most responsible for the emotional impact of   4
the disaster is the one known at first simply as "the man in the
water." (Balding, probably in his 50s, an extravagant mustache.)
He was seen clinging with five other survivors to the tail section of
the airplane. This man was described by Usher and Windsor as
appearing alert and in control. Every time they lowered a lifeline
and flotation ring to him, he passed it on to another of the passengers. "In a mass casualty, you'll find people like him," said Windsor. "But I've never seen one with that commitment." When the
helicopter came back for him, the man had gone under. His selfless-
ness was one reason the story held national attention; his anonym-
ity another. The fact that he went unidentified invested him with a
universal character. For a while he was Everyman, and thus proof
(as if one needed it) that no man is ordinary.

Still, he could never have imagined such a capacity in himself.   5
Only minutes before his character was tested, he was sitting in the
ordinary plane among the ordinary passengers, dutifully listening
to the stewardess telling him to fasten his seat belt and saying

something about the "no smoking sign." So our man relaxed with the others, some of whom would owe their lives to him. Perhaps he started to read, or to doze, or to regret some harsh remark made in the office that morning. Then suddenly he knew that the trip would not be ordinary. Like every other person on that flight, he was desperate to live, which makes his final act so stunning.

For at some moment in the water he must have realized that he would not live if he continued to hand over the rope and ring to others. He *had* to know it, no matter how gradual the effect of the cold. In his judgment he had no choice. When the helicopter took off with what was to be the last survivor, he watched everything in the world move away from him, and he deliberately let it happen. 6

Yet there was something else about the man that kept our thoughts on him, and which keeps our thoughts on him still. He was *there*, in the essential, classic circumstance. Man in nature. The man in the water. For its part, nature cared nothing about the five passengers. Our man, on the other hand, cared totally. So the timeless battle commenced in the Potomac. For as long as that man could last, they went at each other, nature and man; the one making no distinctions of good and evil, acting on no principles, offering no lifelines; the other acting wholly on distinctions, principles and, one supposes, on faith. 7

Since it was he who lost the fight, we ought to come again to the conclusion that people are powerless in the world. In reality, we believe the reverse, and it takes the act of the man in the water to remind us of our true feelings in this matter. It is not to say that everyone would have acted as he did, or as Usher, Windsor and Skutnik. Yet whatever moved these men to challenge death on behalf of their fellows is not peculiar to them. Everyone feels the possibility in himself. That is the abiding wonder of the story. That is why we would not let go of it. If the man in the water gave a lifeline to the people gasping for survival, he was likewise giving a lifeline to those who observed him. 8

The odd thing is that we do not even really believe that the man in the water lost his fight. "Everything in Nature contains all the powers of Nature," said Emerson. Exactly. So the man in the water had his own natural powers. He could not make ice storms, or freeze the water until it froze the blood. But he could hand life over to a stranger, and that is a power of nature too. The man in the 9 water pitted himself against an implacable, impersonal enemy; he fought it with charity; and he held it to a standoff. He was the best we can do.

Questions for Close Reading

1. What is the thesis of the selection? Locate the sentence(s) in which Rosenblatt states his main idea. If he does not state the thesis explicitly, express it in your own words.
2. In the second paragraph, Rosenblatt says that people saw "no failure at all, but rather something successful . . . " in the accident. How did this plane crash come to include elements of success?
3. What made this accident, just one of many plane crashes, unusual and attention-getting?
4. Why, according to the author, do we "not even really believe the man in the water lost his fight" even though he died?
5. Refer to your dictionary as needed to define the following words in the selection: *emblemized* (paragraph 1), *aesthetic* (1), and *implacable* (9).

Questions about the Writer's Craft

1. This essay does not at first seem to be argumentation-persuasion, but rather narration or description. At what point did you realize you were being persuaded to hold a certain viewpoint about the man in the water? To what extent and in what places does Rosenblatt use *pathos*, or emotional appeals, to achieve his purpose?
2. In the first paragraph, Rosenblatt underplays the accident and holds off identifying the flight number until the end of paragraph 2. What is the effect of his maintaining "there was nothing very special in any of it"? How does this way of beginning prepare us emotionally for the point he is going to make?
3. At what point does Rosenblatt take us inside the mind of our unknown man? How does this change in point of view affect our perception of the man in the water?
4. The author points out that this accident embodied "two forms of nature in collision: the elements and human character." There are a number of other contrasts and oppositions presented in the essay. Locate some of them. How do these contrasts help us to appreciate "human character"?

Questions for Further Thought

1. Do you agree that the man in the water is a hero? Is he more of a hero than the other three "acknowledged heroes"? What seems to be the author's definition of heroism?

2. The author writes that the unknown man gave "a lifeline to those who observed him." What does he mean by this? Why do we, the observers, need such a lifeline?

3. Reread the concluding paragraph. Why is this unknown man "the best we can do"? What does Rosenblatt mean by the man's "natural powers"? Why is "a standoff" our best result in our fight against nature?

4. The will to live, to survive at all costs, is usually considered to be our strongest instinct. What even stronger motivation might the man in the water have had? Do you think anything could ever motivate you to give up your own life?

Writing Assignments Using Argumentation-Persuasion as a Method of Development

1. Some experts argue that qualities like heroism can be attributed to genetic makeup; that is, either people are born with the trait or they are not. Other experts, like Lawrence Kohlberg, contend that we humans acquire such virtues if — as children — we are given opportunities to learn about and practice desirable behaviors. Remembering to cite the opposing view, support the proposition that we can *or* cannot be taught to act morally. Develop your argument through specific reference to your own experiences and observations.

2. Rosenblatt writes that for a while the unknown "was Everyman, and thus proof . . . that no man was ordinary." Take as your thesis the idea that no person is ordinary, and write an essay arguing that even the most average person has the potential for heroism. Use the introduction to establish the opposing view: that the mundane nature of everyday life makes heroic action unlikely. Develop your argument by drawing on your own or others' experience. Your essay could focus on any of the following:

   • A person who risked his or her life for others.
   • An athlete who plays on despite pain or injury.
   • A person who perseveres in spite of overwhelming obstacles.
   • A person who overcomes a disability and leads a fulfilling life.

Writing Assignments Using Other Methods of Development

3. Write an essay defining your concept of heroism by explaining what a hero is *not*. Consider at least several of the following possible heroes: politicians and elected officials, celebrities, sports stars, political activ-

ists and protesters, soldiers, the handicapped, parents, and rebels and nonconformists. The final section of the paper should reveal who you think the real heroes are.

4. Many movie and TV series feature heroes. How do these heroes differ from the man in the water? Write an essay that compares and/or contrasts one or more typical movie or TV heroes with the man in the water. Come to some conclusion about the true nature of heroism and the image of human nobility conveyed by the media.

Mark Twain

Mark Twain is a central figure in American literature. The Adventures of Huckleberry Finn, *his finest work, is the story of a journey down the Mississippi by two memorable figures, a white boy and a black slave. Twain was born Samuel Langhorne Clemens in 1835 and was raised in Hannibal, Missouri. During his early years, he worked as a riverboat pilot, newspaper reporter, printer, and gold prospector. Although his popular image is as the author of such comic works as* The Adventures of Tom Sawyer, Life on the Mississippi, *and* The Prince and the Pauper, *Twain had a darker side that may have resulted from the bitter experiences of his life: financial failure and the deaths of his wife and daughter. His last writings are savage, satiric, and pessimistic. The following selection is taken from* Letters From the Earth, *one of his later works.*

The Damned Human Race

Did today's newspaper contain a headline about people—Irish, Lebanese, Salvadoran—fighting somewhere in the world? Most likely, it did. In the following selection, Mark Twain concludes that the combative and cruel nature of human beings makes them the lowest of creatures, not the highest. With scathing irony, he supplies a startling reason for humans' warlike nature.

I have been studying the traits and dispositions of the "lower 1
animals" (so-called), and contrasting them with the traits and dispositions of man. I find the result humiliating to me. For it obliges me to renounce my allegiance to the Darwinian theory of the Ascent of Man from the Lower Animals; since it now seems plain to me that that theory ought to be vacated in favor of a new and truer one, this new and truer one to be named the *Descent* of Man from the Higher Animals.

In proceeding toward this unpleasant conclusion I have not   2
guessed or speculated or conjectured, but have used what is commonly called the scientific method. That is to say, I have subjected
every postulate that presented itself to the crucial test of actual
experiment, and have adopted it or rejected it according to the
result. Thus I verified and established each step of my course in its
turn before advancing to the next. These experiments were made in
the London Zoological Gardens, and covered many months of
painstaking and fatiguing work.

Before particularizing any of the experiments, I wish to state   3
one or two things which seem to more properly belong in this place
than further along. This in the interest of clearness. The massed
experiments established to my satisfaction certain generalizations,
to wit:

1. That the human race is of one distinct species. It exhibits
   slight variations — in color, stature, mental caliber, and so
   on — due to climate, environment, and so forth; but it is a
   species by itself, and not to be confounded with any other.
2. That the quadrupeds are a distinct family, also. This family
   exhibits variations — in color, size, food preferences and so
   on; but it is a family by itself.
3. That the other families — the birds, the fishes, the insects,
   the reptiles, etc. — are more or less distinct, also. They are
   in the procession. They are links in the chain which
   stretches down from the higher animals to man at the bottom.

Some of my experiments were quite curious. In the course of   4
my reading I had come across a case where, many years ago, some
hunters on our Great Plains organized a buffalo hunt for the entertainment of an English earl — that, and to provide some fresh meat
for his larder. They had charming sport. They killed seventy-two of
those great animals; and ate part of one of them and left the sev-
enty-one to rot. In order to determine the difference between an
anaconda and an earl — if any — I caused seven young calves to be
turned into the anaconda's cage. The grateful reptile immediately
crushed one of them and swallowed it, then lay back satisfied. It
showed no further interest in the calves, and no disposition to harm
them. I tried this experiment with other anacondas; always with the

same result. The fact stood proven that the difference between an earl and an anaconda is that the earl is cruel and the anaconda isn't; and that the earl wantonly destroys what he has no use for, but the anaconda doesn't. This seemed to suggest that the anaconda was not descended from the earl. It also seemed to suggest that the earl was descended from the anaconda, and had lost a good deal in the transition.

I was aware that many men who have accumulated more millions of money than they can ever use have shown a rabid hunger for more, and have not scrupled to cheat the ignorant and the helpless out of their poor servings in order to partially appease that appetite. I furnished a hundred different kinds of wild and tame animals the opportunity to accumulate vast stores of food, but none of them would do it. The squirrels and bees and certain birds made accumulations, but stopped when they had gathered a winter's supply, and could not be persuaded to add to it either honestly or by chicane. In order to bolster up a tottering reputation the ant pretended to store up supplies, but I was not deceived. I know the ant. These experiments convinced me that there is this difference between man and the higher animals: he is avaricious and miserly, they are not.

In the course of my experiments I convinced myself that among the animals man is the only one that harbors insults and injuries, broods over them, waits till a chance offers, then takes revenge. The passion of revenge is unknown to the higher animals. 5

Roosters keep harems, but it is by consent of their concubines; therefore no wrong is done. Men keep harems, but it is by brute force, privileged by atrocious laws which the other sex were allowed no hand in making. In this matter man occupies a far lower place than the rooster. 7

Cats are loose in their morals, but not consciously so. Man, in his descent from the cat, has brought the cat's looseness with him but has left the unconsciousness behind — the saving grace which excuses the cat. The cat is innocent, man is not. 8

Indecency, vulgarity, obscenity — these are strictly confined to man; he invented them. Among the higher animals there is no trace of them. They hide nothing; they are not ashamed. Man, with his soiled mind, covers himself. He will not even enter a drawing room with his breast and back naked, so alive are he and his mates to indecent suggestion. Man is "The Animal that Laughs." But so 9 does the monkey, as Mr. Darwin pointed out; and so does the Australian bird that is called the laughing jackass. No — Man is the Animal that Blushes. He is the only one that does it — or has occasion to.

At the head of this article we see how "three monks were burnt   10
to death" a few days ago, and a prior "put to death with atrocious cruelty." Do we inquire into the details? No; or we should find out that the prior was subjected to unprintable mutilations. Man — when he is a North American Indian — gouges out his prisoner's eyes; when he is King John, with a nephew to render untroublesome, he uses a red-hot iron; when he is a religious zealot dealing with heretics in the Middle Ages, he skins his captive alive and scatters salt on his back; in the first Richard's time he shuts up a multitude of Jew families in a tower and sets fire to it; in Columbus's time he captures a family of Spanish Jews and — but *that* is not printable; in our day in England a man is fined ten shillings for beating his mother nearly to death with a chair, and another man is fined forty shillings for having four pheasant eggs in his possession without being able to satisfactorily explain how he got them. Of all the animals, man is the only one that is cruel. He is the only one that inflicts pain for the pleasure of doing it. It is a trait that is not known to the higher animals. The cat plays with the frightened mouse; but she has this excuse, that she does not know that the mouse is suffering. The cat is moderate — unhumanly moderate: she only scares the mouse, she does not hurt it; she doesn't dig out its eyes, or tear off its skin, or drive splinters under its nails — man-fashion; when she is done playing with it she makes a sudden meal of it and puts it out of its trouble. Man is the Cruel Animal. He is alone in that distinction.

The higher animals engage in individual fights, but never in   11
organized masses. Man is the only animal that deals in that atrocity of atrocities, War. He is the only one that gathers his brethren about him and goes forth in cold blood and with calm pulse to exterminate his kind. He is the only animal that for sordid wages will march out, as the Hessians did in our Revolution, and as the boyish Prince Napoleon did in the Zulu war, and help to slaughter strangers of his own species who have done him no harm and with whom he has no quarrel.

Man is the only animal that robs his helpless fellow of his   12
country — takes possession of it and drives him out of it or destroys

him. Man has done this in all the ages. There is not an acre of ground on the globe that is in possession of its rightful owner, or that has not been taken away from owner after owner, cycle after cycle, by force and bloodshed.

Man is the only Slave. And he is the only animal who enslaves. 13 He has always been a slave in one form or another, and has always held other slaves in bondage under him in one way or another. In our day he is always some man's slave for wages, and does that man's work; and this slave has other slaves under him for minor wages, and they do *his* work. The higher animals are the only ones who exclusively do their own work and provide their own living.

Man is the only Patriot. He sets himself apart in his own 14 country, under his own flag, and sneers at the other nations, and keeps multitudinous uniformed assassins on hand at heavy expense to grab slices of other people's countries, and keep *them* from grabbing slices of *his*. And in the intervals between campaigns he washes the blood off his hands and works for "the universal brotherhood of man" — with his mouth.

Man is the Religious Animal. He is the only Religious Animal. 15 He is the only animal that has the True Religion — several of them. He is the only animal that loves his neighbor as himself, and cuts his throat if his theology isn't straight. He has made a graveyard of the globe in trying his honest best to smooth his brother's path to happiness and heaven. He was at it in the time of the Caesars, he was at it in Mahomet's time, he was at it in the time of the Inquisition, he was at it in France a couple of centuries, he was at it in England in Mary's day, he has been at it ever since he first saw the light, he is at it today in Crete — as per the telegrams quoted above — he will be at it somewhere else tomorrow. The higher animals have no religion. And we are told that they are going to be left out, in the Hereafter. I wonder why? It seems questionable taste.

Man is the Reasoning Animal. Such is the claim. I think it is 16 open to dispute. Indeed, my experiments have proven to me that he is the Unreasoning Animal. Note his history, as sketched above. It seems plain to me that whatever he is he is *not* a reasoning animal. His record is the fantastic record of a maniac. I consider that the strongest count against his intelligence is the fact that with that record back of him he blandly sets himself up as the head animal of the lot: whereas by his own standards he is the bottom one.

In truth, man is incurably foolish. Simple things which the 17 other animals easily learn, he is incapable of learning. Among my experiments was this. In an hour I taught a cat and a dog to be friends. I put them in a cage. In another hour I taught them to be friends with a rabbit. In the course of two days I was able to add a fox, a goose, a squirrel and some doves. Finally a monkey. They lived together in peace; even affectionately.

Next, in another cage I confined an Irish Catholic from Tip- 18 perary, and as soon as he seemed tame I added a Scotch Presbyterian from Aberdeen. Next a Turk from Constantinople; a Greek Christian from Crete; an Armenian; a Methodist from the wilds of Arkansas; a Buddhist from China; a Brahman from Benares. Finally, a Salvation Army Colonel from Wapping. Then I stayed away two whole days. When I came back to note results, the cage of Higher Animals was all right, but in the other there was but a chaos of gory odds and ends of turbans and fezzes and plaids and bones and flesh — not a specimen left alive. These Reasoning Animals had disagreed on a theological detail and carried the matter to a Higher Court.

One is obliged to concede that in true loftiness of character, 19 Man cannot claim to approach even the meanest of the Higher Animals. It is plain that he is constitutionally incapable of approaching that altitude; that he is constitutionally afflicted with a Defect which must make such approach forever impossible, for it is manifest that this defect is permanent in him, indestructible, ineradicable.

I find this Defect to be *the Moral Sense*. He is the only animal 20 that has it. It is the secret of his degradation. It is the quality *which enables him to do wrong*. It has no other office. It is incapable of performing any other function. It could never have been intended to perform any other. Without it, man could do no wrong. He would rise at once to the level of the Higher Animals.

Since the Moral Sense has but the one office, the one capacity 21 — to enable man to do wrong — it is plainly without value to him. It is as valueless to him as is disease. In fact, it manifestly *is* a disease. *Rabies* is bad, but it is not so bad as this disease. Rabies enables a man to do a thing which he could not do when in a healthy state: kill his neighbor with a poisonous bite. No one is the better man for having rabies: The Moral Sense enables a man to do wrong. It enables him to do wrong in a thousand ways. Rabies is an innocent disease, compared to the Moral Sense. No one, then, can be the better man for having the Moral Sense. What, now, do we find the Primal Curse to have been? Plainly what it was in the beginning: the infliction upon man of the Moral Sense; the ability to distinguish good from evil; and with it, necessarily, the ability to *do* evil; for there can be no evil act without the presence of consciousness of it in the doer of it.

And so I find that we have descended and degenerated, from some far ancestor — some microscopic atom wandering at its pleasure between the mighty horizons of a drop of water perchance — insect by insect, animal by animal, reptile by reptile, down the long highway of smirchless innocence, till we have reached the bottom stage of development — namable as the Human Being. Below us — nothing.   22

Questions for Close Reading

1. What is the thesis of the selection? Locate the sentence(s) in which Twain states his main idea. If he does not state the thesis explicitly, express it in your own words.
2. Humans are usually called the highest animal, on the basis of intelligence. What are the specific traits that make humans the lowest animal for Twain?
3. How does the story of the earl who hunted down seventy-two buffalo prove that an anaconda is superior to an earl?
4. What does Twain mean when he points out that humankind is the only animal that "has occasion to" blush? What are some of the occasions for blushing he highlights in the essay?
5. Refer to your dictionary as needed to define the following words used in the selection: *confounded* (paragraph 3), *anaconda* (4), *wantonly* (4), *chicane* (5), *heretics* (10), *constitutionally* (19), *ineradicable* (19), and *smirchless* (22).

Questions about the Writer's Craft

1. Most writers do not tell the reader outright the reasoning process they used to arrive at their essay's proposition. But Twain, with scathing irony, states that he reached his conclusion about human beings inductively — through the use of the "scientific method." Why does Twain make this claim?
2. Where in the essay does Twain try to shock the audience? What might be his purpose in using this technique?

3. In some paragraphs Twain piles on the examples of political and religious atrocities. Wouldn't one or two examples be enough? Why does he supply so many?

4. Black humor is defined as "the use of the morbid and the absurd for comic purposes." What elements of the morbid and the absurd do you find in Twain's essay? Would you say "The Damned Human Race" is an example of black humor?

Questions for Further Thought

1. Twain wrote this essay in the early 1900s. Is what he says about humans true today? Have people improved in a century's time? If Twain were writing today, what events and situations would he include in this essay as proof of humanity's lowness?

2. After reading this satire, are you incensed at humanity's failures — or at Mark Twain for taking this approach to exposing them? Has Twain gone overboard here? Or do we humans deserve this attack?

3. If a person behaved like the cat with a mouse that Twain describes in paragraph 10, would that person be evil, or innocent like the cat? Is it really behavior that is the problem for Twain? Or something else?

4. Twain's essay hinges on an idea most of us take for granted — that the human species tops a hierarchy of creatures. We are, we assume, the ultimate creature, the end result of nature's evolutionary process. What would happen if we became aware that we were not the cleverest, most powerful creature in the universe? What beliefs, habits, actions of ours might change?

Writing Assignments Using Argumentation-Persuasion as a Method of Development

1. Twain focuses on the atrocities committed by human beings in order to show that we are desperately flawed. Write an essay arguing it is our everyday meannesses, unkindnesses, and cruelties that make us the "lowest animal." Use real incidents as your examples, and include whatever description and dialogue you wish. Some situations you might choose include:

> Violence or abuse toward children.
> Neglectful or abusive behavior toward animals.
> Insults or prejudice of a racial, sexist, or religious nature.
> Indifference to homeless or injured people.
> Sarcasm and jesting that humilates people, friends, family.

Use the introduction or conclusion of the essay to acknowledge briefly the opposing viewpoint.

2. In an essay, argue that human beings are worthy of being considered the "highest animal." The paper should acknowledge and then refute Twain's charges that people are miserly, vengeful, foolish, and so on. To support your proposition, use specific examples of how human beings can be kind, caring, generous, and peace-loving.

Writing Assignments Using Other Methods of Development

3. What failings of human decency do you see around you every day in your town, on your campus, or at your job? Write an essay showing that inhumanity resides not just in atrocities but also in ordinary life. You may wish to use a sarcastic or bitter tone, as Twain does, and include some "one-liners" or absurd statements.

4. How could humans become less cruel? Write an essay outlining a new process for raising children or "recivilizing" adults — processes, which if instituted, would improve the morality of humanity. You may wish to approach the essay seriously, or you may take a humorous tone.

Thomas Tutko and William Bruns

Thomas Tutko is a professor at San Jose State University, specializing in sports psychology. Born in Pennsylvania, he received a Ph.D. from Northwestern University and has coauthored a number of sports-related books, including Psychology of Coaching *(1971) and* Sports-Psyching *(1976). William Bruns is a freelance writer with an M.A. in journalism from UCLA. His work has appeared in such magazines as* Life, People, *and* Money. *A reporter for* Time *at the 1984 Summer Olympics, Bruns has written or coauthored fifteen books on sports and fitness. The following selection is taken from a book written by Tutko and Bruns,* Winning Is Everything and Other American Myths *(1976).*

To Win or Not to Win:
That Is the Question

Most likely, you have spent — and will spend — much of your life competing. You may compete in sports, but you will also compete for grades, jobs, promotions, even dates and marriage partners. Our free enterprise system is based on competition. Is this why Monday night football is a sacred ritual, why newspapers devote dozens of pages to sports results, why fans battle and brawl over their favorite teams? In this essay, Thomas Tutko and William Bruns explore what amounts to a national obsession with winning, with being "Number One."

One effect of this country's sports craze is that the owners, coaches, players, and fans all suffer from the same delusions. We thirst for whatever tangible evidence we can find that says, "We're a winner. We're Number One!" The athlete or coach who is near the bottom always feels, "I'll win and that'll mean something. I'll be worthwhile, loved, honored, and obeyed." This fundamental faith in the goodness of sports was typified by George Raveling when he took over as head basketball coach at Washington State with the

1

618

goal of helping to end UCLA's dominance in the Pacific Eight conference and in the country. When Raveling was asked how he thought he could succeed where so many had fallen short before, he answered: "I just rely on that saying that the struggle to the top is a rugged one but the view from the top is beautiful. I want that view, and we'll work as hard as we can to get there."

I like Raveling; I think he's a model young coach. But what   2 realistically will happen if, by chance, he knocks off UCLA and wins the NCAA title? What happens when *anybody* reaches the top in sports? Can they relax and savor that moment? Of course not. They have to do it again the next year, and the year after that. . . . Even if you are John Wooden and you win seven consecutive NCAA championships, your fans grumble when you fail to win an eighth. In individual sports like swimming and track and field, breaking records only leaves new records to be broken. No matter at what level we compete and in whatever sport, when we attain a goal we simply move it up another notch, hunting for a perfection that is always just out of reach.

Winning, in fact, is like drinking salt water; it will never   3 quench your thirst. It is an insatiable greed. There are never enough victories, never enough championships or records. If we win, we take another gulp and have even greater fantasies.

From their inception in 1960, the Dallas Cowboys went   4 twelve frustrating years without winning the National Football League championship. They had outstanding talent and they came close on several occasions, but they never could win "the big one." When they finally did win the Super Bowl in 1972, owner Tex Schramm went on television in the midst of his celebrating players and boasted that Dallas would now build a *dynasty*! That's what happens when you drink salt water instead of champagne.

Individual athletes are caught up in the same competitive   5 madness. In 1974, 22-year-old Jimmy Connors suddenly blasted his way to the top of the tennis world by winning Wimbledon and Forest Hills and over $200,000. By September there was no denying his number one ranking. Yet he was never able to relax and enjoy his time on top, something he had trained for from the time he was three years old. A week after winning at Forest Hills he won a tournament in Los Angeles and then was practically forced into playing in San Francisco, two nights later. Furthermore, reporters began asking him what he would do for an encore in 1975. "Well, I

plan to just have another great year," he told them, "Do it all over
again. Pancho Gonzales told me the other day, 'Jim, you proved
this year you're a *good* player. But you'll have to do it a lot of times
to prove you're a great one.'" . . .

Freud would have clearly defined our behavior as a repetition   6
compulsion because there is no moment where the winner can feel,
"I've made it." In *Meat on the Hoof*, Texas football player Gary
Shaw wrote: "A clear-cut victory leads only to another challenge in
a perpetual rat race. As long as there is an attempt to hold on to this
simple view of life as a series of challenges and victories with a few
winners and many losers, then we will be trapped in an anxious and
basically frustrating existence." . . .

The craze in this country that demands that your success in   7
sports is measured only by winning, that you are nothing until
you're Number One, was crystallized by Vince Lombardi's dictum
"Winning isn't everything. It's the only thing." Years later, the
famous football coach claimed he had been misquoted, that what
he had actually said was, "Winning is not everything — but making
the effort to win is."

In fact, the "winning" quote apparently originated with an-   8
other football coach, the late Red Sanders, when he was at Vanderbilt in 1940. The phrase later surfaced, inevitably, in a John Wayne
movie, *Trouble Along the Way*. Wayne plays a tough ex-professional
football coach who is trying to keep custody of his only daughter
while at the same time whipping a small college team into a national powerhouse. Donna Reed, an employee of the child welfare
bureau, asks him one day, "Is winning everything to you?" The
Duke replies, "No, ma'am. Winning isn't everything. It's the only
thing."

This drive to compete and to be a "winner" has always been   9
part of the American psyche. Our early ancestors were aggressive
and competitive to begin with. They knew they were pitted against
amazing odds, but they also felt they were a select and chosen
group. They defied their mother country and were successful. Later
came the "frontier spirit," the belief in survival of the fittest, and
the growing American fetish for figures, statistics, records, and
winners. Over forty years ago, John R. Tunis wrote, in *The American Way in Sport*: "We worship the victors. But why? The Dutch
don't especially, nor the Swedes, neither do the Danes, the Swiss, or
the English, and they all seem fairly civilized people." We devised
an international "scoreboard" to chart our successes in the Olym-

pics as well as in our wars, an obsession that was tragically reflected in our approach to Vietnam, where both President Johnson and President Nixon vowed that they were not going down in history as "the first American President who lost a war."

The competitive instinct that permeates the American spirit is   10 one of the most highly prized values in the country, emanating from our presidents on down. But it is not just competition that is important — it is who *wins* that really matters. When Gerald Ford was vice-president, he wrote in *Sports Illustrated*: "It has been said that we are losing our competitive spirit in this country, the thing that made us great, the guts of the free-enterprise system. I don't agree with that; the competitive urge is deep-rooted in the American character." Fair enough, but then he goes on to say: "We have been asked to swallow a lot of home-cooked psychology in recent years that winning isn't all that important anymore, whether on the athletic field or in any other field, national and international. I don't buy that for a minute. It is not enough to just compete. Winning is very important. Maybe more important than ever." Later, when he was president, Ford continued to plug winning as a great American tradition. "What about winning?" he asked. "How about a good word for the ultimate reason any of us have for going into a competitive sport? As much as I enjoyed the physical and emotional dividends that college athletics brought me, I sincerely doubt if I ever suited up, put on my helmet . . . without the total commitment of going out there to win, not to get exercise, gold or glory, but simply to win."

Gerald Ford is just one of many defenders of the winning   11 creed, as the following quotations will show. . . .

Texas football coach Darrel Royal: "The only way I know how   12 to keep football fun is to win. That's the only answer. There is no laughter in losing." (Read *Meat on the Hoof* to confirm that Royal is not joking.)

Former Kansas City Chiefs coach Hank Stram: "It's only a   13 game when you win. When you lose it's hell." (Especially when it costs you your job.)

Former Boston Bruins coach Bep Guidolin: "Winning is the   14 name of the game. The more you win the less you get fired." (This statement was made before Guidolin lost his job when his Bruins lost in the seventh game of the 1974 Stanley Cup play-off finals to Philadelphia.)

The late Alabama football coach Bear Bryant, asked what he   15 most wanted to be remembered for: "I'd like if it'd be for winning . . . That's our approach: If it's worth playing, it's worth paying the price to win." . . .

Former Dallas quarterback Roger Staubach: "In pro football   16
winning is all there is. If you don't win, you haven't done what the game is about." (Staubach is an active member of the Fellowship for Christian Athletes. Does he feel that Christ was a winner or a loser?)

Norman Vincent Peale: "I once asked Ty Cobb, 'Why do you   17
put such an emphasis on winning? It's only a game.' He said, 'That's the reason I'm out there. Why play if you don't play to win?'" (What about camaraderie and the joy of simply playing a game?) . . .

The late Hubert Humphrey, in the Minnesota Vikings dress-   18
ing room, after a club official pointed out he never shows up after a losing game: "That's true. Frankly, I love being around winners. When you win, you win. And when you lose, you lose. And winning is a lot more fun."

Why has winning taken on such importance? Why have we   19
become obsessed with winning at all costs? For one thing, we play our games against the backdrop of an intensely competitive culture. A high premium is placed on achievement and success. Americans measure everything in terms of progress, or pseudo progress; we always have to feel that we're moving up. In a society that is preoccupied with competition, the average person needs something to latch on to that says, "I'm really *worthwhile*, too." Winning can provide that boost, even if it means that a person is living vicariously through a sports team like the old Green Bay Packers or basking in the triumphs of a once-heroic Arnold Palmer.

Secondly, we are heirs to the Judeo-Christian ethic, which   20
states in principle that man should work hard to succeed, that if a person does his best, works unceasingly, and makes the right sacrifices, he will win. The assumption is that somehow the winner does everything right and the loser does everything wrong. All too often, the message that comes through to those who lose or who fail to reach the top is that obviously they didn't work hard enough and that they're not as worthwhile as the winners. Our tendency is to excuse the shortcomings of a winner—to gloss over his human frailties. But when a person starts to lose, we begin to question his character. Winners and losers are actually seen as good and bad

people. If the athlete manifests certain behavior that leads to success, we say he has "courage," he's a "competitor," he's "mentally
tough." Those who fail to demonstrate the same behavior are
"losers," "flakes," "gutless," or "chokers." Our winning sports
heroes even begin to appear sexually superior; they are "better
looking" and more appealing. Their faces sell products on television, although it's interesting to note that the faces change as the
level of success changes. . . .

Perhaps we could justify this obsession with winning if, at the 21
end of the road, it led to a better and a more wholesome life. If
when you won a trophy or the championship or set a record, you
became a more contented person. Or people used you as a mature
model. Or something meaningful happened to you beyond making $100,000 a year and being in demand on the meat loaf circuit.
Unfortunately, when you finally do win the whole ball of wax, not
only do you have to win it again, but you become a marked man.
Everybody wants to beat you. You accumulate enemies simply
because you have won. When U.S. backstroke swimmer John
Naber handed East Germany's Roland Matthes his first defeat in
seven years, Naber acknowledged his dilemma: "I wanted his
record more than anything. Now all I'll get is the headache of
people trying to beat me simply because I was the one who beat
him."

Countless other athletes have struggled to the top only to find 22
that winning is a hollow trip. In fact, the higher up the scale they
go, the worse the pressures become: the incredible strain to keep
winning; the clamoring public that demands autographs; banquet
appearances and business deals; the insatiable news media that
hunger for "fresh" quotes and every possible insight into the athlete's personal life, and the athlete's own internal demands to
maintain the conditioning and training that brought him to the
top in the first place. Small wonder that many top athletes finally
confide, "What the hell is it all about?" Said tennis heroine Chris
Evert: "It's tough being on top. It's lonely there. It's lonely because
the other players are so competitive. If you want to be the best, you
can't be best friends with everybody."

Another contributing pressure is the realization that an athlete 23
can be a winner one day and a complete bum the next. Unless he is
consistent, he runs the risk of being classified as a loser and facing
the wrath of all his "loyal" fans. Ferguson Jenkins won 20 games or

more for seven consecutive seasons. When he finally came up short — winning "only" 14 games in 1973 — his fans in Chicago started booing him, and his owner proceeded to trade him to one of the worst teams in baseball (where, ironically, he won 25 games the following season).

The final irony is that if an athlete or a team wins *too* consist- 24
ently, many of their fans will start getting bored if records are not broken or the winning margin is not overwhelming. Let a team win too much, like the New York Yankees of old or the UCLA basketball team, and many people are unhappy — from the critics who lament, "Break up the dynasty! They're ruining the game" to disgruntled players who have to ride the bench when they could be starting on any other team. Fans begin to form a strange alliance. It is not that they are *for* a team but against the other team. . . . Even when John Wooden was in the midst of UCLA's 88-game winning streak, he and his wife, Nell, found very little contentment. More often it was a life of aggravation and smoldering pressure. Late in the streak, Mrs. Wooden told a reporter:

> These should have been the best years of our lives. But they haven't been. Nine national championships in ten years is great. So are the winning streaks. But the fans are so greedy. They've reached the point where they are unhappy if John wins a championship game by five points. If he ever loses a game they're going to say that he's too old and he's lost his touch. They can stretch the rules and let him stay until he's sixty-seven, but I wonder if it would be worth it. What more does my husband have to prove?

The UCLA fans were indeed voracious winners. Yet by this 25
stage in John Wooden's career, his own drive for success had become an obsession. Four months later, after UCLA had been upset by North Carolina State in the NCAA finals, Wooden made an unprecedented three recruiting trips to Salt Lake City in order to finally tie down seven-foot Brett Vroman, a player he felt the Bruins needed to win even more championships in the coming years. Here was the greatest basketball coach in college history, a 64-year-old man with a heart problem, pursuing a 17-year-old hotshot who might help keep a basketball machine humming for another three or four years. Is any clearer testimony needed to show us where our fanaticism has brought us?

Questions for Close Reading

1. What is the thesis of the selection? Locate the sentence(s) in which Tutko and Bruns state their main idea. If they do not state the thesis explicitly, express it in your own words.
2. The authors discuss several different types of winners. What are they? Which sports are mentioned most often? Why?
3. What reasons do the authors give for the American obsession with winning?
4. According to Tutko and Bruns, athletes suffer more and more pressures as they rise to success. What are these pressures? Do they undermine the rewards of winning?
5. Refer to your dictionary as needed to define the following words in the selection: *insatiable* (paragraph 3), *permeates* (10), *emanating* (10), *camaraderie* (17), and *clamoring* (22).

Questions about the Writer's Craft

1. Locate three places where Tutko and Bruns discuss the causes of our competitive madness, and three places where they discuss its effects. What other methods of development do the authors use in arguing their proposition?
2. What is the purpose of including so many quotations? Examine paragraphs 11–17. What does listing these quotations accomplish? Why do the authors follow them with remarks in parentheses? What is the tone of these parenthetical comments?
3. Tutko and Bruns use the phrase "sports craze" at the start of their essay. What other descriptive terms do they use to refer to Americans' high esteem of winning? Are these objective terms?
4. "Winning," the authors write, "is like salt water. . . ." How does this comparison clarify the problem the authors find in competitive sports? What is the thirst that sports competition cannot quench? How is this comparison (also known as a simile) an irony?

Questions for Further Thought

1. The title of the essay is a variation on a quotation from Shakespeare's *Hamlet*. Do sports players really have a choice, "to win or not to win"? Do you agree that this is really "the question"?
2. "An athlete can be a winner one day and a complete bum the next," write Tutko and Bruns. Why are fans so fickle? Do you think booing is an acceptable behavior at sports events?
3. The authors cite the Vietnam war as an example of how the compulsion to win has affected us as a nation. Do you see other signs of the "winning mania" in the political goals and programs of today?

4. Sports are set up to foster competition, but should the rest of life be competitive too? Should we strive instead to make our society more cooperative rather than competitive? Why or why not?

Writing Assignments Using Argumentation-Persuasion as a Method of Development

1. In your experience, have you found that the intense drive to come out on top has been helpful or destructive? Write an essay persuading readers that competition has been either a destructive or constructive force in your life or the lives of people you know. One section of the paper — it may be the introduction — should present the opposing viewpoint.

2. An American engineering professor teaching at a university in the Middle East discovered that the homework handed in by his students was always identical. His students met, discussed, and agreed on solutions to the homework problems, and all handed in the same answers. How would students in America benefit from being more cooperative with each other? Write an essay arguing that American education should be reformed to emphasize cooperation. Support your essay by explaining the benefits to students, faculty, and society in general of abolishing competition in education.

Writing Assignments Using Other Methods of Development

3. How does the craze to win affect areas of American life other than sports? Notice references to winning as you go about your daily life. Keep track of where the need to win crops up: in news reports about politics; in references to religious beliefs; in advertising; in popular books about self-help, dieting, and so on. Write an essay showing how this drive to win pervades many parts of our lives.

4. Read "Japan: The Productivity Challenge" (pp. 306–316). Then write an essay comparing the American and Japanese approaches to achievement. Which style do you believe is more effective in the long run? Why?

Frank Trippett

Now senior editor of Time *magazine, Frank Trippett (1926–) has had a lifelong career in journalism. He has served as a writer and editor at such national publications as* Look *and* Newsweek *and is the author of three books:* The States: United They Fall *(1967),* The First Horseman *(1974), and* Child Ellen *(1975). The following essay first appeared in* Time.

A Red Light for Scofflaws

You drive 60 in a 55 mph zone. You fib a bit on your income tax return and your job application. You hide beer in your jacket and bring it into the stadium, although alcohol is prohibited. Are you a criminal? Of course not, you say; everybody does these little things and no one gets hurt. In "A Red Light for Scofflaws," Frank Trippett takes a wider view of what happens when individuals bend small laws for their own convenience.

Law-and-order is the longest-running and probably the best-loved political issue in U.S. history. Yet it is painfully apparent that millions of Americans who would never think of themselves as lawbreakers, let alone criminals, are taking increasing liberties with the legal codes that are designed to protect and nourish their society. Indeed, there are moments today—amid outlaw litter, tax cheating, illicit noise and motorized anarchy—when it seem as though the scofflaw represents the wave of the future. Harvard Sociologist David Riesman suspects that a majority of Americans have blithely taken to committing supposedly minor derelictions as a matter of course. Already, Riesman says, the ethic of U.S. society is in danger of becoming this: "You're a fool if you obey the rules."

Nothing could be more obvious than the evidence supporting Riesman. Scofflaws abound in amazing variety. The graffiti-prone turn public surfaces into visual rubbish. Bicyclists often ride as though two-wheeled vehicles are exempt from all traffic laws. Litterbugs convert their communities into trash dumps. Widespread flurries of ordinances have failed to clear public places of high-decibel portable radios, just as earlier laws failed to wipe out the beer-soaked hooliganism that plagues many parks. Tobacco addicts remain hopelessly blind to signs that say NO SMOKING. Respectably dressed pot smokers no longer bother to duck out of public sight to pass around a joint. The flagrant use of cocaine is a festering scandal in middle- and upper-class life. And then there are (hello, Everybody!) the jaywalkers.

The dangers of scofflawry vary wildly. The person who illegally spits on the sidewalk remains digusting, but clearly poses less risk to others than the company that illegally buries hazardous chemical waste in an unauthorized location. The fare-beater on the subway presents less threat to life than the landlord who ignores fire safety statutes. The most immediately and measurably dangerous scofflawry, however, also happens to be the most visible. The culprit is the American driver, whose lawless activities today add up to a colossal public nuisance. The hazards range from routine double parking that jams city streets to the drunk driving that kills some 25,000 people and injures at least 650,000 others yearly. Illegal speeding on open highways? New surveys show that on some interstate highways 83% of all drivers are currently ignoring the federal 55 m.p.h. speed limit.

The most flagrant scofflaw of them all is the red-light runner. The flouting of stop signals has got so bad in Boston that residents tell an anecdote about a cabby who insists that red lights are "just for decoration." The power of the stoplight to control traffic seems to be waning everywhere. In Los Angeles, red-light running has become perhaps the city's most common traffic violation. In New York City, going through an intersection is like Russian roulette. Admits Police Commissioner Robert J. McGuire: "Today it's a 50-50 toss-up as to whether people will stop for a red light." Meanwhile, his own police largely ignore the lawbreaking.

Red-light running has always ranked as a minor wrong, and so it may be in individual instances. When the violation becomes habitual, widespread and incessant, however, a great deal more than a traffic management problem is involved. The flouting of basic rules of the road leaves deep dents in the social mood. Innocent drivers and pedestrians pay a repetitious price in frustration, inconvenience and outrage, not to mention a justified sense of mortal peril. The significance of red-light running is magnified by its high visibility. If hypocrisy is the tribute that vice pays to virtue, then furtiveness is the true outlaw's salute to the force of law-and-order. The red-light runner, however, shows no respect whatever for the social rules, and society cannot help being harmed by any repetitious and brazen display of contempt for the fundamentals of order.

The scofflaw spirit is pervasive. It is not really surprising when   6 schools find, as some do, that children frequently enter not knowing some of the basic rules of living together. For all their differences, today's scofflaws are of a piece as a symptom of elementary social demoralization — the loss by individuals of the capacity to govern their own behavior in the interest of others.

The prospect of the collapse of public manners is not merely a   7 matter of etiquette. Society's first concern will remain major crime, but a foretaste of the seriousness of incivility is suggested by what has been happening in Houston. Drivers on Houston freeways have been showing an increasing tendency to replace the rules of the road with violent outbreaks. Items from the Houston police department's new statistical category — freeway traffic violence: (1) Driver flashes high-beam lights at car that cut in front of him, whose occupants then hurl a beer can at his windshield, kick out his tail lights, slug him eight stitches' worth. (2) Dump-truck driver annoyed by delay batters trunk of stalled car ahead and its driver with steel bolt. (3) Hurrying driver of 18-wheel truck deliberately rear-ends car whose driver was trying to stay within 55 m.p.h. limit. The Houston Freeway Syndrome has fortunately not spread everywhere. But the question is: Will it?

Americans are used to thinking that law-and-order is threat-   8 ened mainly by stereotypical violent crime. When the foundations of U.S. law have actually been shaken, however, it has always been because ordinary law-abiding citizens took to skirting the law. Major instance: Prohibition. Recalls Donald Barr Chidsey in *On and Off the Wagon:* "Lawbreaking proved to be not painful, not even uncomfortable, but, in a mild and perfectly safe way, exhilarating." People wiped out Prohibition at last not only because of the alcohol issue but because scofflawry was seriously undermining the authority and legitimacy of government. Ironically, today's scofflaw spirit, whatever its undetermined origins, is being encouraged unwittingly by government at many levels. The failure of police to enfore certain laws is only the surface of the problem: they take their mandate from the officials and constituents they serve. Worse, most state legislatures have helped subvert popular compliance with the federal 55 m.p.h. law, some of them by enacting puny fines that trivialize transgressions. On a higher level, the Administration in Washington has dramatized its wish to nullify civil rights laws simply by opposing instead of supporting certain court-ordered desegregation rulings. With considerable justification, environmental groups, in the words of *Wilderness* magazine, accuse the Administration of "destroying environmental laws by failing to enforce them, or by enforcing them in ways that deliberately encourage noncompliance." Translation: scofflawry at the top.

The most disquieting thing about the scofflaw spirit is its   9
extreme infectiousness. Only a terminally foolish society would sit still and allow it to spread indefinitely.

Questions for Close Reading

1. What is the thesis of the selection? Locate the sentence(s) in which Trippett states his main idea. If he does not state the thesis explicitly, express it in your own words.

2. According to Trippett, what is the most dangerous and common kind of "scofflawry" today? Why is it so dangerous?

3. What does the author mean by "hypocrisy is the tribute vice pays to virtue"?

4. What more serious problem underlies the looseness with which Americans adhere to traffic rules? Why is this skirting of the law more than just "poor etiquette"?

5. Refer to your dictionary as needed to define the following words in the selection: *illicit* (paragraph 1), *blithely* (1), *derelictions* (1), *flouting* (5), *brazen* (5), *incivility* (7), and *nullify* (8).

Questions about the Writer's Craft

1. At what point in this essay did you realize that Trippett was concerned with more than just traffic violators? Do you feel Trippett proves that scofflawry will spread "indefinitely"? Or is his argument founded on a fallacy?

2. Where does Trippett support his argument with statistics? Are these statistics convincing? Where else might he have used facts and figures effectively?
3. Why does Trippett add "(hello, Everybody!)" in the middle of a sentence in paragraph 2? Who is his intended audience?
4. Examine Trippett's conclusion. Why is it so short? What effect does this conclusion have on you? What conclusion strategy is he using?

Questions for Further Thought

1. Is scofflawry the major danger to law-and-order in this country? What other kinds of antisocial behavior might be just as or even more dangerous?
2. Do you agree with the sayings, "You're a fool if you obey the rules" and "Rules are made to be broken"? What sound arguments are there against these maxims?
3. Should police do more to curb minor infractions on the road, on subways, on streets? How could we help bring this about?
4. One kind of lawbreaking is the deliberate organized resistance to unjust laws known as civil disobedience. It has been practiced in India to win independence, in the American South to overturn segregation, to name just two instances. Is this kind of lawbreaking justifiable? Does widespread scofflawry undermine the effectiveness of civil disobedience?

Writing Assignments Using Argumentation-Persuasion as a Method of Development

1. Write an essay from the point of view of a scofflaw arguing that some laws are worthless and should be ignored. Support your argument in one of two ways: (1) provide reasons why the laws are of no value, citing examples of what you mean, or (2) examine in depth three examples of faulty laws that should be ignored.
2. Trippett contends that driving violations are the worst form of scofflawry. Think of another form you feel is just as destructive—for example, drug abuse, environmental damage, noise pollution, cheating, or some other type of lawbreaking. Argue that if this type of behavior continues, society will be in equally great danger.

Writing Assignments Using Other Methods of Development

3. Identify some law or restriction that people tend to ignore. You might focus on dorm regulations, library rules, speeding restrictions on our

highways, and so on. In an essay, illustrate the consequences of ignoring these regulations and then describe the advantages that would result if the regulations were honored.

4. Research the term *civil disobedience* by looking it up in an encyclopedia and the *Readers' Guide*. Write an essay that defines civil disobedience, using for support the material you researched. Then show how civil disobedience could be an effective force for change in a current situation that needs remedying. The situation could be on campus, in your hometown, or on the national or international scene.

Margaret Mead

Trained as an anthropologist at Barnard College and Columbia University, Margaret Mead wrote extensively about tribal peoples and American customs. She was born in Philadelphia in 1901, and began her anthropological work in the 1920s. Her seminal studies, Coming of Age in Samoa *and* Growing Up in New Guinea, *made her one of the most well-known scholars in her field. In later years, Mead wrote extensively for popular magazines and analyzed Western culture with the same intensity she had devoted to Pacific tribespeople. She wrote and worked in her office in the American Museum of Natural History in New York right up until her death in 1978. The following essay first appeared in* The New York Times.

One Vote for This
Age of Anxiety

For years, experts have warned us that our century is an age of anxiety, ready to take its toll on our health, our mental stability, and our very future. In the following selection, famed anthropologist Margaret Mead surprises us with another view about anxiety. She advises us to consider the advantages of anxiety over the terrors of primitive peoples or the empty frettings of neurotics. Ultimately, Mead sees in anxiety some benefits for us as individuals and for society as a whole.

When critics wish to repudiate the world in which we live today, one of their familiar ways of doing it is to castigate modern man because anxiety is his chief problem. This, they say, in W. H. Auden's phrase, is the age of anxiety. This is what we have arrived at with all our vaunted progress, our great technological advances, our great wealth — everyone goes about with a burden of anxiety so enormous that, in the end, our stomachs and our arteries and our skins express the tension under which we live. Americans who have   1 lived in Europe come back to comment on our favorite farewell which, instead of the old goodbye (God be with you), is now "Take it easy," each American admonishing the other not to break down from the tension and strain of modern life.

Whenever an age is characterized by a phrase, it is presumably 2 in contrast to other ages. If we are the age of anxiety, what were other ages? And here the critics and carpers do a very amusing thing. First, they give us lists of the opposites of anxiety: security, trust, self-confidence, self-direction. Then, without much further discussion, they let us assume that other ages, other periods of history, were somehow the ages of trust or confident direction.

The savage who, on his South Sea island, simply sat and let 3 breadfruit fall into his lap, the simple peasant, at one with the fields he ploughed and the beasts he tended, the craftsman busy with his tools and lost in the fulfillment of the instinct of workmanship — these are the counterimages conjured up by descriptions of the strain under which men live today. But no one who lived in those days has returned to testify how paradisiacal they really were.

Certainly if we observe and question the savages or simple 4 peasants in the world today, we find something quite different. The untouched savage in the middle of New Guinea isn't anxious; he is seriously and continually *frightened* — of black magic, of enemies with spears who may kill him or his wives and children at any moment, while they stoop to drink from a spring, or climb a palm tree for a coconut. He goes warily, day and night, taut and fearful.

As for the peasant populations of a great part of the world, they 5 aren't so much anxious as hungry. They aren't anxious about whether they will get a salary raise, or which of the three colleges of their choice they will be admitted to, or whether to buy a Ford or Cadillac, or whether the kind of TV set they want is too expensive. They are hungry, cold and, in many parts of the world, they dread that local warfare, bandits, political coups may endanger their homes, their meager livelihoods, and their lives. But surely they are not anxious.

For anxiety, as we have come to use it to describe our charac- 6 teristic state of mind, can be contrasted with the active fear of hunger, loss, violence, and death. Anxiety is the appropriate emotion when the immediate personal terror — of a volcano, an arrow, the sorcerer's spell, a stab in the back and other calamities, all directed against one's self — disappears.

This is not to say that there isn't plenty to worry about in our 7
world of today. The explosion of a bomb in the streets of a city
whose name no one had ever heard before may set in motion forces
which end up by ruining one's carefully planned education in law
school, half a world away. But there is still not the personal, immediate, active sense of impending disaster that the savage knows.
There is rather the vague anxiety, the sense that the future is unmanageable.

The kind of world that produces anxiety is actually a world of 8
relative safety, a world in which no one feels that he himself is
facing sudden death. Possibly sudden death may strike a certain
number of unidentified other people — but not him. The anxiety
exists as an uneasy state of mind, in which one has a feeling that
something unspecified and undeterminable may go wrong. If the
world seems to be going well, this produces anxiety — for good
times may end. If the world is going badly — it may get worse.
Anxiety tends to be without focus; the anxious person doesn't
know whether to blame himself or other people. He isn't sure
whether it is the current year or the Administration or a change in
climate or the atom bomb that is to blame for this undefined sense
of unease.

It is clear that we have developed a society which depends on 9
having the *right* amount of anxiety to make it work. Psychiatrists
have been heard to say, "He didn't have enough anxiety to get
well," indicating that, while we agree that too much anxiety is
inimical to mental health, we have come to rely on anxiety to push
and prod us into seeing a doctor about a symptom which may
indicate cancer, into checking up on that old life-insurance policy
which may have out-of-date clauses in it, into having a conference
with Billy's teacher even though his report card looks all right.

People who are anxious enough keep their car insurance up, 10
have the brakes checked, don't take a second drink when they have
to drive, are careful where they go and with whom they drive on
holidays. People who are too anxious either refuse to go into cars at
all — and so complicate the ordinary course of life — or drive so
tensely and overcautiously that they help cause accidents. People
who aren't anxious enough take chance after chance, which increases the terrible death toll of the roads.

On balance, our age of anxiety represents a large advance over 11
savage and peasant cultures. Out of a productive system of technol-

ogy drawing upon enormous resources, we have created a nation in which anxiety has replaced terror and despair, for all except the severely disturbed. The specter of hunger means something only to those Americans who can identify themselves with the millions of hungry people on other continents. The specter of terror may still be roused in some by a knock at the door in a few parts of the South, or in those who have just escaped from a totalitarian regime or who have kin still behind the Curtains.

But in this twilight world which is neither at peace nor at war, 12 and where there is insurance against certain immediate, downright, personal disasters, for most Americans there remains only anxiety over what may happen, might happen, could happen.

This is the world out of which grows the hope, for the first time 13 in history, of a society where there will be freedom from want and freedom from fear. Our very anxiety is born of our knowledge of what is now possible for each and for all. The number of people who consult psychiatrists today is not, as is sometimes felt, a symptom of increasing mental ill health, but rather the precursor of a world in which the hope of genuine mental health will be open to everyone, a world in which no individual feels that he need be hopelessly broken-hearted, a failure, a menace to others or a traitor to himself.

But if, then, our anxieties are actually signs of hope, why is 14 there such a voice of discontent abroad in the land? I think this comes perhaps because our anxiety exists without an accompanying recognition of the tragedy which will always be inherent in human life, however well we build our world. We may banish hunger, and fear of sorcery, violence, or secret police; we may bring up children who have learned to trust life and who have the spontaneity and curiosity necessary to devise ways of making trips to the moon; we cannot — as we have tried to do — banish death itself.

Americans who stem from generations which left their old 15 people behind and never closed their parents' eyelids in death, and who have experienced the additional distance from death provided by two world wars fought far from our shores are today pushing away from them both a recognition of death and a recognition of the tremendous significance — for the future — of the way we live our lives. Acceptance of the inevitability of death, which, when faced, can give dignity to life, and acceptance of our inescapable role in the modern world, might transmute our anxiety about making the right choices, taking the right precautions, and the right risks into the sterner stuff of responsibility, which ennobles the whole face rather than furrowing the forehead with the little anxious wrinkles of worry.

Worry in an empty context means that men die daily little 16 deaths. But good anxiety—not about the things that were left undone long ago, but which return to haunt and harry men's minds, but active, vivid anxiety about what must be done and that quickly—binds men to life with an intense concern.

This is still a world in which too many of the wrong things 17 happen somewhere. But this is a world in which we now have the means to make a great many more of the right things happen everywhere. For Americans, the generalization which a Swedish social scientist made about our attitudes on race relations is true in many other fields: anticipated change which we feel is right and necessary but difficult makes us unduly anxious and apprehensive, but such change, once consummated, brings a glow of relief. We are still a people who—in the literal sense—believe in making good.

Questions for Close Reading

1. What is the thesis of the selection? Locate the sentence(s) in which Mead states her main idea. If she does not state the thesis explicitly, express it in your own words.
2. According to Mead, what is the difference between anxiety and fear? What are the fears of primitive people?
3. What does Mead mean by "good anxiety"? How is it a sign of hope?
4. Why is the modern American's sense of safety and distance from death still a problem, according to Mead? What connection does Mead draw between accepting death and becoming more responsible?
5. Refer to your dictionary as needed to define the following words used in the selection: *repudiate* (paragraph 1), *castigate* (1), *vaunted* (1), *inimical* (9), and *transmute* (15).

Questions about the Writer's Craft

1. Locate several places where Mead acknowledges other points of view in order to refute them. How effective is this tactic in developing her argument?

2. What is Mead's attitude toward critics of the modern world? What words and phrases in the two introductory paragraphs convey this attitude?

3. Today, few anthropologists would use "savage" or "peasant" to describe non-Western peoples. What are the connotations of these words? Why do you think Mead, a pioneering anthropologist who herself spent years among non-Western societies, chose to use them in 1956?

4. Mead refers to a bomb exploding in a foreign street that disrupts someone's law education (paragraph 7) and to a Swedish social scientist who wrote about American race relations (paragraph 17). Do you know what she is referring to in these paragraphs? Why doesn't she bother to be more specific about what she means? What audience is she writing for?

Questions for Further Thought

1. Do you agree that we are still as sheltered from the reality of death as Mead says? Are Americans more aware of death now than when this essay was written? Why or why not?

2. What anxieties have you noticed among today's college students? To what extent are they related to material possessions and future income?

3. Mead says, " . . . we now have the means to make a great many more of the right things happen everywhere." Do you see evidence that we are using our resources for the "right things"?

4. Do you see signs of anxiety "over what may happen, might happen, could happen" among people you know? Would you say these anxieties are a positive or negative force in their lives?

Writing Assignments Using Argumentation-Persuasion as a Method of Development

1. Mead defends anxiety, a quality which is usually considered a negative influence on our lives. Write an essay defending another quality or condition that is usually criticized. For example, you might defend disobedience, failure, shyness, being a follower, being pushy, and so on. Begin, as Mead does, by explaining how critics think about your topic, and then go on to disprove their contentions.

2. Our anxiety-ridden world, for Mead, represents an advance in civilization. After acknowledging Mead's view, take issue with her position. Argue the point that "vague anxiety, the sense that the future is unmanageable" can be a *counterproductive* force in human life. Support your proposition through reference to your own and others' experiences.

Writing Assignments Using Other Methods of Development

3. There are three kinds of people in the world, Mead implies in paragraph 10: those who are sufficiently anxious, too anxious, and not anxious enough. Write an essay discussing these three types, giving examples based on people you know and the behavior shown by each. Or you may discuss three kinds of worries: those things that people do worry about and shouldn't, those things that people don't worry about and should, and those things that people do worry about and should. Again, provide vivid examples to illustrate each kind of worry.

4. In 1956, America basked in post-war prosperity, world preeminence, and optimism. But times have changed. Write an essay explaining what new anxieties have developed for people to worry about today. The tone of the essay may be serious or light. If you believe Americans worry too much about the trivial, you may wish to use a humorous tone and focus on such modern worries as whether you set your VCR timer to record David Letterman or whether you remembered to put taco chips on the grocery list.

Additional Writing Topics
ARGUMENTATION-PERSUASION

General Assignments

Using argumentation-persuasion, develop any of the following topics. After choosing a topic, think about your purpose and audience. Remember that the paper's thesis should state the issue under discussion as well as your position on the issue. As you work on developing evidence, you might want to do some outside research. Keep in mind that effective argumentation-persuasion usually means that some time should be spent acknowledging and refuting opposing points of view. Be careful not to sabotage your argument by organizing your case around a logical fallacy.

1. Mercy killing
2. Hiring quotas
3. Giving birth control devices to teenagers
4. Prayer in the schools
5. Living off campus
6. The drinking age
7. Spouses sharing housework equally
8. Smoking in public places
9. Big-time sports in college
10. Music videos
11. Mothers of young children going out to work
12. Acid rain
13. Mandatory seat belt use and air bag equipment
14. Registering for the draft
15. Making personal computers mandatory for all college students
16. 55 mile per hour speed limit
17. Putting elderly parents in nursing homes
18. An optional pass/fail system for courses
19. Dress codes
20. Nonconformity in a neighborhood: allowing a lawn to go wild, keeping many pets, painting a house an odd color, or some other atypical behavior.

Assignments with a Specific Audience and Purpose

1. Your supervising editor at *Time* magazine has given you an important assignment: choosing the "Man or Woman of the Year" to be featured on the cover of the December 31 issue. Make your decision and write a report to your boss arguing in favor of this choice.

2. Your eighteen-year-old son or daughter sent off a college application but was rejected because of low SAT scores. Write to the college admissions director, arguing that an injustice has been done. Give reasons why the SAT scores are not a fair indicator of your child's abilities and potential.

3. You and your parents don't agree on some aspect of your romantic relationship (you want to live with your boyfriend/girlfriend and they don't approve; or you want to get married and they want you to wait; or they simply don't like your partner; or any other conflict). Write your parents a letter explaining why your preference is reasonable. Try hard to win them over to your side.

4. As a member of a high school faculty, you support the adoption of a controversial behavior code for students. Write an article for the school newspaper, justifying this new rule to the student body. The rule might be "no radios in school," "no T-shirts," "no food in class," "no smoking on school grounds," or any other rule you think appropriate.

5. Your parents are convinced that the music you listen to is nothing more than deafening noise. Write an essay proving to your parents that your music has value. Use specific examples of lyrics, groups, or musical styles to support your points.

6. You are part of a minority group (racial, ethnic, female teenagers, college students, the elderly, or any other group). On a recent television show or in a TV advertisement, you saw something that depicts your group in an offensive way. Write a letter (to the network or the advertiser) expressing your feelings and explaining why you feel the material should be taken off the air.

FOR
FURTHER
READING

Alice Walker

Alice Walker (1944–   ) was the eighth child of Georgia sharecroppers. After studying at Spelman College in Atlanta, she graduated from Sarah Lawrence College in New York. Before becoming a college teacher, Walker worked in the civil rights movement helping to register black voters and teaching in Mississippi's Head Start program. In recent years, she has built a reputation as a sensitive chronicler of the black experience in America. Her works include the following: a biography, Langston Hughes, American Poet *(1973); poetry,* Revolutionary Petunias and Other Poems *(1973); short stories, collected in* In Love & Trouble *(1973) and* You Can't Keep a Good Woman Down *(1981); and novels, including* Meridian *(1976). Another novel,* The Color Purple *(1982), won a Pulitzer Prize and the American Book Award and was made into a feature film. The following selection comes from her 1983 collection of essays,* In Search of Our Mothers' Gardens.

Beauty: When the Other Dancer Is the Self

A disfiguring injury can seriously effect anyone's self-esteem. Alice Walker sustained such an injury as a child. In this essay, she describes what happened to her and provides glimpses of her Southern childhood and the people who changed her life for better or worse. Walker's experience is a commentary on the role of good looks in a girl's life, and on the importance of good sense in gaining self-acceptance and esteem as an adult.

It is a bright summer day in 1947. My father, a fat, funny man   1
with beautiful eyes and a subversive wit, is trying to decide which of
his eight children he will take with him to the county fair. My
mother, of course, will not go. She is knocked out from getting
most of us ready: I hold my neck stiff against the pressure of her

knuckles as she hastily completes the braiding and then beribbon-
ing of my hair.

My father is the driver for the rich old white lady up the road.   2
Her name is Miss Mey. She owns all the land for miles around, as
well as the house in which we live. All I remember about her is that
she once offered to pay my mother thirty-five cents for cleaning her
house, raking up piles of her magnolia leaves, and washing her
family's clothes, and that my mother — she of no money, eight
children, and a chronic earache — refused it. But I do not think of
this in 1947. I am two and a half years old. I want to go everywhere
my daddy goes. I am excited at the prospect of riding in a car.
Someone has told me fairs are fun. That there is room in the car for
only three of us doesn't faze me at all. Whirling happily in my
starchy frock, showing off my biscuit-polished patent-leather shoes
and lavender socks, tossing my head in a way that makes my ribbons bounce, I stand, hands on hips, before my father. "Take me,
Daddy," I say with assurance; "I'm the prettiest!"

Later, it does not surprise me to find myself in Miss Mey's   3
shiny black car, sharing the back seat with the other lucky ones.
Does not surprise me that I thoroughly enjoy the fair. At home that
night I tell the unlucky ones all I can remember about the merry-
go-round, the man who eats live chickens, and the teddy bears,
until they say: that's enough baby Alice. Shut up now, and go to
sleep.

It is Easter Sunday, 1950. I am dressed in a green, flocked,   4
scalloped-hem dress (handmade by my adoring sister, Ruth) that
has its own smooth satin petticoat and tiny hot-pink roses tucked
into each scallop. My shoes, new T-strap patent leather, again
highly biscuit-polished. I am six years old and have learned one of
the longest Easter speeches to be heard that day, totally unlike the
speech I said when I was two: "Easter lilies/pure and white/blos-
som in/the morning light." When I rise to give my speech I do so
on a great wave of love and pride and expectation. People in the
church stop rustling their new crinolines. They seem to hold their
breath. I can tell they admire my dress, but it is my spirit, bordering
on sassiness (womanishness), they secretly applaud.

"That girl's a little *mess*," they whisper to each other, pleased.   5

Naturally I say my speech without stammer or pause, unlike   6 those who stutter, stammer, or, worst of all, forget. This is before the word "beautiful" exists in people's vocabulary, but "Oh, isn't she the *cutest* thing?" frequently floats my way. "And got so much sense!" they gratefully add . . . for which thoughtful addition I thank them to this day.

It was great fun being cute. But then, one day, it ended.   7

I am eight years old and a tomboy. I have a cowboy hat,   8 cowboy boots, checkered shirt and pants, all red. My playmates are my brothers, two and four years older than I. Their colors are black and green, the only difference in the way we are dressed. On Saturday nights we all go to the picture show, even my mother; Westerns are her favorite kind of movie. Back home, "on the ranch," we pretend we are Tom Mix, Hopalong Cassidy, Lash LaRue (we've even named one of our dogs Lash LaRue); we chase each other for hours rustling cattle, being outlaws, delivering damsels from distress. Then my parents decide to buy my brothers guns. These are not "real" guns. They shoot "BBs," copper pellets my brothers say will kill birds. Because I am a girl, I do not get a gun. Instantly I am relegated to the position of Indian. Now there appears a great distance between us. They shoot and shoot at everything with their new guns. I try to keep up with my bow and arrows.

One day while I am standing on top of our makeshift   9 "garage" — pieces of tin nailed across some poles — holding my bow and arrow and looking out toward the fields, I feel an incredible blow in my right eye. I look down just in time to see my brother lower his gun.

Both brothers rush to my side. My eye stings, and I cover it   10 with my hand. "If you tell," they say, "we will get a whipping. You don't want that to happen, do you?" I do not. "Here is a piece of wire," says the older brother, picking it up from the roof; "say you stepped on one end of it and the other flew up and hit you." The pain is beginning to start. "Yes," I say. "Yes, I will say that is what happened." If I do not say this is what happened, I know my brothers will find ways to make me wish I had. But now I will say anything that gets me to my mother.

Confronted by our parents we stick to the lie agreed upon.   11 They place me on a bench on the porch and I close my left eye while they examine the right. There is a tree growing from underneath the porch that climbs past the railing to the roof. It is the last thing my right eye sees. I watch as its trunk, its branches, and then its leaves are blotted out by the rising blood.

I am in shock. First there is intense fever, which my father tries   12
to break using lily leaves bound around my head. Then there are chills: my mother tries to get me to eat soup. Eventually, I do not know how, my parents learn what has happened. A week after the "accident" they take me to see a doctor. "Why did you wait so long to come?" he asks, looking into my eye and shaking his head. "Eyes are sympathetic," he says. "If one is blind, the other will likely become blind too."

This comment of the doctor's terrifies me. But it is really how I   13
look that bothers me most. Where the BB pellet struck there is a glob of whitish scar tissue, a hideous cataract, on my eye. Now when I stare at people — a favorite pastime, up to now — they will stare back. Not at the "cute" little girl, but at her scar. For six years I do not stare at anyone, because I do not raise my head.

Years later, in the throes of a mid-life crisis, I ask my mother   14
and sister whether I changed after the "accident." "No," they say, puzzled. "What do you mean?"

What do I mean?   15

I am eight, and, for the first time, doing poorly in school,   16
where I have been something of a whiz since I was four. We have just moved to the place where the "accident" occurred. We do not know any of the people around us because this is a different county. The only time I see the friends I knew is when we go back to our old church. The new school is the former state penitentiary. It is a large stone building, cold and drafty, crammed to overflowing with boisterous, ill-disciplined children. On the third floor there is a huge circular imprint of some partition that has been torn out.

"What used to be here?" I ask a sullen girl next to me on our   17
way past it to lunch.

"The electric chair," says she.   18

At night I have nightmares about the electric chair; and about   19
all the people reputedly "fried" in it. I am afraid of the school, where all the students seem to be budding criminals.

"What's the matter with your eye?" they ask, critically.   20

When I don't answer (I cannot decide whether it was an "acci-   21
dent" or not), they shove me, insist on a fight.

My brother, the one who created the story about the wire,   22
comes to my rescue. But then brags so much about "protecting"
me, I become sick.

After months of torture at the school, my parents decide to   23
send me back to our old community, to my old school. I live with
my grandparents and the teacher they board. But there is no room
for Phoebe, my cat. By the time my grandparents decide there *is*
room, and I ask for my cat, she cannot be found. Miss Yarborough,
the boarding teacher, takes me under her wing, and begins to teach
me to play the piano. But soon she marries an African — a
"prince," she says — and is whisked away to his continent.

At my old school there is at least one teacher who loves me. She   24
is the teacher who "knew me before I was born" and bought my
first baby clothes. It is she who makes life bearable. It is her presence
that finally helps me turn on the one child at the school who
continually calls me "one-eyed bitch." One day I simply grab him
by his coat and beat him until I am satisfied. It is my teacher who
tells me my mother is ill.

My mother is lying in bed in the middle of the day, something I   25
have never seen. She is in too much pain to speak. She has an abscess
in her ear. I stand looking down on her, knowing that if she dies, I
cannot live. She is being treated with warm oils and hot bricks held
against her cheeks. Finally a doctor comes. But I must go back to
my grandparents' house. The weeks pass but I am hardly aware of
it. All I know is that my mother might die, my father is not so jolly,
my brothers still have their guns, and I am the one sent away from
home.

"You did not change," they say.   26

Did I imagine the anguish of never looking up?   27

I am twelve. When relatives come to visit I hide in my room.   28
My cousin Brenda, just my age, whose father works in the post
office and whose mother is a nurse, comes to find me. "Hello," she
says. And then she asks, looking at my recent school picture, which
I did not want taken, and on which the "glob," as I think of it, is
clearly visible, "You still can't see out of that eye?"

"No," I say, and flop back on the bed over my book.   29

That night, as I do almost every night, I abuse my eye. I rant   30
and rave at it, in front of the mirror. I plead with it to clear up before

morning. I tell it I hate and despise it. I do not pray for sight. I pray for beauty.
"You did not change," they say.   31

I am fourteen and baby-sitting for my brother Bill, who lives in   32
Boston. He is my favorite brother and there is a strong bond between us. Understanding my feelings of shame and ugliness he and his wife take me to a local hospital, where the "glob" is removed by a doctor named O. Henry. There is still a small bluish crater where the scar tissue was, but the ugly white stuff is gone. Almost immediately I become a different person from the girl who does not raise her head. Or so I think. Now that I've raised my head I win the boyfriend of my dreams. Now that I've raised my head I have plenty of friends. Now that I've raised my head classwork comes from my lips as faultlessly as Easter speeches did, and I leave high school as valedictorian, most popular student, and *queen*, hardly believing my luck. Ironically, the girl who was voted most beautiful in our class (and was) was later shot twice through the chest by a male companion, using a "real" gun, while she was pregnant. But that's another story in itself. Or is it?
"You did not change," they say.   33
It is now thirty years since the "accident." A beautiful journalist comes to visit and to interview me. She is going to write a cover story for her magazine that focuses on my latest book. "Decide how you want to look on the cover," she says. "Glamorous, or whatever."

Never mind "glamorous," it is the "whatever" that I hear.   35
Suddenly all I can think of is whether I will get enough sleep the night before the photography session: if I don't, my eye will be tired and wander, as blind eyes will.

At night in bed with my lover I think up reasons why I should   36
not appear on the cover of a magazine. "My meanest critics will say I've sold out," I say. "My family will now realize I write scandalous books."

"But what's the real reason you don't want to do this?" he   37
asks.

"Because in all probability," I say in a rush, "my eye won't be   38
straight."

"It will be straight enough," he says. Then, "Besides, I   39
thought you'd made your peace with that."

And I suddenly remember that I have.   40
I remember: 41
I am talking to my brother Jimmy, asking if he remembers   42
anything unusual about the day I was shot. He does not know I
consider that day the last time my father, with his sweet home
remedy of cool lily leaves, chose me, and that I suffered and raged
inside because of this. "Well," he says, "all I remember is standing
by the side of the highway with Daddy, trying to flag down a car. A
white man stopped, but when Daddy said he needed somebody to
take his little girl to the doctor, he drove off."
I remember: 43
I am in the desert for the first time. I fall totally in love with it. I 44
am so overwhelmed by its beauty, I confront for the first time,
consciously, the meaning of the doctor's words years ago: "Eyes
are sympathetic. If one is blind, the other will likely become blind
too." I realize I have dashed about the world madly, looking at this,
looking at that, storing up images against the fading of the light.
But I might have missed seeing the desert! The shock of that
possibility — and gratitude for over twenty-five years of sight —
sends me literally to my knees. Poem after poem comes — which is
perhaps how poets pray.

On Sight   45

> *I am so thankful I have seen*
> *The Desert*
> *And the creatures in the desert*
> *And the desert Itself.*
>
> *The desert has its own moon*
> *Which I have seen*
> *With my own eye.*
> *There is no flag on it.*
>
> *Trees of the desert have arms*
> *All of which are always up*
> *That is because the moon is up*
> *The sun is up*
> *Also the sky*
> *The stars*
> *Clouds*
> *None with flags.*
>
> *If there were flags, I doubt*
> *the trees would point.*
> *Would you?*

But mostly, I remember this: 46
   I am twenty-seven, and my baby daughter is almost three.   47
Since her birth I have worried about her discovery that her mother's
eyes are different from other people's. Will she be embarrassed? I
think. What will she say? Every day she watches a television program called "Big Blue Marble." It begins with a picture of the earth
as it appears from the moon. It is bluish, a little battered-looking,
but full of light, with whitish clouds swirling around it. Every time
I see it I weep with love, as if it is a picture of Grandma's house. One
day when I am putting Rebecca down for her nap, she suddenly
focuses on my eye. Something inside me cringes, gets ready to try to
protect myself. All children are cruel about physical differences, I
know from experience, and that they don't always mean to be is
another matter. I assume Rebecca will be the same.

   But no-o-o-o. She studies my face intently as we stand, her   48
inside and me outside the crib. She even holds my face maternally
between her dimpled little hands. Then, looking every bit as serious
and lawyerlike as her father, she says, as if it may just possibly have
slipped my attention: "Mommy, there's a *world* in your eye." (As
in, "Don't be alarmed, or do anything crazy.") And then, gently,
but with great interest: "Mommy, where did you *get* that world in
your eye?"

   For the most part, the pain left then. (So what, if my brothers   49
grew up to buy even more powerful pellet guns for their sons and to
carry real guns themselves. So what, if a young "Morehouse man"
once nearly fell off the steps of Trevor Arnett Library because he
thought my eyes were blue.) Crying and laughing I ran to the
bathroom, while Rebecca mumbled and sang herself off to sleep.
Yes indeed, I realized, looking into the mirror. There *was* a world in
my eye. And I saw that it was possible to love it: that in fact, for all it
had taught me of shame and anger and inner vision, I *did* love it.
Even to see it drifting out of orbit in boredom, or rolling up out of
fatigue, not to mention floating back at attention in excitement
(bearing witness, a friend has called it), deeply suitable to my personality, and even characteristic of me.

   That night I dream I am dancing to Stevie Wonder's song   50
"Always" (the name of the song is really "As," but I hear it as
"Always"). As I dance, whirling and joyous, happier than I've ever
been in my life, another bright-faced dancer joins me. We dance
and kiss each other and hold each other through the night. The
other dancer has obviously come through all right, as I have done.
She is beautiful, whole and free. And she is also me.

James Thurber

American humorist James Thurber (1894–1961) is perhaps best known as the author of "The Secret Life of Walter Mitty." Thurber often wrote about people's longings, using his skill as a satirist to portray the humor and poignance of the human condition. He was able to give his wit — which often bordered on the acerbic — full play during his long career at The New Yorker, *where he wrote satiric essays and drew cartoons. He also wrote several humorous books, including the following:* Is Sex Necessary? *(1929), which he coauthored with E. B. White;* Fables for Our Time *(1940);* My World and Welcome to It *(1942); and* Thurber Country *(1953). This selection first appeared in* My Life and Hard Times *(1933).*

University Days

University catalogs depict higher education as one of life's loftier experiences, with confident undergrads strolling eagerly toward ivy-covered lecture halls. But in this hilarious essay, James Thurber takes the pomp and circumstance out of higher education. He reveals the bumbling, the incompetence, and the embarrassment that frequently beset him and his fellow students at Ohio State University. He shows professors with gritted teeth trying to educate the ineducable and coach the uncooperative. Even back in the 1930s, college life was far from the idealized image depicted in the catalogs.

I passed all the other courses that I took at my university, but I 1 could never pass botany. This was because all botany students had to spend several hours a week in a laboratory looking through a microscope at plant cells, and I could never see through a microscope. I never once saw a cell through a microscope. This used to enrage my instructor. He would wander around the laboratory pleased with the progress all the students were making in drawing the involved and, so I am told, interesting structure of flower cells, until he came to me. I would just be standing there. "I can't see anything," I would say. He would begin patiently enough, explaining how anybody can see through a microscope, but he would always end up in a fury, claiming that I could *too* see through a microscope but just pretended that I couldn't. "It takes away from the beauty of flowers anyway," I used to tell him. "We are not concerned with beauty in this course," he would say. "We are concerned solely with what I may call the *mechanics* of flars." "Well," I'd say, "I can't see anything." "Try it just once again," he'd say, and I would put my eye to the microscope and see nothing at all, except now and again a nebulous milky substance — a phenomenon of maladjustment. You were supposed to see a vivid, restless clockwork of sharply defined plant cells. "I see what looks like a lot of milk," I would tell him. This, he claimed, was the result of my not having adjusted the microscope properly, so he would readjust it for me, or rather, for himself. And I would look again and see milk.

I finally took a deferred pass, as they called it, and waited a year   2
and tried again. (You had to pass one of the biological sciences or you couldn't graduate.) The professor had come back from vacation brown as a berry, bright-eyed, and eager to explain cell-structure again to his classes. "Well," he said to me, cheerily, when we met in the first laboratory hour of the semester, "we're going to see cells this time, aren't we?" "Yes, sir," I said. Students to right of me and to left of me and in front of me were seeing cells; what's more, they were quietly drawing pictures of them in their notebooks. Of course, I didn't see anything.

"We'll try it," the professor said to me, grimly, "with every   3
adjustment of the microscope known to man. As God is my witness, I'll arrange this glass so that you see cells through it or I'll give up teaching. In twenty-two years of botany, I —" He cut off abruptly for he was beginning to quiver all over, like Lionel Barrymore, and he genuinely wished to hold onto his temper; his scenes with me had taken a great deal out of him.

So we tried it with every adjustment of the microscope known   4
to man. With only one of them did I see anything but blackness or the familiar lacteal opacity, and that time I saw, to my pleasure and amazement, a variegated constellation of flecks, specks, and dots. These I hastily drew. The instructor, noting my activity, came back from an adjoining desk, a smile on his lips and his eyebrows high in

hope. He looked at my cell drawing. "What's that?" he demanded, with a hint of a squeal in his voice. "That's what I saw," I said. "You didn't, you didn't, you *didn't*!" he screamed, losing control of his temper instantly, and he bent over and squinted into the microscope. His head snapped up. "That's your eye!" he shouted. "You've fixed the lens so that it reflects! You've drawn your eye!"

Another course that I didn't like, but somehow managed to pass, was economics. I went to that class straight from the botany class, which didn't help me any in understanding either subject. I used to get them mixed up. But not as mixed up as another student in my economics class who came there direct from a physics laboratory. He was a tackle on the football team, named Bolenciecwcz. At that time Ohio State University had one of the best football teams in the country, and Bolenciecwcz was one of its outstanding stars. In order to be eligible to play it was necessary for him to keep up in his studies, a very difficult matter, for while he was not dumber than an ox he was not any smarter. Most of his professors were lenient and helped him along. None gave him more hints in answering questions or asked him simpler ones than the economics professor, a thin, timid man named Bassum. One day when we were on the subject of transportation and distribution, it came Bolenciecwcz's turn to answer a question. "Name one means of transportation," the professor said to him. No light came into the big tackle's eyes. "Just any means of transportation," said the professor. Bolenciecwcz sat staring at him. "That is," pursued the professor, "any medium, agency, or method of going from one place to another." Bolenciecwcz had the look of a man who is being led into a trap. "You may choose among steam, horse-drawn, or electrically propelled vehicles," said the instructor. "I might suggest the one which we commonly take in making long journeys across land." There was a profound silence in which everybody stirred uneasily, including Bolenciecwcz and Mr. Bassum. Mr. Bassum abruptly broke this silence in an amazing manner. "Choo-choo-choo," he said, in a low voice, and turned instantly scarlet. He glanced appealingly around the room. All of us, of course, shared Mr. Bassum's desire that Bolenciecwcz should stay abreast of the class in economics, for the Illinois game, one of the hardest and most important of the season, was only a week off. "Toot, toot, too-toooooot!" some student with a deep voice moaned, and we all looked encouragingly at Bolenciecwcz. Somebody else

5

gave a fine imitation of a locomotive letting off steam. Mr. Bassum himself rounded off the little show. "Ding, dong, ding, dong," he said, hopefully. Bolenciecwcz was staring at the floor now, trying to think, his great brow furrowed, his huge hands rubbing together, his face red.

"How did you come to college this year, Mr. Bolenciecwzc?" asked the professor. "*Chuffa* chuffa, *chuffa* chuffa."   6

"M'father sent me," said the football player.   7

"What on?" asked Bassum.   8

"I git an 'lowance," said the tackle, in a low, husky voice, obviously embarrassed.   9

"No, no," said Bassum. "Name a means of transportation. What did you *ride* here on?"   10

"Train," said Bolenciecwcz.   11

"Quite right," said the professor. "Now, Mr. Nugent, will you tell us — "   12

If I went through anguish in botany and economics — for different reasons — gymnasium work was even worse. I don't even like to think about it. They wouldn't let you play games or join in the exercises with your glasses on and I couldn't see with mine off. I bumped into professors, horizontal bars, agricultural students, and swinging iron rings. Not being able to see, I could take it but I couldn't dish it out. Also, in order to pass gymnasium (and you had to pass it to graduate) you had to learn to swim if you didn't know how. I didn't like the swimming pool, I didn't like swimming, and I didn't like the swimming instructor, and after all these years I still don't. I never swam but I passed my gym work anyway, by having another student give my gymnasium number (978) and swim across the pool in my place. He was a quiet, amiable blond youth, number 473, and he would have seen through a microscope for me if we could have got away with it, but we couldn't get away with it. Another thing I didn't like about gymnasium work was that they made you strip the day you registered. It is impossible for me to be happy when I am stripped and being asked a lot of questions. Still, I did better than a lanky agricultural student who was cross-examined just before I was. They asked each student what college he was in — that is, whether Arts, Engineering, Commerce, or Agriculture. "What college are you in?" the instructor snapped at the youth in front of me. "Ohio State University," he said promptly.   13

It wasn't that agricultural student but it was another a whole   14 lot like him who decided to take up journalism, possibly on the ground that when farming went to hell he could fall back on newspaper work. He didn't realize, of course, that that would be very much like falling back full-length on a kit of carpenter's tools. Haskins didn't seem cut out for journalism, being too embarrassed to talk to anybody and unable to use a typewriter, but the editor of the college paper assigned him to the cow barns, the sheep house, the horse pavilion, and the animal husbandry department generally. This was a genuinely big "beat," for it took up five times as much ground and got ten times as great a legislative appropriation as the College of Liberal Arts. The agricultural student knew animals, but nevertheless his stories were dull and colorlessly written. He took all afternoon on each of them, on account of having to hunt for each letter on the typewriter. Once in a while he had to ask somebody to help him hunt. "C" and "L," in particular, were hard letters for him to find. His editor finally got pretty much annoyed at the farmer-journalist because his pieces were so uninteresting. "See here, Haskins," he snapped at him one day, "why is it we never have anything hot from you on the horse pavilion? Here we have two hundred head of horses on this campus — more than any other university in the Western Conference except Purdue — and yet you never get any real lowdown on them. Now shoot over to the horse barns and dig up something lively." Haskins shambled out and came back in about an hour; he said he had something. "Well, start it off snappily," said the editor. "Something people will read." Haskins set to work and in a couple of hours brought a sheet of typewritten paper to the desk; it was a two-hundred-word story about some disease that had broken out among the horses. Its opening sentence was simple but arresting. It read: "Who has noticed the sores on the tops of the horses in the animal husbandry building?"

Ohio State was a land grant university and therefore two years   15
of military drill was compulsory. We drilled with old Springfield rifles and studied the tactics of the Civil War even though the World War was going on at the time. At 11 o'clock each morning thousands of freshmen and sophomores used to deploy over the campus, moodily creeping up on the old chemistry building. It was good training for the kind of warfare that was waged at Shiloh but it had no connection with what was going on in Europe. Some people used to think there was German money behind it, but they

didn't dare say so or they would have been thrown in jail as German spies. It was a period of muddy thought and marked, I believe, the decline of higher education in the Middle West.

As a soldier I was never any good at all. Most of the cadets were   16
glumly indifferent soldiers, but I was no good at all. Once General Littlefield, who was commandant of the cadet corps, popped up in front of me during regimental drill and snapped, "You are the main trouble with this university!" I think he meant that my type was the main trouble with the university but he may have meant me individually. I was mediocre at drill, certainly — that is, until my senior year. By that time I had drilled longer than anybody else in the Western Conference, having failed at military at the end of each preceding year so that I had to do it all over again. I was the only senior still in uniform. The uniform which, when new, had made me look like an interurban railway conductor, now that it had become faded and too tight made me look like Bert Williams in his bellboy act. This had a definitely bad effect on my morale. Even so, I had become by sheer practice little short of wonderful at squad maneuvers.

One day General Littlefield picked our company out of the   17
whole regiment and tried to get it mixed up by putting it through one movement after another as fast as we could execute them: squads right, squads left, squads on right into line, squads right about, squads left front into line, etc. In about three minutes one hundred and nine men were marching in one direction and I was marching away from them at an angle of forty degrees, all alone. "Company, halt!" shouted General Littlefield. "That man is the only man who has it right!" I was made a corporal for my achievement.

The next day General Littlefield summoned me to his office.   18
He was swatting flies when I went in. I was silent and he was silent too, for a long time. I don't think he remembered me or why he had sent for me, but he didn't want to admit it. He swatted some more flies, keeping his eyes on them narrowly before he let go with the swatter. "Button up your coat!" he snapped. Looking back on it now I can see that he meant me although he was looking at a fly, but I just stood there. Another fly came to rest on a paper in front of the general and began rubbing its hind legs together. The general lifted the swatter cautiously. I moved restlessly and the fly flew away. "You startled him!" barked General Littlefield, looking at me se-

verely. I said I was sorry. "That won't help the situation!" snapped the General, with cold military logic. I didn't see what I could do except offer to chase some more flies toward his desk, but I didn't say anything. He stared out the window at the faraway figures of co-eds crossing the campus toward the library. Finally, he told me I could go. So I went. He either didn't know which cadet I was or else he forgot what he wanted to see me about. It may have been that he wished to apologize for having called me the main trouble with the university; or maybe he had decided to compliment me on my brilliant drilling of the day before and then at the last minute decided not to. I don't know. I don't think about it much any more.

Jonathan Swift

The satirist Jonathan Swift (1667–1745) is most famous as the author of Gulliver's Travels *(1726). Born in Ireland, Swift moved to London at a young age and in 1694 became an Anglican priest. In 1713 he was appointed the dean of St. Patrick's Cathedral in Dublin, a position he held until his death. For most of his life, Swift was an outspoken public figure, writing satiric poems, plays, and essays aimed at political and religious targets. Some of his major works include* A Tale of a Tub *(1704) and* The Battle of the Books *(1704). Later, outraged by the British government's treatment of the Irish people, Swift wrote "A Modest Proposal," the classic essay reprinted here.*

A Modest Proposal

In 1729, Ireland was in tragic condition. Poverty was widespread, a devastating famine was in its third year, and people were starving. Moreover, the British government, which ruled Ireland, imposed high taxes on the already impoverished populace. Angered by these injustices, Swift wrote a powerful satire attacking the English and wealthy Irish who ignored the existence of the suffering masses. Speaking not as himself but in the guise of a disinterested observer, Swift suggested an outrageous solution to Ireland's problems, a solution in keeping with the inhumanity he saw rampant in Ireland.

It is a melancholy object to those who walk through this great town[1] or travel in the country, when they see the streets, the roads, and cabin doors, crowded with beggars of the female sex, followed by three, four, or six children, all in rags and importuning every passenger for an alms. These mothers, instead of being able to work for their honest livelihood, are forced to employ all their time in strolling to beg sustenance for their helpless infants, who, as they

1

[1]Dublin.

grow up, either turn thieves for want of work, or leave their dear native country to fight for the Pretender in Spain, or sell themselves to the Barbadoes.[2]

I think it is agreed by all parties that this prodigious number of children in the arms, or on the backs, or at the heels of their mothers, and frequently of their fathers, is in the present deplorable state of the kingdom a very great additional grievance; and therefore whoever could find out a fair, cheap, and easy method of making these children sound, useful members of the commonwealth would deserve so well of the public as to have his statue set up for a preserver of the nation.   2

But my intention is very far from being confined to provide only for the children of professed beggars; it is of a much greater extent, and shall take in the whole number of infants at a certain age who are born of parents in effect as little able to support them as those who demand our charity in the streets.   3

As to my own part, having turned my thoughts for many years upon this important subject, and maturely weighed the several schemes of other projectors, I have always found them grossly mistaken in their computation. It is true, a child just dropped from its dam may be supported by her milk for a solar year, with little other nourishment; at most not above the value of two shillings, which the mother may certainly get, or the value in scraps, by her lawful occupation of begging; and it is exactly at one year old that I propose to provide for them in such a manner as instead of being a charge upon their parents or the parish, or wanting food and raiment for the rest of their lives, they shall on the contrary contribute to the feeding, and partly to the clothing, of many thousands.   4

There is likewise another great advantage in my scheme, that it will prevent those involuntary abortions, and that horrid practice of women murdering their bastard children, alas, too frequent among us, sacrificing the poor innocent babes, I doubt, more to avoid the expense than the shame, which would move tears and pity in the most savage and inhuman breast.   5

The number of souls in this kingdom being usually reckoned one million and a half, of these I calculate there may be about two hundred thousand couples whose wives are breeders, from which number I subtract thirty thousand couples who are able to main-   6

[2]Many poor Irish were leaving the country to try to find a living elsewhere.

tain their own children, although I apprehend there cannot be so many under the present distress of the kingdom; but this being granted, there will remain an hundred and seventy thousand breeders. I again subtract fifty thousand for those women who miscarry, or whose children die by accident or disease within the year. There only remain an hundred and twenty thousand children of poor parents annually born. The question therefore is, how this number shall be reared and provided for, which, as I have already said, under the present situation of affairs, is utterly impossible by all the methods hitherto proposed. For we can neither employ them in handicraft nor agriculture; we neither build houses (I mean in the country) nor cultivate land. They can very seldom pick up livelihood by stealing till they arrive at six years old, except where they are of towardly parts;[3] although I confess they learn the rudiments much earlier, during which time they can however be looked upon only as probationers, as I have been informed by a principal gentleman in the county of Cavan, who protested to me that he never knew above one or two instances under the age of six, even in a part of the kingdom so renowned for the quickest proficiency in that art.

I am assured by our merchants that a boy or a girl before twelve   7
years old is no salable commodity; and even when they come to this age, they will not yield above three pounds, or three pounds and half a crown at most on the Exchange; which cannot turn to account either to the parents or the kingdom, the charge of nutriment and rags having been at least four times that value.

I shall now therefore humbly propose my own thoughts,   8
which I hope will not be liable to the least objection.

I have been assured by a very knowing American of my ac-   9
quaintance in London, that a young healthy child well nursed is at a year old a most delicious, nourishing, and wholesome food, whether stewed, roasted, baked, or boiled; and I make no doubt that it will equally serve in fricassee or a ragout.

I do therefore humbly offer it to public consideration that of   10
the hundred and twenty thousand children, already computed, twenty thousand may be reserved for breed, whereof only one fourth part to be males, which is more than we allow to sheep, black cattle, or swine; and my reason is that these children are seldom the

[3]Prematurely developed.

fruits of marriage, a circumstance not much regarded by our savages, therefore one male will be sufficient to serve four females. That the remaining hundred thousand may at a year old be offered in sale to the persons of quality and fortune through the kingdom, always advising the mother to let them suck plentifully in the last month, so as to render them plump and fat for a good table. A child will make two dishes at an entertainment for friends; and when the family dines alone, the fore or hind quarter will make a reasonable dish, and seasoned with a little pepper or salt will be very good boiled on the fourth day, especially in winter.

I have reckoned upon a medium that a child just born will   11
weigh twelve pounds, and in a solar year if tolerably nursed increaseth to twenty-eight pounds.

I grant this food will be somewhat dear, and therefore very   12
proper for landlords, who, as they have already devoured most of the parents, seem to have the best title to the children.

Infant's flesh will be in season throughout the year, but more   13
plentiful in March, and a little before and after. For we are told by a grave author, an eminent French physician,[4] that fish being a prolific diet, there are more children born in Roman Catholic countries about nine months after Lent, than at any other season; therefore, reckoning a year after Lent, the markets will be more glutted than usual, because the number of popish infants is at least three to one in this kingdom; and therefore it will have one other collateral advantage, by lessening the number of Papists among us.

I have already computed the charge of nursing a beggar's child   14
(in which list I reckon all cottagers, laborers, and four fifths of the farmers) to be about two shillings per annum, rags included; and I believe no gentleman would repine to give ten shillings for the carcass of a good fat child, which, as I have said, will make four dishes of excellent nutritive meat, when he hath only some particular friend or his own family to dine with him. Thus the squire will learn to be a good landlord, and grow popular among the tenants; the mother will have eight shillings net profit, and be fit for work till she produces another child.

Those who are more thrifty (as I must confess the times re-   15
quire) may flay the carcass; the skin of which artifically[5] dressed will

---

[4]Francois Rabelais, a sixteenth-century comic writer.
[5]Skillfully.

make admirable gloves for ladies, and summer boots for fine gentlemen.

As to our city of Dublin, shambles[6] may be appointed for this purpose in the most convenient parts of it, and butchers we may be assured will not be wanting; although I rather recommend buying the children alive, and dressing them hot from the knife as we do roasting pigs.

A very worthy person, a true lover of his country, and whose virtues I highly esteem, was lately pleased in discoursing on this matter to offer a refinement upon my scheme. He said that many gentlemen of his kingdom, having of late destroyed their deer, he conceived that the want of venison might be well supplied by the bodies of young lads and maidens, not exceeding fourteen years of age nor under twelve, so great a number of both sexes in every county being now ready to starve for want of work and service; and these to be disposed of by their parents, if alive, or otherwise by their nearest relations. But with due deference to so excellent a friend and so deserving a patriot, I cannot be altogether in his sentiments; for as to the males, my American acquaintance assured me from frequent experience that their flesh was generally tough and lean, like that of our schoolboys, by continual exercise, and their taste disagreeable; and to fatten them would not answer the charge. Then as to the females, it would, I think with humble submission, be a loss to the public, because they soon would become breeders themselves; and besides, it is not improbable that some scrupulous people might be apt to censure such a practice (although indeed very unjustly) as a little bordering upon cruelty; which, I confess, hath always been with me the strongest objection against any project, how well soever intended.

But in order to justify my friend, he confessed that this expedient was put into his head by the famous Psalmanazar,[7] a native of the island Formosa, who came from thence to London above twenty years ago, and in conversation told my friend that in his country when any young person happened to be put to death, the executioner sold the carcass to the persons of quality as a prime dainty; and that in his time the body of a plump girl of fifteen, who

16

17

18

---

[6]Slaughterhouses.
[7]A Frenchman, Georges Psalmanazar, who fooled London society into thinking he was from the exotic land of Formosa.

was crucified for an attempt to poison the emperor, was sold to his Imperial Majesty's prime minister of state, and other great mandarins of the court, in joints from the gibbet, at four hundred crowns. Neither indeed can I deny that if the same use were made of several plump young girls in this town, who without one single groat to their fortunes cannot stir abroad without a chair,[8] and appear at the playhouse and assemblies in foreign fineries which they never will pay for, the kingdom would not be the worse.

Some persons of a desponding spirit are in great concern about   19
that vast number of poor people who are aged, diseased, or maimed, and I have been desired to employ my thoughts what course may be taken to ease the nation of so grievous an encumbrance. But I am not in the least pain upon that matter, because it is very well known that they are every day dying and rotting by cold and famine, and filth and vermin, as fast as can be reasonably expected. And as to the younger laborers, they are now in almost as hopeful a condition. They cannot get work, and consequently pine away for want of nourishment to a degree that if any time they are accidentally hired to common labor, they have not strength to perform it; and thus the country and themselves are happily delivered from the evils to come.

I have too long digressed, and therefore shall return to my   20
subject. I think the advantages by the proposal which I have made are obvious and many, as well as of the highest importance.

For first, as I have already observed, it would greatly lessen the   21
number of Papists, with whom we are yearly overrun, being the principal breeders of the nation as well as our most dangerous enemies; and who stay at home on purpose to deliver the kingdom to the Pretender, hoping to take their advantage by the absence of so many good Protestants, who have chosen rather to leave their country than to stay at home and pay tithes against their conscience to an Episcopal curate.

Secondly, the poorer tenants will have something valuable of   22
their own, which by law may be made liable to distress,[9] and help to pay their landlord's rent, their corn and cattle being already seized and money a thing unknown.

---

[8]A groat was a coin worth several pennies; a chair was a sedan chair in which a person was carried by servants.

[9]Seizure for the payment of debts.

Thirdly, whereas the maintenance of an hundred thousand 23
children, from two years old and upwards, cannot be computed at
less than ten shillings a piece per annum, the nation's stock will be
thereby increased fifty thousand pounds per annum, besides the
profit of a new dish introduced to the tables of all gentlemen of
fortune in the kingdom who have any refinement in taste. And the
money will circulate among ourselves, the goods being entirely of
our own growth and manufacture.

Fourthly, the constant breeders, besides the gain or eight shill- 24
ings sterling per annum by the sale of their children, will be rid of
the charge for maintaining them after the first year.

Fifthly, this food would likewise bring great custom to tav- 25
erns, where the vintners will certainly be so prudent as to procure
the best receipts for dressing it to perfection, and consequently
have their houses frequented by all the fine gentlemen, who justly
value themselves upon their knowledge in good eating; and a skillful cook, who understands how to oblige his guests, will contrive to
make it as expensive as they please.

Sixthly, this would be a great inducement to marriage, which 26
all wise nations have either encouraged by rewards or enforced by
laws and penalties. It would increase the care and tenderness of
mothers toward their children, when they were sure of a settlement
for life to the poor babes, provided in some sort by the public, to
their annual profit instead of expense. We should see an honest
emulation among the married women, which of them could bring
the fattest child to the market. Men would become as fond of their
wives during the time of pregnancy as they are now of their mares in
foal, their cows in calf, or sows when they are ready to farrow; nor
offer to beat or kick them (as is too frequent a practice) for fear of a
miscarriage.

Many other advantages might be enumerated. For instance, 27
the addition of some thousand carcasses in our exportation of
barreled beef, the propagation of swine's flesh, and improvements
in the art of making good bacon, so much wanted among us by the
great destruction of pigs, too frequent at our tables, which are no
way comparable in taste or magnificence to a well-grown, fat, year-
ling child, which roasted whole will make a considerable figure at a
lord mayor's feast or any other public entertainment. But this and
many others I omit, being studious of brevity.

Supposing that one thousand families in this city would be 28 constant customers for infants' flesh, besides others who might have it at merry meetings, particularly weddings and christenings, I compute that Dublin would take off annually about twenty thousand carcasses, and the rest of the kingdom (where probably they will be sold somewhat cheaper) the remaining eighty thousand.

I can think of no one objection that will possibly be raised   29 against this proposal, unless it should be urged that the number of people will be thereby much lessened in the kingdom. This I freely own, and it was indeed one principal design in offering it to the world. I desire the reader will observe; that I calculate my remedy for this one individual kingdom of Ireland and for no other that ever was, is, or I think ever can be upon earth. Therefore, let no man talk to me of other expedients: of taxing our absentees at five shillings a pound: of using neither clothes nor household furniture except what is of our own growth and manufacture: of utterly rejecting the materials and instruments that promote foreign luxury: of curing the expensiveness of pride, vanity, idleness, and gaming in our women: of introducing a vein of parsimony, prudence, and temperance: of learning to love our country, in the want of which we differ even from Laplanders and the inhabitants of Topinamboo[10]: of quitting our animosities and factions, nor acting any longer like the Jews,[11] who were murdering one another at the very moment their city was taken: of being a little cautious not to sell our country and conscience for nothing: of teaching landlords to have at least one degree of mercy toward their tenants: lastly, of putting a spirit of honesty, industry, and skill into our shopkeepers; who, if a resolution could now be taken to buy only our native goods, would immediately unite to cheat and exact upon us in the price, the measure, and the goodness, nor could ever yet be brought to make one fair proposal of just dealing, though often and earnestly invited to it.

Therefore, I repeat, let no man talk to me of these and the like   30 expedients, till he hath at least some glimpse of hope that there will ever be some hearty and sincere attempt to put them in practice.

But as to myself, having been wearied out for many years with   31

---

[10]A place in the Brazilian jungle.
[11]Rival factions were at war within Jerusalem when the city was seized by the Romans in 70 A.D.

offering vain, idle, visionary thoughts, and at length utterly despairing of success, I fortunately fell upon this proposal, which, as it is wholly new, so it hath something solid and real, of no expense and little trouble, full in our own power, and whereby we can incur no danger in disobliging England. For this kind of commodity will not bear exportation, the flesh being of too tender a consistence to admit a long continuance in salt, although perhaps I could name a country which would be glad to eat up our whole nation without it.

After all, I am not so violently bent upon my own opinion as to reject any offer proposed by wise men, which shall be found equally innocent, cheap, easy, and effectual. But before something of that kind shall be advanced in contradiction to my scheme, and offering a better, I desire the author or authors will be pleased maturely to consider two points. First, as things now stand, how they will be able to find food and raiment for an hundred thousand useless mouths and backs. And secondly, there being a round million of creatures in human figure throughout this kingdom, whose sole subsistence put into a common stock would leave them in debt two millions of pounds sterling, adding those who are beggars by profession to the bulk of farmers, cottagers, and laborers, with their wives and children who are beggars in effect; I desire those politicians who dislike my overture, and may perhaps be so bold to attempt an answer, that they will first ask the parents of these mortals whether they would not at this day think it a great happiness to have been sold for food at a year old in this manner I prescribe, and thereby have avoided such a perpetual scene of misfortunes as they have since gone through by the oppression of landlords, the impossibility of paying rent without money or trade, the want of common sustenance, with neither house nor clothes to cover them from the inclemencies of the weather, and the most inevitable prospect of entailing the like or greater miseries upon their breed forever. 32

I profess, in the sincerity of my heart, that I have not the least personal interest in endeavoring to promote this necessary work, having no other motive than the public good of my country, by advancing our trade, providing for infants, relieving the poor, and giving some pleasure to the rich. I have no children by which I can propose to get a single penny; the youngest being nine years old, and my wife past childbearing. 33

Martin Luther King, Jr.

Martin Luther King, Jr. (1929–1968), was the most influential voice of the American civil rights movement in the 1950s and 1960s. Born in Atlanta, Georgia, he went on to earn doctorates from Boston University and Chicago Theological Seminary. He served as pastor of a church in Montgomery, Alabama, and was the founder and director of the Southern Christian Leadership Conference. Using a philosophy of nonviolent resistance to injustice, he staged bus boycotts, marches, and sit-ins to protest racial segregation. These actions led to the passage of the 1964 Civil Rights Act and the Voting Rights Act of 1965. King's efforts on behalf of racial injustice and his larger concern for world peace won him international recognition, and he was awarded the Nobel Peace Prize in 1964. The following selection is from King's book, Where Do We Go From Here: Community or Chaos? *(1967), published not long before he was assassinated on April 4, 1968.*

Where Do We Go From Here: Community or Chaos?

Political leaders present convincing arguments for military aggression. They advocate supplying weapons to countries that are fighting communist insurgents; they urge the stockpiling of deadly warheads as a defense strategy; they argue for the funding of nuclear missiles euphemistically called "peacekeepers." But to Dr. King the belief that war can lead to peace is absurd. In this essay, he maintains that only nonviolent methods can bring stability and peace to a troubled world.

A final problem that mankind must solve in order to survive in the world house that we have inherited is finding an alternative to war and human destruction. Recent events have vividly reminded us that nations are not reducing but rather increasing their arsenals of weapons of mass destruction. The best brains in the highly developed nations of the world are devoted to military technology. The proliferation of nuclear weapons has not been halted, in spite of the limited-test-ban treaty.

In this day of man's highest technical achievement, in this day 2 of dazzling discovery, of novel opportunities, loftier dignities and fuller freedoms for all, there is no excuse for the kind of blind craving for power and resources that provoked the wars of previous generations. There is no need to fight for food and land. Science has provided us with adequate means of survival and transportation, which make it possible to enjoy the fullness of this great earth. The question now is, do we have the morality and courage required to live together as brothers and not be afraid?

One of the most persistent ambiguities we face is that every- 3 body talks about peace as a goal, but among the wielders of power peace is practically nobody's business. Many men cry "Peace! Peace!" but they refuse to do the things that make for peace.

The large power blocs talk passionately of pursuing peace 4 while expanding defense budgets that already bulge, enlarging already awesome armies and devising ever more devastating weapons. Call the roll of those who sing the glad tidings of peace and one's ears will be surprised by the responding sounds. The heads of all the nations issue clarion calls for peace, yet they come to the peace table accompanied by bands of brigands each bearing unsheathed swords.

The stages of history are replete with the chants and choruses 5 of the conquerors of old who came killing in pursuit of peace. Alexander, Genghis Khan, Julius Caesar, Charlemagne and Napoleon were akin in seeking a peaceful world order, a world fashioned after their selfish conceptions of an ideal existence. Each sought a world at peace which would personify his egotistic dreams. Even within the life span of most of us, another megalomaniac strode across the world stage. He sent his blitzkrieg-bent legions blazing across Europe, bringing havoc and holocaust in his wake. There is grave irony in the fact that Hitler could come forth, following nakedly aggressive expansionist theories, and do it all in the name of peace.

So when in this day I see the leaders of nations again talking 6 peace while preparing for war, I take fearful pause. When I see our country today intervening in what is basically a civil war, mutilating hundreds of thousands of Vietnamese children with napalm, burning villages and rice fields at random, painting the valleys of that small Asian country red with human blood, leaving broken bodies in countless ditches and sending home half-men, mutilated mentally and physically; when I see the unwillingness of our government to create the atmosphere for a negotiated settlement of this awful conflict by halting bombings in the North and agreeing unequivocally to talk with the Vietcong—and all this in the name of pursuing the goal of peace—I tremble for our world.[1] I do so not only from dire recall of the nightmares wreaked in the wars of yesterday, but also from dreadful realization of today's possible nuclear destructiveness and tomorrow's even more calamitous prospects.

Before it is too late, we must narrow the gaping chasm between our proclamations of peace and our lowly deeds which precipitate and perpetuate war. We are called upon to look up from the quagmire of military programs and defense commitments and read the warnings on history's signposts. 7

One day we must come to see that peace is not merely a distant goal that we seek but a means by which we arrive at that goal. We must pursue peaceful ends through peaceful means. How much longer must we play at deadly war games before we heed the plaintive pleas of the unnumbered dead and maimed of past wars? 8

President John F. Kennedy said on one occasion, "Mankind must put an end to war or war will put an end to mankind." Wisdom born of experience should tell us that war is obsolete. There may have been a time when war served as a negative good by preventing the spread and growth of an evil force, but the destructive power of modern weapons eliminates even the possibility that war may serve any good at all. If we assume that life is worth living and that man has a right to survive, then we must find an alternative to war. In a day when vehicles hurtle through outer space and guided ballistic missiles carve highways of death through the stratosphere, no nation can claim victory in war. A so-called limited war will leave little more than a calamitous legacy of human suffering, political turmoil and spiritual disillusionment. A world war will leave only smoldering ashes as mute testimony of a human race whose folly led inexorably to ultimate death. If modern man con- 9

[1]Only after more than 58,000 Americans had been killed did the United States withdraw from Vietnam. The civil war then continued until the North Vietnamese, aided by the Vietcong, took over all of Vietnam.

tinues to flirt unhesitatingly with war, he will transform his earthly habitat into an inferno such as even the mind of Dante could not imagine.

Therefore I suggest that the philosophy and strategy of non- 10 violence become immediately a subject for study and for serious experimentation in every field of human conflict, by no means excluding the relations between nations. It is, after all, nationstates which make war, which have produced the weapons that threaten the survival of mankind and which are both genocidal and suicidal in character.

We have ancient habits to deal with, vast structures of power, 11 indescribably complicated problems to solve. But unless we abdicate our humanity altogether and succumb to fear and impotence in the presence of the weapons we have ourselves created, it is as possible and as urgent to put an end to war and violence between nations as it is to put an end to poverty and racial injustice.

The United Nations is a gesture in the direction of nonvio- 12 lence on a world scale. There, at least, states that oppose one another have sought to do so with words instead of with weapons. But true nonviolence is more than the absence of violence. It is the persistent and determined application of peaceable power to offenses against the community — in this case the world community. As the United Nations moves ahead with the giant tasks confronting it, I would hope that it would earnestly examine the uses of nonviolent direct action.

I do not minimize the complexity of the problems that need to 13 be faced in achieving disarmament and peace. But I am convinced that we shall not have the will, the courage and the insight to deal with such matters unless in this field we are prepared to undergo a mental and spiritual re-evaluation, a change of focus which will enable us to see that the things that seem most real and powerful are indeed now unreal and have come under sentence of death. We need to make a supreme effort to generate the readiness, indeed the eagerness, to enter into the new world which is now possible, "the city which hath foundation, whose Building and Maker is God."

It is not enough to say, "We must not wage war." It is neces- 14 sary to love peace and sacrifice for it. We must concentrate not merely on the eradication of war but on the affirmation of peace. A fascinating story about Ulysses and the Sirens is preserved for us in Greek literature. The Sirens had the ability to sing so sweetly that sailors could not resist steering toward their island. Many ships were lured upon the rocks, and men forgot home, duty and honor as they flung themselves into the sea to be embraced by arms that drew them down to death. Ulysses, determined not to succumb to the Sirens, first decided to tie himself tightly to the mast of his boat and his crew stuffed their ears with wax. But finally he and his crew learned a better way to save themselves: They took on board the beautiful singer Orpheus, whose melodies were sweeter than the music of the Sirens. When Orpheus sang, who would bother to listen to the Sirens?

So we must see that peace represents a sweeter music, a cosmic melody that is far superior to the discords of war. Somehow we must transform the dynamics of the world power struggle from the nuclear arms race, which no one can win, to a creative contest to harness man's genius for the purpose of making peace and prosperity a reality for all the nations of the world. In short, we must shift the arms race into a "peace race." If we have the will and determination to mount such a peace offensive, we will unlock hitherto tightly sealed doors of hope and bring new light into the dark chambers of pessimism.

Joan Didion

*Known for her taut prose style and sharp social commentary,
Joan Didion (1934–   ) graduated from the University of
California at Berkeley. Her essays have appeared in* The
Saturday Evening Post, The American Scholar, *and* The
National Review, *as well as in two collections:* Slouching
Towards Bethlehem *(1969) and* The White Album
(1979). Salvador *(1983) is a book-length essay about a 1982
visit to Central America. She has also written several novels,
including* River Run *(1963),* Play It As It Lays *(1971),* A
Book of Common Prayer *(1977), and* Democracy *(1984).
The following essay is taken from* The White Album.

In Bed

*Perhaps you are skeptical of people who take to bed with a bad
headache, or maybe you use the term "migraine" to describe
your own occasional discomfort. If so, reading this essay will
put you in your place. A chronic migraine sufferer since childhood, Joan Didion frequently falls victim to bouts of debilitating pain. Brace yourself for some excruciating details; you'll
never use the term "migraine" loosely again.*

Three, four, sometimes five times a month, I spend the day in   1
bed with a migraine headache, insensible to the world around me.
Almost every day of every month, between these attacks, I feel the
sudden irrational irritation and flush of blood into the cerebral
arteries which tell me that migraine is on its way, and I take certain
drugs to avert its arrival. If I did not take the drugs, I would be able
to function perhaps one day in four. The physiological error called
migraine is, in brief, central to the given of my life. When I was
fifteen, sixteen, even twenty-five, I used to think that I could rid
myself of this error by simply denying it, character over chemistry.
"Do you have headaches *sometimes? frequently? never?*" the application forms would demand. "Check one." Wary of the trap, wanting whatever it was that the successful circumnavigation of that

particular form could bring (a job, a scholarship, the respect of mankind and the grace of God), I would check one. "*Sometimes,*" I would lie. That in fact I spent one or two days a week almost unconscious with pain seemed a shameful secret, evidence not merely of some chemical inferiority but of all my bad attitudes, unpleasant tempers, wrongthink.

For I had no brain tumor, no eyestrain, no high blood pressure, nothing wrong with me at all: I simply had migraine headaches, and migraine headaches were, as everyone who did not have them knew, imaginary. I fought migraine then, ignored the warnings it sent, went to school and later to work in spite of it, sat through lectures in Middle English and presentations to advertisers with involuntary tears running down the right side of my face, threw up in washrooms, stumbled home by instinct, emptied ice trays onto my bed and tried to freeze the pain in my right temple, wished only for a neurosurgeon who would do a lobotomy on house call, and cursed my imagination.

It was a long time before I began thinking mechanistically enough to accept migraine for what it was: something with which I would be living, the way some people live with diabetes. Migraine is something more than the fancy of a neurotic imagination. It is an essentially hereditary complex of symptoms, the most frequently noted but by no means the most unpleasant of which is a vascular headache of blinding severity, suffered by a surprising number of women, a fair number of men (Thomas Jefferson had migraine, and so did Ulysses S. Grant, the day he accepted Lee's surrender), and by some unfortunate children as young as two years old. (I had my first when I was eight. It came on during a fire drill at the Columbia School in Colorado Springs, Colorado. I was taken first home and then to the infirmary at Peterson Field, where my father was stationed. The Air Corps doctor prescribed an enema.) Almost anything can trigger a specific attack of migraine: stress, allergy, fatigue, an abrupt change in barometric pressure, a contretemps over a parking ticket. A flashing light. A fire drill. One inherits, of course, only the predisposition. In other words I spent yesterday in bed with a headache not merely because of my bad attitudes, unpleasant tempers, and wrongthink, but because both my grandmothers had migraine, my father has migraine, and my mother has migraine.

No one knows precisely what it is that is inherited. The chemis-   4
try of migraine, however, seems to have some connection with the
nerve hormone named serotonin, which is naturally present in the
brain. The amount of serotonin in the blood falls sharply at the
onset of migraine, and one migraine drug, methysergide, or San-
sert, seems to have some effect on serotonin. Methysergide is a
derivative of lysergic acid (in fact Sandoz Pharmaceuticals first
synthesized LSD-25 while looking for a migraine cure), and its use
is hemmed about with so many contraindications and side effects
that most doctors prescribe it only in the most incapacitating cases.
Methysergide, when it is prescribed, is taken daily, as a preventive;
another preventive which works for some people is old-fashioned
ergotamine tartrate, which helps to constrict the swelling blood
vessels during the "aura," the period which in most cases precedes
the actual headache.

Once an attack is under way, however, no drug touches it.   5
Migraine gives some people mild hallucinations, temporarily
blinds others, shows up not only as a headache but as a gastrointestinal disturbance, a painful sensitivity to all sensory stimuli, an
abrupt overpowering fatigue, a strokelike aphasia, and a crippling
inability to make even the most routine connections. When I am in
a migraine aura (for some people the aura lasts fifteen minutes, for
others several hours), I will drive through red lights, lose the house
keys, spill whatever I am holding, lose the ability to focus my eyes
or frame coherent sentences, and generally give the appearance of
being on drugs, or drunk. The actual headache, when it comes,
brings with it chills, sweating, nausea, a debility that seems to
stretch the very limits of endurance. That no one dies of migraine
seems, to someone deep into an attack, an ambiguous blessing.

My husband also has migraine, which is unfortunate for him   6
but fortunate for me: perhaps nothing so tends to prolong an
attack as the accusing eye of someone who has never had a headache. "Why not take a couple of aspirin," the unafflicted will say
from the doorway, or "I'd have a headache, too, spending a beautiful day like this inside with all the shades drawn." All of us who
have migraine suffer not only from the attacks themselves but from
this common conviction that we are perversely refusing to cure
ourselves by taking a couple of aspirin, that we are making ourselves sick, that we "bring it on ourselves." And in the most imme-

diate sense, the sense of why we have a headache this Tuesday and not last Thursday, of course we often do. There certainly is what doctors call a "migraine personality," and that personality tends to be ambitious, inward, intolerant of error, rather rigidly organized, perfectionist. "You don't look like a migraine personality," a doctor once said to me. "Your hair's messy. But I suppose you're a compulsive housekeeper." Actually my house is kept even more negligently than my hair, but the doctor was right nonetheless: perfectionism can also take the form of spending most of a week writing and rewriting and not writing a single paragraph.

But not all perfectionists have migraine, and not all mi-   7
grainous people have migraine personalities. We do not escape heredity. I have tried in most of the available ways to escape my own migrainous heredity (at one point I learned to give myself two daily injections of histamine with a hypodermic needle, even though the needle so frightened me that I had to close my eyes when I did it), but I still have migraine. And I have learned now to live with it, learned when to expect it, how to outwit it, even how to regard it, when it does come, as more friend than lodger. We have reached a certain understanding, my migraine and I. It never comes when I am in real trouble. Tell me that my house is burned down, my husband has left me, that there is gunfighting in the streets and panic in the banks, and I will not respond by getting a headache. It comes instead when I am fighting not an open but a guerrilla war with my own life, during weeks of small household confusions, lost laundry, unhappy help, canceled appointments, on days when the telephone rings too much and I get no work done and the wind is coming up. On days like that my friend comes uninvited.

And once it comes, now that I am wise in its ways, I no longer   8
fight it. I lie down and let it happen. At first every small apprehension is magnified, every anxiety a pounding terror. Then the pain comes, and I concentrate only on that. Right there is the usefulness of migraine, there in that imposed yoga, the concentration on the pain. For when the pain recedes, ten or twelve hours later, everything goes with it, all the hidden resentments, all the vain anxieties. The migraine has acted as a circuit breaker, and the fuses have emerged intact. There is a pleasant convalescent euphoria. I open the windows and feel the air, eat gratefully, sleep well. I notice the particular nature of a flower in a glass on the stair landing. I count my blessings.

GLOSSARY

Abstract and concrete language refers to two different qualities of words. Abstract words and phrases convey concepts, qualities, emotions, and ideas which we can think and talk about but not actually see or experience directly. Examples of abstract words are *conservatism, courage, avarice, joy,* and *hatred.* Words or phrases whose meanings are directly seen or experienced by the senses are concrete terms. Examples of phrases using concrete words are *split-level house, waddling penguin,* and *short pink waitress uniform.*

Adequate — see *Evidence.*

Ad Hominem Argument — see *Logical Fallacies.*

Analogy refers to an imaginative comparison between two subjects that seem to have little in common. Often a complex idea or topic can be made understandable by comparing it to a more familiar subject, and such an analogy can be developed over several paragraphs or even an entire essay. For example, to explain how the economic difficulties of farmers weaken an entire nation, a writer might create an analogy between failing farms and a cancer that slowly destroys a person's life.

Argumentation-Persuasion tries to encourage readers to accept a writer's point of view on some controversial or significant issue. In *argumentation*, a writer uses objective reasoning, facts, and hard evidence to demonstrate the soundness of a position. In *persuasion*, the writer uses appeals to the readers' emotions and value systems, often in the hope of encouraging them to take a specific action. Argumentation and persuasion are frequently used together in an essay. For example, a writer might argue for the construction of a highway through town by pointing out that the road would bring new business, create new jobs, and lighten traffic. The writer also might try to persuade readers to vote for a highway appropriations bill by appealing to their emotions, claiming that the highway would allow people to get home faster, thus giving them more time for family life and leisure activities. A whole essay can be organized around argumentation-persuasion, or an essay developed chiefly through another mode may contain elements of argumentation-persuasion.

Assertion refers to the *thesis* of an *argumentation-persuasion* essay. The assertion, or *proposition*, is a point of view or opinion on a controversial issue or topic. The assertion cannot be merely a statement of a fact. Such statements as "Women still experience discrimination in the job market," "General Rabb would make an ideal mayor for our town," and "This university should devote more funds to raising the quality of the food services" are examples of assertions that could serve as theses for argumentation-persuasion essays.

Audience refers to the writer's intended readers. In planning the content and tone of an essay, you should identify your audience and consider its needs. How similar are the members of your audience to you in knowledge and point of view? What will they need to know for you to achieve your *purpose*? What *tone* will make them open to receiving your message? For example, if you were to write a description of a trip to Disney World, you would have to explain a lot more to an eighty-year-old grandmother who had never seen a theme park than to a young parent who had probably visited one. If you wrote about the high cost of clothing for an economics professor, you would choose a serious, analytic tone and supply statistical evidence for your points. If you write about the same topic for the college newspaper, you might use a tone tinged with humor and provide helpful hints on finding bargain clothing.

Begging the Question — see *Logical Fallacies*.

Brainstorming is a technique used in the *prewriting* stage. It helps you discover the limited subject you can successfully write about and also generates raw material — ideas and details — to develop that subject. In brainstorming, you allow your mind to play freely with the subject. You try to capture fleeting thoughts about it, no matter how random, minor, or tangential, and jot them down rapidly before they disappear from your mind.

Causal Analysis — see *Cause-Effect*.

Causal Chain refers to a series of causes and effects, in which the result or effect of a cause becomes itself the cause of a further effect, and so on. For example, a person's alarm clock failing to buzz might begin a causal chain by causing the person to oversleep. Oversleeping then causes the person to miss the bus, and missing the bus causes the person to arrive late to work. Arriving late causes the person to miss an important phone call, which causes the person to lose a chance at a lucrative contract.

Cause-Effect, sometimes called *causal analysis,* involves analyzing the reasons for or results of an event, action, decision, or phenomenon. Writers develop an essay through an analysis of causes whenever they attempt to answer such questions as "Why has this happened?" or "Why does this exist?" When writers explore such questions as "What happens or would happen if a certain change occurs?" or "What will happen if a condition continues?" their essays involve a discussion of effects. Some cause-effect essays concentrate on the causes of a situation, some focus on the effects, and others present both causes and effects. Causal analysis can be an essay's central pattern, or it can be used to help support a point in an essay developed primarily through another mode.

Characteristics — see *Formal Definition*.

Chronological Sequence — see *Narrative Sequence* and *Organization*.

Circularity is an error in *formal definition* resulting from using variations of the to-be-defined word in the definition. For example, "A scientific hypothesis is when a scientist makes a hypothesis about the results of an experiment," is circular because the unknown term is used to explain itself.

Class — see *Formal Definition*.

Comparison-Contrast means explaining the similarities and/or differences between events, objects, people, ideas, and so on. The comparison-contrast format can be used to meet a purely factual purpose ("This is how *A* and *B* are alike or different"). But usually writers use comparison-contrast to make a judgment about the relative merits of the subjects under discussion. Sometimes a writer will concentrate solely on similarities *or* differences. For instance, when writing about married versus single life, you would probably devote most of your time to discussing the difference between these lifestyles. Other times, comparison and contrast are found together. In an essay analyzing two approaches to U.S. foreign policy, you would probably discuss the similarities *and* the differences in the goals and methods characteristic of each approach. Comparison-contrast can be the dominant mode of development in an essay, or it can be used as a supplemental pattern in an essay developed chiefly through another mode.

Conclusion refers to the one or more paragraphs that bring an essay to an end. Effective conclusions give the reader a sense of completeness and finality. Writers often use the conclusion as a place to reaffirm the *thesis* and to express a final thought about the subject. Methods of conclusion include summarizing main points, using a quotation, predicting an outcome, or recommending an action.

Conclusion — see *Deduction*.

Conflict creates tension in the readers of a *narration*. It is produced by the opposition of characters or other forces in a story. Conflict can occur between individuals, between a person and society or nature, or within a person. Readers wonder how a conflict will be resolved and read on to find out.

Connectives signal the relationships among ideas in your essay. They help the reader follow the train of thought from sentence to sentence and from paragraph to paragraph. There are three types of connectives. *Transitions* are words that briefly indicate the coming flow of meaning. They can signal an additional or contrasting point, an enumeration of ideas, the use of an example, or other movement of ideas. For a list of transitional devices, see page 41. *Linking sentences* summarize a point just made and then introduce a follow-up point. *Repeated words, synonyms, and pronouns* create a sense of flow by keeping important concepts in the mind of the reader.

Connotative and Denotative Language describes the ability of language to emphasize one or another aspect of a word's range of meaning. *Denotative language* stresses the dictionary meaning of words. *Connotative language* emphasizes the echoes of feeling that cluster around some words. For example, the terms *weep, bawl, break down* and *sob* all denote the same thing: to cry. But they have different associations and call up different images. A writer employing the connotative resources of language would choose the term among these which suggested the appropriate image.

Controlling Idea — see *Thesis*.

Deductive Reasoning is a form of logical thinking in which general statements believed to be true are applied to specific situations or cases. The result of deduction is a conclusion or prediction about the specific situation. Deduction is often expressed in a three-step pattern called a *syllogism*. The first part of the syllogism is a general statement about a large class of items or situations, the *major premise*. The second part is the *minor premise*, a more limited statement about a specific item or case. The third part is the *conclusion* about that specific case or item drawn from the major premise. Deductive reasoning is very common in everyday thinking. For example, you might use de-duction when car shopping:

In an accident, large cars are safer than small cars.
(Major premise)

The Chevy Cruiser is a large car.
(Minor premise)

In an accident, the Chevy Cruiser will be safer than a small car.
(Conclusion)

Definition explains the meaning of a word or concept. The brief formal definitions found in the dictionary can be useful if you need to clarify or restrict the meaning of a term used in an essay. In such cases, the definition is short and to the point. But you may also use an *extended definition* in an essay taking several paragraphs, even the entire piece, to develop the meaning of a term. You may use extended definition to convey a personal slant on a well-known term, to refute a commonly held interpretation of a word, or to dissect a complex or controversial issue. Definition can be the chief method of development in an essay, or it can be used as a supplemental mode in an essay organized around another pattern.

Definition by Negation is a method of defining a term by first explain-ing what it is not, and then going on to explain what it is. For example, you might begin a critical essay about television with a definition by negation: "Television, far from being a magical medium of light entertainment and immediate information, actually disseminates a distorted view of how Americans live and what they want from life, their government, and society." *Definition by negation* can provide a stimulating introduction to an essay.

Description involves the use of vivid word pictures to express what the five senses have experienced. The subject of a descriptive essay can be a person, place, object, or event. Description can be the dominant pat-tern in an essay, or it can be used as a supplemental method in an essay developed chiefly through another pattern.

There are two main types of description. In an *objective descrip-tion*, a writer provides details about a subject without conveying the emotions the subject arouses. For example, if you were involved in a traffic accident, your insurance agent might ask you to write an objec-tive description of the events leading up to and during the crash. But in a *subjective description*, the writer's goal is to evoke in the reader the emotions felt during the experience. For example, in a cautionary letter to a friend who has a habit of driving dangerously, you might write a subjective description of your horrifying close call with death during a car accident.

Development — see *Evidence*.

Dialogue is the writer's way of directly presenting the exact words spoken by characters in a *narration*. By using dialogue, writers can convey people's individuality and also add drama and immediacy to an essay.

Directional Process Analysis — see *Process Analysis*.

Division-Classification refers to a logical method for analyzing a single subject or several related subjects. Though often used together in an essay, division and classification are separate processes. *Division* involves breaking a subject or idea into its component parts. For instance, the concept "an ideal vacation" could be divided according to its destination, accommodations, or cost. *Classification* involves organizing a number of related items into categories. For example, in an essay about the overwhelming flow of paper in our everyday lives, you might classify the typical kinds of mail most people receive: personal mail (letters, birthday cards, party invitations), business mail (bills, bank statements, charge card receipts), and junk mail (flyers about bargain sales, solicitations to donate, contest announcements). Division-classification can be the dominant pattern in a paper, or it may be used to support a point in an essay organized chiefly around another pattern of development.

Dominant Impression refers to the purpose of a descriptive essay. While some descriptive essays have a thesis, some do not; instead, they convey a dominant impression or main point. For example, one person writing a descriptive essay about New York City might use the architectural diversity as a focal point. Another person writing a description of Manhattan might concentrate on the overpowering sense of hustle and speed about everyone and everything in the city. Both writers would select only those details that supported their dominant impressions.

Dramatic License refers to the writer's privilege, when writing a narrative, to alter facts or details to strengthen the support of the *thesis* or *narrative point*. For example, a writer is free to flesh out the description of an event whose specific details may be partially forgotten or to modify or omit details of a narrative that do not contribute to the meaning the writer wishes to convey.

Emphatic Sequence — see *Organization*.

Ethos refers to the necessity for a writer to establish an image of reliability or credibility in the readers of an *argumentation-persuasion* essay or piece. This is done by using reason and logic to argue points, by being moderate in any appeals to the emotions, and by demonstrating overall knowledgeability of the subject. Effective argumentation-persuasion should possess *ethos*, *logos*, and *pathos*.

Etymology refers to the history of a word or term. All English words have their origins in other, usually ancient, languages. Giving a brief etymology of a word can help a writer establish the context for developing an *extended definition* of the word. For example, the word *criminal* is derived from a Latin word meaning "accusation/accused." Today, our word *criminal* goes beyond the concept of "accused" to mean "guilty."

Evidence lends substance to your main idea and so assists the reader to accept your viewpoint. Evidence should meet three criteria. First of all, it should be *unified*, in the sense that all supporting ideas and details should relate directly to the point you are making. Second, the evidence should be *adequate*; there should be enough evidence to convince the reader to agree with your thesis. Third, evidence should be *specific*, that is, vivid and detailed, rather than vague and general. The bulk of an essay is devoted to supplying evidence. Supporting the thesis with solid evidence is the third stage of a writing process.

Exemplification, at the heart of all effective writing, involves using concrete specifics to support generalizations. In exemplification, writers provide examples or instances that support or clarify broader statements. You might support the thesis statement, "I have a close-knit family," by using such examples as the following: "We have a regular Sunday dinner at my grandmother's house with at least ten family members present"; "My sisters and brothers visit my parents every week"; "I spend so much time on the phone talking with my sisters that sometimes I have trouble finding time for my new college friends." Exemplification may be an essay's central pattern, or it may supplement an essay developed mainly around another pattern.

Extended Definition — see *Definition*.

Fallacies — see *Logical Fallacies*.

Figures of Speech are imaginative comparisons between two things usually thought of as dissimilar. Some major figures of speech are *simile, metaphor*, and *personification*. *Similes* are comparisons that use the signal words *like* or *as*: "Superman was as powerful as a locomotive." *Metaphors*, which do not use signal words, directly equate unlike things: "The boss is a tiger when it comes to landing a contract." "The high-powered pistons of the boxer's arms pummeled his opponent." *Personification* attributes human characteristics to inanimate things or nonhuman beings: "The angry clouds unleashed their fury on the town"; "The wind caressed the trees," "The turtle shyly poked his head out of his shell."

First Draft refers to the writer's first try at producing a basic, unpolished version of the whole essay. It is often referred to as the "rough" draft, and nothing about it is final or unchangeable. The process of writing the first draft often brings up new ideas or details. Writers sometimes break off writing the draft to *brainstorm* or *freewrite* as new ideas occur to them, and then return to the draft with new inspiration. You shouldn't worry about spelling, grammar, or style in the first-draft stage; instead, you should keep focused on casting your ideas into sentence and paragraph form. Writing the first draft is the fifth stage in the writing process.

Flashback — see *Narrative Sequence*.

Flashforward — see *Narrative Sequence*.

Formal Definition involves stating a definition in a three-part pattern of about one-sentence in length. In presenting a formal definition a writer puts the *term* in a *class* and then lists the *characteristics* that separate the term from other members of its class. For example, a formal definition of a word processor might be, "A word processor (term) is an electronic machine (class) that is used to write, edit, store, and produce typewritten documents (characteristics)." Writers often use a formal definition to prepare a reader for an extended definition that follows.

Freewriting can help a writer during the *prewriting* stage in coming up with ideas for developing the limited topic. To use this method, you should write nonstop for five or ten minutes about everything your topic brings to mind. Disregard grammar, spelling, and organization as you keep your pen and mind moving. Freewriting is similar to *brainstorming*, except that the result is a rambling, detail-filled paragraph rather than a list.

Generalization — see *Logical Fallacies*.

Inductive Inference is the term for a conclusion based on *inductive reasoning*. Because the reasoning behind specific cases may not be simple, there is usually an element of uncertainty in an inductive conclusion. Choosing the correct explanation for specific cases is a matter of carefully weighing and selecting alternative conclusions.

Inductive Reasoning is a form of logical thinking in which specific cases and facts are examined in order to draw a wider-ranging conclusion. The result of inductive reasoning is a generalization that is held to apply to situations or cases similar to the ones examined. Induction is typical of scientific investigation and of everyday thinking. For example, on the basis of specific experiences, you may have concluded that when you feel chilly in a room where everyone else is comfortable, you are likely to develop a cold and fever in the next day or two. In an *argumentation-persuasion* essay, the conclusion reached by induction would be your *assertion* or *thesis*.

Informational Process Analysis — see *Process Analysis*.

Introduction refers to the first paragraph or several paragraphs of an essay. The introduction serves three purposes. It informs readers of the general subject of the essay, it catches their attention, and it presents the controlling idea or thesis. The methods of introducing an essay include the use of an anecdote, a quotation or surprising statistic or fact, or questions. Or you may narrow your discussion down from a broad subject to a more limited one.

Irony occurs when writers or speakers say the opposite of what they actually mean. The listener or reader is able to comprehend the true meaning because of the style, the tone, or context of the ironic statement. Author Betty Rollin describes a simple example of verbal irony (also known as *sarcasm*) in "Allene Talmey" (page 195). When her boss at *Vogue* asked her, "What are you trying to say, dear?" Rollin understood that her boss really meant "moron," not "dear."

Linking Sentences — see *Connectives*.

Logical Fallacies are easily committed mistakes in reasoning that writers must be on guard against, especially when writing *argumentation-persuasion* essays. There are many kinds of logical fallacies.

Hasty generalizations are unsound *inductive inferences* based on too few instances of a behavior, situation, or process. For example, it would be a hasty generalization to conclude that you are allergic to a food such as curry because you once ate it and became ill. There are several other possible explanations for your illness, and only repetitions of this experience or a lab test could prove conclusively that you are allergic to this spice.

Post hoc thinking results when you presume that one event caused another just because it occurred first. For instance, if your car broke down the day after you loaned it to your brother, you would be committing the post hoc fallacy to blame him, unless you knew he did something to your engine.

Ad hominem argument occurs when you attack a person's point of view by criticizing the person, not the issue. Often called "mudslinging," ad hominem arguments try to invalidate a person's ideas by revealing unrelated, past or present, personal or ethical flaws. For example, to claim a person cannot govern the country well because it can be proven he has had an extramarital affair is to use an ad hominem argument.

Begging the question is a fallacy in which the writer assumes something that should be proven and directs the reader's attention to an opinion that is usually easier to prove. To argue that "A law should be passed to require that dangerous pets like German shepherds and Doberman pinschers be restrained by fences, leashes, and muzzles at all times" would be to beg the question of whether such dogs are always dangerous.

Logos is a major factor in creating an effective argument. It refers to the soundness of *argumentation*, as created by the use of facts, statistics, information, and commentary by authoritative sources. The most effective arguments involve an interplay between *logos, pathos*, and *ethos*.

Major Premise — see *Deduction*.

Minor Premise — see *Deduction*.

Narration means recounting an event or a series of related events to make a point. Narration can be an essay's principal mode of development, or it can be used to supplement a paper organized primarily around another pattern. For instance, to persuade readers to avoid drug use, a writer might use the narrative mode by recounting the story of an abuser's addiction and recovery.

Narrative Point refers to the meaning you intend to convey to your reader by telling a certain story. This narrative point might be a specific message or lesson, or it might be a feeling about the situation, people, or place of the story. This underlying meaning is achieved by presenting details that support it and editing out any that are nonessential. For example, in an essay about friendship, a writer's point might be that friendships change when one of the friends acquires a significant partner of the opposite sex. The writer would focus on the details of how her close female friend had less time for her, changed their habitual times of getting together, and confided in her less. The writer would omit judgments of the friend's choice of boyfriend and her declining grades, because these details, while real for the writer, would distract the reader from the main narrative point.

Narrative Sequence refers to the order in which a writer recounts events. When you follow the order of the events as they happened, you are using *chronological sequence*. This sequence, in which you begin at the beginning and end with the last event, is the most basic and commonly used narrative sequence. If you interrupt this flow to present an event that happened before the beginning of the narrative sequence, you are employing a *flashback*. If you skip ahead, to an event later than the one that comes next in your narrative, you are using the *flashforward* technique.

Objective Description — see *Description*.

One-Side-at-a-Time Method refers to one of the two techniques for organizing a *comparison-contrast* essay. In using this method, a writer discusses all the points about one of the compared and contrasted subjects before going on to the other. For example, in an essay titled, "Single or Married?" a writer might first discuss single life in terms of amount of independence, freedom of career choice, and companionship. Then the writer would discuss married life in terms of these same three subtopics. The issues the writer discusses in each half of the essay would be identical and presented in the same order. See also *Point-by-Point Method*.

Organization refers to the process of arranging your evidence to support your thesis in the most effective way. In organizing, you decide what ideas come first, next, and last. In *chronological* sequence, you arrange details according to occurrence in time. In *spatial* sequence, details appear in the order in which they occur in space. In *emphatic* sequence, ideas are sequenced according to importance, with the most significant, outstanding, or convincing evidence being reserved for last. Organizing is the fourth stage of the writing process.

Outlining is making a formal plan before writing a *first draft*. Writing an outline helps you determine whether your supporting evidence is logical and adequate. As you write, you can use the outline to keep yourself on track. Many writers use the indentation system of roman numerals, letters, and arabic numbers to outline; sometimes writers use a less formal indented list. Outlining is done during the fourth stage of the writing process.

Paradox refers to a statement that seems impossible, contrary to common sense, or self-contradictory, yet that can after consideration be seen to be plausible or true. For example, Oscar Wilde produced a paradox when he wrote that "When the gods wish to punish us, they answer our prayers." The statement does not contradict itself because often, Wilde believes, that which we wish for turns out to be the very thing that will bring us the most pain. Another example of paradox occurs when Loren Eiseley responds "I do," to a boy's question, "Do you live here, Mister?" (see page 353). His answer is a paradox because while Eiseley does not literally live there, in some deeper sense the place is his home.

Pathos refers to the emotional power of an *argumentation-persuasion* essay. By appealing to the needs, values, and attitudes of readers and by using highly *connotative language*, writers can increase the chances that readers will come to agree with the ideas in an essay. Writing very strong in *pathos* is usually persuasive in *purpose*, but all effective argumentation-persuasion essays are built upon the three factors, *pathos, logos*, and *ethos*.

Plan of Development refers to a useful but not essential means of supplying the reader with a brief map of the main points to be covered. If used, the plan of development occurs as part of the *thesis* or in a sentence following the thesis. In it, the main ideas are mentioned in the order they will appear in the supporting paragraphs. Longer essays and term papers usually need a plan of development to maintain unity, but shorter papers may do without.

Point-by-Point Method refers to one of the two techniques for organizing a *comparison-contrast* essay. A writer using this method covers each point of comparison or contrast in relation to each subject of the comparison before going on to the next point. For example, in an essay titled, "Single or Married?" a writer might first discuss the amount of independence a person has when single and when married. Then, the writer might go on to discuss how the single or married state affects career choice. Finally, the writer might discuss the amount of companionship available in each of the two lifestyles. See also *One-Side-at-a-Time Method*.

Point of View refers to the perspective a writer chooses when writing about a subject. In *narration*, the point of view should be consistent throughout. If you narrate events as you experienced them, you are using the first-person point of view. You might say, for example, "I noticed jam on the child's collar and holes in her shirt." If you relate the events from a distance, as if you know about them but did not experience them, you are using the third-person point of view. For example, "Jam splotched the child's collar and her shirt had several holes in it."

Post Hoc Thinking—see *Logical Fallacies*.

Prewriting is the first stage of the writing process. During prewriting, you jot down rough ideas about your subject without yet moving to writing a draft of your essay. Your goals at this stage are to (1) understand the boundaries of the assignment, (2) discover the limited subject you could write well about, (3) generate raw material about the limited subject, and (4) organize the raw material into a very rough *scratch outline*. If you keep in mind that prewriting is "unofficial," it can be a low-pressure, even enjoyable activity.

Process Analysis refers to writing that explains the steps involved in doing something or the sequence of stages in a recurring event or behavior. There are two types of process analysis. In *directional process analysis*, readers are shown how to do something step-by-step. Cookbook recipes, tax form instructions, and how-to books are some typical uses of instructional process analysis. In *informational process analysis*, the writer explains how something is done or occurs, without expecting the reader to attempt the process. "A Senator's Road to Political Power," "How a Bee Makes Honey," and "How a Convict Gets Paroled" would be titles of essays developed through informational process analysis. Process analysis can be the dominant mode in an essay, as in these examples, or it may be used in an essay of another mode to support a point. For example, in a cause-effect essay that explores the impact of the two-career family, process analysis might be used to explain how parents arrange for day care.

Proofreading involves rereading your final draft carefully to catch any errors in spelling, grammar, punctuation, or typing that have slipped by to this stage. While such errors are minor, a significant number of them can seriously weaken the effectiveness of your essay. Proofreading is the last step of the writing process.

Proposition—see *Assertion*.

Purpose is the reason you have in mind for writing a particular essay. Usually writers frame their purposes in terms of the effect they wish to have on their *audience*. They may wish to express themselves, explore a subject or experience, explain an idea or process, provide information, influence opinion, or entertain. Many essays have more than one purpose. As a writer, you will find you will be most effective if you establish one primary purpose for your essay and plan it accordingly.

Refutation of the Opposition is an important strategy in *argumentation-persuasion*. In refutation, writers acknowledge that there are opposing views on the subject under discussion, and go on to do one of two things. They may admit the opposing views are somewhat valid, but assert that their own position has more merit and devote their essay to demonstrating that merit. For example, a writer might assert, "While many business majors graduate to find interesting and lucrative jobs, liberal arts graduates have many more advantages in the job market in the long run, because they think better, learn faster, and communicate more successfully." This writer would concentrate on proving the advantages liberal arts graduates have. On the other hand, writers may choose to argue actively against the views held by the opposition before going on to support their own thesis. Such refutation of opposing views can help strengthen the writer's own arguments.

Repeated Words, Synonyms, and Pronouns—see *Connectives*.

Revision means, literally, "reseeing" your *first draft* with a fresh eye, as if you were a new reader. In revising, you make whatever changes are necessary to increase the essay's effectiveness. You might eliminate weak phrasing or examples, change the organization, add transitions, or rework whole paragraphs. Such changes often make the difference between mediocre and superior writing. Revision is the last stage of the writing process.

Satire is a humorous form of social criticism usually aimed at society's institutions or human behavior. Often irreverent as well as witty, satire is serious in purpose: to point to evil, injustice, and absurdity and bring about change through an increase in awareness. Satire ranges widely in tone: it may be gentle or biting; it may sarcastically describe a real situation or use fictional characters and events to spoof reality. Satire often makes use of *irony*. Examples of satire in this book include "In Depth, but Shallowly," "How to Live to Be 200," and "A Modest Proposal."

Scratch Outline refers to your first informal plan for an essay, devised at the end of the *prewriting* stage. In making a scratch outline, you select ideas and details from your raw material for inclusion in your essay and discard the rest. You also arrange these ideas into an order that makes sense and that will help you to achieve your *purpose*. A scratch outline is tentative and flexible, and can be reshaped as needed.

Sensory Description vividly evokes the sights, smells, taste, sounds, and physical feelings of a scene or event. It allows the reader to feel imaginatively present. For example, if a writer carefully chooses words and images, readers can see the vibrant reds and oranges of falling leaves, taste the sourness of an underripe grapefruit, hear the growling of motorcycles as a gang sweeps through a town, smell the spicy aroma of a grandmother's homemade tomato soup, and feel the pulsing pain of a jaw after Novocaine wears off. Sensory description is particularly important in writing *description* or *narration*.

Sentence Variety adds interest to the style of an essay or paragraph. In creating sentence variety, writers mix different kinds of sentences and sentence patterns. For example, you might make sure some of your sentences are short and some long, some simple, some complex, and some compound-complex, and that your sentences use a number of different transitional and opening phrases. Repetitive sentence patterns tend to make readers pay less attention.

Spatial Sequence — see *Organization*.

Specific — see *Evidence*.

Stipulative Definition is a way of restricting a term for the purposes of discussion. Many words have multiple meanings which can get in the way of clarity when a writer is creating an extended definition. For example, you might stipulate the following definition of *foreign car*: "While many familiar American cars these days use parts or even whole engines made in foreign countries by foreign car manufacturers, for the purposes of discussion, 'foreign car' refers only to those automobiles wholly designed and manufactured by a company based in another country. By this definition, a Volkswagen made in Pennsylvania is a foreign car."

Subjective Description — see *Description*.

Support — see *Evidence*.

Syllogism — see *Deduction*.

Term — see *Formal Definition*.

Thesis is the central idea in any essay, usually expressed in a one- or two-sentence thesis statement. Writers accomplish two things by providing a *thesis* statement in an essay; they indicate the essay's limited subject and express an attitude about that subject. Also called the *controlling idea*, the *thesis statement* consists of a particular slant, angle, or point of view about the limited subject. Stating the thesis is the second stage of the writing process.

Tone conveys a writer's attitude toward a subject. It is similar to tone of voice in speaking, in that a reader detects tone more through how writers say something than through what they say. Your tone in writing can be serious, sarcastic, humorous, analytic, critical, angry, and so on.

Topic Sentence is the term for the sentence or two that conveys the main idea of a paragraph. Such sentences are often, but not always, found at the start of a paragraph. They provide a statement of the subject to be discussed and an indication of your attitude toward that subject. Writers concern themselves with topic sentences during the writing of the first draft, the fifth stage of the writing process.

Transitions — see *Connectives*.
Unified — see *Evidence*.

THEMATIC
CONTENTS

COMMUNICATION AND LANGUAGE

COMPETITION AND CONFLICT

692

CONTEMPORARY ISSUES

EDUCATION

FAMILY AND CHILDREN

GOVERNMENT AND LAW

HEALTH AND MEDICINE

HUMAN GROUPS AND SOCIETIES

HUMOR AND SATIRE

MEANING IN LIFE

MEMORIES AND AUTOBIOGRAPHY

NATURE AND SCIENCE

WORK

INDEX

To the Student
From the Authors

By now, you realize that almost all writing goes through a series of revisions. The same was true for this book. *The Macmillan Reader* has been reworked a number of times, with each revision taking into account student and instructor reaction to drafts of material.

Before we prepare the next edition of *The Macmillan Reader*, we'd like to know how you, the student, feel about the book. We hope you'll spend a few minutes completing this brief questionnaire. You can be sure that your responses will help shape subsequent editions. Please send your completed survey to the College English Editor, Macmillan Publishing Company, 866 Third Avenue, New York, New York 10022.

Thanks for your time.

College _____ City and state _____

Course title _____ Instructor _____

DESCRIPTION	I really liked.	It was okay.	I didn't like.	I didn't read.
Woiwode, *Wanting an Orange*	____	____	____	____
Baker, *In My Day*	____	____	____	____
Trillin, *The Bubble Gum Store*	____	____	____	____
White, *Once More to the Lake*	____	____	____	____
Anderson, *Children's Hospital*	____	____	____	____

	I really liked.	It was okay.	I didn't like.	I didn't read.
NARRATION				
Orwell, *Shooting an Elephant*	___	___	___	___
Greene, *Handled with Care*	___	___	___	___
Watkins, *Little Deaths*	___	___	___	___
Hughes, *Salvation*	___	___	___	___
Sizer, *Horace's Compromise*	___	___	___	___
EXEMPLIFICATION				
Packard, *Children at Risk*	___	___	___	___
Rollin, *Am I Getting Paid for This?*	___	___	___	___
Lindbergh, *Channelled Whelk*	___	___	___	___
Nilsen, *Sexism and Language*	___	___	___	___
Cowley, *The View From 80*	___	___	___	___
PROCESS ANALYSIS				
Leacock, *How to Live to Be 200*	___	___	___	___
Hubbell, *The Beekeeper*	___	___	___	___
Mitford, *The American Way of Death*	___	___	___	___
Roberts, *How to Say Nothing in 500 Words*	___	___	___	___
McWilliams, *Selecting a Word Processing Computer*	___	___	___	___
COMPARISON-CONTRAST				
LeBoeuf, *Japan: The Productivity Challenge*	___	___	___	___
Lurie, *Male and Female*	___	___	___	___

	I really liked.	It was okay.	I didn't like.	I didn't read.
Spikol, *High Noon*	___	___	___	___
Rodriguez, *Workers*	___	___	___	___
Eiseley, *The Brown Wasps*	___	___	___	___

CAUSE-EFFECT

Gallup, Jr., *The Faltering Family*	___	___	___	___
Farb, *In Other Words*	___	___	___	___
Wolfe, *O Rotten Gotham*	___	___	___	___
Schwartz, *Communication in the Year 2000*	___	___	___	___
Thomas, *The Health Care System*	___	___	___	___

DEFINITION

Cole, *Entropy*	___	___	___	___
Chase, *A Very Private Utopia*	___	___	___	___
Syfers, *Why I Want a Wife*	___	___	___	___
Mencken, *The Politician*	___	___	___	___
Winn, *TV Addiction*	___	___	___	___

DIVISION-CLASSIFICATION

Barry, *In Depth, but Shallowly*	___	___	___	___
Zinsser, *College Pressures*	___	___	___	___
Hilfiker, *Making Medical Mistakes*	___	___	___	___
McClintock, *Propaganda Techniques*	___	___	___	___
Morris, *Individual and Group Identity*	___	___	___	___

ARGUMENTATION-PERSUASION

	I really liked.	It was okay.	I didn't like.	I didn't read.
Marzollo, *My Pistol-Packing Kids*	——	——	——	——
Fussell, *The Boy Scout Handbook*	——	——	——	——
Krents, *Darkness at Noon*	——	——	——	——
Wainwright, *A Little Banning*	——	——	——	——
Rosenblatt, *The Man in the Water*	——	——	——	——
Twain, *The Damned Human Race*	——	——	——	——
Tutko and Bruns, *To Win or Not to Win*	——	——	——	——
Trippett, *A Red Light for Scofflaws*	——	——	——	——
Mead, *One Vote for This Age of Anxiety*	——	——	——	——

FOR FURTHER READING

Walker, *Beauty: When the Other Dancer Is the Self*	——	——	——	——
Thurber, *University Days*	——	——	——	——
Swift, *A Modest Proposal*	——	——	——	——
King, *Where Do We Go From Here: Community or Chaos?*	——	——	——	——
Didion, *In Bed*	——	——	——	——

Any general comments or suggestions?

Name ——————————— Date ———————————

Address ————————————————————————

THANKS AGAIN!